The Blackwell Companion to the Study of Religion

Blackwell Companions to Religion

The Blackwell Companions to Religion series presents a collection of the most recent scholarship and knowledge about world religions. Each volume draws together newly-commissioned essays by distinguished authors in the field, and is presented in a style which is accessible to undergraduate students, as well as scholars and the interested general reader. These volumes approach the subject in a creative and forward-thinking style, providing a forum in which leading scholars in the field can make their views and research available to a wider audience.

Published

Forthcoming

The Blackwell Companion to the Study of Religion

Edited by Robert A. Segal

WILEY-BLACKWELL

A John Wiley & Sons, Ltd., Publication

This edition first published 2009
© 2009 Blackwell Publishing Ltd except for editorial material and organization © 2006 Robert A. Segal; except for Chapter 18 © 2006 Jeffrey J. Kripal

Edition history: Blackwell Publishing Ltd (hardback, 2006)

Blackwell Publishing was acquired by John Wiley & Sons in February 2007. Blackwell's publishing program has been merged with Wiley's global Scientific, Technical, and Medical business to form Wiley-Blackwell.

Registered Office
John Wiley & Sons Ltd, The Atrium, Southern Gate, Chichester, West Sussex, PO19 8SQ, United Kingdom

Editorial Offices
350 Main Street, Malden, MA 02148-5020, USA
9600 Garsington Road, Oxford, OX4 2DQ, UK
The Atrium, Southern Gate, Chichester, West Sussex, PO19 8SQ, UK

For details of our global editorial offices, for customer services, and for information about how to apply for permission to reuse the copyright material in this book please see our website at www.wiley.com/wiley-blackwell.

The right of Robert A. Segal to be identified as the author of the editorial material in this work has been asserted in accordance with the Copyright, Designs and Patents Act 1988.

Library of Congress Cataloging-in-Publication Data

The Blackwell companion to the study of religion / edited by Robert A. Segal.
      p.   cm.—(Blackwell companions to religion)
   Includes bibliographical references and index.
   ISBN-13: 978-1-4051-8598-1 (pbk : alk. paper)   1. Religion.   I. Segal, Robert Alan.   II. Series.
   BL48.B53 2006
   200′.7—dc22

                                                        2005015487

A catalogue record for this book is available from the British Library.

Set in 11 on 13.5 pt Photina
by SNP Best-set Typesetter Ltd, Hong Kong
Printed in Singapore by Utopia Press Pte Ltd
1   2009

Dedicated to
John Clayton (1943–2003) – colleague, friend,
and the original editor of this Companion

and to
Catherine Bell (1953–2008) – distinguished
authority on ritual, contributor to this
Companion, and friend

Contents

[†]Deceased

Contributors

Catherine Bell[†] was Professor Emerita of Religious Studies, Santa Clara University, Santa Clara, California, USA

Gustavo Benavides, Associate Professor, Department of Theology and Religious Studies, Villanova University, Villanova, Pennsylvania, USA

Fiona Bowie, Senior Lecturer and Head of Department of Archaeology and Anthropology, University of Bristol, UK, and Senior Research Fellow, Carter G. Woodson Institute for African American and African Studies, University of Virginia, Charlottesville, USA

Steve Bruce, FBA, FRSE, Professor of Sociology, University of Aberdeen, Scotland

Colin Campbell, Professor of Sociology, University of York, UK

Simon Coleman, Professor of Anthropology, University of Sussex, UK

[†]Deceased

Lawrence S. Cunningham, John A. O'Brien Professor of Theology, University of Notre Dame, Notre Dame, Indiana, USA

Grace Davie, Professor of Sociology, University of Exeter, UK

Douglas J. Davies, Professor in the Study of Religion, University of Durham, UK

G. Scott Davis, Lewis T. Booker Professor of Religion and Ethics, University of Richmond, Virginia, USA

Lorne L. Dawson, Director, Laurier-Waterloo, Ph.D. in Religious Studies and Professor of Sociology and Realism Studies, Department of Sociology, University of Waterloo, Canada

Mark Juergensmeyer, Professor of Sociology and Religious Studies and Director, Global and International Studies, University of California, Santa Barbara, California, USA

Jeffrey J. Kripal, J. Newton Rayzor Professor of Religious Studies, Rice University, Houston, Texas, USA

Roderick Main, Senior Lecturer in Psychoanalytic Studies and Director, Centre for Psychoanalytic Studies, University of Essex, Colchester, UK

Ian Markham, Dean and President, Virginia Theological Seminary, Alexandria, USA

Henry Munson, Professor of Anthropology, University of Maine, Orono, USA

Stephen Prickett, FAHA, FEA, Margaret Root Brown Professor of English and Director, Armstrong Browning Library, Baylor University, Waco, Texas, USA

Richard H. Roberts, Emeritus Professor of Religious Studies, University of Lancaster, UK, and Honorary Professor of Religious Studies, University of Stirling, Scotland

Paul Roscoe, Professor of Anthropology, University of Maine, Orono, USA

Jeffrey Burton Russell, Professor Emeritus of History, University of California, Santa Barbara, California, USA

Thomas Ryba, Notre Dame Theologian in Residence and Adjunct Professor of Philosophy, Purdue University, West Lafayette, Indiana, USA

Robert A. Segal, Sixth Century Chair in Religious Studies, University of Aberdeen, Scotland, UK

Rodney Stark, University Professor of the Social Sciences, Baylor University, Waco, Texas, USA

Charles Taliaferro, Professor of Philosophy, St. Olaf College, Northfield, Minnesota, USA

Introduction

Robert A. Segal

What Makes Religious Studies a Discipline?

What is meant by calling religious studies a discipline? According to one view, religious studies, to qualify as a discipline or a field, must have a distinctive method. Yet most disciplines harbor no distinctive method. Many either share a method – notably, the so-called "scientific method" – or else employ a variety of methods – for example, quantitative as well as qualitative approaches or textual analysis as well as fieldwork. Still, does religious studies possess a method of its own? Many of the classical defenders of religious studies as a discipline invoke phenomenology as the distinctive method of the discipline. In his entry in this Companion on the phenomenology of religion, Thomas Ryba expertly works out the goal of this approach to religion. But at least as practiced, phenomenology of religion amounts to no more than data gathering, if also the classification of the data gathered. In other words, the touted method of religious studies turns out to be taxonomy. And it is taxonomy at the descriptive level. It is the classification of professedly religious beliefs, practices, and objects.

If a discipline must have a distinctive method, and if data gathering and classification are all that religious studies offers, then the field is on shaky grounds. Not only are data gathering and classification common to all other fields, but the other fields that claim to study religion happily utilize the data and classifications provided by religious studies. Anthropologists of religion, sociologists of religion, psychologists of religion, and economists of religion all rely on the findings of specialists in religious studies. What social scientists proceed to do with those findings seemingly distinguishes them from those who toil in religious studies. For social scientists seek to *explain* the data amassed and organized, and they seek to explain them in their own disciplinary ways – anthropologically, sociologically, psychologically, and economically. Unless religious studies, whether or not the phenomenology of religion in particular, not merely *describes* certain beliefs, practices, and objects as religious but also *explains* them religiously, it serves as a mere underlaborer.

The second defense of religious studies as a discipline is that the field does in fact explain religion "religiously" rather than anthropologically, sociologically, psychologically, or economically. To explain religion from any perspective is to account for both its origin and its function. An anthropological explanation of religion accounts for religion as a case of culture. A sociological explanation of religion accounts for religion as a case of society. And so on. According to "religionists," as I dub defenders of its disciplinary autonomy, religious studies accounts for religion not as a case of anything else but in its own right – as religion. The origin and function of religion are therefore distinctively, or irreducibly, religious.

Now for religionists, no less than for anthropologists, sociologists, psychologists, and economists, religion is a human, not a divine, creation. Religious beliefs and practices are concocted by humans, not revealed from on high. But humans purportedly concoct them in order to make contact with God. That is the irreducibly religious origin and function of religion. Humans do not happen to seek contact with God. They *need* to do so. Just as they come into the world with a need for food and for love, so they come into the world with a need for God. That need, like the need for food or love, is innate. Religion arises and serves to fulfill it.

How religion fulfills the need varies from religionist to religionist. For Mircea Eliade, the most influential contemporary religionist, religion provides contact with God through myths and rituals. Myths carry one back to the time when, so it is believed, God was closest to humans. Rituals offer a place where God has once appeared to humans and so, it is believed, is likeliest to appear anew.

The difficulties with this second defense of the autonomy of religious studies are several. To begin with, what is the evidence of any need to encounter God? Religionists infer from the existence of religion a need for contact with God, but the social sciences profess to be able to account for the existence of religion in terms of secular circumstances and secular needs, which range from the need for crops to the need for meaningful-ness. If religion reflects an innate need to encounter God, how can there be any individuals or cultures that are not religious? The rejoinder by religionists such as Eliade is that religion is still present in them, simply not overtly or even consciously so.

Yet even if religion can be shown to be universal, and even if religion can be shown to fulfill a need for God, why must that need be innate? Why can the need not be a mere means to some other end, including some underlying secular need? No social scientist denies or must deny that reli-gion serves to make contact with God. What social scientists want to know is why humans seek – let us even say need – to make that contact. Making contact is deemed a means to another end. Religion may be a useful means to that end, may even be the best means, or may yet be an indispensable means, as it is for Emile Durkheim, for whom religion serves to unify members of society. But no social scientist is prepared to take the need for contact as an end rather than a means. None is prepared to take a yearn-ing for God as a sufficient explanation of religion.

Take Sigmund Freud, perhaps the most unabashed of reductionists. In *Totem and Taboo* Freud maintains that the guilt felt by sons toward their fathers over the sons' parricidal wishes causes them to create a cosmic, divine father to try to love and obey, thereby placating their guilt toward their human fathers. In *The Future of an Illusion* Freud maintains that the protection that fathers had given their sons and daughters alike in chil-dren is restored through the creation of a cosmic, divine father, who now shields them from the world at large. Freud hardly denies that adult adher-ents yearn to get close to God. He denies that that yearning explains itself. Rather, it is the consequence of pre-religious, childhood experiences or fantasies. Religion is an adult response to a nonreligious need. Religion is a means to a nonreligious end.

The issue is not whether Freud's explanation of religion is convincing. Many objections can be noted. If, according to *Totem and Taboo*, adult sons create God to give themselves a second chance at obedience toward their fathers, how does Freud account for female adherents? How does he account for those religions, the existence of which he acknowledges, in which the chief god is female or in which there are multiple gods of either gender or in which the gods are animals, plants, or even inanimate entities like the sun? If, according to *The Future of an Illusion*, sons and daughters alike create God to restore the security their childhood fathers provided, how does Freud account for those religions in which God is cruel, capri-cious, or indifferent rather than paternal? How does he account for those religions, which in fact means all religions, in which God fails to fend off the travails of life?

The issue at hand is not, however, whether Freud's explanation of reli-gion, in either of his main works on religion, is convincing but whether it subsumes the religionist one under itself. Surely it means to do so. What

Freud wants to explain is the relationship of humans to God. He may be skewing the relationship, seeing it as he does either as one of hatred, love, guilt, and penance (*Totem and Taboo*) or as one of protection from the elements (*The Future of an Illusion*), but religion for him is still basically a relationship to God.

C. G. Jung, Freud's great rival, may stand closer to the religionist notion of the relationship. In his *Psychology and Religion* Jung actually cites phenomenologist Rudolf Otto's characterization of religion as at heart the experience of God, and of an awesome, overpowering God. Jung simply translates that relationship into psychological terms – into the encounter of ego consciousness with the unconscious. Jung, too, may be skewing the relationship, seeing it as he does as one of virtual possession by God, but religion for him is still at base an encounter with God. Even if, for Jung, God seeks out adherents more than they seek out God, closeness to God is the aim of religion, just as it is for religionists.

Not only Freud and Jung but all other social scientists as well start with the religionist perspective – that is, with religion as religion. Social scientists start with the beliefs and practices aimed at effecting the ideal relationship to God. But unlike religionists, social scientists venture beyond that perspective. They want to know why adherents seek a relationship to God. They rely on scholars of religion to document the fact of the quest for God. But that quest becomes the phenomenon to be explained, not the explanation itself. The claim by religionists to possess their own sufficient explanation of religion thus fails.

The third defense of religious studies as an independent discipline is the appeal to other disciplines, especially to literary studies. It is argued that just as the study of literature is autonomous because of the irreducibly literary nature of literature, so the study of religion should be autonomous because of the irreducibly religious nature of religion. By the distinctively literary quality of literature is meant aspects of a work like genre, symbolism, plot, character, and point of view – all elements in the interpretation of a work of literature. By the distinctively religious character of religion is meant not only the interpretation of its meaning but also the determination of its origin and function. Still, the parallel to literary study is intended to argue that religious studies has the same claim to independence as literary studies.

Alas, the appeal fails. Literary critics do not merely declare that literature is literature but attempt to prove it – by showing that the interpretation of a literary work depends on the analysis of its literary aspects. By contrast, religionists simply declare that God is God and not a father or an archetype. That, once again, Freud and Jung and other social scientists do not deny that God is God but instead want to account for that distinctively religious side of religion is a point continually missed. To match their counterparts in literary studies, religionists would have to show that God cannot be accounted for psychologically. Instead, they tend to declare, not that psychologists or other social scientists dare not even try.

The religionist appeal to literature is not only vain but also ironic. For in recent decades literary studies has become the most contested of fields. New Criticism, which reigned supreme in the English-speaking world in the 1940s and 1950s, came closest to literary nonreductionism. But its heyday has long passed, and it has been succeeded by an array of reductionistic approaches – for example, feminist, black, gay and lesbian, and New Historicist brands of literary criticism, as they consider themselves to be. And long before them there existed Freudian, Jungian, and Marxist varieties of literary criticism, all of which continue to exist. It is not anti-literary outsiders but literary critics themselves who employ these approaches. Like their nonreductionistic fellow critics, they grant that the texts they scrutinize are manifestly literary. But unlike their nonreductionistic kin, they maintain that those texts are latently sociological, political, psychological, and historical. What for nonreductionists in literary studies is the end point of the study of literature is for reductionists – though this term is not used – the starting point. Reductionistic approaches to literature are intended to account for the irreducibly literary level, not to deny it, just as reductionistic approaches to religion are intended to account for the irreducibly religious level, not to deny it.

At the same time the parallel of religious studies to literary studies shows that the quest for autonomy is by no means confined to religious studies. Just as today literary critics such as Harold Bloom and Frank Kermode seek to defend the study of literature against its collapse into cultural studies and other fields, so, for example, the philosopher Arthur Danto seeks to argue against the collapse of art into philosophy. Decades ago the philosopher R. G. Collingwood argued that history is not to be collapsed into a natural science. Not only established disciplines but also new ones must defend their turf. At the turn of the last century Durkheim asserted the autonomy of sociology by differentiating it from psychology. Psychology asserted its independence by differentiating itself from philosophy.

For me, at least, religious studies does not require either a distinctive method or a distinctive explanation to be worthy of disciplinary status. I prefer to compare it with an area studies, albeit one covering a worldwide area! To me, religious studies is a subject matter, open to as many approaches as are prepared to study it. On the one hand none of the approaches is likely to exhaust the subject. On the other hand not all approaches are compatible with one another. What counts is that the subject matter – religion – be connected to the rest of human life – to culture, society, the mind, the economy – rather than separated from it by the siege-like defensiveness of religionists. For religionists, religion is what is left standing when everything else to which religion might be linked has been eliminated. For me, religion is best deciphered when it is connected to as much of the rest of human life as possible. Contrary to religionists, religion does not thereby lose its distinctiveness. Rather, it becomes a distinctive, irreducibly religious part of other domains of life.

The Companion

The twenty-four chapters in this Companion are divided into approaches and topics. There are nine approaches and fifteen topics. Other topics and perhaps even other approaches could have been added, but the twenty-four chosen surely cover much of the way that religion is currently studied.

The nine approaches cover eight disciplines: anthropology (Fiona Bowie), economics (Rodney Stark), literature (Stephen Prickett), phenomenology (Thomas Ryba), philosophy (Charles Taliaferro), psychology (Roderick Main), sociology (Steve Bruce), and theology (Ian Markham). The ninth approach is the comparative method (Paul Roscoe). The authors of the disciplinary approaches are professionals in those fields. They present the ways that their fellow anthropologists, economists, literary critics, and so on have analyzed religion. (Two exceptions need to be noted: Rodney Stark is by profession a sociologist, and Roderick Main is by profession a scholar of religion.) By no means do all or even any of the authors raise the issue of reductionism or worry about the collapse of religious studies into their disciplines. On the contrary, all seek to show what their disciplines have contributed to the understanding of the phenomenon of religion.

Two of the entries, on phenomenology of religion and on theology, deal with approaches that are by nature nonreductionistic. While Ryba traces the application of philosophical phenomenology to the study of religion, he shows that phenomenology of religion arose at least in part as a reaction to the reductionism of the social sciences. While Ian Markham presents the various cultural influences on theology, he shows how theology has incorporated them, not how they have incorporated theology. Still, neither Ryba nor Markham contends that the approach each presents should be immune to influences from other domains.

The fifteen topics vary in their origins. Most clearly hail from religious studies: "death and afterlife" (Douglas Davies), "fundamentalism" (Henry Munson), "heaven and hell" (Jeffrey Russell), "holy men/holy women" (Lawrence Cunningham), "magic" (Gustavo Benavides), "mysticism" (Jeffrey Kripal), "new religious movements" (Lorne Dawson), "pilgrimage" (Simon Coleman), "myth" (Robert Segal), "ritual" (Catherine Bell), and "secularization" (Steve Bruce). Other categories clearly come from elsewhere: "body" (Richard Roberts), "ethics" (Scott Davis), "modernity and postmodernity" (Colin Campbell), and "nationalism" (Mark Juergensmeyer). Some of the categories are old, and some of them are new – obviously, "new religious movements" and, if not "modernity," then "postmodernity." The concept of "secularization" arose in the late nineteenth century, as Steve Bruce shows. Mark Juergensmeyer explains that the notion of nationalism, which originally meant secular nationalism, arose only in reaction to the Enlightenment. Henry Munson notes that the term "fundamentalism" was coined only in 1920. Jeffrey Kripal observes that, as a category, "mysticism" arose only in the twentieth century. Catherine Bell notes that "ritual," while not a new term, came into its own only in the nineteenth century, when it was separated from religion. I myself contend that the status of "myth" was transformed when, in the twentieth century, it was likewise largely uncoupled from religion. Conversely, Gustavo Benavides shows in detail the inseparability of "magic" from "religion" – and, even more, vice versa.

Whether or not these categories derive from religious studies or are applied to it, all of them undergo change, as the contributors repeatedly demonstrate. Categories that come from outside religious studies are altered when applied to religion. Categories that come from within religious studies are altered when applied to different religions, periods, or places. For me, the malleability that characterizes the categories evinces their value rather than their limitations. The openness of the categories is part of the openness of the overall study of religion.

Part I

Approaches

— Chapter 1 —

Anthropology of Religion

Fiona Bowie

The study of religion has been central to anthropology since its inception. As an inclusive, comparative study of human societies, from their prehistoric origins to the present, anthropology has sought to describe, classify, and explain religious beliefs and practices. At the same time the term "religion" is elusive and problematic. While some early missionaries denied that the "savage" peoples they encountered had any religion at all, others saw religion everywhere. There has also been a tendency to label anything we do not understand in other cultures, past or present, as religious. The term often lacks even an approximate translation in non-Western languages, and scholars often fall back on the "I know it when I see it" line of argument.

Descriptions of the history of anthropology of religion commonly follow a chronological scheme that divides scholars and their views into broad theoretical categories, or "isms": evolutionism, functionalism, structural-functionalism, structuralism, poststructuralism, deconstructionism, feminism, postmodernism, and so on. While these schemes have their uses, they can also prove misleading. For example, the earlier ones set up an evolutionary framework that was then so often dismissed as a nineteenth-

century aberration. Yet while we today undoubtedly build on the achievements and seek to avoid the perceived mistakes of our forebears, we are
also following a circular or spiral road along which we repeatedly return
to the same points of orientation.

When it comes to religion, I am persuaded that we are often describing
different parts of the same elephant. When the psychologically oriented
theory of Bronislaw Malinowski, who believed that religion enables people
to cope with life's vicissitudes, is contrasted to that of his rigidly sociological contemporary Alfred Reginald Radcliffe-Brown, who saw religion as
part of the structure of society, helping to keep it in some kind of equilib-
rium, one scholar is examining the elephant's leg and the other its ear.
The contention that religion has both a psychological and a social aspect,
that it can both unsettle and stabilize, can be both illogical and rational,
can be both formalistic and spontaneous, and can be both devoid of personal significance and deeply meaningful, does not necessarily mean confusion or fundamental disagreement among scholars. Rather, it may
reflect the complexity of the phenomenon "religion."

My own approach is to move around the elephant, pointing out some
of its features on the way, with the aid of some of the scholars whose
works have helped us understand particular features of this creature we
choose to call "religion." I begin with a survey of definitions and the context in which they originate, and then consider some of those features of
religion that stir interest in a slightly different guise in each generation:
the origin of religious thinking; the nature of religious experience; and
the existence of different "mentalities," or forms of thought. These topics
reflect the engagement of scholars with the boundaries that separate
human beings from the rest of the animal kingdom (or so we assume);
with the differences between scientific, Enlightenment thinking and religious or "mystical" thinking; and at times with the divide between Western
and non-Western societies.

Definitions and Perspectives

Attempts to define religion inevitably reflect the theoretical orientation of
the writer. An early and influential attempt at definition was Edward
Burnett Tylor's "belief in spiritual beings." Tylor (1832–1917) held the
first professorship in anthropology in the world at the University of Oxford.
It was created for him in 1896. Although raised as a Quaker, Tylor saw
himself as a scientific rationalist. All religious ideas had developed, in his
view, out of a primitive belief in the animate nature of natural phenomena ("animism"). Traces of earlier beliefs and practices could be seen in
contemporary religions through a process of "survivals." For Tylor, all
religion is a mistaken attempt to make sense of the physical world in which

we live, as rational as science but simply erroneous. More recently, Robin Horton has concurred with Tylor's "intellectualist" view of religion, regarding African religions as explanatory attempts to link causes and events in much the same way as scientific practice, but based on inadequate or faulty information.

Malinowski (1884–1942), sometimes considered the founding father of fieldwork in anthropology through his pioneering work in the Trobriand Islands off Papua New Guinea in the early years of the twentieth century, focused on the individual, psychological function of religion. For Malinowski (1948), religion arose as a response to emotional stress. When technical knowledge proved insufficient, human beings turn to magic and religion in order to achieve their ends, and as a form of catharsis. By mimicking or anticipating the desired goal, rituals assert order in an unpredictable universe.

A third approach to religion is associated with scholars who take what is referred to as a symbolist view of society. The French sociologist Émile Durkheim (1858–1917), drawing on data from Australian aboriginal societies, saw society rather than the individual as the source of both profane, everyday norms and sacred ones. In *The Elementary Forms of the Religious Life* (1912), Durkheim describes religion not as an individual response to life crises but as the embodiment of society's highest goals and ideals. Religion acts as a cohesive social force and adds up to more than the sum of its parts. It is real in that it exists in people's minds and impels them to heed societal dictates, but what is perceived as external to society – God – is in fact a projection and reflection of society.

Clifford Geertz, a contemporary American anthropologist, has offered a definition of religion that combines Durkheim's symbolic functionalism – religion as a collective social act – with Max Weber's concern for meaning – religion as a system for ordering the world. Unlike Tylor, Geertz does not define religion in terms of belief in God but rather as a symbolic system, the meaning of which can be decoded. Religion for Geertz is: "(1) a system of symbols which acts to (2) establish powerful, pervasive, and long-lasting moods and motivations in men by (3) formulating conceptions of a general order of existence and (4) clothing these conceptions with such an aura of factuality that (5) the moods and motivations seem uniquely realistic" (Geertz 1973, p. 4).

Geertz's definition has been extensively criticized by Talal Asad, who sees Geertz's emphasis on the symbolic as too abstract, as too far removed from the social, historical, and political context that gives a symbol its meaning. Asad challenges the assumption that religion can even be studied as a cross-cultural category. He concludes that "there cannot be a universal definition of religion, not only because its constituent elements and relationships are historically specific, but because that definition is itself the historical product of discursive processes" (Asad 1993, p. 29).

Gavin Flood, an English scholar of religion, while "acknowledging that religion is impossible to define in any definitive sense" (Flood 1999, p. 47), argues that it is legitimate for scholars to construct definitions of religion to suit their different purposes. Without claiming universal applicability, Flood describes religions as "value-laden narratives and behaviours that bind people to their objectivities, to each other, and to non-empirical claims and beings" (Flood 1999, p. 47). For Flood, "religions are less about truth claims and more about identity, less about structures and more about texts, less about abstraction and more about tradition or that which is passed on" (Flood 1999, p. 47). By his definition, religion is more or less equivalent to a world view, and thereby allows a great deal to be included within the field of study.

The English anthropologist Mary Douglas, particularly in *Purity and Danger* (1966) and *Natural Symbols* (1970), has focused on the relationship between social form and religious expression. Her approach is more systematic than Geertz's. She looks for predictive patterns that link social structure (grid) and group pressures – or lack of these features – to a social cosmology that justifies the pattern of that society. For example, a society with clearly defined social boundaries and strong social pressures (high grid and high group) is likely to be formalistic, pietistic, and pro-active in policing its boundaries, and to have a category of rejects. As a practising Catholic, she might well have had the pre-Vatican II Roman Catholic Church in mind. At the other extreme a hermit would be low grid and low group, and would be free to develop a more individualistic, idiosyncratic, and inclusive cosmology.

 While many, if not most, anthropological approaches to religion are either agnostic or atheistic – wishing to study the beliefs and practices of others in emic, or indigenous, terms but without according them objective veracity – there are some scholars of religion who adopt a more explicitly anti-religious position in the name of science. Here the errors inherent in a religious mindset appear so egregious that to give them any credence at all in any society is seen as dangerously unscientific. James Lett, an American anthropologist of religion, for instance, rejects the "bracketing out" of questions of belief characteristic of a phenomenological approach, as exemplified in E. E. Evans-Pritchard's oft-quoted dictum that "there is no possibility of [the anthropologist] . . . *knowing* whether the spiritual beings of primitive religions or of any others have any existence or not, and since that is the case he cannot take the question into consideration" (Evans-Pritchard, quoted in Lett 1997, p. 17). For Lett, "Considerations of disciplinary integrity, public welfare, and human dignity demand that religious claims be subjected to anthropological evaluation. . . . [A]nthropologists have an intellectual and ethical obligation to investigate the truth or falsity of religious beliefs" (Lett 1997, pp. 104–5). Lett's scientific approach to the study of religion leads him to conclude that "we know that no religious belief is true because we know that all religious beliefs are either nonfalsifiable or falsified" (Lett 1997, p. 116). Scholars of religion have a duty to proclaim that fact. While Lett's sense of obligation to separate the study of religion from science represents a marginal position within the anthropology of religion, a generally materialist view of the universe and a nontranscendental, nonrevelatory view of religion is nevertheless common. The interpretive difficulties this view can pose for the ethnographer who has participated in the religion being depicted are discussed in the penultimate section of this chapter.

The Origins of Religion

When Charles Darwin (1809–82) published *The Descent of Man* in 1871, the Church was outraged. Darwin appeared to be claiming that human beings are descended from apes, leaving no room for God's direct creation of humans. Where was the order in creation, if a random interaction between the natural environment and biological organisms had led to the present variety of living creatures? While Darwin's ideas appeared as an affront to religious belief, the notion of social evolution, later known as Social Darwinism, was well established by the 1870s, and proved much less objectionable. The leading Social Darwinian was the British social and political thinker Herbert Spencer (1820–1903). He propounded the theory that all things, animate and inanimate, move from simpler to more differentiated complex forms, from homogeneity to heterogeneity. In *The Principles of Sociology* (1876) he developed his thesis of universal evolution, which included his notion of the "survival of the fittest." This view of human society was more flattering to the Victorian mind. After all, human beings represented the grand climax of evolution, and Great Britain, leader of the industrial revolution, was arguably the most complex society in the world and therefore stood at the peak of the evolutionary pyramid. Unlike some of his contemporaries, who could see little kinship between themselves and "rude and savage peoples," Spencer believed that all human beings, however simple their technology, are rational.

According to Spencer, religion arose from the observation that in dreams the self can leave the body. The human person therefore has a dual aspect, and after death the spirit or soul continues to appear to living descendants in dreams. The ghosts of remote ancestors or prominent figures eventually acquired the status of gods – an idea known as Euhemerism, after the Sicilian writer Euhemerus, c. 315 BCE. The widespread practice of pouring libations on the graves of ancestors and offering them food developed into sacrifices for the gods. Ancestor worship was therefore at the root of religion.

Tylor agreed with Spencer's social evolutionary views and in part with his notion of the dream origin of religion but preferred to emphasize the role of the soul in his account of religious origins. Hence "animism," from the Latin *anima*, or "soul." According to Tylor, our earliest ancestors believed that animate and inanimate objects as well as human beings have a soul, life force, or personality. The term "animism," while used by Tylor as synonymous with religion *per se*, is still used with different nuances for "primitive," "indigenous," or "tribal" religions.

Tylor formulated a concept of culture, still influential in anthropology, which defined it as a complex whole, including knowledge, belief, art, morals, law, custom, and any other acquired social habit, not least religion. Some cultural elements or traits were transmitted across time and space in a process known as diffusion. Where these traits commonly coincided, they were referred to as adhesions. Supposedly primitive traits found in a more "advanced" society were mere fossil-like "survivals" from an earlier evolutionary stage, and indeed provided proof of social evolution. Among such survivals Tylor listed many regional folk customs such as Midsummer bonfires and the Breton peasants' All Souls supper for the spirits of the dead. The oldest survivals were to be seen in language. The myths, stories, and sayings of today betray half-forgotten beliefs in phenomena such as the augury of birds, still visible in the saying "a little bird told me."

There was considerable debate in the nineteenth century between those who saw all or most human culture as resulting from the diffusion of ideas through population movement and those who believed that cultures evolved independently of one another. Those who espoused "independent invention" maintained that because all human beings have a similar psychological make-up, they tend to come up on their own with the same solutions to cultural problems.

James George Frazer (1854–1941), a Scottish classicist who became an anthropologist, was one of Britain's best-known scholars of religion. Drawing on classical sources and the reports of missionaries and explorers, Frazer compiled a multi-volume compendium in which he attempted to construct a universal theory of magic, religion, and society, published under the title *The Golden Bough* (1890, 1900, 1911–15). Frazer believed that magic preceded religion. As magic was increasingly perceived to be fallacious, people looked for other means of psychological support and concocted the illusion that spiritual beings could help them. When in turn people eventually realized that religion does not work, they turned to science. Both science and magic are based on the manipulation of natural laws, whereas religion is based on belief in personalities, or gods.

Evans-Pritchard eloquently described the intellectualist positions of scholars like Spencer, Tylor, and Frazer as the "if I were a horse" fallacy and described their tales on the origins of religion as "Just So" stories analogous to Rudyard Kipling's "How the leopard got its spots." Lacking any real evidence, Spencer, Tylor, and Frazer resorted to asking themselves what they would have done had they been "primitives." As Evans-Pritchard points out, if these scholars were correct, as civilization progressed, fallacious reasoning would die out, yet instead animistic and magical views of the world, ancestral cults, and beliefs in a Supreme Being all continue to exist, even in otherwise secular, scientific industrialized settings.

Malinowski, as one of the founders of the functionalist school of anthropology, paid less attention to evolutionary origins and the notion of survivals. Society was seen by him as a self-regulating system in which religion, economic organization, and kinship formed parts of an organic whole. For Malinowski, whatever exists today does so because it continues to serve a function. Were it a mere "survival," it would die out. Like Frazer, Malinowski (1948) distinguished magic from religion. A religious act aims at something beyond itself. Its object is not the performance of the rite. The rite is an act of worship, or propitiation, directed at a higher being, whose response to the rite cannot be wholly assumed or anticipated. Magic is a more technical procedure and is an end in itself. It is believed to be effective if performed correctly. A curse will strike its victim if the right words are uttered and the right actions performed.

In actuality, it is difficult to distinguish religious ritual from magical actions. While the division between religion and magic proposed by Malinowski may hold good in some circumstances, in the majority of occasions religious and magical elements appear intertwined, and the motivations of the participants similarly mixed. A mortuary ritual, for instance, is intended to release the soul and to prevent its return to haunt the living. By performing the banishing ritual correctly, survivors ensure that the soul will continue its journey to the other life. The same ritual can be taken either as a magical act, as an efficacious action in itself, or as a religious ceremony, in which a higher being is invoked to spur or receive the departing spirit and to comfort the living.

As different as magic and religion are, according to Malinowski they serve the same psychological function: the alleviation of anxiety in the face of life's uncertainties. But as Evans-Pritchard observed, while emotions, desires, and impulses undoubtedly play a part in religion, it is not the case that the performance of a religious or magical act automatically produces the psychological effects that Malinowski supposes. We really have here another example of the "if I were a horse" argument: "If we were to perform rites such as primitives do, we suppose that we would be in a state of emotional turmoil, for otherwise our reason would tell us that the rites are objectively useless" (Evans-Pritchard 1965, p. 43).

Anthropology in North America followed a rather different course from that in Europe, drawing on elements of both continental and British scholarship but with a specific emphasis on the notion of culture. A key figure was the German-born Franz Boas (1858–1942), who emigrated to the United States and there developed a school of anthropology that stressed cultural differences. His historical particularism, as it is sometimes known, combined Durkheim's emphasis on the social with Malinowski's stress on individual psychology. Both material culture and personality define a characteristic cultural style unique to each society. Boas was not particularly interested in the social functioning of institutions, which developed into a major theme of British social anthropology under Radcliffe-Brown in the United Kingdom. Like Durkheim, Boas had an interest in totemic systems and in the way in which symbols linked religious activities with other aspects of social life.

Alfred Reginald Radcliffe-Brown (1881–1955) was one of the first British social anthropologists to engage in fieldwork. At Cambridge University, Radcliffe-Brown studied psychology under W. H. R. Rivers (1864–1922) who had taken part in the Torres Straits Expedition of 1898 with another founding figure of Cambridge anthropology, Alfred C. Haddon. From 1906 to 1908 Radcliffe-Brown carried out research in the Andaman Islands in the Bay of Bengal. The resulting monograph, *The Andaman Islanders* (1922), is primarily an account of Andamanese religious beliefs and ceremonies. It represents one of the first fieldwork monographs in the anthropology of religion. The Andamanese were "tribal" hunter-gatherers who had remained relatively isolated until a penal settlement was established on South Andaman Island in 1858. They were therefore held up as representatives of "racial purity" and their society seen as a kind of living fossil that could reveal something about the origins of religion. Radcliffe-Brown asserted that the Andaman Islanders' main supernatural beings were spirits of the dead, which were associated with the sky, forest, and sea, and nature spirits, which were personifications of natural phenomena. He applied a Durkheimian analysis to his Andaman material, looking for correlations between Andamanese religion and social structure. Although usually referred to as a functionalist because of his interest in the ways in which institutions present an organic picture of society, Radcliffe-Brown also anticipated the kind of structural analysis pioneered by Claude Lévi-Strauss. He divided Andamanese cosmology into a tripartite schema: sea/water, forest/land, and sky/trees, with spiritual agencies, dietary restrictions, ceremonies, subsistence activities, flora, and fauna all corresponding to one of these three categories.

Arthur Maurice Hocart (1883–1939), educated at Oxford, carried out extensive fieldwork in the South Seas. He adopted Boas' detailed fieldwork methods, while continuing to hold a basically evolutionary perspective. He was not interested in finding the origin of religion, which he held to be an impossible task, although he did concern himself with the origins of monotheism. He rejected Malinowski's individual psychological approach, favoring Durkheim's view of sociological religion. According to Hocart, "The facts are that our earliest records show us man worshipping gods, and their earthly representatives – namely kings" (Hocart 1952, p. 67). This view led him to a rather contemporary conclusion, one developed by Maurice Bloch in his work on Madagascar, that "religion and politics are inseparable, and it is vain to try to divorce them. . . . Monarchists must necessarily uphold the Church and ardent believers in one God will help build up large nations. The belief in a Supreme God or a Single God is no mere philosophical speculation; it is a great practical idea" (Hocart 1952, p. 76).

Claude Lévi-Strauss (1908–) was born in Belgium but has spent most of his working life in France. He is one of the founders of structuralism, an intellectual movement derived from linguistic theory that focuses on the structures of societies, texts, languages, and cultural life. The relations among elements in the present are stressed, at the expense of historical change. The solution to the origins of religion and society proposed by Lévi-Strauss is totally different from any historical explanation. Lévi-Strauss has been unswerving in his search for the universal structures of human thought and social life. Taking his cue from structural linguistics, in particular the work of Noam Chomsky and Ferdinand de Saussure, together with the Russian formalists such as Vladimir Propp, Lévi-Strauss has sought to decipher a grammar of the mind. He proposes a kind of universal psychology with a genetic base, which gives rise to social structures. Just as there are limits to linguistic variation, so there are certain basic innate patterns of culture based on a series of binary oppositions. Thus all societies distinguish between the raw and the cooked, the raw standing for both nature and women and the cooked standing for both culture and men. Myths reveal common story lines that can be used to understand the limited number of ways in which human beings interpret the world.

While structural theory was popular in Britain and America for a period in the 1960s and 1970s, its influence within English-speaking social and cultural anthropology has been less marked than that of the Durkheimian symbolist approach. As with the earlier search for universals, the innate structures proposed by Lévi-Strauss remain speculative. As with Frazer, there is a danger of simply amassing data that repeat an argument without actually strengthening it. For Lévi-Strauss, individual experience and emotions such as love, hate, fear, and desire are subsidiary to the basic underlying structures that give rise to society, and those structures are innate. Many critics have in the end found that this approach leaves too many important questions unanswered. We may unravel the structures of the mind and of society, but do we know what it is to live and feel as a human being? If history and agency take a back seat, can we still see ourselves as self-determining individuals, and can we grasp the complexity of interactions between humans and their world?

The search for origins has largely fallen out of favor in anthropology, which in its social and cultural forms has become increasingly the study of human beings in their local context. There are exceptions to this rule. In his recent work *Religion Explained: The Evolutionary Origins of Religious Thought* (2001) Pascal Boyer looks to cognitive psychology to provide a theory of religion, which is seen to derive from mental templates that are in turn the result of an evolutionary process which favors certain forms of cultural transmission over others:

Some concepts happen to connect with inference systems in the brain in a way that makes recall and communication very easy. Some concepts happen to trigger our emotional programs in particular ways. Some concepts happen to connect to our social mind. Some of them are represented in such a way that they soon become plausible and direct behaviour. The ones that do *all* this are the religious ones we actually observe in human societies. They are most successful because they combine features relevant to a variety of mental systems. (Boyer 2001, p. 50)

In approaching the question of origins ontologically rather than temporally, Boyer can be seen as a successor of Noam Chomsky, with his search for a universal grammar in the structure of the human mind. For Boyer, it is our biology that holds the answer to the question of the origin of religion. Religion is hard-wired into our brains and is reproduced in newborns as they are socialized into language and culture.

Thomas Csordas, in an article entitled "Asymptote of the Ineffable: Embodiment, Alterity and the Theory of Religion" (2004), presents an argument that shares certain features with that of Boyer. It too eschews lengthy discussion of what we mean by religion or a focus on its particular manifestations, in order to ask more fundamental questions. Both the phenomenological, existential approach favored by Csordas and the psychological one proposed by Boyer reject historical explanations of religion. For them, religion can never be replaced by science, as Marx or Malinowski might have imagined, or explained away as an epiphenomenon of power and privilege, pace Michel Foucault. Csordas' elegant and simple explanation for the origin of religion is that it is based on a fundamental embodied alterity – the "phenomenological kernel of religion" (Csordas 2004, p. 3) – and that "insofar as alterity is part of the structure of being-in-the-world – an elementary structure of existence – religion is inevitable, perhaps even necessary" (Csordas 2004, p. 3). The self, following Maurice Merleau-Ponty, is both subject and object. It contains "presences" that are both hidden from us and part of us. We can never wholly know ourselves or others. The asymptote of the essay title – the lines that never quite meet – represent this alterity. The desire for oneness or unity can never be consciously achieved. As we approach others or ourselves, we become strangers. For Csordas, embodied otherness replaces Roy Rappaport's (1995) formulation of the origin of religion in the "fall from grace" that accompanied the emergence of language, creating "an originary rupture, a profound alterity" (Rappaport, quoted in Csordas 2004, p. 5) and a profound alienation of parts of the psyche from one another.

While espousing what is today a minority voice within anthropology, with their interest in a search for the origins of religion, Csordas, Rappaport, and Boyer represent at the same time a conventional materialism within the anthropological study of religion. There is a "policing" of the boundaries between religion and theology and of the kind of religion deemed to be a suitable object of anthropological attention. Simon Coleman found that he had to justify his decision to study evangelical Christians in Sweden to colleagues, who assumed that he "must be a sympathiser of the group when [he] didn't condemn it," which rather suggests that "some cultures and belief systems are . . . more acceptable to the anthropological community than others" (Bowie 2003, p. 140). The gibe or fear that one's colleagues might "go native" and thereby lose the critical outsider's perspective, which is deemed identical with a social scientific approach to religion, is something with which all field-working ethnographers are familiar.

Religious Experience

E. E. Evans-Pritchard (1902–73), Professor of Anthropology at Oxford from 1946 to 1970, is rightly remembered for his studies of the Azande peoples of Central Africa, with whom he lived between 1926 and 1930. Throughout his work he presents Zande oracles, magic, and witchcraft as a logical, coherent set of beliefs and practices. Evans-Pritchard came to regard the consulting of an oracle before undertaking an action as a sensible way of ordering one's affairs – no better or worse than any other. He was happy to enter into discussions of rationality with his Zande informants, and never patronized them by assuming that they were incapable of making sound judgments or defending their beliefs and practices. An example was his encounter with witchcraft. According to the Azande, moving lights emanate from the body of the sleeping witch as the activated witchcraft substance stalks its prey. Evans-Pritchard writes:

> I have only once seen witchcraft on its path. I had been sitting late in my hut writing notes. About midnight, before retiring, I took a spear and went for my usual nocturnal stroll. I was walking in the garden at the back of my hut, amongst banana trees, when I noticed a bright light passing at the back of my servants' huts towards the homestead of a man called Tupoi. As this seemed worth investigation I followed its passage until a grass screen obscured the view. I ran quickly through my hut to the other side in order to see where the light was going to but did not regain sight of it. I know that only one man, a member of my household, had a lamp that might have given off so bright a light, but next morning he told me that what I had seen was witchcraft. Shortly afterwards, on the same morning, an old relative of Tupoi and an inmate of his homestead died. This event fully explained the light I had seen. I never discovered its real origin, which was possibly a handful of grass lit by someone on his way to defecate, but the coincidence of the direction along which the light moved and the subsequent death accorded well with Zande ideas. (Evans-Pritchard 1976, p. 11)

In reflecting afterwards on the event, Evans-Pritchard sought to reassert his own Western, scientific outlook. The alternative would have been to accept an Azande view of the world based on the belief that human beings can be witches and can project a visible witchcraft substance which has to the power to kill other human beings. While not wishing to go this far, Evans-Pritchard did not simply dismiss the world view of his Zande informants as primitive or inferior. He allowed himself to be drawn into its logic and to reason from within Zande categories of thought.

This movement from skepticism to shared experience with those in the culture studied, and then back to some external point of reference, is common among anthropologists working on religious themes. Tanya Luhrmann (1989), studying urban witchcraft in London in the 1980s, was similarly drawn into the worlds of her informants, yet without ultimately accepting their underlying cosmology. Luhrmann describes humor and play as attitudes basic to witchcraft. In an evocative description of a "maypole" ritual performed by her coven in an urban room, she shows how humor and play can awaken a sense of wonder in those participating. A cord attached to the ceiling served as a maypole, and the participants used strings of colored yarn instead of ribbons. The dancers' intention was to weave into the "maypole" those things that they wished to weave into their lives. Apparently, an even number of participants is needed to wind a maypole successfully, but as there were eleven persons present, the coven chose to disregard this requirement rather than to leave anybody out:

> The result, to begin with, was chaos and confusion. Everyone was laughing as we dodged in and out, creating a tangled knot of yarn. It was scarcely a scene of mystical power; a ritual magician would have blanched pale and turned in his wand on the spot. But an odd thing began to happen as we continued. The laughter began to build a strange atmosphere, as if ordinary reality was fading away. Nothing existed but the interplay of colored cords and moving bodies. The smiles on faces that flashed in and out of sight began to resemble the secret smiles of archaic Greek statues, hinting at the highest and most humorous of Mysteries. We began to sing; we moved in rhythm and a pattern evolved in the dance – nothing that could ever be mapped or plotted rationally; it was a pattern with an extra element that always and inevitably would defy explanation. The snarl of yarn resolved itself into an intricately woven cord. The song became a chant; the room glowed, and the cord pulsed with power like a live thing, an umbilicus linking us to all that is within and beyond. At last the chant peaked and died; we dropped into trance. When we awoke, all together, at the same moment, we faced each other with wonder. (Luhrmann 1989, pp. 334–5)

Some anthropologists have gone further, not only participating in the rituals of others and sharing the emotions that arise but outrightly accepting the cosmological stance of informants. Paul Stoller studied as a "sorcerer's apprentice" among the Songhay of Niger in West Africa and recorded that "The Songhay world challenged the basic premises of my scientific training. Living in Songhay forced me to confront the limitations of the Western philosophical tradition. My seventeen-year association with Songhay reflects the slow evolution of my thought, a thought profoundly influenced by Songhay categories and Songhay wisdom" (Stoller and Olkes 1989, p. 227). Stoller, unlike so many others who have studied religion or ritual in other cultures, did not manage, or perhaps wish, to shrug off a Songhay world view on his return to the familiarity of American culture. Perhaps fear had fundamentally reshaped his understanding of reality, for he fled Niger when he believed himself under attack by another sorcerer.

For Edith Turner, participation in a healing ritual among the Ndembu of Zambia, in which she had been invited by a healer called Singleton to act as one of the "doctors," was equally an experience of transformation, although an altogether happier one. The ritual, known as Ihamba, involved the removal of a deceased hunter's tooth from the back of a sick woman. Turner had witnessed the Ihamba before, earlier on the same visit in 1985, and also with her late husband, anthropologist Victor Turner, when they had lived with the Ndembu in the 1950s. But she had not previously been a central participant in the ritual. The saying of "words" to clear the air was an important prelude to what happens in this kind of healing, in which the participation of relatives and significant community members is key. Having brought various grievances, including her own, into the open, Turner writes:

> I felt the spiritual motion, a tangible feeling of breakthrough going through the whole group. . . . Suddenly Meru [the patient] raised her arm, stretched it in liberation, and I *saw* with my own eyes a giant thing emerging out of the flesh on her back. This thing was a large gray blob about six inches across, a deep gray opaque thing emerging as a sphere. I was amazed – delighted. I still laugh with the realization of having seen it, the ihamba, and so big! We were all just one in triumph. The gray thing was actually out there, visible, and you could see Singleton's hands working and scrabbling on the back – and then the thing was there no more. Singleton had it in his pouch, pressing it in with his other hand as well. The receiving hand was ready; he transferred whatever it was into the can and capped the castor oil leaf and bark lid over it. It was done. (Turner 1992, p. 149)

I suspect that the divide among scholars of religion is not primarily between those who are happy to go along with fieldwork experience without seeking to analyze it and those who participate in it while retaining firmly in mind the difference between a "primitive," "mystical" mentality and a scientific, rationalistic one. The main distinction is probably between those who have experienced something extraordinary, moving, or profound that makes sense within the context of the people performing the ritual – even if that something is at odds with the ethnographer's own rational understanding – and those who have simply not had such an experience. There are, after all, skeptics and believers within all societies, so why not among anthropologists, too? Even Tibet's Dalai Lama is able to leave open a window of doubt concerning his own reincarnated status, however central this belief may be to his own identity and to the faith of the Tibetan people. Anthropology is distinguished by its method, and since the days of Baldwin Spencer and Frank Gillen's participation in aboriginal ceremonies in Queensland at the end of the nineteenth century, and of Malinowski's espousal of participant observation in the Trobriands a few decades later, ethnographers have understood that surveys, statistics, interviews, and the collection of material objects cannot yield the same interpretive depth as that which comes from sharing in the lives of those being observed.

Edith Turner is no less concerned than any other Western-trained observer with the status of the tooth that Singleton later produced from the can in which the ihamba spirit was imprisoned. But like the Kwakiutl shaman Quesalid, who started off as a skeptic set on disclosing the trickery involved in shamanic healing but ended up becoming a great healer, Turner came to understand the difference between the outer appearance of objects and their essence, material or immaterial. There is a Buddhist story concerning a pilgrim who promised to bring his elderly Tibetan mother a relic of the Buddha. On his return from India, he realized that he had not fulfilled his promise. He picked up a dog's tooth from beside the road and presented it to his mother as a tooth of the Buddha. The old woman made a shrine and prayed in front of the "relic" with great devotion. After a while the pilgrim was amazed to see a yellow glow emanating from the shrine. The tooth had taken on an aura of sacrality. Similarly, Quesalid found that while he might have concealed objects in his mouth to "suck out" of patients, his healing was still effective. Having seen the gray blob come out of Meru, Edith Turner was convinced of the reality of the ihamba spirit, and she was able to appreciate the distinction made by many peoples the world over between the inner spirit form and the house or casing which represents and contains it. Concealing an object in the mouth or producing a tooth is thus not "trickery" but the giving of outward, visible expression to the normally invisible, but nevertheless palpable, action of the spirits. Missionaries and anthropologists who used to assert that Africans mistook their "fetishes" for animate objects failed to understand that a consecrated statue becomes a powerful object not because it is worshiped as a god (or devil) but because it has the power to attract and contain spiritual forces. According to Christian Eucharistic theology, the elements of bread and wine are ritually transformed into the body and blood of Jesus Christ in a "hypostatic union," while retaining their outward appearance. The so-called fetishes and sacred objects of African peoples are more akin to the tabernacle that contains the god than to the god itself.

In general, the gap between Western and non-Western conceptions of the instances of spiritual forces in the material world is much narrower than many assume. Pilgrimage cults that gather around weeping or moving plaster statues of the Virgin Mary in contemporary Irish Catholicism, for instance, attest to not dissimilar beliefs in the embodied immanence of the supernatural. Like shamans, stigmatists use their body as an inscription or a container of divine presence.

Modes of Thought

Anthropologists of religion have frequently returned to the question of modes of thought. When discussing religious experience, for instance, an anthropologist is often asking implicitly whether "the other" is fundamentally like "us." Is there a conceptual dividing line between pre-scientific and scientific thinking? If there are different mentalities, or ways of thinking, are they present in each one of us, in all societies, or in different measure in different societies? When asked whether he accepted Zande ideas of witchcraft, Evans-Pritchard gave the kind of "yes and no" answer that must be familiar to many field anthropologists:

> In my own culture, in the climate of thought I was born into and brought up in and have been conditioned by, I rejected, and reject, Zande notions of witchcraft. In their culture, in the set of ideas I then lived in, I accepted them; in a kind of way I believed them. . . . If one must act as though one believed, one ends in believing, or half-believing as one acts. (Evans-Pritchard 1976, p. 244)

One scholar who spent his life pondering the question of mentalities was the philosopher Lucien Lévy-Bruhl (1857–1939). Like his French contemporary Durkheim, Lévy-Bruhl thought that religion was socially based, but he increasingly distanced himself from the Durkheimian school. He stressed the need to see each culture as a whole in order to uncover the relationships and assumptions that govern it. He put forward, but later modified, the notion that primitive and modern cultures exhibit distinct kinds of mentalities, one "mystical" and pre-logical, the other objective and logical.

Nineteenth-century evolutionary theorists such as Spencer, Tylor, and Frazer shared three assumptions: (1) the idea of progress, (2) an unquestioned faith in the efficacy of the comparative method, and (3) the notion of a "psychic unity" among all peoples. If left on their own, all societies would pass through the same stages of social evolution. Eventually, all societies would reach the same peak of rational, civilized thought and behavior that characterized Victorian Britain.

Lévy-Bruhl challenged the third of these assumptions. He concluded that the formal rules of logic that governed rational thought do not actually apply in many simpler societies. According to Lévy-Bruhl, the West has an intellectual tradition based on the rigorous testing and analysis of hypotheses, so that Westerners are logically oriented and tend to look for natural explanations of events. But the "collective representations" of "primitive" peoples tend to be "mystical." In *How Natives Think* (1910) Lévy-Bruhl stated that "the reality surrounding the primitives is itself mystical. Not a single being or object or natural phenomenon in their collective representations is what it appears to be to our minds" (Lévy-Bruhl 1985, p. 38). He concluded that differences in ways of thought preclude the existence of a psychic unity of human beings and that in simple societies Aristotelian logic, such as the law of noncontradiction, simply does not apply.

Lévy-Bruhl's ideas were subjected to a storm of criticism. He was a philosopher with a background in psychology rather than a fieldwork anthropologist, and many of his data were shown to be inadequate. He was also understood to be saying that "primitive" peoples are not able to make objective causal connections between events. His critics maintained that any rigid line drawn between "primitives" and "us" is indefensible. In fact, Lévy-Bruhl never denied that all people everywhere use logical thought in relation to practical and technical matters. He claimed only that the pre-logical interpretation of an event will always predominate in a "primitive mentality." Against Lévy-Bruhl, it was argued that the notion of faith in a Western context similarly depends upon believing something that cannot be proved and similarly invokes the language of paradox and mystery.

In his search for a comparative understanding of "mentalities," Lévy-Bruhl sought to challenge both the intellectualist school of Tylor and Frazer, who assumed that mental processes are everywhere the same, and the cultural relativists like Franz Boas, who rejected any attempt to make generalizations about peoples. Lévy-Bruhl rejected Malinowski's search for individual, psychological explanations of human behavior, preferring the collectivist approach of Durkheim. For Lévy-Bruhl, "primitives" perceive and conceive the world as they do because their perceptions and in turn conceptions are shaped by their "collective representations" – a concept that he took from Durkheim.

Lévy-Bruhl came to accept that the division he had sought to make between different types of thinking in different types of societies was too rigid, and by the 1930s he no longer sought to defend this position. In his *Carnets*, or *Notebooks*, he proposed:

let us entirely give up explaining participation by something peculiar to the human mind, either constitutional (in its structure and function) or acquired (mental customs). In other words, let us expressly rectify what I believed correct in 1910: there is not a primitive mentality distinguishable from the other by *two* characteristics which are peculiar to it (mystical and prelogical). There is a mystical mentality which is more marked and more easily observable among primitive peoples than in our own societies, but it is present in every human mind. (Lévy-Bruhl 1975, pp. 100–1)

Lévy-Bruhl's conclusion – that there are different kinds of thinking, "logical" and "mystical," in all societies, even if found in different degrees – has continued to engage the attention of anthropologists interested in cognition.

Byron Good (1994), an American medical anthropologist, is among those who have recently revisited the "mentalities debate." For Lévy-Bruhl, religion belongs to pre-logical thinking, characterized as it is by the experience of non-material realities, whereas medicine would be classified as part of logical thinking, as a response to the empirical world. For Good, by contrast, there is a close relationship between science, including medicine, and religious fundamentalism. He seeks to collapse the distinction between the realm of the sacred (religion) and the realm of the profane (science). The relationship between them turns in part on our concept of "belief":

For fundamentalist Christians, salvation is often seen to follow from belief, and mission work is conceived as an effort to convince the natives to give up false beliefs and take on a set of beliefs that will produce a new life and ultimate salvation. Ironically, quite a-religious scientists and policy makers see a similar benefit from correct belief. Educate the public about the hazards of drug use, our current Enlightenment theory goes. . . . [G]et them to believe in the right thing and the problem will be licked. Educate the patient, medical journals advise clinicians, and solve the problems of noncompliance that plague the treatment of chronic disease. . . . [G]et people to believe the right thing and our public health problems will be solved. Salvation from drugs and from preventable illness will follow from correct belief. (Good 1994, p. 7)

Evans-Pritchard distinguished between what Azande "believe," as in "Azande believe that some Azande are witches," and what they "know," or their medical knowledge of diseases and healing. Thus Evans-Pritchard organized his monograph on Zande witchcraft "around a distinction between those ideas that accord with objective reality . . . and those that do not; the language of knowledge is used to describe the former, the language of belief the latter" (Good 1994, p. 13). Good turns to the Canadian

scholar of religion Wilfred Cantwell Smith in order to explore the etymology of the term "belief," concluding that our understanding of the term
is relatively recent. In Old English "to believe" meant to "hold dear." For
Chaucer, it was "to pledge loyalty." Belief in God was not therefore a claim
to hold to something that could not be proved but a promise to live one's
life in the service of God, like a bondsman to his lord. Only by the end of
the seventeenth century did "belief" indicate a choice between possible
explanations or propositions, so that "I believe in God" implied a choice
between believing that God exists and claiming that God is merely a
human creation. As Evans-Pritchard indicated, for the Azande to "believe"
in witchcraft was a very different proposition than it was for him. As in
pre-Enlightenment Europe, so for the Azande, there was a single, hegemonic world view. The possibility that witches might not exist was not
part of Zande "collective representations," to use Lévy-Bruhl's phrase,
which itself comes from Durkheim. Both medical scientists and fundamentalist Christians, according to Good, use "belief" in this contemporary
sense of choosing between options, one true and one false. The notion of
"correct belief" is central, implying as it does the choice between a right
and a wrong way of seeing the world.

The concept of belief as currently understood and used in English may
be difficult or impossible to translate into other languages. Mary Steedly
(1993), an American anthropologist who has worked among the
Karobatak in Sumatra, reported that her hosts kept posing a question that
she interpreted as "Do you believe in spirits?" Steedly did not want to say
"no," to avoid damaging her relations with the people, but felt unable to
lie by answering "yes." Only after some months did she realize the
Karobatak were not asking her "Do you believe spirits exist?" but "Do you
trust the spirits?" They wanted to know whether she maintained a relationship with them. Medieval Christians who asserted belief in God did not
proclaim God's existence, which was presupposed, but their loyalty to God.
The key difference between both Evans-Pritchard and Mary Steedly as
moderns on the one hand and the Azande, Karobatak, and medieval
European Christians on the other is the presence of alternative views of
the world.

Good contrasts the biomedical world view, limited but self-confident, to
the much more tentative and questioning approach of anthropology,
referring to Clifford Geertz's description of the Western "salvational
belief in the powers of science" (Geertz 1988, p. 146). However untried,
untested, or illogical a medical procedure or scientific hypothesis may
be, there is considerable investment in *believing* that it is rational and
wholly different from the claims of religion and thought worlds of "primitive" peoples. Most anthropologists would agree with Lévy-Bruhl's later
conclusions, that there are different ways of thinking common to all
peoples. There is a scientific way of thinking that tests hypotheses against
everyday reality and experience, essential to technical advances, and a

more "mystical" or nonlogical mode of thought that works through metaphor and analogy to make sense of the complexity of human existence. In practice, these may not be distinguishable from one another, or may both come into play in the same situation. Philosophers and theologians, for instance, have argued for the rationality of belief in God, and supposedly irrational beliefs such as witchcraft may appear to be supported by empirical evidence.

Mary Douglas is a strong advocate of the view that there is a psychic unity to human beings. For her, both primitive rituals and secular rites serve as focusing mechanisms or mnemonics. Obsessively packing and repacking a suitcase before a holiday will not make the weekend come any sooner but can help the traveler focus on the pending departure. In the same way a Dinka herdsman who knots a bundle of grass at the wayside as he hurries home to supper does not expect the action alone to get him home in time. The knotted grass helps focus his mind, and he redoubles his efforts to be home on time (see Douglas 1966, pp. 63–4). In both of these examples what might seem to be irrational activities in fact have a practical, rational effect – once that effect is correctly identified. To draw too tight a distinction between modes of thought is to misunderstand human behavior. For Douglas, as for Good, "The right basis for comparison is to insist on the unity of human experience and at the same time to insist on its variety, on the differences which make comparison worth while" (Douglas 1966, p. 77). It is the greater the choices available to us that really distinguish modern from simpler societies.

There are other ways of distinguishing modes of thought besides Lévy-Bruhl's. According to Douglas, there is a difference between personalized and impersonal thinking. Some cosmologies, including those of China as well as of Sub-Saharan Africa, relate the universe directly to human behavior. Geomancy and *feng shwe*, for instance, work on the assumption that the earth and human fortune are intimately related to each other. We should not forget the impact of the Enlightenment on Western thought, including European Christianity. As the New Zealand anthropologist Paul Gifford states:

> The supernaturalistic has largely disappeared (we will use this term to distinguish between the realm of demons, spirits, witches and so on from the supernatural – God, heaven, prayer, the resurrection of Christ, sacraments – which has largely persisted in the Western churches). . . . Reality is generally not experienced in terms of witches, demons and personalised spiritual powers, and Christianity has changed to take account of this. . . . In Africa most Christians operate from a background little affected by the European Enlightenment; for most Africans, witchcraft, spirits and ancestors, spells and charms are primary and immediate and natural categories of interpretation. . . . Most Africans have an "enchanted" worldview. (Gifford 1998, pp. 327–8)

In the mainstream Christian churches in Africa, preachers publicly espouse Enlightenment thinking, while most lay persons hold to a much more "traditional," supernaturalistic view of the world, one common in Europe prior to the Enlightenment. The fastest-growing churches in Africa, as in Latin America, are those that preach a prosperity Gospel: if you believe (and give or "seed" money to the church), you will be blessed with health and wealth. These newer Pentecostal churches reject traditional culture yet also have a traditional vision of reality with a discourse between God and the Devil, with miraculous interventions, and with an instrumental understanding of religion. Prosperity Gospel churches are also expanding in the West, often controlling considerable financial resources and making use of the latest media and Internet technology to spread their message. We are reminded of Clifford Geertz's (1988) assertion that there are local ways of being global. Thus the values of Western commercial market economies, supernaturalism, and a rather mechanical, materialistic view of religion (give money to the Church and you will automatically receive the "hundredfold" in material blessings) readily adapt themselves to many different local contexts.

The English historian Robin Horton (1994) has long contrasted the "closed" nature of African traditional thought, in which there is only one belief system available, to the "open" world view of modern Europe and America, where there are alternative belief systems. We have already seen that Tylor, Malinowski, and others were wrong to assume that science would eventually put paid to both magic and religion. In actuality, science merely provides one more element, albeit an immensely powerful and significant one, in the cosmological choices available. It is clear that not everyone can cope with the developing awareness of alternatives, which erode certainties and absolute values. According to Horton:

> These people still retain the old sense of the absolute validity of their belief-systems, with all the attendant anxieties about threats to them. For these people, the confrontation is still a threat of chaos of the most horrific kind – a threat which demands the most dramatic measures. They respond in one of two ways: either by trying to blot out those responsible for the confrontation, often down to the last unborn child; or by trying to convert them to their own beliefs through fanatical missionary activity. . . . Some adjust their fears by developing an inordinate faith in progress towards a future in which "the Truth" will be finally known. But others long nostalgically for the fixed, unquestionable beliefs of the "closed" culture. They call for authoritarian establishment and control of dogma, and for the persecution of those who have managed to be at ease in a world of ever-shifting ideas. Clearly, the "open" predicament is a precarious, fragile thing. (Horton 1994, pp. 256–7)

We can probably all think of examples of both kinds of reactions, from blind faith in science and progress to the restrictive Islam of Afghanistan's

Pentacostalism and "prosperity gospel"

Taliban and Christian fundamentalists convinced that they alone are "saved." The competing marketplace of ideas that constitutes modernity is the home less of rational, scientific thought than of a jumble of assorted ideas, some compatible, others contradictory. Scientific rationality is just one of the options. Where the developed world differs from that of indigenous peoples is in its proselytization. Traditional peoples rarely try to convince others of the rightness of their world view. It is self-evident. Once choice is introduced, so is uncertainty. Being social animals, we react to doubt by attempting to recruit others to our side, finding security in numbers or, failing that, drawing ever tighter boundaries that exclude the outside world with its "wrong" way of seeing. It is also possible, however, for different world views to coexist, within a society or even within an single individual. One can be both a believer and a scientist, or both an academically trained anthropologist and an initiated witch. How these apparently incompatible world views are reconciled depends on the nature of the society in question and of the individual – the individual's experiences, intellectual predilections, and personality. For the field-working ethnographer, the issue of experience and the interpretation of that experience cannot be ignored. What almost all the varied contributions of anthropologists to the study of religion share are a depth and a complexity that arise from embodied knowledge and a dialogical relationship with the subject of study. Religion is not just "out there" but simultaneously observed and experienced from within.

Bibliography

Asad, Talal. *Genealogies of Religion: Discipline and Reasons of Power in Christianity and Islam*. Baltimore, MD: Johns Hopkins University Press, 1993.

Bowie, Fiona. *The Anthropology of Religion*. Oxford: Blackwell, 2000.

Bowie, Fiona. "Belief or Experience: The Anthropologist's Dilemma," in *Contemporary Conceptions of God: Interdisciplinary Essays*, ed. Cyril G. Williams. Lewiston, ME: Edwin Mellen, 2003, pp. 135–60.

Boyer, Pascal. *Religion Explained: The Evolutionary Origins of Religious Thought*. New York: Basic Books, 2001.

Csordas, Thomas. "Asymptote of the Ineffable: Embodiment, Alterity, and the Theory of Religion," *Current Anthropology* 42 (2004): 1–23.

Douglas, Mary. *Purity and Danger*. London: Routledge and Kegan Paul, 1966.

Douglas, Mary. *Natural Symbols*, 1st edn. Harmondsworth: Penguin, 1970.

Durkheim, Emile. *The Elementary Forms of the Religious Life* [1912], tr. Joseph Ward Swain. London: Allen and Unwin, 1915.

Evans-Pritchard, E. E. *Theories of Primitive Religion*. Oxford: Oxford University Press, 1965.

Evans-Pritchard, E. E. *Witchcraft, Oracles and Magic among the Azande* [1937]. Abridged edn, ed. Eva Gillies. Oxford: Clarendon Press, 1976.

Flood, Gavin. *Beyond Phenomenology: Rethinking the Study of Religion*. London: Cassell, 1999.

Frazer, James George. *The Golden Bough*, 1st edn, 2 vols. London: Macmillan, 1890. 2nd edn, 3 vols. London: Macmillan. 3rd edn, 12 vols. London: Macmillan, 1911–15.

Geertz, Clifford. "Religion as a Cultural System," in *Anthropological Approaches to the Study of Religion*, ed. Michael Barton. London: Tavistock, 1973, pp. 1–46.

Geertz, Clifford. *Local Knowledge: Further Essays in Interpretive Anthropology*. New York: Basic Books, 1988.

Gifford, Paul. *African Christianity: Its Public Role*. London: Hurst, 1998.

Good, Byron J. *Medicine, Rationality and Experience: An Anthropological Perspective*. Cambridge: Cambridge University Press, 1994.

Hocart, Arthur Maurice. *The Life-giving Myth and other Essays*, ed. Lord Raglan. London: Methuen, 1952.

Horton, Robin. *Patterns of Thought in Africa and the West*. Cambridge: Cambridge University Press, 1994.

Lett, James. "Science, Religion, and Anthropology," in *Anthropology of Religion: A Handbook*, ed. Stephen D. Glazier. Westport, CT: Greenwood, 1997, pp. 103–20.

Lévy-Bruhl, Lucien. *The Notebooks on Primitive Mentality* [1949], tr. Peter Rivière. Oxford: Blackwell, 1975.

Lévy-Bruhl, Lucien. *How Natives Think* [1910], tr. Lilian A. Clare, with introduction by C. Scott Littleton. Princeton, NJ: Princeton University Press, 1985 [original publication of tr. 1926].

Luhrmann, Tanya. *Persuasions of the Witch's Craft*. Oxford: Blackwell, 1989.

Malinowski, Bronislaw. *Magic, Science and Religion and Other Essays*, ed. Robert Bedfield. Garden City, NY: Doubleday, 1948.

Radcliffe-Brown, A. R. *The Anaman Islanders*. Cambridge: Cambridge University Press, 1922.

Rappaport, Roy A. "Logos, Liturgy, and the Evolution of Humanity," in *Fortunate the Eyes That See: Essays in Honor of David Noel Freedman*, eds. Astrid Beck et al. Grant Rapids, MI: Eerdmans, 1995, pp. 601–32.

Steedly, Mary Margaret. *Hanging Without a Rope: Narrative Experience in Colonial and Neocolonial Karoland*. Princeton, NJ: Princeton University Press, 1993.

Stoller, Paul, and Cheryl Olkes. *In Sorcery's Shadow*. Chicago: University of Chicago Press, 1989.

Turner, Edith. *Experiencing Ritual: A New Interpretation of African Healing*. Philadelphia: University of Pennsylvania Press, 1992.

Tylor, Edward Burnett. *Primitive Culture*, 2 vols. 1st edn. London: Murray, 1871.

— Chapter 2 —

The Comparative Method

Paul Roscoe

Applied with varying degrees of analytical rigor, the comparative method has been a staple of Western thought since the days of Herodotus. In biology, it achieved an early prominence in Darwin's comparison of different species to support his theory of evolution. More recently, biologists have used the method to illuminate organic function, specie morphology, primate-troupe structure, and the processes of biological evolution. Comparison came later to the social sciences, but it is now widely employed in sociology, economics, political science, psychology, and anthropology.

In religious studies, comparison has a distinguished ancestry in the work of William Robertson Smith and, more recently, of Mircea Eliade. Notwithstanding this pedigree, scholars of religion now tend to spurn the comparative method, not least because of their unease over the excesses they see in the work of two early practitioners, Robertson Smith himself and, even more, J. G. Frazer. As Robert Segal (2001) has argued, these concerns may be misplaced. Still, there remain a large number of further issues – in particular, statistical and epistemological questions – that have largely escaped the attention of scholars of religious studies. By contrast, these issues have received extensive airing in anthropology, the social science that has as its enduring goal a holistic understanding of all human societies and that consequently has made by far the greatest use of the comparative method.

Yet in anthropology, too, comparativism has had a controversial history. On the one hand are those in the "scientific" wing of the discipline. They trace their intellectual history to the 1930s and 1940s and specifically to George P. Murdock's comparative work at Yale's Institute of Human Relations. Scientifically minded anthropologists argue that anthropological knowledge can best be advanced with the help of formal, statistically rigorous comparisons of samples of the world's known societies (see C. Ember 1996; M. Ember 1991). On the other hand are those in the humanist wing of the discipline. They include interpretivists, poststructuralists, and postmodernists. Humanistically inclined anthropologists have focused a withering fire on comparativism, objecting that cultures, by their nature, cannot be compared; that ethnographies, which purport to describe these cultures, are actually fictional texts composed in the imagination of "observers"; that classification and generalization are the product of Western hegemony – an antiquated, unethical, positivist power play that seeks to encapsulate and thereby control the Other; and that there are no sociological laws and therefore no possibility for theoretical generalization (see Geertz 1973, p. 25; Holy 1987). Taken to its extreme, as Thomas Gregor and Donald Tuzin (2001, p. 5) observe, this radical critique portends the end of anthropology – exactly as its more nihilistic critics would wish.

This chapter attempts to illuminate some of the issues that have emerged in this fractured debate. It first examines some of the statistical issues associated with the comparative method and discusses the problems raised by the difficulty of defining in any defensible way what constitutes a sampling universe. Second, it argues that debates about the comparative method are often covert debates not about methodology but about theoretical axioms concerning the nature of human beings and society. As a result, adherents and opponents of comparison tend to talk past, rather than engage, one another, restating their axioms under the guise of methodological critique.

The Comparative Method

To begin with, we should recognize that comparison is an inescapable and unobjectionable aspect of reasoning. Benson Saler nicely summarizes what cognitive psychologists have long known: that comparison is an inescapable part of cognition because the unfamiliar can be conceptually assimilated only in terms of the familiar. Writes Saler: "We regularly monitor the world, and in doing so we creatively and selectively compare newly encountered phenomena to established representational structures" (Saler 2001, p. 268). As Gregor and Tuzin elegantly state for anthropology:

> At its most basic level, *all* anthropology is comparative. There is no way to talk about other cultures and their institutions without, at least implicitly, comparing them to other cultures. . . . [C]omparison is the bread and butter of anthropology. It is inherent in the act of classification, by which we identify unfamiliar behaviors, describe institutions, and communicate the results of our work to others. We cannot describe one society without having others in mind, for comparison is the recurring element of our basic analytical tools. (Gregor and Tuzin 2001, pp. 2,7; see also Segal 2001)

Even opponents of comparison are closet comparativists. No matter how emphatically they oppose comparison, no matter how forcefully they insist that their aim is to study another culture "in its own terms," they have no option but to render their descriptions in Eurocentric terms if their descriptions are to remain intelligible to the anthropological community.

The issue, however, goes beyond the description of other cultures. If we do not seek also to draw generalizations by comparing how cultures are the same and how they are different, the purpose of describing other cultures in the first place is thrown into question. As A. R. Radcliffe-Brown observed, "Without systematic comparative studies, anthropology will become only historiography and ethnography" (Radcliffe-Brown 1951, p. 16). "Comparison elevates the level of our work to the quest for principles of human life that transcend any one culture, even as it accepts the importance of culture in forming people's interests and the views they have of others" (Gregor and Tuzin 2001, p. 7).

Ironically, the comparative method is almost certainly not what either its proponents or its opponents say it is. Supporters of comparison advocate it as part of a "scientific" approach to society, but too often this assertion rests on unsophisticated conceptions of what constitutes the scientific method. In opposing comparativists' claims to the mantle of "science," "humanistic" critics frequently make an equally basic error: they covertly equate a science of society with positivism and then, by pointing to the obvious failings of positivism, assume that they have disposed of a science of society (see Roscoe 1995).

As the relevant experts – the historians, philosophers, and sociologists of science – now routinely tell us, most presentations of the scientific method bear scant resemblance to what scientists do in practice. In actuality, science is a highly complex, interpretive endeavor that, as yet, is only poorly understood. In light of present understandings, scientific practice might best be described as a subjective juggling and modification of interpretations in terms of subjectively perceived consistency and problematicity. Scientific advance is, then, the interpretive capacity to render rival hypotheses implausible (see Roscoe 1995, pp. 494–7). The same is true of the comparative method. What is deemed to be the comparative method is almost certainly not what is actually being done. Like the scientific method, it is probably a complex and poorly understood interpretive process.

Still, let us sketch some of the essential elements of the comparative method. As commonly described, comparison starts with an interest in some phenomenon such as biological speciation or male initiation. A hypothesis or theory is then proposed that relates variation in some observable aspect of this phenomenon (X) to one or more other observable conditions (Y, Z). For example, Darwinians propose an evolutionary theory that the different species of the world (X) are the product of the different physical environments (Y) in which they are found. In a paper that began the formalization of the comparative method in the social sciences, Edward Burnett Tylor tabulated data on 282 societies to show that the "comic custom" of ritual avoidance of the mother-in-law (X) was related to matrilocal postmarital residence (Y) (see Tylor 1889). John Whiting and his colleagues proposed that the occurrence of genital mutilation (X) in male initiation was the product of tropical environments (Y) and of societies with patrilocal postmarital residence (Z) (see Whiting *et al.* 1958; Whiting 1964). A cross-species or cross-cultural sample is then assembled and analyzed to see whether, as predicted, trait X occurs in and only in the presence of Y and Z. In actuality, comparison is often conducted far less formally, and it may be used for a variety of other purposes as well – for example, as an exploratory tool to examine whether phenomenon X is universal or to investigate the properties of phenomenon X.

What is perhaps more interesting than the manner in which comparison is deployed is the theoretical presumption upon which it is grounded: an assumption that the observable variations in X are either the manifestations or the products of the operation of observable conditions (Y, Z) on one or more underlying, unobservable or unobserved entities or processes. In the case of evolutionary theory the different species of the world are the (observed) manifestations of different (observed) physical environments acting through the phenotype to influence the transmission down the generations of genes, a process directly observable neither in its operation nor in the way it affects phenotypes. Tylor theorized that, in matrilocal societies (an observed trait), mother-in-law avoidance (another observed trait) culturally marks the difference between the wife's family and the "stranger" husband who has intruded into their household. In the case of genital mutilation Whiting and his colleagues argued, among other things, that the warmth of tropical climates results in exclusive mother–infant sleeping arrangements, which thereby foster a dependence of the son on the mother. In patrilocal societies this dependence is considered inimical to adult masculinity and respect for the father, and genital mutilation emerges as a psychological means of severing the bond. In this hypothesis the presence or absence of genital mutilation is the (observed) manifestation in patrilocal societies (an observed social trait) of climate (an observed factor) acting on several unobserved or unobservable factors (including intensity of the mother–son bond, conceptions of adult masculinity, and the psychological effects of incising the penis).

Presented thus, the comparative method seems unobjectionable, and it is difficult to understand why the method should so often provoke controversy. The reason, I suggest, is that debates about the comparative method are not really about the validity of the *method* at all. Rather, they are disputes about the validity of the comparativist assumption that the surface manifestations to be explained are all expressions of the same underlying, obscure or obscured explanatory entity or process. Comparativists assert this uniformity. Their critics demur. Obscured by disputes about "method," in other words, are implicit quarrels about the nature of humanity and of cultural processes.

Early American cultural anthropology formulated the initial reservation. Franz Boas, in an early objection to Tylor's method of comparison, complained that the endeavor was undermined by the problem of convergent evolution: "The identical result [i.e., cultural trait] may have been reached on . . . different lines of development and from an infinite number of starting points" (Boas 1940). If this is the case, then comparison ends up erroneously counting as instances of the same thing traits that are the product of quite different processes. Many other anthropologists were to echo Boas' objection (see Benedict 1959, pp. 37–8, 242–5; Evans-Pritchard 1965).

In *Patterns of Culture* Ruth Benedict sought to expand on Boas' point in a way that foreshadowed subsequent interpretivist objections to comparison. As she framed the issue, the significance of a cultural trait depends on the way in which that trait has merged with other traits from different fields of experience (see Benedict 1959, pp. 37–44). The trait cannot therefore be extracted from these experiential fields and compared with a similar trait in another culture because the contexts render the traits different. To grasp the significance of Benedict's argument, one must note her somewhat idiosyncratic view of the nature of humans and their cultures. Drawing on gestalt theories then current in psychology, she argued that just as individual psychologies are patterned to interpret the world and act in it in different ways – for example, entrepreneurial, pessimistic, paranoid – so, too, are cultures patterned around distinctive themes – a Dionysian pattern in one society, an Apollonian configuration in another. Therefore the same trait – for example, the ritual consumption of human flesh – might be used in one way by one culture – in a Dionysian culture, perhaps to denigrate enemies by turning them into feces – and another way by another culture – in an Apollonian culture, perhaps as a positive expression of kinship. To count the occurrences of ritual cannibalism as instances of the same trait would thus be as meaningless as comparing a flag with a brightly colored table cloth on the grounds that they are both pieces of cotton fabric.

In sum, Boas and Benedict protested that what might look like the same cultural trait in two different societies might actually be two quite different traits with different origins and different meanings. The validity of these objections, however, rests on the acceptance of particular theoretical assumptions about the nature of humans and their cultures. If one accepts Benedict's contention that cultural traits are seamlessly organized into distinctive gestalts, for instance, then certainly it is problematic to extract them from this matrix and compare them in isolation. But if one questions the assumption, then Benedict's objections are moot. Her real objection is not to the use of comparison but to what can rightfully be compared.

Much of the current criticism of comparativism in social science rests on the same misstated grounds: objections ostensibly lodged at the method turn out to be assertions about what is and is not comparable, and these assertions in turn reflect covert assumptions about the nature of humans and their cultures. In broad terms, the humanistic critiques of the method seem to be based on the premise that humans are thoroughly hermeneutic beings – suspended, as Clifford Geertz, following Max Weber, puts it, in webs of significance that they themselves have spun (see Geertz 1973, p. 5). Humanistic social scientists seek to understand culture from the "inside," to represent cultures "in their own terms," and their interest is in cultural differences. They are interested in faithfully translating cultural difference into Western terms. By so doing, they seek to expose the constructed, as opposed to natural, character of Western cultural categories. To this camp, beliefs, ideas, and reasons are causes. Indeed, some of the more extreme critiques of comparativism seem to represent mental phenomena as the *irreducible* causes of behavior. The human genetic heritage and common practical exigencies such as subsistence and military defense seemingly do not exist – or at least are irrelevant, trivial, or uninteresting in comprehending human behavior. With this emphasis on mental phenomena as the foundation for explaining human affairs, there is little sympathy for the idea that aspects of human culture can be characterized as manifestations of underlying entities or processes common to humanity and culture. Hence the hostility among humanistic social scientists to comparativism and to the "totalizing" theories and "metanarratives" produced by so-called "positivistic" or "scientific" social scientists.

The "scientific" social scientists, by contrast, conceptualize humans as sharing capacities that transcend cultural differences. This camp recognizes the existence of cultural differences but is interested in why societies exhibit cultural similarities as well as cultural differences. If humanistic social scientists are interested in culture from the "inside," their "scientific" colleagues are interested in culture from the "outside." They presume the existence of unobserved or unobservable commonalities in humans and in culture that are manifest in similar ways in some physical and social contexts and in different ways or not at all in others. Hence their interest in the comparative method. Most "scientific" social scientists recognize the importance of humans' interpretive capacity, and many would allow that reasons alone can be causes. A few, however, deny the notion that ideational phenomena shape human behavior in significant ways. In limiting themselves to genetic explanations of human behavior to the exclusion of ideational causes, some sociobiologists and evolutionary psychologists present a mirror image of the one-sided position of some "humanistic" social scientists.

Having sketched this conceptual landscape, I now want to consider more closely the details of the positions staked out in contemporary social science for and against the comparative method. I shall consider first the scientific wing of social science. The criticisms that occupy its attention tend to the methodological and the technical: how best to apply the comparative method to ensure the most accurate results. I shall then consider the position of the humanistic wing of social science. The criticisms here tend to the theoretical rather than the methodological.

Formal Comparison and Its Problems

Rigorous proponents of the formal or "scientific" comparative method insist that the research problem be clearly stated, that the theory or hypothesis under test be made explicit, that the method of testing and the results of the study be sufficiently clear to be replicable, that the data used be shown to be valid and reliable, that the societies under study be clearly defined, that an objective sampling procedure be specified, that the data be made available to other researchers, and that appropriate statistical tests be employed (see M. Ember 1991; C. Ember 1996). These are demanding criteria, and only a few studies ever fulfill them. Many other social scientists adopt less rigorous procedures in practice, sometimes because available data or funding are insufficient to meet all of the requirements, sometimes because of objections to one or more of the criteria themselves.

The scope of comparison

The scope of comparison is limited by both logical and pragmatic constraints. First of all, the method can only be used to test hypotheses about cultural traits that vary in some way across human societies. Either the traits must vary in their occurrence, being present in some societies and absent from others, or, if they are universal, they must vary in their intensity or elaboration. We can imagine any number of hypotheses that explain why human kinship systems recognize connections of substance between mother and child (usually common "blood"). Perhaps the connection is the result of infant dependency (committing the mother to caring for her offspring) or of a need to assign offspring to particular families. But because there are no societies in which infants are independent or in which there are no families, these hypotheses are impossible to test.

Theories about universal traits can be tested comparatively if the hypothesis can be phrased in proportional terms and if the data to test it are measurable on an ordinal (i.e., ranked) rather than a nominal (presence/absence) scale. Although incest avoidance, for example, is quasi-universal, some hypotheses about its origins can be tested because its strength is variable and, in principle at least, measurable across societies (say, by the frequency of infractions). The Westermarck hypothesis is testable, for example, because it links the intensity of incest avoidance to the degree of co-socialization in childhood (which can be measured using variables such as the proportion of their childhood that siblings have lived apart).

Constrained by matters of logic, this first issue has attracted little controversy. A more provocative issue concerns the advantages and disadvantages of worldwide, or "holocultural," comparisons, as opposed to regional, or "controlled," ones. Worldwide comparative studies sample all known world cultures to test theories or to generate hypotheses. Regional studies, by contrast, sample an areal subset of the world's cultures – for example, the cultures of New Guinea or the pastoral societies of East Africa. The avowed advantage of worldwide comparisons is exactly that the findings can be held true of all known societies rather than of just a portion of them. Worldwide comparisons are also less vulnerable to sampling biases introduced by "Galton's problem" – a point to be considered later.

The major cost of worldwide comparison is control of the quality of the data. A human community is a complex structure, and documentation of this structure is often fragmentary and fragile. Furthermore, much of the documentation is a product of colonialism, written by agents such as missionaries, colonial officers, and anthropologists, each with its own interests. Often documentation is limited to the colonial history of the community. Consequently, one must try to reconstruct from these documents what a community was like before it was significantly affected by the colonial presence. To extend this exercise to the world as a whole is all but impossible. Inevitably, the quality of the data employed in worldwide comparisons suffers.

Where comparison is limited to a single region of the world, skills ensuring the quality of the data become more feasible. Furthermore, a regional comparison can be "controlled" (see Eggan 1954; Boas 1940; Evans-Pritchard 1965; Borgerhoff Mulder *et al.* 2001). Because of their shared histories, it is argued, the cultures of a region are likely to have been shaped by similar processes, permitting the effects of a number of potentially confounding variables to be controlled and thereby revealing more clearly the causes of some aspect of cultural variation. For example, the comparative analysis of the hypothesis that male initiation severs mother–son bonds in patrilocal societies is less likely to be confounded by external variables such as differences in subsistence economy, in the degree of religious or political engagement with colonial powers, and in the articulation with the wider world economy.

Sampling and statistical significance

Formal cross-cultural surveys place great emphasis on the statistical significance of their results – an issue that arises because it is impossible to use all human societies to test a theory. Despite the best efforts of archeologists, there will always be many prehistoric human communities about which either nothing is known or too little is known to be useful. Even if we were to limit attention to existing societies, there would remain many about which we know little. Finally, even if all societies, past and present, were known in detail, there would remain for some theorists the issue of the hypothetical sampling universe. Physicists measuring the gravitational constant, for example, run a series of experiments that sample a hypothetical population comprising the infinite number of these experiments that could be run. Likewise, the argument goes, social scientists need to sample a hypothetical population comprising an infinite number of societies that could have happened – for example, if the physical universe were run over and over again. In short, no matter how broad our comparisons, they cannot embrace all human societies. Inevitably, we are restricted to samples – a restriction that automatically raises a host of statistical issues.

If the conclusions derived from a sample are to be reliable, two conditions must be satisfied. First, the sample must be drawn in a way that avoids *systematic* bias. Were one interested, for example, in studying how kinds of spiritual systems are distributed across the cultures of the world, it would make little sense to use the cold-calling telephone techniques common to market or political surveys. Most of the people in lesser developed countries like New Guinea, for example, have no access to a telephone. Consequently, one would likely draw the erroneous conclusion that human spirit systems are overwhelmingly monotheistic or polytheistic – the systems found in most industrial states – when in fact the religious systems of many, if not most, societies of the world are dominated by ancestor spirits. Even if the level of telephone ownership were equal across world cultures, one still would end up over-sampling industrial states, since the populations of these societies and therefore the numbers of their telephones are greater by several orders of magnitude than the populations and numbers of telephones in the small-scale cultures of the so-called "tribal" world.

The usual method of avoiding systematic bias is to draw a *random* sample, but this method is difficult to apply to human societies. Since little is known of many past and present societies, it would be pointless to include them in a cross-cultural sample. Rather, sampling is usually limited to the one thousand or so "adequately described" societies found in sources such as the *Ethnographic Atlas* and the *Human Relations Area Files*. But because large, complex societies such as the Maya and the Mesopotamian and Hawaiian kingdoms are more visible in the archeological and documentary record than smaller, less complex "tribal" communities, this condition automatically and unavoidably introduces a systematic bias into sampling. Moreover, language and colonial histories have resulted in some "adequately described" societies being sampled more often than others. Social science being largely a Western enterprise, societies colonized by Western nations feature disproportionately in cross-cultural work. For example, African societies are more commonly included than those in regions once under Soviet control. Even in regions colonized by the West, language barriers have skewed sampling. Societies described in Dutch ethnographies, for instance, are less often sampled than societies described in English-language ethnographies.

These problems can be avoided. The inadequate representation in cross-cultural samples of non-English ethnographies and of societies under non-Western influence is surmountable, in principle, by more conscientious research. The problem that larger, more complex societies are more visible can be overcome by drawing a stratified rather than a purely random sample. Suppose, for example, one wished to test a hypothesis that the religious system of a society is affected by the level of the political centralization of the society. It would then be legitimate to divide up the population of "adequately described" societies by level of political centralization – for example, into egalitarian, Big-man, chief, and state societies; to draw randomly the same number of societies from each stratum; and to use this stratified sample to test the hypothesis at issue.

A number of comparativists, George P. Murdock in particular, struggled heroically to provide ethnographic databases constructed to ease these many sampling problems. Murdock went as far as to claim that "a carefully drawn sample of around 200 cases essentially exhausts the universe of known and adequately described culture types" (Murdock and White 1969, p. 337). Yet even his "Standard Cross-Cultural Sample" rested on a number of debatable, subjective premises (see Murdock and White 1969, p. 332).

Even if one assumes that systematic sampling bias can be dealt with satisfactorily, there remains the problem of *random* bias in a sample. Although many known human societies revere ancestor spirits, it is possible that a randomly chosen sample still could be skewed by the luck (or, rather, bad luck) of the draw. By sheer chance a random sample of all known human religious systems still could end up comprising only, or mainly, monotheistic systems. The probability is relatively low, but it exists and could lead to erroneous conclusions about human religious systems. There is no way of avoiding altogether random bias. All that can be done is to calculate the *significance* of the result. In other words, we calculate the probability that our sample might be so badly skewed as to lead us to draw an erroneous conclusion, and we then ask whether we are confident with that probability. Do we want to feel 95 percent confident in our results? 99 percent confident? 99.9 percent confident? A wide range of techniques exists for testing the significance of different kinds of data.

Galton's problem

Unfortunately, the application of these techniques to human societies is bedeviled by "Galton's" problem – a problem that has attracted more technical attention from formal comparativists than any other issue. Strictly speaking, Galton's problem was not that of Francis Galton but that of Edward Burnett Tylor. After Tylor had presented his paper dealing with ritual avoidance of the mother-in-law to the Royal Anthropological Institute, Galton rose to comment on what he considered a serious statistical problem in Tylor's "social arithmetic." Tylor's trait tallies, he suggested, might be artificially inflated by having counted the same trait several times over. The Malaysian islands provided Galton his ethnographic case in point. Tylor had tallied each island as a separate case. But Galton pointed out that these islands shared a cultural heritage, and he asked whether the islands really therefore should count as several cases rather than just one case.

The issue Galton raised is central to statistical procedure because these methods presume that the events or cases in a sample are drawn entirely independently of one another. Galton was pointing out that, because human cultures may not be independent of one another, a sample of these cultures may not constitute entirely independent cases. For example, if two neighboring societies both practice ritual cannibalism, they could hardly be counted as independent cases for sampling purposes if both were descended from a parent society that had also practiced ritual cannibalism. Even if the two societies shared no parentage, it would still be inappropriate to count them as separate cases if, say, one had adopted ritual cannibalism from the other or if one had forcibly imposed ritual cannibalism on the other. Galton insisted that, for statistically valid comparison, the traits involved have to be "independently invented, not copied" (Galton, quoted in Tylor 1889, p. 270).

There is considerable disagreement over the degree to which Galton's problem *is* a problem. More than a few studies simply ignore it, arguing that if societies speak mutually unintelligible languages, their cultures are likely to be unrelated. Other studies, however, suggest the effects of common phylogeny can exert a huge influence on the validity of statistical methodology, particularly where regional rather than worldwide comparisons are involved (see Ember and Otterbein 1991, pp. 222–5; Borgerhoff Mulder *et al.* 2001).

Anthropologists have developed two principal methods to try to compensate for the lack of statistical independence among the societies of the world. One approach has been called the *sifting method*. Rather than sample the societies of the world at random to test a hypothesis, one samples *areas or regions* of culture. If evidence suggests that the Swazi, Xhosa, and Zulu peoples derive from a recent common source, one does not sample them as three separate cases but instead as representatives of just one – the Nguni people. The problem with sifting, however, is the absence of any obvious method for establishing the boundaries of the culture areas or regions that should be sampled. In testing her hypothesis that the presence or absence of sorcery beliefs is a function of the presence or absence of superordinate systems of justice, for example, Beatrice Whiting sifted her original sample of fifty randomly selected societies into twenty-six areas that, she claimed, were generally recognized as having cultural unity (see B. B. Whiting 1950). An immediate problem, of course, is that the recognition of cultural unity is hostage to advances in knowledge of prehistory: what is "generally recognized" as a culture area in one generation of scholarship may change radically in the next. But Raoul Naroll pointed to a further problem: the diffusion of a cultural trait cannot legitimately be expected to stop at the boundary of a culture area or even of a continent (see Naroll 1970, p. 978).

Naroll was especially taken with Galton's problem and together with his students devised a second set of methods to deal with its effects (see Narroll 1970). Commonly known as *propinquity* or *spatial autocorrelation* techniques, these methods assume that diffusion is a function of geographical propinquity. In other words, cultural traits are more likely to have diffused between societies adjacent to each other than between societies separated by great distances. Adjacent societies are also more likely to share historical parentage than societies separated from one another. Propinquity methods operate by counting similarities between neighboring societies as the consequence of diffusion or common ancestry and by counting similarities between distant societies as more likely reflecting independent invention. When they were first introduced, propinquity methods were tedious and time-consuming to apply, but with the advent of computer-based statistical programs their use is now relatively effortless.

Comparison and the issue of sample units

There lurks a further, currently unresolved problem in cross-cultural anthropological analysis that, taken to its logical conclusion, would greatly complicate not only the solution to Galton's problem but also the application of statistical methods to cross-cultural data. The issue concerns the units making up a sample, and the problem arises because the nature of these units differs fundamentally between the social world and the physical world, which statistical methods were developed to analyze.

The physical world is divided into units that can be legitimately distinguished from one another. The elements of the periodic table and the materials they give rise to in the natural world are manifestly distinct from one another. Likewise oak trees are manifestly different from elms: there are mutually exclusive morphological differences in leaf type, bark, and height. Since species by definition do not interbreed, only with human intervention can intermediate hybrids occur to blur these boundaries. It is therefore unproblematic to define the population of cases or events to be sampled and then to draw the sample. But "societies," "cultures," and "cultural units" do not appear to exist "out there" as distinct units in the way that elements or floral and faunal species do. Sampling thus becomes problematic.

Formal comparativists usually define a "society," "culture," or "cultural unit" in terms of language. Melvin Ember and Carol Ember, for example, define the cultural unit of comparison as "a population that more or less contiguously inhabits a geographic area and speaks a language not normally understood by people in neighboring societies" (Ember and Ember 1994, p. 188; see also Borgerhoff Mulder *et al.* 2001, p. 1063). One problem with this approach is the presumption that language and culture are somehow coterminous, so that there is a one-to-one correspondence between a particular language and a particular set of cultural traits. But this is not the case. In New Guinea, the graveyard of many a methodology and a theory, significant cultural differences exist not only at the level of language but also at the level of dialect. The Boiken "language" of the Sepik region, for example, is spoken by people adapted to such different environments as islands, coasts, thin-soiled mountains, fertile foothills, and infertile grass plains. To claim that the speakers of Boiken share a culture is absurd. Subsistence depends on fishing and sago in some areas, on gardening and sago in others, and on hunting and sago in yet others. Preferred marriage patterns range from sister exchange to marriage with the father's mother's brother's son's daughter. In some areas competitive exchange focuses on domesticated pigs; in others, on long yams; in still others, on giant yams, sago, turtles, or wild pigs. In others yet, there appears to be no competitive exchange at all. The Boiken language can be divided into seven "dialects," some of which are mutually unintelligible, and even within a dialect area there can be considerable cultural heterogeneity. The Western Yangoru Boiken copied the initiation houses and long-yam cults of their neighbors, the Kaboibus Arapesh and Eastern Abelam, and culturally seemed at least as similar to these non-Boiken speakers as to the Central Yangoru Boiken, who spoke the same Yangoru dialect yet exchanged pigs and had a quite different, high-fenced initiation enclosure. Conversely, there are groups in the Sepik region that exhibit no significant linguistic differences at all yet differ markedly in their cultures. The language of the Torembi Iatmul, who live inland from the Sepik River, is 100 percent cognate with that of the Iatmul, who live on the river itself, yet culturally the two groups differ significantly, not least in their primary subsistence activities – fishing among the riverine folk; sago-gathering and cultivation among the Torembi.

The more serious problem with defining a cultural unit for the purposes of comparison is the very assumption that there exist natural social units that are somehow separated off or at least separable from one another geographically, socially, or temporally – in other words, that there exist units of culture that can be distinguished, sampled, and compared. This idea of discrete cultural units can be attributed to Boas (1940), but it is difficult to defend either temporally or spatially. Over time, humans and the cultures they bear give rise to other culture-bearing humans in a process that is continuous, not discrete. Except in the case of whole human groups going extinct, it is impossible to divide up this developmental process in such a way as to be able to determine when one "cultural unit" ended and another began. Spatially, at any one point in time, there is constant interaction among humans to the geographic limits of their social relationships. Even before globalization, for example, most of the people in New Guinea were related directly or indirectly to one another through vast networks of relations based on trade, marriage, and war. Through the peoples of the Torres Straits, New Guineans were ultimately enmeshed in networks that included many Australian aboriginal communities. Within these capacious spheres of interaction, it is impossible to identify any "naturally" occurring discrete cultural units. To do so would be as arbitrary as identifying discrete colors within the visible spectrum. To be sure, we divide this spectrum up into different colors, but these distinctions are arbitrary impositions on a frequency continuum of electromagnetic radiation. It would obviously be going too far to suggest that there *are* no cultural differences, for manifestly there are. Rather, the point is that cultural difference varies in a continuous fashion, whereas statistical method presumes that the cases or events forming a population are discrete.

The Humanistic Critique of Comparison

These technical issues concerning comparativism emanate from the "scientific" wing of social science. The other kinds of criticisms of comparison come largely from those in the "humanistic" wing, which opposes the method altogether. Many of the same complaints have been voiced also by students of religion (see Segal 2001, p. 348).

Comparative deductions are obvious

Among the most deceptive and least consequential claims against comparison is that its results are "meager and controversial" (Evans-Pritchard 1965, p. 27) or "banal or empty," "commonplace or vacant" (Geertz 1973, p. 25). These criticisms are extensions of an old complaint about the findings of social science in general: in contrast to the physical sciences, it is said, generalizations in the social sciences turn out to be obvious. Whether leveled at social science in general or at the comparative method in particular, these claims are at best debatable, at worst absurd.

The findings of social science appear obvious because, unlike atoms and molecules, humans have introspective access to the grounds of their behavior. It should therefore not surprise us if social scientific generalizations seem obvious – once they have been pointed out. For example, American visitors to the United Kingdom are often puzzled and frustrated to find themselves bumping into other pedestrians on the sidewalk. Once the reason is pointed out – that pedestrians tacitly follow the rules of their respective roads, walking to the left in the United Kingdom, to the right in the United States – it becomes "obvious." But the reason is obvious only in hindsight, *once* the cross-cultural explanation has been pointed out. Moreover, one can point to any number of comparative conclusions that it would be absurd to characterize as obvious. There is nothing obvious or banal about Alvin Wolfe's (1969) finding that African communities in which people live in large villages made up of several clans or other political divisions produce significantly more visual art than those in which people belong to a single large clan or tribe and live in small, dispersed homesteads.

Inadequacies in the data used

More substantial objections to comparison center on the claim that, in some way or another, the method distorts the data it compares. Questions are commonly raised about variations in the breadth, depth, nature, and interpretation of the ethnographic work on which comparisons are based. The data for one cultural unit may be based on intensive fieldwork by a trained anthropologist, whereas that for another might derive from the fleeting observations of a passing missionary. The presumption, of course, is that intensive fieldwork will provide more reliable data than fleeting observation. Perhaps, but the reverse can also be true. For the purpose of comparing unacculturated communities, the fleeting observations of a passing missionary making first contact may be of much greater value than intensive fieldwork by a trained anthropologist decades after that contact, during which time the community has been affected by the contact. Either way, the objection would remain that the comparative method affords equal weight to all data.

The use of coded data in comparative studies – that is, of ethnographic data transformed into numbers, rankings, letters, or categories such as present/absent – comes in for especially stern criticism. Coding, it is charged, is inescapably reductive, obscuring cultural variation. Coding cannibalism as "present" or "absent," for example, erases the different purposes that might motivate it – denigration of an enemy, absorbing the strength of an enemy, communing with the deceased, or some mixture of these motives. All get counted as instances of the same category. At the same time many phenomena escape coding altogether. For example, some studies have attempted to correlate childhood socialization with attitudes toward sexuality. But attitudes can be ambivalent. For instance, people may react emotionally against homosexuality and yet feel that it should be permitted, but this ambivalence would escape a present/absent dichotomy. Comparative studies also frequently fail to make clear what exactly has been coded: is it behavior or informants' statements about behavior? The difference may be crucial: statements asserting an ideology of individual autonomy and egalitarianism, for example, may be proclaimed most loudly in precisely those societies where autonomy and egalitarianism are most threatened.

All of these objections are fair. They raise proper cautions about the weight to be afforded the conclusions from a comparative study, though, to be fair, the authors of comparative studies are themselves often quite explicit about the frailties of their data. Less warranted is the common strategy of using these objections, some of which, after all, apply as well to non-comparativist studies of individual cultures, to dismiss out of hand the conclusions of a particular comparative study or, more egregiously, to reject comparison *per se*.

The issue of comparable traits

Critics have often argued that the cultural traits that comparativists compare may in fact be incomparable. This is a variant of Boas' and Benedict's already cited objection to comparison. Broad comparisons, protested Evans-Pritchard, fail to ensure that the cultural traits being compared are of equivalent value (see Evans-Pritchard 1965, p. 19). Are "monogamy" among the Veddahs of Ceylon and "monogamy" in Western Europe units of the same kind? If not, then how can we compare them?

Mark Hobart (1987) offers a more recent version of this objection. He asserts that the objects compared are prejudged to be similar, yet no standards are advanced for declaring them equivalent. In fact, Hobart claims, even so-called cultural universals are in actuality culturally unique. He asks, seemingly rhetorically, "Everywhere animals and people eat. Is this not a universal which underwrites all translation?" (Hobart 1987, p. 39). Not according to Hobart. In Bali, he argues, there are at least eight terms for "eating," and not only the terms but also the concept of eating vary with caste, politeness, personal health, and familiarity with the eater.

In reply, one must note a certain intellectual legerdemain here: to support his case that "eating" is a different act depending on the cultural context, Hobart proceeds to equate eight Balinese terms with "eating." It is difficult to fathom his methodology, but he appears to have taken eight terms that, to be sure, differ significantly in their full meaning but that nonetheless all refer to the act of putting edible commodities in the mouth and swallowing them. If this is so, then all that Hobart has shown is that eating in Bali is associated with meanings that differ *in part* in different contexts, not that eating is seen as an utterly different act in each case.

Hobart's criticism is founded on an axiom common to critiques of comparativism: that human cultures are entirely incomparable with one another, that they constitute mutually exclusive universes of meaning. If this position were accepted, cross-cultural research would be forced to a dead stop. But Hobart's position rests on the same untenable assumption that undermines the application of statistical techniques to comparison: the presumption that human cultures exist as separable and separate units, hermetically sealed from one another into unique semantic universes.

Comparative data, meaningful context, and categorical imposition

Perhaps the most common of all "humanistic" objections to the comparative method is a combination of the two forgoing complaints. By its nature, it is claimed, comparison extracts behaviors and beliefs from their meaningful context, thereby radically distorting them. A related complaint is that the categories that comparativists deploy are external impositions – of a religiously or Eurocentrically imperialistic kind – that distort or obliterate contextual significance. For example, in comparing initiation rites across the world, comparativists assume that they are comparing local manifestations of a transcultural category – "initiation rites" – much as one might compare oranges, tangerines, and grapefruits, assuming them all to be different manifestations of the transpecies category "citrus fruits."

In fact, critics contend, comparativists are comparing apples with oranges and are erroneously calling them both citrus fruits. In anthropology, the favorite targets of this criticism are Tylor and Frazer. Students of religion prefer to place Frazer and Robertson Smith in the crosshairs. But the criticisms are the same.

The point that cultural traits should be neither extracted from their meaningful context nor subject to the imposition of external categories is well taken, but who would demur? As Segal has pointed out, even Frazer, seemingly the worst offender, insisted that the best data for comparison are those collected by observers who have lived many years with the people, who are fully conversant in their language, and who describe their life "as if no other people existed on the face of the earth" – in other words, in the full complexity of its own, meaningful terms (Frazer 1931, p. 246; see Segal 2001, p. 351).

What opponents of comparison appear to object to is less comparison itself than the way comparativists *conduct* comparison. There is nothing about the process of comparison that precludes the inclusion of any amount of meaningful context along with some cultural trait or another. In fact, opponents of comparison frequently prove this point in their own work. Notwithstanding their expostulations against the comparative method, they themselves frequently use informal comparisons to advance their particular views of culture. What many critics of comparison seem really to be complaining about is that comparativists do not take *enough* meaningful context into account. But the issue depends on one's theoretical premises – on the degree to which one holds that human belief and behavior are determined by hermeneutic, as opposed to non-hermeneutic, forces and processes. It is a theoretical disagreement over how comparisons should fruitfully proceed, not over whether to compare at all.

Comparativists in turn have legitimate complaints against the way critics deploy their own comparisons. First, anti-comparativists like Geertz blithely disregard sampling issues and Galton's problem in their own work to the extent that their conclusions are often pointless. Arguments supported by casual comparisons of two or three cultures, selected by unspecified criteria, are hardly persuasive, regardless of how much "meaningful" context is imported. Second, the complaint that cultural traits should not be extracted from their meaningful context is often pushed to a ludicrous extreme. Grounded in an assumption that meanings are explanation, the objection frequently seems to presume that meanings are the *only* explanation, that human behavior responds solely to mental phenomena, as though the parameters of the physical world and pan-human concerns such as putting food on the table and defending against attack by predators were irrelevant to understanding human beliefs and behaviors. It is as bearers of a culture, to be sure, that we learn the world around us, and this cultural learning dictates our behavior in that world. But some of these learned meanings have been shaped *by* the world. Humans inculcated in a culture that does not recognize food or recognize the mechanical and gravitational forces governing the construction of weaponry, for example, are unlikely to be around for very long to perpetuate that culture.

Meaning is surely of importance in understanding many aspects of cultural difference – for example, why in some New Guinea male initiation rites initiates should be infused with semen anally in one community, by fellatio in another, and by anointment in yet another. But many beliefs and behaviors amount to universals or quasi-universals – for example, incest avoidance – or to high-frequency occurrence – for example, the occurrence of initiation *per se* in politically uncentralized communities and the strong correlation of headhunting ritual complexes with large, politically uncentralized, river-dwelling communities. These occurrences are difficult to attribute to meanings alone since meanings would presumably generate variability rather than similarity. In light of these commonalities it is difficult to see why meanings must constitute the only explanations, as even the most committed interpretivist anthropologists have sometimes reluctantly conceded. When similar belief-and-behavior complexes recur in numerous communities widely distributed in space and time, one must draw one of three conclusions. First, perhaps remarkable coincidence is at work. Second, perhaps researchers have been fooled by the operation of multiple end-point probability – the fact that *some* similar characteristic can always be found within a finite set of cases if one looks hard enough, in much the same way that, given infinite time, twenty-five people in a room can always find something they all share, such as the same birthday or a favorite song. Third, perhaps meaning is not the sole determinant of human culture. If we allow this last possibility, then we allow the possibility of comparison.

Conclusion

This assessment of the comparative method has reviewed a range of technical and nontechnical issues that merit attention, but two issues stand out as stark object lessons for scholars in other fields. First, the fieriest disputes about the comparative method are anything but debates about methodology. Social scientists have wasted an inordinate amount of time and ink talking past one another about comparativism. Generally, these discussions have gone nowhere because in actuality they are covert exercises in asserting and defending *a priori* assumptions about the nature of humanity and of cultural processes. These assumptions are well worth airing and discussing, but what could have been a worthwhile debate about them has been displaced by specious discussions of methodology. The reason, one suspects, is that the models of humanity at stake and the research programs predicated upon them are vulnerable to significant criticism.

Second, the insistence by formalists on rigorous statistical tests and on auto-correlation techniques to correct for Galton's problem will remain a misplaced technicalism until or unless a more persuasive basis can be established for constituting "cultural units" or for sampling a universe of cultural traits that varies continuously, not discretely, across space and time. But issues related to sampling and to Galton's problem cannot thereby be ignored, and the informal and unspecified sampling procedures that interpretivists often employ are not thereby justified. To choose cases simply because they happen to corroborate a pet hypothesis is indefensible no matter what one's epistemology. Any comparison needs to justify the sample it draws and to make some attempt to evaluate the possible effects on the sample of shared histories or cultural contacts.

And how, in light of these lessons, should the comparativist – whether social scientist or student of religion – proceed? Quite simply, we should proceed pragmatically: rather than endlessly discussing the comparative method, we should get on and do it, and see what results seem to work in getting us along, in helping us understand the social worlds around us. Lest this seem a disappointingly aimless program of action, let me defend it by returning to a point raised earlier – that, regardless of what they claim to be doing in the name of the scientific method, physical scientists operate in just this way in generating knowledge of the natural world.

It is highly significant, I think, that the physical sciences advance in the virtual absence of debate and disagreement about method. To be sure, there are manifold disputes about whether *particular* methods and technologies of observation generate what their proponents claim they generate. In the past decade, for example, there have been widely divergent views among climatologists about whether satellite data are indeed showing global warming or merely reflect the manner in which sensing equipment samples the regions of the earth and the structure of the atmosphere. But these are technical debates, ones akin to debates over the significance of Galton's problem.

By contrast, debates over how or whether to deploy the scientific method are conspicuous by their absence. In fact, most scientists have an all-encompassing, well-established, and largely unquestioned ideology about what it is that they are doing. This "positivist" methodological ideology serves them well, and yet it is patently false both as a prescription for, and as a description of, scientific method (see Roscoe 1995, pp. 494–6). Rather, its value lies in diverting physical scientists from endless discussions about what they are doing – discussions that almost inevitably would be unproductive because the method they actually use is still so poorly understood. In a celebrated article Stephen Brush argued that the history of science should be X-rated to shield young and impressionable students from the violence that would be done to their development as scientists were they to realize how science actually does get done (see Brush 1974).

Thoroughly hermeneutic and subjective though their method is in actuality, physical scientists get on and do what they do with results that seem remarkable in their power – theories that seem to work ever better in allowing humans to understand and control the physical world. Oblivious to what they are actually doing, physical scientists nevertheless are able to produce impressive results. In science, pragmatism rules: all discussions and disagreements are thrown out of the window once something is found that seems to work.

There are undeniable differences in studying cultural rather than physical worlds. The physical world, for example, is ubiquitous and on a human scale unchanging. By contrast, social worlds differ from one another and change with every moment of time, hindering the replication of observation. Still, if students of society are to generate knowledge that allows them better to understand and influence social worlds, there is no reason in principle that the same pragmatism should not serve them as well. Useful theories are unlikely to result from insisting, covertly or overtly, on the superiority of one set of *a priori* assumptions about humans over another, or from epistemological debates over what "method" to apply to their study. These debates will continue to be vacuous and unproductive. Results will come rather from getting on and studying humans and their cultures, including their religions, with whatever resources are to hand. Comparison – whatever it is and however it actually works – is one such resource, and there are few better ones.

Bibliography

Benedict, Ruth. *Patterns of Culture* [1934]. Boston: Houghton Mifflin, 1959.

Boas, Franz. "The Limitations of the Comparative Method of Anthropology" [1896], in his *Race, Language and Culture*. New York: Macmillan, 1940, pp. 270–80.

Borgerhoff Mulder, Monique, Margaret George-Cramer, Jason Eshleman, and Alessia Ortolani. "A Study of East African Kinship and Marriage Using a Phylogenetically Based Comparative Method," *American Anthropologist* 103 (2001): 1059–82.

Brush, Stephen. "Should the History of Science Be X-Rated?" *Science* 183 (1974): 1164–72.

Eggan, Fred. "Social Anthropology and the Method of Controlled Comparison," *American Anthropologist* 56 (1954): 743–6.

Ember, Carol. "Cross-Cultural Research," in *Encyclopedia of Cultural Anthropology*, eds. David Levinson and Melvin Ember. New York: Holt, 1996, vol. I, pp. 261–5.

Ember, Melvin. "The Logic of Comparative Research," *Behavior Science Research* 25 (1991): 143–53.

Ember, Melvin, and Carol R. Ember. "Cross-Cultural Studies of War and Peace: Recent Achievements and Future Possibilities," in *Studying War: Anthropological Perspectives*, eds. S. P. Reyna and R. E. Downs. Langhorne, PA: Gordon and Breach, 1994, pp. 185–208.

Ember, Melvin, and Keith F. Otterbein. "Sampling in Cross-Cultural Research," *Behavior Science Research* 25 (1991): 217–33.

Evans-Pritchard, E. E. "The Comparative Method in Social Anthropology," in *The Position of Women in Primitive Societies and Other Essays in Social Anthropology*, ed. E. E. Evans-Pritchard. New York: Free Press, 1965, pp. 13–36.

Frazer, James George. *Garnered Sheaves*. London: Macmillan, 1931.

Geertz, Clifford. *The Interpretation of Cultures*. New York: Basic Books, 1973.

Gregor, Thomas A., and Donald Tuzin. "Comparing Gender in Amazonia and Melanesia: A Theoretical Orientation," in *Gender in Amazonia and Melanesia: An Exploration of the Comparative Method*, eds. Thomas A. Gregor and Donald Tuzin. Berkeley: University of California Press, 2001, pp. 1–16.

Hobart, Mark. "Summer's Days and Salad Days: The Coming of Age of Anthropology?" in *Comparative Anthropology*, ed. Ladislav Holy. Oxford: Blackwell, 1987, pp. 22–51.

Holy, Ladislav, ed. *Comparative Anthropology*. Oxford: Blackwell, 1987.

Murdock, George P., and Douglas R. White. "Standard Cross-Cultural Sample," *Ethnology* 8 (1969): 329–69.

Naroll, Raoul. "Galton's Problem," in *A Handbook of Method in Cultural Anthropology*, eds. Raoul Naroll and Ronald Cohen. New York: Columbia University Press, 1970, pp. 974–89.

Radcliffe-Brown, A. R. "The Comparative Method in Social Anthropology," *Journal of the Royal Anthropological Institute* 81 (1951): 15–22.

Roscoe, Paul B. "The Perils of 'Positivism' in Cultural Anthropology," *American Anthropologist* 97 (1995): 492–504.

Saler, Benson. "Comparison: Some Suggestions for Improving the Inevitable," *Numen* 48 (2001): 267–75.

Segal, Robert A. "In Defense of the Comparative Method," *Numen* 48 (2001): 339–73.

Tylor, Edward Burnett. "On a Method of Investigating the Development of Institutions; Applied to Laws of Marriage and Descent," *Journal of the Royal Anthropological Institute* 18 (1889): 245–72.

Whiting, Beatrice B. *Paiute Sorcery*. New York: Viking Fund, 1950.

Whiting, John W. M. "Effects of Climate on Certain Cultural Practices," in *Explorations in Cultural Anthropology*, ed. Ward H. Goodenough. New York: McGraw-Hill, 1964, pp. 511–44.

Whiting, John W. M., Richard Kluckholn, and Albert S. Anthony. "The Function of Male Initiation Ceremonies at Puberty," in *Readings in Social Psychology*, eds. Eleanor E. Maccoby, Theodore M. Newcomb, and Eugene L. Hartley. New York: Holt, 1958, pp. 359–70.

Wolfe, Alvin W. "Social Structural Bases of Art," *Current Anthropology* 10 (1969): 3–29.

Chapter 3

Economics of
Religion

Rodney Stark

In his classic work *The Wealth of Nations* (1776) Adam Smith, the founder of modern economics, published some remarkable insights about religion. Among them were the proposition that state churches will always be lax and lazy and the recognition that the solution to religious conflict is to have not fewer religious groups but more (see Smith 1981). Nevertheless, the "economic" approach to religion is new and has mainly been the work of sociologists, not economists (see Young 1997). Indeed, given their narrow focus on "commerce," most economists have found Smith's work on religion so irrelevant that the chapters he devoted to the topic are omitted from all but one of the available editions of his masterpiece.

Until recently, what little work was done on religion by card-carrying economists has seldom strayed from such mundane matters as the effects of free time on church attendance and the tendency for high-income congregations to substitute money for time, using paid services rather than relying on member volunteers. Fortunately, this narrow focus seems to be changing: a number of young economists recently have been showing interest in the economic approach to religion as developed by sociologists. In 2004 an organization of economists interested in doing research on religion was formed. (I was one of the founders.)

Meanwhile, in 1980, when William Sims Bainbridge and I launched what has since come to be called the economic approach to religion, we knew nothing of Adam Smith's work. His name is not even in the index of our *The Future of Religion* (1985). Two years later, when we published *A Theory of Religion*, we had intended to add the subtitle *An Economics of Intangibles*, but the publisher objected. Even then, we mentioned Smith only as an example of a deductive theorist and still knew nothing of his work on religion. I became aware of Smith's contributions only several years ago, after having independently reached many of the same conclusions.

In any event, as developed by sociologists, the economic approach is not mainly about money, about prices, or even about good works as an investment in heavenly pay-offs. Rather, it can be characterized as an economic approach because when it analyzes religion at the *individual* level, it emphasizes *exchange relations* between humans and the supernatural. At the *collective* level the economic approach to religion rests on the fundamental concepts of *supply* and *demand*. Of course, the other social scientific approaches to religion also stress *demand*, usually calling it "need," and propose that people are driven to faith by social deprivations, thwarted desires, neurosis, ignorance, fear, the Oedipus complex, false consciousness, or some other human shortcoming. The economic approach, by contrast, takes a "normal" view of demand and assumes that religious behavior can be as reasonable as any other form of human activity. Of even greater importance in distinguishing the economic approach from all others is its emphasis on *supply* and on the fundamental insight that most variations in the expressed demand for religion are the result of variations in the effectiveness and diversity of religious suppliers. In turn, these variations are the product of the overall religious situation: do many religions groups *compete* for followers, or does the state collaborate with one group in an effort to impose a *monopoly*?

To illustrate how fundamental is the shift of emphasis from demand to supply, consider that when confronted with major shifts in the religious composition of societies – as when the Methodists grew so rapidly in the United Kingdom – proponents of the other approaches usually pose the basic question as: *Why did people's religious preferences change?* That seems an entirely reasonable question. Yet when posed this way, we are directed to seek our answer in shifting demand and therefore to conclude that these changes occur because people suddenly develop new, unmet religious needs and turn to or produce new religious institutions able to meet these needs. By a similar logic, the very low level of religious participation in Sweden, for example, is attributed to a decline in demand: people there have supposedly lost their need for religion, perhaps because the socialist state has adequately provided for whatever need religion had formerly fulfilled.

Not only do I think that these are the wrong answers; I also think that they answer the wrong question. There is considerable evidence that, although it may often be latent, religious demand is very stable over time and that religious change is instead largely the product of supply-side transformations (see Stark and Finke 2000; Stark 2003). In effect, religious demand remains relatively constant, whereas suppliers rise and fall, and the overall level of religious participation is a function of the diversity and the energy of suppliers. Hence my colleagues and I would pose the fundamental question this way: *Why do religious organizations change so that they no longer enjoy mass appeal?* Specifically, what went wrong with the Church of England, and why has the Swedish state church made so little effort to attract and hold an active membership? As will be seen, the "economic" answers offered to these questions are not limited to practical or purely organizational concerns. Rather, since the objects of interest are *religious* organizations, serious and extensive attention is given to the *contents* of religion – to doctrine, to what people *believe*, and to what the religious organizations *teach*.

For reasons that I shall never fully understand, a number of critics have chosen to misrepresent the application of economic ideas and terms to religion as a descent into vulgar materialism (see Bruce 1999). In his review of *The Churching of America, 1776–1990*, Martin E. Marty proclaimed that Roger Finke and I had reduced religious life to mere "winning and losing," presenting a "world [that] contains no God or religion or spirituality, no issue of truth or beauty or goodness" (Marty 1993, p. 88). Had he even read the dust jacket summary, Marty could scarcely have failed to grasp that the central argument in that book is that doctrine holds the key to organizational health. On the first page of that book we wrote: "to the degree that denominations rejected traditional doctrines and ceased to make serious demands on their followers, they ceased to prosper. The churching of America was accomplished by aggressive churches committed to vivid other-worldliness" (Finke and Stark 1992, p. 1). As with the first page, so with the last and so with most pages in between, our message was that *vague* and *permissive doctrines* are what turn religious groups into "losers." In my judgment it is precisely the focus on belief, not the use of economic principles, that really upsets ultra-liberal and anti-religious opponents and motivates their misleading claims and their outlandish rhetoric, such as Steve Bruce's attack on "the malign influence of a small clique of U.S. sociologists of religion" and his presumption that he is up to the task of driving "the stake through the vampire's chest" (Bruce 1999, pp. 1–2).

In this chapter I shall sketch the basic insights gained thus far by the economic approach to religion. Far fuller treatment is to be found in some of my recent publications (see Stark and Finke 2000; Stark 1996, 2003, 2004, 2005).

The economic approach to religion is based on nine fundamental principles: (1) the core of all religions is belief; (2) the basis of all religious practice involves exchanges with the supernatural; (3) individual religious tastes vary along a spectrum of intensity; (4) people are as rational in making their religious choices as in making their secular decisions; (5) religious doctrines differ greatly in their ability to inspire commitment; (6) religion is a collective enterprise; (7) religious groups that ask the most of members are enabled thereby to give them the most, thus sustaining the highest levels of rank-and-file commitment; (8) most new religious groups begin as high intensity faiths, and the more successful ones gradually reduce their levels of intensity; (9) competition among religious organizations in any society stimulates effort, thus increasing the overall level of religious commitment and causing the demise of faiths lacking sufficient market appeal. As I discuss each of these principles, I will sketch the amazing number of conclusions that can be deduced from this simple set of assumptions, and I will cite some of the extensive evidence in support of each. These studies are very disproportionately American, not because I do not know of research done elsewhere but because, unfortunately, at least nine of ten studies in the social scientific study of religion and in social science generally have been done by Americans, usually using data on Americans.

For the sake of clarity, the discussion will be organized on the basis of the above list.

1. *Religion consists of explanations of existence based on supernatural assumptions, including statements about the nature of the supernatural and about ultimate meaning* (see Stark 2004).

The core of all religions is that they tell us the meaning of life, if any, and what the supernatural is like. The term "supernatural" is much broader than the term "god." I define the "supernatural" as forces or entities, conscious or otherwise, that are beyond or outside nature and that can suspend, alter, or ignore physical forces. Gods are *conscious supernatural beings.* This definition of religion leaves room for "godless" religions such as the elite forms of Confucianism and Taoism, in which the supernatural is conceived of as a divine "essence," lacking consciousness or concerns. It should be noted, however, that godless religions fail to appeal to the general public and that the popular forms of Confucianism and Taoism include a substantial pantheon of gods – most of them of small scope and of dubious character. *Magic* is excluded by this definition since it does not concern itself with ultimate meaning and typically does not offer explanations even of its own mechanisms, let alone of more profound matters.

It is, of course, obvious that there is more to religion than belief. But once we know what religion *is*, then and only then can we distinguish those actions and feelings that are religious from those that are not. A High Mass and a Nazi Party rally both qualify as rites, and both can inspire deep emotions in participants. Only by noting which one is grounded in supernatural assumptions and which one is not can they be distinguished. When I refer to religious rites, for example, I mean rites that are performed for religious reasons. Using "religion" as a modifier makes it possible to incorporate all aspects of religion and the religious life without the use of complex definitions.

2. *The core of religious practice involves exchange relations between humans and the supernatural.*

When the supernatural is conceived of as merely an unconscious essence, religious practice lacks intensity and focus. Because there is no conscious being to pray to, appeals to the Tao, for example, take the form of blind appeals to luck, as in the use of mechanical prayer wheels or writing requests for good fortune on slips of paper and tying them to a wire to blow in the wind. It is questionable whether these actions should be called praying, any more than gamblers blowing on the dice and saying "Come on, gimme an eighter from Decatur" should be considered praying.

Consequently, godless religions are limited to small elites, and even in "godless" Asia most people orient their religious practice to gods. In godly religions two questions dominate the religious life: What do the gods want, and what can the gods give? The answers define and direct the entire range of religious culture and behavior. Stripped to essentials, godly religions consist of exchange relations with the gods, and all questions as to why people perform any given sacred activity are answered: "Because it pleases the gods." Why do people wish to please gods? To gain benefits and avoid harm. Granted, people often develop strong emotional bonds to gods and gladly worship them without any thought of benefits. Yet even then the exchange relationship remains basic, and religious people are not reluctant to acknowledge that exchange is the central message of most hymns and ritual prayers. Moreover, as will be seen, the ability of a religion to generate commitment depends on the perceived reliability and scope of its gods – that is, on the perceived value of the rewards that they can plausibly offer.

That beliefs about the nature of the supernatural are a more basic feature of religion than is ritual has been demonstrated by research, both anthropological and experimental, showing that in exchanges with the supernatural, the emphasis on the perfect execution of rituals is a function of the powers attributed to the supernatural agency to which the rituals are directed (see Lawson and McCauley 1990). At one extreme is ritual magic, which is directed to supernatural entities lacking consciousness or to supernatural beings of very limited capacities, such as imps or demons. Here it is assumed that each ritual must be performed with extreme precision because the supernatural agency lacks the capacity to know the intent of those performing the ritual and is unable to see beyond errors in ritual performance. At the other extreme are the omnipotent gods of the great monotheisms. From them blessings may be granted as a result of impromptu prayers virtually devoid of ritual character because such gods are fully aware of the intentions of the supplicant. Consequently, relatively little emphasis is given to precision even in conducting formal rituals directed to these gods: no one thinks that transubstantiation will fail to occur during a mass if the priest mixes up the words.

3. *In every society, people differ in their religious tastes.*

Were we to rank people according to the intensity of their religious preferences, the result would approximate a bell-shaped curve: some people want
high-intensity religion, some want little to do with religion at all, and most
people want a faith that offers them valuable rewards in exchange for various
requirements, but want the requirements to be moderate in both number
and cost.

The importance of diversity in religious tastes is that all societies therefore
include a set of relatively stable market *niches*, or sets of persons sharing
distinctive religious preferences, needs, tastes, or expectations. The existence
of these niches has profound consequences for religious suppliers: no single
supplier can satisfy the full array of niches since no organization can be at
once intense and lax, worldly and otherworldly. The natural state of religion
in any society is thus one of *pluralism* – the existence of an array of suppliers, each appealing to a particular niche or narrow set of niches. Consequently, religious organizations can be located along an axis of religious
intensity, with *sects* being high-intensity groups and *churches* being those
offering lower intensity. As will be seen, market forces tend to limit the formation of new religious groups to sects and to tempt newly formed sects to
reduce their initial level of tension in order to appeal to larger niches. I identify pluralism as the *natural* state of religion in societies, but not as the *usual*
state. Typically, pluralism has been suppressed in favor of religious
monopolies.

Religious monopolies are artificial, existing only to the extent that *coercive
force* is utilized to prevent competition. Coercion need not involve naked
force. Many governments in contemporary Europe employ less brutal techniques to place all religious groups other than the "state church" at severe
disadvantages. But however pluralism is impeded, the result is religious dissatisfaction, apathy, and antagonism since the religious preferences of most
market niches thereby go unmet. As will be seen, this failure to satisfy
demand explains the low levels of religious participation in much of Europe
despite the high levels of belief (see Davie 1994). These same forces arising
from unmet demand stimulate heresies and religious wars (see Stark
2003).

4. *People are as rational in making religious choices as in making secular
    decisions.*

Claims that religion stems from ignorance or irrationality reveal more about
those who make them than about human behavior. Two issues are involved
here. The first concerns the so-called "rational choice" assumption: that
humans tend to seek rewards and to avoid costs. Although some social scientists imply that to make this assumption is tantamount to signing a pact
with the devil, it is obvious that, within clear limits, humans *are reasonable*

beings who act accordingly. Of course, everyone acknowledges that human behavior is not *always* rational, subject as it is to error and impulse. But the best starting assumption is that behavior *is* rational in that people usually attempt to pursue what they perceive to be the best option for achieving their goals, and these goals need not be either selfish or admirable. Stated with proper qualifications, the rational choice premise reads: *In pursuit of rewards (what are deemed desirable or valuable), people attempt to make rational (effective and efficient) choices, limited by their information, by the available options, and by their understanding of what is involved.* What it is that people deem rewarding differs, being shaped by culture and socialization. Allowance must also be made for character. Laziness often influences choices, impulsiveness and passion may short-circuit calculations, and moral concerns may rule out many options.

Despite the complaints by postmodernists and other opponents of reason, there is nothing radical or new about the assumption that human behavior generally makes sense and is therefore relatively predictable. From the moment our earliest ancestors achieved consciousness, this has been the assumption that all humans make about others, withdrawing it only when forced to do so by clear cases of madness. Were our behavior substantially irrational, not only would social science be invalid, but social life would be impossible: if the behavior of others were utterly unpredictable, we could not interact. Fortunately, within the suggested limits, humans generally act in reasonable ways, *at least as they see it*. This qualifying clause reminds us that, as the great American sociologist James Coleman put it, "much of what is ordinarily described as nonrational or irrational is merely so because observers have not discovered the point of view of the actor, from which the action *is* rational" (Coleman 1990, p. 18).

The second issue is the claim that while most kinds of human behavior meet the standard of rationality, religious behavior does not, being rooted in ignorance and neurosis. This view goes back to the beginnings of social science. Thomas Hobbes, one of the celebrated founders of social science, dismissed all religion as "credulity," "ignorance," and "lies" and dismissed gods as "creatures of . . . fancy" (Hobbes 1956, I, p. 98). A century later, David Hume echoed Hobbes, dismissing all miracles as limited to "ignorant and barbarous nations" (Hume 1962, p. 123). During the nineteenth century August Comte coined the word "sociology" to identify a new field that would replace religious "hallucinations" as the guide to morals (Comte 1896, II, p. 554). Then Ludwig Feuerbach "discovered" that humans create gods in their own image (see Feuerbach 1957). That thesis was appropriated (without acknowledgment) by Emile Durkheim, who taught that society itself is always the true object of religious worship: "god . . . can be nothing else than [society] itself, personified and represented to the imagination" (Durkheim 1995, p. 206). This view of religion continues. On the first page of his book *Mystical Experience* Ben-Ami Scharfstein, an Israeli psychologist, reveals that "mysticism is . . . a name for the paranoid darkness in which

unbalanced people stumble so confidently" and goes on to identify the supernatural as a "fairy tale" (Scharfstein 1973, pp. 1, 45).

Research makes a mockery of all these claims (see Stark and Finke 2000).
A mountain of trustworthy studies reveals that religion is positively associated with mental health. Religious people are substantially less prone to
neurosis, anxiety, depression, and other forms of psychological problems. In
many nations the more educated that people they are, the more likely they
are to attend church, and among university faculty, those in the physical
and natural sciences are more religious than are their colleagues in other
fields. High-intensity religious movements usually have been based primarily on the upper classes rather than on the poor or the peasantry (see Stark
1996, 2004). Finally, there is overwhelming evidence that people in both
premodern and modern societies weigh their religious decisions carefully
(see Stark and Finke 2000).

5.   *Religions differ greatly in their ability to inspire commitment.*

The image of the supernatural on which a religion is based determines how
that religion is practiced and the requirements that it can impose on followers. Consider godless religions. Their followers may have things to pray *for*,
but they have no one to pray *to*. Neither the Tao nor the liberal Christian
"ground of our being" is conscious, and non-beings, divine or not, can be
the object of only meditation and introspection since they neither hear nor
care.

The nature and duration of exchange relationships between humans and
gods are determined by the scope of the gods. Where there are believed to
be many gods, each of relatively limited scope, exchanges will be *short term*,
involving an immediate offering in hopes of a rapid response, such as in the
case of rain dances. Where there exists an extensive pantheon, supplicants
often shop around for a god thought to specialize in their current needs: good
crops, safe voyages, better health, love, victory, and so on. Then the appropriate ritual will be performed, often including a sacrifice, and the desired
outcome eagerly awaited. Gods who fail are often discarded for those thought
more dependable. In Chinese folk temples disappointed petitioners have been
known to beat the statue of a god with sticks or even smash the statue when
the desired boon did not come.

Obviously, then, polytheism is unable to generate *exclusive, long-term*
exchange relations. On the contrary, faced with a pantheon of gods, the
sensible person will construct a religious portfolio to spread the risks of
nonfulfillment (see Iannaccone 1995). Long-term exchange relations with
a single god are found only within monotheism. It is not merely that belief
in One True God eliminates alternatives but also that only gods of this
immense scope offer rewards (and punishments) of sufficient value to motivate a life-long exchange relationship. The truly priceless religious rewards
are not to be obtained in the here and now but in another "place," usually

after death. No cash-and-carry exchanges bring rewards of this magnitude. They are reserved for the faithful, for those who regularly fulfill their obligations to God, typically over their entire lifetimes. Hence only monotheism can generate intense and durable commitment from the general public, as opposed to dedicated priests.

Even within monotheism, there is considerable variation in the levels of commitment. To the extent that a particular religious group presents God as benign and relatively undemanding, members will respond with low levels of participation, and religion will tend to be of little consequence in their daily lives. For example, among Americans, images of God as *powerful* are highly correlated with obeying the law, whereas images of God as *affectionate* produce no similar correlations (see Stark 2004). There is now a very large literature unanimously showing that strict churches are strong churches in terms of member commitment because the value of the rewards available from religion tends to be a function of cost: the more that is asked, the more that can be given and plausibly promised (see Stark and Finke 2000).

6. *Religion is a collective enterprise.*

Only the mad, and then very rarely, pursue a private faith. Even ascetic hermits are motivated and sustained by a collective faith. To create a plausible and satisfying religious culture is no easy task and typically is the product of collective and successive creation. Moreover, as with most other important cultural products, religion is best served by specialists. Thus religious specialists are among the first to appear as societies become more complex, and their primary function is as "middle men" between humans and gods, gaining their living from transactions (see Stark and Bainbridge 1987).

In search of a noun that is not culture-bound, the way the term "priest" is, I choose to identify these specialists as *ecclesiastics*. Specifically, ecclesiastics assume responsibility for the formation and promulgation of doctrine, for the conduct of rituals, and especially for religious socialization, whether through initiations or through Sunday schools. The overall "health" of religion in any society will depend upon the energy expended by religious specialists, especially in socializing the young. Thus the recent decline in religious activity in the United Kingdom and some other European nations was preceded by a decline in the religious socialization of children.

That religion is a social activity provides a key solution to the primary religious problem: the risk that religion is nothing but "fairy tales." Put another way, the universal problem of religion is one of *confidence*. No exchanges with the gods will occur until or unless people are sufficiently confident that it is wise to expend these costs. Like all other investors, people contemplating religious commitments will seek assurance. An individual's confidence in religion is strengthened to the extent that *others express* their confidence in it. Throughout our lives we rely on the wisdom and experience of others to help us make good choices. Moreover, we learn to place greater faith in the testimony of some people over others. Therefore religious groups will be able to instill greater confidence among participants to the extent that they are linked by social bonds such as family and friendship. Other things being equal, small, intimate religious groups will generate higher levels of confidence and therefore of commitment than larger groups (see Stark and Finke 2000).

Confidence is also strengthened by participation in religious activities such as ritual and prayer. I do not suggest that confidence building is the primary reason that people engage in religious activities. They do so mainly because the activities are believed to be proper forms of exchange with the divine. But neither do I suggest that the confidence that these activities provide is an unconscious "function" that escapes individual notice. It is very common for people to pray for strengthened faith – "Lord, I believe; help thou mine unbelief" (Mark 9:30) – and to believe that they have received the same. The "peace of mind" that comes from prayer is widely acknowledged. As for rituals, social scientists are unanimous that participation in them builds faith. Even Durkheim admitted that the "*apparent* function [of ritual] is to strengthen the bonds attaching the believer to his god" (Durkheim 1995, p. 226). Of course, he quickly added that what ritual *really* does "is strengthen the bonds attaching the individual to society, since god is only a figurative expression of society" (Durkheim 1995, p. 226).

Although prayer and ritual participation build confidence in religion, personal testimony is the primary means by which people reassure one another that religion is true. In addition to asserting their personal certainty about otherworldly rewards, people often enumerate miracles as proof of their religion. How they recovered from cancer, how they overcame alcoholism or drug abuse, how they became reliable and faithful spouses, how they survived a catastrophic accident, or how their prayers for a dying child were answered are all cited as evidence that a religion "works," that its promises come true. People often testify about their own experiences of God as proof that religious explanations are valid. In the case of groups that engage in various forms of collective "ecstatic" experiences, they offer one another direct *demonstrations* of the existence of God.

As noted, testimonials are especially effective when they come from a trusted source. Thus friends are more persuasive than mere acquaintances, and testimonials are even more persuasive when those testifying have little to gain and perhaps much to lose. For this reason laity are often more persuasive than ecclesiastics, who have a vested interest in promoting religious commitment. At the same time confidence in a religion also will be greater to the extent that its ecclesiastics display a level of commitment greater than that expected of followers.

There are several ways in which ecclesiastics can demonstrate superior commitment. They can *do* more, and they can *do without* more. Ecclesiastics do more by excelling in objective forms of commitment. For example, Spirit baptism, or speaking in tongues, is required of those seeking to become ministers of the Assemblies of God but is not required of ordinary members. Of perhaps even greater impact is the extent to which ecclesiastics do without by making personal sacrifices. Celibacy and poverty are common forms of self-sacrifice, and to the extent that ecclesiastics are known to pay these costs on behalf of their faith, they will have more influence.

This conclusion may seem inconsistent with the prevalence of rich priests serving opulent temples. But what too long has been overlooked is that in these cases there tends also to be a relatively low level of mass commitment and a high level of antagonism toward ecclesiastics. It probably is true that the clergy in modern Scandinavia and Germany are the highest paid in the world, yet nowhere is organized religious participation lower, although subjective commitment, in terms of belief in basic religious concepts, remains high. Public antagonism toward priestly luxury surely played an important role in both the Reformation and the Counter-Reformation.

The practice of burnt offerings arose as a way of assuring people that their sacrifices went to the gods rather than to priest. Indeed, other things being equal, well-paid clergy are never a match for lay preachers or impoverished ascetics in head-to-head credibility contests. This factor explains why a powerful ascetic current persists in all religious traditions: it offers competitive advantages vis-à-vis credibility. Ecclesiastics who do not sacrifice can still effectively motivate their flocks, but they must offset the absence of sacrifice by demonstrating a high level of commitment in other ways – often by very effective displays of *subjective* commitment.

Finally, confidence is the key not only to high levels of commitment but also to *conversion*, which is best defined as *a shift from one religious tradition to another* – for example, from Islam to Hinduism – rather than from one organization to another within a tradition – as from Lutheranism to Methodism, which is an example of *reaffiliation*. The long-held assumption that conversions occur in response to the attractions of a religious ideology, as an effort to satisfy unmet needs, is not supported by research. Instead, as many studies have demonstrated, the necessary factor is for a person to have or to form close personal ties to those who already belong to the new faith (see Lofland and Stark 1965; Stark and Bainbridge 1985; Stark 1996). Long before they even know much about the beliefs involved in the religion to which they are converting, people gain confidence in them because people they trust testify to their validity. As a result, conversion is achieved mainly by the rank and file, as they spread their faith to others in their social networks – to relatives, friends, neighbors, and associates. Hence religious groups attain high rates of conversion to only the extent that members are sufficiently committed to proselytize.

It also should be noted that, regardless of their social ties to converts, not all are equally likely to convert. The more committed they are to one faith, the less likely they are to shift to another. Thus converts are overwhelmingly recruited from the ranks of those having no prior religious commitment or having only a nominal commitment. For example, most Americans who say their parents had no religion have themselves joined a religious group. Americans from nonreligious Jewish homes are extremely over-represented in new religious movements. They also have a high probability of converting to Christianity (see Stark and Finke 2000).

7. *Religious groups that ask the most of members are enabled thereby to give the most: Within limits, stricter churches are stronger.*

Here we confront one of the most important and disputed issues in the social scientific study of religion: *Why do they do it?* Why are people willing to make the very high levels of sacrifice required by higher-tension religious organizations? Traditionally, social scientists have answered this question in terms of irrationality, claiming that people pay high prices for their religion because they do not recognize an alternative, having been socialized to regard a high level of commitment as both normal and necessary. However, the evidence is overwhelming that people *do* weigh the costs and benefits of religious commitment. Indeed, there is considerable evidence from around the world that, *other things being equal*, people will seek to minimize and delay payment of religious costs – that they will go as far as to "cheat" the gods (see Stark and Finke 2000). If this is so, why does *anyone* belong to a sect? Why don't Jehovah's Witnesses, Primitive Baptists, and Nazarenes flock to the far less expensive religion offered by low-tension bodies such as the Anglicans and Unitarians?

The answer can be found in elementary economics. Price is only one factor in any exchange. Quality is the other. Combined, they yield an estimate of *value*. Herein lies the secret of the strength of higher-tension religious groups: despite being expensive, they offer greater value. In fact, they are able to do so partly *because* they are expensive. Membership in any religious organization involves both religious rewards and social ones. That is, in addition to those things promised via religious means are the ordinary pleasures of belonging to a group. On both counts, higher-tension groups excel.

The association of *religious rewards* with tension rests upon differences in the conception of God and of otherworldly rewards. As noted, all *exclusive* religious organizations conceive of a *dependable* God of *great scope* who is capable of providing *otherworldly rewards*. They differ over the vividness of these conceptions, the confidence generated in them, and the degree to which God is thought to be *responsive*. The lower their tension, the more religious groups tend to conceive of God as a distant, impersonal, rather *unresponsive* entity. Of course, no religious organization is entirely godless, and even in the most liberal Western divinity schools many faculty and students affirm some kind of God. Many of the rank and file in the most liberal Protestant churches continue to worship more traditional visions of

God, rejecting the modern revisions and resenting the revisionists sent to them as clergy. Nevertheless, compared with a God who notes the fall of every sparrow and is brimming with concern and generosity, the God presented by lower-tension groups is much less suitable as an exchange partner. For example, the very influential American theologian Paul Tillich proclaimed that "you must forget everything traditional you have learned about God, perhaps even the word itself" in order to comprehend that "the word *God* means" the "depth of existence" (Tillich 1962, p. 63). No conscious "being" for Tillich. Not surprisingly, most who have followed Tillich's lead have ended with no god of any kind, being or otherwise. Cambridge theologian Don Cuppitt's book title says it all: *After God: The Future of Religion* (1997).

But how can a religion without God have a future? In my judgment Cupitt's prescription amounts to expecting people to continue to buy football tickets and gather in the stands to watch players who, for lack of a ball, just stand around. If there are no supernatural beings, then there are no miracles, there is no salvation, prayer is pointless, the commandments are but ancient wisdom, and death is the end. In that case a rational person would have nothing to do with church. Or more accurately, a rational person would have nothing to do with a church *like that*.

To the extent that one seeks religious value, one must prefer a higher-priced supplier. Not only do more expensive religious groups offer a far more valuable product, but in doing so they generate levels of commitment needed to maximize individual levels of confidence in the religion – in the truth of its fundamental doctrines, in the efficacy of its practices, and in the certainty of its otherworldly promises. This increase in commitment occurs in two ways: by example and by exclusion.

People take their cues from the *example* set by typical others. To the extent that most people around them display high levels of commitment and express their confidence that their religion is true and effective, people will conform. Just as people join religious groups in response to social influence, so, too, their level of participation responds to that of those around them, especially to that of close friends and family members. It follows that the higher the level of commitment expected by the group, as displayed by the average member and as justified by the group's doctrines, the higher the average level of confidence and of commitment.

Consider a church where every Sunday seems like Christmas. Nearly everyone always attends and helps "make a joyful noise unto the Lord." The collection plates overflow, and there are far more volunteers than needed to perform needed functions. It would be difficult for most people to maintain a low level of commitment in this environment. Compare this church with one where most people fail to attend on the average Sunday, where those who do attend display little enthusiasm, and where the pastor devotes the sermon to social justice and seems to say as little as possible about Christ. Because no one volunteers, a substantial portion of available church funds must be spent on janitorial and clerical services and on maintenance. Consequently, the church must struggle with budgetary problems, which get worse each year as membership declines. If one responded here to the example of others, one would attend only occasionally and would have little confidence in the religion.

One way to prevent such a congregation like this from developing is to eliminate the deadwood, to prevent those of little commitment from setting the example. Here we encounter a growing theoretical literature on the "free-rider problem." The initial insight involves the creation of collective or public goods, from which everyone benefits. The rational person would withhold contributing to the creation of a public good, enjoying the benefits while avoiding the costs. For example, any given individual is better off benefiting from flood prevention dams, highways, or military security without contributing time or money to these collective enterprises. People who act this way are free-riders. To protect society from being exploited in this fashion, governments must coerce citizens to pay their proper share. Of course, the problem is not limited to public works. All collective activities face potential exploitation by free-riders to the degree that benefits created by the group cannot be withheld from nonparticipants.

Returning to our two hypothetical congregations, we can easily see that the low-commitment congregation is the victim of free-riding. Religious organizations are especially vulnerable to free-riding because some of the most important features of religion are collective goods. They exist only insofar as some individuals pool their resources to provide the physical setting within which religious activities can occur and engage in the collective activities themselves. Religious rituals such as worship services, weddings, and funerals are collective "goods." The norms of religious groups, especially of lower-tension religious groups, make it difficult to justify withholding these collective goods from anyone. The result is a substantial amount of free-riding. For example, it is a form of free-riding to show up only for services at Christmas and Easter, expecting them to occur despite the fact that one has relied on others to keep things going the remainder of the year. Free-riders would expect to draw upon the congregation for weddings, funerals, and christenings, even if they take part in these ceremonies only when they are directly involved. Even if these people do make an appropriate financial contribution, it does not offset the drain upon the average level of group commitment caused by their inactivity. Couched in contemporary jargon, these folks are bad role models.

Considering this state of affairs, Laurence R. Iannaccone noticed that free-riding could be prevented in religious groups by requiring high costs of everyone, so that "potential members are forced to choose whether to participate fully or not at all" (Iannaccone 1994, p. 1188). In this way potential free-riders are excluded and thereby prevented from exploiting the group. High costs make membership sufficiently unattractive to chase away the apathetic, but in doing so high costs make the rewards of belonging far more intense. Thus in our hypothetical high-commitment congregation, as each person pays the high cost of membership, each receives greater religious value because of the increased capacity of the group to create a religious product that is undiluted by low-commitment "members."

Think of a congregation in which individual levels of religious commitment fluctuate on a scale from one to ten. Suppose there is the same number of people at each level, which yields an average commitment level of five. Now suppose this congregation imposes a rule requiring a commitment level of five or above in order to remain a member. The immediate result is an average level of commitment of 7.5. Moreover, people who had previously scored five and thus had been average members in terms of commitment now find themselves at the bottom. Many of these are likely to respond by increasing their level of commitment in order to become average members once again. As they do so, the average level of commitment also rises, and the returns on their investments increase correspondingly. Obviously, there are limits to this reciprocal relationship between cost and value. One easily recognizes religious groups too expensive to grow substantially. But costs must be sufficient to exclude potential free-riders.

Of course, active congregations do not provide religion alone. They also produce substantial worldly gratifications. It is a common observation that people in high-tension churches have a lot of fun in church. Moreover, these groups offer very substantial levels of emotional and even material security. Because of their capacity to generate high levels of commitment, the early Christian communities were bastions of mutual aid in a world almost entirely lacking in social services. The early Christians tended the sick and elderly and provided for widows and orphans (see Stark 1996). No wonder early Christianity was so successful in winning converts. Many higher-tension religious groups do the same today.

Commitment is energy. Members of higher-tension churches do not expend all of their energy doing directly religious things. After the worship service is over, after the prayers are said, there is much energy remaining for more mundane, but organizationally vital, activities. For example, Mormons are asked to tithe not only financial support but also their time. The average Mormon congregation receives 400 to 600 hours of voluntary labor per week, or the equivalent of ten to fifteen full-time employees. The result is that all functions necessary for operating the local ward are performed by unpaid volunteers – including the role of bishop (pastor), which typically requires from twenty to forty hours per week. But after the clerical, janitorial, and other maintenance jobs are done, there still is a huge supply of labor remaining, which Mormons deploy to perform social services for one another. Volunteers paint and repair the homes of the elderly and disabled. Volunteers do childcare. Volunteers transport people to church, to medical and dental appointments, and to the supermarket. Mormon charity and volunteer social services provide for members who otherwise would go on the welfare rolls. In similar fashion, volunteer crews of Jehovah's Witnesses build all of their churches, often over a single weekend, and the Witnesses also rely entirely on volunteers to lead and maintain their congregations. Similar patterns exist in all of the higher-tension religious groups. Not surprisingly, these resources translate into growth.

8. *Most new religious groups begin in a high state of tension (as sects), and the more successful ones gradually lower their level of tension, becoming more church-like.*

Organizations are easier to form insofar as they can be sustained by a small number of very highly committed founding members. There are two reasons that this is the case. First, the smaller the number needed, the easier it will be for a founder or founders to attract the necessary number – to attract twenty followers rather than, say, 2,000. Second, small groups can much more easily reduce free-riding by better monitoring of members' contributions and by being better able to motivate their members. Hence the smaller the group, the greater the proportional per capita contributions. Consequently, it takes amazingly few people to sustain a religious group, *if* they are sufficiently committed. In the late 1970s, of 417 American-born sects, about 30 percent had fewer than 500 members and more than half had fewer than 2,000 (see Stark and Bainbridge 1985). There are many sects able to own a church building despite having fewer than two dozen members. These groups exist because each member makes a substantial contribution of both time and money. Therefore most religious groups will begin in a relatively high state of tension. They will be sects.

However, people who can be motivated to the extent required to sustain the birth of a sect make up a relatively small market niche. Consequently, those sects that achieve a large following have relaxed their demands to some extent. The trick is to become sufficiently accommodated to society to grow, yet without becoming so undemanding as no longer to generate a high level of commitment. Keep in mind that all of today's fading liberal Protestant bodies (Methodists, Congregationalists, Lutherans, etc.) began as high-tension sects and over the centuries accommodated their way to weakness.

It also should be noted that most sects never reduce their initial level of tension and do not grow. Consequently, therefore, the high-tension end of the church–sect spectrum abounds in small, unsuccessful religious organizations. That is, most sects are dead ends. They start small, remain small, and slowly wither away.

There are many reasons that most sects fail. As with all other organizations that face the marketplace, sects often fail for want of a sufficiently attractive or distinctive product. Others fail because of ineffective marketing. Still others fail because of internal fights or lack of effective leadership. Sometimes sects begin with a level of tension that virtually precludes much recruitment. Many sects are created by the efforts of one person. They form around a leader having exceptional interpersonal skills, which some call charisma. In many of these instances initial growth ceases as the leader becomes smothered in intragroup relationships and no longer has the capacity to form new attachments with outsiders.

Finally, the success or failure of many sects stems from lack of a sufficient market opening. As a result of over-production, sects face fierce competition. Of course, this competition occurs only where the formation of new religious groups and competition among all religious groups is permitted. Where competition is prohibited or greatly impeded by government regulation, not only will there be few religious choices, but many people will reject those available to them. This rejection of the limited available choices explains the low levels of religious participation in most of Europe, even though levels of belief remain high.

9. *Competition among religious organizations in any society stimulates effort, thus increasing the overall level of religious commitment and causing the demise of faiths lacking sufficient market appeal.*

Until very recently, the continuing vigor of religion in the United States was dismissed by advocates of the secularization thesis as "American exceptionalism." Much was written to explain why the United States was failing to accompany the more "mature" and "sophisticated" European nations as they became fully modern, irreligious societies – the consensus being that there was something seriously defective about American culture. Even Iceland was said to have achieved an advanced state of secularization, whereas the United States continued to display the religious vigor deemed appropriate only for backward nations.

However, as so often happens, history failed to cooperate. In recent years modernization in Africa, Latin America, and parts of Asia has been accompanied by a remarkable intensification and spread of religion. In light of these massive developments, it is Europe that now appears to be the exception in need of explanation. As Peter Berger put it:

> I think what I and most sociologists of religion wrote in the 1960s about secularization was a mistake. Our underlying argument was that secularization and modernity go hand in hand. With more modernization comes more secularization. It wasn't a crazy theory. There was some evidence for it. But I think it's basically wrong. Most of the world today is certainly not secular. It's very religious. So is the U.S. The one exception to this is Western Europe. One of the most interesting questions in the sociology of religion today is not, How do you explain fundamentalism in Iran? but, Why is Western Europe different? (Berger 1997, p. 974)

This shift took the secularization faithful by surprise, leaving them with little to offer as an explanation of European exceptionalism other than to repeat their tired refrains about the incompatibility of religion with modernity. However, advocates of the economic approach to religion have said all along that low levels of religion in Europe have nothing to do with modernity or the implausibility of faith. Rather, the apathy of Europeans toward religious organizations is the expected result of highly regulated and constrained religious markets that effectively prevent healthy competition. Protected and subsidized churches tend to be inefficient, with the result that general religiousness suffers. Europeans are reluctant to express their religious beliefs in action, proponents of the economic approach argue, because Europe's dominant churches (Lutherans in the North, Catholics in the South, and Anglicans across the Channel) have long done little to attract them. Indeed, one place secularization clearly has made significant inroads among Europeans has been among clergy staffing the protected monopoly firms, many of whom are not merely unable but unwilling to minister actively to the public. Virtual atheism is quite commonly and openly expressed by leading church figures in many European nations, especially in Protestant societies (see Stark and Finke 2000). By contrast, when Americans confront denominations and church leaders of this sort – and they do – they have many attractive alternatives. So, rather than cease going to church, as Europeans have done, Americans simply cease going to *those* churches and switch their affiliations. The point is that people will switch rather than quit wherever churches *actively compete* for their support.

These principles are most readily applied within the context of a *religious economy*, which consists of all the religious activity going on in a society: a "market" of current and potential adherents, one or more organizations ("firms") seeking to attract or retain adherents, and the religious culture ("product") offered by the organization(s). To sum up the relevant elements of the religious economy theory: (1) If government regulation of religious markets suppresses competition, the authorized religious groups will make little effort to attract rank-and-file support or to meet religious "demand." (2) Moreover, the authorized churches will tend to be controlled and staffed by careerists, often quite lacking in religious motivation. (3) The result will be widespread public religious alienation and apathy. (4) In addition, lacking effective religious socialization and congregational support, religious beliefs will become tentative, vague, and somewhat eclectic. (5) If deregulation occurs, the eventual result will be a religious revival, as religious organizations begin to compete for public support. (6) Participation in organized faiths will rise. (7) Religious beliefs will become more definite and more widely held.

There is considerable evidence that this model fits recent religious developments in much of the world. The massive religious revival in Latin America began as Protestant faiths gained a sufficient foothold to challenge the negligent Catholic monopoly, thereby not merely converting millions to intense forms of Christianity but eventually stimulating vigorous Catholic responses. In Africa, literally thousands of indigenous Protestant sects now compete for members, not only vis-à-vis one another but also in competition with an aggressive Catholicism and in many places with militant Islamic groups. Indeed, the Islamic revival rests upon serious, sometimes bloody, competition among its many sects and factions.

Many studies support the predictions from the religious economy theory as applied to Western Europe (see Stark and Finke 2000). Of particular interest is that the recent and remarkable deregulation of religion in Italy has rapidly been followed by an equally remarkable religious revival: levels of church attendance and of traditional belief have risen substantially, especially among people under thirty (see Introvigne and Stark, 2005).

Conclusion

So this is what is meant by the "economic" approach to religion. Although I have not read any of the other chapters included in this book, I am certain that this chapter is very different from the rest, not only in its "answers" but even in many of the questions that are addressed. I suggest there primarily are two reasons for these differences. First, many of those attracted to the "social scientific study" of religion are not scientific to any detectable extent. They would much prefer to be called humanists and to concern themselves with themes, metaphors, discourses, morals, feelings, transcendence, symbols, archetypes, and so on. Second, even among those with scientific intentions, most are drawn to the topic of religion out of a deep animosity toward the phenomenon. They study religion in hopes of stamping it out, agreeing with Sigmund Freud, who explained on *one* page of his famous psychoanalytic exposé of faith – *The Future of an Illusion* – religion is an "illusion," a "sweet – or bittersweet – poison," a "neurosis," an "intoxicant" and "childishness to be overcome" (Freud 1961, p. 88).

I am content to assume that the billions of people who embrace religion are as sane as the members of the Psychoanalytic Society, and rather less strange. If you agree, then you accept the most fundamental axiom of the economic approach to religion.

Bibliography

Berger, Peter L. "Epistemological Modesty: An Interview with Peter Berger," *Christian Century* 114 (1997): 972–8.
Bruce, Steve. *Choice and Religion: A Critic of Rational Choice Theory*. Oxford: Oxford University Press, 1999.
Coleman, James S. *Foundations of Social Theory*. Cambridge, MA: Belknap Press of Harvard University Press, 1990.
Comte, Auguste. *The Positive Philosophy* [1830], ed. and tr. Harriet Martineau. London: Bell, 1896.

Cupitt, Don. *After God: The Future of Religion.* New York: Basic Books, 1997.

Davie, Grace. *Religion in Britain Since 1945: Believing Without Belonging.* Oxford: Blackwell, 1994.

Durkheim, Emile. *The Elementary Forms of the Religious Life* [1912], tr. Karen E. Fields. New York: Free Press, 1995.

Feuerbach, Ludwig. *The Essence of Christianity* [1841], tr. George Eliot. New York: Harper Torchbooks, 1957.

Finke, Roger, and Rodney Stark. *The Churching of America, 1776–1990: Winners and Losers in Our Religious Economy.* New Brunswick, NJ: Rutgers University Press, 1992.

Freud, Sigmund. *The Future of an Illusion* [1927], tr. W. D. Robson-Scott, rev. James Strachey. Garden City, NY: Doubleday, 1961.

Hobbes, Thomas. *Leviathan* [1651]. Chicago: Regnery, 1956.

Hume, David. *Inquiry Concerning Human Understanding* [1748]. New York: Macmillan, 1962.

Iannaccone, Laurence R. "Why Strict Churches Are Strong," *American Journal of Sociology* 99 (1994): 1180–211.

Iannaccone, Laurence R. "Risk, Rationality, and Religious Portfolios," *Economic Inquiry* 33 (1995): 285–95.

Introvigne, Massimo, and Rodney Stark. "Religious Competition and Revival in Italy," *Interdisciplinary Journal of Research on Religion* 1 (2005): www.bepress.com/ijrr.

Lawson, E. Thomas, and Robert N. McCauley. *Rethinking Religion: Connecting Cognition and Culture.* Oxford: Oxford University Press, 1990.

Lofland, John, and Rodney Stark. "Becoming a World-Saver: A Theory of Conversion to a Deviant Perspective," *American Sociological Review* 30 (1965): 862–75.

Marty, Martin E. "Churches as Winners, Losers," *Christian Century* (January 27 1993): 88–9.

Scharfstein, Ben-Ami. *Mystical Experience.* Indianapolis: Bobbs-Merrill, 1973.

Sherkat, Darren E., and John Wilson. "Preferences, Constraints, and Choices in Religious Markets: An Examination of Religious Switching and Apostasy," *Social Forces* 73 (1995): 993–1026.

Smith, Adam. *An Inquiry into the Nature and Causes of the Wealth of Nations* [1776]. 2 vols. Indianapolis: Liberty Fund, 1981.

Stark, Rodney. *The Rise of Christianity: A Sociologist Reconsiders History.* Princeton, NJ: Princeton University Press. 1996.

Stark, Rodney. *For the Glory of God: How Monotheism Led to Reformations, Science, Witch-Hunts, and the End of Slavery.* Princeton, NJ: Princeton University Press, 2003.

Stark, Rodney. *Exploring the Religious Life.* Baltimore, MD: Johns Hopkins University Press, 2004.

Stark, Rodney. *The Victory of Reason: How Christianity Led to Freedom, Capitalism, and Western Success.* New York: Random House, 2005.

Stark, Rodney, and William Sims Bainbridge. *The Future of Religion: Secularization, Revival, and Cult Formation.* Berkeley: University of California Press, 1985.

Stark, Rodney, and William Sims Bainbridge. *A Theory of Religion.* New York: Peter Lang, 1987.

Stark, Rodney, and Roger Finke. *Acts of Faith: Explaining the Human Side of Religion*. Berkeley: University of California Press, 2000.

Tillich, Paul. *The Courage to Be*. London: Collins, 1962.

Young, Lawrence A., ed. *Rational Choice Theory and Religion: Summary and Assessment*. New York: Routledge, 1997.

— Chapter 4 —

Literature and Religion

Stephen Prickett

Whether or not the study of literature has any *intrinsic* link with the study of religion is not a question that would even have been asked before the end of the eighteenth century. But like many other Romantic questions about hidden connections, once asked, it refuses to go away. Partly as a result, the words "religion" and "literature" have themselves both undergone radical changes of meaning within the past two hundred years. Yet behind those changes lies the much older historical question of the connections between religion and writing itself. If at first glance it seems obvious that any links must be accidental – more to do with the historical evolution of civilization in general than with any necessary connection – that apparent coincidence has persisted ever since ancient Egypt.

We start, therefore, with two other words that have long been associated with religion in all its forms: "sacred" and "spiritual." While no definition will ever be adequate for the most deeply felt and most complex of human experiences, some form of the sacred seems common to almost all societies, whereas spirituality is more usually associated with literate cultures. In his ground-breaking book *Orality and Literacy* (1982) the Japanese-American Jesuit Walter J. Ong points out that oral cultures are *static*. While orality does not preclude change – all literate cultures were once oral – oral cultures find it difficult to *conceptualize* change, which is typically either gradual and so unnoticed or unanticipated, bewildering, and even catastrophic. The normative task for an oral society is not innovation but *remembering*. Bruce Chatwin's *The Songlines* illustrates how Australian aboriginals must learn their tribal songs in order to survive in the harsh desert conditions of the Outback. Encoded in songs for each area is vital information about the location of water, food, and possible dangers. To cross the territory of another tribe, it is a matter not just of courtesy but of survival to learn their songs first. Elsewhere in the world elders are charged with the task of acting as the tribal memory bank, recalling genealogies, medicines, and emergency diets in times of famine.

Here the concept of "tradition" is profoundly different from that in Western Judeo-Christian cultures. Where oral tradition represents the collected wisdom of all time – the equivalent of the contents of all our libraries combined – accuracy of repetition is paramount. Changes may be suicidally dangerous. Tradition as blind repetition can, of course, persist even in semi-literate societies. In Muslim schools students memorize from written sources the seventh-century Arabic of the Koran; Rabbinic schools teach Hebrew to modern American Jews; many illiterate medieval European Christians learned passages from the Vulgate. In literate societies, however, a different concept of tradition has also existed for millennia, where *midrash*, or an ongoing tradition of exegesis and comment, has always accompanied the teaching of the sacred texts. "What is the Torah?" runs one Jewish catechism, with its answer, "It is midrash Torah" – it is the Law *and* its associated tradition (Wadsworth 1981, p. 8). The Law, sacred as it is, is incomplete without its ongoing tradition of comment and exegesis. For T.S. Eliot, this idea of an ever evolving text became the distinctive quality of the great European literary tradition: its capacity for innovation. For him, only the new could truly be *traditional*. But this notion of tradition *as change* presupposes a firm grasp on what is being changed. The New Testament rejection of Jewish dietary rules needs also the original prescriptions themselves. Records of debate and change are possible only in a literate and textually based society.

Associated with this new meaning of tradition was also a new kind of internalization – a new sense of interior mental space. Reading was once quite as noisy a process as consulting the tribal memory man. To read was to read aloud. In some early English manuscripts the injunction to "rede" can mean either to read for one's own personal edification or to *recite* for the benefit of all. The difference was one not so much of vocalization as of volume. Exactly when people started reading silently, to themselves, and "internalizing" what they were reading is unclear, but it was associated with devotional and religious exercises. St. Augustine records his astonishment as a young man when, unexpectedly visiting St. Ambrose in his cell, he found him studying a book *without moving his lips.* The fact that the literate and educated Augustine had never before seen such a phenomenon is as significant as his immediate conviction that it was a product of the most advanced spirituality (see Manguel 1996, p. 42). At what point internalizing became the norm is unclear, but records of the noise created by hardworking school classes suggest that it persisted into the eighteenth century, and so-called "blab schools" in the United States still existed in the early nineteenth.

Meanwhile, a second source of internalization had transformed both author and readership: the invention of the movable-type printing press. Protestantism was the product of advanced technology. Not for nothing was the first book published by Gutenberg in Mainz a Bible. Within two hundred years – by the middle of the seventeenth century – the vast majority of Protestants could read the Bible in the privacy of their own homes. But by becoming a commercial artifact, the Bible had passed forever beyond the institutional control of the Church, whether Protestant or Catholic. Just as readers were free to read the Bible directly in terms of their own contexts and circumstances, so, too, were they free, and even encouraged, to internalize its message as speaking directly to them.

The "sacred" in Rudolf Otto's (1923) classic sense of the "holy" – the fear of a semi-magical, numinous, even ghostly quality – is probably universal, but it is often below or beyond the threshold of articulation. The sacred adheres to places, to rituals, even sometimes to beliefs that cannot be challenged. The "spiritual," by contrast, is something to be internalized, adhering more to people, ideas, and written texts than to particular places and rituals. A tradition of spirituality is at once communal and personal, commonly associated with the particular holy books, be they Zoroastrian, Buddhist, Jewish, Christian, or Islamic, and often within the ethos of a religious movement – Essenes, Tibetan mystics, Sufis, or Christian organizations as diverse as the Benedictines, the Orthodox, and the Quakers. To the degree that it is psychological, internal, and literary, spirituality is also essentially dynamic – usually described by initiates not in terms of goals or even of states of mind but as a "way," a "path," or a "journey."

This distinction between the spiritual and the sacred also reveals much about the evolution of the idea of "religion" in that religious groups usually describe their activities in the internalized and dynamic terms of a literate tradition – not merely through attachment to specific "holy" books but also through a sense of history and identity created by debate, conflict, and even persecution. The European idea of "religion" has its origins as much in politics as in semantics. As the Australian historian Peter Harrison has argued, our word "religion" acquired its modern meaning of a systematized code of belief and practice only in England during the seventeenth century, as the religious upheavals of the sixteenth-century Reformation allowed people, for almost the first time, to see that *more* than one such system could exist. Only then could "a religion" be perceived as one system among several that could be studied, as it were, objectively, from the outside. Only then did the word acquire a possible plural form. In that sense, Harrison argues, our concept of religion is itself only about three hundred years old (see Harrison 1990). That new meaning was, moreover, born of irreconcilable conflict. As the philosopher John Locke put it in one of his more ironic and deadpan moments, the kings and queens of post-Reformation England had been "of such different minds in point of religion, and enjoined thereupon such different things," that no "sincere and upright worshipper of God could, with a safe conscience, obey their several decrees" (Locke 1965, p. 191).

The distinction also allowed generalizations about what different religions had in common. For the eighteenth-century Scottish divine Hugh Blair, some form of "religion" was self-evidently a universal human phenomenon:

> Cast your eyes over the whole earth. Explore the most remote quarters of the east or the west. You may discover tribes of men without policy, or laws, or cities, or any of the arts of life: But no where will you find them without some form of religion. In every region you behold the prostrate worshipper, the temple, the altar, and the offering. Wherever men have existed, they have been sensible that some acknowledgement was due, on their part, to the Sovereign of the world. If, in their rudest and most ignorant state, this obligation has been felt, what additional force must it acquire by the improvement of human knowledge, but especially by the great discoveries of the Christian revelation? Whatever, either from reverence or from gratitude, can excite men to the worship of God, is by this revelation placed in such a light, as one should think were sufficient to overawe the most thoughtless, and to melt the most obdurate mind. (Blair 1824, vol. I, p. 3)

This Enlightenment assumption was to be challenged from an unexpected quarter. David Collins, author of one of the earliest books on Australia, remarked in his *Manners and Customs of the Natives of New South Wales* that "It has been asserted by an eminent divine that no country has yet been discovered where no trace of religion was not to be found. From every observation and enquiry that could be made among these people, they appear to be an exception to this opinion" (Collins 1804, p. 354). Since the tribe in question was later effectively exterminated, we have no means of knowing whether this claim was correct, but relevant here is what Collins *believed*. It is a nice irony that Blair, Collins' "eminent divine," was not merely Minister of the High Church of Edinburgh but also Professor of Rhetoric and Belles Lettres at the University – in effect, the world's first Professor of Literature.

Collins' assertion that under Blair's definition the Australian aborigines had no religion was, however, to be taken up by the young Friedrich Schleiermacher, already translator of Blair's *Sermons* in German and now at work in Berlin simultaneously on two immensely ambitious projects. The first was his *On Religion* (1799) – a challenge to the free-thinking assumptions of what he calls the "cultured despisers" of religion: his circle of self-styled "Romantic" acquaintances, including his friend Friedrich Schlegel, who had specifically urged him to produce such a *Kampfschrift* (or "fighting book") at a surprise birthday party held for Schleiermacher in the previous November. The second was a translation of Collins' *History* into German.

What had started as a commissioned translation for a Berlin publisher was finally abandoned not because of loss of interest but because of its length. The final product overflowed into two volumes – an enormous size, given the paucity of information then available, and far more than the dismayed publisher or was prepared to finance. Though most of this work is now lost, the portion that survives reveals much about what was going on in Schleiermacher's mind at this period, and helps to explain the central thesis of *On Religion*, one of the most extraordinary and influential theological books of the age.

"Religion," Schleiermacher declared, does not depend upon there being a God at all. It is, rather, a matter of the "direction of the imagination," which is "the highest and most original element in us." Expanding on his fragment 350 in the *Athenaeum*, written more or less at the same time, he explains that "it is your imagination that creates the world for you, and . . . you can have no God without the world. . . . In religion, therefore, the idea of God does not rank as high as you think" (Schleiermacher 1988, p. 138). This stress on the primacy of the "imagination" may look as if it is merely repeating Kant, but the word Schleiermacher uses is *fantasie*, not the *Einbildungskraft* normally used by Kant and the other Romantics for "imagination." Like the English word "fantasy," "imagination" here connotes something more personal, subjective, and even idiosyncratic than the synthetic imagination of the philosophers. To make it the prime instrument in religion was therefore startlingly original. So far from returning to a sense of the pre-literate sacred as a basis for religion, Schleiermacher draws on a most sophisticated literary tradition of spirituality to inform, through the imagination, the most basic sense perception. Religion, in Schleiermacher's sense, is far wider than anything assumed by Blair. It depends not on any conscious metaphysical beliefs at all but on a kind of joyful innocence of perception potentially common to all humanity:

> Religion's essence is neither thinking nor acting, but intuition and feeling. It wishes to intuit the Universe. . . . Thus religion is opposed to these two in everything that makes up its essence and in everything that characterises its effects. Metaphysics and morals see in the whole universe only humanity as the centre of all relatedness, as the condition of all being and the cause of all becoming; religion wishes to see the

infinite, its imprint and its manifestation, in humanity no less than in all other individual and finite forms. . . . Religion shows itself to you as the necessary and indispensable third next to those two, as their natural counterpart, not slighter in worth and splendour than what you wish of them. (Schleiermacher 1988, p. 102)

To find the bases of religion in the primal act of imaginative sense perception is to extend the favorite Romantic concept of the "noble savage." According to this view, not merely was this participation common to all humanity, but primal participation was most powerful in the most primitive and therefore most uncorrupted peoples. The apparent "degradation" of the aborigines, even their lack of gods and incomprehension of death, could be stood on its head and seen as a quality of innocence lost to uncomprehending Europeans. If this view is phrased in the language of Romantic aesthetics, common alike to the poetry of Hölderlin and Wordsworth, its prime example was now to be found in Collins' aborigines.

That this was an overtly aesthetic definition of religion is made clear by the implied parallel to art. Even the purpose of religion, to "intuit the universe" (or, as Schleiermacher says later in the same piece, to provide an "intuition of the infinite"), follows similar descriptions of art. Though art and religion are different, there is, Schleiermacher insists, a "passing over" from one to the other. Art is unfulfilled if it is separated from its natural concomitant, religion. Any doubts as to the literary nature of this parallel could be and were quickly dispelled by cross-reference to his friend Friedrich Schlegel's novel *Lucinde*, written when its author was living with Schleiermacher and published in 1799, the same year as *On Religion*. Widely denounced as obscene at the time, the novel has long, even tedious, descriptions of vague undifferentiated states of being that seem almost to have been written as an illustration of the principles of religion being adumbrated by his flat-mate (see Schlegel 1971).

Despite some toning-down of this argument in revisions to subsequent editions of *On Religion*, Schleiermacher's new definition of religion was to gain increasing currency in the nineteenth and twentieth centuries. When, in the famous obscenity trial of the 1960s, we find D. H. Lawrence's *Lady Chatterley's Lover* being defended as an essentially "religious" work, the idea might have exasperated some of the book's detractors on the prosecution bench, very few people, least of all those familiar with Lawrence, found it a wholly new or even blasphemous meaning of the word.

Schleiermacher's new definition of religion also reflected a new definition of literature and of art. While explicitly rejecting the idea that religion depended on a written tradition or indeed on an idea of God at all, what one might call Schleiermacher's "aesthetics of presence" was, of course, not merely dependent on a literary tradition but also dependent specifically on a Romantic philosophic tradition going back to Kant. Kant's Third Critique, the *Critique of Judgment*, had given a wholly new prominence to aesthetics. Though its arguments were, and remain, sometimes obscure and controversial – profound or unsatisfactory, according to taste – it was to change radically the subsequent development of literary and artistic theory.

Hegel's assertion that "in our time, the theory of art is much more important than any actual examples of its practice" reiterated a fundamental tenet of the Jena group – with which both Schlegel brothers and Schleiermacher were associated (see Bowie 1990, p. 135). As two recent French critics have put it:

> Because it establishes a period in literature and in art, before it comes to represent a sensibility or style (whose "return" is regularly announced), romanticism is first of all a *theory*. And the *invention* of literature. More precisely, it constitutes the inaugural moment of literature as *production of its own theory* – and of theory that thinks itself as literature. With this gesture, it opens the critical age to which we still belong. (Lacoue-Labarthe and Nancy 1988, pp. xxi–xxii)

This concept of "literature" as of inherent value over and above its ostensible subject rapidly became common to Romanticism throughout Europe at this period. The *Oxford English Dictionary* lists this value-added variant as the third and most modern meaning of "literature," defining it as "writing which has a claim to consideration on the ground of beauty of form or emotional effect" – adding that it is "of very recent emergence in both France and England."

In Germany, however, the problems of how we know reality raised by Kant meant that the idea of literature was to take on an even higher status than in either England or France, for literature could be seen as in some sense *the* mediator of reality. It was even possible for extreme Kantians to hold that poetic or literary descriptions, as aesthetic constructs, were actually *more* real than direct sense-data, which provide no certain access to things-in-themselves. "Art first becomes true art," wrote Hegel, "in this freedom it has, when it has placed itself in the same sphere as Religion and Philosophy, and becomes merely another way of making conscious and expressing the godlike, the deepest interests of man, and the most comprehensive truths of the Spirit" (Hegel 1975, vol. 1, pp. 11–12; see also Ashton 1980, p. 116). The distinctive addition made by the Schlegels and their circle was that it was, or should be, impossible to distinguish between this theory of literature and its actual practice. The result in much of the Romantic writing of the period is a kind of theoretical synaesthesia linking poetry, the novel, philosophy, and frequently theology as well. Discussing Schelling's philosophy, for example, Friedrich Schlegel wrote: "Philosophy . . . is the result of two conflicting forces – of poetry and practice. Where these interpenetrate completely and fuse into one, there philosophy comes into being; and when philosophy disintegrates, it becomes mythology or else returns to life. The most sublime philosophy, some few surmise, may once again turn to poetry" (*Athenaeum* Fragment 304: Schlegel 1971).

The meaning of such statements (and there are many) is complicated by fundamental differences between the development of the English and the development of the German language since the middle of the eighteenth century. The American theologian Hans Frei has noted how the rise of modern historicism in Germany did not lead toward a greater interest in historical realism or particularity, and he attributes this fact in part to the universalizing tendency that began with Herder and that "reached its philosophical epitome in Hegel's descriptive explanation of spirit or reason as the unitary moving force of history. In a more moderate form this spiritualizing, universalizing tendency, for which life, spirit, self-consciousness, or some other mode of man's self-grasp as generically unique is the subject of culture and history, has remained the same ever since" (Frei 1974, pp. 213–14).

This trend in Germany was further complicated by two contingent factors. The first was the lack of appropriate native artistic models for the German literary theorists. The novel was still a low-status art form in late eighteenth-century Germany. There was little before Wieland and Goethe. Even for poetry, critics tended to cite French and English examples as frequently as they did German ones. Shakespeare dominated the German critical scene more than he did even in England, and much English nineteenth-century bardolatry actually came from Germany. The second factor was that German has two adjectives, both of which are covered by the single English word "poetic." That from poetry, *dichterisch*, refers specifically to verse and imaginative writing in a technical sense, corresponding to the English use of the word in such phrases as "poetic criticism." The second, *poetisch*, came increasingly to refer to the universal, abstract, and spiritualized meaning referred to by Frei – a meaning that in English would be implied by such phrases as "poetic landscape," especially in painting, or even "poetic justice," in drama.

Together, the terms suggest the enormous cultural force possessed by the idea of the "poetic" to the German Romantics. Schlegel praises Goethe's prose novel, *Wilhelm Meister*, as "all poetry – high, pure poetry. Everything has been thought and uttered as though by one who is both a divine poet and a perfect artist" (Wheeler 1984, p. 64). Nor was this terminology confined to those Romantics who, like Schleiermacher and Schlegel, are now remembered as philosophers and critics. The poets Tieck and Novalis equally blur the line between philosophy and art. Comparing Cervantes with Shakespeare, Tieck declares *Don Quixote* "genuine poetry," which "set the tone for the whole age. . . . Cervantes, with great understanding and the most delicate and graceful touch, was trying to provide poetry in its orphaned state with a safe course and steady support in real life" (Wheeler 1984, p. 120). Even more disconcerting for English readers, Novalis praises Schlegel's *literary criticism* as poetry: "Schlegel's writings are philosophy as lyric. His [essays on] Forster and Lessing are first-rate minor poetry, and resemble the Pindaric hymns" (Wheeler 1984, p. 92). In this cultural climate, prose could only come across as a minor and technically uninteresting sub-genre of an idea of literature dominated by an all-embracing concept of "poetics."

Though the commonality of religion and literature was most extensively theorized by German Romantics like the Schlegels, Schleiermacher, and Novalis, it was not confined to Germany. In France the Revolutionary skepticism of Volney's *Ruins of Empires* (1791) – an attempt to historicize and explain Christian mythology in terms of Egyptian and Babylonian sources for the Bible – was countered by Chateaubriand's *Genius of Christianity* (1802). For Chateaubriand, the very qualities of traditional religion which had earned Volney's contempt as its weakest points were to be extolled as its essential qualities. Regardless of historical sequence, Christianity for Chateaubriand became the "ur-religion," as it were – the Platonic form by which all others were to be understood and against which all others were but shadowy reflections. The irrationality and emotion of Christianity, its ancient mythology, its capacity to inspire the most childish and naive devotion – all were now adduced as proof of its imaginative and psychological depth, its unique capacity to satisfy the whole person. This view was contrasted to what was portrayed as the shallow intellectualism of the Enlightenment skeptics. Chateaubriand's counter-thesis was nothing less than that

> the Christian religion, of all the religions that ever existed, is the most humane, the most favourable to liberty and to the arts and sciences; that the modern world is indebted to it for every improvement, from agriculture to the abstract sciences – from the hospitals for the reception of the unfortunate to the temples reared by the Michael Angelos and embellished by the Raphaels . . . that nothing is more divine than its morality – nothing more lovely and more sublime than its tenets, its doctrine, and its worship; that it encourages genius, corrects the taste, develops the virtuous passions, imparts energy to the ideas, presents noble images to the writer, and perfect models to the artist; that there is no disgrace in being believers with Newton and Bossuet, with Pascal and Racine. (Chateaubriand 1856, pp. 48–9)

For Chateaubriand, the mythologies of other, earlier religions, so far from being the source of later Christian doctrines, which he instead believed had been revealed, nevertheless point *toward* them, as dim intuitions of transcendent truth. Chateaubriand happily admits that ideas of the future life and of the immortality of the soul are present in older religions, but in their Christian form they are transformed by being no longer selective or culture specific: "The heaven and hell of the Christians are not devised after the manners of any particular people, but founded on the general ideas that are adapted to all nations and to all classes of society" (Chateaubriand 1856, pp. 203–4). Unlike the classical Elysium, heaven admits children, slaves, and "the lower classes of men." Unlike the Norse Valhalla, Christians do not specify either the weather or social activities. Unlike the mystery religions on which it has drawn, Christianity has no esoteric secrets: "What the brightest geniuses of Greece discovered by a last effort of reason is now publicly taught in every church; and the labourer, for a few pence, may purchase, in the catechism of his children, the most sublime secrets of the ancient sects" (Chateaubriand 1856, p. 204).

This blatantly appropriative argument climaxes with Part II, "The Poetic of Christianity," which argues not merely that Christianity has far outshone the pagan world in its capacity to inspire the arts, especially poetry, but also that Christianity is in its essence even *more* poetic than the arts that it inspires. Whatever the beauties of Homer and his fellow Greeks, they are occluded by the grandeur and sublimity of the Bible. By comparison with the Christian moderns, moreover, the ancients fail even where they might have been expected to excel: "whatever may be the genius of Homer and the majesty of his gods, his *marvellous* and all his grandeur are nevertheless eclipsed by the *marvellous* of Christianity" (Chateaubriand 1856, p. 330).

Yet Chateaubriand is concerned less with making comparisons than with developing a critical theory that will account for the *literary* superiority of Christian civilization over its antecedents:

> Christianity is, if we may so express it, a double religion. Its teaching has reference to the nature of intellectual being, and also to our own nature: it makes the mysteries of the Divinity and the mysteries of the human heart go hand-in-hand; and, by removing the veil that conceals the true God, it also exhibits man just as he is. Such a religion must necessarily be more favourable to the delineation of *characters* than another which dives not into the secret of the passions. The fairer half of poetry, the dramatic, received no assistance from polytheism, for morals were separated from mythology. (Chateaubriand 1856, p. 232)

If Chateaubriand glories in the new sense of Christian individuality, he is no less conscious of the moral and social dimensions raised by it: "Christianity, . . . by mingling with the affections of the soul, has increased the resources of drama, whether in the epic or on the stage" (Chateaubriand 1856, p. 299). Pagan antiquity had little interest in an afterlife, and classical tragedy ended simply with death. In Racine's *Phèdre*, however, the tragic tension is increased because, as a Christian wife, Phèdre is also jeopardizing her immortal soul. These examples typify a trend among Romantics in England, France, and Germany away from classical and toward biblical literary models. Chateaubriand claimed that this new

sense of individuality and inner space produced by Christianity had transformed poetry. Not merely did Dante or Milton owe their sublimity to the
Bible, but so had the subsequent Romantic aesthetic, which sees that their
true value is neither contingent nor merely fashionable but the *necessary*
and *inevitable* outcome of a Christian civilization. Moreover, the development of this "modern" sensibility enables us to look back on the past and
appropriate from it qualities that could hardly have been appreciated or
even recognized in earlier or non-Christian societies: "The growth of
descriptive poetry in modern times enables us to see and appreciate the
genius of the poets of Job, Ecclesiastes, and the Psalms" (Chateaubriand
1856, p. 380). The development of a modern historical and literary consciousness was not merely an outcome of Christianity. We understand
Christianity itself differently, and more comprehensively, as a result. Our
religion has, in short, given us the tools more fully to comprehend it.

Despite the fact that Chateaubriand's book was written in England
during his exile from revolutionary France, the idea of Christianity as the
creator of its own, primarily literary aesthetic was developed mainly in
Germany and France, and found few echoes in the United Kingdom, where
in the wake of the French Revolution, for the first three decades of the
nineteenth century Continental ideas were treated with paranoid
suspicion. Even though Samuel Taylor Coleridge had studied contemporary Romantics in Germany, and even though many of his works, including the first *Lay Sermon, The Friend*, and *Aids to Reflection* all revolve around
the relationship between literature and religion, he was nevertheless to be
accused by a later generation of Germanists, such as Thomas Carlyle and
Thomas de Quincey, of cowardice in expounding his views (see Ashton
1980, pp. 27–61). Typically, his own insights were scattered and unsystematic, to be found as often in footnotes and appendices as in the main
texts.

Thus in an appendix to the *Lay Sermons*, Coleridge describes the
Scriptures as:

> the living *educts* of the imagination; of that reconciling and mediatory
> power, which incorporating the Reason in images of the Sense, and
> organising (as it were) the flux of the Senses, by the permanence and
> self-circling energies of the Reason, gives birth to a system of symbols,
> harmonious in themselves, and consubstantial with the Truths, of
> which they are the conductors. . . . Hence . . . The Sacred Book is wor-
> thily intitled *the* WORD OF GOD. (Coleridge 1972, pp. 28–9)

Here Coleridge is at his most Kantian in doing what Kant never did: supplying in place of aesthetic abstractions the texts of the Bible as a bridge
between the world of the "Understanding" (the Kantian "Practical
Reason") and the world of "Reason" ("Pure Reason"). Hence for Coleridge
the poetic symbol is essentially *bi-focal*:

It is characterised by a translucence of the special in the Individual, or of the General in the Especial, or of the Universal in the General. Above all by the translucence of the Eternal through and in the Temporal. It always partakes of the Reality which it renders intelligible; and while it enunciates the whole, abides itself as a living part in the Unity, of which it is the representative. (Coleridge 1972, p. 80)

A symbol is the opposite of a generalization. Generalizations are a kind of lowest common denominator, deduced by the understanding from outward events according to what Coleridge elsewhere described as the dead arrangement of a mechanical philosophy. By contrast, a "symbol" is described by the metaphor of a lens. It is "translucent." It allows the light – by implication, even that of divine inspiration – to flow unimpeded through it and, by focusing on the concreteness of a particular example, to illuminate the universal of which it is an organic part.

Poetry, Coleridge explains in a parallel discussion written about the same time, "brings the whole soul of man into activity . . . reconciling opposite of discordant qualities" into a new and health-giving harmony (Coleridge 1907, vol. II, p. 12). We recognize the authenticity of biblical inspiration from the evidence of its poetic power on ourselves rather than from any external authority. This view does not mean that the Bible is *merely* to be apprehended as aesthetic or that the huge Romantic extension of the idea of the "poetic" means that *all* prose is poetic: "The first chapter of Isaiah (indeed a very large proportion of the whole book) is poetry in the most emphatic sense; yet it would be not less irrational than strange to assert that pleasure, and not truth, was the immediate object of the prophet" (Coleridge 1907, vol. II, p. 11). "Pleasure" and "instruction," the traditional Aristotelian ends of poetry, are not, however, to be abandoned now that "truth" is more a matter of inward "recognition" (in the Platonic sense) than of external instruction. On the contrary, there is an inherent *psychological* link between the two. In Coleridge's theory of the imagination, all knowledge is acquired by an actively integrating mental process. Thus in reading poetry, or the Scriptures, we are not passively receiving something "given" but are *participators* in it (see Prickett 1976, pp. 19–22). When Coleridge writes of the Bible that "there is more that *finds* me than all other books put together" (Coleridge 1849, p. 13), he is using the image of dialogue: the process of call and response that he sees as the hallmark of God's dealings with humans from Genesis to Acts, as a metaphor of the process of reading itself. Poetry is, as it were, characterized by this image of "election" in the theological sense. The Bible is "*the* WORD OF GOD" because it exemplifies most openly what is everywhere true of poetry. The *logos* is poetic.

Like many of Coleridge's other definitions, including that of "imagination," this distinctive meaning of "poetic," with its implications of psychological and Platonic truth, was not taken up by his nineteenth-century successors. Though there had been attempts to popularize Coleridgean and German Romantic ideas – notably, by the Hare brothers' *Guesses at Truth*, which went through five editions between 1827 and 1872 – the general notion of "imaginative" and "poetic" by the middle of the century was more likely to be *contrasted* to empirical, scientific truth than to suggest the poetic sort. Moreover, wherever this Romantic tradition was followed, the trail was often deliberately and tactically obscured.

For Søren Kierkegaard, in the Denmark of the 1830s, only a break with the grand narrative of Hegelianism could reassert the particularity central to actual literature, a particularity that had been lost in generalizations about literature. In the concreteness and irony of religious narrative he found writ large the fundamental irony at the center of all narrative. Kierkegaard went further than any of his contemporaries in seeing irony not merely as present within our narratives of the world but as *essential* to them. Within two years of completing his doctoral dissertation on *The Concept of Irony* (1841), he had published the two volumes of *Either/Or* (in February 1843), his *Three Edifying Discourses* (May 1843), and what has become his best-known book, *Fear and Trembling*, together with *Repetition* (October 1843). In the course of this astonishing burst of creativity, he was to elaborate the complex and dialectical triad that was to lie at the heart of much of his subsequent thinking.

In *Fear and Trembling* Kierkegaard describes three levels, or stages, in the development of the biblical Abraham toward what Kierkegaard calls the "knight of faith": the "aesthetic," the "ethical," and the "religious." Each prior stage is good in itself but is fatally and ironically undermined by the next. Thus what he calls "the beautiful story" of Abraham and his son Isaac on Mount Moriah must stand criticism from the ethical standpoint: is it *ever* right to practice human sacrifice, let alone of the firstborn, and at an age of understanding? But in turn the ethical standpoint is undermined by the religious, in which God's will, however mysterious, must prevail. Each level is wholly incommensurable with the others, yet as each higher stage is reached, the earlier stages, which originally looked like ultimate values in themselves, are reinterpreted and revalued. But for Kierkegaard, the aesthetic can never be subsumed into the ethical, or the ethical into the religious. Their values are not overturned or denied. They are simply *incommensurable*. Plurality and irony are not so much the result of imperfect understanding as part of the very fabric of existence.

If this was a difficult doctrine, Kierkegaard was well aware of its difficulties. To tell and re-tell the story of Abraham and Isaac is to highlight its insolubly problematic status, and if readers are not troubled by the feeling that this story is really not beautiful or ethical or religious, then they have not yet begun to struggle with its meaning. "Though Abraham arouses my admiration," writes Kierkegaard, "he at the same time appalls me." Any version of the story that sidesteps the impossibility of grasping his actions would "leave out the distress, the dread, the paradox" (Kierkegaard

1989a, pp. 71, 75). Not merely do such paradoxes in reading the Scriptures seem to belong to a different universe from the certainties of earlier pious or skeptical interpretations, but they also illustrate more clearly than ever before the Romantic assumption of the universal need for hermeneutics. No text is ever completely self-explanatory.

John Henry Newman, perhaps the least recognized Romantic of the nineteenth century, had other reasons for distancing himself from the Romantic aesthetic tradition. This slow, agonizing movement from Anglicanism to Roman Catholicism, described so graphically in his auto-biography, *Apologia Pro Vita Sua* (1865), was as much an emotional as an intellectual quest (see Prickett 1976). At its center was a search for what constituted "the Church." The delicately ironic title of his 1850 *Lectures on Certain Difficulties Felt by Anglicans in Submitting to the Catholic Church* barely conceals his contempt for the lack of organic self-consciousness of his old communion: "As a thing without a soul, it does not contemplate itself, define its intrinsic constitution, or ascertain its position. It has no traditions, it cannot be said to think; it does not know what it holds and what it does not; it is not even conscious of its own existence" (Newman 1850, p. 7). For Newman, the true analogy to the Church is now neither a grain of mustard seed nor yet a vine but a sentient human being.

Yet even as Newman begins to elaborate his metaphor, there occurs a typically Romantic shift of perspective. Just as Wordsworth, in his Preface to the *Lyrical Ballads*, had answered his own question, "What is a Poem?," by defining the nature of a poet, so Newman answers his own question, "What is the Church?," by shifting from anthropomorphic imagery of the institution to the mind of the individual who is doing the imagining:

> Thus it is that students of the Fathers, antiquarians, and poets, begin by assuming that the body to which they belong is that of which they read in time past, and then proceed to decorate it with that majesty and beauty of which history tells, or which there genius creates. . . . But at length, either the force of circumstance or some unexpected accident dissipates it; and, as in fairy tales, the magic castle vanishes when the spell is broken, and nothing is seen but the wild heath, the barren rock, and the forlorn sheep-walk: so it is with us as regards the Church of England, when we look in amazement on that which we thought so unearthly, and find so common-place or worthless. (Newman 1850, pp. 6–7)

The allusion to Keats' *La Belle Dame Sans Merci* is obvious. Keats' letters were not yet known to the general public, but there is a striking echo here of his belief that "The Imagination may be compared to Adam's dream: he awoke, and found it true."

What the Anglican Church could never satisfy was Newman's *imagina-tion*. Though Newman ignored Chateaubriand, regarded the Germans with hostility, and once even denied having read Coleridge, his quest for an emotionally fulfilling and unified faith that satisfied not merely his intellect but also his imagination belongs to the mainstream Romantic tradition. How, then, could he describe that richness of historical tradition, of language, ritual, and emotional association that he experienced in the life of the Catholic Church? Newman repeats the answer that he had already given in a different context in an earlier essay on the poet and critic John Keble: the life of the Church is *poetic*. "The Church herself is the most sacred and august of poets" (Newman 1846, vol. II, p. 442). If the language of the Church is "poetic," it is because the Church itself, the body of Christ, is the model from which we learn what a "poet" is. Almost fifty years after Chateaubriand, and thirty years after Coleridge, Newman, also a poet, is not so much defining literature in terms of the Church as defining the Church in terms of literature. Christianity is an essentially literary religion.

Ironically, Matthew Arnold, perhaps the most widely read English critic of the later part of the nineteenth century, would have agreed. But that, it turned out, was proof not of its essential truth but only of its essential wish fulfilment. Arnold's most popular theological works, *Literature and Dogma, God and the Bible*, and *St. Paul and Protestantism*, are often treated as if they were principally attempts to introduce German theology, especially the Higher Criticism of Feuerbach and Lessing, to an English audience. In many respects, however, his theological and critical stance is closer to that of the philosopher John Stuart Mill, whose *Autobiography* was published in 1873, the same year as *Literature and Dogma*. After his severe breakdown in early manhood, Mill had been forced to admit the emotional and healing power of poetry – especially, as it happened, the poetry of such "religious" writers as Wordsworth and Coleridge. Yet as an avowed and lifelong agnostic, Mill could hardly subscribe to their beliefs. His solution was the notion of "two truths": the idea that while poetry offered no accurate descriptions of the "real world" – science did that – it did offer "emotional truth" about human states of mind. The trick was to see that poetry and science referred to different areas of experience. In his essay on *What is Poetry?* (1833) Mill explains that poetry is neither more nor less than "feeling" or emotion, to be "distinguished from what Wordsworth affirms to be its logical opposite, namely not prose, but matter of fact or science" (Mill 1965, p. 104).

As Arnold presumably knew, Wordsworth never actually made this statement (see Prickett 1986, pp. 62–5), but Arnold, like Mill, believed that poetry was the language of emotion and not of fact. Similarly, there was no verifiable public cognitive content to the language of religion. It was, he insisted, "poetic." It was a product of that familiar phenomenon of *Aberglaube*, which Arnold translates as "extra-belief": the encrustation of miraculous legend, superstition, and fairy tale that had grown up around the basic moral truths of Christianity and which by the nineteenth century were in danger of strangling them. "*Aberglaube*," he explains, "is the poetry of life" that results from a process of innocent collective self-deception rather than deliberate fraud:

> That men should, by help of their imagination, take short cuts to what they ardently desire, whether the triumph of Israel or the triumph of Christianity, should tell themselves fairy-tales about it, should make those fairy-tales the basis for what is far more sure and solid than fairy-tales, the desire itself – all this has in it, we repeat, nothing which is not natural, nothing blameable. (Arnold 1895, p. 80)
> [Nevertheless] We have to renounce impossible attempts to receive the legendary and miraculous matter of scripture as grave historical and scientific fact. We have to accustom ourselves to regard henceforth all this part as poetry and legend. In the Old Testament as an immense and poetry growing round and investing an immortal Truth, "the secret of the Eternal": *Righteousness is salvation*. In the New, as an immense poetry growing round and investing an immortal truth, the secret of Jesus: *He that will save his life shall lose it, he that will lose his life shall save it*. (Arnold 1960, p. 370)

The question is what Arnold, the poet and man of letters, means here by "poetry." He is not asserting that "poetry" is simply a decorative fiction which is untrue, for he is also committed to the view that poetry embodies profound truths. Yet in the last resort "poetry," or a "feeling," must be separated from "truth" – here, clearly, ethics. The kernel can be extracted from its shell. Poetry – to continue his own image of a nut – is the husk that protects the seed, carries it safely to its destination, and nourishes it. But in order that the seed of truth may grow, the husk must eventually be dispensed with. It must break down or decay. If at first poetry gives life to new truths, it can become a source of confusion, misunderstanding, of "delusion and error." Poetry is not itself "untrue," for it was never about ideas in the first place. Poetry is merely a *mode* of expression – figurative, unscientific, and primitive. For Arnold, the tragedy of modernity is that "soon enough will the illusion which charmed and aided man's inexperience be gone; what have you to give him in the place of them?" (Arnold 1960, p. 378).

The real paradox of Arnold as poet-theologian is that he was to *narrow* the concept of the "poetic" more radically than any of his predecessors – including Mill, the utilitarian atheist. For Mill, at least the whole of religion, considered as "feelings of devotion," was poetic. Because Arnold was determined to salvage *some* ethical and cognitive kernel from that feeling, he was forced in the end to define "poetry" as the useless residue. Worse, as a poet, he found himself forced to consign almost everything that is attractive in religion to that residue. Like Keats' knight-at-arms or some strict Lockean who had discovered the unreality of secondary qualities or some Kantian forbidden to take pleasure in moral duty, Arnold finally boxed himself into a corner where "reality" was totally stripped of human emotion. As the ex-Jesuit and Catholic Modernist, George Tyrrell acutely observed that what Arnold had really "hoped for was, roughly speaking, the preservation of the ancient and beautiful husk after the kernel had been withered up and discarded" (Tyrrell 1902, p. 60).

Though Tyrrell himself had begun from a position not dissimilar to Arnold's, he was more sensitive to what Schleiermacher had seen as the roots of religion in primal perception itself. "All language," Tyrrell wrote in 1907, "is poetical in origin. It tries to express the whole inner state – not merely the truth, but the emotions and feelings in which truth is embedded; for the so-called 'faculties' – mind, will, feeling – have not yet been marked off from one another by abstract thought" (Tyrrell, quoted in Sagovsky 1983, p. 56). Nevertheless, for much of the twentieth century, as for the nineteenth, the English-speaking world remained perplexed by the problems of emotion versus truth that had fixated Mill and Arnold, and it failed to develop the original perspectives of the German Romantics. For this failure twentieth-century political history was partly responsible. Though Tyrrell's own approach deserves perhaps more study (see Sagovsky 1983; Prickett 1986) in the hands of this tradition, any approach to religion through literature remained a bi-focal and an often sadly pedestrian affair, lacking any clear theoretical rationale and frequently relying on strained comparisons between secular fiction and biblical books from which their authors garnered a few useful quotations.

Only in the second half of the century have the initial Kantian problems of the place of aesthetics in religion and of Kierkegaard's insistence on the inevitable irony of all literature been fruitfully re-examined. The German Catholic theologian Hans Urs von Balthazar's attempt to approach God by way of Kant's Third Critique, on aesthetic judgment, was startlingly at odds with the conventional Thomism of Catholic thought when it first appeared in the middle of the century, but it was to prove prophetic. "Great works of art," writes Balthazar, "appear like inexplicable eruptions on the stage of history. Sociologists are as unable to calculate the precise day of their origin as they are to explain in retrospect why they appeared when they did. . . . [Art's] unique utterance becomes a universal language; and the greater a work of art, the more extensive the cultural sphere it dominates will be" (Balthazar 1973, pp. 20–1).

In the Anglo-American world the assumed antithesis between scientific and religious language was so strong that when it was actually challenged from the scientific side, that challenge was largely ignored. Yet while Michael Polanyi's *Personal Knowledge* (1958) was written in English, he was himself Hungarian – part of that huge diaspora of European intellectuals created by Hitler which so enriched the English-speaking world. For Polanyi, writing as a scientist and a philosopher trained in the then current Anglo-American traditions of mechanism and linguistic skepticism, and with no apparent theological connections, language itself becomes in effect a crypto-theological device – a position that not even German Romantics had defended. Ever since Augustine, discussions of language had started with the idea of the Fall. For post-lapsarian humanity, after the catastrophe of Babel, language could never be more than an imperfect and muddied medium. While Enlightenment philosophers were less enamoured with theories of divine origin, from Locke to Leibniz the shadow of the Fall was transmuted into assumptions of the insufficiency of language and the hopelessly chaotic nature of metaphor. Indeed, the first claim that the structure of language itself might have a hidden metaphysical agenda was made not by a theologian but by a philosopher who wanted to get rid of what he regarded as covert and illegitimate theology. "I fear we are not getting rid of God," wrote Nietzsche, only partly tongue-in-cheek, "because we still believe in grammar" (Nietzsche 1968, p. 38).

Polanyi's theory of language, which for him comprises not merely verbal systems but all forms of symbolic description and measurement, including mathematics, started from a radical philosophical subjectivism. What makes it truly radical, however, is that this very personal quality of language opens a door to the possibility of universal communication. In the logic of discovery, for instance, he suggests that:

> even though we have never met the solution, we have a conception of it in the same sense as we have a conception of a forgotten name so that in some mysterious sense we will "recognise" the outcome as right when we finally arrive at it. Our heuristic cravings imply, like our bodily appetites, the existence of something which has the properties required to satisfy us, and . . . the intuitions which guide our striving express this belief. But the satisfier of our cravings has in this case no bodily existence . . . but when it comes we will believe it because "It arrives accredited in advance by the heuristic craving which evoked it." [He quotes the mathematician Polya:] "When you have satisfied yourself that the theorem is true, you start proving it." (Polanyi 1958, pp. 129–31)

Echoes of Plato are obvious in this conception of "truth," and Polanyi was refreshingly quick to acknowledge the metaphysical underpinnings of his epistemological system. But though "truth" may have a metaphysical as well as a physical reality, in the end that physical reality is a constant check. "Reality" in this very practical sense is not the unknowable ultimate Kantian "thing-in-itself" but a construct in which we are active and cooperative partners. The inability of living ordinary human language to maintain itself as a totally closed system is what Polanyi means by "indeterminacy." It is here that we find what might be called his "scientific subjectivism," pointing toward conclusions that are inescapably theological rather than merely linguistic. Insofar as formal languages work with terms that are totally defined in advance, they are incapable of describing anything not so defined. For Polanyi, the converse is that "only words of indeterminate meaning can have a bearing on reality" (Polanyi 1958, p. 251). "To speak a language is to commit ourselves to the double indeterminacy due to our reliance both on its formalism and on our continual reconsideration of this formalism in its bearing on our experience" (Polanyi 1958, p. 95).

But while it is theoretically possible to construct a "closed" language which is based upon unsound premises and which therefore lies, a closed language is impossible with the open-endedness of living language, which is constantly open to the check of reality. It is presumably possible to tell lies in any language. What is not possible, Polanyi believed, is to imagine a living language so constituted that lies could not in the end be detected and be shown to be lies if the appropriate evidence were brought forward. The concept of a lie can exist only in a context where we also know what truth means. However languages may differ in their ways of describing the world, all languages are ultimately subject to the idea of truth in some ultimate and therefore theological sense. Language may thus bear witness to the existence of God.

Though this conclusion appears to follow from Polanyi's whole argument, his hesitation in drawing it suggests doubts as to whether it is a legitimate inference from his psycho-biological premises. The English literary theorist George Steiner had no such inhibitions in his *Real Presences* (1989). Here he combines Polanyi's idea of the truth-value of language (unacknowledged) with von Balthazar's reanimation of the Kantian value of the aesthetic. Steiner, like the German Romantics and their French structuralist successors, is overwhelmed by the limitless possibility of language and in particular by the formal indeterminacy of any sentence. In Saussurian terminology he allows that "There is always . . . 'excess' of the signified beyond the signifier" (Steiner 1989, p. 84). The greater the gap between what is said and what can be said about it, the greater the *literary* value of the text in question (Steiner 1989, p. 83). This notion of "literature" as a text that invites comment and elucidation echoes Clifford Geertz's notion of "thick descriptions," for language which is richer and more culturally dense because of the resonances particular actions or feelings have within a certain culture (see Geertz 1983, ch. 1) – a definition which articulates the bond between literature and theology.

It is therefore no surprise to find Steiner differing sharply from the French theorists Roland Barthes and Jacques Derrida or their Swiss mentor, Ferdinand de Saussure, over the question of "meaning." Do words have innate historical stability in addition to their power of creating new meaning, or are they no more than algebraic terms, unrooted in the things they stand for and charged only with meaning by their context? The theoretical epitome of this position Steiner finds, not surprisingly, in "the deconstructionist post-structuralist counter-theology of absence" (Steiner 1989, p. 122).

Against this view Steiner:

> proposes that any coherent understanding of what language is and how language performs, that any coherent account of the capacity of human speech to communicate meaning and feeling is, in the final analysis, underwritten by the assumption of God's presence. I will put forward the argument that the experience of aesthetic meaning in particular, that of literature, of the arts, of musical form, infers the necessary possibility of this "real presence." (Steiner 1989, p. 3)

He offers what he calls, after Pascal's famous wager on God's existence, "a wager on transcendence," arguing that there is, in a genuinely great work of art and in its reception "a presumption of presence" (p. 214) – a word here used, almost defiantly, in a sense made popular by Derridian deconstructionists. "Presence" signifies that unattainable postlapsarian condition in which a text or word stands fully and completely for what it represents. In other words, Steiner is reasserting with an ironic postmodern boldness that all great art is ultimately religious art. It is not in what Derrida calls "grammatology" but in poetry that we encounter God.

Yet Steiner, who is Jewish by birth, nowhere commits himself to any specific theology. "Presence" and "transcendence" are, perhaps wisely, as far as he will allow himself. Questions remain: can we *define* "genuinely great art" or just recognize it? One pragmatic historical test stipulates that a work must, first, have survived several changes of fashion with its reputation intact – thus Shakespeare and Mozart are more visible now than in their own time – and that a work must have caused us to see and experience the world differently, and so changed the subsequent course of aesthetic expression. Both criteria are, of course, openly Romantic. But so is the whole notion of "great art." The Romantic "re-invention" of the Bible by Chateaubriand, Coleridge, Schleiermacher, and others drew on just these assumptions (see Prickett 1996). But it is one thing to believe that religious experience is in the twenty-first century inescapably literary and aesthetic or, conversely, that great literature presents "transcendent" experience. It is quite another to insist on equivalence. Only by returning to the Kierkegaardian paradox of incommensurables, I suspect, can we begin to address this question. That question, in one form or another, may well turn out to be the major calling for twenty-first-century theology.

Bibliography

Arnold, Matthew. *Literature and Dogma* [1873]. London: Macmillan, Popular edn, 1895.

Arnold, Matthew. *God and the Bible* [1875], ed. R. H. Super. Ann Arbor: University of Michigan Press, 1971.

Ashton, Rosemary. *The German Idea: Four English Writers and the Reception of German Thought, 1800–1860*. Cambridge: Cambridge University Press, 1980.

Balthazar, Hans Urs von. *Two Say Why*, tr. John Griffiths. London: Search Press, 1973.

Balthazar, Hans Urs von. *The Glory of the Lord*, ed. and tr. John Riches, 7 vols. Edinburgh: Clark, 1982–9.

Blair, Hugh. *Sermons*, 2 vols. London: Baynes, 1924.

Bowie, Andrew. *Aesthetics and Subjectivity from Kant to Nietzsche*. Manchester: Manchester University Press, 1990.

Chateaubriand, François René Auguste de. *The Genius of Christianity* [1802], tr. Charles White. Baltimore, MD, 1856.

Chatwin, Bruce. *The Songlines*. New York: Penguin, 1987.

Coleridge, Samuel Taylor. *Confessions of an Inquiring Spirit*, 2nd edn, ed. H. N. Coleridge, 1849.

Coleridge, Samuel Taylor. *Biographia Literaria* [1817], ed. John T. Shawcross, 2 vols. Oxford: Oxford University Press, 1907.

Coleridge, Samuel Taylor. *Lay Sermons* [1816–17], ed. R. J. White. Princeton, NJ: Princeton University Press, 1972.

Collins, David. *An Account of the English Colony of New South Wales* [1796], 2nd edn. London, 1804.

Eliot, T. S. "Tradition and the Individual Talent" [1919], in his *Selected Essays*. London: Faber, 1932, pp. 13–22.

Frei, Hans W. *The Eclipse of Biblical Narrative: A Study in Eighteenth and Nineteenth Century Hermeneutics*. New Haven, CT: Yale University Press, 1974.

Geertz, Clifford. *The Interpretation of Cultures*. New York: Basic Books, 1973.

Harrison, Peter. *"Religion" and the Religions in the English Enlightenment*. Cambridge: Cambridge University Press, 1990.

Hegel, Georg Wilhelm Friedrich. *Aesthetics: Lectures on Fine Art* [1835–8], tr. T. M. Knox, 2 vols. Oxford: Clarendon Press, 1975.

Kierkegaard, Søren. *The Concept of Irony, with Continual Reference to Socrates* [1841], eds. and trs. Howard V. Hong and Edna H. Hong. Princeton, NJ: Princeton University Press, 1989a.

Kierkegaard, Søren. *Fear and Trembling*, tr. Walter Lowrie [1941]. Princeton, NJ: Princeton University Press, 1989b.

Lacoue-Labarthe, Philippe, and Jean-Luc Nancy. *The Literary Absolute: The Theory of Literature in German Romanticism* [1978], trs. Philip Barnard and Cheryl Lester. Albany: State University of New York Press, 1988.

Locke, John. *A Letter Concerning Toleration* [1689], in his *Treatise of Civil Government and A Letter Concerning Toleration*, ed. Charles L. Sherman. New York: Appleton Century Crofts, 1965.

Manguel, Alberto. *A History of Reading*. New York: HarperCollins, 1996.

Mill, John Stuart. "What Is Poetry?" in *Mill's Essays on Literature and Society*, ed. J. B. Schneewind. New York: Collier Books; London: Collier-Macmillan, 1965, pp. 102–17.

Nietzsche, Friedrich. *The Twilight of the Idols and the Anti-Christ*, ed. and tr. R. J. Hollingdale. Penguin, 1968.

Newman, John Henry. *Essays Critical and Historical*, 2 vols. London: Longmans Green, 1846.

Newman, John Henry. *Lectures on Certain Difficulties Felt by Anglicans*, 2nd edn. London: Burns and Lambert, 1850.

Newman, John Henry. *Apologia Pro Vita Sua*. London: Longmans Green, 1864.

Ong, Walter J. *Orality and Literacy: The Technologizing of the Word*. London: Methuen, 1982.

Otto, Rudolf. *The Idea of the Holy: An Inquiry into the Non-rational Factor in the Idea of the Divine and its Relation to the Rational* [1917], tr. John W. Harvey. London: Oxford University Press, 1923.

Polanyi, Michael. *Personal Knowledge: Towards a Post-Critical Philosophy*. London: Routledge, 1958.

Prickett, Stephen. *Romanticism and Religion: The Tradition of Wordsworth and Coleridge in the Victorian Church*. Cambridge: Cambridge University Press, 1976.

Prickett, Stephen. *Words and the Word: Language, Poetics, and Biblical Interpretation*. Cambridge: Cambridge University Press, 1986.

Prickett, Stephen. *Origins of Narrative: The Romantic Appropriation of the Bible*. Cambridge: Cambridge University Press, 1996.

Prickett, Stephen. *Narrative, Religion and Science: Fundamentalism versus Irony 1700–1999*. Cambridge: Cambridge University Press, 2002.

Sagovsky, Nicholas. *Between Two Worlds: George Tyrrell's Relationship to the Thought of Matthew Arnold*. Cambridge: Cambridge University Press, 1983.

Schlegel, Friedrich. *Lucinde and the Fragments* [1799], tr. Peter Firchow. Minneapolis: University of Minnesota Press, 1971.

Schleiermacher, Friedrich. *On Religion: Speeches to its Cultured Despisers* [1799], tr. Richard Crouter. Cambridge: Cambridge University Press, 1988.

Steiner, George. *Real Presences: Is There Anything In What We Say?* London: Faber, 1989.

Tyrrell, George. *The Faith of the Millions: A Selection of Past Essays*. 2nd series. London: Longmans Green, 1902.

Wheeler, Kathleen M. (ed.), *German Aesthetic and Literary Criticism*. Cambridge: Cambridge University Press, 1984.

Chapter 5

Phenomenology of Religion

Thomas Ryba

About twenty years ago, I ran across a description in *Openings*, the US list of positions in religious fields. It read something like this: "A small college in the Eastern United States is looking for a candidate to teach introductory courses in Western religions and courses in her/his religion of specialization at the upper undergraduate level. Phenomenologists of religion need not apply." No explanation was provided for this pointed proscription.

A few years later, at temporal distance insufficient to heal the smart of that job announcement, I had a friendly argument with a senior colleague about the usefulness of the phenomenological method in the academic study of religion. During that argument he tossed off a remark that hit me squarely between the eyes. He said, "The trouble with you phenomenologists is that you spend so much damned time tinkering with the recipe that you never get around to baking the cake." With that quip the conversation ended abruptly, but the injustice of it stayed with me, especially since my interest in religious phenomenology had been spurred by the opposite experience. What had drawn *me* to religious phenomenology was that some of its practitioners had spent too much time baking very bad cakes with no discernible recipes.

The first anecdote, I think, illustrates the hard times on which religious phenomenology has fallen in the past twenty years, hard times particularly unforgiving of a religious science that held so much promise in its vigorous youth but that has proven so sterile in middle age. The second of these anecdotes is more directly symptomatic of the intellectual malaise of our *Zeitgeist*. Among phenomenologies there is indeed an unresolved contradiction between theory and practice, and the legitimacy of religious studies itself has been challenged in the past thirty years. Practitioners have shared a gnawing perplexity about objects and methods of research. This perplexity has been exacerbated by methodological diversity and theoretical disunity during a period in which the reign of grand theory has meant critical irreflexivity, practical sterility, and – despite postmodern disclaimers – the total hegemony of theory.

If a cake's proof is its taste, then there are delicious, intuitively baked cakes, just as there are many speculative recipes awaiting realization as delicious cakes. Likewise there are sound religious phenomenologies that are developed impressionistically, just as there are ideas of phenomeno-logical method that would result in sound phenomenologies, if they were realized. The problem lies with phenomenologies that, either because of their *ad hoc* composition or because of their unrealistic theoretical architectonics, are only *half-baked*. A second problem is the variety of phenomenological approaches. The proliferation of phenomenologies – baked, half-baked, or simply imagined – has meant that the very phrase "phenomenology of religion" has become equivocal and confusing (see Ryba 1991; Gilhus 1994, p. 20; Jensen 1993, pp. 109–33). But I will argue that phenomenologies possess sufficient similarities to be treated as a family of related approaches.

A third problem is the disparity between religious phenomenological and philosophical phenomenological methods. Each camp of practitio-ners has learned little from the other, and to the disadvantage of both groups. I am not suggesting this divide is absolute. As we shall see, reli-gious phenomenologies fall on a spectrum defined by their reliance on philosophical themes.

My purpose in this chapter is to clarify what religious phenomenology is and ought to be, in light of how it has been imagined and historically realized and also in light of the contemporary challenges it faces and must answer. What are wanted are guidelines about how to make it a service-able method in religious studies. My purpose is to suggest features of philosophical phenomenology that can be used to augment religious phe-nomenology, and to do so by *alluding* to the complex history of both.

What "Phenomenology" Means

Although it is anachronistically medieval to begin with an etymology to explain what something is, Martin Heidegger's discussion of "phenomenology" provides a model of etymology put to good philosophical use, even though we will not follow him in all his conclusions.

"Phenomenology" is formed from the Greek words *phainomena* and *logike*. *Phainomenon* is the noun formed from the passive inflection *phainomai* of the verb *phaino*. The Greek root *pha-* and its Sanskrit cognate *bha-* both mean "to shine bright or luminous, to be splendid, beautiful or eminent, to appear as, seem, look like, pass for, to show, exhibit or manifest" (Liddell and Scott 1846, p. 1589). According to Heidegger, this "showing" is made known *through* the phenomenon and is paradigmatic of signification. All "indications, presentations, symptoms and symbols have this fundamental formal structure of appearing" (Heidegger 1962, p. 29). This root contributes to the ambiguity of the meaning of *phainomenon* because it indicates a middle position between the subjective and the objective contributions of consciousness. Etymologically, "phenomenon" denotes any possible object of experience as it seems or can be perceived.

O- is the suffix of combination used to form compound words. *Logos* rarely means a mere written or verbal sign but rather means the outer sign *as expressing* the inner word or concept. Like its Latin cognate *ratio*, it also refers to the inner concept, with both words referring to "language, discourse, dialogue, principle, essence, reasonable arrangement, definition, proportion, analogy, ratio, reasonable ground, etc." (Liddell and Scott 1846, pp. 862–3). *O-* joined to *logikê/logia*, as in *–ologikê* or *-ologia*, means specifically analytic or scientific discourse about the word prefixed to it. But readings that thematize the suffix phrases *ho logos* or *ho logia* are also possible. According to the first thematization, the *logos – ho logos –* of something is most singularly its inner nature. According to the second thematization, *–ologia* signifies *the* singular concept (or science) thematized by the noun standing before it. When both thematizations are telescoped together, phenomenology is construed as a science of essences disclosed by phenomena. Heidegger notes that the *logos* as manifestation (*apophainesthai*) displays verbally what is partially or fully occluded by the appearance. When rigorous discourse becomes proof, then *logos* as manifestation becomes demonstration (*apophansis*) or scientific proof (*apodeixis*) (see Heidegger 1962, p. 56). Putting the two *etuma* together, we get a preliminary definition:

> *Phenomenology is scientific or analytic discourse about anything that appears subjectively and objectively to consciousness as pointing to something else; as such, it is about the very nature of those appearances but especially as they refer to or reveal an underlying, invariant structure or essence.*

Joining this definition to the Peircean taxonomy of signs, we can specify three species of phenomenological appearances: (1) indices, (2) icons, and (3) presentations (see Peirce 1974, vol. 5, pp. 140–2; vol. 2, pp. 156–75).

Indexic appearances are causally connected to their objects. They are phenomena like wind in the tree tops, Geiger counters and miracles. Iconic appearances bear homologies to their objects. They are phenomena like shadows, blueprints, and religious statuary. Presentational appearances make their objects really present. They are phenomena like the shared formality of concept and thing in St. Thomas' epistemology, the Jewish Tetragrammaton and the Roman Catholic Eucharist.

This threefold classification is a bit misleading insofar as *all* appearances are to some degree indexic, iconic, or presentational. *All* appearances are connected to their objects through causal chains or instrumentalities; *all* appearances possess features homologous to their objects; and *all* appearances present features of their objects. A sign's classification is determined by the immediacy and predominance of these features – whether the causal connection is proximate or distant, whether the homology is rich or minimal, or whether the presence is full or limited.

No appearance is free-floating, or entirely disconnected from any object, except in thought experiments. Even mirages and illusions signify some objects. To do phenomenology is to take the signal nature of appearances seriously. Unlike researchers who see their work done when the *purported* object behind an appearance is proven illusory, the phenomenologist of religion sees this step as the beginning of a new research project: discovering the *real* object behind what amounts to a Foucauldian symptomology (see Foucault 1975, pp. 88–106). Because phenomena always signify objects, phenomenologists greet illusions as opportunities to establish their proper attribution.

Another feature of appearances is that their ability to signal can be gauged according to their connectedness to objects. Thus one can say that a phenomenon is "over-determined," or polysemous, if its signification and accompanying interpretations are many. A phenomenon is "uni-semously determined" if there is a singular signification and interpretation. Finally, when phenomena are connected to objects in vague, puzzling, or mysterious ways, thus forcing extensive contextual investigations to discover any signification, these phenomena may be said to be "underdetermined."

Finally, we can study phenomena according to the efficacy with which they deliver their objects, that is, whether they signify their objects as semblances encouraging either error or access to their signaled objects. For example, phenomenology done to show that some phenomena are manipulated by political or ecclesial authorities to deceive a population about their true significance would be a methodological part of ideological criticism (see Ryba 2000, pp. 168–89).

Phenomena manifest two varieties of objects: (1) objects of the external world and (2) objects of the internal world. Objects of the external world exist outside of our bodies. We experience them as independent of our powers, wills, or personalities. Objects of the internal world exist inside our bodies. They depend on our physical, volitional, or personal existence. Objects of the external world are accessible to a community of observers in a way that internal objects are not. Objects of the internal world are more directly, though not infallibly, accessible through internal sensation. Internal sensations are signs given in embodied self-awareness.

Phenomenology is a reading of regular features of appearances intended to disclose related, underlying objects with certainty. The history of phenomenology, in its philosophical and religious varieties, is the history of a search for reliable methods of disclosure and for taxonomies of disclosed objects. Phenomenology is a realization of the Western scientific project, not with respect to inductive models of reasoning but with respect to the search for essential structures and their axiomatic arrangement according to the logics of parts and wholes, inclusion and exclusion, and dependence and independence. A phenomenological analysis of appearance thus more closely resembles set theory than inductive science. Even though it finds its field of investigation in the appearances of the physical world, the phenomenological quest is for the invariant structures that lie behind appearances. Appearances themselves are like symptoms rather than causes.

How Phenomenology Generally Proceeds

Following these preparatory descriptions, an example will make clear how phenomenology proceeds. This example comes from the practice of meditative prayer.

In the Roman Catholic tradition, the practice of meditative prayer has a long history and is described in detail by Louis of Granada, Theresa of Avila, Ignatius Loyola, Alphonsus Liguori, John Baptiste de Salle, and others. Its purpose is to fix on a passage in Christian Scriptures – the mysteries of the life and death of Jesus Christ, for example – for the purpose of discursively grasping the meaning of that passage, to come to certainty about its value, to love that value, and then to apply it in practice. Here an understanding of the meaning of the text is not what is primarily sought but rather a commitment to it which will issue in action. Although different lists of steps for its accomplishment are provided by different spiritual writers, there are at least six: (1) discursive prayer for grace to aid the meditation; (2) the minute *composition of place*, or reconstruction of the passage of the scripture in imagination; (3) reflection on the imaginative reconstruction resulting in conclusions and applications; (4) a discursive resolution of will to act according to these conclusions; (5) a conversation with God about the discoveries; and (6) a concluding prayer of thanksgiving, oblation, or petition.

A phenomenological analysis of meditative prayer would be interested in establishing both its conditions of possibility and its necessary and sufficient features. On the basis of the reports of meditators, phenomenologists would attempt to understand the intended end of the meditation, the focus (or intentionality) of each step as well as the background consciousness attending each. They would try to describe the feeling of presence (the presentational appearance) attendant upon the rehearsal of the imaginative reconstruction (iconic appearance), for example. They would try to describe which phenomena signal the transition from one step to another and how conscious focus changes with each. They would try to determine how conscious perceptions (the indexic appearances) cue the meditator that grace was operative in aiding the imaginative reconstruction, conclusions, and resolutions, and whether there was a relationship between the power of the meditative insights and the practice of the virtuous resolutions. They would try to determine whether certain imaginative reconstructions were more effective at revealing the value of the text and which ones enkindled commitment to the values expressed. In short, phenomenologists would attempt to understand whether each step was grounded on the previous step, which steps were in the conscious control of the meditator, which steps were (apparently) influenced by factors outside of conscious experience, and which steps were indispensable to the results sought. They would be interested in the necessary and sufficient features of this kind of prayer to be able to say what it essentially is.

More broadly, phenomenologists would be interested in showing whether the conscious acts connected with meditative prayer shared features with the other varieties of prayer (vocal-liturgical, affective and contemplative), as the Roman Catholic tradition claims, or stands apart as something distinct. Even more generally, phenomenologists would be interested in looking across religious traditions to see whether meditative practice with similar conscious acts occurs in other traditions and whether it delivers similar results and under what conditions (of dependence) it emerges relative to the historical development of those traditions.

Finally, the features identified in Roman Catholic meditative prayer might also be compared with secular techniques of visualization to see whether the techniques and results are the same or as effective apart from the meditator's claim that supernatural aid is required. The comparative goal of the phenomenological analysis of meditative prayer would be to provide a thick description as an end in itself and for comparison with other religious and secular descriptions in order to discover common necessary and sufficient structures.

Empirical science differs from phenomenology in that it (1) provides reductive explanations and (2) uses those reductive explanations to make predictions. It does both these things from a theoretical frame that is *not* that of adherents to a religion, that is not the theoretical frame relative to a religion.

Whereas empirical psychology might be interested in explaining the physiology of such meditation, or in providing a reductive explanation of *why* similar techniques of visualization lead to effective action, and then to use such reductive explanations to make predictions, the phenomenological technique is only secondarily directed to these ends. Whereas some methods of the empirical sciences proceed – in the short run – by simplifying and ignoring anomalous data, phenomenological analysis is interested in the thick description of these data and the way they form meaningful, ideal wholes.

Phenomenology is not interested in the reductive explanation of religion or in making predictions, though its descriptions may be useful in assisting reductions or predictions. In fact, many of the phenomenologists of the nineteenth century say that phenomenology is the first part of the empirical sciences. Phenomenology is a method of pure description concerned not with *material* causation but with the logic of parts and wholes, logical dependence and independence. Its interest is in establishing necessary and sufficient conditions *relative to the religious theoretical frame*. It looks for the essential structures that lie behind religious phenomena not because it wants to explain them in terms of simpler causes or in terms of a more scientific theory but because it wants to understand how the world view of the believer logically coheres.

Sometimes the investigation of the relations within the claims of the tradition means that inconsistencies are observed, but then the question is first put to the religious experts as to whether these inconsistencies are real or only apparent. If apparent, the phenomenological description is adjusted. If the experts provide no correction for an inconsistency, then the essential description is taken as more accurate to the phenomenon (relative to that tradition) than even the responses of the religious experts.

We must be clear that phenomenology stands not in opposition to empirical analysis but as a part of it. Its proponents claim that, as a superior method of description, it is an observational method which is a necessary complement to scientific explanation and forms the first part of empirical science. However, phenomenological analysis does throw down a gauntlet in the face of the reductive orientation of empirical sciences. In that phenomenology issues in a rich set of descriptions that coheres as a system, each description in this system calls for an explanation.

Philosophical Phenomenology Provides One
of the Theoretical Frames for
Religious Phenomenology

The development of philosophical phenomenology would not have been possible had natural science not rehabilitated phenomena. In developing phenomenological methods for religious studies, scholars of religion were influenced by descriptive methods in the sciences, even when their borrowings from philosophical phenomenology were indirect or unconscious. For this reason, Western science, philosophical phenomenology, and religious phenomenology are mutually imbricated and cannot be discussed in isolation from one another.

Pre-Husserlian philosophical phenomenology

Seven philosophers figure importantly in the pre-Husserlian development of philosophical phenomenology: Johann Heinrich Lambert (1728–77), Immanuel Kant (1724–1804), John Robison (1739–1805), Georg Friedrich Hegel (1770–1831), Sir William Hamilton (1788–1856), William Whewell (1794–1866), and Charles Sanders Peirce (1839–1914). It is possible to summarize the themes of these pre-Husserlian theoreticians of phenomenology as they anticipate Husserlian ideas. First, they accomplish their work against the background of Western science. Second, they thematize phenomena as *objects* of scientific reflection. Third, they propose *methods* by which phenomena can be described scientifically. Fourth, they theoretize the disciplinary *placement* of phenomenology among known sciences.

Philosophical phenomenology and
Western science

The historical origins of phenomenology are complex. In any consideration of its patrimony, Platonic dialectic, analysis and colligation, Aristotelian syllogistic, Skeptic and Neoplatonic notions of "suspension," Augustinian criteriology, Galilean empirical science, and Cartesian hyperbolic doubt all figure as influences. Though first conceived by Johann Heinrich Lambert in 1764 as a new instrument (*organon*) to supplement the deductive method of Aristotle and empiricist method of Bacon, it arrived late on the Western intellectual scene. It marks a transition from sciences excessively determined by deductive *a priori* assumptions to models allowing for the grounding of science in experience, a transition marked by the assumption that appearances are inherently intelligible.

The philosophical understanding of phenomena

The philosophical theoreticians of phenomenology construe phenomena with an expansiveness that includes all possible objects. All seven of the theoreticians are in agreement that phenomena may be taken as objects of science, but they differ over what they conceive phenomena to be.

For Lambert, phenomena are the false aspects of anything and can be classified according to three categories of experience: physical, psychological, and moral experience (see Lambert 1764, vol. 2, pp. 229–30). The purpose of phenomenology is the separation of appearance and error from truth, truth being the conformity of thought with what exists (see Lambert 1764, vol. 2, pp. 217–18). Robison leaves phenomena relatively undefined, presuming them to be pure *qualia* present in perception, metaphysically unconnected, with mind supplying the causal connection between them (see Robison 1798, p. 587). For Kant, undetermined sensation is mere appearance. Sensation becomes experience, if sensation is thought through the categories of understanding. But Kant allows that experience can be examined, descriptively, according to its pure sensuality. These would be phenomena prior to any determinative judgment (see Kant 1985, pp. 476–8). Hegel, the absolute idealist, more radically subjectivizes phenomena by understanding them as coextensive with mind. Initially and unconsciously, they are given as unconstructed and unintelligible: they *are*, but in what sense they are cannot be described. Conceptualized through the conscious distinctions that accompany the Hegelian dialectic, they attain intelligibility (see Hegel 1967, p. 94).

Hamilton's notion of phenomena resembles those of his predecessors in a variety of ways. Like Lambert, Hamilton divides phenomena into three classes – cognitions, feelings and conations – that roughly correspond to the Lambertian divisions (see Hamilton 1877, vol. 1, pp. 183–4). And like Robison and Kant, Hamilton places phenomena outside of causal relations, causation being a constructive capacity of consciousness. There is a duality in the way Whewell understands phenomenology that reflects both empiricist and idealist influences. On the one hand phenomena are the *a posteriori* qualities of objects studied by individual sciences. On the other hand phenomena are only intelligible because they are structured by paired *a priori* ideas ("syzygies" or couplings) that make them scientific objects (see Whewell 1967, vol. 1, pp. 17–24). Finally, for Peirce, phenomena (or *phaenerons*) populate the field of possible objects of consciousness, a field of objects "directly open to observation" and complexly stratified like the Husserlian notion of experience but dependent upon constitutive categories of firstness (monadicity characterized by noumenal unconnectedness), secondness (dyadicity characterized by struggle, resistance, effort, causation, force, and surprise), and thirdness (triadicity characterized by transuasion, understanding, and law) (see Peirce 1974, vol. 5, p. 28; vol. 1, pp. 141–3).

The philosophical understanding of "phenomenology"

Two distinctively different notions of phenomenology are formulated by its pre-Husserlian philosophical architects. By one notion, phenomenology gives access to *a priori* conditions of appearance in any human experience. The philosophical phenomenologies of Lambert, Kant, Hegel, and Hamilton are primarily oriented to this project. By the other notion, phenomenology is directed to *a posteriori* classification of empirical data according to resemblances and differences. This is the project of Robison's phenomenology. Sometimes, as with Whewell and Peirce, phenomenology is associated with both the project of understanding experience and the project of classifying data (see Ryba 1991, pp. 213–30; James 1995, pp. 28–9).

The place of phenomenology within the sciences

The pre-Husserlian phenomenologists articulate phenomenology in relation to other sciences variously, according to whether they think it a method or a free-standing science. Those thinkers – Lambert, Robison, and Hamilton – who discuss science in the abstract, as a method of attaining certain knowledge without associating it with a specific discipline, are inclined to articulate phenomenology as a part of a generalizable scientific method. Lambert makes phenomenology follow the methods of logic and alethiology (science of truth) because each provides supplements that enable phenomenology to distinguish false appearance (*Schein*) from truth. By contrast, Robison puts phenomenology before the methods of taxonomy and etiology (science of causes) because, following Humean empiricist assumptions, classification and the postulation of causation follow upon accurate description. Akin in his reasoning to Robison, Hamilton places phenomenology before nomology (science of laws) and ontology (science of being) because the scientific description of cognitions, feelings, and conations must precede an understanding of their law-like connection, refinement, and theoretical employment.

Kant, Hegel, Whewell, and Peirce presume phenomenology to be science in a disciplinary sense, not simply a method. For Kant, phenomenology is a sub-discipline which is a part of the metaphysical foundations of the natural sciences, a science that describes the contents but not the forms of the experiences of motion. Although Kant never speaks about religious phenomenology *per se*, his philosophy affects its development by profoundly influencing nineteenth-century philosophy of science. Later, Kant's ideas enter religious studies when religionists like Rudolf Otto and

Anders Nygren appropriate his epistemology to theoretize the category of the Holy. Hegel makes phenomenology a foundation of philosophy construed as the model science. It is the first part in the encyclopedia of the philosophical sciences and the basis upon which Hegelian logic, philosophy of nature, and philosophy of mind are developed. Whewell uses the term phenomenology ambiguously. Secondarily, he understands it as designating the "palaetiological sciences": historical, descriptive sciences such as geology, paleontology, and uranology. Primarily, however, he understands it as a method for studying the origins, methods, and goals of the disciplinary sciences. As such, it is a part of philosophy of science.

Finally, Peirce makes phenomenology a separate discipline standing between pure mathematics and the inductive sciences. It mediates between these sciences by taking the logical forms of pure mathematics and showing that they are implicit in observational data. Peirce allows phenomenology to meddle in the inductive sciences at will. There can be phenomenologies of physics, chemistry, sociology, and – one would presume – religion inasmuch as all of these scientific domains possess empirical data that can be organized according to formal structures.

Husserlian phenomenology

Despite the claims of Herman Spiegelberg and Dermot Moran, Husserl cannot be said to be the creator of phenomenology (see Moran 2000, p. 60). As we have seen, it existed in wide variety in the late eighteenth and throughout the nineteenth century. However, the interests of most pre-Husserlian phenomenologists – perhaps with the exception of Peirce – were not so narrowly focused on the development of phenomenological method and its minute application as was Husserl. For the rigor that he brought to phenomenology, Husserl's name is deservedly connected with the twentieth-century movement. Husserlian philosophy is an intellectual watershed upstream from all twentieth-century phenomenologies as well as from those postmodern philosophies engaged in the paradoxical deconstruction of the very Husserlian techniques and goals that made them possible.

Husserl's "perfectionism, pride and great insecurity" contributed to his "over-confidence" on the one hand and to an "almost masochistically self-disparaging humility" on the other, so that Husserl's system, like Theseus' ship, was a project in a constant process of construction and renovation (see McCall 1983, p. 55). It is a live question whether there is a single Husserlian phenomenology or several incompatible Husserlian approaches (see Moran 2000, pp. 56–66).

Among the distinct purposes of Husserlian phenomenology are: (1) the critique of the knowledge founding logic, (2) the description of the grounding structures of experience, (3) the description of the role of the mind in the constitution of experience, (4) the creation of "a unified theory of science and knowledge," (5) the provision of a non-naturalistic ground for worldhood, and (6) the realization of a "complete descriptive philosophy" (see Farber 1968, p. 152). What follows highlights those purposes that have direct significance for religious phenomenology.

Phenomena in Husserlian phenomenology

Like that of Peirce, the Husserlian phenomenon is any possible object of consciousness. But unlike Peirce, Husserl does not posit a world external to consciousness. Consciousness and possible consciousness exhaust all that is or that can be thought. The phenomenal field is a structured, stratified network formed of conscious acts and meanings, any part of which can be thematized as phenomenological object. One of the most potentially fruitful (yet neglected) phenomenological techniques, the Husserlian mereology (*meros* + *logike* = "science of parts"), is presented in the *Logical Investigations* (see Husserl 1970, vol. 2, pp. 435–89). There Husserl shows how the logic of dependence and independence, of part and whole, can be used to describe the essential features of any object. He maintains that this logical technique is applicable to any stratum of experience.

Initially, Husserl sought universal knowledge through a method that would ground certainty, first, in monadic consciousness and, second, inter-monadically (see Husserl 1976, p. 156). In the years following the *Cartesian Meditations*, this search was frustrated. The new hope that emerged was that certain knowledge could be grounded in a pre-given, intersubjective manifold of appearances that he termed the "Lifeworld" (see Husserl 1973, pp. 136–7). Whether the *genesis* of experience is primarily rooted in the ego or in the Lifeworld, the Husserlian phenomenology takes the *subjective analysis* of objective experience as the method by which evidences are brought to certainty. It is in his desire to return to ordinary experiences that his motto "Back to the sources" has its meaning. And it is on this score that his phenomenology is particularly criticized by the postmoderns (see Flood 1999, pp. 91–116).

Consciousness as object-constituting

From Brentano, Husserl adopted the notion that all experience is intentional, or directed toward objects. But for Brentano, following the Thomists, this intentional relation delivers a real object external to consciousness, whereas for Husserl the intention delivers the object as an act and object *within* consciousness. For Husserl, there is no outside to consciousness. Even when the object is understood as transcendent, it is not transcendent to all possible consciousnesses, only transcendent to *a* consciousness in its finitude.

For Husserl, object-consciousness possesses a unique intentional structure consisting of the mental act that intends the object (*noesis*) and the essential qualities of the intended object (*noema*). Both of these structures are known within an organized context of previous mental acts – a *noetic* horizon – and of previous possible transformations of the object – a *noematic* horizon. Thus even in the midst of experience of a dynamic object, intentionality of consciousness is fixed on what is invariant in the object as it streams through consciousness. The intention "tracks" it and preserves its identity (see Husserl 1937, p. 700a).

The steps in the Husserlian phenomenological technique

The distinctive feature of Husserlian phenomenology, in contrast to its predecessors, is its technique. Tied to the ends of Husserlian phenomenology enumerated by Farber above, Husserlian phenomenology aims to be an essential (*eidetic*) science of "indissoluble essential structures . . . which persist through all imaginable modifications" (see Husserl 1976, pp. 11–12). It is directed to bring the phenomenologist to a preconceptionless and indubitable experience of appearances and, on the basis of this experience, to uncover the essential typologies manifest through these appearances.

Because Husserl obsessively tinkered with them, it is impossible to establish a precise set of steps for his method. Even so, it is possible to describe some of the most important steps, which are repeated in different works. They are: (1) *epochē*, (2) phenomenal reduction, (3) contemplative modalization, (4) essential reduction, and (5) transcendental reduction.

The germ of Husserl's idea for the *epochē* ("suspension" or "bracketing") of phenomena can be attributed – minus their skepticism – to Sextus Empiricus and the Neoplatonic Academicians Arcesilaus and Carneades (see Ryba 1991, pp. 208–11). For Husserl, the *epochē* is neither the denial of the existence of a being nor Cartesian hyperbolic doubt. Rather, it is the suspension of judgment about a phenomenological object so that it presents itself denuded before consciousness (see Husserl 1976, pp. 107–11). Bracketing transforms the natural conscious attitude by putting quotidian interpretations of appearance out of play to reveal phenomena as they are. The effect of this phenomenal transvaluation is to reduce objects to pure phenomenological data as the matter for the next step, phenomenological reduction.

The aim of *phenomenological reduction* is to reveal parts and wholes that comprise phenomena. It is complete when a thought whole can be shown to be necessarily dependent on its constituent parts, according to the Husserlian mereological relations. This is equivalent to saying that the relation between phenomenal parts and wholes is presented to consciousness as adequate, indubitable, distinct, and clear.

Contemplative modalization is the step preparatory to the eidetic reduction and consists of (a) an intuition that decides the limits to the phenomenon, (b) a variation of its internal features to determine the admissible limits to its typification, and (c) a variation of the limits to its relative determination by other objects. The point of contemplative modalization is to ground the whole, first, with respect to internal parts and then with respect to external phenomena (see Husserl 1973, pp. 103–5).

Eidetic reduction is accomplished by subjecting the immediate founding parts of an object to imaginative variation to arrive at unchangeable features that are structurally characteristic. The sub-step of eidetic annihilation completes eidetic reduction. Here various features are imaginatively disengaged from the object. If disengagement makes the object incomprehensible, then these are its essential features (see Husserl 1973, pp. 103–5).

Husserl claims that this technique can be applied to anything thinkable. It is in this context that Husserl's reduction to the Lifeworld and the transcendental reduction have meaning. They are applications of these technical steps, but with specific objects. The reduction to the Lifeworld attempts to describe the essential features of a pre-given intersubjective world as it grounds human consciousness. The transcendental reduction uses the same method in an attempt to define human individuality (the self or transcendental ego) as that which remains when the Lifeworld is put out of play.

A description of philosophical phenomenology

It is now possible to provide a general description of philosophical phenomenology that joins its pre-Husserlian to its Husserlian features. The objects of phenomenology are phenomena understood as any possible object of consciousness. The purpose of phenomenology is twofold: (1) the exhaustive diachronic and synchronic description and formalization of unchanging phenomenal qualities and relations, and (2) the taxonomic arrangement of these qualities and relations. The distinctive methods of phenomenology consist of unprejudiced observation and description, especially phenomenological reduction, essential reduction, and taxonomy conducted according to mereological rules. Phenomenology does not exist as a separate science but is an observational method that is part of every science. Its object domain is dictated by the science of which it is part.

Phenomenology of Religion

Though the scholasticism of the phenomenology of religion has been most pronounced in the Netherlands, Scandinavia, Germany, the United

Kingdom, and the USA, my focus will be on what Jacques Waardenburg has called "classical religious phenomenology," the approach closely connected with the Dutch school in the first half of the twentieth century (see Waardenburg 1978, pp. 23–44). I choose this school as my focus because there religious phenomenology had its origin and achieved its most distinctive formulation.

Chantepie's religious phenomenology

About one hundred years after Lambert coined the term "phenomenology," the Dutch religious historian Pierre Daniel Chantepie de la Saussaye invented the term "religious phenomenology" in his *Manual for the Study of Religion* (1891). This phrase designates a component of religious science directed to the arrangement of religious conceptions so that "important sides and aspects" are brought into resolution (Chantepie 1891, p. 6). Four components are requisite to this science: (1) "metaphysical, psychological, and historical" methodologies; (2) a philosophy of history of civilizations; (3) specific backgrounds (archaeology, philology, ethnology, psychology, mythology, and folklore); and (4) an orientation to study religion in its *essence* and *manifestation* (see Chantepie 1891, pp. 3–8; Ryba 2001, p. 311).

Chantepie cites Hegel's *Lectures on the Philosophy of Religion* as the basis for the first set of requisite features. Only metaphysical and psychological methodologies are formally philosophical. History, while treated as the material of philosophical analysis, is not. The investigation of the *essence* of religion corresponds to the philosophy of religion, which is subdivided into the metaphysics, or objective investigation, of religion and the psychology, or subjective investigation, of religion. The investigation of the *manifestation* of this essence corresponds to the history of religion, which is subdivided into ethnology and history. Taxonomy, or the systematization of religious phenomena, bridges the philosophy and the history of religion (see Ryba 2001, p. 312; James 1995, p. 42). Though Chantepie intends to purge everything except the historical from his *Manual*, he retains phenomenology despite its muddying of methodological boundaries.

Phenomenology in the *Manual* is primarily taxonomic and historical. Phenomena are arranged according to the "necessary division[s]" in the evolution of consciousness reflecting the unity of religion, the many-faceted manifestations of religion, and the relationship between its unity and variety (see Chantepie 1891, pp. 50–1). This arrangement identifies the originating ideas of religions, but because genetic approaches are inadequate, it also organizes *forms* of essential features, forms not unlike the Whewellian syzygies: true-false, natural-revealed, popular-personal, mythological-dogmatic, rationalistic-aesthetic-ethical, ecstatic-depressed, particular-universal, and natural-moral. Though Chantepie defers to the "accurate definition" of religious phenomena by philosophy, and avows contentment with historical and ethnographic classification, his deference is at odds with his execution (see Chantepie 1891, p. 67; Ryba 2001, p. 315).

Tiele's religious phenomenology

By the time Cornelius Petrus Tiele wrote the *Elements of the Science of Religion* (1896–8), the idea of a science of religion had been sufficiently established to allow him to claim that it was one of the "sciences of the human mind" (Tiele 1899, vol. 1, p. 2). Tiele never claimed to be offering an exact definition of the essence of religion since that definition could only be the result of arduous scientific labors (see Tiele 1899, vol. 1, p. 4). Nevertheless, a heuristic definition was needed. Tiele provides it in recursive form as "the aggregate of all those phenomena invariantly . . . termed religious, in contradistinction to ethical, aesthetical, political" phenomena (Tiele 1899, vol. 1, p. 4). In other words, the essence of religion consists of "manifestations of the human mind in words, deeds, customs and institutions" testifying to the "belief in the superhuman" and serving "to bring [one] . . . in relation with it (Tiele 1899, vol. 1, p. 4). Here the operative words are "manifestations" and "belief." Tiele has no intention of extending his understanding of the phenomena of this science to supernatural objects, *per se*. Religious phenomena are "historical-psychological, social and wholly human" thematizations of the supernatural (Tiele 1899, vol. 1, pp. 4–5). Even so, he does not consider this science reductively naturalistic either (see Tiele 1899, vol. 1, pp. 15–16).

Tiele's approach to the discovery of the essence of religion is empirical and works toward that essence through an "unprejudiced" but "sound and critical" scientific "investigation" of its concrete phenomena (Tiele 1899, vol. 1, pp. 5, 9). Science here possesses four features: (a) an object domain with sufficient breadth; (b) a unifying theme for the facts of that domain; (c) an ordered system of these facts as the data for inferences; and (d) fruitful results on the basis of a, b, and c (see Tiele 1899, vol. 1, p. 6). The object domain of religious science is the set of all human manifestations of religion. The *unity* of this domain is the historical continuity of human psychology refracted through these phenomena in different developmental stages. The *ordered system* of facts is the scientific taxonomy of religious phenomena. The eventual *fruitfulness* of its results is presaged by the importance of the study (see Tiele 1899, vol. 1, p. 6). The very structure of Tiele's *Essay* corresponds to the outward and the inward objects of this science. The outward objects are addressed in the morphological, or *ontic*, section, which deals with "the constant changes of form resulting from an ever-progressing evolution." The inward objects/unity are addressed in the ontological section, which deals with "the unalterable element in transient and ever-altering forms" that constitute "the origin and very nature of religion" (Tiele 1899, vol. 1, p. 27).

Tiele places religious phenomenology at the point of convergence between the historical study of religion, "which observes, collects, combines, compares and classifies facts in their order of development," and special theologies, which legitimate religious belief (see Tiele 1899, vol. 1, p. 13). The crowning achievement of the science of religion – the discovery of origins and essences – cannot be achieved by either alternate study. Tiele's phenomenology is a special science in a way that Chantepie's is not, though it is profoundly philosophical because it penetrates to the foundation of religious phenomena (see Tiele 1899, vol. 1, pp. 13–15).

Tiele describes the methods of his science with greater clarity than Chantepie. Not exclusively positivist-empirical, genetic-speculative, or metaphysical, the phenomenology of religion employs as its chief method an *a posteriori* deductive movement. Its premises are the inductive conclusions of the proximate empirical sciences. It moves deductively from their empirical conclusions to common religious psychology or being, the goal here being an explanation of religious consciousness that can be tested by facts (see Tiele 1899, vol. 1, pp. 18–20).

Tiele's phenomenology constructs a taxonomy divided between morphological and ontological features. Morphological taxonomy proceeds according to vitalist laws of growth and progress reminiscent of John Henry Newman's marks of development: religion preserves a unity despite its developmental polymorphism; religious change is not capricious but law-like, with later stages emerging out of earlier; religion is an *entelechy*, with its final form present potentially in its earliest stage; each stage is valuable, important, and rightly existent; each stage is sublimated in a succeeding stage; and last, religion preserves its *sui generis* status against other cultural sectors (see Tiele 1899, vol. 1, pp. 29–31; see also Ryba 2001, p. 321).

Like human growth, religious growth can be either continuous or discontinuous, either stagnant or dynamic, either progressive or regressive, either short-lived or long-lived, and either culturally dependent or culturally independent (see Tiele 1899, vol. 1, pp. 31–2). Religions develop like the radiation of animal species. Each germ-form radiates into multiple branches, each branch being a "one-sided elaboration of one leading religious [root] idea" leading to its "utmost consequences" conditioned by the historical circumstances in which it grows (Tiele 1899, vol. 1, p. 55). History compels variation in the root idea of religion – an idea not unlike that of Husserlian perspectival variation. Against Chantepie's sympathies, Tiele rejects the Hegelian classification of religions, calling it "a failure" and "useless," and settles on a general distinction between nature and ethical religions, but admits that all classifications are fuzzy and provisional at best (see Tiele 1899, vol. 1, p. 58).

Because the ontology of religion employs a historical equivalent of the Husserlian perspectival variation, the essence of religion is manifest through historical forms, but not as repetitions of the same stages for each religion. Individual forms have different histories, and the transversal comparison of these histories leads to a universal changeless essence. Because most evolved religious adaptations best manifest religious potential, they are instructive more about the essence of religion than about primitive adaptations (see Tiele 1899, vol. 1, pp. 53–4; vol. 2, p. 188).

Kristensen's religious phenomenology

A measure of the acceptance of this new religious science was that when the Norwegian William Brede Kristensen succeeded C. P. Tiele at the University of Leiden in 1901, the new chair was named "History and Phenomenology of Religion" (see James 1995, p. 141). Though adopting features of Chantepie's phenomenology, Kristensen rejects Tiele's evolutionism (see James 1995, pp. 141, 148–9). He also rejects traditional comparative religion as insufficiently scientific because it is pitched apologetically to demonstrate the superiority of Christianity (see Kristensen 1960, p. 2). Because religious phenomenology favors neutral observation, it constitutes a new kind of comparison, one that is without triumphalist and developmentalist presumptions. Its focus is narrower than that of previous approaches. Instead of comparing religions "as large units," it extracts similar minute phenomena from "their historical setting[s]" to "bring them together" and study them in classes to "shed light" on one another (Kristensen 1960, p. 2). How these classes are determined is something of a hermeneutical circle. Kristensen does not discount taxonomic difficulties but thinks that these may be circumvented by closer scrutiny of minute data working toward the essences lying behind them (see Kristensen 1960, pp. 8–9).

Because similar motivations determine similar practices, Kristensen believes that broad data sets within religious categories like sacrifice, prayer, ritual, oracle, and world order can correct false conclusions drawn from familiarity with a single religion (see Kristensen 1960, p. 3). Phenomena that present themselves as inter-traditionally "nearly identical" are most intriguing, the purpose of phenomenology being to get at the universal value, "thought, idea or need" that they present (Kristensen 1960, p. 2). Here value plays a role different than in comparative religion. The concern of religious phenomenology is not with comparing the excellence of religions but with understanding why a particular thing is valued *within* a religion (see Kristensen 1960, p. 2). Phenomenology of religion begins by attempting to understand religion from its "own standpoint . . . that is how it is understood by its own adherents" (Kristensen 1960, p. 6). Then "Phenomenology [of Religion] tries to gain an over-all view of the ideas and motives which are of decisive importance in all of History of Religion" (Kristensen 1960, pp. 2–3), and it does so according to their historical and ideal connections.

Like Rudolf Otto, Kristensen takes the Holy as the *sui generis* category of religion, a category that is not susceptible to "intellectual, ethical or aesthetic" reduction. The Holy is a category populated by phenomena that arouse awareness of "spontaneous factors which are infinite and absolute" (Kristensen 1960, pp. 15–16). The philosophy of religion takes the idea of the Holy as a concept for criticism and refinement, but religious phenomenology tries to capture it as experienced. This approach puts the Holy beyond rational criticism because *as* experience it is "self-subsistent and absolute." The challenge that faces religious phenomenology is to grasp the Holy from within the believer's religious experience and then to formulate accurate descriptions of it (Kristensen 1960, p. 23).

None of this is to say that other approaches to religion are useless. Rather, they are simply less than ideal (see Kristensen 1960, p. 6). Comparative religion fails because it valorizes a religion. The history of religion is objectively too distant. The philosophy of religion is focused on idealities (see Kristensen 1960, pp. 6–7, 9). The belief commitments smuggled into comparative religions bias its conclusions. The objectively empathetic method of history – which is incapable of delivering the "existential' nature" of religion – falls short of imaginative entry into religion. The essential method of philosophy does not search out religious facts (see Kristensen 1960, p. 9). Religious phenomenology charts a middle course among these three approaches (see Kristensen 1960, p. 6). In doing so, it employs data provided by comparative religion, the history of religion, and the philosophy of religion alike. In turn, these disciplines stand in "mutual relation" to it and freely borrow from it (Kristensen 1960, p. 9). From comparative religion, religious phenomenology accepts some typological categories. From history of religion, it accepts the empathetic method and historical facts. From philosophy, it accepts the definition of the essence of religion. But to these gleanings phenomenology adds the "personal touch," an "indefinable sympathy" (or intuition) for alien religious data which grows through scientific discovery while being grounded in our own experience of what religion is (see Kristensen 1960, p. 10). While not denying religious phenomenology its scientific objectivity, Kristensen introduces a theological cause for its fruitfulness: religious phenomenology "without doubt, takes place by the illumination of a Spirit who extends above and beyond our spirit" (Kristensen 1960, p. 10).

Kristensen accepts the Chantepean placement of religious phenomenology between the philosophy of religion and the history of religion but enlarges its precise conception (see James 1995, p. 142). He is skeptical that this architectonic can be built systematically or logically because anticipations, presumptions, and intuition – the core of personal or subjective intentionality – are its constituent materials (see Kristensen 1960, p. 10).

Van der Leeuw's religious phenomenology

Not in execution but in theory, Gerardus van der Leeuw's phenomenology in *Religion in Essence and Manifestation* (1986) comes closest to being a realization of the Husserlian method and, some would say, the high-water mark of phenomenology in religious studies. There are, however, serious questions about how extensively Husserl's method informs this work, coming as the application of Husserl's method does as an afterthought in the epiglomena of van der Leeuw's work.

Van der Leeuw's characterization of religious phenomena is curiously at odds with his Husserlian method and betrays Hegel's influence (through Chantepie) and Heidegger's influence (through Bultmann) (see Waardenburg 1978, pp. 187–247). The van der Leeuwian notion of phenomenon follows Greek etymology: it indicating something neither completely object nor completely subject. Here the phenomenon appears inseparable from the person to whom it appears, but without the object modifying the subject or vice versa. It is a mediator between subjectivity and objectivity. Its essence is *in* its appearance, and that appearance is given *for* someone (see van der Leeuw 1986, p. 672; see also Ryba 2001, p. 179). However, like the Husserlian phenomenon, the van der Leeuwian phenomenon is an image the perspectives and facets of which are perceptibly and structurally, but non-causally and non-factually, connected to other phenomena. This notion of phenomenon resembles Otto's and Eliade's ideograms and Hegel's unconceptualized representation. Its constellation of structural features – related to persons, situations, or religions – consists of eternal, irreal, and ahistorical objects which van der Leeuw terms "ideal types" (van der Leeuw 1986, p. 673; see also Ryba 2001, p. 180).

All phenomena may be disclosed according to a threefold sequence: (1) as mediating concealment, (2) as gradual revelation, and (3) as iconic mediation of essence. Each corresponds to a level of life: experience, understanding, and testimony. Like the Kantian manifold of appearances or Peircean firstness, experience is incomprehensible except as consciously structured in understanding. Meaning is connected with testimony but is not reducible to objectivity or to subjectivity of understanding. This distinction mirrors the Hegelian evolutionary schema for religion, for that schema begins in objectivity, moves to subjectivity, and results in the synthesis of the two. The meaning of a phenomenon is like an intuitive revelation. Essential meaning is disclosed through phenomenal adumbrations, but this disclosure is possible only because the subject already possesses a series of similar experiences that allow its interpolation. For essential meaning to manifest itself through phenomena, its distinctive facets must be related to a wider horizon of meanings (see van der Leeuw 1986, pp. 672–4).

What differentiates the experience of religious phenomena for the scholar from that of the believer is that the believer experiences the power of the phenomenon as an uncanny something the uniqueness of which is vivid, whereas the phenomenologist thematizes the phenomenon against its field of relations to reveal its essence or meaning (see van der Leeuw 1986, pp. 23–8).

Van der Leeuw's phenomenological method possesses six steps: (1) names are associated with phenomena; (2) the phenomenon is imaginatively and sympathetically *interpolated* into consciousness; (3) the phenomenon is focused on (bracketed) to the exclusion of others, so that essential features may be observed; (4) the regular structural relationships between the phenomenon and a wider field of phenomena are clarified; (5) the *logos*/meaning of the phenomenon is distilled; and (6) the disclosed structure is those in and corrected by other researches such as archeology and philology (see van der Leeuw 1986, pp. 674–7).

Van der Leeuw describes the disciplinary placement of phenomenology by saying what it is not. It is not the poetry of religion, for poetry is the imaginative creation of meaning. It is not the history of religion, for history attempts to establish what actually happened. It is not the psychology of religion, for psychology attempts to understand the mechanics of conscious and unconscious processes. It is not the philosophy of religion, for philosophy takes religion as a set of premises to be tested and reasoned about. And finally, it is not theology, for theology refers to God himself by way of revelation, not appearance. Religious phenomenology is related to all and does not eschew their various contributions but has its own, unique purpose: the description of religious essences. It is not concerned with the origin of religion or religious development but operates in relative freedom from all non-phenomenological researches (see van der Leeuw 1986, pp. 685–9).

A Description of Religious Phenomenology

A general description of *classical* religious phenomenology is now possible. Phenomenology is a method of entry into the inner, historically conditioned, self-understanding of religions in order to provide structural descriptions and explanations of religious experiences, concepts, doctrines, myths, ethics, rituals, and institutions (see Ryba 1991, p. 236). The objects of religious phenomenology are any religious ideas, acts, or customs presented to consciousness either directly or as mediated by artifacts and communication. (Here "religious" is susceptible to a variety of provisional definitions. An essence of "religion," if it can be discovered at all, is the end of a long project, not its beginning.) Religious phenomenol-

ogy applies methods of philosophical phenomenology to concrete historical phenomena. From regular structures, it produces typological/essential
descriptions of phenomena, diachronically and synchronically, intra-
traditionally and inter-traditionally. Its method consists of empathetic
entry (interpolation) into phenomena that involves bracketing religious
truth, demands, and values to produce (relatively) unprejudiced essential
descriptions. Arriving at that meaning of religion in its particularity and
universality, it continually tests this meaning against data from cognate
fields.

Religious phenomenology is hardly a free-standing science. At present,
it exists as part of methodologically heterogeneous religious studies.
Should religious studies someday achieve a stable disciplinary structure,
then, on analogy with the hard sciences, phenomenology would become
a part of its observational methods.

Recent Critiques of Phenomenology

Many critiques have been leveled at phenomenology since it achieved its
maximum influence about the middle of the twentieth century. These critiques have come from various camps and, again, can be distinguished
by whether they are directed at philosophical or religious phenomenology, even though many of the critiques first leveled at philosophical
phenomenology have been appropriated by the critics of religious
phenomenology.

Critiques of philosophical phenomenology

Martin Heidegger, Husserl's research assistant and an early and important
critic, repudiated Husserl's transcendental idealism and his scientific pre-
tensions, though he used the Husserlian notion of the Lifeworld and *epochê*
(restyled as *Destruktion*/deconstruction) as springboards to develop a phenomenology of the historicity and concreteness of human existence. The
Heideggerian appropriation of Husserlian phenomenology works off of
both ends of this project, developing ideas from both Husserl's early realist
period and his later anthropological orientation.

In Heidegger's *Being and Time* this re-orientation is especially evident in
the absence of Husserlian terminology and method. Heidegger emphatically repudiates Husserlian method. Indeed, he repudiates any *single* phenomenological method, following Aristotle (*On the Parts of Animals*, 639^{b}
1–640^{a}) in declaring that all methods of study are determined from the
side of their objects. For Heidegger, the primary phenomenological object/
phenomenon is being, but in Husserlian phenomenology being is bracketed for the sake of objectivity. The restoration of being raises the question

of the relation between *being* and *being intended*, a question more appropriate to Thomism than to Husserlian phenomenology and probably indicative of Heidegger's Roman Catholic theological training (see Moran 2000, p. 232). Even so, Heidegger's "solution" is radically subjective, anthropocentric, and non-Thomist. For him, the most basic intentionality is human practical comportment as concretely lived. Practical comportment already occurs against a horizon of being that establishes its possibilities. Thus when the question of being is raised, it has already been decided in the notion of worldhood we have inherited. This "hermeneutical circle" is not, however, vicious. The question of being in the philosophical sense addresses us in liminal experiences that indicate transcendence. Among these are anxieties about death, meaninglessness, quotidian existence with others, restlessness, and rootlessness (see Heidegger 1962, pp. 228–35).

There is in Heidegger a peculiar ambivalence toward science with implications for the claims of phenomenology. Because scientific intentionality turns lived existence into abstractions, it distorts lived immediacy. However, the very anxieties and distortions of human nature produced by science and technology, together with its transcendent orientation toward truth, can also become the subject of philosophical reflection and become entrees into being.

In the last half of the twentieth century the other major critic of Husserlian phenomenology was Jacques Derrida, the philosopher whom Michel Foucault called an *"obscurantisme terroriste"* because of his tendency to accuse and mock instead of argue (see Searle 1993, pp. 178–9). The difficulty and subtlety – some would say chicanery – of Derrida's critique make it difficult to summarize, so that it can be described here in only the sketchiest terms.

Derrida pitched his philosophy as a kind of anti-phenomenology against both Husserlian and Heideggerian thought. Although Derrida learned radical questioning and deconstruction from Heidegger, he found both procedures to be insufficiently rigorous (see Moran 2000, p. 461). His philosophy proceeds on the basis of a critique of the spatialization and temporalization of presence (see Ryba 1999–2000, p. 167). All presence is undercut by an inherent *differance* (a French neologism meaning "to differ" + "to defer") because every now-moment or spatial-point is presented to consciousness through an intentional content; but if presented through an intentional content, it must be mediate and not present. Additionally, intentional content always mediates anterior and posterior conscious acts, but philosophies of presence (presumably) require these to be immediate for the reliability of representation to be secured. Thus representations cannot be brought to phenomenological certainty because they do not *present* but mediately *re-present*. Each representation differs from its signified, so that the achievement of meaning is always deferred (see Ryba 1999–2000).

Derrida proposes an alternative to the Husserlian view of consciousness, arguing that consciousness is a semiotic process based on accidental, non-transcendent relationships between signifier and signified. For Derrida, nothing exists except signifiers, so that all signifieds are simply signifiers-signified-by-signifiers. Humankind is thus sealed within a "fly bottle" of signifiers which refer to nothing outside the bottle. Conscious representation is simply a special case of this idea. It is here that Derrida introduces the notion of the "trace" to explain how representation occurs.

The "trace" is a sign that mediates identity between representations by first displacing and then erasing each predecessor. Traces are non-identical carriers of meaning that mediate other signs by displacing them with a new meaning and thereby deferring the completion. The identity of meaning is an illusion. Each subsequent thought about a purportedly identical theme is an illusory distortion. Deconstruction is the project of close textual readings to reveal how texts exist intrinsically in opposition to themselves, that is, to reveal the *differance* active in meaning. Thus all human communication possesses an inherent slippage. It is incapable of delivering a self-same meaning, presence, or being. Derrida employs this critique of presence to undermine two features of the Husserlian and Heideggerian phenomenologies, which he imagines to be at the root of the Western philosophical tradition: its logocentrism (its focus on rationality) and its ontotheologism (its focus on the presence of being as pointing toward transcendence) (see Ryba 1999–2000).

Critiques of religious phenomenology

When classical religious phenomenologies appropriate methods and assumptions from philosophical phenomenologies, it is a simple matter to turn the critiques of the latter into critiques of the former. Thus it is not uncommon to find the religious phenomenology criticized along the lines proposed by Heidegger and Derrida. But from within religious studies, phenomenology has also been subjected to a series of critiques independent of philosophical critiques. Three critiques merit brief treatment here.

The first critique is that phenomenology of religion, in framing its object domain, begins with an inadmissible *a priori* assumption of a *sui generis* domain such as *the Sacred* or *the Transcendent*. Russell McCutcheon, among others, has suggested that this specification of the object field is a strategy to reserve a unique disciplinary space and identity for religious studies. The desire to reserve this domain is connected with theological, social, and political motivations to control the manufacture of scholarly discourse about religion and to control its disciplinary borders (see McCutcheon 1997, p. 73). We are told that religious science, which presumes the existence of a governing motif for religion like the Whewellian governing motifs for the inductive sciences, is not based upon defensible research but functions as an ideological legitimation to preserve an elite's control. And even if the *sui generis* nature of religious objects were not politically driven, this *sui generis* status could only be proved after many years of research. It cannot be asserted *a priori*. Some, like the sociobiologist E. O. Wilson, who points to the convergence of sciences in our own time, predict that this claim to unique governing motifs may very shortly become indefensible for any discipline, let alone for a science of religion.

A second, related critique is that religious phenomenology is an apologetics for the theology of its practitioners. According to this critique, the ideological assumptions of its practitioners contradict its claims to objectivity. Examples are the way Tiele couples phenomenology with an evolutionary schema to make Christianity a "higher" religion and the assertion by Kristensen that the academic study of religion results in spiritual growth and is guided by a gracing Spirit of sympathy. Most recently, Ivan Strenski has traced the historical origins of the idea of religion as a *sui generis* category to the Remonstrant assumptions of Dutch religious phenomenologists (see Strenski 2004, pp. 5–16). In each case the suspicion is raised that phenomenology is not so much the means for arriving at unbiased description as the opposite: a means to establish the superiority of Christianity.

A third critique of religious phenomenology is that the goal of objectivity is a pipe dream, as are all supposed methods of its delivery. At best, objectivity can only be approached sporadically in religious research. More appropriate is a dialogical method. Two variations on this theme have been recently proposed. Although he admits that a phenomenology of religious doctrines has merit, Raimon Panikkar has declared that the *epochê* is "psychologically impracticable, phenomenologically inappropriate, philosophically defective, theologically weak and religiously barren" applied to inter/intra-religious dialogue (Panikkar 1999, p. 76). According to Panikkar, religious dialogue is an engagement of the whole person. It will not do to force bracketing and Cartesian doubt upon those individuals for whom thought and faith are inseparable. Religious dialogue – unlike phenomenology – involves an element of risk: dialogical openness must involve the possibility of conversion (see Panikkar 1999, pp. 77–83).

More directly informed by postmodern thought, Gavin Flood's recent critique of religious phenomenology raises a number of issues originally broached by Heidegger and Derrida, but it is in his insistence on religious study that is historicist, that involves reflective dialogue, and that is anthropologically centered that he is most critical of religious phenomenology (see Flood 1999, pp. 235–6). Although not engaged in a critique of rationality *per se*, Flood suggests that naturalist or Cartesian assumptions foreclose discovery. He advocates an approach to religion that privileges "hermeneutics over epistemology and sees explanation as a form of interpretation" (Flood 1999, pp. 89–90). Because both naturalism and

Cartesian rationalism construe human identity, motivation, and intentionality according to absolutist assumptions, they are not, for Flood, sufficiently open to be informed by other views. In the case of naturalism its metatheoretical perspective is a view from nowhere. The Husserlian version of religious phenomenology takes its metatheoretical perspective from the position of the solipsistic transcendental ego (see Flood 1999, pp. 89–90, 115). Flood argues that both metaphysical positions are insufficiently critical of their own historical locations and are possible only against an unquestioned set of assumptions and preapprehensions. By contrast, the dialogical researcher engages texts and other religious phenomena with an awareness of historical location. One moves dialectically from outside to inside religious meaning, actively creating a new narrative in which dialogue partners struggle to reach mutual understanding. Here communication and intersubjectivity, in their locality, are the presupposed conditions of understanding, not some monadic contemplative ego (see Flood 1999, pp. 143–68).

Evaluation of the Critiques of Philosophical and Religious Phenomenology

Because the critiques of philosophical phenomenology also apply in part to religious phenomenology – insofar as the methods of philosophical phenomenology are sometimes telescoped into those of religious phenomenology – they can be answered together.

It is far from certain that Heidegger's critique of Husserl is fatal. Certainly, it corrects Husserlian narrowness and dead ends, but it *is* anticipated within Husserl's phenomenological project. Heidegger supplements the Husserlian project (1) by reintroducing the problem of being as a theme, (2) by enlarging its characterization of philosophical rationality, and (3) by accomplishing a phenomenological reduction of the Lifeworld. The first two achievements are equivalent to a partial ontological and epistemological reorientation of phenomenology. The third is the application of phenomenological reduction to the solution to a specific descriptive problem that Husserl never solved. Heidegger also provided a phenomenological analysis of anxiety and the liminal with important implications for interpreting religious belief and practice.

At the same time Derrida's critiques of phenomenology have not been so productive. It is clear that opposition to the metaphysics of presence places Derrida outside of the scope of Western science and rationality, but it is also clear that Derrida has not ascended to an Archimedean foothold from which he can dislodge this project. Apart from opponents of Derrida who question whether he is really arguing anything meaningful or important – or even arguing at all – there is a more substantive backlash to his anti-phenomenology (see Searle 1993, p. 178). First, scholars such as Terry Eagleton have shown that *Derridistas* and their kin are guilty of the same essentialism that they damn in their superficial collapsing of all Western philosophies under the tags "Platonic," "essentialist," "ontotheo-logical," or "logocentric." Second, J. Claude Evans and John M. Ellis among others, have even argued that Derrida *intentionally* misread Husserl's semantics and Sassure's semiotics in order to bring them into conformity with his own presuppositions. Finally, although any approach that makes phenomenologists re-examine their assumptions is valuable, it is difficult to see how a philosophy that undercuts the possibility of entry into the meaning of another text (or another life) can have productive results for any science interested in interpretation. With Derrida the possibility of interpretation, empathy, and sympathy are banished as meaningful human actions.

The following answers may be given to the remaining critiques of reli-gious phenomenology. First, the definition of religious objects that collects them under a *sui generis* category may well be an attendant feature of religious phenomenology with ideological underpinnings, but an atten-dant feature is not a necessary feature. For this critique to have teeth, one must demonstrate that this category is both a necessary and a sufficient condition for the practice of religious phenomenology. And that demon-stration, of course, presupposes that one has shown the Holy or the Transcendent to be empty categories, something that, despite all the talk about manufacturing religion, has not to my knowledge been accom-plished. Simply put: religious phenomenology and the Holy or the Transcendent are accidentally related. Phenomenology of religion does not require the Transcendent or the Holy to do its work. Phenomenological method may be turned to any phenomenon relevant to religious studies, supernatural or otherwise.

Second, the charge that phenomenology is theologically contaminated has teeth only when it can be shown that phenomenology cannot help but distort any possible object. Apart from Derridistas, no one to my knowledge has made the claim that all phenomenology is thus contami-nated, only that religious phenomenology is. If this contamination is simply about the objects studied by religious phenomenology, then theo-logical decontamination is accomplished by separating the method from these objects. Moreover, if one argues from theological origins to present theological contamination, one commits the genetic fallacy.

Third, there is no doubt that dialogical engagement with religious traditions can improve understanding. Dialogue has its own logic, which is not the logic of phenomenology. Nevertheless, this distinctiveness does not preclude a place for phenomenology among the inventory of religious methodologies. Perhaps everything that Panikkar says about inter-religious dialogue is true. Frank and open struggle often produces understanding. This fact does not prevent phenomenological analysis of the dialogue itself as an object in order to determine which engagements are more convincing and are productive of conversion, thus coming to certainty about its dynamic. If one does not prohibit a rhetorical analysis of dialogue, why disallow a phenomenological analysis?

Flood's arguments are more sophisticated, but the same question of phenomenology as a supplement may be posed. If he does not preclude empiricist methods as supplements to dialogical religious studies, why does he preclude the phenomenological method? There is no reason to assume that discoveries resulting from phenomenological or eidetic reduction (or the passive empathetic entry into the meaning of another religion) should not be brought to the dialogical table as a point of discussion. Someone else's characterization of our unreflective behavior is sometimes the means to reflective awareness. Psychoanalysis provides an analogue. There is no reason to assume that a suitably modified phenomenology could not likewise be illuminating.

Flood's criticism of Husserlian phenomenology is *metonymic*. It damns the whole on the basis of selective criticism of the parts, and it neglects those parts that are open to improvement. It does not imagine the phenomenology that might be. Also, it uncritically accepts postmodern positions that are in fact as metaphysically freighted as any of Husserl's – Derrida's theory of signification, for example.

Finally, although the historical locality of human thought and consciousness indubitably condition interpretation, there is new evidence from cognitive psychology to support Darwin's thesis that humans may be adaptively "hard-wired" perceptually, semiotically, and hermeneutically (see Mehler and Dupoux 1994; Pyysiäinen 1999–2000). The ability to gauge and attribute emotions and intentions may correspond to the reality of those states. There may be an adaptive causal shaping of human nature constitutive of a deep intersubjectivity beyond the empty play of signifiers. What phenomenology seeks in indubitable evidence may be first delivered instinctually. This does not eliminate the phenomenological task. It simply re-orients that task toward the description of how these empirical discoveries compel certainty for consciousness. Here signification – in the Peircean sense – becomes a natural feature of the world efficiently active beyond our reflective awareness of it.

Prospects for the Phenomenology of Religion

In this chapter I have traced the contours of philosophical and religious phenomenologies to say something about their common features. I have also examined, and answered, some criticisms of each method. The task of devising a workable, generalizable recipe for religious phenomenological method remains a task for the future. Its recipe still requires tinkering. Although there have been creative advances in religious phenomenology in the last half of the twentieth century, they have been made by continental philosophers such as Emmanuel Levinas and Jean-Luc Marion. As a kind of postmodern metaphysics, these religious phenomenologies most closely resemble fundamental theologies – or, to use the older term, "apologetics" – of Judaism and Christianity. For this reason they lie outside the scope of classical religious phenomenology. Religious phenomenologies, following the classical recipe, might be valuably informed by these philosophies, but they cannot adopt their discoveries and methods *tout court* without becoming theologically partisan.

Perhaps more important for the augmentation of classical religious phenomenology are recent formulations of phenomenological method by philosophers of cognitive science like Hubert Dreyfus and Daniel Dennett. Dennett's discussion of *heterophenomenology* has much to recommend it to religious phenomenologists interested in the relationship among intersubjectivity, intentionality, and religious world building (see Dennett 1991, pp. 43–98). Also, the modification of the Husserlian reduction to the Lifeworld is an available method employed by phenomenological anthropologists like Michael Jackson in their fieldwork. It provides a means of entry into alien and otherwise inaccessible social worlds.

For now, the practice of religious phenomenology within religious studies has entered a period of dormancy, but not on account of any critical wound. No critique thus far has proven fatal to the phenomenological project, and some critics have even shown the way to its improvement. A few things are clear. Future phenomenologists of religion will ignore the discoveries of previous philosophical phenomenologists at their peril. Religious phenomenologists will do well to pay attention to an appropriately modified version of Husserlian method. But this reliance on Husserlian phenomenology should not be tantamount to servitude. The objects of religious studies and its non-theological orientation will dictate a unique inflection for future phenomenological method. In turn, the method itself will provide descriptions of phenomena that will change philosophy of religion and will shape its assumptions.

In its rehearsal of the many varieties of phenomenological method and its attempt to provide a description of their shared features, this chapter may seem to be just another example of phenomenological recipe-tinkering. But it is intended to be more. It is intended to be an invitation for a new generation of religionists to engage the classical recipes of phenomenology, to test them, and to realize their promise in new scholarly confections. *Back to the recipes!*

Bibliography

Chantepie de la Saussaye, Pierre Daniel. *Manual of the Science of Religion* [1887], tr. Beatrice Colyer-Fergusson. New York: Longmans, Green, 1891.

Dennett, Daniel. *Consciousness Explained.* New York: Little, Brown, 1991.

Farber, Marvin. *The Foundation of Phenomenology: Edmund Husserl and the Quest for a Rigorous Science of Philosophy.* 3rd edn. Albany: State University of New York Press, 1968.

Flood, Gavin. *Beyond Phenomenology: Rethinking the Study of Religion.* London: Cassell, 1999.

Foucault, Michel. *The Birth of the Clinic: An Archaeology of Medical Perception* [1963], tr. A. M. Sheridan Smith. New York: Vintage, 1975.

Gilhus, Ingvild Saelid. "Is a Phenomenology of Religion Possible? A Response to Jeppe Sinding Jensen," *Method and Theory in the Study of Religion* 6 (1994): 163–71.

Hamilton, Sir William. *Lectures on Metaphysics and Logic,* eds. Henry Mansel and John Veitch. 2 vols. Edinburgh: Blackwood, 1877.

Hegel, Georg W. F. *The Phenomenology of Mind* [1807], tr. J. B. Baillie. New York: Harper and Row, 1967.

Heidegger, Martin. *Being and Time* [1927], trs. John Maquarrie and Edward Robison. New York: Harper and Row, 1962.

Husserl, Edmund. "Phenomenology," *Encyclopaedia Britannica.* 14th edn. [1927], vol. 17., pp. 699b–702b.

Husserl, Edmund. *Logical Investigations* [1900], tr. John N. Findlay. 2 vols. London: Routledge and Kegan Paul, 1970.

Husserl, Edmund. *Experience and Judgment* [1948], trs. J. S. Churchill and Karl Ameriks. Evanston, IL: Northwestern University Press, 1973.

Husserl, Edmund. *Ideas* [1913], tr. W. R. Boyce Gibson. New York: Humanities Press, 1976.

James, George Alfred. *Interpreting Religion: The Phenomenological Approaches of Pierre Daniel Chantepie de la Saussaye, W. Brede Kristensen, and Gerardus van der Leeuw.* Washington, DC: Catholic University of America Press, 1995.

Jensen, Jeppe Sinding. "Is a Phenomenology of Religion Possible? On the Ideas of a Human and Social Science of Religion," *Method and Theory in the Study of Religion* 5 (1993): 109–33.

Kant, Immanuel. *Metaphysical Foundations of Natural Science* [1790–1803] in *Philosophy of Material Nature,* tr. James W. Ellington. Indianapolis, IN: Hackett, 1985.

Kristensen, William Brede. *The Meaning of Religion,* tr. John B. Carman. The Hague: Martinus Nijhoff, 1960.

Lambert, Johann Heinrich. *Neues Organon.* 2 vols. Leipzig: Johann Wendler, 1764.

Leeuw, Gerardus van der. *Religion in Essence and Manifestation: A Study in Phenomenology* [1933], tr. J. E. Turner. Princeton, NJ: Princeton University Press, 1986.

Liddell, Henry George, and Robert Scott. *A Greek-English Lexicon.* New York: Harper, 1846.

McCall, Raymond J. *Phenomenological Psychology*. Madison: University of Wisconsin Press, 1983.

McCutcheon, Russell T. *Manufacturing Religion: The Discourse on Sui Generis Religion and the Politics of Nostalgia*. Oxford: Oxford University Press, 1997.

Mehler, Jacques, and Emmanuel Dupoux. *What Infants Know: The New Cognitive Science of Early Development* [1990], tr. Patsy Southgate. Oxford: Blackwell, 1994.

Moran, Dermot. *Introduction to Phenomenology*. London: Routledge, 2000.

Panikkar, Raimon. *The Intrareligious Dialogue*. New York: Paulist Press, 1999.

Peirce, Charles Sanders. *Collected Papers*, eds. Charles Hartshorne and Paul Weiss. Vol. 1: *Principles of Philosophy*. Vol. 2: *Elements of Logic*. Vol. 5: *Pragmatism and Pragmaticism*. Cambridge, MA: Harvard University Press, 1974.

Pyysiäinen, Ilkka. "Phenomenology of Religion and Cognitive Science: The Case of Religious Experience," *Temenos* 35–36 (1999–2000): 125–54.

Robison, John. "Philosophy," *Encyclopaedia Britannica*. 3rd edn. [1798], one-volume edition, pp. 586–8.

Ryba, Thomas. *The Essence of Phenomenology and its Meaning for the Scientific Study of Religion*. New York: Peter Lang, 1991.

Ryba, Thomas. "Why Revisit the Phenomenology of Religion?" *Temenos* 35–36 (1999–2000): 155–82.

Ryba, Thomas. "Manifestation." In *Cassell's Guide to the Study of Religion*, eds. Russell McCutcheon and Willi Braun. London: Cassell, 2000, pp. 168–89.

Ryba, Thomas. "Comparative Religion, Taxonomies and 19th Century Philosophies of Science: Chantepie de la Saussaye and Tiele," *Numen* 48 (2001): 309–38.

Searle, John. "The World Turned Upside Down," In *Working through Derrida*, ed. Gary B. Madison. Evanston, IL: Northwestern University Press, 1993, pp. 170–83.

Strenski, Ivan. "Original Phenomenology of Religion: A Theology of Natural Religion," In *The Comity and Grace of Method*, eds. Thomas Ryba, George Bond, and Herman H. Tull. Evanston, IL: Northwestern University Press, 2004, pp. 5–16.

Tiele, Cornelius Petrus. *Elements of the Science of Religion*. 2 vols. London: Blackwood, 1899.

Waardenburg, Jacques. *Reflections on the Study of Religion*. The Hague: Mouton, 1978.

Whewell, William. *The Philosophy of the Inductive Sciences Founded on Their History* [1840]. 2 vols. New York: Johnson Reprint Company, 1967.

—— Chapter 6 ——

Philosophy of Religion

Charles Taliaferro

Philosophy plays an indispensable role in the study and practice of religion. Students of religion as well as religious believers operate with some understanding of the nature of reality and the legitimacy of human convictions. This understanding is itself a philosophy of human nature. And when we study this philosophy historically, anthropologically, sociologically, and theologically, we implicitly rely on a philosophy about the methods employed. For example, a historical method that rules out in principle religious experiences such as an incarnation, an avatar, or miracles is probably a reflection of the philosophy called naturalism. An in-depth assessment of this historical method and its reliability would have to involve an investigation into the credibility of naturalism. Roughly, "naturalism" holds that reality can be either completely or at least fundamentally described and explained by the physical sciences. Naturalism rules out in principle any appeal to God or Brahman or some nonphysical, transcendent dimension of the cosmos.

The study of religion, to be complete, needs to address basic philosophical questions about what exists (metaphysics), about what can be known (epistemology), and about what is valuable (value theory and ethics). This undertaking would at some point involve exploring naturalism as well as the many alternatives to it. Philosophy is hard to avoid. Even the radical dismissal of philosophy involves a philosophy. For example, someone may dismiss philosophy as futile on the grounds of a severe skepticism about human cognition, but this rationale is itself a philosophy.

This chapter consists of four sections: (1) the meaning of religious beliefs and practices, (2) the coherence of theism, (3) arguments for and against belief in God, and (4) religious pluralism. Although this chapter does not address the philosophy of history and science, it addresses the philosophical issues that have a direct bearing on the historical and scientific study of religion. If, for example, theistic and non-theistic religious concepts of the sacred turn out to be demonstrably meaningless, then the pathway is clear for a thoroughly secular, naturalistic history and the scientific study of the Bible and the Vedas. But if some non-naturalist religious concepts of the world turn out to be coherent and plausible, then the inquiry into religion needs to be open to recognizing religious claims as true rather than the immediate dismissal of them as superstition.

The Meaning of Religious Beliefs and Practices

In the mid twentieth century there was an important philosophical movement called positivism, alternatively referred to as *logical positivism* or *verificationism*. This movement was heavily influenced by twentieth-century natural science. The success of science was expected to herald a new age for philosophy, in which the more speculative work on God, the soul, and ethics was to be subject to a vigorous empirical critique. There were many versions of the empiricism promoted by the positivists, but the following empiricist principle is representative: for a propositional claim (statement) to be logically meaningful, either it must be about the bare formal relations between ideas, such as those enshrined in mathematics and analytic definitions ("A is A," "triangles are three-sided"), or there must in principle be perceptual experience that provides evidence for the truth or falsity of the claim. Ostensibly factual claims that have no implications for our empirical experience are empty of content. In line with this form of positivism, A. J. Ayer (1910–89) and others claimed that religious beliefs are meaningless. How might one empirically confirm that God is omnipresent or loving or that Krishna is an avatar of Vishnu? In an important debate in the 1950s and 1960s, philosophical arguments about God were likened to debates about the existence and habits of an unobservable gardener. The idea of a gardener who is not just invisible but also undetectable by any sensory faculty seemed nonsense. Using this garden analogy and others crafted with the same design, Antony Flew made the case that religious claims do not pass the empirical test of meaningfulness. The field of philosophy of religion was largely an intellectual battlefield where the debates centered on whether religious beliefs are meaningful.

Empirical verificationism is by no means dead. Some critics of the belief in an incorporeal God continue to advance the same critique as that of Flew and Ayer, albeit with refinements. Michael Martin and Kai Nielsen are representative of this approach. Still, empiricist challenges to the meaningfulness of religious belief are now deemed less impressive than they once were.

Perhaps the most damaging charge against positivism was that it is self-refuting. The empiricist criterion of meaning itself does not seem either to involve the formal relation between ideas, as with tautologies, or to be empirically verifiable. How might one determine whether the principle is correct? At best, the principle of verification seems to be a recommendation as to how to describe those statements that positivists are prepared to accept as meaningful. But then how might a dispute about which other statements are meaningful be settled in a non-arbitrary fashion? To religious believers, for whom talk of "Brahman" and "God" is at the center of meaningful discourse, the use of the principle of empirical verification seems arbitrary and question-begging. If the positivist principle is tightened up too far, it seems to threaten various propositions that at least appear to be highly respectable, such as scientific claims about physical processes and events that are not publicly perceptible. For example, what are we to think of states of the universe prior to all observation or physical strata of the cosmos that cannot be observed even indirectly but can only be inferred as part of an overriding scientific theory? Or what about the mental states of other persons, which may ordinarily be reliably judged but which, some argue, are under-determined by external, public observation? One's subjective states – how one feels – can be profoundly elusive to external observers and even to oneself. Can I empirically observe your sense of happiness? Obviously under ordinary conditions we would reply in the affirmative, but appearances can be deceiving, and we can readily imagine cases where an individual's happiness or some other subjective state must be inferred on the basis of behavior, testimony, or brain states. And yet all this evidence is fallible. Our judgments about the subjective states of other persons rely on the mediated, indirect nature of our awareness of others. The conscious states of persons seem to resist air-tight verification (see Taliaferro 1994, 2005).

The strict empiricist account of meaning was also charged with lacking a solid empirical foundation on the grounds that there is no coherent, clear, basic level of experience with which to test propositional claims. The experiential "given" is simply too malleable, often reflecting prior conceptual judgments. Incompatible philosophical frameworks can be used to describe what seems to be the same "empirical experiences." For example, one may describe experience in terms of enduring substantial objects or, as some Buddhists do, in terms of a series of distinct, momentary states without enduring substantial objects. Mystics in different religions and different times have claimed to experience the reality of a spirit everywhere present. When Ayer allowed that in principle mystical experience might give meaning to religious terms, there then appeared to be a slippery slope leading from empirical verificationism to mystical verificationism (see Ayer 1936, pp. 180–1). A growing number of philosophers in the 1960s and 1970s were led to conclude that the empiricist challenge was not decisive. Critical assessments of positivism have been offered by Alvin Plantinga, Richard Swinburne, and John Foster, among others. Ronald Hepburn summarizes a widely held present-day conviction: "There can be no short-cut in the philosophy of religion past the painstaking examination and re-examination of problems in the entire field. . . . No single, decisive verification-test, no solemn Declaration of Meaninglessness, can relieve us of the labor" (Hepburn 1963, p. 50). Ayer himself conceded that the positivist account of meaning was unsatisfactory (see Taliaferro 2005, pp. 337–61).

With the retreat of positivism, several movements have emerged in philosophy of religion. The majority of work in the field has been realist in the sense that it has treated religious beliefs about God, Brahman, the soul, karma, and so on as beliefs about reality. Given the substantiality of this work, most of this chapter assumes a realist outlook. That is, God either exists or does not exist. But some philosophers inspired by Ludwig Wittgenstein have either rejected realism or at least called for its radical reconfiguration. Their views are important to consider, as they address the issue of the very meaning of religious belief and practice.

Wittgenstein launched an attack on what has been called the picture theory of meaning, according to which statements may be judged true or false depending upon whether reality matches the picture represented by the belief. This understanding of truth and beliefs – essentially the correspondence theory of truth in which the statement "God exists" is true if and only if God exists – seemed to Wittgenstein to be misguided. According to Wittgenstein, it gives rise to insoluble philosophical problems, and it misses the whole point of having religious beliefs, which is that their meaning is to be found in the life in which they are employed. By shifting attention away from the referential meaning of words to their use, Wittgenstein introduced the idea that we should attend to what he called *forms of life*. As this shift has been applied to religious matters, a range of philosophers have either denied or at least downplayed the extent to which religious forms of life involve metaphysical claims. Peter Winch, B. R. Tilghman, and D. Z. Phillips have all espoused this approach to religion. It may be considered *nonrealist* in the sense that it does not treat religious beliefs as straightforward metaphysical claims about reality that can be adjudicated philosophically as either true or false concerning an objective reality. By this view the traditional metaphysics of theism actually got what it deserved when it came under attack in the mid twentieth century by positivists.

This Wittgensteinian challenge, then, appears to place to one side much of the way that philosophers in the West have traditionally approached religion. When, for example, Descartes, Locke, Leibniz, Berkeley, and Hume argued for and against the justification of belief in God, metaphysics was at the forefront. They were interested in the best possible arguments for and against God's existence. The same preoccupation with the truth or falsehood of religious belief was also central to ancient and medieval philosophical reflections about the Divine. When Aristotle and Thomas Aquinas articulated arguments for God's existence, they were engaged in full-fledged metaphysics.

Several points can be made on behalf of recent nonrealism. First, it has some basis in the practice of religion. Something more than "mere" metaphysical theorizing is at work in religious life. Religion seems pre-eminently to be focused on how we live. Phillips has examined different religious practices such as prayer and the belief in an afterlife, concluding that both are intelligible because the motives behind each can be held intact without any of the metaphysical "baggage" traditionally linked with them. For example, prayer to God by parents for the recovery of a child's health may be understood as an expression of their anguish and an effort to center their hope on the child's getting better, not as an attempt to influence God's will.

A second reason that has been offered is that the classical and contemporary arguments for specific views of God have seemed unsuccessful to many, though not all, philosophers. Some nonrealists contend that the unresolvability of a theism versus atheism debate reveals the vacuity of realism. By relocating beliefs about God to dimensions of human life, one can avoid the traditional project of arguing for or against a religious theory. Phillips writes:

> To ask whether God exists is not to ask a theoretical question. If it is to mean anything at all, it is to wonder about praising and praying; it is to wonder whether there is anything in all that. This is why philosophy cannot answer the question "Does God exist?" with either an affirmative or a negative reply. . . . "There is a God", though it appears to be in the indicative mood, is an expression of faith. (Phillips 1976, p. 181)

While nonrealism has much to commend it, there are also difficulties. First, radical nonrealists such as Don Cupitt, who denies religious language any referential use, seem to undermine religious practice. Consider, for example, the central examples historically and today of petitionary prayer. While there is more going on in such rites than metaphysics, is it plausible to think that prayers for forgiveness, deliverance from evil, or for a birth or death are free of any commitment about whether there actually is some divine or transcendent reality? The penitent person of prayer may be using only an implicit metaphysics, but without *some* view about what there is, prayer seems unintelligible. Prayers that seem addressed to God make little sense if the one praying is convinced that there is no divine reality. Phillips' effort to cut off the possibility of philosophically articulating theistic notions of the mind or consciousness of God seems to some philosophers to be at odds with religious practice. Phillips writes:

> It is not "consciousness," metaphysically conceived, that shows us what is meant by "the mind of God," but the religious practice in which that notion has its application. But do not be drawn into the old confusion: if one finds out what is meant by "the mind of God" and gives heed to it, that is what one is heeding, not the practice. (Phillips 2005, p. 457)

For a range of philosophers, the very practice of prayer in traditional, mainline Judaism, Christianity, and Islam involves addressing what the believer takes to be a divine reality that is loving, just, and compassionate. The person praying is not addressing the practice but something beyond the practice, and if that reality is not conscious or in any way loving or mindful or conscious of creation, there seems little point of addressing prayers to that reality.

Second, nonrealism, as it is practiced in philosophy of religion, still seems committed to substantial views about realist philosophy of religion. For example, Phillips seems committed to holding that religious beliefs about the soul surviving death are either incoherent or false if they are understood as beliefs about what will happen at death. There thus remains a recalcitrant sense in which nonrealism has a stake in what appears to be a realist metaphysics.

The current literature on the meaning of religious language is rich, and it is impossible in this space to highlight the nuances among realists and nonrealists. Cupitt, for example, maintains a thorough nonrealism – an explicit denial of the truth of theism – whereas Phillips' position is more subtle. Phillips does not explicitly claim that there is or is not a God, for the claim is metaphysical. He focuses on the analysis of religious contexts, not on abstract metaphysics. His work is important in encouraging philosophy of religion to be about *religion* and not about a *philosophy* of "ultimate reality" that may or may not be religiously relevant. To secure a position somewhere in between current versions of nonrealism and realism, one would need to see the intelligibility of both raising theoretical questions such as "Is there a God?" or "Does Brahman exist?" and searching out the meaningful practices of faith, praise, meditation, and prayer that give rise to our concepts of God and Brahman.

Debate about the Coherence of Theism

Most philosophy of religion in the West has focused on different versions of theism, the belief that there is a God who has created and sustains the cosmos. Ancient philosophy of religion wrestled with the credibility of monotheism and polytheism vis-à-vis skepticism and primitive naturalistic schemes. For example, Plato argued that the view that God is singularly good should be preferred to the portrait of the gods that was articulated in Greek poetic tradition, according to which there are many gods and they are often imperfect and subject to vice and ignorance. The emergence of Judaism, Christianity, and Islam on a global scale secured the centrality of theism for philosophical enquiry, but the relevance of a philosophical exploration of theism is not limited to those interested in these religions and the cultures in which they flourish. While theism has generally flourished in these three religions, one may be a theist without adopting any specific religion, and one may find theistic elements, however piecemeal, in Confucianism, Hinduism, some versions of Mahayana Buddhism, and the religions of some smaller-scale societies (see Griffiths 1994). The debate over theism also has currency for secular humanism and for religious forms of atheism such as Therevada Buddhist philosophy.

Philosophical inquiry into the concept of God as well as into other significant religious concepts like Brahman, Karma, and reincarnation involves what are called "thought experiments." In a thought experiment a state of affairs is described (pictured, imagined) as a genuine possibility, even if the state of affairs has never been known to obtain. To develop a coherent understanding of God as an omniscient being, one may well begin with modest thought experiments in which a person knows vastly more than any of the rest of us. Once our imagination coaxes us to conceive of a being with immense knowledge surpassing our own, is there any barrier of a logical kind to conclude that a being could not know all that it is possible to know? The reasons for the stipulation about "logic" is that there may be biological, physical constraints on the capacity of any human person or imaginary finite species knowing all that it is possible to know. But not knowing any constraint for finite beings, let alone for a being that is incorporeal and thus without physical limitations, one begins to conceive of the divine attribute of omniscience. Further thought experiments are then introduced to refine the concept of the mode and scope of divine knowledge.

If there is a God, would God's knowledge of the world be akin to ours in every respect? It would seem the height of anthropomorphism to suppose that all cognitive beings must know the world as we do. In classical theism there is often a distinction made between what is meant by saying *that God knows the world* and what is meant when we speak of *how God knows the world.* In the first case the word "to know" may be used univocally – God and you both know 2 + 2 = 4 – but in the second case how God knows this truth and all other truths may be different from the way you do.

Philosophical controversy arises over the mode of divine cognition. Advocates of what is called "concept empiricism" have claimed that in a thought experiment in which we imagine an all-knowing being, the only reasonable way in which to conceive of an omniscient being knowing what something feels like would require that that being have the appropriate feeling. But how could an all-knowing being ever feel what ignorance is like? And if we fill out the picture of God as both omniscient and omnipotent, how could an omnipotent being know fear? These puzzles are usually handled by challenging whether concept empiricism is true of all beings whatsoever. Even if it is true that you would not know fear without being vulnerable, why assume that all conceivable beings are in a similar predicament? Some philosophers have challenged whether concept empiricism is true in our own case. David Hume famously thought that one could grasp the idea of a shade of blue without ever having experienced it. But others have held that God can be all-knowing and all-powerful and yet know ignorance and fear by way of their opposites. Ignorance is the opposite of knowledge; fear of harm is the opposite of certain invulnerability. While interesting work has been done on the mode of divine cognition (see Beaty and Taliaferro 1990), more work has been focused on the scope of omniscience.

Imagine a God who knows the future free action of human beings. If God does know that you will freely do some act X, then it is true that you will indeed do X. But if you are free, are you not free to avoid doing X? Given that it is foreknown that you will do X, it appears that you are not free to refrain from the act. Initially, this paradox seems easy to dispel. If God knows about your free action, then God knows that you will freely do something and that you can refrain from it. God's foreknowing the act does not make it necessary. Perhaps the paradox arises only because we confuse the proposition "Necessarily, if God knows X, then X" with the proposition "If God knows X, then necessarily X." Historically, Boethius, Anselm, Aquinas, and others sought to preserve the reality of freedom along with God's foreknowledge, and this stance is widely represented today. The problem, or at least mystery, is retained, however, when the point is pressed concerning the grounds for foreknowledge. If God does know that you will freely do X, then it appears that there must now be a fact of the matter about what you will and will not do, and thus some residual sense in which your freely doing X is not something that can be altered. If the problem is put in first-person terms, and one imagines that God foreknows that you will freely turn the next page, then an easy resolution of the paradox seems elusive. Imagine that God tells you what you will freely do. Under these conditions is it still intelligible to believe that you have the ability to do otherwise if it is known by God as well as by you what you will indeed elect to do?

Various replies have been given, of which I note three. (1) Some have adopted what is called compatibilism, affirming the compatibility of free will with determinism. Accordingly, foreknowledge is no more threatening to freedom than determinism.

(2) A second position involves adhering to the radically libertarian outlook of insisting that freedom involves a radical, indeterminist exercise of power. Accordingly, God cannot know future free action. What prevents philosophers holding this view from denying that God is omniscient is that they contend that there are no truths about future free actions. Prior to someone's doing a free action, there is no fact of the matter that the person will do a given act. This view is in keeping with Aristotle's philosophy of time and truth. Aristotle thought that it was neither true nor false prior to a given sea battle whether a given side would win. Some theists, such as Richard Swinburne, adopt this line today, holding that the future cannot be known. If the future cannot be known for metaphysical reasons, then omniscience can be read as simply knowing all that it is possible to know. That God cannot know future free action is no more of a mark against God's being omniscient than God's inability to make square circles is a mark against God's being omnipotent.

(3) Other philosophers deny the original paradox. They insist that God's foreknowledge is compatible with libertarian freedom, and they seek to resolve the quandary by claiming that God is not bound in time (God does not so much foreknow the future as know what for us is the future from an eternal viewpoint) and by arguing that the unique vantage point of an omniscient God prevents any impingement on freedom. God can simply know the future without the future's having to be grounded in an established, determinate future. Just as God's knowledge of what is to us the past does not make our past actions determined, so God's knowing what is to us the future does not make our future actions determined.

Eternity

Consider, briefly, two other divine attributes that have generated great philosophical attention: divine eternity and goodness. Can there be a being that is outside time? In the great monotheistic traditions God is conceived of as having no beginning or end. God will never, and can never, cease to be. Some philosophical theists hold that God's temporality is like ours in the sense that there is a before, a during, and an after for God – or a past, present, and future for God. This view is sometimes referred to as the thesis that God is everlasting. Those who adopt a more radical stance claim that God is independent of temporality. They argue either that God is not in time at all or that God is "simultaneously" at or in all times. This position is sometimes called the view that God is eternal, as opposed to everlasting.

Why adopt the more radical stance? One reason, already noted, is that if God is not temporally bound, there may be a resolution to the earlier problem of reconciling freedom with foreknowledge. As Augustine pointed out in *The City of God*, while we pass through time moment by moment, with a past, present, and future, God comprehends all things from His eternal, stable presence (see Augustine, *City of God*, Book XI: 21). It is not that God is restricted to the present moment yet foresees what will take place. Rather, from the standpoint of eternity, God comprehends what for us is the future within God's complete comprehension of all things. If God is outside time, there may also be a secure foundation that explains God's immutability (changelessness), incorruptibility, and immortality. Furthermore, there may be an opportunity to use God's standing outside of time to launch an argument that God is the creator of time.

Those affirming God to be unbounded by temporal sequences face several puzzles which I note without trying to settle. If God is somehow at or in all times, is God simultaneously at or in each? If so, there is the following problem. If God is simultaneous with Rome burning in 410, and also simultaneous with your reading this book, then it seems that Rome must be burning at the same time that you are reading this book. A different problem arises with respect to omniscience. If God is outside of time, can God know what time it is now? Arguably, there is a fact of the matter that it is now, say, midnight on November 1, 2005. A God outside of time might know that at midnight on November 1, 2005, certain things occur, but could God know when it is now that time? The problem is that the more emphasis we place on the claim that God's supreme existence is independent of time, the more we seem to jeopardize taking seriously time as we know it. Finally, while the great monotheistic traditions provide a portrait of the Divine as supremely different from the creation, there is also an insistence on God's proximity or immanence. For some theists, describing God as a person or as person-like (God loves, acts, knows) is not to equivocate. But it is not clear that an eternal God can be personal.

The goodness of God

All known world religions address the nature of good and evil, and all commend ways of achieving human well being, which is conceived of as salvation, liberation, deliverance, enlightenment, tranquility, or an egoless state of Nirvana. Notwithstanding important differences, there is a substantial overlap among many of these conceptions of the good, as witnessed by the commending of the Golden Rule ("Do unto others as you would have them do unto you") in many religions. At the same time some religions construe the Divine as in some respect beyond our human notions of good and evil. In Hinduism, for example, Brahman has been extolled as possessing a kind of moral transcendence, and some Christian theologians have likewise insisted that God is only a moral agent in a highly qualified sense. For them, to call God good is very different from calling a human being good.

Here I note only some of the ways in which philosophers have articulated what it means to call God good. In treating the matter, there has been a tendency either to explain God's goodness in terms of standards that are not those of God's creation and thus in some measure are independent of God's will, or to explain God's goodness in terms of God's will and the standards that God has created – a position known as "theistic voluntarism." A common version of theistic voluntarism is the claim that for something to be good or right is simply to mean that it is willed by God and that for something to be evil or wrong is to mean that it is forbidden by God.

Theistic voluntarists face several difficulties: moral language seems intelligible without having to be explained in terms of the Divine will. Many persons make what they take to be objective moral judgments without making any reference to God. If they are using moral language intelligibly, how can it be that the very meaning of their moral language must be analyzed in terms of Divine volitions? New work in the philosophy of language may be of use to theistic voluntarists. According to a causal theory of reference, "water" necessarily designates H_2O. It is not a contingent fact that water is H_2O, notwithstanding the fact that many use the term "water" without knowing its composition. Similarly, can it not be the case that "good" may refer to that which is willed by God, even though many are not aware of the existence of God or even deny God's existence? Another difficulty for voluntarism lies in accounting for the apparent meaningful content of claims like "God is good." It appears that in calling God good, the believer is saying more than that "God wills what God wills." If so, must not the very notion of goodness have some meaning independent of God's will? Also at issue is the worry that if voluntarism is accepted, the theist has threatened the normative objectivity of moral judgments. Could God make it the case that moral judgments are turned upside down – for example, making cruelty good? Arguably, the moral universe is not so malleable. In reply, some voluntarists have sought to understand the stability of the moral laws in light of God's immutably fixed, necessary nature.

By understanding God's goodness in terms of God's being, as opposed to God's will alone, we come close to the nonvoluntarist stand. Aquinas and others hold that God is essentially good by virtue of God's very being. All these positions are nonvoluntarist insofar as they do not claim that what it means for something to be good is that God wills it to be so. The goodness of God may be articulated in various ways, either by arguing that God's perfection requires God's being good as an agent or by arguing that God's goodness can be articulated in terms of other Divine attributes such as those just outlined. For example, because knowledge is in itself good, omniscience is a supreme good. God has also been considered good insofar as God has created and conserves in existence a good cosmos. Debates over the problem of evil – if God is indeed omnipotent and perfectly good, why is there evil? – have poignancy precisely because they challenge this chief judgment of God's goodness. The debate over the problem of evil is taken up in the next section.

The choice between voluntarism and the view of God's very being as good is rarely strict. Some theists who oppose a full-scale voluntarism allow for partial voluntarist elements. According to one such moderate stance, while God cannot make cruelty good, God can make morally required or morally forbidden *some* actions that otherwise would be morally neutral. Arguments for this view have been based on the thesis that the cosmos and all its contents are God's creation. Theories spelling out why and how the cosmos belongs to God have been prominent in all three monotheistic traditions. Plato defended the notion, as did Aquinas and Locke (see Brody 1974 for a current defense).

Arguments For and Against God's Existence

In some introductory philosophy textbooks and anthologies, the arguments for God's existence are presented as ostensible proofs which are then shown to be subject to various objections. For example, an argument from the apparent order and purposive nature of the cosmos will be criticized on the grounds that, at best, the argument establishes that there is a purposive, designing intelligence at work in the cosmos but not that there is a designer of omnipotence, omniscience, and omnibenevolence. But two comments need to be made at the outset. First, that "meager" conclusion alone would be enough to disturb a scientific naturalist, who wishes to rule out *all transcendent intelligence*. Second, few philosophers today advance a single argument as a proof. Customarily, a design argument is advanced alongside an argument from religious experience, together with the other arguments to be considered. It is increasingly common to see philosophies – scientific naturalism or theism – advanced with cumulative arguments, with a whole range of considerations, and not with a supposedly knock-down, single proof. Good philosophy, I suggest, involves comparing positions of comparative strength and weakness. Interesting philosophical arguments rarely, if ever, achieve, irresistible, coercive assent from all rational parties.

The arguments for God's existence that have received the most attention in contemporary philosophy of religion are the arguments from religious experience and from miracles and the ontological, cosmological, and design arguments. The arguments against God's existence have taken three forms: arguments that theism is incoherent (the divine attributes are incoherent), that the positive case for theism is unsuccessful and some nontheistic alternative preferable, and that the extensive scope and depth of evil in the cosmos are evidence that there is no God.

Theistic arguments

Caroline Franks, Jerome Gellman, Keith Yandell, William Alston, and others have contended that the ostensible experience of God (or the divine) is evidence that there is indeed a God (or divine reality). The arguments are constructed on the grounds of an analogy with the ostensible experience of material objects in the world. Each philosopher has worked either to harmonize what appear to be incompatible religious experiences or to argue for the primacy of some experiences over others. Of course, if there are powerful reasons for thinking that there can be no God or divine reality, the evidential force of such experiences is negligible. Advocates of religious experience therefore often appeal to other arguments to set up a framework favorable to theism. Arguments for and against the rational acceptability of religious experiences depend very much on the overall force of one's background assumptions about what is plausible. (For a good defense of the argument from religious experience, see Alston 1991; for a good critique, see Sobel 2004.)

There are various versions of the cosmological argument. Some argue that the cosmos had an initial cause outside it, a First Cause in time. Others argue that the cosmos has a necessary, sustaining cause from instant to instant. The two versions are not mutually exclusive, for it is possible both that the cosmos had a First Cause and that it currently has a sustaining cause.

The cosmological argument relies on the intelligibility of the notion of something which is not itself caused to exist by anything else. This could be either the all-out necessity of supreme pre-eminence across all possible worlds used in versions of the ontological argument or a more local, limited notion of a being that is uncaused in the actual world. If successful, the argument would provide reason for thinking that there is at least one being of extraordinary power responsible for the existence of the cosmos. At best, it may not justify a full picture of the God of religion, for a First Cause would be powerful but not necessarily omnipotent. Even so, a plausible cosmological argument would challenge naturalism.

Both versions of the argument ask us to consider the cosmos in its present state. Is the world as we know it something that necessarily exists? At least with respect to ourselves, earth, the solar system, and the galaxy, it appears not. With respect to these items in the cosmos, it makes sense to ask why they exist rather than not. In relation to scientific accounts of the natural world, these enquiries into causes make abundant sense and are perhaps even essential presuppositions of the natural sciences. Some proponents of the argument contend that we know *a priori* that if something exists, there is a reason for its existence. So why does the cosmos exist? If we explain the contingent existence of the cosmos (or states of the cosmos) only in terms of other contingent things – earlier states of the cosmos, say – then a full cosmic explanation will never be attained. At this point the two versions of the argument divide. Arguments to a First Cause in time contend that a continuous temporal regress from one contingent existence to another would never account for the existence of the cosmos, and the conclusion is that it is more reasonable to accept that there was a First Cause than to accept either a regress or the claim that the cosmos just came into being from nothing. Arguments to a sustaining cause of the cosmos claim that explanations of why something exists now cannot be adequate without assuming a present, contemporaneous sustaining cause. The arguments have been based on the denial of all actual infinities or on the acceptance of some infinities – for instance, the coherence of supposing there to be infinitely many stars – combined with the rejection of an infinite regress of explanations solely involving contingent states of affairs.

This last position has been described as a vicious regress, as opposed to one that is benign. There are plausible examples of vicious infinite regresses that do not generate explanations. For instance, imagine that I explain my possession of a book by reporting that I got it from A, who got it from B, and so on to infinity. This account would still not explain how I got the book. Alternatively, imagine a mirror with light reflected in it. Would the presence of light be successfully explained if one claimed that the light was a reflection of light from another mirror, and the light in that mirror came from yet another mirror, and so on to infinity? Consider a final case. You come across a word that you do not understand – say, "ongggt." You ask its meaning and are given another word which is unintelligible to you, and so on, forming an infinite regress. Would you ever know the meaning of the first term? The force of these cases is to show how similar they are to the regress of contingent explanations.

It has been objected that both versions of the cosmological argument are based on an inflated picture of what explanations are reasonable. Why should the cosmos as a whole need an explanation? If everything in the cosmos can be explained, albeit through infinite, regressive accounts, what is left to explain? One may reply either by denying that infinite regresses actually do satisfactorily explain or by charging that the failure to seek an explanation for the whole is arbitrary. The question "Why is there a cosmos?" seems perfectly intelligible. If there are accounts for individual things in the cosmos, why not of the whole? The argument is not built on the fallacy of treating every whole as having all the properties of its parts.

But if everything in the cosmos is contingent, it seems as reasonable to believe that the whole cosmos is contingent as to believe that if everything in the cosmos is invisible, the cosmos as a whole is invisible.

Another objection is that rather than explaining the contingent cosmos, the cosmological argument introduces a mysterious entity of which we can make very little philosophical or scientific sense. How can positing at least one First Cause provide a better account of the cosmos than simply concluding that the cosmos lacks an ultimate account? In the end the theist seems bound to admit that the question why the First Cause was created at all is a contingent matter. If, on the contrary, the theist has to claim that the First Cause had to do what it did, would not the cosmos be necessary rather than contingent?

Some theists come close to concluding that it was indeed an essential feature of God that creation had to occur. If God is supremely good, there had to be some overflowing of goodness in the form of a cosmos. But most theists reserve some role for the freedom of God and thus seek to retain the idea that the cosmos is contingent. Defenders of the cosmological argument still contend that its account of the cosmos has a comprehensive simplicity lacking in alternative views. God's choices may be contingent, but not God's existence. The Divine choice of creating the cosmos can be understood to be profoundly simple in its supreme, overriding action, namely to create something good. Swinburne has argued that accounting for natural laws in terms of God's will provides for a simple, overarching framework in terms of which to comprehend the order and purposive character of the cosmos. At this point we move from the cosmological to the teleological arguments.

Defenders of the cosmological argument include Richard Swinburne, Richard Taylor, Hugo Meynell, Bruce Reichenbach, William Rowe, Alexander Pruss, and Richard Gale. Prominent opponents include Howard Sobel, Michael Martin, Graham Oppy, and J. L. Mackie.

Teleological arguments focus on characteristics of the cosmos that seem to reflect the design or intentionality of God or, more modestly, of one or more powerful, intelligent God-like agents. Part of the argument may be formulated as providing evidence that the cosmos is the kind of reality that would be produced by an intelligent being and then arguing that positing this source is more reasonable than either agnosticism or the denial of it. As in the case of the cosmological argument, the defender of the teleological argument may want to claim to be giving us only some reason for thinking that there is a God. Note the way that the various arguments might then be brought to bear on each other. If successful, the teleological argument may provide some reason for thinking that the First Cause of the cosmological argument is purposive, whereas an argument from religious experience may provide reasons to seek further support for a religious conception of the cosmos and to question the adequacy of naturalism.

One version of the teleological argument will depend on the intelligibility of purposive explanation. In the case of human agency it appears that intentional, purposive explanations are legitimate and can truly account for the nature and occurrence of events. In thinking about an explanation for the ultimate character of the cosmos, is it more likely for the cosmos to be accounted for in terms of a powerful, intelligent agent or in terms of a naturalistic scheme of final laws with no intelligence behind them? Theists who employ the teleological argument draw attention to the order and stability of the cosmos, the emergence of vegetative and animal life, the existence of consciousness, the existence of morality, and the existence of rational agents in an effort to identify what might plausibly be seen as purposively explicable features of the cosmos. Naturalistic explanations, whether in biology or physics, are then cast as being comparatively local in application when held up against the broader schema of a theistic metaphysics. Darwinian accounts of biological evolution will not necessarily assist us in thinking through why there are either any laws or any organisms to begin with. Arguments supporting and opposing the teleological argument will then resemble arguments about the cosmological argument, with the negative side contending that there is no need to move beyond a naturalistic account and the positive side aiming to establish that failing to go beyond naturalism is unreasonable.

In assessing the teleological argument, we can begin with the objection from uniqueness. We cannot compare our cosmos with others, determining which "cosmoses" have been designed and which not. If we could, then we might be able to find support for the argument. If we could compare our cosmos with those we knew to be designed, and if the comparison were closer than with those we knew to be undesigned, then the argument might be plausible. Without comparisons, however, the argument fails. Replies to this line of attack have contended that were we to insist that inferences in unique cases were out of order, then we would have to rule out otherwise perfectly respectable scientific accounts of the origin of the cosmos. Besides, while it is not possible to compare the layout of different cosmic histories, it is in principle possible to envisage worlds that seem chaotic, random, or based on laws that cripple the emergence of life. We can envisage an intelligent being creating these worlds, but through considering their features, we can articulate some marks of purposive design to help us judge whether the cosmos was designed rather than created at random.

Some critics appeal to the possibility that the cosmos has an infinite history to bolster and reintroduce the uniqueness objection. Given infinite time and chance, it seems likely that something like our world will come into existence, with all its appearance of design. If so, why should we take it to be so shocking that our world has its apparent design, and why should explaining the world require positing one or more intelligent designers? Replies repeat the earlier move of insisting that if the objection were to be decisive, then many seemingly respectable accounts would also fall by the wayside. It is often conceded that the teleological argument does not demonstrate that one or more designers are required. It seeks rather to establish that positing such purposive intelligence is reasonable and preferable to naturalism. Defenders of the argument this century include George Schlesinger and Richard Swinburne. It is rejected by J. L. Mackie and Michael Martin.

The problem of evil

If there is a God who is omnipotent, omniscient, and completely good, why is there evil? The problem of evil is the most widely considered objection to theism in both Western and Eastern philosophy. There are two general versions of the problem: the deductive or logical version, which asserts that the existence of any evil at all, regardless of its role in producing good, is incompatible with God's existence; and the probabilistic version, which asserts that given the quantity and severity of evil that actually exists, it is unlikely that God exists. The deductive problem is currently less commonly debated because it is widely acknowledged that a thoroughly good being might allow or inflict some harm under certain morally compelling conditions, such as causing a child pain when removing a splinter. More intense debate concerns the likelihood or even the possibility that there is a completely good God, given the vast amount of evil in the cosmos. Consider human and animal suffering caused by death, predation, birth defects, ravaging diseases, torture, rape, oppression, and "natural disasters." Consider how often those who suffer are innocent. Why should there be so much gratuitous, apparently pointless evil?

In the face of the problem of evil, some philosophers and theologians have denied that God is all powerful and all knowing. John Stuart Mill took this line, and panentheist theologians today also question the traditional treatments of Divine power. For these theologians, God is immanent in the world, suffering with the oppressed and working to bring good out of evil, although in spite of God's efforts, evil will invariably mar the created order. Another response is to think of God as being very different from a moral agent. Brian Davies and others have contended that what it means for God to be good is different from what it means for an agent to be good. Those who think of God as *Being* as opposed to *a being* have some reason to adopt this position. A more desperate strategy is to deny the existence of evil, but it is difficult to reconcile traditional theism with moral skepticism. Also, insofar as we believe there to be a God worthy of worship and of human love, the appeal to moral skepticism carries little weight. The idea that evil is a privation of the good, a twisting of something good, may have some currency in thinking through the problem of evil, but it is difficult to see how it *alone* can go very far to vindicate belief in God's goodness. Searing pain and endless suffering seem altogether real even if they are analyzed as philosophically parasitic on something valuable.

The three main monotheistic traditions, with their ample insistence on the reality of evil, offer little reason to try to defuse the problem of evil by this route. Indeed, classical Judaism, Christianity, and Islam are so committed to the existence of evil that a reason to reject evil would be a reason to reject these traditions themselves. What would be the point of Judaic teaching about the Exodus (God's liberating the people of Israel from slavery) or Christian teaching about the incarnation (Christ's revealing God as love and releasing a Divine power that will in the end conquer death), or the Islamic teaching of Mohammed (the holy prophet of Allah who is all just and all merciful) if slavery, hate, death, and injustice do not exist?

In part, the magnitude of the problem of evil for theism depends on one's commitments in other areas of philosophy, especially ethics, epistemology, and metaphysics. If, in ethics, you hold that *there should be no preventable suffering for any reason, no matter what the cause or consequence*, then the problem of evil will conflict with accepting traditional theism. Moreover, if you hold that any solution to the problem of evil should be evident to all persons, then again traditional theism is in jeopardy, for clearly the "solution" is not evident to all. Debate has largely centered on the legitimacy of adopting some position in the middle: a theory of values that would preserve a clear assessment of the profound evil in the cosmos as well as some understanding of how this evil might be compatible with the existence of an all-powerful, completely good Creator. Can there be reasons that God would permit cosmic ills? If we do not know what those reasons might be, are we in a position to conclude that there are none or that there cannot be any? Exploring different possibilities will be shaped by one's metaphysics. For example, if you do not believe that there is free will, then you will not be moved by any appeal to the positive value of free will and its role in bringing about good as offsetting its role in bringing about evil.

Theistic responses to the problem of evil distinguish between a *defense* and a *theodicy*. A defense seeks to establish that rational belief that God exists is still possible (when the defense is employed against the logical version of the problem of evil) and that the existence of evil does not make it improbable that God exists (when used against the probabilistic version). According to the defense response, no creature should expect to be able to solve the problem of evil. It is beyond our epistemic capacities to stand in judgment here. Some have adopted the defense strategy while arguing that we are in a position to have rational beliefs in the existence of evil and in a completely good God who hates this evil, even though we are unable to see how these two beliefs are compatible. A theodicy is more ambitious and is typically part of a broader project, arguing that it is reasonable to believe that God exists in light of the good as well as the evident evil of the cosmos. In a theodicy the project is not to account for each and every evil but to provide an overarching framework within which to understand at least roughly how the evil that occurs is part of some overall good – for instance, the overcoming of evil as itself a great good. In practice, a defense and a theodicy often appeal to similar factors, the foremost being what many call the Greater Good Defense.

In the Greater Good Defense it is contended that evil can be understood as either a necessary accompaniment to bringing about greater goods or an integral part of these goods. Thus, it is proposed that free creatures who are able to care for each other and whose welfare depends on each other's freely chosen action constitute a good. For this good to be realized, it is argued, there must be the *bona fide* possibility of persons harming each other. According to the Greater Good case, evil provides an opportunity to realize great values, such as the virtues of courage and the pursuit of justice. Peter Van Inwagen (1998), Richard Swinburne (1979), and others, have also underscored the good of a stable world of natural laws in which animals and humans learn about the cosmos and develop autonomously, independent of the certainty that God exists. Some atheists accord value to the good of living in a world without God, and these views have been used by theists to back up the claim that God might have reason to create a cosmos in which Divine existence is not overwhelmingly obvious to us. If God's existence were overwhelmingly obvious, then motivations to virtue might be clouded by self-interest and by the fear of offending an omnipotent being. Further, there may even be some good to acting virtuously even if circumstances guarantee a tragic outcome. John Hick so argues in *Evil and the God of Love* (1966), in which he develops what he construes to be an Irenaean approach to the problem of evil. On this approach it is deemed good that humanity develops the life of virtue gradually, evolving to a life of grace, maturity, and love. By contrast, there is the theodicy associated with St. Augustine, according to which God created us perfect and then allowed us to fall into perdition, only to be redeemed later by Christ. Hick thinks the Augustinian model fails, whereas the Irenaean one is credible.

Some have based an argument from the problem of evil on the charge that this is not the best possible world. If there were a supreme, maximally excellent God, surely God would bring about the best possible creation. Because this is not the best possible creation, there is no supreme, maximally excellent God. Following R. M. Adams, many now reply that the whole notion of a best possible world, like that of the highest possible number, is incoherent. For any world that can be imagined with such and such happiness, goodness, virtue and so on, a higher one can be imagined. If the notion of a best possible world is incoherent, would this fact not count against belief that there could be a supreme, maximally excellent being? It has been argued on the contrary that Divine excellences admit of upper limits or maxima that are not quantifiable in a serial fashion. For example, Divine omnipotence involves the ability to do anything logically or metaphysically possible but does not require actually doing the greatest number of acts or a series of acts of which there can be no more.

Those concerned with the problem of evil clash over the question of how one assesses the likelihood of Divine existence. Those who reportedly see no point to the existence of evil or no justification for God to allow it seem to imply that if there were a point, they would see it. Note the difference between seeing no point and not seeing a point. In the cosmic case is it clear that if there were a reason justifying the existence of evil, we would see it? William Rowe thinks some plausible understanding of God's justificatory reason for allowing the evil should be detectable but grants that there are cases of evil that are altogether gratuitous. Defenders like William Hasker and Steve Wykstra reply that these cases are not decisive counter-examples to the claim that there is a good God. These philosophers hold that we can recognize evil and grasp our duty to be to prevent or alleviate it. But we should not take our failure to see what reason God might have for allowing evil to count as grounds for thinking that there is no reason. (For a sophisticated treatment of these issues, see Rowe 2004.)

Some portraits of an afterlife seem to have little bearing on our response to the magnitude of evil here and now. Does it help to understand why God allows evil even if all victims will receive happiness later? Still, it is difficult to treat the possibility of an afterlife as entirely irrelevant. Is death the annihilation of persons or an event involving a transfiguration to a higher state? If you do not think that it matters whether persons continue to exist after death, then speculation is of little consequence. But suppose that the afterlife is understood as being morally intertwined with this life, with opportunity for moral and spiritual reformation, transfiguration of the wicked, rejuvenation and occasions for new life, perhaps even reconciliation and communion between oppressors seeking forgiveness and their victims. Then these considerations might abet a defense against arguments based on the existence of evil. Insofar as one cannot rule out the possibility of an afterlife morally tied to our life, one cannot rule out the possibility that God brings some good out of cosmic ills.

Work on the problem of evil and many other areas that bear on the plausibility of theism is at the heart of contemporary philosophy of religion.

Religious Pluralism

While the majority of this chapter has highlighted the case for and against the theistic philosophy that has emerged from Judaism, Christianity, and Islam, there is today an expanding literature in the English-speaking world that covers a wider range of religions. There is now a growing, philosophically rich literature on Hinduism, Buddhism, Daoism, Confucianism, religion in Africa and, most recently, Native American religions. This growth has taken place alongside a greater openness by philosophers within Judaic, Christian, and Islamic traditions to engage in fruitful exchange with one another as well as with nonmonotheistic traditions. This expansion has led to a great deal of work on the compatibility of different religions, the definition of religion, and the role of religion in pluralistic democracies.

There are two major positions in comparative philosophy of religion. One holds that the great world religions may all be seen as offering different perspectives on the same reality. This view, sometimes called "perspectivalism" or simply "pluralism," is advanced by John Hick, who describes the ultimate reference point of all religions in terms of what he calls "the Real":

> May it not be that the different concepts of God as Jahweh, Allah, Krishna, Param Atma, Holy Trinity, and so on; and likewise the different concepts of the hidden structure of cosmic process culminating in Nirvana, are all images of the divine, each expressing some aspect or range of aspects and yet none by itself fully and exhaustively corresponding to the infinite nature of the ultimate reality? (Hick 1973, p. 140)

Since the early 1970s Hick has refined the answer "yes." His position would bolster the argument from religious experience insofar as it challenges an objection that religious experiences would justify incompatible religions. In Hick's framework, Buddhist and Muslim mystics all testify to the same divine reality, the Real. Hick's view is opposed by an opposing camp that stresses the differences among religions. Paul Griffiths, Keith Yandell, and others argue that "the Real" is either incoherent or religiously irrelevant. These philosophers further insist on the thesis that the great world religions contain contradictory treatments of ultimate reality. For example, a Buddhist concept of Nirvana involves the dissolution of the individual self in a cosmos with no God, whereas a Christian concept of salvation involves the individual in relation to other individuals, including God. The debate between Hick and his opponents is substantial, involving different philosophies of truth, belief, and justification. (For a fascinating study of comparative religion, see Sessions 1994.)

The definition of religion and the role of religion in pluralistic democracies are of current concern to philosophers. Some forms of political liberalism today require that no laws or policy making be justified by exclusively religious reasons. John Rawls, Robert Audi, and others hold that comprehensive religious doctrines may rightly motivate political action but that in terms of justifying laws, only secular reasons are permissible. Reasonable citizens may adhere to incompatible religions or no religion whatever, and it is unfair to impose legislation that is religiously based on those who do not share the religion. The reason that this issue ties in with the definition of religion is that if the aim is to exclude religion, what is it that makes Christianity and Buddhism religions yet excludes as religions a devout commitment to supposedly nonreligious ideals like utilitarianism, a free market economy, and a reverence for nature? Definitions of religion that insist on a concept of God do not work insofar as one recognizes Theravada Buddhism as a religion.

Philosophical reflection on religion in political philosophy and on the definition of religion remain important areas of inquiry. (For a handsome collection of papers on this topic, see Quinn and Meeker 2000.)

The philosophy of religion is one of the fastest growing areas in the field of philosophy, with a range of journals, institutions, and conferences providing forums for ongoing dialogue. Among cutting-edge work that it has not been possible to document here, readers may find rich resources on feminist philosophy of religion and work by philosophers on religious approaches to the environment, race, science, literature and the arts, religious rites, and more. (See Quinn 1997, as well as Wainwright 2005, for a wide survey of issues, including philosophy of religion informed by continental and feminist philosophies. For a wider narrative history, see Taliaferro 2005, chs. 7–9).

Bibliography

Alston, William. *Perceiving God.* Ithaca, NY: Cornell University Press, 1991.

Ayer, A. J. *Language, Truth and Logic.* London: Gollancz, 1936.

Beaty, Michael, and Charles Taliaferro. "God and Concept Empiricism," *Southwest Philosophy Review* 6 (1990): 97–105.

Brody, Baruch. "Morality and Religion Reconsidered," in *Readings in the Philosophy of Religion*, ed. Baruch Brody, 2nd edn. Englewood Cliffs, NJ: Prentice Hall, 1992, pp. 491–503.

Griffiths, Paul. *On Being Buddha.* Albany: State University of New York Press, 1994.

Hepburn, Ronald W. "From World to God," *Mind* 72 (1963): 40–50.

Hick, John. *Evil and the God of Love.* 1st edn. London: Macmillan, 1966.

Hick, John. *God and the Universe of Faiths.* London: Macmillan, 1973.

Mackie, John L. *The Miracle of Theism.* Oxford: Clarendon Press, 1985.

Martin, Michael. *Atheism.* Philadelphia, PA: Temple University Press, 1990.

Mitchell, Basil, ed. *The Philosophy of Religion.* Oxford: Oxford University Press, 1971.

Morris, T. V., ed. *The Concept of God.* Oxford: Oxford University Press, 1987.

Phillips, D. Z. *Religion Without Explanation.* Oxford: Blackwell, 1976.

Phillips, D. Z. "Wittgensteinianism: Logic, Reality, and God," in *The Oxford Handbook of Philosophy of Religion*, ed. William Wainwright. Oxford: Oxford University Press, 2005, pp. 447–71.

Plantinga, Alvin. *God and Other Minds*. Ithaca, NY: Cornell University Press, 1967.

Plantinga, Alvin. *The Nature of Necessity*. Oxford: Oxford University Press, 1974.

Quinn, Philip L., and Charles Taliaferro, eds. *The Blackwell Companion to Philosophy of Religion*. Oxford: Blackwell, 1997.

Quinn, Philip L., and Kevin Meeker eds. *The Philosophical Challenge of Religious Diversity*. Oxford: Oxford University Press, 2000.

Rowe, William. "The Problem of Evil and Some Varieties of Atheism," *American Philosophical Quarterly* 16 (1979): 335–41.

Rowe, William. *Can God Be Free?* Oxford: Clarendon Press, 2004.

Sessions, Lad. *The Concept of Faith: A Philosophical Investigation*. Ithaca, NY: Cornell University Press, 1994.

Sobel, Howard. *Logic and Theism*. Cambridge: Cambridge University Press, 2004.

Swinburne, Richard. *The Coherence of Theism*. Oxford: Clarendon Press, 1977.

Swinburne, Richard. *The Existence of God*. Oxford: Clarendon Press, 1979.

Swinburne, Richard. *Providence and the Problem of Evil*. Oxford: Oxford University Press, 1998.

Taliaferro, Charles. *Consciousness and the Mind of God*. Cambridge: Cambridge University Press, 1994.

Taliaferro, Charles. *Contemporary Philosophy of Religion*. Oxford: Blackwell, 1998.

Taliaferro, Charles. *Evidence and Faith: Philosophy and Religion since the Seventeenth Century*. Cambridge: Cambridge University Press, 2005.

Van Inwagen, Peter. "The Magnitude, Duration, and Distribution of Evil: A Theodicy," *Philosophical Topics* 16 (1998): 161–87.

Wainwright, William, ed. *The Oxford Handbook of Philosophy of Religion*. Oxford: Oxford University Press, 2005.

Yandell, Keith. *The Epistemology of Religious Experience*. Cambridge: Cambridge University Press, 1993.

Chapter 7

Psychology of Religion

Roderick Main

The psychology of religion is the application of the theories and methods of psychology to understanding religion. In principle, psychologists of religion can practice their discipline without the consent of adherents and without regard to their own beliefs. But this straightforward account in fact simplifies the situation. The very terms "psychology" and "religion" have often meant different things to psychologists of religion. Some approaches to psychology, such as the depth psychological ones, can be characterized as primarily subjective and interpretive. Other approaches, especially those from mainstream scientific psychology, are more nearly objective and empirical. The differing presuppositions and methods of these approaches yield different kinds of data and understanding about religion. From the earliest days there have been attempts to combine subjective with objective approaches in order to enrich each, but it seems improbable that psychology of religion will ever operate with a single, unified body of theory and method. In referring to the "psychology of religion," one therefore must specify which psychology is involved in any particular case.

Of religion, a similar caution is necessary. Most of the early studies in psychology of religion generalized from the case of modern Protestant

Christianity in Europe and North America. But it is debatable whether findings about this tradition apply to traditions that are other than Protestant, Christian, Western, or modern. The term "religion" applies to hundreds, even thousands, of traditions. Recent work in the field has become more sensitive to the diversity among religious traditions, to the differing sets of cultural beliefs and behaviors in which these traditions are found, and indeed to the difficulty of defining satisfactorily the term "religion" itself.

In addition to the complexities of the terms psychology and religion, the relationship between the fields designated by these terms is also less than straightforward. The phrase "psychology of religion" suggests a one-way relationship, with psychology as the *method* of study and religion as the *object* of study. In practice, however, the relationship between psychology and religion has often been more reciprocal, with religion explicitly or implicitly asserting its viewpoint alongside or even against that of psychology. One must be alert to the presence of this reciprocity in understanding the psychology of religion.

In this chapter, the early contexts and origins of psychology of religion, in particular the early flowering of the discipline in the United States between about 1880 and 1930, will first be discussed. Then depth psychological approaches to religion, focusing on the theories of Freud and Jung but also looking at some later contributions, will be considered. Next, the more objective, empirical approaches that stem from mainstream scientific psychology will be reviewed. Finally, some of the ways in which religion and psychology have stood in a more reciprocal relationship will be examined.

The Beginnings of Psychology of Religion

In late nineteenth-century Europe and America the success and professionalization of science, together with the rise of secular educational, welfare, and legal institutions, led to the lessening importance of traditional religion both as a social force and as a source of intellectually satisfying explanations of human nature and the world. Previously, religious phenomena had been studied almost exclusively from a committed Christian theological perspective. Now there emerged attempts to account for these phenomena in purely naturalistic terms and to consider non-Christian religions as well as Christianity. Out of these developments there arose several new disciplines, including the history of religion, or comparative religion. Concurrently, there developed naturalistic rather than theological attempts to account for the human mind. On the one hand mental states were correlated with, even reduced to, physiological states, giving rise to the discipline of psychophysiology. On the other hand a possible unconscious dimension of the human mind was ever more considered, giving rise to the early depth psychologies. The simultaneous appearance of these scientific approaches toward the study of religious phenomena and the human mind made it inevitable that there would also emerge attempts to study scientifically the states of mind specifically associated with religion. It is largely from this confluence of factors that the discipline of psychology of religion arose (see Heisig 1989, pp. 57–8).

Yet this new discipline was not merely concerned with the disinterested application of scientific methods to generate naturalistic knowledge about religion. Many of those involved in the discipline in the early days also had specific agendas – pro-religious or anti-religious – and sought to enlist psychology either to re-frame religion in a form that would be acceptable to modern, scientific sensibilities or to disprove it once and for all. Both the multiple origins of psychology of religion and the contrasting motivations of its practitioners have continued to influence the field.

A number of distinctive but interconnected traditions of psychological work on religion appeared at roughly the same time. One tradition, in the German-speaking world, included the work of above all Sigmund Freud and Carl Gustav Jung. Another, in the French-speaking world, included the work of Pierre Janet and Théodore Flournoy. However, the most decisive tradition for the early identity of the field was the Anglo-American one, which included the work of G. Stanley Hall, James Leuba, Edwin Starbuck, James Pratt, and above all William James (see Wulff 1997, pp. 21–48).

Hall, Leuba, and Starbuck

The first landmark event in the psychology of religion was the publication in 1902 of William James' *The Varieties of Religious Experience*, based on the Gifford Lectures that he had delivered in Edinburgh in 1901 and 1902. But James was not the first major US researcher of the field. A claim to that distinction could be made for G. Stanley Hall (1844–1924). Hall was trained in theology but later turned to psychology, studying with the German psychologist Wilhelm Wundt in Leipzig and with James at Harvard. Against the trend of his time he promoted experimental over philosophical methods in psychology and pioneered the empirical study of individual religious experience. His main focus was on religious development and in particular on conversion, which he viewed as a phenomenon occurring primarily in adolescence. Though he emphasized the biological basis of religious experience and attempted to recast the meaning of religion in wholly psychological terms, he did so in a spirit of deep commitment to the Christian tradition. At the same time the function or main beneficial effect of religion was for him social adjustment. Hall's influence came variously from his own research and publications; from his position as President of Clark University, where he established what became known as the "Clark School of Religious Psychology"; from his founding of *The American Journal of Religious Psychology and Education* (1904–11); from his introduction of psychoanalysis to the United States through the invitation of Freud and Jung to a conference at Clark University in 1909; and from the inspiration and guidance he provided to his students, notably, James Leuba and Edwin Starbuck (see Wulff 1997, pp. 49–62).

James Leuba (1868–1946) was born in Switzerland but emigrated to the United States. Under Hall's direction he used a combination of questionnaires and personal interviews to conduct the first academic study of the psychology of conversion as well as a study of religious beliefs among scientists and psychologists. He found that the belief in God among scientists declined with the knowledge that they had about matter, society, and mind; with their peer-rated eminence; and with the recency of their response to his questionnaire (see Wulff 1997, p. 209), all of which could be taken to indicate that advance in science leads to a decline in religiosity. Leuba's approach was empiricist, reductive, and anti-religious. He held that mystical experiences were not qualitatively different from ordinary or pathological psychological experiences. And he even prefigured Freud in emphasizing the importance of sexual impulses and symbols in religion. Leuba published prolifically and became the recognized leader of the psychology and religion movement that emerged in the United States in the early decades of the twentieth century (see Beit-Hallahmi 1974, p. 85).

Edwin Starbuck (1866–1947) studied under James at Harvard and under Hall at Clark University, where he remained. It was Starbuck who first used the phrase "psychology of religion," as the title of a book published in 1899. In his book he reported the results of his questionnaire studies of conversion and of the less extreme development of religious beliefs, which he termed "gradual growth." His approach involved collecting large bodies of data and quantifying them to reveal general trends. By this means he demonstrated the correlation of conversion with the onset of puberty. Unlike Leuba, he maintained a positive attitude toward religion. His work is now judged to have been theoretically naïve, and his continuing claim to fame is that his data on conversion provided one of the principal sources used by James (see Beit-Hallahmi 1974, pp. 85–7; Wulff 1997, pp. 26–7).

James and Pratt

Although William James (1842–1910) was an influence on Hall, Leuba, and Starbuck, his own principal work in the psychology of religion, *The Varieties of Religious Experience* (1902), was written only after the three of them had already made significant contributions to the field. James had a broad education in the arts, philosophy, and science. He began his academic career by teaching physical psychology at Harvard after the manner of Wundt. Later he shifted to philosophy, though he remained largely concerned with psychological topics. He took a naturalistic view of religious phenomena but carefully avoided reductionism, viewing religion as something universal and not in itself abnormal. He believed that all religions point to a transcendent world that influences this world (see James 1902, pp. 498–509). In anticipation of the emerging depth psychological approaches to religion, he located the origin of the sense of transcendence that characterizes religious experience in a subliminal consciousness, a part of the mind not directly accessible to intentional observation (see James 1902, pp. 501–3).

Rather than attempting to make statistical generalizations based on quantitative data, as had Leuba and Starbuck, James offered systematic descriptive accounts of unique cases in which he combined considerations from scientific empiricism with introspective analysis. His focus was on personal religious experience, which he considered to be the heart of religion. He defined religion, with acknowledged arbitrariness, as "the feelings, acts, and experiences of individual men in their solitude, so far as they apprehend themselves to stand in relation to whatever they may consider the divine" (James 1902, pp. 31–2). Not himself prone to these experiences, James presented and analyzed numerous personal documents variously collected from religious literature, from Starbuck's questionnaire surveys, and from friends and acquaintances.

Although he shared the Protestant bias of many of the early US researchers into religion, James was sensitive to the great variety of ways, some of them contradictory, in which religion can manifest itself. He developed a rudimentary typology, in which he distinguished between the religion of the "healthy-minded" and the religion of the "sick soul." Healthy mindedness is "the tendency which looks on all things and sees that they are good" (James 1902, p. 86). James also refers to persons of this optimistic disposition as the "once-born," since their happy contentment with the way the world is does not lead them to seek to be re-born into any other world or state of awareness. "Sick souls," by contrast, are those persuaded that "the evil aspects of our life are of its very essence, and that the world's meaning most comes home to us when we lay them most to heart" (James 1902, p. 128). Sick souls wish to be redeemed from this world and be re-born into a spiritual reality or awareness. They are therefore "twice-born." Like Hall, Leuba, and Starbuck, James directs a considerable amount of attention to conversion experiences (see James 1902, pp. 186–253). Unlike Hall and his students, he also gives close consideration to saintliness and to mystical experiences, whose four principal characteristics he identifies as ineffability, noetic quality, transience, and passivity (see James 1902, pp. 370–420).

James makes two kinds of judgments about religious phenomena: "existential judgments," which concern the origin and history of the phenomena, and "spiritual judgments," which concern the significance and meaning of the phenomena. In the *Varieties* he is especially concerned with a spiritual judgment concerning the "fruits" of religion for life – in particular, like Hall, the effectiveness of religion in promoting social adaptation.

James' work on religion has been criticized for its neglect of institutional and historical factors, for its overestimation of the role of feeling, for its inclusion of pathological cases, and for its appeal to unknowable subconscious processes (see Wulff 1997, pp. 499–503). Among James' critics was his student and friend the philosopher James Pratt (1875–1944), whose work *The Religious Consciousness* (1920) gained a prestige within the field second only to that of the *Varieties*. Pratt rejected his teacher's pragmatic approach to religion in favor of a critical realist approach, according to which the truth or falsehood of religious claims can be evaluated in terms of their cogency in accounting for reality rather than in terms of their consequences for behavior and health. Like James, Pratt was sympathetic to religion, and his work is similarly descriptive. Unlike James, Pratt focused on ordinary rather than exceptional religiosity, on gradual "moral" conversion rather than sudden highly emotional conversion, and on mild rather than extreme religious experiences. Pratt also contributed to widening awareness of Eastern religions, about which he had considerable knowledge.

The work in the United States of Hall, Leuba, Starbuck, James, and Pratt, as well as that of others such as George Coe and Edward Ames, has been taken to constitute a distinctive psychological movement that arose around 1880 and declined around 1930 (see Beit-Hallahmi 1974). Among the reasons suggested for the decline of the movement are its lack of independence from theology and from the philosophy of religion; its lack of a comprehensive theory; its poor methods of data-collection; the existence of conflicts within both researchers and subjects because of their personal investments in religion; the focus of the developing social sciences on phenomena more amenable to "objective" study; the rise of behaviorism within academic psychology; and the perceived greater promise of psychoanalytic approaches to the study of religious phenomena (see Beit-Hallahmi 1974, pp. 87–8).

Depth Psychological Approaches

Concurrent with these developments in the US was the emergence in Europe of psychological theories that emphasized the importance of the unconscious mind. Drawing their insights mainly from the clinical consulting room, depth psychologies provided richly articulated theories of the structure and dynamics of a part of the mind that is normally inaccessible to consciousness but that nevertheless influences human experience, belief, and behavior. Depth psychologists emphasized the role of <u>instincts</u> and of early childhood experiences in the formation of this hidden part of the mind. Most notable among these approaches were Sigmund Freud's (1856–1939) psychoanalysis and Carl Gustav Jung's (1875–1961) analytical psychology. Each of these psychologists applied his theory extensively to religious phenomena but arrived at strikingly different conclusions.

Janet and Flournoy

Again, however, these two most famous figures in their field were not necessarily the first. The French psychologist Pierre Janet (1859–1947), who coined the term "subconscious" and developed a theory of psychological dissociation, was concerned with religious phenomena throughout his career. He wrote about the genesis and function of the idea of God, which he considered to be the core of religion. He studied such experiences as conversion, ecstasy, and spirit possession, especially in the case of one exceptional patient, "Madeleine." <u>Predicting the demise of religion, he recommended scientific psychotherapy as a secular alternative.</u> Janet was a <u>significant influence on both Freud and Jung</u>, even if not fully credited by either, and <u>also on Leuba</u> (see Heisig 1987, p. 60; Wulff 1997, p. 38).

Another important figure was the Swiss philosopher and psychologist Théodore Flournoy (1854–1920). A friend of James and later of Jung, Flournoy switched from the study of theology to the study of medicine. He believed that for some persons it was necessary to <u>liberate themselves from religious dogma in order to experience an authentic inner religious life.</u> This position, together with some of the principles he maintained for doing psychology of religion, found resonance with Jung and with many subsequent workers in this field. For instance, Flournoy emphasized the importance of excluding one's own presuppositions about the reality of the supposed objects of religion (the "Principle of the Exclusion of the Transcendent"), although he recognized the appropriateness of observing people's feelings about these supposed objects. His own writings exemplify the possibility of providing nonreductionistic depth psychological understanding of exceptional religious experience, as in his case study of the modern mystic Cécile Vé (see Wulff 1997, pp. 41–3).

Freud

Freud was raised and educated in Vienna and spent all but the last year of his life there. Unable to obtain a research position as a neurologist, he took up the practice of psychiatry and, in collaboration with the Viennese physician Joseph Breuer, <u>became interested in</u> <u>hysterical patients.</u> Freud concluded that the symptoms of these patients stemmed not from physiological factors but from emotional, specifically sexual, traumas suf-fered in infancy. Later he rejected this position for the view that not actual experiences but conflicts arising from the child's instinct-driven sexual fantasies are responsible for the symptoms. Above all, Freud maintained that the male child's wish to have sex with his mother conflicts with his fear that he will consequently be punished by castration by his possessive father. The child both adores the father, on whom he so much depends, and feels murderously competitive with him. Freud termed this uncon-scious fantasy the "Oedipus complex." It was Jung, not Freud, who coined the term "Electra complex" for the female version of the complex, in which the girl wishes to have sex with her father and is envious of her mother.

[margin note: Oedipus complex and Castration anxiety]

With varying degrees of success the Oedipus complex may be "resolved" through the child's identification with his father – or, in the girl's case, mother. Failure to resolve the complex is, in Freud's view, the prime cause of neurosis. The main task of psychoanalysis is to cure neurosis by provid-ing an understanding of the complex. The unacceptable incestuous and murderous wishes that compose this fantasy are prevented from entering consciousness by powerful defense mechanisms. Therefore the uncon-scious has to be approached obliquely through a combination of tech-niques, which include free association, the interpretation of dreams, and the re-enactment of childhood fantasies in a transference relationship with an analyst.

Freud wrote five main works that provide psychoanalytic perspectives on religion: "Obsessive Actions and Religious Practices" (1907), *Totem and Taboo* (1913), *The Future of an Illusion* (1927), *Civilization and Its Discontents* (1930), and *Moses and Monotheism* (1939) (see Freud 1990, 1991). His method involves generalizing from individual cases to the psyche of all humans, and from clinical observations to cultural manifestations, includ-ing religion. For his knowledge of religion he relies primarily on anthro-pological texts, supplemented by introspective insights and a good measure of historical speculation. His approach is decidedly interpretive rather than empirical.

Among the topics that Freud discusses are religious behavior in the form of ritual and sacrifice; religious experience in the form of mysticism and the "oceanic feeling"; and religious belief in the form of taboos, God images, and general religious aspirations. Governing all his discussions is the view that religious phenomena originate from the human psyche and are the projection onto God and the world of infantile sexuality and intra-familial conflicts, most often the Oedipus complex. For instance, he com-pares religious rituals with the obsessive and compulsive behavior of neurotics – behavior aimed at the repression of instinctual impulses. He concludes that religion itself is a "universal obsessional neurosis" (Freud 1990, p. 40). Alternatively, he derives religious needs from "the infant's helplessness and the longing for the father aroused by it" (Freud 1991, p. 260). God images are the projection of idealized images of the omniscient and omnipotent father experienced in childhood (see Freud 1991, p. 199). By contrast, the mystic's "oceanic feeling" of unbounded unity is a projection of yet earlier primary narcissism – an infantile condition in which libido is not yet oriented toward real objects in the outer world but is directed inward toward the ego (see Freud 1991, pp. 251–60). Elsewhere the appeal of sacrifice in religion stems from its offering release from the guilt of patricide, both as fantasized within the dynamics of the Oedipal situation and as a "deed" actually committed in pre-history, when the dominant father of a primal horde was murdered and eaten by his envious sons. The guilty memory of this deed, Freud asserts, has been transmitted by heredity to all subsequent humans (see Freud 1990, pp. 159–224).

Freud acknowledges that religion has played an important role in the development of civilization through helping persons come to terms with both the outer forces of nature and the internal forces of instinctual life. Above all, religion has helped persons to repress anti-social incestuous and aggressive desires. But these benefits have been obtained at the cost of guilt and neurosis (see Freud 1990) and of living in a state of illusion, where religious phenomena have been valued because they have been wished for, not because they have been demonstrated to be real. In fact, religion has the effect of keeping persons in a state of child-like dependence, in which they are unable to face reality. For Freud, a maturer attitude would be the scientific one, in which one accepts reality for what it is and in which one consciously restrains anti-social desires because it is necessary to do so for the maintenance of civilization. Freud therefore welcomed the decline of religion as a sign of humanity's advance toward adulthood (see Freud 1991, pp. 179–241).

Freud's psychology of religion has been vigorously criticized. In both *Totem and Taboo* and *Moses and Monotheism* he relies on dubious anthropological and historical speculations – for example, about the universality of totemism and about the life of Moses. He adopts as a basic assumption Lamarck's discredited notion of the inheritance of acquired characteristics, such as the guilt that the sons felt in the primal parricide. He focuses on a narrow selection of religious phenomena and fails to do justice to the complexity and multi-dimensionality of religion. His claim that God images stem primarily from longing for an omnipotent father is contradicted by the many empirical studies which have demonstrated the greater role played by the mother in the formation of God images. Again, while there are undoubtedly strong parallels between the compulsive behavior of neurotics and the performance of religious rituals, the inference that religious rituals may simply be a widespread and culturally sanctioned instance of neurotic actions is challenged by empirical data which show that engagement in religious rituals often correlates positively with sound mental health (see Palmer 1997, pp. 60–81; Wulff 1997, pp. 309–18).

In spite of these limitations and errors, Freud's theory has remained immensely influential. It provides a coherent and detailed psychological account of religion that addresses not only conscious dynamics but also unconscious ones such as projection, sublimation, and displacement. It provides a means of understanding the rich content of religious symbols, myths, and rituals. Some of Freud's suggestions have received a measure of empirical support – for instance, that of the influence of early relationships on the way a person conceives of God. Even in his own day, Freud's own negative evaluation of religion was deemed separable from his psychoanalytic method, and pastors and theologians, especially Freud's friend Oskar Pfister, were among those who used his insights to offer a positive view of religion.

Jung

Jung, the son of a Protestant pastor, was raised and educated in Basel, Switzerland, and spent all of his working life in or near Zurich. He trained as a psychiatrist and worked for nine years at Zurich's prestigious Burghölzli Mental Hospital before devoting himself exclusively to his private practice. Between 1906 and 1913 he allied himself to Freud and was prominent in the development of the psychoanalytic movement. However, various theoretical and personal differences between Freud and Jung led to their acrimonious separation. Important among the theoretical differences were their views on religion.

After splitting with Freud, Jung more fully developed his own distinctive psychology. Where Freud emphasized a repressed unconscious and universal complexes stemming from instinctual conflicts, Jung emphasized a "collective unconscious" and universal "archetypes" as inherited forms of psychic functioning. Where Freud was mostly concerned with the causes and effects of psychic phenomena, Jung attended equally to their purpose, or teleology. He postulated that psychic development was governed by an autonomous archetypal process ("individuation") that aimed at integration rather than division between the unconscious and the conscious aspects of the psyche and at the realization of a unifying centre of the personality (the "self") (see Jung 1969, pp. 3–105). Where for Freud symbols are disguised references to purely instinctual processes, for Jung they are the best possible expressions of unknowable processes that are as much nonmaterial, or spiritual, as bodily. Jung's method of interpreting symbols includes a process of "amplification," which involves finding mythic, historical, and cultural parallels to the symbolic images at hand. Religious imagery from diverse traditions provided one of the richest sources of these parallels.

Jung's principal writings on religious topics are gathered in *Psychology and Religion: West and East* (1969), one of the volumes of his Collected Works. His psychology of religion, like Freud's, consists largely of a straightforward application of his general psychology, though Jung was much more explicitly influenced *by* religion in the development of his general psychology. Also like Freud, Jung bases his insights on generalizations from a small number of clinical cases, together with wide-ranging but unsystematic textual research and bold speculation. Unlike Freud but like Flournoy, Jung aims to withhold judgment about the truth of religious beliefs and devotes his attention to religious phenomena as they present themselves as psychological facts (see Jung 1969, pp. 5–6).

Jung's main focus in his psychology of religion is on spontaneous experiences – in particular, on dreams and fantasies that seem charged with a special quality of heightened emotionality ("numinosity") (see Jung 1969, pp. 5–105). He does also discuss formal beliefs and practices – for example, the dogma of the Trinity and the rite of the Mass – but for him these beliefs and practices either stem from or bear on individual experience (see Jung 1969, pp. 107–200, 201–96). Like Freud, Jung locates the origin of religious phenomena in the unconscious psyche. For Jung, however, the unconscious consists not only of personal contents but even more of collectively inherited archetypes. Key here is the archetype of God, which Jung sometimes presents as virtually equivalent to the unconscious, hence to the totality of archetypes, but at other times characterizes as the central, highest archetype, which orders the other archetypes (see Jung 1969, pp. 81, 468–9).

Although the human psyche is thus imprinted with an archetype of God, that archetype, like any other, can never be known directly but only through its diverse expressions as archetypal imagery, all of which will be colored by personal and cultural associations. While there is a single archetype of God – whatever its status vis-à-vis the other archetypes – we can never know the full meaning of this archetype but can gain only an approximate understanding of it from its manifestations of Yahweh, Brahman, Tao, the Absolute, Zeus, Krishna, and so on, all with their attendant imagery and range of interpretations. For Jung, images of the archetype of the self are functionally indistinguishable from images of the archetype of God. Hence Jung's process of individuation leads to realization of "the God within" (see Jung 1969, p. 58).

For Jung, antithetically to Freud, the presence of religiosity is not usually a sign of neurosis. On the contrary, the *absence* of religiosity, especially in the second half of life, may be a prime *cause* of neurosis. Jung even declares that the recovery of the religious dimension of experience is precisely what is required by many of his older patients (see Jung 1969, p. 334). Religion for Jung also has a social significance. It can provide the individual with a source of authority strong enough to counterbalance the forces, particularly totalitarian forces, that tend toward de-individualization, or "mass-mindedness."

Some critics of Jung's psychology of religion have targeted his psychology *per se*. For instance, the existence of a collective unconscious and of universal archetypes has been considered implausible and untestable. Also criticized has been Jung's analysis of religious traditions, which he sometimes seems to present as but instances of his psychological concepts, as in his equation of the Hindu concept of Atman-Brahman with his understanding of the self (see Parsons 2001, p. 235). Above all, and in spite of his positive attitude toward religion, Jung has frequently been accused of reducing religion to psychology, principally because of his insistence that psyche is the only immediately experienced reality (see Palmer 1997, pp. 166–96). Nevertheless Jung's attempts to apply his psychology to religion have been immensely influential, both in the illuminating perspectives that they have provided on religious symbols, myths, and rituals and in the impetus that they have given to comparativist dialogues, to humanistic and transpersonal psychology, and to various formulations of psychology *as* religion.

Unlike the early US researchers, both Freud and Jung provide rich theories of religion. Their theories share many premises, such as the origin of religious phenomena in the unconscious mind, the fundamental role of projection, and the need to interpret religious content symbolically. But these shared premises are mixed with other assumptions about which they radically disagree, with the result that their overall evaluations of the role of religion in psychic life are almost antipodal.

Other psychoanalytic contributions: Winnicott, Kohut, Erikson

Where Freud considered religious phenomena to be projections of the Oedipus complex and in particular of an omnipotent father, some later psychoanalysts attached greater importance to the pre-oedipal stages of development. Central here are the infant's libidinous relationship to its primary caregiver, usually its mother, and also its libidinous relationship to its own self in a state before it is aware of its separation from others – the state of "primary narcissism." Consideration of these pre-oedipal phases has allowed Freudian psychoanalytic theory to account for a wider range of religious phenomena, especially for the extent to which maternal and self-oriented relationships, and not merely paternal relationships, may contribute to religious imagery (see Wulff 1997, pp. 320–70).

One influential development for the psychology of religion has been the theory of the English pediatrician Donald Winnicott (1896–1971). Winnicott was concerned with the processes by which the infant emerges into the social world. An important role, he believed, is performed by an "intermediate area" of experience, neither wholly inner and imaginary nor wholly outer and real. It is the area, epitomized by play, in which a child can make believe and can experiment safely with new and creative ways of relating to the world. It is also typically the location of a child's "transitional object," such as a teddy bear or piece of blanket, that helps ease the child away from its fantasy of omnipotence (the belief that it can make things happen merely by thinking) toward acceptance of objective reality. The intermediate area is a realm of illusion, but of illusion understood as something necessary and positive for healthy and creative living, not as delusion. Winnicott suggests that this intermediate area remains of relevance in adult life and is the location of culture and religion since these, too, are "transitional phenomena" that help throughout life to bridge inner and outer realities. He thus agrees with Freud that religion is illusion but removes the pejorative connotations from this characterization. Later writers, such as Paul Pruyser, W. W. Meissner, and Ana-Maria Rizzuto, have applied Winnicott's theories to religion much more extensively than he himself did (see Wulff 1997, pp. 339–46; Capps 2001, pp. 205–40).

In classical Freudian theory, the persistence of narcissism into adulthood was almost invariably considered pathological. Indeed, the condition was usually considered untreatable by means of psychoanalysis because the narcissistic personality, incapable as it is of establishing relations with external objects, is unable to enter into a transference relationship with the analyst. However, the Chicago psychoanalyst Heinz Kohut (1913–81) proposed that, in addition to the classical developmental pathway that leads from narcissism to object-relatedness, or relating to other persons, there is a pathway that leads from primitive narcissism to mature narcissism. Mature narcissism involves the transference of libido from the self to self-transcending ideals and is characterized by qualities such as creativity, empathic understanding, humor, and wisdom. Although Kohut, like Winnicott, was not himself directly concerned with religion, many subsequent researchers have found value in his insights, especially for understanding forms of religion in which the emphasis is not on obedience to a numinous object (God) or on communion or union with that object but on self-realization, as in Zen Buddhism and contemporary "self-spirituality" (see Wulff 1997, pp. 346–61; Capps 2001, pp. 241–304).

Another influential development in psychoanalytic theory was Erik Erikson's (1902–94) model of psychosocial development. Erikson postulated an eight-stage life cycle, each stage of which represents a crisis in human relationships that generates virtues and vices, affects later stages, and is evinced in religious behavior. This encompassing stage model itself bears comparison with religious world views. Erikson believed that religious attitudes largely have their origin in the mother–child relationship, but he did not thereby consider religious attitudes immature. On the contrary, he considered that the religious life can be psychologically healthy and even necessary for growth into full psychological and social maturity (see Wulff 1997, pp. 371–413; Capps 2001, pp. 121–203). Erikson applied his theories to the biographies of two major religious thinkers, Martin Luther and Mohandas Gandhi (see Erikson 1958, 1969).

The theories of Winnicott, Kohut, and Erikson may seem closer to Jung than to Freud in the positive view of religion that they foster. Still, all of these post-Freudian thinkers remain firmly grounded in Freud's naturalistic view of the origins of religion. By contrast Jung, while eschewing metaphysical assertion, still keeps the door open to the possible reality of a divine source for religious phenomena (see Wulff 1997, pp. 637–8).

Empirical Approaches

Although depth psychologists such as Freud and Jung insisted that their methods were empirical because of their basis in careful observation, most academic psychologists would maintain that an empirical approach to psychology requires not just observation but also experimentation, measurement, repeatability, and prediction. It is in this stronger sense that empiricism is understood here. But this kind of empiricism has its limitations and has often been criticized for its inability to yield data that illuminate the deeper issues of religion. This inability may have partly contributed to the early ascendancy of the explanatorily richer depth psychological theories of religion. Still, from around 1950, there has been a progressive resurgence of interest in empirical approaches to the psychology of religion, much of it characterized by the search for methods capable of yielding data that are empirically sound yet nontrivial.

Empirical psychology of religion has almost always been undertaken from within departments of psychology since researchers in departments of religious studies rarely have the necessary scientific training or resources. But departments of psychology have largely been dominated by behaviorist approaches that are suspicious of religion, and this suspicion has both inhibited work and colored the work that has been done. Nevertheless, psychology of religion has gradually gained recognition as a subdiscipline within psychology, and various psychological methodologies have been adapted to the task of gaining understanding of religion. These methodologies have so far mostly been either experimental or correlational, both of them aimed at obtaining quantitative data.

Methodology

The ideal in experimental investigations is to have sufficient control over the variables involved to be able to establish clear causal connections between them. Because of the highly subjective and complex nature of most religious phenomena, this ideal is often difficult for psychologists of religion to realize. Nevertheless, in laboratories and other highly controllable environments there have been investigations of the physiological states of meditating or praying subjects as well as observations of subjects in whom religious experiences have been induced by the use of drugs, sensory deprivation, hypnosis, and other techniques (see Beit-Hallahmi and Argyle 1997, pp. 85–9). There have also been some successful field experiments, such as John Darley and Daniel Batson's "Good Samaritan" experiment. Here students who had just read the parable of the Good Samaritan were sent on an errand and *en route* encountered someone in need of help. It was found that the students who had recently been exposed to the parable were no more likely to offer help than a control group of students who had not been recently exposed to the parable. At the same time, whether or not the students had been told to hurry on their errand did make a difference (see Batson and Ventis 1982, pp. 291–2).

One way of getting round the limitations of laboratory experiments and other attempts artificially to recreate the conditions in which religious phenomena occur has been to make use of real-life circumstances in what have been called "quasi-experiments." For example, researchers can develop hypotheses about what will happen among the members of a religious group if a prophecy due for fulfillment on a specified date is not fulfilled. When the date passes, the researchers can observe the behavior of the group members and thereby test their hypotheses (see Beit-Hallahmi and Argyle 1997, p. 48).

Because of the difficulty of establishing definite causal connections between religious phenomena and the various biological, personal, social, cultural, and other factors with which they may be associated, the empirical psychology of religion makes great use of correlational studies. These studies test whether variables within a complex situation – for example, peer-rated eminence within a field of science and belief in a God who answers prayer – are found to occur together with a frequency that is statistically significant. The data for the statistical analyses involved in correlational studies are mostly acquired through questionnaires and surveys (see Hood *et al.* 1996, pp. 38–9).

A major impetus to the resurgence of psychology of religion was given by the work of the Harvard psychologist Gordon Allport (1897–1967), author of the influential book *The Individual and his Religion* (1950). An authority in personality and social psychology, Allport, like James, was sensitive to the diversity and complexity of religious phenomena and advocated what he called "ideographic" research methods, which focus on individual case studies. But he was also strongly committed to rigorous scientific techniques aimed at establishing general laws – techniques that he called "nomothetic" methods – and in his own studies tended to employ these (see Wulff 1997, pp. 584–5). Allport was particularly concerned to differentiate between more and less mature forms of religiousness (see Wulff 1997, pp. 586–9). Partly in order to explore this distinction, he and some colleagues developed questionnaire scales to quantify the religious trends of a personality. The most influential of these is the Religious

Orientation Scale, which measures the extent to which a person's faith is extrinsic (valued because useful to the self's personal and social interests) or intrinsic (valued in itself and superordinate to the self's other interests). Allport associates intrinsic faith with greater religious maturity (see Wulff 1997, pp. 231–7, 593–4). An alternative scale to Allport's is Batson's Religious Life Inventory, designed some years later. This scale includes measures of religiousness not only as a means and as an end, as did Allport's scale, but also as a quest, involving qualities not discernible from Allport's scale, such as complexity, doubt, and tentativeness (see Batson and Ventis 1982, pp. 137–70). The informativeness of these scales, and of others like them, has been disputed, but they continue to be widely used.

Other methods used in empirical psychology of religion include the structured interview and projective techniques. But these methods introduce a much greater subjective element. Even when the interview is tightly structured according to a predetermined list of questions, there is an inevitable interplay between the interviewer and the interviewee that may affect the responses in ways that are difficult to monitor or control (see Spilka 2001, p. 39). Similarly, projective techniques, such as asking children to draw pictures of God and then analyzing what thoughts and feelings they have projected into their picture, allow room for the researcher's subjectivity to influence the selection, organization, and interpretation of the data obtained (see Spilka 2001, p. 38).

Religious phenomena

Empirical studies in the psychology of religion have attempted to gain understanding of the whole range of religious phenomena. Among the many forms of religious behavior studied are participation in group worship, prayer, reading of Scriptures, use of religious language, sacrifice, making of donations to support religious activities, keeping of dietary laws, healing, and choosing of religion as a career. These phenomena are on the whole relatively easy to observe and measure, and they seem to provide a good indication of religious motivation and commitment, though caution is obviously needed in handling the self-reports by which so many of the data about religious behavior are obtained (see Spilka 2001, p. 35).

Much work has also been done on religious beliefs, especially by means of questionnaires and interviews. Almost every facet of religious belief has been addressed, not least the fundamental question of belief in God. Studies have attempted to ascertain how many persons believe in God in specific communities, what they believe about God, how they have acquired their beliefs, how and why their beliefs may change, and how the incidence and nature of belief in God vary according to nationality, gender, social class, personality, profession, and age group (see Beit-Hallahmi and Argyle 1997, pp. 97–185).

Although religious experience, as the most private and least easily verbalized dimension of religion, might seem the least amenable to empirical investigation, considerable informative work has been done in this area, much of it through, again, the use of questionnaires. The range of religious experiences reported is extremely diverse and includes conversion, mysticism, visions, voices, healing, near-death experiences, states of peace, awe, enlightenment, timelessness, love, remorse, forgiveness, and release from the fear of death (see Hood *et al.* 1996, pp. 185–8).

Origins of religion

Another issue that empirical studies have addressed is the possible psychological origin of religion. Various hypotheses have been proposed, locating the origin of religion in neural factors, cognitive needs and styles, adjustment to anxiety, fear of death, effects of early childhood, various kinds of projection, and sexual motivation (see Beit-Hallahmi and Argyle 1997, pp. 11–24; Hood *et al.* 1996, pp. 12–23). The most strongly supported hypotheses would seem to be the projection hypotheses (see Beit-Hallahmi and Argyle 1997, p. 255). The projection can take various forms. Religious phenomena can be the projection of individual factors, such as early relations with caregivers, or of social factors, such as the way a society is organized. Religious phenomena can either directly parallel these individual and social phenomena or stand in a compensatory or disguised relation to them (see Beit-Hallahmi and Argyle 1997, pp. 19–20). But there is also compelling evidence for the role of social learning in the origin and maintenance of religious attitudes (see Beit-Hallahmi and Argyle 1997, pp. 24–5).

Effects of religion

Considerable empirical research has focused on the psychological effects of religion. The effects include, at the individual level, how religion contributes to people's happiness, physical and mental health, moral and sexual behavior, and attitudes toward death (see Beit-Hallahmi and Argyle 1997, pp. 184–207). At a social level, researchers have studied the effects of religion on fertility, divorce, crime and deviance, work and achievement, prejudice and ethnocentrism, political involvement, and social integration or exclusion. Among the findings are that religious involvement, especially intrinsic religious involvement, generally does correlate positively with happiness, optimism, the tendency to work harder, the ability to cope with stress, diminished fear of death, greater marital stability, lower crime rates, and more charitable work. Yet religious involvement

surprisingly does not seem to correlate with increased honesty. Furthermore,
some forms of religious involvement, especially the most intrinsic, also
correlate positively with prejudice, authoritarianism, and a loss of freedom
to think. Indeed, some of the evidence suggests that many of the apparent
benefits of religion are gained at the cost of hostility toward groups other
than one's own (see Beit-Hallahmi and Argyle 1997, pp. 208–29).

Evaluation of the empirical approach

Notwithstanding the vast amount of empirical work that has been undertaken on the psychology of religion and the many informative results that
have been obtained, there remain problems with empirical approaches.
One problem is that empirical psychological work tends to focus on persons
rather than on contents – symbols, myths, and rituals. As a result, it is
often insensitive to the complex history and rich connotative meaning of
these contents (see Wulff 1997, pp. 256–7).

Another problem is that the sought-after objectivity of the empirical
approaches can do violence to the subjective quality of many religious
phenomena. In experimental and quasi-experimental studies the scientific
ends are likely to interfere with the religious engagement of the subjects,
 yet if there is no effective entry into the religious sphere by the subjects,
then the behavior and experiences investigated will not be religious (see
Wulff 1997, p. 252). Again, in correlational studies based on questionnaires, quantifiable data can usually be obtained only when the possible
responses are standardized and simplified. Yet standardization and simpli-
 fication often leave both respondents and historians of religion dissatisfied
at the loss of important distinctions (see Wulff 1997, p. 253).

An increasing number of researchers are coming to appreciate that
subjectivity cannot be excluded altogether from the psychology of religion. Even with questionnaire studies, for example, while the use of standardized questions and statistical techniques for analyzing results can
exclude the subjectivity of the researcher, it does so by shifting the subjective element in the study onto the subjects. These subjects, if they are
adequately to answer the probing questions about their practices, beliefs,
and experiences, are implicitly expected to engage in often quite deep and
subtle levels of introspection, for which in most cases they will not have
been trained (see Wulff 1997, pp. 254–6). Recognizing this problem,
some researchers have begun to explore more qualitative psychological
research methods, in which the researcher's subjectivity is not just
acknowledged but actively used as a research instrument – for example,
in interviews and participant observation studies. These methods can
complement the more objective and quantifiable empirical approaches.
They also provide a point of rapprochement with psychoanalytical
approaches, for acknowledgment and use of subjectivity, especially in the

dynamics of transference and countertransference, are one of the analyst's core investigative methods.

Some consider that the success of empirical psychology of religion has been modest and has been hampered by its lack of a governing theory (see Hood *et al*. 1996, pp. 446–52). While it is admittedly difficult to operationalize and to test many of the most interesting theoretical insights in psychology of religion, it is also the case that effective measurement without an adequate theoretical framework is liable to be trivial and uninformative. As Ralph Hood and his colleagues aptly observe, there is a need for "theory congruent with the passion and interest elicited by religion" (Hood *et al*. 1996, p. 446). Even in the current state of the field, however, informative data have been obtained by empirical means, and certainly the more objective empirical approaches need to be pursued if psychologists of religion wish not only to formulate theories and construct hypotheses but also to test them.

Religion and Psychology

Although the psychology of religion in the strict sense involves the application of a psychological theory to the elucidation of religious phenomena, the field has been greatly influenced by various ways in which the relationship between psychology and religion has been less straightforward.

Theology, psychology, and psychotherapy

In some cases religion has explicitly taken the initiative in relation to psychology by appropriating psychological insights and practices for its own ends. For example, the years between 1930 and 1960 saw, particularly in America, a period of productive dialogue between theology and psychology, when a number of prominent theologians welcomed the challenging new perspectives that psychological and psychoanalytical thinking provided on traditional religion, seeing in these styles of thinking an opportunity to enrich their own theology (see Homans 1989, pp. 69–71). A notable and influential representative of this trend was the Protestant theologian Paul Tillich (1886–1965), who not only included psychoanalytic insights in his theological works but also explicitly attempted to synthesize the Christian tradition with psychoanalysis as well as with Marxism and existentialism. He attempted this synthesis largely through his "correlational method," whereby theological questions were illuminated in a sophisticated way by being re-framed in terms of modern cultural discourses. For example, he saw neurotic conflict and neurotic anxiety as a means of avoiding existential awareness of one's finitude – a failure to engage with ultimate realities, to recognize one's freedom, and to find "the courage to be" (see Tillich 1952). Developments in psychology and psychoanalysis also encouraged the emergence of pastoral counseling, where ministers employed the new psychological and therapeutic understanding to help them in their pastoral practice (see Heisig 1989, pp. 64–5).

Religious and anti-religious agendas

In other cases the effect of religious, or anti-religious, commitments has had a more covert influence on the engagement of psychology with religion. For example, Freud's work in this area is not merely a disinterested application of psychoanalytic theory to religion. It is motivated by a conscious anti-religious attitude. Jung's theory is also not neutral toward religion but, contrary to Freud, is influenced by the desire to re-frame some of the main concerns of religion in terms more acceptable to modern consciousness. Within empirical psychology of religion, some have suggested that subjective-empirical approaches tend to be pursued by more conservative religionists, whereas objective-empirical approaches tend to be pursued by more liberal religionists (see Spilka 2001, p. 31). Others, however, argue that the questionnaires used in objective correlational studies "have tended to define religion in literalistic terms" and that "much research of this type has been carried out in defense of more or less conservative views" (Wulff 1997, p. 635). In each of these cases the kind of psychology of religion practiced is arguably influenced by a prior agenda.

Humanistic and transpersonal psychology

Prior agendas also influence research and practice in humanistic and transpersonal psychology. Although many previous researchers, such as James, Jung, and Allport, can be said to be in the humanistic tradition, the approach is most often associated with the work of Abraham Maslow (1908–70), especially his book *Religions, Values, and Peak Experiences* (1964). According to Maslow, human beings have a "hierarchy of needs." In addition to physiological needs, safety needs, belongingness needs, and self-esteem needs, humans have a need for "self-actualization." Indicators of progress toward self-actualization include greater acceptance of reality, deeper relationships, philosophical humor, moral elevation, and, most famously, "peak experiences." Peak experiences are basically mystical experiences presented as universally occurring naturalistic events, not unique to any religion but rather the common core uniting them all (see Wulff 1997, pp. 604–16). Humanistic psychology resembles the depth psychological approaches in its emphasis on human subjectivity and direct inner experience but resembles the empirical approaches in its attempt to investigate religious phenomena, especially religious experience, through observation, experiment, and measurement.

Researchers in humanistic psychology, including Maslow himself, increasingly focused their attention on those aspects of psychology that seemed to transcend personal boundaries, such as the experiences of unitive, spiritual, and transcendent states of consciousness, and this emphasis gave rise to the distinctive movement known as transpersonal psychology (see Wulff 1997, pp. 616–23). Researchers in this area such as Charles Tart, Robert Ornstein, and Ken Wilber have been particularly concerned with Eastern religious experience, meditation, and the search for new paradigms that can integrate religion with science – or, even more boldly, to account for the whole of reality.

Although purporting to apply the most rigorous scientific methods, humanistic and transpersonal psychologies are both usually pursued by researchers sympathetic to claims for a transpersonal dimension of human experience, and their experiments have often been criticized for being designed less to test than to confirm transpersonal assumptions. In this sense the religious or transcendental orientation of the researchers has reciprocally influenced the kind of psychology of religion that those researchers do. They are not simply operating with a body of mainstream psychological theory and applying it to the phenomena of religion. Rather, they are crediting the claims for mystical and religious experience and are attempting to devise psychological methods and theories adequate to the investigation and explanation of such phenomena.

Psychology and comparativist approaches to religion

Another area in which religion has forced a reconsideration of some of the assumptions governing its psychological investigation is in comparativist religious studies. Although there was a definite Christian and Protestant bias in much of the early work in the psychology of religion, several prominent researchers did look to other traditions, especially Eastern ones. James discussed Muslim, Hindu, and Buddhist experiences. Pratt wrote knowledgeably about Hinduism and Buddhism, traveling to the East specifically in order to learn more. Freud referred to Hinduism when discussing the mystic's "oceanic feeling." Jung traveled to India and Africa and wrote on Indian Yoga, Chinese Taoism, both Tibetan and Zen Buddhism, and many other non-Christian traditions. To be sure, all of this work can be criticized for its orientalizing tendencies and its limited knowledge of the traditions being studied, but it set in motion a fruitful trend in contemporary psychology of religion (see Parsons 2001). As this trend has developed, the parochialism of the early psychology of religion has been challenged by awareness both of the great diversity of world religions and of the existence of sophisticated models of psychological understanding – Hindu, Buddhist, Taoist, Kabbalistic, or Sufi – very different from those that were developed in Europe and the United States in the late nineteenth and early twentieth centuries.

Psychology as religion

There have been various suggestions, ranging from the scathing to the enthusiastic, that psychology itself might be a new form of religion. Here psychology and religion would be related through neither subordination nor dialogue but partial merging. The kind of psychology involved in this position is primarily either humanistic or phenomenological – in both cases concerned with the exploration of psychic depths and the realization of hidden potentials through aligning oneself with those depths. The kind of religion involved here is noninstitutional and nondogmatic spirituality. The influence of theorists such as Jung, Maslow, and Wilber has contributed to what is arguably the most conspicuous form of "psychology as religion": the New Age Movement, with its highly psychologized form of nonaffiliated spirituality (see Barnard 2001).

The existence of these less straightforward relationships has led some researchers to prefer to place their work within a more broadly defined field of "psychology *and* religion" or "religion and psychological studies" rather than within "psychology *of* religion" (see Homans 1989; Jonte-Pace and Parsons 2001). Psychology of religion would, then, be a subdiscipline or specific approach within this broader field.

Conclusion

The psychology of religion is a complex field involving a diverse range of psychological theories, ways of understanding religion, and relationships between psychology and religion. This complexity ensures that the field will continue to develop in more than one direction, with various approaches challenging and enriching one another. In particular, there is scope for more explicit crossovers among psychoanalytical, empirical, and humanistic approaches as well as among those involved in the psychology of religion in the strict sense and those involved in the relationship between religion and psychology more broadly. The bold theories of psychoanalysis, for example, have been able to yield at least some testable hypotheses, and more should become possible as empirical methods increase in sophistication. Furthermore, the shift within academic psychology toward the inclusion of qualitative methods in addition to quantitative methods provides scope for closer engagement with depth psychological and other hermeneutic approaches. Recent developments within specific branches of academic psychology, including social psychology, cognitive psychology, developmental psychology, and evolutionary psychology, could also prove fruitful for the study of religion (see Hood *et al.* 1996, pp. 449–50).

Whatever the approach, the standard of work in the psychology of religion can certainly be enhanced by psychologists learning more about religion and by religionists learning more about psychology. More work also needs to be done to counteract the biases that arguably have entered the field from the localized provenance of the data. For example, the majority of empirical work has been done in North America and very often, for convenience of data collection, on US university campuses. While some of the findings appear to be safely universalizable, others almost certainly are not (see Beit-Hallahmi and Argyle 1997, pp. 230–1). Like other areas in the study of religion, psychology of religion also needs to pay more attention to the gender biases embedded in both its history and its current practice (see Jonte-Pace 2001).

The development of the psychology of religion as a field was long hampered by mutual suspicion between psychology and religion – an inheritance largely from the science-versus-religion debates of the late nineteenth and early twentieth centuries. As levels of awareness both within and between these disciplines continue to become more sophisticated, plural, and self-reflexive, there is less of a sense either that psychology necessarily is reductive of religion or that religion necessarily is intolerant of the aims of psychology. The psychology of religion is now a well-established, vibrant field that can help both students and adherents to understand more deeply some of the many factors influencing religiosity.

Bibliography

Allport, Gordon. *The Individual and his Religion: A Psychological Interpretation.* New York: Macmillan, 1950.

Barnard, G. William. "Diving into the Depths: Reflections on Psychology as a Religion," in *Religion and Psychology: Mapping the Terrain*, eds. Diane Jonte-Pace and William Parsons. London: Routledge, 2001, pp. 297–318.

Batson, C. Daniel, and W. Larry Ventis. *The Religious Experience: A Social-Psychological Perspective.* New York: Oxford University Press, 1982.

Beit-Hallahmi, Benjamin. "Psychology of Religion 1880–1930: The Rise and Fall of a Psychological Movement," *Journal of the History of the Behavioral Sciences* 10 (1974): 84–90.

Beit-Hallahmi, Benjamin, and Michael Argyle. *The Psychology of Religious Behaviour, Belief and Experience.* London: Routledge, 1997.

Capps, Donald, ed. *Freud and Freudians on Religion: A Reader.* New Haven, CT: Yale University Press, 2001.

Erikson, Erik H. *Young Man Luther: A Study in Psychoanalysis and History.* New York: Norton, 1958.

Erikson, Erik H. *Gandhi's Truth.* New York: Norton, 1969.

Freud, Sigmund. *The Origins of Religion*, tr. James Strachey, Penguin Freud Library, vol. 13 (1907–39). London: Penguin, 1990.

Freud, Sigmund. *Civilization, Society and Religion*, tr. James Strachey, Penguin Freud Library, vol. 12 (1908–33). London: Penguin, 1991.

Heisig, James. "Psychology of Religion," in *Encyclopedia of Religion*, ed. Mircea Eliade. 1st edn. New York: Macmillan; London: Collier Macmillan, 1989, vol. 12, pp. 57–66.

Homans, Peter. "Psychology and Religion Movement," in *Encyclopedia of Religion*, ed. Mircea Eliade. 1st edn. New York: Macmillan; London: Collier Macmillan, 1989, vol. 12, pp. 66–75.

Hood, Ralph, *et al. The Psychology of Religion: An Empirical Approach* [1985]. 2nd edn. New York: Guilford Press, 1996.

James, William. *The Varieties of Religious Experience*, 2nd edn. New York: Longman, Green, 1902.

Jonte-Pace, Diane. "Analysts, Critics, and Inclusivists: Feminist Voices in the Psychology of Religion", in *Religion and Psychology: Mapping the Terrain*, eds. Diane Jonte-Pace and William Parsons. London: Routledge, 2001, pp. 129–46.

Jonte-Pace, Diane, and William Parsons, eds. *Religion and Psychology: Mapping the Terrain*. London: Routledge, 2001.

Jung, C. G. *Psychology and Religion: West and East*, [1958], 2nd edn. Collected works of C. G. Jung, eds. Sir Herbert Read et al., trs. R. F. C. Hull et al. Princeton, NJ: Princeton University Press. London: Routledge, 1969.

Maslow, Abraham. *Religions, Values, and Peak Experiences*. Columbus: Ohio State University Press, 1964.

Palmer, Michael. *Freud and Jung on Religion*. London: Routledge, 1997.

Parsons, William. "Themes and Debates in the Psychology – Comparativist Dialogue," in *Religion and Psychology: Mapping the Terrain*, eds. Diane Jonte-Pace and William Parsons. London: Routledge, 2001, pp. 229–53.

Pratt, James. B. *The Religious Consciousness: A Psychological Study*. New York: Macmillan, 1920.

Spilka, Bernard. "Psychology of Religion: Empirical Approaches," in *Religion and Psychology: Mapping the Terrain*, eds. Diane Jonte-Pace and William Parsons. London: Routledge, 2001, pp. 30–42.

Tillich, Paul. *The Courage to Be*. New Haven, CT: Yale University Press, 1952.

Wulff, David. *Psychology of Religion: Classic and Contemporary*, 2nd edn. New York: Wiley, 1997.

— Chapter 8 —

Sociology of Religion

Grace Davie

The discipline of sociology is about patterns. More specifically, and in common with other social sciences, it is concerned both with identifying and with explaining the nonrandom ways that individuals, communities, and societies order their lives. The sociology of religion aims to discover the patterns of individual and social living associated with religion in all its diverse forms. It is not concerned with the competing truth claims made by religions.

To indicate that the many and varied aspects of religious life form patterns does not imply that they are *caused*, either directly or indirectly, by the different variables that appear to correlate with them. For example, in large parts of the Christian West women appear to be more religious than men – an obvious and pervasive example of a pattern. Why this should be so moves us to the level of explanation, and in more ways than one. For we have to consider not only why women are more religious than men but also why this difference was ignored for so long in the sociological literature.

In light of these issues this chapter is organized as follows. The first section deals first with the evolution of the sociology of religion since the time of the founding fathers: Karl Marx, Max Weber, and Emile Durkheim.

The association between the early development of sociology and the European context from which it emerged is central to these discussions. The same factor (or rather its absence) accounts for the very different directions that the sociology of religion has taken elsewhere in the world.

The second section outlines the contrasting trajectories of the sociology of religion, above all in Europe and the United States. Particular attention is paid to the complex relationships that exist among the different ways of being religious, the various theoretical perspectives that emerge to explain what is happening, and the different topics that as a result dominate the agenda.

Selected examples of these topics are the focus of the third section. Western Europeans, for example, are significantly less active religiously than contemporary Americans. Hence the stress among sociologists on secularization in Western Europe but on religious activity in the United States. Generalizability from either region to the rest of the world should not be assumed.

The final section concerns sociological method. Here the variety of methodological approaches within the subdiscipline is outlined. The stress is on the complementary nature of the work being done. The section concludes with a note on cognate disciplines.

The Founding Fathers

The beginnings of sociology are rooted in the transformation of European society, as the constituent nations of the continent embarked, each in its own way, on the process of industrialization. Marx, Weber, and Durkheim were at once participants in and observers of this massive upheaval. All three sought not only to understand the processes that were taking place but also to establish a discipline that would enhance this understanding. What was happening? Why was it happening in some places rather than others? And what were the likely consequences for different groups of people? All three concluded that religion was a central feature in explaining what was happening, why it was happening, and what the consequences were.

Karl Marx (1818–83) lived a generation earlier than Weber and Durkheim. There are two key elements in the Marxist perspective on religion. One is descriptive, the other evaluative. Marx describes religion as a dependent variable: religion depends on economics. Nothing about religion can be understood apart from the economic order and the relationship of the capitalist and the worker to the means of production. But religion is also to be condemned. It is a form of alienation – a symptom of social malformation which disguises the exploitative relationships of capitalist society by persuading believers that these relationships are natural and therefore acceptable. Religion at once masks alienation and compounds it. The real causes of social distress cannot be tackled until the religious element in society has been stripped away. Everything else is a distraction.

Debates over Marx's approach to religion have to be approached with care. It has become increasingly difficult to distinguish Marx's own analysis of religion from that of subsequent schools of Marxism and from the invocation of "Marxism" as a political ideology. The enduring point to grasp from Marx himself is that religion cannot be understood apart from the social world of which it is part. This insight remains central to the evolution of the sociology of religion. It needs, however, to be distinguished from an over-deterministic interpretation of Marx which postulates the dependence of religion on economic forces in mechanical terms – that is, the notion that different forms of religion can simply be "read off" from different forms of the economy.

An additional caution is more political. It may indeed be the case that one function of religion is to disguise and thereby perpetuate the very evident hardships of this world. Marx was correct to point this out. Nowhere, however, does Marx justify the active destruction of religion by those Marxist regimes which maintain that the only way to reveal the true injustices of society is by destroying the religious element within them. Examples abound prior to the fall of communism in the former Soviet Union. Only recently has the policy begun to shift in China. Marx himself took a longer-term view, claiming that religion would disappear of its own accord with the advent of the classless society. Quite simply it would no longer be necessary and so would fade away.

The inevitable confusions among Marx, Marxism, and Marxist regimes have, however, had a profound effect on the reception of Marx's ideas in the twentieth century. The total, abrupt, and unforeseen collapse of Marxism as an effective political creed in 1989 is but the latest twist to a considerably longer tale. The extraordinary events of this *annus mirabilis* may not invalidate the theory itself, but they do lead us to wonder whether Marxism can ever again become a viable political doctrine.

In many ways Max Weber's (1864–1920) contribution to the sociology of religion should be seen in this light. Rather than simply refuting Marx, Weber vindicates much of what Marx himself suggested, as opposed to the vulgarizations of Marx's later disciples. Weber stresses the multi-causality of social phenomena, not least of religion. In so doing, he argues against the one-sidedness of "reflective materialism," according to which religion does no more than reflect the economy. But the causal sequence is not simply reversed. In fact, the emergence of what Weber calls "elective affinities" – the mutual attraction or affinity between material and religious interests – is entirely compatible with Marx's own understanding of ideology. Still, for Weber, the process by which these affinities come into being must be case by case and cannot be assumed to be uniform world-wide. For Weber, in contrast to Marx, the attraction can run in both directions: not only from the material to the religious but also from the religious to the material.

Weber's influence spread to every corner of sociology, not least the sociology of religion. His writings on secularization, on religious change, on religious organizations (the difference between church and sect), on vocations, on religious roles, on authority, on leadership, and on theodicy and on soteriology continue to provoke debate. Only the first two of these issues – secularization and religious change – will be considered here.

Central to Weber's understanding of religion is the conviction that religion is something other than, or separate from, society or "the world." In other words, religion has an existence in its own right – an existence driven by the content of a belief system, or an "ethic," that does not simply mirror the context in which it exists. Three points follow. First, the relationship between religion and the world is contingent and variable: how a particular religion interacts with the surrounding context varies with time and place. Second, this relationship must be researched and cannot simply be assumed. Third, the relationship between religion and society is steadily weakening in modern society. This weakening, to the point that religion has ceased to be an effective force in society, lies at the heart of the process known as "secularization," as a result of which the world has become progressively "disenchanted."

Questions of definition lie beneath these statements. Despite his well-known unwillingness to provide a formal definition of religion, it is clear that at least in practice Weber is working with a *substantive* definition of religion. He is concerned with the ways in which the *content* of a particular religion, or more precisely of a religious ethic, influences both individual and collective behavior. This definition underpins his *Sociology of Religion* (1922), a comparative study of the major world faiths and their impact on everyday life – a hugely impressive undertaking. If religious beliefs influence the way that individuals behave, it follows that changes in belief generate changes in behavior that in turn have an impact beyond the religious sphere. Weber's most celebrated example is found in *The Protestant Ethic and the Spirit of Capitalism* (1904–05/1920), one of the most widely read texts in all of sociology.

For Weber, the relationships between ethic and context and between religion and the world must be examined case by case. There are complex links between a set of religious beliefs and the particular social stratum, which becomes either the source or the carrier of the beliefs in any society. Not everyone has to be convinced by the content of religious teaching for the influence of this ethic to be felt outside the religious sphere. Indeed, a central task of the sociologist is the identification of the particular individuals or groups of individuals who, at a given moment in history, are instrumental in this process.

Working out these relationships, of which elective affinities are but one example, is a crucial task of the sociologist of religion.

Emile Durkheim (1858–1917), who was the contemporary of Weber, began from a different position. Working from a study of totemic religion among Australian aborigines, he became convinced that religion binds members of society. He writes from a functional rather than, like Weber, from a substantive perspective. Durkheim is concerned with what religion does socially. What, then, will happen when time-honored forms of society begin to mutate so fast that traditional patterns of religion are increasingly under strain? How will the function of religion still be fulfilled? This situation confronted Durkheim in France in the early part of the twentieth century. Durkheim responded as follows: the religious aspects of society should be allowed to evolve alongside everything else, in order that the symbols of solidarity appropriate to the developing social order – in this case incipient industrial society – may emerge. New forms of society require new forms of religion. Religion will always exist, for it performs an indispensable function. But the precise nature of religion will vary from place to place and from period to period in order to achieve an appropriate "fit" between religion and the prevailing social order.

Of the early sociologists, Durkheim was the only one to provide an explicit definition of religion. As he puts it in his key work on religion, *The Elementary Forms of the Religious Life* (1912), "[A] religion is a unified system of beliefs and practices relative to sacred things, that is to say, things which are set apart and forbidden – beliefs and practices which unite into one single moral community called a Church, all those who adhere to them" (Durkheim 1965, p. 47). First, he distinguishes between the sacred – that which is set apart – and the profane – everything else. Religion here is being defined *substantively*. The sacred, however, possesses a *functional* quality not possessed by the profane. It has the capacity to unite the collectivity in a set of beliefs and practices that are focused on the sacred object. Acting as a group is for Durkheim of greater sociological importance than the object of worship. The uncompromisingly "social" aspects of Durkheim's thinking are both an advantage and a disadvantage. The differentiation of the social from the psychological ensures that the group is not reduced simply to individuals, as Weber's sociology ultimately does, but the emphasis on society as a reality *sui generis* brings with it the risk of a different kind of reductionism. For taken to its logical conclusion, religion becomes nothing more than the symbolic expression of social experience. This conclusion disturbed many of Durkheim's contemporaries and remains problematic.

While the evolution of the sociology of religion cannot be understood without knowledge of the founding fathers, the availability of their writing should not simply be assumed. It has depended and still depends on competent and available translations. Jean-Paul Willaime (1995), for example, argues that the arrival of Weberian thinking in French sociology only in the early post-World War II period offered significant alternatives to those who were trying to understand the changes in the religious life of France at this time. Weber's work, or parts of his work, had been available in English almost a generation earlier (for example, *The Protestant Ethic and the Spirit of Capitalism* in 1930). What was available to whom in the development of sociological thinking must be investigated and cannot simply be assumed.

Subsequent Developments: Old World and New

Almost half a century passed before the second wave of activity in the sociology of religion took place. The second wave came, moreover, from a very different quarter: from the churches rather than from the social scientific community. But this activity took a different form on each side of the Atlantic. In the United States, where religious institutions remained relatively buoyant and where religious practice continued to grow, sociologists of religion in the early twentieth century were largely motivated by the social gospel, or the notion that the churches should be active agents in alleviating the problems of society. A second, less positive theme ran parallel in the United States: religion became increasingly associated with the social divisions of US society. H. Richard Niebuhr's *The Social Sources of Denominationalism* (1929) typifies this trend.

By the 1950s, however, the principal focus of US sociology lay in the normative functionalism of reigning American sociologist Talcott Parsons, who stressed above all the integrative role of religion. Religion, a functional prerequisite for society, was deemed central to the complex models of social systems and social action elaborated by Parsons. In bringing together social systems with social action, Parsons was drawing on both Durkheim and Weber. At the same time functionalism reflected his American background. It emerged from a social order entirely different from either the turbulence that motivated the founding fathers or the long-term confrontations between church and state in the Catholic nations of Europe, especially France. Post-World War II United States represented a settled period of industrialism in which consensus appeared not only desirable but also possible. The assumption that the social order should be underpinned by religious values was widespread. Parsons' influence can be seen in subsequent generations of scholars, notably, the American Robert Bellah and the German Niklas Luhmann.

This optimism did not last, either in the United States or anywhere else. As the 1950s gave way to a far less confident decade, the sociology of religion shifted once again – this time to the social construction of meaning systems. The key theorists here were Peter Berger and Thomas Luckmann (see Berger and Luckmann 1966). Both inverted the Parsonian model:

social order exists, but it is constructed from below rather than from above. It comes from the struggles by individuals to make sense of their lives. So constructed, religion offers believers crucial meanings by which to orient their existence, not least during times of personal or social crisis. Hence Berger's (1967) notion of religion as a "sacred canopy," which shields both individual and society from an otherwise purposeless existence. The mood of the later 1970s, profoundly shaken by the oil crisis and its effect on the economy, reflects the search for meaning. In the 1970s religion became increasingly prominent – not only in the United States but world-wide. That shift was epitomized by the religiously inspired Iranian revolution in 1979.

One point remains clear: Americans themselves continue to be religious. Just *how* religious they are, it is not always easy to say (see Hadaway et al., 1998), but in the present-day United States, the notion that pluralism necessarily generates religious decline, in that it erodes the sacred canopy or shared belief system, becomes increasingly difficult to sustain. Quite simply, secularization has not happened. The evolution of Berger's thinking is crucial in this respect. In the 1960s, Berger was a firm advocate of the theory of secularization – a tradition that goes back to Weber (see Berger 1967, 1969). In the decades since, in light of not only the continued religious activity of many Americans but also the increasing salience of religion in almost all parts of the developing world, Berger has radically revised his thinking. Secularization is for him no longer a worldwide theory but a theory with limited application, above all suited to the European case (see Berger 1999).

An alternative theory, one that sees pluralism as contributing to the growth rather than the decline of religion, has emerged in the United States. Known as rational choice theory (RCT), it is advocated above all by the American sociologists Rodney Stark and William Sims Bainbridge, with important contributions by Roger Finke and Larry Iannaccone. RCT is quintessentially American in that it assumes both the presence and the desirability of choice – in this case the choice of religion. The theory postulates that individuals are naturally religious and will activate their religious choices, just like all other choices, in order to maximize gain and minimize loss. In arguing in these terms, RCT draws both on economic ways of thinking and on elements of exchange theory taken from psychology. The theory works in terms of supply rather than demand: religious activity will increase wherever there is an abundant supply, or marketplace, of religious choices, offered by a wide range of religious "firms," and will diminish wherever supplies are limited, as in the quasi-religious monopolies of Western Europe.

The assumptions of European sociologists of religion are radically different from those of their American counterparts. The concern of Europeans has been with religious decline rather than growth. Hence the distinctively European preoccupation with secularization. Also different are the post-World War II points of departure, which are nicely exemplified in the titles published in France in the early years of the war. The most celebrated of these, Henri Godin and Yvan Daniel's *La France, pays de mission* (1943), evinces the mood of a growing group of French Catholics increasingly worried by the weakening position of the Church in French society. For the situation to be remedied, accurate information was essential. Hence a whole series of enquiries, under the direction of Gabriel Le Bras, aimed at identifying exactly what characterized the religion of the people – or lived religion (*la religion vécue*), as it became known.

Accurate information acquired a momentum of its own, which led to certain tensions. There were those, in France and elsewhere, whose work remained motivated by pastoral concern. Others felt that knowledge was valuable for its own sake and resented the ties to the Catholic Church. There eventually emerged an independent section within the Centre National de la Recherche Scientifique, the Groupe de Sociologie des Religions. The change in title was significant: "religious sociology" became "the sociology of religions" in the plural. Yet there was continuity as well as change. The initial enthusiasm for mapping, which had begun with Fernand Boulard and Gabriel Le Bras on rural Catholicism, and had continued through the work of Fernand Boulard and Jean Rémy on urban France, culminated in François-André Isambert's and Jean-Paul Terrenoire's magnificent *Atlas de la pratique religieuse des catholiques en France* (1980). Here were deep explanations for the significant regional differences that had emerged.

Jean-Paul Willaime (1995, pp. 37–57) and Danièle Hervieu-Léger and Willaime (2001) tell in detail this primarily French or, more accurately, francophone story: the story of the emergence of accurate and careful documentation motivated primarily by pastoral concerns, the establishment of the Groupe de Sociologie des Religions in Paris in 1954, the gradual extension of the subject matter beyond Catholicism, the development of a distinctive sociology of Protestantism, the methodological problems encountered along the way, and finally the emergence of an international organization and the "déconfessionalisation" of the sociology of religion. The evolution from Conférence international de sociologie religieuse, founded in Leuven, Belgium, in 1948, through the Conférence internationale de sociologie des religions, organized in 1981, to the present Société internationale de sociologies des religions, which dates from 1989, highlights this story. It marks a shift from a group primarily motivated by religion to one motivated by social science. It is, however, a story that emerges, and could only have emerged, from a particular intellectual context: that of Catholic Europe. This context has led to preoccupations that are not always shared by scholars from other parts of the world.

The British case forms an interesting hybrid within this bifurcation of French and American thinking. British sociologists of religion draw considerably on the literature of their fellow English-speaking Americans, but they operate in the distinctively European context of low levels of religious activity. In many ways the British face in two directions at once. They have been more influenced by American-like pluralism than are most of their Continental colleagues. Hence a long-term British preoccupation with new religious movements rather than with popular religion. The parameters of religious activity in the United Kingdom are, however, very different from those in the United States, and here the work of American scholars has proved less helpful. American theories, developed to explain relatively high levels of activity, do not fit the UK case, where nominal membership remains the norm.

Still, most, if not quite all, American and British scholars share a further, here lamentable characteristic: an inability to "access" the sociological literature in any language other than their own. Hence their dependence on each other. Many Continental scholars can do better, leading to a noticeable imbalance in sociological writing. Most Continental sociologists make reference to the English-speaking literature in their work, but the reverse is seldom the case, at least until a translation appears.

The subject that does unite British with Continental rather than American sociologists of religion is religious decline, or the process of secularization. Strictly, "secularization" does not mean the disappearance of religion. Rather, it means the loss of the social significance of religion (see Wilson 1982; Bruce 2002). No one disputes that in Western Europe the indices of active religiosity point downwards. This trend is particularly true of the Protestant nations of Northern Europe, a pattern beginning to be repeated in some, though not all, of the Catholic countries further south. This downward trend is not, however, the whole story. Two further features are crucial. First, there is the continuing resonance of the historic traditions of Europe in latent rather than active forms. Large numbers of Europeans, for example, continue to be members of mainstream churches, even if they rarely practice their faith. Relatively few have no contact whatsoever with these churches. Second, there is a growing religious diversity in Europe, brought about by the arrival of populations, both Christian and non-Christian, from other parts of the world for economic reasons. In short, there are important qualifications to be made to the theory of secularization even in Europe.

Still more important is the need to escape from the notion that secularization offers a "general theory" of religion in the modern world. The experience of the European churches is unique (see Berger 1999; Davie 2002). In Western Europe industrialization, which is almost always associated with urbanization, has had serious consequences for the traditional churches because of the particularities of Europe religious history. European religious life has long been linked not only to political power but also to the application, indeed the legitimation, of this power at the local level, not least in the parish. European religion is rooted in localities.

Herein lies both its strength and its weakness. Religion can still evoke powerful instincts, clearly illustrated in local celebrations and feast days. The Spanish examples come quickly to mind. Conversely, the parish unit was profoundly disturbed at the time of the industrial revolution – a shock from which the mainstream religions of Europe have still not fully recovered.

Secularization theorists are right to note this critical disjunction in the evolution of religious life in Europe. Too quickly, however, have they drawn the wrong inference: that religion and modern, primarily urban, life are incompatible. Secularization did not happen in the United States, where pluralism appears to have stimulated rather than inhibited religious activity, and not least in cities. Nor has secularization happened in the developing world – a point discussed in the following section.

Some Illustrations

The examples that follow are far from exhaustive. They have been selected simply to exemplify the material already set out. One further theme concerns the persistent dilemmas *within* the sociology of religion itself and their effect on the agenda that has emerged. The discussion of mainstream and margins confronts this issue.

Mainstream and margins

Of the material published in the subdiscipline of the sociology of religion, one point is immediately apparent: the distribution of scholarship in this field is not determined by the size of the constituencies involved, particularly among Europeans. Indeed, the reverse is to a large extent the case. In the United Kingdom, for example, very significant attention has been paid to minority religions, especially to new religious movements, and by a distinguished group of sociologists – Eileen Barker, James Beckford, Roy Wallis, and Bryan Wilson, to name the most eminent. Their work dates for the most part from the late 1960s and 1970s and constitutes an attempt to understand the fragmentation of religious belief that took place as one result of the revolution of the 1960s. A number of their studies have become classics – for example, Beckford's study of Jehovah's Witnesses (1975) and Barker's study of the Moonies (1984). The genre has been continued by a growing group of research students.

Some twenty years later, attention was drawn to a rather different form of "alternative" religion: the New Age, as opposed to new religious movements. The two kinds of religions in fact overlap – some new religious movements manifest the tendencies of the New Age – but the fields are distinct. Studies of new religious movements inevitably reflect the organ-

izational issues that arise from these groups: both internal questions about
leadership and external questions about the relationship of new religious
movements to the wider society. The New Age, by contrast, is more accurately described as a collection of tendencies – green issues, alternative
health therapies, and techniques of training and management – that
together constitute a movement. Paul Heelas (1996) has offered a percep-
tive overview of this somewhat amorphous set of ideas. For him, the New
Age is at once an extension of modernity into the religious domain and a
reaction to the more materialistic aspects of modern living. The movement
maintains a strong emphasis on both the self and "holism," by which is
meant the indissolubility of the links among mind, body, and spirit in the
individual and between creator and created in the cosmos.

New
Age

That so much sociological attention, especially in the United Kingdom,
has been concentrated on so few has had both positive and negative consequences. On the positive side an enormously rich body of data has
emerged from the field, aspects of which raise crucial issues for democracy
– for example, the relationship of pluralism to tolerance. New religious
movements in particular become highly sensitive indicators of more
general attitudes: precisely which religious groups modern societies are
prepared to tolerate and which groups not.

Rather more negative, however, has been the relative *lack* of sociological
attention to the religious mainstream. That problem has been compounded
by the assumption of secularization as the dominant paradigm, especially
in Europe. Each of these tendencies exacerbates the other: why study
something considered to be in terminal decline, given that more interesting things are going on at the margins? Yet an alternative formulation of
the question can lead to more interesting outcomes. It is this. Do new
religious movements constitute a challenge to secularization in that they
tend to attract disproportionate numbers of adherents from the heart of
modernity – namely, the technical elite? Or are they, by their very nature,
evidence of the marginalization of religion from the center of modern or
modernizing societies? Opinions differ.

One point remains clear: the answers to all these questions vary from
place to place. What emerges in fact is a complex interaction between
particular new religious movements and the societies of which they are
part. New religious movements are not simply multi-nationals that can
put down roots anywhere. Rather, they choose their locations with care
and adapt themselves accordingly. Some societies, moreover, are clearly
more welcoming than others. In recent decades one issue has increasingly
dominated the literature: the marked lack of tolerance toward new religious movements in France, compared with that in all other Western
European countries. Why should this be so, given the evident democratic
ideals of the French nation?

The answers exemplify the strengths of sociological analysis. It is not
so much the beliefs and practices of new religious movements – or "sects,"

as they are known in the French case – that cause the problem as the
incapacity of the French system to accommodate religious groups that do
not fit existing categories (see Hervieu-Léger 2001). Two opposing forces
dominate the religious field in France: the Catholic Church and the secular
state. The secular state is underpinned by the distinctively French notion
of *laïcité* – a term that denotes the absence of religion in public space,
especially the state and public school system. *Laïcité* becomes in fact an
alternative source of collective identity for French people. It is precisely
this identity that Durkheim was seeking to promote in his search for a
form of "religion" suited to a modern industrial economy.

It became increasingly clear in the later decades of the twentieth century
that neither side in this somewhat confrontational system could cope with
the fragmented nature of religion that was ever more a part of late modern
society, not least in Europe. That situation has led to a negative, many
would say repressive, attitude toward certain religious minorities. Those
proscribed, and subsequently harassed by the authorities, have included
many new religious movements. Elsewhere in Europe the same groups
provoke considerably less hostility, with the notable exception of Scientology.
Interestingly, those parts of Europe formerly under Communist domination are now displaying tendencies rather similar to the French case, and
for the same reasons. Minority groups do not fit easily into the categories
defined by history, especially in the Orthodox countries of Eastern
Europe.

The attention to context has a further positive outcome. Sociologists are
once again becoming aware of the continuing importance of mainstream
religion, even in Europe. The historic churches may be smaller than they
once were, but they still attract considerable numbers of people – far more
than many secular equivalents. The loss in membership in both trade
 unions and political parties should be seen as parallel trends, brought
about for the same reasons as religious decline: the changing nature of
society – a shift that has serious implications for any group that depends
on committed and regular attendance. Within this changing situation, I
myself have paid attention to the enduring legacies of Europe's Christian
churches. Europeans continue to manifest some kind of religious belief,
even if they do not attend church with any regularity (see Davie 1994).
European populations are for the most part content that churches continue to exist in order to function "vicariously" – that is, that an active
minority continue to operate on behalf of a largely sympathetic, if not
practicing, majority (see Davie 2000). Martyn Percy (2001) has strongly
endorsed this conclusion.

A second, equally important emphasis lies in the increasing attention
paid to the growing number of non-Christian faith communities in Europe.
That topic undoubtedly draws on the work on new religious movements,
especially the emphasis on religious tolerance, yet at the same time it goes
further. Unlike many new religious movements, these religions can

scarcely be considered fragmentations of existing religions. The growing presence of other faiths reflects an entirely different kind of pluralism, brought about for economic reasons – employment-driven immigration. The arrival above all of a sizable Muslim presence has demanded sociological attention. Careful documentation of the incoming groups themselves is an important part of this work, not least their evolution over several generations. Even more significant is the interaction between Islam and the host societies of Western Europe, where the evident capacity of the growing Muslim communities to alter some of the basic understandings of European life is becoming more and more apparent. For example, Islam – simply by being there – challenges the European tendency to relegate both religion and religious issues to the private sphere.

Both the attention to historic deposits and the work on other faith communities have clearly undermined at least some aspects of the secularization thesis. The "theory" remains strong, however, and continues to dominate significant aspects of the sociological agenda (see Brown 2001; Bruce 1996, 2002). Even more important, secularization – indeed, secularism – constitutes a pervasive and "popular" world view in the European context. Secularism can be seen, for example, in the media portrayals of religion. It is a point developed at some length by Martyn Percy (2001), a British scholar with both theological and sociological training. One of Percy's aims is to rediscover the place not only for religion but also for theology in public debate. With considerable robustness he combats the assumptions of a still dominant secular elite.

[handwritten margin note: Note also that the secular worldview is developing and progressing]

The situation in the United States is both similar and different. On the one hand the secular elites of both Europe and the United States have much in common. Peter Berger (1999) notes the presence of a global elite able to move easily from country to country, from faculty club to faculty club, safely cocooned from the realities of everyday life. On the other hand the higher level of religiosity in the United States prompts greater attention to the mainstream in sociological studies of religion. Nancy Ammerman's magisterial *Congregation and Community* (1997) exemplifies this approach, relating the shifting nature of religious congregations to the continually evolving communities of which they are a part. Her work also provides rich evidence of the nature of religion in the modern United States. Even her table of contents demonstrates persistence, relocation, adaptation, and innovation in combinations that would be hard to match in Europe. There is, in other words, more of a forward movement in America than would be possible in the Old World, and in an astonishingly wide variety of cases. That variety spurs inquiry.

In short, it is the task of sociologists of religion both to document and to explain the differences between the Old World and the New. Increasingly, however, the developing as well as the developed world is also demanding scholarly attention, prompting a new set of questions.

Pentecostalism

Some cases in point are the extraordinarily rapid growth of Pentecostalism across the developing world, the presence of Catholicism as a *global* religion (the majority of Catholics now live in Latin America), and the increasing visibility of world faiths other than Christianity. The truly global nature of Catholicism, for example, was strikingly evident in April 2005, as the world acknowledged the death of Pope John Paul II and the election of his successor, Benedict XVI. How was it possible to account for the evident popularity of the late Pope, whose teaching was sharply critical of Western relativism? And how, in the twenty-first century, can the Catholic Church find ways to "manage" its very different constituencies? It is clear that shifts in religious demography have far-reaching consequences for both theology and organization.

Rightly or wrongly, much of the study of other faiths, especially of Islam, has been subsumed under the rubric of "fundamentalism," an important but problematic term. Particularly in popular usage, and particularly since 9/11, fundamentalism has become a pejorative word. Consequently, even scholars of religion have been paying too much attention to conservative forms of religion in the modern world, and to their negative side. Fundamentalism is seen as a means of resistance, sometimes very violent, to a supposedly secular modernity. There is considerably less scholarly attention to varieties of religions, both Christian and other, that not only allow believers to take full part in modern society but even enhance their capacity to do so.

Hence the concentration in this section on Pentecostalism, generally agreed to be the fastest-growing form of Christianity. Despite the conservative nature of its teaching, Pentecostalism is distinct from fundamentalism, particularly from the organic or statist versions of fundamentalism (see D. Martin 2002). Unlike fundamentalism, Pentecostalism looks up rather than down, and out rather than in. Above all, it empowers the individual through the "gifts of the spirit," enabling not only survival but success even in difficult economic circumstances. It is by nature fissiparous, encouraging by its very existence the extension of both voluntarism and competitive pluralism. And to quote David Martin, "In those parts of the world where Pentecostalism is most expansive, notably Latin America and Africa, any extension of pluralistic voluntarism is arguably a manifestation of modernity" (D. Martin 2002, p. 1).

Pentecostal growth began in Latin America in the 1960s, when, ironically, the secularization thesis in the West was at its most popular. Pentecostalism has penetrated some parts of Latin America more than others, a pattern that demonstrates once again the complex interaction between innovation in religion and the context in which innovation arises. In subsequent decades Pentecostalism has spread to large parts of English-speaking Africa and to the Pacific Rim, especially to the Philippines and

South Korea, and increasingly to China. Conversely, Pentecostalism in its more innovative forms has made little headway in the developed world, and almost none in Europe. Why Europe has proved unusually hostile territory is an important sociological question, one still to be answered. The relationship with America is more complex, given an already existing evangelical presence (see D. Martin 2002, pp. 33–42).

The first point to grasp is the difficulty that the pioneers in the field encountered in trying to get their work accepted at all, a discussion that worked at several levels (see D. Martin 1990). The first reaction to the serious study of Pentecostalism was to deny that anything significant at all was taking place (see D. Martin 1990). How could it, given the dominant paradigm which postulated that modernization means secularization, not the exponential growth of forms of religion with a distinctively emotional element? Gradually, the debate shifted to accounting for a phenomenon that could no longer be denied. The initial explanation was that American missionaries were, wittingly or not, acting as agents of American imperialism by persuading significant sections of the population in Latin America to adopt American forms of religion. American imperialism proved an attractive explanation, particularly for those who had difficulty acknowledging the fact that growing numbers of marginalized people were opting for Pentecostalism rather than for liberation theology, the favored option of European intellectuals. But the data failed to support the theory. The evidence revealed that Pentecostal churches in Latin America were indigenous and were growing despite missionary influence rather than because of it.

How, then, to account for the increasing numbers of people all over the modernizing world attracted to Pentecostalism? Is there anything in the sociological repertoire to explain this phenomenon? If the sociology of religion is to retain its credibility, it must be able to explain what manifestly *is* there, not what theoretically ought to be.

Steve Bruce (1996) considers Latin American Pentecostalism within the secularization thesis, to which he stands committed. He argues that the conditions in Latin America and elsewhere are similar to those experienced in Europe some two hundred years earlier: the rootlessness of the population in light of extraordinarily rapid economic changes, including a dramatic movement of population away from rural areas to the mega-cities. According to Bruce, Pentecostalism is a form of religion that provides support – economic, social, and spiritual – just as Methodism had done in the early years of the Industrial Revolution in Britain. For Bruce, the secularization thesis remains intact: it would be undermined only if significant numbers of previously secular populations returned to religion, which, Bruce argues, is not the case in Latin America.

Undeniably there are historical parallels between Methodism and Pentecostalism. More problematic are attempts to apply the secularization thesis to Latin American Pentecostalism. A theory that postulates a necessary link between modernization and secularization has been damaging

to sociological inquiry in this part of the world: why else was the phenomenon of Pentecostalism denied for so long? The answer lies in the power
of the theoretical paradigm. Quite simply, Western sociologists would not
see what theory forbade. Only gradually has the sheer weight of the data
begun to demand a revision, not only in the thesis itself but also in the
research agenda that ensues.

So much for the approach of a prominent European to the question.
Can American rational choice theory (RCT) do better? RCT came late to
Latin America, though the somewhat innovative use of the theory by
Anthony Gill (1998) demonstrates both the potential in the theory itself
and the need to take into account the growing presence of Pentecostalism
in this part of the world. Gill seeks explanations for the contrasting positions of the Catholic Church on social issues in terms of the context in
which they are working, not simply in terms of the theological corpus. His
analysis is not, however, hostile to theology. It is more a question of
explaining why the policies of the Catholic Church vary from country
to country, more precisely from Chile to Argentina. The extent of
Pentecostalism as an alternative possibility for poorer people is a significant factor in the analysis. In Chile, where both evangelical and socialist
movements are present, the Catholic Church was very critical of the
Pinochet regime. In neighboring Argentina the traditional accommodation between church and state to a large extent continued. In other words,
where the Catholic Church faces competition in the recruitment of believers, the Catholic authorities will oppose authoritarian regimes in order to
maintain credibility with the poor.

The crucial point lies deeper – in the need to find theoretical approaches
that can explain the evident compatibility of innovative forms of religion
with modern ways of living. The assumption that religion and modernity
are necessarily in conflict derives from the European sociological heritage
and the founding fathers. These connections, however, are seriously under
pressure as the sociological horizons widen to encompass both new areas
of enquiry and a greater diversity of geographical regions. The concept of
"multiple modernities" is becoming increasingly salient in this respect.
According to Shmuel Eisenstadt, modernity is a multiple, as opposed to a
unitary, concept. It is sometimes associated with secularization, but not
inevitably (see Eisenstadt 2000). Consequently, neither Europe nor indeed
the markedly more religious United States should be considered a lead
society, so that the forms of religion found in either should not be assumed
to herald their replication elsewhere.

Religion and the everyday

The third example in this section illustrates an entirely different way of
working. It is concerned with the life cycle of both individuals and communities. It pays particular attention to gender, to age, and to death.

Traditionally considered the province of anthropology at least as much as of sociology, these topics have reinvigorated sociological thinking in recent decades.

The attention to gender is particularly welcome, given the centrality of this variable in any inquiry about Christianity in the Western world. Here, moreover, there is a similarity in the findings on Europe, the United States, and Latin America: in all three cases, women not only are consistently more religious than men but also express their religiousness differently from men (see Woodhead 2002). Given the persuasiveness of the data, it is remarkable that until recently, convincing explanations for these differences remained noticeably difficult to come by. Once again, it is the lack of prior sociological attention to these findings as much as the findings themselves that requires explanation. A similar lacuna can be found in ecclesiastical circles, where the predominance of women in religious organizations is very often expressed negatively – as the under-representation of men.

The lack of attention within the churches can be partially explained by an understandable preoccupation in recent decades with the *absence* of women in the priesthood rather than their *presence* in the pews. The disproportionate religiousness of lay women requires, however, both documentation and explanation. Are women more inclined to be religious because of who they are or because of the expectations that society places on them? If the answer is nurture, then the situation may well change in the foreseeable future. If the answer is nature, then the imbalance may continue for some time despite the rapid evolution in the roles of women in most Western societies.

A second point is also important: the lack of attention to the same question on the part of secular feminists. Here the reasoning is somewhat similar to the debates surrounding the secularization thesis: feminist scholars have had difficulty coming to terms with data that fail to fit their theories. The fact that women appear to frequent disproportionately the very institutions that are responsible for their "oppression" challenges many feminist assumptions. The case of Pentecostalism in the developing world proves especially problematic. Here the presence of women is equally evident, perhaps more so, yet the theological thrust is markedly conservative. Churches here endorse traditional patterns of family life, including male headship – a point repeatedly emphasized by anthropologists and missiologists but ignored by sociologists (see B. Martin 2002).

A considerably more creative approach can be found in the work of Linda Woodhead (2002), who takes seriously the question of gender but permits women to make the choices that suit them best. What emerges is a wide range of possibilities, both for and against religious outcomes, themselves of different types. The data are complex, prompting equally varied explanations: what is liberating for one woman may be oppressive for another. There are differences between the West and the developing world in the ways in which women negotiate their religious lives, differences that reflect the degree to which mainstream religion has or has not been privatized. Whatever the case, the women in question, as autonomous social actors, must decide and speak for themselves.

The life cycle, the aging process, and the inevitability of death are part of what it means to be human. After decades of silence, comparable with the Victorian distaste for talking about sex, both society and sociologists have become increasingly preoccupied with death. Those interested in religion have a particular part to play in this debate – unsurprisingly, given that the offering of solutions to the mystery of death is one of the traditional *functions* of religion. What happens, then, in a modern and supposedly secular society, when the time-honored explanations are no longer considered convincing but where death remains as unavoidable as ever before? All that can be said about modern societies is that death can be put off for longer – hence the parallel preoccupation with aging – and that we die in greater comfort than in previous generations. But die we still do.

The work of Tony Walter (1994) is central here. He describes the evolution of death from traditional to modern to "neo-modern" societies. Parts of the story are by now commonplace: death has changed from primarily a public event embedded in community to a private affair, and one discussed in medical rather than religious terms. Antibiotics are of greater use for most of our ailments than cycles of prayer. Yet as dissatisfaction with the modern way of death has increased, so has the pressure for change. According to Walter, there are two possibilities. On the one hand "late-modern" revivalists assert the right of individuals to know that they are dying and to express how they feel. On the other hand the postmodern revival is both more radical and more conservative. Individuals must be allowed to choose: to know that they are dying or not to know; to grieve in an expressive manner or not to do so. Whatever works for the individual is considered the right thing to do.

Beneath these questions lies a powerful subtext: both the dying and the grieving individual must be considered as a person, not simply as a bundle of symptoms or sorrows. Walter drives the argument to a provocative conclusion: that holistic care has entered the mainstream of medicine as a response to the needs of dying people. The issues that he raises go far beyond the immediate subject matter of his book. They challenge both the institutional arrangements of modern societies and the theoretical implications of some aspects of the secularization theory. Increasing specialization which is a key tenet of this theory, is obliged to give way, as "holy" and "whole" reacquire their common root. The set apart – for Durkheim, the sacred – becomes once again integral to the well being of both individual and collective life. Religion is rediscovered in the everyday.

A Methodological Note

The introductory section of this chapter emphasized the defining feature of sociological study of religion: that it is about discerning and explaining the diverse and complex patterns to be found in the religious aspects of human living. In order to accomplish these tasks, the discipline has drawn on a wide variety of methods, some of which have been noted and each of which yields particular kinds of data. The methods used are complementary. Taken together, they enable the researcher to build up as complete a picture as possible of the phenomenon at hand. This final section brings together the principal methodologies found in the sociological study of religion.

There is a distinction, first of all, between quantitative and qualitative data. Quantitative data rely heavily on statistical analyses, whether of existing data sets or of material generated by the sociological inquirer in search of a pattern. That pattern can stretch over time or place. Good examples of this way of working can be found in the contrasting trends found in Europe and the United States concerning religious activity or in the measuring of the nature of Pentecostal growth in the developing world since the 1960s.

Large-scale statistical enquiries are enhanced by smaller qualitative studies, concentrating on fewer persons but in more depth. These studies are particularly useful in investigating religious minorities, which are too small to produce meaningful data in any large-scale survey. Two or three members of a new religious movement may be present in a national survey, but rarely more. Hence the need for alternative ways of working: the purposive sample; the in-depth interview; or the classic ethnographic tool, that of participant observation. Sources of qualitative data, moreover, are diverse. Increasingly, they include text and discourse, or art and artifacts, as well as encounters with people. Researchers must, in addition, draw from the past as well as the present. Explanations for comparative difference almost always reside in the past – a point already exemplified in the comparison between different European societies and their attitudes to new religious movements.

History and sociology clearly overlap. Equally porous are the lines between sociology and psychology, between sociology and anthropology, and between sociology and political science. Each field is nevertheless distinct, defined partly in terms of subject matter but also by preference for one form of inquiry over another. Rather more problematic is the relationship of sociology, in fact of all the social sciences, with theology. Theology is concerned with truth claims and as such is resistant to any discipline that relativizes the religious message. Two somewhat opposed points of view have emerged in recent discussion. The first, held by John

Milbank (1990), maintains that sociology and theology are incompatible discourses. Sociology, an inevitably secular science, should not encroach upon the sublime. David Martin (1997) argues the opposite: that sociology, appropriately understood and carefully employed, *can* contribute to theological understanding without the compromising of either discipline.

For Martin, theological insights and the context from which they emerge are necessarily linked. For example, the Christian calling, both individual and collective, is to be "in the world but not of it." In Martin's mixing of sociological with theological language, between the specificities of each situation and the exigencies of the gospel lies "an angle of eschatological tension." Documenting and explaining the sharpness of the angle are sociological tasks. So are suggestions of possible resolution, if the tension becomes unbearable. Theologies of baptism provide one illustration. Modes of initiation that fitted the state churches of northern Europe no longer fit, either socially or theologically, as the basis of membership in those churches mutates from ascription to voluntarism. New understandings are required, and they are more likely to succeed if the sociological shifts are not only taken into account but also properly understood.

Bibliography

Ammerman, Nancy. *Congregation and Community.* New Brunswick, NJ: Rutgers University Press, 1997.

Barker, Eileen. *The Making of a Moonie: Choice or Brain/washing?* Oxford: Blackwell, 1984.

Beckford, James. *The Trumpet of Prophecy.* Oxford: Blackwell, 1975.

Berger, Peter L. *The Sacred Canopy: Elements of a Sociological Theory of Religion.* Garden City, NY: Doubleday, 1967.

Berger, Peter L. *A Rumor of Angels: Modern Society and the Rediscovery of the Supernatural.* Garden City, NY: Doubleday, 1969.

Berger, Peter L., ed. *The Desecularization of the World: Resurgent Religion and World Politics.* Grand Rapids, MI: Eerdmans, 1999.

Berger, Peter L., and Thomas Luckmann. *The Social Construction of Reality: A Treatise on the Sociology of Knowledge.* Garden City, NY: Doubleday, 1966.

Brown, Callum. *The Death of Christian Britain.* London: Routledge, 2001.

Bruce, Steve. *Religion in the Modern World: From Cathedrals to Cults.* Oxford: Oxford University Press, 1996.

Bruce, Steve. *God Is Dead.* Oxford: Blackwell, 2002.

Davie, Grace. *Religion in Britain Since 1945.* Oxford: Blackwell, 1994.

Davie, Grace. *Religion in Modern Europe.* Oxford: Oxford University Press, 2000.

Davie, Grace. *Europe, the Exceptional Case.* London: Darton, Longman and Todd, 2002.

Durkheim, Emile. *The Elementary Forms of Religious Life* [1912], tr. Joseph Ward Swain. London: Allen and Unwin; New York: Free Press, 1965 [1915].

Eisenstadt, Shmuel. "Multiple Modernities," *Daedalus* 120 (2000): 1–30.

Gill, Anthony. *Rendering unto Caesar.* Chicago: University of Chicago Press, 1998.

Godin, Henri, and Yvan Daniel. *La France, pays de mission.* Paris: Les Éditions du Cerf, 1943.

Hadaway, Kirk, Penny Marler, and Mark Chaves. "A Symposium on Church Attendance," *American Sociological Review* 63 (1998): 111–45.

Heelas, Paul. *The New Age Movement: The Celebration of the Self and the Sacralization of Modernity.* Oxford: Blackwell, 1996.

Hervieu-Léger, Danièle. *La Religion en miettes ou la question des sectes.* Paris: Calman-Lévy, 2001.

Hervieu-Léger, Danièle, and Jean-Paul Willaime. *Sociologies et religion.* Paris: Presses Universitaires de France, 2001.

Isambert, François-André, and Jean-Paul Terrenoire. *Atlas de la pratique religieuse des catholiques en France.* Paris: Presses de la Fondation nationale des sciences politiques; Editions du CNRS, 1980.

Martin, Bernice. "The Pentecostal Gender Paradox: A Cautionary Tale for the Sociology of Religion," in *The Blackwell Companion to the Sociology of Religion,* ed. Richard Fenn. Oxford: Blackwell, 2002, pp. 52–66.

Martin, David. *Tongues of Fire.* Oxford: Blackwell, 1990.

Martin, David. *Reflections on Sociology and Theology.* Oxford: Clarendon, 1997.

Martin, David. *Pentecostalism: The World Their Parish.* Oxford: Blackwell, 2002.

Milbank, John. *Theology and Social Theory: Beyond Secular Reason.* Oxford: Blackwell, 1990.

Niebuhr, H. Richard. *The Social Sources of Denominationalism,* New York: Holt, 1929.

Percy, Martyn. *The Salt of the Earth: Religious Resilience in a Secular Age.* Sheffield: Sheffield Academic Press, 2001.

Walter, Tony. *The Revival of Death.* London: Routledge, 1994.

Weber, Max. *General Economic History,* tr. Frank. H. Knight. London: Allen and Unwin, 1927.

Weber, Max. *The Protestant Ethic and the Spirit of Capitalism* [1904–05/1920], tr. Talcott Parsons. London: Allen and Unwin, 1930.

Weber, Max. *The Sociology of Religion* [1922], tr. Ephraim Fischoff. Boston: Beacon Press, 1963.

Willaime, Jean-Paul. *Sociologie des religions.* Paris: Presses Universitaires de France, 1995.

Wilson, Bryan R. *Religion in Sociological Perspective.* Oxford: Oxford University Press, 1982.

Woodhead, Linda. "Women and Religion," in *Religions in the Modern World,* eds. Linda Woodhead, Paul Fletcher, Hiroko Kawanami, and David Smith. London: Routledge, 2002, pp. 332–56.

Chapter 9

Theology

Ian Markham

"Theology" comes from two Greek words. *Theos* means God; *logos* means word. Literally, then, theology means "words about God," or perhaps more helpfully, "study" of God. At least within the academic world, theology is largely confined to an attempt to arrive at a "systematic" account of God and of God's relations with the world. Theology tends to focus on "what is believed," although of course there are beliefs about practices. Theology is grounded within a tradition. So one often speaks of "Christian theology," "Jewish theology," or "Islamic theology" but never of theology as such.

This chapter looks first at some of the different ways in which the word "theology" is used. Next the focus is on Christian theology, with links made to other traditions. Then the chapter considers (a) sources for theology, (b) the impact of modernity on theology, and (c) the likely future directions for theology.

The Word "Theology" in Use

It was Ludwig Wittgenstein (1889–1951) who famously suggested that the best way to ascertain the meaning of a word is to look at its use, or uses. One should not be searching for an all-embracing definition that covers every way in which the word gets used but should instead recognize that given the dynamic nature of human nature, words end up with multiple meanings (see Byrne and Clarke 1993). The word "theology" is no exception. There are four major meanings in the current literature.

The first meaning was presented at the outset of the chapter: the *attempt to arrive at a systematic account of God and of God's relations with the world*. Most religious traditions have certain beliefs about the nature of ultimate reality and about the way that ultimate reality impinges on our world. These beliefs are the domain of theology. The task of theology is not only to articulate those beliefs but also explain and justify them. Explanation means providing a coherent account of the beliefs. Justification means explaining why a tradition thinks its beliefs true. Given the complexity of the subject matter, it is not surprising that many believers resort to "mystery" and "paradox," but even here one finds that much theology is devoted to showing how certain understandings of the mystery are appropriate or inappropriate.

The second usage of theology is *an attempt to determine the implications of God for a given subject area*. We find Christian theologians referring to a "theology of work" or a "theology of sexuality." In fact, one can have a theology of anything – as long as the purpose is to explicate the implications of belief in God for that topic. For work, for example, we find Christian theologians engaging with the thought of Augustine (354–430), Aquinas (1225–74), Luther (1483–1546), and Calvin (1509–64) and bringing out the differences among them (see Volf 1991; Ledbetter 2001). A theologian might point out that Augustine tended to see work as a consequence of sin, whereas Aquinas had a greater sense of the intrinsic value of work. Luther and Calvin both placed much more emphasis on turning one's secular work into a task intended to serve God. In each case the theologian will examine the link between the overall faith as grounded in Scripture and the application to work. After embarking on this historical study, the theologian might then suggest an alternative account that relates the sources of faith to the issue of work.

A third, pejorative usage of theology is *the introduction of unresolvable issues and needless complexity*. This usage is found primarily among secularists, atheists, and those who dislike elaborate metaphysical speculation. UK Prime Minister Harold Wilson was fond of dismissing certain political debates and questions as "theological," by which he meant that there was no point discussing the issue because it had no practical implications. Exponents of this view of theology will often cite the famous medieval debate about the number of angels who can dance on a head of a pin. Underpinning this view of theology as pointless is a major methodological question: how can human beings have knowledge of the ultimate realm? Immanuel Kant (1724–1804) suggested that it is impossible for us to know about the noumenal world – the world as it is in itself – and that we must resign ourselves to knowing the phenomenal world – the world as it appears to us. According to Kant and to many others, we cannot get outside our heads and find out what the world really is like. The consequence for theology is that we should admit our epistemological limitations and thereby make more room for faith.

The fourth usage of theology is popular among an anti-intellectual strand of evangelical Christianity. Here theology is deemed *the elevation – the unwarranted elevation – of human reason over the simple demands of faith*. Theology is here deemed to be an act of hubris. This view of theology goes back to the growth in European liberal theology of the nineteenth and twentieth centuries. For many Christians, the critical study of the Bible has been destructive to their understanding of the "Word of God." To them, it seems as if mere human beings are presuming to judge the Word of God. Theology that simply explicates the Word of God is for them acceptable. Theology that goes beyond explication to evaluation is suspect.

For the rest of this chapter, I shall use the first definition. As a theologian, I have a positive view of the task of theology. The last two definitions do, however, raise a legitimate question: on what basis do we decide what is true in theology? After all, there are many beliefs about God and God's relations even within each religion, much less among religions. How, then, do we decide which beliefs are true? How do we resolve disagreements in theology? To answer these questions we shall now turn to the different sources in theology. The focus will be the Christian tradition, although links will be made to non-Christian traditions.

Sources for Systematic Theology

All religions concede that humans on their own cannot arrive at a knowledge of God. For most traditions God is an entity who created the world and brought everything into being. But it is difficult to see how humans, who are a small part of the created order, can have knowledge of the creator. Therefore all religious traditions rely on revelation – a text or a person revealing God to us. It is possible to have a partial knowledge of God from other sources – for example, the fact there is a world may enable us to infer that there is a creator of the world – but any certainty on detail about the nature of that God depends on revelation.

Therefore we start with the first and primary form of revelation – Scripture. Each religion has a different book or sets of books. Muslims have the Qur'an; Christians, the Bible; Jews, the Hebrew Bible; Hindus, the Vedas; Buddhists, the Tripitaka. Yet upon closer investigation, the matter proves more complicated.

Muslims believe that the Holy Qur'an is literally the dictated words of God to an illiterate prophet living in the seventh-century Mecca and Medina in present-day Saudi Arabia. The Qur'an is considered infallible.

Much is made of the beauty of the original Arabic text as evidence for its divine origin. Although some conservative evangelical Christians might make a comparable claim for the Bible, there is one major difference. The Qur'an starts each chapter, or *sura*, with the declaration that what follows are the dictated words of God, whereas the Christian's claim to divine authorship is much more opaque. 2 Timothy 3:16 is the most often cited verse: "for all Scripture is given by inspiration of God and is profitable for doctrine, reproof, correction, and instruction in all righteousness." Although the word "inspiration" does mean "God-breathed," it refers to the Hebrew Bible (the Christian Old Testament) and not to the New Testament. In addition, the Hebrew Bible does not read like the "words of God." The phrase "the Lord says" introduces a statement from God in a third-party story about the growth of a nation. Moreover, other works clearly do not purport to relay God's words. For example, the Psalms are words spoken *to* God, not *from* God.

For these reasons most Christian theologians maintain that the Bible *contains* the Word of God rather than *is* the Word of God. For example, Karl Barth (1886–1968), the famous Swiss theologian, insisted that technically the Word of God for Christians is Jesus. Thus in the opening chapter of the Gospel of John, it is Jesus who is described as the *logos* – the word – who in eternity was with God. Barth argued the Bible becomes the Word of God when it witnessed to the Word, which is Jesus. This view of Scripture contrasts sharply to the one found in Islam.

The second source for theology is the believing community, of which the theologian is a part. The term "tradition" describes the way in which the community develops an interpretation of Scripture over time. This community provides the rules for interpreting the text, as the English philosopher Alasdair MacIntyre argues in his *Whose Justice? Which Rationality?* (1988). For MacIntyre, interpretations are grounded in a tradition. There are certain rules surrounding the development of a tradition. The texts are interpreted and then modified as a result of engagement with other traditions.

The third source for theology is "reason." The importance of reason, or rationality, varies from tradition to tradition. In the West two expectations are central to rationality: coherence and justification. A coherent belief is one that is not self-contradictory. Most contradictions in religion are not obvious. They often arise as a result of the implications of two beliefs. For example, a religion might affirm both that "humans have free will" and that "God determines everything that happens." If human free will means that human behavior is not determined, then how can God determine human behavior? It is theology that seeks to reconcile these beliefs, such as by suggesting that God simply has foreknowledge of the decisions that humans will freely make.

The place of reason varies from tradition to tradition. Some strands of most religions insist that human reason is important, but other strands equally insist that the mysteries of religion cannot be fathomed by reason. MacIntyre seems to suggest that "theoretical rationality" is itself tradition-constituted and that the "laws of logic" are not binding on every religion. But, exactly what MacIntyre means is not clear, for he seems to be opposed to the kind of relativism that his stress on the autonomy of traditions suggests.

For example, MacIntyre was the leading opponent of the English philosopher Peter Winch, who wrote:

> criteria of logic are not a direct gift of God, but arise out of, and are only intelligible in the context of, ways of living or modes of social life as such. For instance, science is one such mode and religion is another; and each has criteria of intelligibility peculiar to itself. . . . But we cannot sensibly say that either the practice of science itself or that of religion is either illogical or logical; both are non-logical. (Winch 1958, pp. 100–1)

MacIntyre had two major objections to this position. First, Winch's cultural relativism makes it difficult to explain historical transitions. For example, seventeenth-century Scotland witnessed a transition from a culture that believed in witches to one that did not. Those involved in this transition had "arguments" that made the transition from one culture that believed in witches to a culture that was more scientific intelligible. For those living through the transition, the world view with witches made less sense than the world view without witches. Therefore it is not the case that each world view has its own internal rationality. Winch's analysis cannot, then, be right.

Second, Winch makes "translation" difficult to understand. MacIntyre puts it thus:

> Consider the statement made by some Zande theorist or by King James VI and I, "There are witches," and the statement made by some modern sceptic, "There are no witches." Unless one of these statements denies what the other asserts, the negation of the sentence expressing the former could not be a translation of the sentence expressing the latter. Thus if we could not deny from our own standpoint and in our own language what the Azande or King James asserts in theirs, we should be unable to translate their expression into our language. Cultural idiosyncrasy would have entailed linguistic idiosyncrasy and cross-cultural comparison would have been rendered logically impossible. But of course translation is not impossible. (MacIntyre 1970, p. 129)

The English theologian Keith Ward makes the same point about the necessity of assuming a shared rationality:

> There are some very basic rational criteria which can be brought to bear upon all claims to truth, in religion as elsewhere. Rationality involves

the use of intelligent capacities, including the capacity to register information correctly, to compare similar pieces of information, to deduce and infer in accordance with rules of logic and relate means to ends effectively. A rational person can act on a consciously formulated principle in order to attain an intended goal. . . . Such simple forms of reasoning are necessary to any form of intelligently ordered social life. They are not, and cannot be, culturally relative. (Ward 1994, p. 319)

The last traditional source for systematic theology is "experience," by which is meant the experience of God. For some theologians, experience is the core of religion. The German theologian Friedrich Schleiermacher (1768–1834) insisted that the heart of the Christian religion is the experience of "dependence" on God. This experience drives our subsequent reflection on God. Certain more progressive forms of theology have argued that the experience of the people of God, especially those who are oppressed, is important in making sure that our theological understanding of the world takes the issue of justice seriously. Feminist theology, for example, asserts that the experience of God by women has been overlooked. Black theology makes an equally important point that the dominant white narrative has been oppressive. The experience of God among the slave owners contrasted markedly to the experience of God among the slaves.

We have, then, four primary sources of theology: Scripture, community, reason, and experience. The four are woven together differently from tradition to tradition. Furthermore, most religions have a range of sub-traditions that reflect the diversity of possible options. While it is true that Islam makes the Qur'an central, such forms of Islam as Sufism make the mystical experience central. In Christianity the main divide is over the relationship of Scripture to the Church. For Roman Catholics, the Council of Trent in the sixteenth century insisted that the Christian Scriptures need the Church to interpret the text. By contrast, Martin Luther, one of the founders of Protestantism, argued that it is the "plain sense" of Scripture which should be binding on the Church. Therefore "by Scripture alone" (*sola Scriptura*) is the authority for the Church in Protestantism.

Another illustration of the different ways in which the sources work together is found around the question of the status of reason. Anglicans, influenced by Richard Hooker (1554–1600), talk of religion as a three-legged stool, with Reason as the third leg alongside Scripture and Tradition. Since the Enlightenment, progressive Christians have given special weight to "reason." Arguments that are simply grounded in "authority" were challenged by the discoveries of science. Critics of this way of thinking insist that "reason" has thereby been set up as a judge of Christian doctrine. Defenders of reason respond by pointing out that Galileo was proved right and the Bible wrong.

Another important debate is over the place of history. There is a difference between the treatment of the past by, for example, the author of

Chronicles or even the authors of the Gospels and our modern-day expectations. For Chronicles, the task of history is to explain the significance of
the past for the present. The author is interested in the status of the
Temple. The four kings who are given the most sustained treatment in the
book are David (for bringing the Ark of the Covenant to Jerusalem),
Solomon (for building the temple), and two reformers of the Temple (Josiah
and Joash). Many other kings who ruled for a much longer period of time
and, judged by modern criteria, were more significant are given much less
attention. For the Chronicler, however, the task of describing the past is
to inform and shape debates in the present.

By contrast, our modern historical sensitivity has made us especially
attuned to the question of what exactly happened. For us the past must
be understood on its own terms. A legacy of the Enlightenment has been
the "objective" study of history. Instead of using the past to inform debates
about the present, we seek to "work out" what happened in the past and
"why" those involved acted as they did. In short, the modern historical
task is to give an account of the past that the figures and groups involved
would recognize.

The discussion of the sources and the ways in which they combine
has introduced us to the topic of the next section: namely, the impact
of modernity of the study of theology. It is to this theme that I turn
next.

Modernity and Theology

For those theologians who consider that the Enlightenment has significantly transformed our understanding of ourselves and our place in the
universe, this historical sensitivity is key. The English New Testament
scholar Leslie Houlden famously remarked that "we must accept our lot,
bequeathed to us by the Enlightenment, and make the most of it" (Houlden
1977, p. 125). Denis Nineham (1976) has expounded the implications for
Christian theology at some length. He argues that our historical sensitivity
has made us aware of the vast differences between all previous ages and
ours. There is a real sense in which we cannot believe a doctrine in the
same way our forbears did. To take an obvious example, the doctrine of
the Ascension in a three-tier universe involves Jesus' "ascending" into a
heaven above the clouds. In a post-Copernican universe this notion of
heaven is not an option. As the American astronomer Carl Sagan apparently informed Bishop John Shelby Spong, had Jesus launched off from
earth at the speed of light, then even two thousand years later he would
still not have left our solar system (see Spong 1998, pp. 40–1). For conservative Christians, one modifies the doctrine to involve an elevation up
several miles (to explain the biblical text) followed by a departure into a

parallel universe (to use the language of the New Physics). The point is that this modified belief in the ascension is not the same as the one held by those who included the phrase "he ascended into heaven" to the creeds.

The debate over the significance of history is a key one in modern theology. Our postmodern sensitivities have complicated the picture. Where the practice of modernism involved seeking "what precisely happened," postmodern sensitivities have challenged the legitimacy of the question itself. The capacity to stand outside time and to interrogate the past as a detached observer has increasingly come to be viewed as impossible. Instead, a different picture has evolved. The past comes to us, primarily, in the form of texts. All texts require interpretation. Precisely what a text meant to those who first heard it not only is difficult to determine but also assumes a capacity on our part to transcend our own cultural location. We cannot bridge the centuries in between the text and us. Modernity assumed that Truth – an accurate description of the way things are – was possible. However, for theologians shaped by postmodernism, there is no such thing as "uninterpreted data." To take an illustration used by Nineham, in a thirteenth-century European culture the likely interpretation of a person's suffering from a fit would have been demon possession. In the twenty-first century the likely interpretation would be epilepsy. The sense data – the image hitting the eyes – has not changed. The interpretation of the data has.

This heightened sense to interpretation has given birth to certain distinctive insights. Liberation and feminist theologians make much of the fact that the "economic" and "gender" vantage point is an important key in making sense of the text. Liberation theology emerged in Latin America within the Roman Catholic Church and observed that when one "reads" the story of the Exodus in Exodus 3 or the parables of Jesus in Luke, one does not conclude that all that matters is individual salvation, sexual propriety, and "caring for your soul." On the contrary, the poor in the slums in Brazil identify themselves with the drama of Exodus and with the promise of a God who will liberate his people from slavery. Similarly, Jesus' declaration that "rich people find it difficult to enter the Kingdom of God" is linked to real "rich people" who use their power to keep all the resources for themselves.

Feminist theologians examine Scripture from the standpoint of power. Like liberation theologians, they are disturbed with the ease with which Christianity has supported wealth and patriarchy. Historically, rich males have had all the options, with women often finding themselves exploited, abused, raped, and even killed. Feminist theology has set itself the hard task of understanding how Christianity has permitted, even sanctioned, this treatment.

Sometimes a passage in a religious text serves to espouse patriarchy explicitly. 1 Timothy argues that because Adam was first created and because Eve was the first to sin, the authority of the male over the female is justified. Women are even forbidden to teach men. At other times the service to patriarchy is more indirect. Referring to God as "father" may seem benign, but when there are only men – for example, in a celibate world of monks – the masculine nature of God can become an unthinking assumption.

One widespread narrative that underpins much feminist theology is the conviction that the Christian commitment to two significant dualisms stemming from the Greco-Roman period is responsible for much implicit patriarchy. The first is the dualism between God and matter. The second is the dualism between spirit and body. The argument goes thus: the dualism between God and the world, in which God is totally distinct from the world, is responsible for the denigration of matter, of which the world is made, over spirit, of which God is composed. God antedates the world and will survive the end of the world. The world is a passing entity. Therefore the physical world has limited value. It is thus not surprising that the Christian West is indifferent to the environmental crisis facing our planet.

Add to this dualism the doctrine that the body will pass away and that only the "spirit" or "soul" of a person will survive, and we have a deeply anti-body religion. The consequences for patriarchy are significant. One almost unconscious cultural assumption is that men, by virtue of their rationality and power, are closer to God and that women are closer to nature. Men resemble God because of the dominance of masculine images for God and because gender stereotypes of the male stress "rationality" and "power," which are traditional divine attributes. Meanwhile women are linked with Mother nature partly because both are agents of reproduction. Hence the taboo against menstruation in the Hebrew Bible (Leviticus 15:19–23). Men fear the reproductive capacity of women. In addition, the female form generates sexual desire in men, thereby exacerbating uncontrollable passion. With these almost unconscious cultural assumptions, the argument goes, we have an implicit justification for the rule of men. The institution of marriage is deemed the social institution in which men are the "head of the house." Consequently, opportunities for women to become leaders in the Church or the world are limited.

The feminist critique of religion provides what I have called a "suggestive narrative" (see Markham 2004, p. 95) – one that makes sense of certain puzzling preoccupations of, in this case, the Christian community and, more broadly, Western culture. For example, given that Jesus hardly mentions the topic of sex, why is sex a major preoccupation of the churches? Why are people so attached to masculine descriptions of God, especially given that all theologians concede that God in "Godself" is beyond gender? The feminist suggestive narrative offers answers to these questions.

But seen from the vantage point of, say, India, the narrative is less persuasive. For the corollary of the feminist narrative is that if Christianity rethinks its account of God, perhaps along the lines suggested by the American theologian Sallie McFague (1993), then our culture will be less patriarchal and less environmentally unfriendly. Yet while India has a monistic account of God with many female deities, it too, has both a patriarchal society and a poor environmental record. Kwok Pui-lan, in her *Introducing Asian Feminist Theology* (2000), argues that Western feminists must be careful not to universalize their criticism of Christianity: "While Western feminists must either challenge the uneasy connections between women and nature, or reclaim positive dimensions of women's embodiment and their closeness to nature, Asian feminist theologians are faced with the glorification of nature in their cultures, while their own bodies are denigrated" (Pui-lan 2000, p. 115).

Thus far, our engagement with modernity has concentrated on the historical sensitivity generated by the Enlightenment, a sensitivity that in turn created sensitivity to "interpretation," which further created the "hermeneutics of suspicion," or the focus on whose interests an interpretation of religion serves. Liberation and feminist theology are two illustrations of this process, which are very much shaped by the Enlightenment sensitivity to history.

Running parallel with this historical sensitivity has been the emergence of modern science. In the popular mind science has been the major challenge to religion. Both the persecution of Galileo (1564–1642), who dared to challenge the cosmology accepted by the Roman Catholic Church, and the fierce antagonism to Darwin's (1809–82) theory of natural selection typify the conflict between religion and science. Modern opponents of religion attribute this conflict to the displacement of religious explanations of the world by scientific ones. Planets once believed to be sustained in their orbit by the hand of God are now known to be sustained by gravity. Natural disasters, once considered the judgment of God, are now explained by science. The English biologist Richard Dawkins puts the point bluntly:

> We know approximately when the universe began and why it is largely hydrogen. We know why stars form, and what happens in their interiors to convert hydrogen to the other elements and hence give birth to chemistry in a world of physics. We know the fundamental principles of how a world of chemistry can become biology through the arising of self-replicating molecules. We know how the principle of self-replication gives rise, through Darwinian selection to all life including humans.

> It is science, and science alone, that has given us this knowledge and given it, moreover, in fascinating, overwhelming, mutually confirming detail. On every one of these questions theology has held a view that has been conclusively proved wrong. Science has eradicated smallpox, can immunise against most previously deadly viruses, can kill most previously deadly bacteria.

Theology has done nothing but talk of pestilence as the wages of sin. Science can predict when a particular comet will reappear and, to the second, when the next eclipse will occur. Science has put men on the moon and hurtled reconnaissance rockets around Saturn and Jupiter. Science can tell you the age of a particular fossil and that the Turin Shroud is a medieval fake. Science knows the precise DNA instructions of several viruses and will, in the lifetime of many present readers of the Independent, do the same for the human genome.

What has "theology" ever said that is of the smallest use to anybody? When has "theology" ever said anything that is demonstrably true and is not obvious? I have listened to theologians, read them, debated against them. I have never heard any of them ever say anything of the smallest use, anything that was not either platitudinously obvious or downright false. (Dawkins in Markham 2000 pp. 22–3)

Although in the popular mind this picture of science standing in opposition to religion has been influential, in the academy the polarity has been more nuanced. Many physicists in the twentieth century argued that some of the insights emerging, in particular from the New Physics, are compatible with a theological description of the world. Two physicists have been especially significant. Paul Davies (1983) has argued for a form of deism or belief in a nonpersonal creator God, and John Polkinghorne (1991) has defended all the key doctrines of orthodox Christianity. According to both Davies and Polkinghorne, the New Physics of Einstein and Heisenberg has opened up a universe that is fundamentally open and unpredictable and that is therefore one in which purpose and free will make more sense.

Ultimately, science needs theology. The underlying assumptions of science require a universe that is intelligible and orderly. Given that science seeks explanations for the world, it is an obviously legitimate question to seek an explanation for the assumptions that science as a discipline is forced to make. According to the philosopher Richard Swinburne, any adequate explanation of the world has to be theistic, so that science needs religion (see Swinburne 1979, pp. 139–41). In the meantime our historical sensitivity has created a new way of looking at the world – one that focuses on the cultural context of any beliefs. "Why is something believed at a particular time?" is now an inescapable question.

Future Directions in Theology

Theology operates in two domains: in the academy and in faith communities. In this concluding section I shall look first at the trends within the academy – mainly, the Anglo-American academy – and then at trends in faith communities.

In the academy there are four key trends. The first is the continuing growth of postliberal theologies. The term "postliberal" was used by the American theologian George Lindbeck in his *The Nature of Doctrine: Religion and Theology in a Postliberal Age* (1984). There he argues for a cultural-linguistic approach to religion: instead of seeing theology either as a set of propositions that are straightforward assertions about a timeless reality (the traditional conservative view) or as an articulation of one's feelings about life (the nonrealist, liberal view), one should see theology as part of the life of a believing community that expresses itself through rituals, prayers, worship, and a "form of life." Doctrines express rather than depict the life of a community.

One significant development of Lindbeck's work has been the movement known as "Radical Orthodoxy," of which the English theologian John Milbank is the chief figure. In *Theology and Social Theory* (1990) he sets out to "deconstruct" modernity by exposing its hidden assumptions. His dense and difficult argument is ably summarized by Fergus Kerr:

> Historically, according to Milbank, in seventeenth-century thinkers such as Grotius and Hobbes, the concepts of sovereignty, autonomy, property, power, and so on, which were to generate the new "secular" disciplines of political theory, economics and sociology, emerged from the late-medieval theological matrix of an effectively non-Trinitarian theism which celebrated a notion of the absolute will of the divine monarch. The "anthropology" which celebrates human beings as atomistic individuals, with their individuality defined essentially as will, would thus be the spin-off of a (distinctly non-Thomist!) voluntarist monotheism. The modern liberal-individualist conception of the human person would thus be a product of a heretical (because barely if at all Trinitarian) conception of God. (Kerr in Gill 1996, p. 432)

According to Milbank, seemingly secular categories like "individual" and "social" in fact derive from theology. The secular, on which the social sciences are parasitic, "had to be invented as the space of 'pure power'" (Milbank 1990, p. 12). Therefore disciplines such as the "sociology of religion" ought to disappear because "secular reason claims that there is a 'social' vantage point from which it can locate and survey various 'religious' phenomena. But it has turned out that the assumptions about the nature of religion help to define the perspective of this social vantage" (Milbank 1990, p. 139). Sociology has no privilege over theology. Insofar as sociology can continue, "it must redefine itself as a 'faith'" (Milbank 1990, p. 139).

Having deconstructed secularism, Milbank then constructs an account of Christianity as "a true Christian metanarrative realism" (Milbank 1990, p. 389). For him, Christianity is the only possible response to Nietzsche's nihilism. Following Augustine's two cities, we now have a cosmic contrast. Where the secular world is built on an ontology of violence, Christianity is committed to an ontology of peace. Milbank concludes the book: "[T]he absolute Christian vision of ontological peace now provides the only alternative to a nihilistic outlook" (Milbank 1990, p. 434).

The theological task for those sympathetic to Radical Orthodoxy is to explain the nature of God and of God's relations with the world using a form of reasoning that has shaped by the community of the Church. With sympathizers such as the American Stanley Hauerwas and Gregory Jones, the movement will clearly continue to attract attention.

The second trend in contemporary theology is the growth of "identity theologies." We have already seen how liberation theology was an inspiration to feminist theologies. Over the past thirty years other identity theologies have emerged. With Malcolm X and Martin Luther King the United States has sought to come to terms with the racism in its past. Given the deeply religious nature of the American people, it is not surprising that this effort has provoked an important theological conversation. Probably the best-known advocates of "black theology" are James Cone and Cornel West.

In recent years we have seen the emergence of a "womanist" theology, led by the American womanist theologian Kelly Delaine Brown Douglas, who writes:

> Black women in the United States have given voice to a new theological perspective: womanist. Although the meaning of the term "womanist" originated with Alice Walker's interpretation of the Black cultural expression, "You acting womanish," it goes beyond her words. It points to the richness and complexity of being Black and female in a society that tends to devalue both Blackness and womanhood. (Douglas 1993, p. 290)

The theological challenge is to make sense of this double oppression in order to spur liberation.

Along with black theology, there have emerged other liberationist theologies, such as Hispanic/Latino theology. Here the task is to make sense of a particular narrative of a people within the American context. While the dominant "civil religion" of the United States, to use the term of sociologist Robert Bellah (1967), employs Puritan images and languages to stress the sense of America as a promised land and a chosen people, the particular Hispanic American account challenges that sense. As Fernando Segovia explains:

> It is clear to me that, while we may not have called upon such [biblical] terminology and symbolism, our image of our neighbor to the north, *al norte*, was not that far removed from such lofty heights of biblical rhetoric. . . . Most people felt great admiration for the United States as a nation and world power, even when they deplored, as many did, the way in which it threw its weight around in the rest of the Americas and

above all in the Caribbean. . . . In sum, the United States was in a very real sense "the promised land," not so much perhaps in religious terms but certainly in terms of progress and modernity. . . . It was with such visions of peace and serenity and such expectations of justice and opportunity that many U.S. Hispanic Americans have, in the long course of the century, left their respective homelands and arrived on these shores – whether by plane, barge, raft, train, car, tunnel, or some other means; whether by walking, climbing, riding, wading, swimming. . . . What many of us ultimately found upon arrival, however, was not quite what we had envisioned, but then utopian expectations are in the end impossible to satisfy and ultimately lead to practices of demythologizing and deconstruction, from the most minor to the most radical. The "promised land" did have its blemishes and imperfections, and some of those concerned us directly. (Segovia 1996, pp. 23–5)

The image of America has clashed with the experience of America, thereby creating the problem that becomes the material for this identity theology.

One last example of the identity theologies that continue to garner attention is the "gay and lesbian" identity theology. The role that abortion played in the culture wars of the 1980s and 1990s has now been succeeded by the debate over gay marriage. The campaign to make homosexuality legal was largely framed in terms of privacy. So, the argument went, the law should not extend to the privacy of the bedroom between consenting adults. But at the start of the twenty-first century the issue has become one of "public recognition." Given that so many of the objections to same-sex relations are theological, it is not surprising that there is a lively theological debate about the issue. In *Just Good Friends* (1995) Elizabeth Stuart argues that the category of friendship is not only the key one for understanding gay and lesbian relationships but also a central theological category that heterosexuals need to appreciate. Sexuality should be shared and celebrated among friends, not confined to an exclusive, patriarchal institution of monogamous marriage.

The third trend in contemporary theology is the "liberal" trend. The term "liberal" is difficult to define. It seems to involve a certain set of commitments that include "reshaping" the faith in the light of a changing culture. The Americans David Tracy and Gordon Kaufman remain the pre-eminent liberal theologians. Various theologians in the United Kingdom have again started to use the word "liberal." For twenty years or so it had been out of fashion. There was widespread feeling that the non-realism of Don Cupitt was the logical outcome of the liberal tradition, so that the term "liberal" become associated with "increasing disbelief." Insofar as religion is in the business of believing things, this association did not bode well for liberalism.

The late 1990s saw a resurgence of liberalism. The form of liberalism varied considerably. For some, "liberal" meant a *critical engagement with the Enlightenment.* The English New Testament scholar Leslie Houlden was part of that 1970s brand of liberalism expressed in the collection of essays called *The Myth of God Incarnate* (see Hick 1977). The English ethicist John Elford's two most recent books, *the Pastoral Nature of Theology* (1999) and *The Ethics of Uncertainty* (2000), are in this tradition. For others, "liberal" has meant recognition *of the epistemological limitations of the theological discourse.* Gareth Jones has provided an eloquent description of this understanding of the liberal theological task in his *Critical Theology* (1995). For yet others, "liberal" represents the *need for engagement* – with science, with other religious traditions, or more broadly with culture. Here lie the English Clive Marsh's delightful *Christianity in a Post-Atheist Age* (2002) and Martyn Percy's *The Salt of the Earth: Religious Resilience in a Secular Age* (2002). The strongest representative of this form of liberalism is the English theologian Keith Ward (1994, 1996). His four-part series setting out an approach to systematic theology that takes into account the insights of other faith traditions stands as a model for this approach to theology. Finally, there are those who want to link liberal theology with *postmodernism* and *liberation theologies.* A good example is J'annine Jobling's *Restless Readings* (2002), in which she starts with the problem of hermeneutics from a feminist perspective and ends up with a strong commitment to the need for a community in which the text is understood.

The last trend in academic theology is the one that most fully overlaps with theology in particular faith traditions. These are the many traditional theologians variously labeled "Barthians," "Evangelicals," or "Catholics." Representative are Colin Gunton and David Ford (both Barthians) in the United Kingdom and Robert Jenson (Lutheran) and Richard John Neuhaus (Roman Catholic) in the United States. Although the precise form or theological inspiration varies considerably, the theological task is much the same: to explicate the various sources of knowledge of God to present a consistent witness to the nature of God and of God's relation with the world.

This last group of academic theologians is significant because it is the one closest to the actual belief systems of people in congregations. The elevated insights of Jacques Derrida do not quite connect with the challenge of preaching to a congregation. And along with Derrida, almost all major progressive theologians disappear as influences on everyday Christians. From this perspective the great theologians of the twentieth century are the Englishmen C. S. Lewis, John Packer, and perhaps John Stott. As Mark Noll puts it:

> In the second half of the twentieth century, a good case could be made that the German Roman Catholic Hans Küng and the Anglican evangelical John R. W. Stott have been among America's most influential popular religious authors. The pattern of significant modern influence from overseas was well established by England's G. K. Chesterton earlier in the century. That pattern has certainly continued, as the tremendous

American fascination with the religious writings of Oxford don C. S. Lewis testifies so powerfully. (Noll 2002, pp. 190–1)

From Stott (a priest) to Lewis (the professor of English) – these are the persons who have made a difference to the religious life of Christians. For it is their books that are read and that shape religious life in ways that the holders of teaching posts in theology in universities will never manage to do.

One startling illustration of this gulf between trends in the academy and trends in the Church is the phenomenal success of the *Left Behind* series. As of 2005, the series had sold more than sixty million copies. *Publishers Weekly* announced that *Desecration* was the best-selling hardcover fiction title in 2001, displacing John Grisham, who had held that slot for the previous seven years. These books are not simply read but shared. They are studied. They are extensively discussed on the Internet. It is these books which preoccupy many Christians around the world.

The books provide a fictional portrayal of the "end times." Grounded in a premillennial dispensationalist theology, they envision a rapture, during which millions of Christians mysteriously disappear, followed by a seven-year tribulation that culminates in the Battle of Armageddon. Starting in the present, the first book begins with the night flight from Chicago to London, midway across the Atlantic, on a Boeing 747 jetliner. Stillness descends upon the cabin, which is then disturbed by an elderly woman discovering that her husband is missing, to be followed by many other passengers complaining that family members have disappeared. The clothes are all that remain of the disappeared. The mysterious disappearance of people on the aircraft is part of a worldwide spontaneous disappearance of millions of people. This event is the "rapture" – the call of the Church out of the world to be saved from the judgment of God that will follow in the tribulation. The first book in the series was called *Left Behind*, followed by *Tribulation Force, Nicolae, Soul Harvest, Apollyon, Assassins, The Indwelling, The Mark, Desecration, The Remnant,* and *Armageddon.* The last one was *Glorious Appearing.*

As one witnesses the extraordinary impact of this fictional series, one realizes that probably the most significant theologian of the nineteenth century was the Irishman John Nelson Darby, the inventor of dispensationalism. It is dispensationalism that provided the framework for the complex web of beliefs surrounding the rapture, the tribulation, and the Last Judgment. While even today Darby continues to have a dramatic impact on the Church, most modern theologians have barely heard of him, let alone read him – a conspicuous example of the divide between academics and ordinary believers.

This gap between theology in the academy and theology in congregations is likely to get wider. The American religious historian Philip Jenkins documents that of which many are already aware: that the Church is going south. He sets out the statistics in his introduction to *The Next Christendom* (Jenkins 2002). While at the beginning of the century, Europe constituted the largest bloc of Christians, the figures in 2025 will have a total of:

> 2.6 billion Christians, of whom 633 million would live in Africa, 640 million in Latin America, and 460 million in Asia. Europe, with 555 million, would have slipped to third place. Africa and Latin America would be in competition for the title of most Christian continent. About this date too, another significant milestone should occur, namely that these two continents will together account for half the Christians on the planet. By 2050, only about one-fifth of the world's 3 billion Christians will be non-Hispanic Whites. Soon, the phrase "a White Christian" may sound like a curious oxymoron, as mildly surprising as "a Swedish Buddhist." Such people exist, but a slight eccentricity is implied. (Jenkins 2002, p. 3)

The precise implications of this trend for the shape of the theological task are difficult to identify. But we can say now with some confidence that the effect is likely to be dramatic and that the *Left Behind* series may find even more readers, leaving the progressive academy increasingly on the periphery.

Bibliography

Bellah, Robert. "Civil Religion in America," *Daedalus* 96 (1967): 1–21.

Byrne, Peter, and Peter Clarke. *Definition and Explanation in Religion.* Basingstoke: Macmillan, 1993.

Davies, Paul. *God and the New Physics.* London: Penguin Books, 1983.

Dawkins, Richard. Letter to *The Independent*, March 20, 1993, reprinted in *A World Religions Reader*, ed. Ian Markham. Oxford: Blackwell, 2000. pp. 22–3.

Douglas, Kelly Delaine Brown. "Womanist Theology: What Is its Relationship to Black Theology?" in *Black Theology*, eds. James H. Cone and Gayraund S. Wilmore. Maryknoll, NY: Orbis, 1993, pp. 290–9.

Elford, R. John. *The Pastoral Nature of Theology.* London: Cassell, 1999.

Elford, R. John. *The Ethics of Uncertainty: A New Christian Approach to Moral Decision-Making.* Oxford: Oneworld, 2000.

Hick, John, ed. *The Myth of God Incarnate.* London: SCM Press, 1977.

Houlden, Leslie. "The Creed of Experience," in *The Myth of God Incarnate*, ed. John Hick. London: SCM Press, 1977, pp. 125–32.

Jenkins, Philip. *The Next Christendom: The Coming of Global Christianity.* Oxford: Oxford University Press, 2002.

Jobling, J'annine. *Restless Readings.* Aldershot: Ashgate, 2002.

Jones, Gareth. *Critical Theology.* Cambridge: Polity Press, 1995.

Kerr, Fergus. "Simplicity Itself: Milbank's Thesis [1992]," reprinted in *Theology and Sociology*, ed. Robin Gill, new edn. London: Cassells, 1996, pp. 429–34.

Ledbetter, Shannon. "Vocation and Our Understanding of God," *Modern Believing* 4 (2001): 38–49.

Lindbeck, George. *The Nature of Doctrine: Religion and Theology in a Postliberal Age*. Philadelphia: Westminister Press, 1984.

MacIntyre, Alasdair. "The Idea of a Social Science," in *Rationality*, ed. Bryan R. Wilson. Oxford: Blackwell, 1970, pp. 112–30.

MacIntyre, Alasdair. *Whose Justice? Which Rationality?* Notre Dame, IN: University of Notre Dame Press, 1988.

Markham, Ian. *A Theology of Engagement*. Oxford: Blackwell, 2004.

Marsh, Clive. *Christianity in a Post-Atheist Age*. London: SCM Press, 2002.

McFague, Sallie. *Models of God*. Minneapolis, MN: Augsburg Fortress Press, 1993.

Milbank, John. *Theology and Social Theory*. Oxford: Blackwell, 1990.

Nineham, Dennis. *The Use and the Abuse of the Bible*. London: Macmillan, 1976.

Noll, Mark A. *The Old Religion in a New World*. Grand Rapids, MI: Eerdmans, 2002.

Percy, Martyn. *The Salt of the Earth: Religious Resilience in a Secular Age*. Sheffield: Sheffield Academic Press, 2001.

Polkinghorne, John. *Reason and Reality*. London: SPCK, 1991.

Pui-lan, Kwok. *Introducing Asian Feminist Theology*. Sheffield: Sheffield Academic Press, 2000.

Segovia, Fernando F. "Aliens in the Promised Land: The Manifest Destiny of U. S. Hispanic American Theology," in *Hispanic/Latino Theology: Challenge and Promise*, eds. Ada María Isasi-Díaz and Fernando F. Segovia. Minneapolis, MN: Fortress Press, 1996, pp. 15–44.

Spong, John Shelby. *Why Christianity Must Change or Die*. San Francisco: HarperSanFrancisco, 1998.

Stuart, Elizabeth. *Just Good Friends: Towards a Lesbian and Gay Theology of Relationships*. London: Mowbray, 1995.

Swinburne, Richard. *The Existence of God*. Oxford: Clarendon Press, 1979.

Volf, Miroslav. *Work in the Spirit: Toward a Theology of Work*. New York: Oxford University Press, 1991.

Ward, Keith. *Reason and Revelation*. Oxford: Oxford University Press, 1994.

Ward, Keith. *Religion and Revelation*. Oxford: Oxford University Press, 1996.

Winch, Peter. *The Idea of a Social Science*. London: Routledge and Kegan Paul, 1958.

Part II

Topics

Chapter 10

Body

Richard H. Roberts

The body is a central theme in recent cultural theory. The body is also a core concern in world religious traditions, and the body as locus of experience, object of desire, source of metaphor, and icon of self-representation is a pervasive preoccupation of Western, especially post-modern, culture. These factors, taken together, make for a high degree of complexity when the "body" is addressed in the study of religion. A review of the literature exposes an unresolved matrix of difficult issues that run like fault lines across the landscape of this endeavor. The key questions that inform this complexity are how and why religion paradoxically reinforces, diminishes, and transmutes the relationship of humankind to its identity as embodied consciousness.

The chapter proceeds as follows. First, the crisis of representation of the body within the social sciences as it touches upon the study of religion is addressed. Second, key features of the depiction of the body in the West are sketched out from their origins in the ancient Near East. Third, a brief exploration of the somatic aspects of non-Western traditions is presented. Fourth, these three perspectives are drawn together as prerequisites for understanding the place of the body in advanced modernity or "postmodernity." Fifth and last, some of the ways in which the contemporary problematics of the body appear in the study of religion are tied back to major concerns in social and cultural theory. It will be argued that religion is an increasingly salient rather than marginal feature of post-modernized societal conditions in advanced modernity that are undergoing progressive, if ambiguous and contradictory, re-enchantment (see Roberts 2001, pp. 269–91; Ward 2003).

Social Scientific Approaches to the Body: A Crisis of Representation

The social scientific study of the body was not, generally speaking, a central concern in the work of the so-called founding fathers of sociology (see Featherstone and Turner 1995). Nevertheless, some important judgments were made about the body and sexuality. For example, Max Weber asserted that "Despite the belief that hostility towards sexuality is an idiosyncrasy of Christianity, it must be emphasised that no authentic religion of salvation had in principle any other view" (Weber 1978, vol. I, p. 606). There has always been a deep-rooted ambivalence about the status of the body.

The situation is complicated by the variety of "bodies" to be found in an era of historical and cultural diversity. As the British sociologist Anthony Synnott has argued:

> At present, there is no consensus on the meaning of the body; in a pluralistic society, no consensus can be expected. Constructions reflect the values not only of the culture, but also of the sub-culture, and of the specific individuals, and they are ever changing. Thus the discourse continues, debating whether and to what degree, and in what ways the body is tomb or temple, loved or hated personal or state property, machine or self. (Synnott 1993, p. 37)

In a revised introduction to his sociology of the body, the English sociologist Bryan Turner juxtaposes a certain nostalgia for the time before the impact of technology:

> The Church is the Body of Christ, the Good Shepherd of wayward sheep. The sharing of bread (*pan*) provided a discourse for all forms of companionship and community. The process of eating is thus transcribed into a discourse of social relationships and exchanges. In contemporary society, with rationalization, secularization and McDonaldization, these

robust metaphors of body as centrepiece of human thinking are now disguised, submerged, or displaced by technology. (Turner. 1996, p. xiv)

Yet recently, an inversion of the historic Western priority of rational soul over sensual body has begun to take place. Michel Foucault has influenced writers in many settings with his analyses of the punishment and disciplining of the body as the central feature of the control of the production of social identities. In his consideration of religion and the body, Turner places selfhood and body in the closest proximity and highlights the difficulties in conceptualizing the religious body. The "body is a project in high modernity" which can be "made, constructed, and endlessly refashioned through the life-cycle." Indeed, "for some writers on the sociology of the body, in modern society the self *is* the body," with the consequence that "these developments represent a definite reversal of the traditional pattern in which the flesh was subordinated to the interests of the soul" (Turner, "The Body in Western Society: Social Theory and Its Perspectives," in Coakley 1997, p. 33). Turner concludes on sociological grounds that "the body, rather than being a naturally given datum, is a socially constructed artefact like other cultural products" (Turner, in Coakley 1997, p. 19).

The difficulties of mainstream sociology with the body were noted early in the twentieth century by Durkheim's associate and nephew, Marcel Mauss, who argued presciently for the importance of somatic analysis (see Mauss 1979). The anthropology of the body as developed from Mauss by such figures as Gregory Bateson (1977), Geoffrey Samuel (1990), and Thomas Csordas (1993, 1997) has begun to offer an alternative interdisciplinary paradigm for the representation of the body and the "sacred" (see Samuel 1990, pp. 1ff.). Furthermore, the "homecoming" of anthropology from its historic pursuit of the distant primitive and the now alien premodern to the study of modernized cultures in the West coincides with the impact of globalization on the body, the "Easternization" of the body and of spirituality in the West, and the hybridization of identities explored in postcolonial theory. Yet even within mainstream anthropology explicit concerns with the body have nonetheless remained for the most part relatively marginal (see Ingold 2002 *ad loc.*).

The general "re-somatization" of contemporary social change is reported in cultural studies through the investigation of, for example, sex therapy, power, body building, childcare, dance, celebrity, food consumption, body image, gender, sexual orientation, and body movement (as in kinesics). Only belatedly have practitioners of sociology and anthropology begun to revise their disciplines in the light of this increased salience of the body. The process has been accelerated by feminist theorists who have, for example, promoted equivalences between women:body and men:mind and have thus articulated a problematic polarization between women and men (see Holdrege 1998, pp. 344–6; Haraway 1997).

The subdiscipline of the sociology of religion has respected the limitations of mainstream sociological theory. For a thirty-year period following the Second World War, the sociology of religion took its main inspiration from theories of secularization. These theories explained the marginalization and decline of religion in the West primarily along functionalist lines and were largely blind to the contingency of the body beyond its role as the object for the numerical quantification of participation in organized religion. The most obvious source of innovation in the study of religion and the body has come from an enhanced body awareness in feminist theory, which has also had a significant impact upon male writers (see Brown 1988; Mellor and Shilling 1997).

The Body in Western Religious Traditions

In their accounts of the early Christian period both Peter Brown and Robin Lane Fox give significance to the body and sexuality and make the early Christian somatic attitudes a defining feature of their accounts (see Brown 1988; Lane Fox 1986). The "angelic way" of early Christians paradoxically at once devalued and reified the body. The Christian life was an eschatological mode of existence rooted beyond the torments of sexuality. Similarly, Brown notes the "disturbing strangeness" of some of the central preoccupations of the Christian men and women of the first five centuries. St. Paul had an unparalleled influence upon Western Latin Christianity. In his Letter to the Romans Paul writes: "For I know that nothing good dwells in me, that is my flesh (*sarx*). . . . I see in my members another Law at war with the Law on my mind. . . . Wretched man that I am! Who will deliver me from this body (*soma*) of death?" (Romans 7:18, 23–4). Brown concludes that Paul

> crammed into the notion of the flesh a superabundance of overlapping notions. The charged opacity of his language faced all later ages like a Rohrsach test: it is possible to measure, in the repeated exegesis of a mere hundred words of Paul's letters, the future course of Christian thought on the human person. . . . A weak thing in itself, the body was presented as lying in the shadow of a mighty force, the power of the *flesh*: the body's physical frailty, its liability to death and the undeniable penchant of its instincts towards sin served Paul as a synecdoche for the state of mankind pitted against the Spirit of God. (Brown 1988, p. 48)

Brown argues that Paul left a "fatal legacy to future ages" in losing touch with the "warm faith shown by contemporary pagans and Jews that the sexual urge, although disorderly, was capable of socialisation and of ordered, even warm, expression in marriage" (Brown 1988, p. 55).

The problematization of the body in the Christian and Western trad- ition heightens the contemporary crisis, in which the body is at once increasingly central in so-called "postmodern" terms to the experience of selfhood and subject to a "modern" commodification of inwardness of identity unparalleled since the days of slavery and the early Industrial Revolution (see Roberts 2001, pp. 36–61). As early as the late first century, the Christian ideal of complete sexual abstinence makes its appearance: "Blessed are they who have kept the flesh pure, for they shall become a temple of God. . . . Blessed are the continent, for to them God will speak" (Acts of Paul and Thecla 4, *New Testament Apocrypha*, vol. II, p. 354). In the second century, extreme followers of the Latin theologian Tatian argued that the sexual joining of Adam with Eve had been instrumental in creating a "false society." Brown concludes that this view broke the "ancient continuity of man and the natural world" and abrogated the "assumption that human society grew organically from natural urges" (Brown 1988, p. 94).

Each generation of (male) Christian theologians struggled with the tradition of continence. Clement of Alexandria, writing at the end of the second century, could build upon pre-established tradition when he pre- sented an austere vision of the "human ideal of continence, . . . that which is set forth by the Greek philosophers, [that] teaches one to resist passion, so as not to be made subservient to it, and to train the instincts to pursue rational goals." Indeed, Christians should a step further: "Our ideal is not to experience desire at all" (Clement, *Stromateis* 3.7.57). The ideal of sexual continence also supported empowerment by the Holy Spirit, as when Tertullian connected suspension of all future sexual activity with the giving of the Spirit: "By continence you will buy up a great stock of sanctity, by making savings on the flesh, you will be able to invest in the Spirit" (Tertullian, *de ieiunio* 1.1, *Corpus Christianorum* 2: 1262, cited in Brown 1988, p. 78). This spiritualized intensity implied no mere division of human being into spirit and body but the need to prepare the body for the Spirit through control and submission, a restraint often associated with the decline in sexual drive that comes with aging. Hence Tertullian depicted Church leaders as a "Spirit-filled gerontocracy" (Brown 1988, p. 79). Only through denial could the body become the instrument upon which the adept learned to play the interior music of the sacred.

In third-century Roman society the continent virgin body came to con- stitute a core value of the community. The "angelic way" of living beyond the body and sexuality had implications for those, who like Origen, took the extreme practical step of self-castration, a practice valued in some Encratite third- and fourth-century Christian circles (see Ranke- Heinemann 1990). As a eunuch, Origen became a "walking lesson in the basic indeterminacy of the body" (Brown 1988, p. 169). The transformed body could thus serve as a visible emblem of spiritual transformation – in eschatological terms a "first instalment" (*arrabon*) of salvation and the end of time. Later, in Milan and Rome, as in the great churches of the East, the virgins of the church functioned as "nothing less than human boundary stones. Their presence defined the Catholic basilica as privileged, sacred space" (Brown 1988 p. 356). Paradoxically, Christian Gnostic circles treasured those incidents in the Gospels that described the close, yet sexless, relations of Christ with the women of his circle, especially those with Mary Magdalene. For a second-century writer, these anecdotes were an image of the sweet and irresistible absorption of the woman, the perpetual inferior, into her guiding principle, the male. Thus in an apocryphal gospel Simon Peter says to the disciples, "Let Mary leave us, for women are not worthy of life." Jesus himself said, "I myself shall lead her and make her male" (Gospel of Thomas, cited in Brown 1988, p. 113).

For the Desert Fathers, sexual desire again performed a metonymic function, now in existential terms, for it "revealed the knot of unsurrendered privacy that lay at the very heart of fallen man." It thus became what Brown describes in an intriguing way as "an ideogram of the unopened heart" (Brown 1988, p. 230). The flight from the body was yet further intensified in Ambrose of Milan's expression of aversion: the believer is urged not to "swerve, get stuck, or sucked into" the treacherous morass of the flesh (Brown 1988, p. 349). For Jerome, the human body remained a darkened forest, filled with the roaring of wild beasts, that could be controlled only by rigid codes of diet and by the strict avoidance of occasions for sexual attraction (see Brown 1988, p. 376).

Augustine's arguments concerning the origins of original sin in concupiscence and the consequent necessity of the Virgin Birth give him pride of place in the development of the connection between body and sexuality in the West. The growing social power of somatic anxiety and intolerance becomes apparent in the first burning of male prostitutes in 390 CE (see Brown 1988, p. 383). The sharp *summa voluptas* of orgasm notoriously escaped conscious rational control, and for Augustine existence in the *flesh* is in essence tragic (see Brown 1988, pp. 418–19). Brown concludes that "Christian notions of sexuality had tended to prise the human person loose from the physical world. . . . Sexuality was not seen as a cosmic energy that linked humans both to the fertile herds and to the blazing stars" (Brown 1988, p. 432).

Over against the primorial celebration of fertility, the emergence of the cult of the Virgin Mary "offered the numinous inversion of the dark myth of shared, fallen flesh" (Brown 1988, p. 445). The ambiguity of Mary's place as the unspotted Virgin yet Primal Mother completed the problematic compact of Christianity with its late Roman setting and in turn early medieval development. Devotion to the Virgin Mary continued this ambivalent juxtaposition of roles as at once deliverer from sexual sinfulness and intercessor for the infertile.

Early Western Christian attitudes toward the body persisted, and feminist scholarship has achieved much in uncovering their subsequent history and ongoing implications. Caroline Walker Bynum (1991) has shown that the inscription of theological truth upon the body of the woman adept, sometimes in forms as literal as through the appearance of the *stigmata* and the travails of "holy anorexics," was central to the somatic experience of women within Western Christendom. European and American feminist scholars continue to explore these continuities. Given the attitude toward the body, it is not surprising that a contemporary Orthodox theologian like Kallistos Ware should attempt to provide an even-handed account of the body in Greek Christianity and strive to deal positively with the infamously misinterpretable Pauline set of contrasts of body (*soma*) to soul (*psyche*) and of flesh (*sarx*) to spirit (*pneuma*). Ware recognizes that the attitude of the Greek Fathers toward marriage is "often less than totally affirmative" (Ware, "My Helper and My Enemy: The Body in Greek Christianity," in Coakley 1997, p. 104). In Orthodox teaching marriage is understood as a witness amounting to martyrdom: hence on their marriage the couple receive the martyr's crown.

In his brief study of the formative phases of the subsequent Reformation, David Tripp investigates the Reformers' attitude toward dancing, taking dancing as a touchstone of their views on the body. The judgment of Richard Baxter upon this "sinful sport" that "bewitcheth and befooleth" is taken as representative (Tripp, "The Image of the Body in the Formative Phases of the Protestant Reformation," in Coakley 1997, p. 144). Tripp is nonetheless valiantly optimistic when he concludes that early exponents of Protestant Christianity "reflect a discovery, however inconsistent and uneven, of a sense of the body in the person, in the general community, in the Eucharist" and that "the popular rediscovery of Protestant roots may combine with our present new emphasis upon corporeity to revive the Reformers' affirmation of the body as gift and sacrament, rather than as burden and threat, in Protestant theory and practice" (Tripp, in Coakley 1997, p. 147).

The sociologists Philip Mellor and Chris Shilling undercut this apologetic attempt to represent the Reformation in positive somatic terms by tracing the continuing denigration of experience of the body in European modernity back to Martin Luther himself:

Luther conceived "by faith alone" while he was sitting on the privy, moving his bowels, in a Wittenberg monastery tower. This evacuation of the body and focus on the mind may, perhaps, be as good as a place as any to chart the birth of modernity. Early modern, Protestant bodies became oriented more towards words and symbols than to the wider sensory potentialities of bodies. (Mellor and Shilling 1997, p. 10)

Mellor and Shilling maintain that the "Protestant desire to live an ordered and rational life . . . was closely associated with an antipathy and anxiety towards human embodiment" (Mellor and Shilling 1997, p. 124). They would appear to follow Weber in attributing much of the banal aridity of the bureaucratized world to Protestantism. It is against this background that contemporary postmodern "baroque moderns" playfully re-engage with sensuality, aestheticization, and visual culture. Correspondingly, the "re-emergence of the sacred in effervescent forms of sociality signals the exhaustion of the moral basis for modern contractarian relationships." Furthermore, "Debates about whether we are living in a modern or postmodern society are giving way to a more serious question about the very possibility of a rational social order" (Mellor and Shilling 1997, p. 190).

As self-consciously male sociologists, Mellor and Shilling adopt a feminist awareness of the body as determinative of self-identity and investigate Western somatic consciousness in order to produce a version of the modern divided self. This consciousness is both "baroque" (floridly expressive, visual, sensual, hence Catholic) and "modern" (fearful of somatic metaphor, verbal, rational, hence Protestant) in ways that afford clarification of the dialectics of contemporary re-somatization, which are now rendered even more complex by the interplay of "real" and "virtual" bodies (see Hailes 1999).

Tripp's implausible claims associated with the representation of the body as justified and "real" because of its Eucharistic reinforcement within Protestantism confront the reader with an uncomfortable paradox at the heart of the Christian doctrine of the Incarnation and "the body" as the Body of Christ, from which the reality, fulfillment, and finality of all contingent human bodies are somehow to be derived. This attitude originates in the earliest stages of the tradition and enjoys strong contemporary sanction in both major Catholic and Protestant strands of Latin Western Christianity. The influential French Roman Catholic theologian Jean-Luc Marion writes of the Eucharist "that the materiality that transubstantiation provokes aims only at uniting us, through the Spirit that brings it about, with the spiritual body of Christ constituted by the Church" and that as a result a spiritual body is "a body infinitely more united, more coherent, more consistent – in a word, more real – than any physical body" (Marion 1991, p. 179).

Western methodological concerns and traditions have so colored the representation of the "bodies" of the religious "other" that some politically aware Westerners declare the *impossibility* of this representation and some non-Westerners its *unacceptability*. All the major traditions of Christianity – Catholic, Protestant, and Orthodox – inherit a difficulty: a powerful metaphorical *imaginaire* of "the Body" that coexists with the negation of contingent bodies. There is in effect no Christian Tantra through which *Eros* might inform and energize *Agape*. As the Swedish theologian Anders Nygren argued, "There is no way, not even that of sublimation, that leads over from Eros to Agape" (Nygren 1953, p. 52). This problematic inheritance reinforces the Cartesian tendency to divorce mind from body. It also, if inadvertently, sanctions the evolution of a pornographic virtual "unhappy consciousness" – an information-technological porn-Eros divorced from the responsibilities of the owned embodiment characteristic of human maturity.

Non-Christian Traditions

Judaism

Over against both patriarchal Roman familial practice and Jewish esteem for the married state, the Christian exaltation of sexual continence even within marriage came to focus and exemplify the radicality of Christian discipleship, a tendency criticized by Jews from earliest times (see Boyarin 1999) down to the closing passages of Franz Rosenzweig's *The Star of Redemption* (1921). In a recent review of Jewish worship, Louis Jacobs has stressed that toward the body there is both the "normal mysticism" of Judaism and the more esoteric practice of the Kabbalah (Jacobs, "The Body in Jewish Worship: Three Rituals Examined," in Coakley 1997, p. 86). Thus the Friday night before the Sabbath is the "special time for marital relations" (Jacobs, in Coakley 1997, p. 80). This endorsement of (hetero)sexual activity in the context of marriage is at radical variance with the view of Western Christianity. In not only ordinary but also mystical traditions of Judaism the body and sexuality are affirmed. Nevertheless, Howard Eilberg-Schwartz has polemically argued against "the sexless God" and the disembodied patriarchy characteristic of the Hebrew Bible:

> As a symbol to be emulated, a sexless father God naturally provides an ideal of male asceticism. To be really like God, a man should have no sexuality. Israel's God thus generates very different consequences for masculinity than a religious system in which the phallus and sexuality of the male gods are the subject of speculation, as in Hinduism, for instance. (Eilberg-Schwartz 1994, pp. 199–200)

Levitical laws of pollution and the corresponding need for ritual purification are likewise perceived, not least by feminist scholars and contemporary activists, as hostile to women's bodies.

Some leading contemporary feminists maintain that patriarchy, both Christian and Jewish, amounts to "necrophilia" (see Daly 1984) and is thus perniciously and incorrigibly resistant to all real embodiment. Men are seen as incapable of embodiment other than that required to secure momentary male gratification and insemination. Patriarchy understood thus as phallocracy (but without a benign phallus) energizes exclusionist

feminism and modes of female embodiment that tend in the partheno-
genic same-sex directions enabled by artificial insemination and new *in
vitro* techniques of reproduction. Here there is a significant affinity between
contemporary social change and debates in the religious field.

Islam, Sufism, and Sikhism

Consideration of the body in Islam is so problematic that there is, for
example, no consideration of the body in Sunni and Shi'ite Islam in Sarah
Coakley's outstanding collection, to which all those concerned with the
body and religion are much indebted (see Coakley 1997). Historically
speaking, views of Islam and the body are overshadowed by debates on
Orientalism and postcolonialism. Western accounts of the body in Islam
have been dominated by "Orientalist" representations of the shrouded
female Muslim body as the locus of exotic but veiled sexuality and of the
male Muslim body as the quintessential expression of unfettered male
corporeal desire, in a tradition that extends from, for example, Mozart's *Il
Seraglio* through Sir Richard Burton's translation of the *Thousand and One
Nights* to the Moor in Stravinsky's *Petrushka*. Against these excesses,
Annemarie Schimmel's study of the subleties and theological significance
of the parallel between the veiling of the female body and that of the Kaaba
in Mekkah, and the corelative involutions of the safeguarding by such
veiling of male gender identity against social disorder (*fitna*) is exemplary
in its even-handedness (see Schimmel 1997). For more scholarly interest
is expressed in the female Muslim body than in that of the male (see
Yegenoglu 1998). World political developments are today entangled in
the dialectical culture politics of the female body: a modesty which entails
that the invisibility of the female Muslim body is the acute converse of the
exposure of women's bodies in globalized pornography. The tension is
heightened by the much publicized postmortem sexual rewards offered to
self-immolating male Islamic "martyrs" and also by American Neo-
Conservative Christian fundamentalist depictions of the conjugal life of
the Prophet Muhammed himself.

In contrast to the differentiated and now much fraught somatic world
of mainstream Islam, eros in Sufi literature and life, as presented in
Annemarie Schimmel's brief study, is full of skillfully wrought ambiguities. Asceticism, ecstasy, a fluid, gender-floating sexual "other" in a society
largely free of a visible female presence, the eventual identification of pain
and joy in "mystical masochism" – all these take us deep into the mysteries of an orgasmic religious experience. Yet even here, as in many other
world religious traditions, there is the banality of world weariness, as
when Ibrahim ibn Adham remarks that "When a man marries he boards
a ship, and when a child is born to him he suffers shipwreck" (Schimmel,
" 'I Take the Dress Off the Body': Eros in Sufi Literature and Life," in Coakley
1997, p. 270). According to Schimmel:

The Sufis experienced time, and again the *Urschauder*, the primordial rapture of love which they date back to the day of the Covenant, the *ruz-i alast*. They experienced it in a mixture of fascination and awe, whether this love was purely "divine" or grew in connection with a human subject. They went back beyond the institutionalized, rigorously legalistic framework of orthodox Islam into the darkness where the true Water of Life can be found. (Schimmel, in Coakley 1997, p. 285)

Sufism offers a path from the Islam of the masses to the ecstatic experience of the primordial. This path energizes the appeal of Sufi practices in the West, where significant numbers likewise seek emancipation from a routinized mass culture – this time that of modernity itself. These Western networks of lineage tend to replicate the exotic and coded secrecy so often necessitated by the fate of Sufis within Muslim societies.

In a useful and well-observed account of the body in Sikhism, Eleanor Nesbitt has explored an example of how a religion may emerge from conflicting alternatives through calculated selective reversals seen in the *panj kakke*, the "five Ks" of uncut hair, comb, wristlet, short sword, and cotton undergarment worn by both men and women as signs of their commitment. Sikh views of the body, as presented by Nesbitt, lack the extreme features to be found in some other religions and spiritual practices, where ambivalence regarding the body and sexuality appears to be systemic (see Nesbitt, "The Body in Sikh Tradition," in Coakley 1997, pp. 289–305).

Hinduism and Buddhism

In her indispensable collection Sarah Coakley places the non-Abrahamic religions apart as "Beyond the West." It is in this setting that Wendy Doniger then sets out from the "quasi-universalism" of the body to consider Hindu medical and mythical constructions of the body. *The Laws of Manu* offer a "chilling image" of the body. A man should "abandon this foul smelling, tormented, impermanent dwelling place of living beings, filled with urine and excrement, pervaded by old age and sorrow, infested by illness, and polluted by passion, with bones for beams, sinews for cords, flesh and blood for plaster, and skin for the roof" (Doniger, "Medical and Mythical Constructions of the Body in Hindu Texts," in Coakley 1997, pp. 169–70). Contrary to some popularly held Western Neo-Tantric images of Hindu belief and practice, the separation and deconstruction of the characteristics of the body and its organs are the price paid for the tolerable cultural management of sexuality. "In both cases, male and female, the genitals pose great dangers as long as they are attached to the human (or divine body); only when they are detached are they safe, indeed the object of worship" (Doniger, in Coakley 1997, p. 180).

In Therevada Buddhism the body may once more be construed in a way that reinforces the point that radical misogyny and male anxiety in the face of the female body and sexuality are not the exclusive possession of monotheistic traditions. The threat of the *vagina dentata* is thus no prerogative of the West. As Steven Collins observes, in the monastic discipline of the *Vinaya* the Buddha remonstrates with an errant monk tempted back into marital intercourse:

> It would be better, foolish man, to put your male organ into the mouth of a terrible and poisonous snake than into a woman. . . . It would be better, foolish man, to put it into a blazing, burning, red-hot charcoal pit than into a woman. Why? On account of *that*, foolish man, you might die, or suffer deathly agony, but that would not cause you to pass, at the breaking up of the body after death, to a lower rebirth, a bad destiny, to ruin, to hell. But on account of *this*, foolish man, [you may]. (Collins, "The Body in Theravada Buddhist Monasticism," in Coakley 1997, p. 185)

The Mahayan Buddhist monastic goal is not simply renunciation of the body and sexuality but once again the aspiration to live beyond passion, for "the Arhat is . . . no longer subject to wet dreams" (Collins, in Coakley 1997, p. 190). That goal is similar to the goal of Clement of Alexandria's desire-free second-century Christian. Collins proceeds to provide a useful summary of body meditation techniques that underlie the juxtaposition of the "*deconstruction* and rejection of the body in meditative analysis with the *construction* of it in social behaviour as unified and valued public object" (Collins, in Coakley 1997, p. 199). Collins is also prepared to suggest grounds of comparison when he draws a parallel between Buddhist and Christian salvation in a kind of "socio-religious theatre" (Collins in Coakley 1997, p. 201). Thus the body becomes the instrument which opens up interiority:

> In so far as salvation is conceived as a spiritual state manifested in both mind and body, the attempt to inhibit (or, perhaps, exorcise) all sexual drives and thoughts, and not merely to prevent overt sexual activity, necessarily induces psychic conflict, a conflict which opens up the interior terrain for which texts and doctrines provide the map. In this private zone of operations the de-sexualised, and thus in one sense the de-socialised, individual can embody in imagination the immateriality posited in the doctrines of Buddhism, and in this way "touch the deathless with the body." (Collins in Coakley 1997, p. 201)

Paul Williams' account of Mahayana Buddhist perspectives on the body takes the reader out of the monastery into the spiritual use of the body open to any aspirant, lay or monastic, who, "far from seeking death or being phobically enfeebled, gains vigour in acting virtuously for others as a *bodhisattva* for the benefit of others" (Williams, "Some Mahayana

Buddhist Perspectives on the Body," in Coakley 1997, p. 214). Buddhist somatic realism can be summed up as follows: "The body is your enemy, for the body can make you constantly miserable and finally kills you," and desire for a person of the opposite sex is pointless, merely "a particularly time-consuming and destructively absurd version of the general desire for the body" (Williams, in Coakley 1997, p. 209).

Suicidal renunciation rightly made for the benefit of others may be valuable and justifiable in Buddhist terms of compassion. Williams expounds tradition with forceful insight and proceeds to develop in outline a doctrine of concern for the other:

> Compassion requires some sort of active embodiment; embodiment is an expression of spiritual attainment, the spontaneous overflow of enlightenment which necessarily flows for the benefit of all sentient beings precisely because it *is* enlightenment. For both Buddha and *bodhisattva* in their different ways the body is an expression of their spiritual being. Their body is their Being-for-others. (Williams, in Coakley 1997, p. 228)

As regards the Far East, in his study on the Taoist body and cosmic prayer Michael Saso claims that there is a unique conjoining of body, mind, heart, and belly in Taoist and Tantric Buddhist practice. He also makes the possibly more contentious claim that the practice of Taoist or Zen meditation is compatible with the maintenance of belief systems other than the traditional partner of Confucianism and that Christians and Muslims can therefore share in the practice (see Saso, "The Taoist Body and Cosmic Prayer," in Coakley 1997, p. 233; Schipper 1993). As regards the migration and inculturation of spiritual body practices under globalized conditions, some are more capable of undergoing cultural translation than others, but the explanation of these differences in affinity is a complex task.

Taoist and other Chinese spiritual body practices have proved to be highly mobile and adaptable in the process of "Easternization." The migration and global dissemination of Far Eastern practices in the martial and healing arts raise important issues (see Ryan 2002). Similarly, difficulties of cultural translation occur in the diffusion and differentiation of Neo-Tantra in Western contexts by, for example, "Sanyasins" – so-called "renunciates" trained at the Rajneesh ashrams at Poona and elsewhere. These cases range in style from the extreme regime of the "Osho Multiversity" in the Netherlands to more gentle esoteric teachers who guide their followers toward the achievement of erotically aware union with the Divine.

The Somatic Complex and the Re-composition of
the Religious Field

Contemporary research on the body in religion takes at least five basic directions. First, largely but not exclusively under the influence of second- and third-wave feminism, the body now enjoys a central place in contemporary cultural theory and in the decipherment of the politics of individual identity (see Butler 1993). Second, phenomenological theory has evolved in ways potentially capable of providing a basis in the interdisciplinary field of religious studies for more effective research into the body (see Waaijman 1993). Third, anthropologists such as the Tibetologist Geoffrey Samuel have developed the Batesonian tradition in ways that allow for a more effective understanding of the relationship between anthropology and biology. Samuel has applied his "multimodal framework" theory to the interface between shamanic phenomena and institutionalized traditions (see Samuel 1990). Fourth, ritual and performance theory has provided a forum for the study of body/mind connection and the association of gesture and movement with altered states of consciousness eminently applicable to the contemporary popular resurgence of ritual activity (see Schechner 1996). Fifth, the investigation of the interface between spiritualities and the varied fields of psychotherapy has provided indispensable insight into the role of the body in psycho-spiritual healing processes (see Csordas 1997; West 2000). Finally, the manipulation and managerial "transformation" of the identities and "spirituality" of employees in managed organizations have become a significant feature of organizational development (see Roberts 2001, pp. 62–85).

Conclusion: Religious Salience and the
Return of the Body

The history of the body in religion is characterized by complex dichotomies in both religions themselves and the methods used to study them. The study of religion today focuses on processes of "re-traditionalization" that can no longer be understood as marginal or peripheral but instead are a function of core processes in the world system, of which the "return of the body" is but one aspect. The full analysis of this situation lie beyond the scope of this chapter. Religious bodies and their representations encode cultural transformations that can only be fully understood through a renewed encounter between mainstream social theory and the contemporary transformations of religion. As the anthropologist Mary Douglas once observed, "Just as it is true that everything symbolises the body, so it is equally true that the body symbolises everything else" (Douglas 1966, p. 122). The body will remain at the heart of religious concerns.

Bibliography

Bateson, Gregory. *Mind and Nature: A Necessary Unity.* London: Wildwood Press, 1977.

Boyarin, Daniel. *Dying for God: Martyrdom and the Making of Christianity and Judaism.* Stanford, CA: Stanford University Press, 1999.

Brown, Peter. *The Body and Society: Men, Women, and Sexual Renunciation in Early Christianity.* New York: Columbia University Press, 1988.

Butler, Judith. *Bodies that Matter.* London: Routledge, 1993.

Bynum, Caroline Walker. *Fragmentation and Redemption: Essays on Gender and the Human Body in Medieval Religion.* New York: Zone Books, 1991.

Coakley, Sarah, ed. *Religion and the Body.* Cambridge: Cambridge University Press, 1997.

Csordas, Thomas J. "Somatic Modes of Attention," *Cultural Anthropology* 8 (1993): 135–56.

Csordas, Thomas J. *The Sacred Self: A Cultural Phenomenology of Healing.* Berkeley: University of California Press, 1997.

Daly, Mary. *Pure Lust: Elemental Feminist Philosophy.* Boston: Beacon Press, 1984.

Douglas, Mary. *Natural Symbols: Explorations in Cosmology.* Harmondsworth: Penguin, 1976.

Eilberg-Schwartz, Howard. *God's Phallus and Other Problems for Men and Monotheism.* Boston: Beacon Press, 1994.

Featherstone, Mike, and Bryan S. Turner. *The Body: Social Process and Cultural Theory.* London: Sage, 1991.

Featherstone, Mike, and Bryan S. Turner. "Body and Society: An Introduction," *Body and Society* 1 (1995): 1–12.

Foucault, Michel. *Discipline and Punish: The Birth of the Prison,* tr. Allan Sheridan. London: Allen Lane, 1977.

Hailes, N. Katherine. *How We Became Posthuman: Virtual Bodies in Cybernetics, Literature and Informatics.* Chicago: University of Chicago Press, 1999.

Haraway, Donna J. *Modest_Witness@Second_Millennium. FemaleMan©_Meets_OncoMouse™.* New York: Routledge, 1997.

Holdrege, Barbara A. "Body Connections: Hindu Discourses of the Body and the Study of Religion," *International Journal of Hindu Studies* 2 (1998): 341–86.

Ingold, Tim, ed. *Companion Encyclopaedia of Anthropology* [1994]. 2nd edn. London: Routledge, 2002.

Lane Fox, Robin. *Pagans and Christians.* London: Viking, 1986.

Marion, Jean-Luc. *God Without Being: Hors-Texte,* tr. Thomas K. Carlson. Chicago: University of Chicago Press, 1991.

Mauss, Marcel. "Body Techniques" [1936], in his *Sociology and Psychology: Essays,* tr. Ben Brewster. London: Routledge and Kegan Paul, 1979, pp. 95–123.

Mellor, Philip, and Chris Shilling. *Re-Forming the Body: Religion, Community and Modernity.* London: Sage, 1997.

Nygren, Anders. *Eros and Agape,* tr. Philip A. Watson. London: SPCK, 1953.

Ranke-Heinemann, Uta. *Eunuchs for Heaven: The Catholic Church and Sexuality,* tr. John Blownjobs. London: Deutsch, 1990.

Roberts, Richard H. *Religion, Theology and the Human Sciences.* Cambridge: Cambridge University Press, 2001.

Rosenzweig, Franz. *The Star of Redemption* [1921], tr. William W. Hallo. London: Routledge and Kegan Paul, 1971.

Ryan, Alexandra E. Our Only Uniform Is the Spirit: Embodiment, Tradition and Spirituality in British Taijiquan. Unpublished PhD dissertation, Lancaster University, 2002.

Samuel, Geoffrey D. *Mind, Body and Culture: Anthropology and the Biological Interface.* Cambridge: Cambridge University Press, 1990.

Schechner, Richard. "The Future of Ritual," in his *The Future of Ritual: Writings on Culture and Performance.* London: Routledge, 1993, pp. 228–65.

Schimmel, Annemarie. *My Soul Is a Woman: The Feminine in Islam.* New York: Continuum, 1997.

Schipper, Kristofer. *The Taoist Body.* Berkeley: University of California Press, 1993.

Synnott, Anthony. *The Body Social: Symbolism, Self and Society.* London: Routledge, 1993.

Turner, Bryan S. *The Body and Society: Explorations in Social Theory* [1984]. London: Sage, 1996.

Waaijman, Wees. "Towards a Phenomenological Definition of Spirituality," *Studies in Spirituality* 3 (1993): 5–57.

Ward, Graham. *True Religion.* Oxford: Blackwell, 2003.

Weber, Max. *Economy and Society: An Essay in Interpretative Sociology,* eds. Guenther Roth and Claus Wittich, trs. Ephraim Fischoff *et al.* 2 vols. Berkeley: University of California Press, 1978.

West, William. *Psychotherapy and Spirituality: Crossing the Line between Therapy and Religion.* London: Sage, 2000.

Yegenoglu, Meyda. *Colonial Fantasies: Towards a Feminist Reading of Orientalism.* Cambridge: Cambridge University Press, 1998.

Chapter 11

Death and Afterlife

Douglas J. Davies

The human drive for meaningfulness is faced with challenges, not the least of which is death. Most religious traditions interpret death as the gateway to destiny and as the fulfillment of life's meaning. To the secular world death remains no less profound a challenge to meaningfulness. This chapter will consider theoretical, then religious, and finally secular approaches to death.

Theoretical Approaches

While no one possesses evidence of a kind that can persuade skeptics that an afterlife awaits them, few ideas are more important if they are actually true. It was that kind of quandary that led the philosopher Blaise Pascal (1623–62) to the idea of a wager to be made with oneself: if one lives a religious life and heaven exists, one wins, and if there is no heaven, one loses nothing; but if one does not live religiously and there is a heaven, one loses. The odds thus come down on living a religious life. Today some might add that if the religious life involves constraints on how one would otherwise prefer to live and, if there is no heaven, then one loses by living a religious life. Pascal's wager points out the close relationship that exists in many cultures among morality, religion, and the afterlife. Plato's concept of a heaven-like ideal world, in which ideas of truth and beauty exist in their fullness, from which the soul comes into the body before birth, and to which it goes after its period of relative imprisonment, has been widely influential.

Psychologically, death has been dealt with in terms of the grief suffered through bereavement. Sigmund Freud (1922) developed the notion of a death instinct, named after the Greek god of death, "Thanatos." The death instinct is the human inclination to return to the state of matter. It is experienced individually as masochism and socially as warfare. Freud also considered death as loss and provided the basis for subsequent psychological studies of "attachment and loss" – studies that consider the identity of the survivor in relation to the deceased.

Anthropological studies have demonstrated a largely universal belief that some form of human identity continues beyond death. The Victorian anthropologist E. B. Tylor (1871) even argued that religion itself evolved from belief in a soul that survives the death of the body. Whether or not religion in fact originated as a response to death, it has certainly been the major means of turning death into a positive event. The anthropologist Bronislaw Malinowski (1948) argued that funeral ritual is a fundamental way in which people "ritualize" their optimism. As death provides opportunity for new leaders to emerge, whether in families or in states, funerary rites, including memorial events, often furnish a pivotal point for renewed endeavor. Economic and political factors are also often embedded in death rites, as issues of inheritance and the transmission of authority arise. In any case the dead are seldom forgotten. Whether as ancestors or as travelers on a path of transmigration to some heaven, they are often believed to maintain relationship with the living.

Three other anthropologists have linked death rites to the identity of the dead and the bereaved. Robert Hertz developed the idea of "double burial," a process that he divided into "wet" and "dry" phases. The first, wet phase deals with the corpse from the moment of death till burial or cremation. It covers the period when the deceased is removed from that person's normal social status. The second phase uses the "dry" remains, whether bones or ashes, to confer a new identity on the deceased: that of ancestor. Throughout this double process the surviving kin also undergo changes of identity as they assume new roles.

Arnold van Gennep (1960) outlined what he called "rites of passage." He maintained that rites of passage involve a threefold scheme: separation from one's present status, transition or set-apartness, and reintegration into society with a new status. He argued that any rite of passage reflects the stage of life in which it occurs. In funerals the emphasis is on the deceased's separation from the living and integration into the afterworld.

The contemporary anthropologist Maurice Bloch (1992) has shown how death is used symbolically as a cultural way of dealing with biological death. While birth, maturity, and death may be considered the natural facts of life, many cultures have not been prepared to let biological death have the last word. Instead, they have used rituals to effect the symbolic death of the natural life and a symbolic rebirth into an eternal life. In Christianity, baptism is said to involve a death to the "natural" person and the birth of a "spiritual" person. Being "born again" is in this sense believed to be a means of overcoming natural death.

Myth, morality, and merit

Myths of traditional societies and doctrines of world religions express opposition to death by deeming it an alien intrusion caused by the stupidity, greed, or misconduct of the first human beings. Entry into an afterlife is often associated with some form of judgment upon the deceased person's life. An individual's identity in life becomes the basis for one's status after death. Insofar as the judgment is of one's adherence to prized social values, death serves to uphold the very foundations of society.

Traditionally, heaven and hell have been taken as the destinations of the good and the wicked. But these notions, especially of hell, have lost popularity in twentieth-century Christianity, at least in liberal Christianity. Similarly, in Judaism, ideas of the afterlife have become less significant. Traditionally, Christianity favored a supernatural division into heaven and hell. So, too, did Islam, which took the Jewish- and Christian-like belief in the resurrection and judgment with great seriousness. In Judaism, Christianity, and Islam death is the pivotal point between phases of human identity, with ethics providing the foundation for destiny. Some criticize this outlook because it seems to provide a way of controlling people's behavior: they will go to heaven only if they are obedient. Making merit is one widespread feature of religion, as important in Buddhism as in Christianity. But sometimes religions react against rigid schemes of merit and the hopelessness that they can breed. Instead, religions invoke the love, acceptance, and grace offered by God.

Religious Perspectives

In religions worldwide the contradiction between the decay of the body and the continuation of the individual is overcome through belief in an eternal soul, in a resurrected body, or in a combination of the two. The human body is often assumed to be powered by a soul, spirit, or life-force that departs at death and continues as an ancestor in touch with the living or else resides in some distant heaven or back on earth through reincarnation in another body. By contrast, resurrection is the belief that the body is reconstituted in some way and brought to life again. The major religions have adopted one or other of these ways through death to an afterlife.

Zoroastrianism is among the oldest religions in the world. It goes back some 3500 years to Persia, with its devotes, subsequently known as Parsees, migrating to India and elsewhere. Its texts speak of the dead whose actions are brought to light by the bridge of judgment over which the deceased must pass to receive rewards or punishments. This tradition believes in an ultimate form of resurrection, even though its funeral practice is to expose dead bodies in special structures, often called towers of silence, where vultures can eat the polluting flesh. The bones go into a central pit. Burial is avoided to prevent corrupting the earth. Cremation is avoided to prevent polluting fire, itself a prime medium of worship. By contrast, ancient Egypt preserved its dead through mummification, yet also believed in a future judgment and resurrected body.

In the biblical period of Judaism there was scant belief in an afterlife. Any notion of an afterlife was vague, referring more to a dark underworld than to any sharp divide between heaven and hell. Rewards and punishments took worldly form. Hence the very worldly catastrophes befalling a Job could not be offset by appeal to compensation after death. Later parts of the Hebrew Bible, perhaps influenced by Persia through Jewish captivity in Babylon, developed fuller ideas of resurrection, judgment, and afterlife. By the time of Jesus, there was a clear divide within Judaism between the Sadducees, who rejected the idea of an afterlife, and the Pharisees, who espoused it.

Christianity became the first world religion centered on the belief in a resurrection, but one without the dominant pressure of an ethical judgment of individuals. For Paul, faith in Jesus frees believers from sin and guarantees their resurrection into an afterlife of joy, whether on a renewed and restored earth or in a heaven. Unlike Zoroastrianism or Judaism, Christianity was not a traditional society grounded in long-established kinship networks but a new association of individuals drawn from different Mediterranean communities. Faith, trust, and a personal sense of union with Christ as the transcendent Lord who forgives sin replaced social law codes that had to be obeyed. When Christianity became the state religion of the Roman Empire, social codes developed as methods for controlling human behavior and encouraging obedience to law. Images of hell and heaven emerged as the destination of the obedient and disobedient. Christianity has subsequently experienced the conflict between the stress on Christ, grace, and resurrection and the stress on law, obedience, and judgment. Wherever Christianity becomes established as the dominant religion, it tends to emphasize obedience and judgment.

Islam followed the broad scheme of the Jewish and Christian emphasis upon obedience to God, or Allah. The growth of entire Islamic communities produced a social base for the new religion. Death came to be associated with judgment and with the rewards and punishments of an afterlife. The notion of paradise was one of a garden of delights for the obedient Muslim. Against this background of law-based living, there have arisen groups that stress the love of Allah and give themselves to mystical forms of worship. Living under the law is here supplanted by the joy of union with the transcendent One.

Hinduism maintains that one's position in life derives from *karma*, a kind of merit based on doing one's duty in previous lives. *Samsara* is the belief in many lives, through which one increases or decreases one's *karma* and, accordingly, gains a better or worse subsequent reincarnation. This inevitable process constitutes a judgment, though without any personal judge. For millennia, this moral control grounded destiny within caste behavior. Yet here, too, the idea of love rather than of duty influenced ideas of death and afterlife. So, too, in Sikhism and Buddhism, which, despite their comparable commitment to the notions of *samsara* and *karma*, developed beliefs in love relationships, focused on savior figures, in addition to mechanical legal codes. For example, the love of the True Guru in Sikhism, the love of Krishna in Hinduism, and the Pure Land form of Buddhism all involve faith in a loving savior figure. Love from god, it is believed, enables devotees to bypass the long circuits of *karma*-driven *samsara* and enter directly into the realm of divine bliss. Sikhism, as a movement of protest against traditional caste-based Hindu society, was not unlike earliest Christianity in its protest against Judaism. Both involved the growth of new communities that transcended traditional forms of kinship and that were inspired by ideas of divine love.

Locating the dead

To inhabit an eternal realm, whether heaven or hell, the dead need a transformed body. Either God will raise the decayed body from its grave and give it new life, or else this transformed body will be reunited with the soul, which has been waiting since the death of the body to form a new unity. Early Christianity emerged out of Judaism, which at the time of Christ was divided into those who did (Pharisees) and those who did not (Sadducees) believe in resurrection. Christians not only adopted the outlook of the Pharisees but also believed that Jesus had himself been resurrected – the first actual case of the general principle. Early Christians, as with many of their successors, believed that the world would soon come to an end with the Second Coming of Christ, when the earth would be transformed, all humanity judged, and the eternal Kingdom of God established. There is an extensive theology called Eschatology, which discusses what are called the "last things." Those judged worthy would live in this new world.

Love, grief, and eternity

Death highlights a widespread religious relationship, sometimes complementary yet more often antagonistic, between love and duty. Having considered duty, which is tied to merit and to rewards and punishments, we now consider love, one of the most powerful of human experiences. Love leads to varying degrees of attachment between persons and becomes radically problematic when someone loved dies. Death challenges attachment. Throughout life we find ourselves attached to parents and close relatives and later become attached to spouse, partners, and friends. These bonds provide a degree of security and enter into our sense of self. Death can bring this secure identity into question, as when the bereaved speak of their "world collapsing around them."

We have seen that religious traditions have provided one of the most extensive means of coping with grief through rituals that seek to relocate the dead, give the dead a new identity, and thereby forge a new relationship between the survivor and the deceased. In many traditional societies the new identity is that of an ancestor. In no religions are the bereaved left to themselves. They are always part of the ongoing transformation of the identity of their dead. The ritual of grief also becomes the ritual process of ongoing maturity after bereavement, as roles are assumed that were once occupied by the dead.

Many world religions also highlight the place of a savior figure, often divine, who stands beyond death and offers a way past death. Hinduism, Buddhism, Christianity, and Islam all have their special groups devoted to what may be called a love-grace union with the savior or god. Through hymns, songs, and prayers devotees express their love of their savior or god. It is inconceivable to devotees that this bond of attachment can be broken even by death. The element of romantic love upsurges within worship, and the relationship between devotee and deity echoes something of the experience of romantic love between human beings. It is no accident that the words used of love toward God by worshipers echo the love songs of a lover to the beloved. The religious experience of a sense of union during life with one who transcends death implies, for some, a continued union with that divine lover after death. This love union clearly goes far beyond the strict ideal of merit gained through obedience to religious rules.

Eternal family life and identity

The ideal of love toward deity has in Christianity, for example, also included the belief that human families themselves will remain together in the afterlife. Though expressive more of popular belief than of formal theology, the idea that families stay together in heaven developed quite considerably within the twentieth century, despite the wedding vow limiting marriage "till death us do part." In a literal sense this point of termination is contradicted by funeral services which often suggest that spouses will be rejoined in heaven.

On earth we know who we are through our bodies and through the relationships we have with others' bodies. In order to "be myself" in heaven or hell I therefore need to retain or regain my body, which is the basis of my identity. But heaven is different from earth, and the Bible refers to a "spiritual body." Just what a "spiritual body" is is hard to say, but somehow it must express my identity.

One building block of this approach lies in the Catholic doctrine that the soul in this life comes to expression through and as a body. Instead of a sharp soul–body divide, the two are intimately associated in this world and also in the next. The future "body" may differ from the present one, but some form of union will ensure that one's real self will be identifiable through my new body. Within this process of continuity there is also a process of change because heaven is different from earth. Heaven involves the presence of God and a new order of being from that known on earth. Sin in particular – that aspect of life that spoils a self and its relations to others – will no longer be a factor. Whether through a period of cleansing transformation in purgatory, as in Catholic tradition, or in a more instantaneous transformation, as generally preferred in Protestant thought, the real self will undergo transformation. Accordingly, the Christian afterlife will involve a changed identity as the old self is revealed anew, freed from sin, and transformed by its new kind of relationship with God and with others.

While Christian theologians often emphasize this kind of argument and reinforce it with the doctrine of the resurrection as the vehicle for providing transformed bodies with a recognizable identity, many ordinary Christians often imagine that the human soul simply leaves the body at death and proceeds to its new life in heaven. This simple view assumes a continuing identity without worrying about any technical account.

Secular Perspectives

From a secular perspective the key questions are whether life can be meaningful without an afterlife and whether belief in an afterlife must be religious. Communism, for example, rejects the belief in an afterlife but offers an ideology to make sense of this life. For secular existentialists, the choice to live without any religious meaning challenges persons to forge their own meaning. The contemporary sociologist Zygmunt Bauman (1992) argues that societies exist to hide its members from the real fact of death as the end of life. For if people realize that life has no meaning, they will lose all hope and will give up on their daily lives.

Some Eastern religions, especially Buddhism, start with the self, with its self-concern and its striving for meaning in a world that seems to be filled with phenomena demanding explanation. But these phenomena turn out to be illusory. They have been produced by over-creative imaginations and are flawed by the lust to preserve the self at all costs. Only by learning that the "self" is not an enduring and "eternal" entity can one live in a way that abandons the striving for meaning and for merely momentory pleasure. The Eastern belief in the nothingness of things has come to be set within a "religious" tradition of compassion for others. By contrast, the Western stare at nothingness is more likely to engender despair, scorn for the "non-self," and indifference to anyone else.

Increasing numbers accept death as a fact of life. Accordingly, new forms of funeral rite are life-focused, celebrating what the deceased has meant to others and has contributed to the world. Various secular associations are happy to engage in rituals for the dead that emphasize this life. Just as many Communist societies in the twentieth century created special rituals for the dead to stress their value to the state, so individual forms of secularism demonstrate the human commitment to this life as meaningful. Death rites confirm this commitment.

Bibliography

Bauman, Zygmunt. *Mortality, Immortality.* London: Polity Press, 1992.

Bloch, Maurice. *Prey into Hunter.* Cambridge: Cambridge University Press, 1992.

Davies, Douglas J. *Death, Ritual and Belief.* London: Continuum, 2002.

Davies, Douglas J. *Anthropology and Theology.* Oxford: Berg, 2002.

Freud, Sigmund. *Beyond the Pleasure Principle* [1920–22], tr. C. J. Hubback. London: International Psychoanalytical Press, 1922.

Hertz, Robert. "A Contribution to the Study of the Collective Representation of Death," [1907] in his *Death and the Right Hand*, eds. and trs. Rodney Needham and Claudia Needham. New York: Free Press, 1960. pp. 27–86.

Jankowiak, William, ed. *Romantic Passion. A Universal Experience?* New York: Columbia University Press, 1995.

Kramer, David. *The Meanings of Death in Rabbinic Judaism.* London: Routledge, 2000.

Malinowski, Bronislaw. *Magic, Science and Religion and Other Essays*, ed. Robert Redfield. Garden City, NY: Doubleday, 1948.

Tylor, E. B. *Primitive Culture* [1871], 2 vols. 5th edn. New York: Harper, 1958 [original pub. of 5th edn. 1913].

Van Gennep, Arnold. *The Rites of Passage* [1908], trs. Monika B. Vizedom and Gabrielle L. Caffee. Chicago: University of Chicago Press, 1960.

— Chapter 12 —

Ethics

G. Scott Davis

What Is Ethics?

"Ethics" and its cognates derive from a Greek root that encompasses "custom," "habit," "disposition," and "character." "Morals" and its cognates derive from the Latin terms used to translate words with that Greek root. While technical distinctions between "ethics" and "morality" have sometimes been drawn, the distinctions have no historical basis or philosophical use beyond that exploited by those who make them. Here they will be used interchangeably.

"Religion," though the Romans themselves disputed its etymology, refers to the scrupulous execution of rights and duties that flow from the awe and fear inspired by the majesty of the divine rather than to any specific set of beliefs or practices. Institutions, practices, and beliefs have usually been identified as religious because of their antiquity, their claims for supernatural origin, or their incorporation into a comprehensive vision of the cosmos and the place of human beings in it. Ethics and religion have always been closely intertwined. Euthyphro, in Plato's dialogue of that name, takes it as given that justice and piety are closely related even if, by the end of the dialogue, Socrates has questioned exactly what that relation might be (see Plato 1997, 14b–15e).

Part of the problem with the relation of ethics to religion lies in the often unarticulated presuppositions and expectations with which people approach the study of ethics. By dividing the discussion that follows into law, character, and economics, I intend to challenge the usefulness of the reigning typology of deontology, teleology, and consequentialism (see Frankena 1973) and the still older one of egoism, utilitarianism, and intuitionism (see Sidgwick 1907). Both William Frankena and Henry Sidgwick, by dissolving the complexity of our moral reflection into technical "isms," make it difficult to see how the language of ethics is connected to the language that we use and to the institutions that we confront in everyday life. The limits of these older typologies become even more apparent when we look at the moral traditions of other times and cultures (see the entries for Buddhism, Islam, China, and Hinduism in Becker and Becker 2001; Singer 1991). Journals such as *Philosophy East and West* and the *Journal of Religious Ethics* now regularly publish articles on Buddhist, Confucian, Hindu, Muslim, and Jewish ethics, all of which incorporate traditions and perspectives not easily accommodated by these older typologies (compare Danto 1972 with Harvey 2000).

The Legal Paradigm

Euthyphro takes for granted what may be called the "legal paradigm," which sees ethics as a matter of following rules. A recognized authority promulgates the law that subjects have a duty to obey. Failure to obey typically results in a finding of guilt unless there are mitigating circumstances. To be upright is to know the law and to exert oneself in fulfilling it.

Examples of the legal paradigm abound. In Jewish tradition God delivered the law, or *Torah*, to Moses, in both written and oral form, on Mt. Sinai. The *Torah* is the culmination of God's legislation for humanity. That legislation began with the prohibitions of Genesis 2:16–18 and includes the Noachide Law of Genesis 9:8–17. The 621 commandments issued to the Israelites were codified by Rabbi Judah the Patriarch into the *Mishnah* in the late second century CE. The *Mishnah*, with its commentary, became the basis of rabbinic tradition.

At perhaps the same time on the Indian subcontinent, the *Laws of Manu* emerged as the pre-eminent manual of conduct for the Hindu tradition. Both the *Manu* and the *Mishnah* draw on much older material that had itself been the subject of much commentary over centuries. Both organize the daily practices of life within a larger cosmic whole. Both begin with an account of the origins of the cosmos, the ranks and relations among the peoples who inhabit the cosmos, and the basic order for living.

Several centuries later, the followers of Muhammad collected the traditions of the prophet, the *hadith*, as a foundation for interpreting what the *Qur'an*, God's final revelation to humanity, implies for the community of the faithful. The *Muslim* is someone who submits to God's will. *Islam* is the way of life made up of the community of believers who have submitted to God's will. For over a thousand years the *Qur'an* and the *hadith* have remained the bases for the orthodox schools of *shari'a*, or Islamic law (see Cook 2000).

For traditions such as these, to which over a third of contemporary humanity adheres, ritual, ethics, and law are mingled so inextricably as to call into question any distinction between ethics and religion. Sex, food, and the various media of exchange cannot be knit together into a worthy life without knowing the divine order of the cosmos. Ritual, or the rules for maintaining that order, is of paramount importance, as evidenced in debates over rabbinic authority in Israel, over caste distinctions in India, and over the role of *shari'a* in the Islamic world.

Medieval Catholicism reflects an interesting development of the legal paradigm. The early Church, in coming to grips with its Jewish origins, distinguished the "Old Law" of the Jews from the "New Law" of Jesus, with its twin injunctions to love God and love thy neighbor. But by the High Middle Ages the various councils of the Church had promulgated canons for Church and social order at least as complicated as the teachings of the Rabbis. From the eleventh century on, "church courts exercised jurisdiction, for example, over marriage and the termination of marriage, the legitimacy of children, all kinds of sexual conduct, commercial and financial behaviour, the legitimate times and conditions of labour, poor relief, wills and testaments, and burial of the dead" (Brundage 1995, p. 71). All of these decisions reflected the principles that the community was expected to maintain on the basis of God's law. In the thirteenth century Thomas Aquinas developed a schema for relating the various forms of *human* law, which was always local, to the *natural* law, or those precepts of action to be adopted by any agents possessed of virtue and right reason, precepts independent of their particular religious commitments.

For Aquinas, the natural law is shorthand for what the mature agent, fully informed and grounded in the natural virtues of prudence, justice, courage, and temperance, would take to be consonant with right reason. Christian ethics perfects nature, through the theological virtues of faith, hope, and charity, without destroying God's created order. From the beginning of the modern period, however, Catholic natural law has tended toward the legal paradigm, with moral duties derived directly from precepts grounded in nature. In the early twentieth century the American moral theologian John A. Ryan (1906) embraced the latest theories of economics and political science to argue that, as a matter of natural law, "the laborer's claim to a living Wage is of the nature of a *right*" (Ryan, quoted in Gustafson 1978, p. 22). Later in the century French Catholic thinkers such as M.-D. Chenu worked to bring the tradition closer to Aquinas' ethics of character.

In the aftermath of the Second Vatican Council (1962–5), new perspectives in Catholic moral theology proliferated. Mary Daly's (1990) feminism and the liberation theology of Gustavo Gutierrez (1973) have had a worldwide impact. Closer to the mainstream, Richard McCormick's (1978) and Charles Curran's (1999) analyses of competing moral and premoral values have freed priests and counsellors to recommend in good conscience actions that, to traditionalists and to those more wedded to the legal paradigm, seemed prohibited by natural law. Curran in particular has found himself at odds with the Vatican on sexual and medical ethics. Without rejecting the natural law tradition, he argues that on issues about which doctrines are not held to have been established infallibly, the theologian is at liberty to follow that teaching which seems most probable. For example, in cases where a pregnancy would put the welfare of a woman or her family in jeopardy, it can be argued that it is both legitimate and faithful to counsel her to use artificial birth control.

Lisa Cahill (1994) is one of a number of younger Catholic moral theologians who have placed the natural law tradition within the larger historical development of Christian moral thinking. While writing as a feminist on matters of gender and family, she takes earlier and competing arguments seriously and makes it her task to place them before the reader. In this sense, regardless of their positions on particular issues, she follows McCormick and Curran in expanding the available forms of argument open to the moral theologian. For all three, a formal, or deductive, legal approach neglects the particulars of individual experience and the history out of which Catholic tradition has emerged.

This moral ecumenism has not gone unchallenged. During the long reign of Pope John Paul II the Vatican attempted to reassert its authority over moral theology. In works such as the papal encyclical *Veritatis Splendor* the legal paradigm is vigorously reaffirmed. Moreover, "this law cannot be thought of as simply a set of norms on the biological level; rather it must be defined as the rational order whereby man is called by the Creator to direct and regulate his life and actions and in particular to make use of his own body" (Wilkins 1994, p. 125). Among the leaders in articulating a new natural law theory are the Australian legal theorist John Finnis and his student, the Princeton political theorist Robert George. When George remarks that the attempts of American bishops to reassert the traditional teachings on sexual and medical ethics "have been constantly undercut by the scandal of theological dissent" and that "it is only a bit of an exaggeration to say that heresy is so widespread that it threatens to become the norm" (George 2001, p. 300), he signals his belief that liberal moral theory, both secular and religious, is an assault on the basic human goods that give substance to natural law.

The Protestant Reformation led half of Europe to jettison the canon law of the Catholic Church, but not the inclination to formulate ethics on the model of the law. The Dutch lawyer and humanist Hugo Grotius led the way in formulating a modern natural law derived solely from the basic condition of the human animal. From the facts that we are self-interested, driven to self-preservation, yet at the same time inclined to sociability, Grotius and those who followed him attempted to generate a system of obligations and prohibitions that could be agreed on across frequently warring religious communities. Grotius continues to be seen as having laid foundations for international law (see Schneewind 1998, pp. 58–81).

The legal paradigm is pushed to, and perhaps beyond, its limits by Immanuel Kant. Kant argued that there is a moral law, binding on all rational agents, but that to be properly moral, it must be promulgated by the autonomous agent himself, to himself, and with a good will free from any taint of self-interest. The test for the purity of these mandates is the "categorical imperative," one formulation of which makes it clear that others are always to be treated as ends in themselves and never as means (see Schneewind 1998, pp. 483–530). Religion remains, but now only as a guarantee that the demands of the moral law will be fulfilled.

This approach has not been without its critics. Elizabeth Anscombe, for example, argued that the legal paradigm does not make much sense "unless you believe in God as a law-giver: like Jews, Stoics, and Christians" (Anscombe 1997, p. 31). For her, the notion of legislating for yourself is a philosopher's fiction designed to preserve the form without retaining the substance that makes it intelligible, namely, the superior power that is entitled to govern its subordinates. If, ethically speaking, all human beings are equally free and autonomous, then this so-called legislation is no different from mere consensus. Understanding how we might justify that consensus requires a different form of argument.

Ethics and Character

For Aristotle, to do ethics is to pursue such questions as "What kind of people should we want to be?" and "What kinds of lives should we try to pursue?" Ethics is part of "politics," by which he means the systematic reflection on how people ought to live together (see Aristotle 1999, 1094a–b). The human animal shares many traits with the rest of earth's animal population, pursuing both food and sex while fleeing both predators and the elements. But humans are distinctive in the extent of their reasoning powers, reflected not only in the complexity of language but also in their ability to control and remake the world around them. At bottom, the point of all this thinking and remaking is to secure happiness.

For Aristotle, happiness is not momentary satisfaction but living in a way that allows individuals to pursue and secure reasonable goods, to enjoy them with others, and to pass them on to future generations. Achieving happiness is in part beyond our control in that we cannot choose to be born into a secure environment, be free from want, and be guaranteed to succeed when we compete with others. But most people have some control over their lives. They develop abilities, habits, and skills that give them a better chance of success than they would otherwise have. Habits that allow an agent to distinguish real from apparent goods and thereby to do the right thing, at the right time, and in the right way are excellent qualities, qualities that come to be called "virtues" (see Aristotle 1985, 1107a–1113b). Habits that tend to inhibit the successful pursuit of reasonable ends are defects, or "vices."

Some forms of excellence, and the habits that contribute to them, are tied to specific beliefs and ends. The ancient Greeks, for example, would have thought it natural and right to take pride in their accomplishments and to express that pride, reasonably, in their actions. Early medieval Christians, or at least those who responded to the teaching of St. Benedict's *Rule*, exalted humility, submitting to the authority of another in ways that would have shocked their Greek forbears. Yet both groups would have agreed that achieving any goods through purposeful action requires some degree of practical wisdom, justice, courage, and self-discipline. These "cardinal virtues," as they have been known since antiquity, are essential to the individual of good character. Friendship between persons of good character is among the most desirable of human goods. It motivates individuals to do noble and beautiful things, and it allows friends to band together and to pursue goods that would be unobtainable by isolated individuals (see Aristotle 1985, 1156b).

Even virtuous persons disagree about which goods to pursue and when, about who is entitled to what, and about which pleasures are reasonable for whom. Thus law is central to organizing and protecting the city state, or *polis*. It shapes individuals by teaching them what their neighbors love and what the members of the *polis* expect from one another. But law is not an end in itself. It is always general and therefore stands always in need of interpretation and application. The point of the law is to secure, in a general way, the common good of the political community. It can succeed only if it is interpreted by persons of good will, guided by practical wisdom. These are qualities that must be developed over time, in interaction with other people. Aristotle's term *epieikeia* (*aequitas* in the Latin of Aquinas) means "decent," or "reasonable." As a virtue, decency must be exercised to correct the law when, as a result of its generality, a strict construction would be unreasonable or unfair (see Aristotle 1985, 1137b). For the Aristotelian, the obvious injustice of "strict constructionism" points up the limits of the legal paradigm.

An ethics of character is not unique to Aristotle or to his Western followers. Herbert Fingarette has argued that Confucius seeks to identify a central Chinese tradition that makes it possible, in a period of social and political chaos, for individuals to see themselves as inherently worthy because they are the vessels of a civilizing tradition (see Fingarette 1972, p. 62). In Fingarette's reconstruction the crude material of humanity is civilized by one's coming to identify oneself with *li*, or what he calls "holy rite." In the process of practicing holy rite, the individual develops *ren*, or character, making it possible for the individual to recognize, appreciate, and negotiate the web of relations that make life worth living and protecting. To do all this is to walk the correct path, or *tao*.

Fingarette puts Confucius' achievement in perspective by contrasting the ways in which a practice may be established and maintained: "By effective command, by common agreement, and by inheritance through accepted tradition" (Fingarette 1972, p. 62). On Fingarette's account, legitimation through the direct authority of the ruler was inherently unstable in a period of warring states and rival strong men. Fear and self-interest shifted unpredictably with the emergence or arrival of new players on the political or military stage. An independent and impartial authority might be found in the law of heaven, but Confucius "was not impressed with the possibilities of metaphysical speculation and 'theology'" (Fingarette 1972, p. 62). What did impress Confucius was the ability of humans to identify themselves with tradition and to cultivate it for its own sake. When ritual, *li*, is respected for its own sake, the person of good character, *ren*, neither exploits knowledge and ability for the person's own ends nor allows practice to degenerate into perfunctory ritualism. The person of good character does not deviate from the path. That person is not unlike Aristotle's *phronimos*, the person of practical wisdom, who knows and does the right thing, in the right way, at the right time (see Aristotle 1985, 1105a–1108b).

The twentieth-century Swiss theologian Karl Barth developed a particularly influential account of character and of the faithful church in the light of God's word. Barth insisted on the primacy of revelation over and against worldly enterprises. The work of the theologian is to interpret God's word to and for the Church. God's word confronts believers and, as Barth puts it in discussing abortion and the Sixth Commandment, "we have first and supremely to hear the great summons to halt issued by the command" (Barth 1961, p. 416). But this summons is only the beginning of the discussion, not the end. "Human life, and therefore the life of the unborn child," he continues, "is not an absolute, so that, while it can be protected by the commandment, it can be so only within the limits of the will of Him who issues it" (Barth 1961, p. 420). To do ethics is to hear the commandment and to act faithfully in the moment. To be able to do so, believers must understand themselves as members of the faithful community and must cultivate the habits of thought and action that witness to the story revealed in Scripture.

The Mennonite theologian John Howard Yoder both criticizes and develops Barth's vision. Trained at Goshen Seminary and the University of Basel, where he attended Barth's lectures, Yoder developed a critical biblical realism with immediate normative implications (see Davis 1999, pp. 278–305). He argued that the Gospel demands the renunciation of violence and coercion by force because they are at odds with the peaceable kingdom proclaimed by Jesus. In numerous writings Yoder embraced the scandalous and counter-intuitive implications of the Gospel: that humanity is not in charge of its own destiny, that it cannot secure justice and progress through its own power, and that faith in the promise of Christ's death and resurrection should guide the expression of Christian witness as social critique (see Yoder 1994, pp. 160–7).

The Methodist theologian Stanley Hauerwas combines the character-centered ethics of Aristotle and Aquinas with Barth's emphasis on revelation and a theological stance shaped by Yoder's account of the peaceable kingdom. For Hauerwas, to be a Christian is to witness to the world the impact of the Gospel on life. To be a theologian is to confront the Christian community with its failure to live up to the demands of the Gospel. And to be a moral theologian is to show the Christian community how that witness can express itself in response to political conflict, problematic pregnancies, and the needs of the handicapped. From this vantage point the careful and eclectic pragmatism of Hauerwas' teacher James Gustafson is a temptation to worldly accommodation. Hauerwas' confrontational stance is part of his sense of the theologian's vocation, though it is also informed by the occasionally apocalyptic language of his sometime colleague Alasdair MacIntyre (see Hauerwas 2001, pp. 267–84).

In *After Virtue*, published in 1981, MacIntyre argues that the general malaise of contemporary modern societies is linked to the loss of a tradition that could make character come alive. According to MacIntyre, the language of morals among the intellectual and professional elite in modern Western societies has become one of individual self-interest, sustained by a bureaucracy designed to facilitate the privately chosen objectives of the ruling class. This situation minimizes any incentive for the haves and the have-nots to see themselves as bound together for the common good. The only hope, MacIntyre seems to say, is for the appearance of a new vision of character that can be implemented through the creation and embrace of meaningful practices and institutions (see MacIntyre 1998, pp. 73–101).

Some have recently taken to calling this position "virtue ethics," but that term is probably misleading. "Virtue" has an unfortunate, Victorian ring not found in Aristotle's *arete*. Certainly what are to count as excellences depends on the kind of persons and communities people set themselves to becoming, so that it is the "ethos," the "character" of individuals, communities, and the kinds of lives to which they aspire that identifies a particular tradition (see Crisp and Slote 1997).

One of the by-products of the renewed interest in character and the virtues is a new approach to comparative religious ethics. Rather than comparing laws or codes, one discovers what matters to a tradition, at a particular time and place, by asking what makes one a saint or a sinner, who the exemplary figures are, and how their stories shape the perceptions of a community (see Hawley 1987). In answering these questions, the historian and the anthropologist may be as helpful as the philosopher and the theologian. The anthropologists Mary Douglas and Clifford Geertz have influenced a generation by bringing the social theories of Durkheim and Weber, respectively, to bear on the results of fieldwork as a means of illuminating the moral imagination at home and abroad. Discussing the notions of pollution held by ancient Israelites and modern Africans, Douglas helps her reader understand why some forms of sexuality are felt, even in twentieth-century England and America, to be not merely deviant but dangerously so. Geertz, by contrasting the ideal types of Indonesian and Moroccan Islam, calls into question the very idea of a single, monolithic Islam and, by extension, the idea of any single, monolithic religious tradition once it has moved beyond its historical and geographic origins (see Douglas 1966; Geertz 1968).

The Economic Paradigm

A third paradigm speaks in terms of values, rights, and principles of fair exchange. The language of economics is both natural and important to any society that develops much beyond the stage of hunting and gathering. But the dramatic expansion of commerce from the late Middle Ages to the modern period saw a rise in the language of rights and values. This language is common to moral theories that, on the surface, seem to be as antithetical as the utilitarianism of Peter Singer is to the Kantian contract theory of John Rawls.

At the end of the eighteenth century the British reformer Jeremy Bentham maintained that all values can be reduced to functions of pleasure and pain. By measuring the total amount of pain and pleasure, and determining how to minimize pain and maximize pleasure, benevolent government can establish a regime that is fair to each and that maximizes the pleasures of all. "Utilitarianism," as Bentham's position came to be known, maintains "the rightness or wrongness of an action depends only on the total goodness or badness of its consequences" (Smart, in Smart and Williams 1973, p. 4). This view assumes that a value can be assigned to a given state of affairs and that, at least in principle, those values can be compared within a single system. When pressed, this stark statement of the theory seems to imply such extremely counter-intuitive results that Bernard Williams finds it hopelessly simpleminded, with "too few thoughts and feelings to match the world as it really is" (Williams, in Smart and Williams 1973, p. 149).

Peter Singer, the most eminent contemporary utilitarian, embraces the seemingly counter-intuitive implications of his position. For Singer, all suffering is to be deplored, including that of animals. Citizens of the developed world should therefore eschew animal farming, with all its cruelties, not only to eliminate animal suffering but also to maximize the production of non-animal foods that can relieve the famine that plague the less developed world. Recognition of animal suffering and the unequal distribution of resources should prompt reconsideration of the apparel industry, medical research, cosmetic testing, and other aspects of day-to-day life (see Singer 1993, pp. 119–34).

Singer's pursuit of a consistent utilitarianism has led him to put forward a number of controversial positions in medical ethics. In his view, not only is abortion, at least at the early stages, a legitimate option for the mother, but in cases of severe genetic defect it may be the right thing to do for the fetus. Allowing newborns with severe disadvantages to die may also be incumbent on the benevolent physician, particularly when the defect will almost certainly lead to suffering and death after only a few days or weeks of life. At the other end of life, euthanasia, including physician-assisted suicide, should be a legal option (see Singer 1993, pp. 202–13).

Singer's utilitarianism has provoked outrage in a variety of corners, but there is nothing philosophically unusual about his reasoning, beyond its consistency. At the philosophical level critics worry about "slippery slope" problems, or situations where allowing what might seem a morally justified exception to generally held rules or prohibitions lowers the bar, making further exceptions more likely until the original rule itself has been discarded. A typical slippery slope argument might begin with the view that it is always wicked to kill the innocent. But then there are those battlefield cases where the good soldier is excruciatingly and fatally wounded, begging his buddy for a quick end to his pain. A "mercy killing" is not really a murder. The buddy was just speeding up an inevitable process, thereby relieving his friend's suffering. But if battlefield mercy killings are acceptable, what about the aging wife, whose husband is dying slowly of advanced prostate cancer, for whom the morphine haze has become an intolerable misery, matched only by the pain without morphine? Can she morally take nonviolent, if illegal, steps to hasten his dying? And if she can, what about the doctor who has just delivered an anencephalic baby? Would it be better for all involved to let the baby die in the delivery room and to record a stillbirth? Even those whose intuitions are clear at any one stage on the slope typically find another point at which they are stymied, making it hard to explain where to draw a line.

On the economic model, the standard way to constrain utilitarian arguments is by providing a theory of rights. "Rights" are entitlements, held by individuals and sometimes groups, to receive certain goods and be protected from certain burdens. At the beginning of the twentieth century Wesley Hohfeld put forward an account of legal concepts that has been extremely influential. For Hohfeld, rights are correlated with duties in a system where a number of other key legal terms, such as privilege, immunity, and liability, divide the field of legitimate action. By arraying these concepts in systematic form, one can distinguish how they at once differ and work together in the legal order. Thus "a right is one's affirmative claim against another, and a privilege is one's freedom from the right or claim of another." Similarly, "a power is one's affirmative 'control' over a given legal relation as against another; whereas an immunity is one's freedom from the legal power or 'control' of another as regards some legal relation" (Hohfeld, "Fundamental Legal Conceptions," in Kent 1970, p. 140). If we can differentiate among powers, duties, and immunities, then we can explain their relative value within the larger system and can achieve fairness in the distribution of goods.

The "contract" theory familiar from Hobbes, Locke, and Rousseau sees politics and the moral order as emerging from a bargaining situation in which one set of rights – those of the strongest in the state of nature – are bargained away in favor of another set of rights – those associated with the security necessary to enjoy a variety of social pleasures free from attack and the fear of attack. John Rawls' *Theory of Justice* (1971) comes out of this tradition. For Rawls, reason dictates that if you don't know where you will end up in the social hierarchy, it is unreasonable to bargain away claims to fair treatment and opportunity on the slim chance of coming out on top. Reasonable persons, when forced to choose the basic structure of their society from behind the "veil of ignorance," will therefore set up the conditions for the pursuit of basic goods in a way that maximizes the opportunities of any given individual to compete successfully while minimizing the burdens that anyone will be called upon to endure for the good of the whole (see Rawls 1999, pt. I).

The resulting system, which Rawls calls "justice as fairness," can be applied to the real world. For example, it might be the case that slavery, the subordination of women, or the euthanasia of substandard newborns might optimize economic return, family stability, or the allocation of medical resources. But given the unpredictability of an individual's place in the human world, it would be irrational for anyone to endorse this system, and it would therefore be unfair for those in power to impose this policy on anyone else. Within the constraints imposed by the concept of justice as fairness, the practical determination of policy choices is not appreciably different from the utilitarian attempt to maximize benefits and minimize burdens for individuals and for society as a whole.

Religious thinkers have embraced the economic model in several ways. Joseph Fletcher's *Situation Ethics* is a form of Christian utilitarianism, where the only norm against which to measure action is whether the action is consistent with Christian love, as applied to a given situation. Because it seems to countenance abortion, euthanasia, and other seriously contested kinds of action, situation ethics was hotly debated through the early 1970s. Natural law thinkers, who tend to see such actions as contrary to justice, question not only the morality of situation ethics but its claim to represent a religious perspective. Others seek to identify the ways in which outcomes and principles can be balanced with religious commitments, even when they do not follow Fletcher into what many see as an uncontrolled relativism (see Outka and Ramsey 1968).

Catholic "proportionalism" is considerably more nuanced than situationism. Richard McCormick has developed the traditional moral doctrine of "double effect," which recognizes that one action may have multiple effects, some of them outside the intention of the agent, to argue that "the traditional distinction between direct and indirect is neither as exclusively decisive as we previously thought, nor as widely dispensable as some recent studies suggest" (McCormick and Ramsey 1978, p. 50). Central to proportionalist justifications is the distinction between moral and premoral goods and evils. While it is never considered legitimate to intend evil, even where good may come, it may be acceptable to tolerate some events that are evil, when they are the indirect results of actions taken toward genuinely good ends.

Many of the most important practical results of this position come in medical ethics. Traditional Catholic teaching rejects any direct abortion as an attack on innocent life. This position holds even where another innocent, the mother, may die. The proportionalist argues for saving the patient even if the doctor knows that the direct result of treatment will be the death of a fetus. As Charles Curran puts it, "Life is certainly the most fundamental and basic premoral good, but all human beings and the Catholic tradition have recognized that life can on occasion be taken as in the case of self-defense" (Curran 1999, p. 156). Particularly when there is honest intellectual dispute about the status of the fetus, a doctor can properly act as a healer on behalf of the patient.

The impact of Rawls' thought on religious ethics has been complex. For Rawls, one of the requirements of public discourse is that it be restricted to a shared vocabulary of justice as fairness. We must therefore both recognize the existence of contemporary pluralism and agree to check our mutually incompatible "comprehensive doctrines" at the door of public reason. In one sense this view seems fair enough. If the Buddhist, the Catholic, and the atheist do not agree to disagree on some fundamental matters, conversation will never get going. But at a deeper level we should expect there to be some logical relation between policies on the allocation of health care in public hospitals and, for instance, the moral status of the fetus or the Alzheimer's sufferer, both of them weak members of the community, whom the Christian is enjoined to protect. It seems unreasonable of Rawls to insist that the very beliefs most deeply held, those which inform someone's thinking at the deepest level, be disregarded in discussing the public good. Liberal theologians such as Douglas Hicks argue that is possible to endorse Rawls' concern for "mutual respect and civility" without "unnecessarily impoverish[ing] the resources for discourse in the public sphere" by excluding theological language (Hicks 2000, pp. 100–1).

A more intractable debate arises where religion, rights, and consequences intersect in cross-cultural contexts. The rights of women and children in particular create conflict when the traditional practices of a culture, or the legal constraints based on religion, lead to situations where human activists recommend intervention against the demands of tradition. The flip side of this tension is the inclination of liberal regimes to grant "group rights" to immigrant and other minorities that exempt them from otherwise applicable statutes. In the United States, for example, the Amish of Lancaster County, Pennsylvania, have received numerous legal exemptions based on their religious convictions. These exemptions include allowing their buggies to drive the country roads, excusing their children from the full requirements of public education, and exempting their men from military service on the grounds of conscientious objection. The argument is that their religious witness is so evident and long-standing that it would be an intolerable assault on their consciences to demand conformity.

In an article that has received considerable attention, Susan Moller Okin has questioned the justice of granting these group rights. She argues, for instance, that "the French accommodation of polygamy illustrates a deep and growing tension between feminism and multiculturalist concern for protecting cultural diversity" (Okin 1999, p. 10). Okin contends that if traditional practices are harmful, then there is no good reason to support them and a very good reason to oppose them. Okin's goal is to push Rawls' "justice as fairness" further by expanding the strictures on which goods may be traded to achieve what ends in a liberal society. As a critic of liberal pluralism, she insists on the urgency of speaking out on behalf of women and others whose voices are often silenced by their own traditions.

Ethics, Religion, and the Twenty-first Century

No typology can capture the complexities of moral discourse. For example, the centrality of the Torah to Jewish life might suggest the dominance of the legal paradigm, but the emphasis on character throughout the history of the tradition makes simple generalizations problematic. Jewish work in medical ethics is particularly complex and well developed. Rabbinic tradition insists, for example, on preference for the mother over the fetus in cases of potentially life-threatening pregnancy, so that direct abortion may, in some instances, be not merely a personal choice but a religious obligation (see Kellner 1978, pp. 257–83; Dorff and Newman 1995, pp. 382–91). The Rabbinic teaching that a woodchopper may be restrained if his work is prolonging the agony of a dying person has led to an extended literature on the scope and legitimacy of euthanasia and the implications of medical technology (see Dorff and Newman 1995, pp. 129–93).

Work in Islamic ethics is similarly complicated by the need to consider philosophical, legal, and religious sources (see Hourani 1971, pp. 1–16). The early development of *shari'a* gave considerable weight to the legal paradigm in determining basic questions of the conduct of life (see Cook 2000). But the intense, if brief, influence of Greek philosophy left a legacy of philosophical questions about the good life and the goal of political organization (see Lerner and Mahdi 1963, pp. 22–186). The sociologist Yvonne Haddad, among others, has shown the interaction of traditional Muslim values, local tradition, and American culture on immigrant communities in the present-day United States (see Haddad and Lummis 1987).

Buddhism, with its many schools and lack of a central institutional authority, has generated many, sometimes competing, perspectives on ethics. All embrace the Buddha's Four Noble Truths, which locate the source of human suffering in desire and its consequences. Likewise all recognize that the end of suffering requires the discipline of the Eightfold Path. But thereafter, the teachings of the different schools diverge. Environmental degradation in Southeast Asia had led to the intensive development of Buddhist environmental thought there. Civil conflict between Hindu Tamils and Buddhist Sinhalese in Sri Lanka has required considerable rethinking of the Western tendency to identify Buddhism with pacifism. The interaction among Buddhism, Confucianism, and indigenous traditions has generated diverse and sometimes incompatible approaches to abortion and medical ethics in contemporary Japan (see Harvey 2000).

Bibliography

Anscombe, Elizabeth. "Modern Moral Philosophy", in *Virtue Ethics*, eds. Roger Crisp and Michael Slote. Oxford: Oxford University Press, 1997, pp. 26–44.

Aristotle. *The Complete Works of Aristotle: The Revised Oxford Translation*, ed. Jonathan Barnes. 2 vols. Princeton, NJ: Princeton University Press, 1985.

Aristotle. *Nicomachean Ethics*, tr. Terence Irwin, 2nd edn. Indianapolis: Hackett Books, 1999.

Barth, Karl. *Church Dogmatics III/4: Doctrine of Creation*, trs. Geoffrey Bromiley and Thomas Torrance. Edinburgh: Clark, 1961.

Becker, Lawrence, and Charlotte Becker, eds. *Encyclopedia of Ethics* [1992], 2nd edn. London: Routledge, 2001.

Brundage, James. *Medieval Canon Law*. London: Longman, 1995.

Cahill, Lisa. *Love Your Enemies: Discipleship, Pacifism, and Just War Theory*. Minneapolis, MN: Augsburg Fortress, 1994.

Cook, Michael. *Commanding Right and Forbidding Wrong in Islamic Thought*. Cambridge: Cambridge University Press, 2000.

Crisp, Roger, and Michael Slote, eds. *Virtue Ethics*. Oxford: Oxford University Press, 1997.

Curran, Charles. *The Catholic Moral Tradition Today*. Washington, DC: Georgetown University Press, 1999.

Daly, Mary. *Gyn/Ecology: The Metaethics of Radical Feminism*. Boston: Beacon Press, 1990.

Danto, Arthur. *Mysticism and Morality: Oriental Thought and Moral Philosophy*. New York: Basic Books, 1972.

Davis, G. Scott. "Tradition and Truth in Christian Ethics," in *The Wisdom of the Cross: Essays in Honor of John Howard Yoder*, eds. Stanley Hauerwas, Chris Hubner, Harry Hubner, and Mark Thiessen Nation. Grand Rapids, MI: Eerdmans, 1999, pp. 278–305.

Doniger, Wendy, and Brian K. Smith, trs. *The Laws of Manu*. Harmondsworth: Penguin Books, 1991.

Douglas, Mary. *Purity and Danger*. London: Routledge and Kegan Paul, 1966.

Douglas, Mary. *Implicit Meanings* [1975], 2nd edn. London: Routledge, 1998.

Fingarette, Herbert. *Confucius: The Secular as Sacred*. New York: Harper and Row, 1972.

Fletcher, Joseph. *Situation Ethics: The New Morality*. Philadelphia, PA: Westminster Press, 1966.

Frankena, William. *Ethics* [1963], 2nd edn. Englewood Cliffs, NJ: Prentice-Hall, 1973.

Geertz, Clifford. *Islam Observed: Religious Development in Morocco and Indonesia*. Chicago: University of Chicago Press, 1968.

Geertz, Clifford. *The Interpretation of Cultures*. New York: Basic Books, 1973.

Geertz, Clifford. *Available Light: Anthropological Reflections on Philosophical Topics*. Princeton, NJ: Princeton University Press, 2000.

George, Robert. *Making Men Moral: Civil Liberties and Public Morality*. Oxford: Oxford University Press, 1993.

George, Robert. *The Clash of Orthodoxies: Law, Religion, and Morality in Crisis*. Wilmington, DE: ISI Books, 2001.

Gustafson, James. *Protestant and Roman Catholic Ethics: Prospects for Rapprochement*. Chicago: University of Chicago Press, 1978.

Gutierrez, Gustavo. *A Theology of Liberation: History, Politics, Salvation*, trs. C. Inda and John Eagleson. Maryknoll, NY: Orbis Books, 1973.

Haddad, Yvonne H., and Adair T. Lummis. *Islamic Values in the United States: A Comparative Study*. Oxford: Oxford University Press, 1987.

Harvey, Peter. *An Introduction to Buddhist Ethics: Foundations, Values and Issues.* Cambridge: Cambridge University Press, 2000.

Hauerwas, Stanley. *The Hauerwas Reader,* ed. John Berkman and Michael Cartwright. Durham, NC: Duke University Press, 2001.

Hauerwas, Stanley, Chris Hubner, Harry Hubner, and Mark Thiessen Nation, eds. *The Wisdom of the Cross: Essays in Honor of John Howard Yoder.* Grand Rapids, MI: Eerdmans, 1999.

Hawley, John Stratton, ed. *Saints and Virtues.* Berkeley: University of California Press, 1987.

Hicks, Douglas. *Inequality and Christian Ethics.* Cambridge: Cambridge University Press, 2000.

Hohfeld, Wesley Newcomb. *Fundamental Legal Concepts as Applied to Judicial Reasoning.* New Haven, CT: Yale University Press, 1919.

Hourani, George F. *Islamic Rationalism: The Ethics of 'Abd Al-Jabbar.* Oxford: Oxford University Press, 1971.

Kent, Edward A., ed. *Law and Philosophy: Readings in Legal Theory.* New York: Appleton-Century-Crofts, 1970.

Lerner, Ralph, and Muhsin Mahdi, eds. *Medieval Political Thought.* Ithaca, NY: Cornell University Press, 1963.

MacIntyre, Alasdair. *After Virtue: A Study in Moral Theory.* 1st edn. London: Duckworth, 1981.

MacIntyre, Alasdair. *The MacIntyre Reader,* ed. Kelvin Knight. Notre Dame, IN: University of Notre Dame Press, 1998.

McCormick, Richard, and Paul Ramsey, eds. *Doing Evil to Achieve Good: Moral Choice in Conflict Situations.* Chicago: Loyola University Press, 1978.

Okin, Susan Moller. *Is Multiculturalism Bad for Women?,* eds. Joshua Cohen, Matthew Howard, and Martha Nussbaum. Princeton, NJ: Princeton University Press, 1999.

Outka, Gene, and Paul Ramsey, eds. *Norm and Context in Christian Ethics.* New York: Scribner's, 1968.

Plato, *Complete Works,* ed. John Cooper. Indianapolis: Hackett Publishing, 1997.

Rawls, John. *A Theory of Justice* [1971], rev. edn. Cambridge, MA: Harvard University Press, 1999.

Ryan, John A. *A Living Wage.* New York: Macmillan, 1906.

Schneewind, Jerome. *The Invention of Autonomy: A History of Modern Moral Philosophy.* Cambridge: Cambridge University Press, 1998.

Sidgwick, Henry. *The Methods of Ethics* [1874], 7th edn. London: Macmillan, 1907.

Singer, Peter, ed. *A Companion to Ethics.* Oxford: Blackwell, 1991.

Singer, Peter. *Practical Ethics* [1979], 2nd edn. Cambridge: Cambridge University Press, 1993.

Smart, J. J. C., and Bernard Williams. *Utilitarianism: For and Against.* Cambridge: Cambridge University Press, 1973.

Wilkins, John, ed. *Considering "Veritatis Splendor."* Cleveland: Pilgrim Press, 1994.

Yoder, John Howard. *The Royal Priesthood,* ed. Michael Cartwright. Grand Rapids, MI: Eerdmans, 1994.

— Chapter 13 —

Fundamentalism

Henry Munson

Once used exclusively to refer to American Protestants who insisted on the inerrancy of the Bible, the term *fundamentalist* has come to be used to refer to an astonishing variety of religious movements. The most influential – and controversial – comparative study of "fundamentalism" has been the monumental Fundamentalism Project, directed by Martin E. Marty and R. Scott Appleby. Sponsored by the American Academy of Arts and Sciences, this project resulted in the publication of five encyclopedic volumes (see Marty and Appleby 1991, 1993a, 1993b, 1994, 1995).

Marty and Appleby describe fundamentalism as primarily the militant rejection of secular "modernity." They stress that fundamentalism is not merely traditional religiosity but rather a religious response to secularization and "modernization." They argue that this response is inherently political, even though the political dimension may be dormant at times. Marty and Appleby exclude from their model of fundamentalism such groups as the Amish, who are neither political nor militant. They contend that fundamentalism contains "a totalitarian impulse" insofar as *"fundamentalists seek to replace existing structures with a comprehensive system emanating from religious principles and embracing law, polity, society,* economy, and culture" (Marty and Appleby 1991, p. 824). Marty and Appleby ascribe to fundamentalists a Manichaean world view, in which fundamentalists "often see themselves as actors in an eschatological drama" (Marty and Appleby 1991, p. 819).

Problems with the Marty–Appleby Model of Fundamentalism

Marty and Appleby have made a great contribution to the comparative study of religion and politics by bringing together many excellent studies of differing forms of twentieth-century religious conservatism. Moreover, they have spurred many scholars to ask how the various movements commonly called fundamentalist are both similar and distinct. But Marty and Appleby themselves focus too much on alleged similarities and not enough on important distinctions. Many scholars have criticized the Fundamentalism Project on this ground (see Juergensmeyer 1993; Munson 1995). The other main criticisms have been as follows. First, the term "fundamentalist" is polemical, for it implies that all those who refuse to dilute the fundamental tenets of their religions are bigoted fanatics. Second, the term is of Protestant origin and distorts the non-Protestant movements to which it is applied. Third, the term is used to refer to a wide range of movements in which religion actually plays quite different roles. In light of these criticisms, many scholars have tended to avoid using the term "fundamentalist" outside its original Protestant context.

We shall attempt to demonstrate that some of these criticisms are warranted by examining the Christian, Jewish, and Muslim movements most commonly called "fundamentalist." To be sure, the various movements that insist on strict conformity both to sacred scripture and to a moral code ostensibly based on it and that reject cultural changes that are seen as contradicting divine law are similar in these key respects. But there are equally important differences. For example, conservative religious movements focused primarily on conformity to a strict moral code must be distinguished from movements like Hindu nationalism, in which religion serves primarily as a badge of national identity and in which insistence on conformity to a strict moral code is absent or relatively insignificant (see Raychaudhuri 1995; Munson 2003). Marty and Appleby, together with Gabriel Almond and Emmanuel Sivan, who appear to endorse their perspective, blur this distinction when they write of "Hindu fundamentalism" (Almond et al. 2003, pp. 122, 135, 404, 469). Hindu nationalism is rooted in the notion that to be a "real" Indian, one must be a Hindu and not a Muslim or a Christian. To label this movement "fundamentalist" is to distort the impulse that led to it.

Christian Fundamentalism in the United States

The word "fundamentalist," traditionally written with an uppercase F, was coined in 1920 to refer to militantly conservative evangelical Protestants ready to fight for the basic tenets presented in *The Fundamentals*, a series of twelve pamphlets published in the United States from 1910 to 1915. The central theme of *The Fundamentals* is that the Bible is the infallible, or "inerrant," word of God. That is, it is without error. Associated with this idea is the belief that believers should live their lives according to a strictly biblically based morality.

Christian fundamentalism, which existed long before the word did, emerged within American evangelical Protestantism. Evangelical Christians believe not only that the Bible is the inerrant word of God but also that one can be saved from eternal damnation only by accepting Jesus Christ as one's savior and that the Christian is obliged to "evangelize," or spread the "good news" of Christ's death and resurrection, for the sake of humanity. The acceptance of Jesus as one's savior is linked to the idea of being "born again" through an experience of the Holy Spirit. Christian fundamentalists have been described as evangelicals who are "angry about something" (Marsden 1991, p. 1). That something is the violation of their beliefs. The term "fundamentalist" thus connotes more dogmatism and militancy than does "evangelical."

Early twentieth-century Christian fundamentalists were outraged by the "higher criticism" of the Bible, which denied that the Bible had been revealed by God and which sought to reconcile Christianity with science and modernity. They also opposed the teaching of evolution and supported the movement to ban the sale and consumption of liquor.

In the nineteenth century, Christian evangelicals of a fundamentalist orientation were politically active on both sides of the slavery issue. They were also politically active in anti-Catholic nativism, in the preservation of the sanctity of Sunday, and in the temperance movement. It is often said that after the disastrous Scopes trial of 1925, Christian fundamentalists avoided the political arena for decades. This assertion is not entirely true. Fundamentalists like Gerald B. Winrod (1900–57) and Gerald L. K. Smith (1898–1976) ran for public office in the 1930s and 1940s on platforms that combined anti-Semitism, anti-communism, and populism with Christian revivalism (see Ribuffo 1983). From the 1950s through the 1970s fundamentalist preachers like Billy James Hargis combined similar themes – minus any explicit anti-Semitism – with opposition to racial integration (see Martin 1996). The Ku Klux Klan also combined Christian fundamentalism with hatred of blacks, Jews, and Catholics (see Marsh 1997, pp. 49–81).

Yet despite all these cases of political activism, it remains true that American Christian fundamentalists largely avoided the political arena from the late 1920s to the late 1970s. This avoidance stemmed in part from the fundamentalists' failure to win control of the major Protestant denominations in the 1920s. It was also rooted in the doctrine of separation from "non-Christians." Christian fundamentalists, like evangelicals in general, generally reserve the term "Christian" for those who have been "born again" by accepting Jesus as their savior. Consequently, Catholics and liberal Protestants do not qualify as Christians.

This issue of separation was one reason for a major split among conservative American Protestants in the 1940s. In 1941 the Reverend Carl McIntire and a relatively small number of fundamentalists who insisted on strict separation from more liberal Christians formed the American Council of Christian Churches. In 1942 a number of prominent evangelicals dissatisfied with both the liberal churches and the strict fundamentalism of people like McIntire established the National Association of Evangelicals. For decades after this split, Christian fundamentalists condemned evangelicals for their willingness to compromise with theological liberalism. By the late 1980s, however, many fundamentalists were calling themselves evangelicals to avoid the negative connotations of the term "fundamentalist."

The debate over the traditional Christian fundamentalist doctrine of separation has clear political implications. Politically active fundamentalists need to work with as many people as possible to achieve their political goals. Fundamentalists have had to work with Catholics and Mormons, groups traditionally condemned and shunned as heretical by fundamentalists. Strict fundamentalists like Bob Jones III still see cooperation with such groups as sinful. More pragmatic fundamentalists like Jerry Falwell believe that political necessity outweighs the traditional insistence on separation.

The apolitical character of most twentieth-century Christian fundamentalists is also rooted in premillennial eschatology. "Premillennialists" believe that Jesus Christ will return before the millennium, or a thousand-year period of perfect peace. There is no point in trying to reform the world now, the premillennialists argue, because it is doomed until Jesus returns and defeats the Antichrist. This attitude is reflected in the common expression "Why polish the brass on a sinking ship?"

By contrast, "postmillennialist" fundamentalists argue that spiritual and moral reform is prerequisite for the millennium, after which Christ will return. Thus where premillennialism seems to lead to political passivity, postmillennialism seems to lead to political activism. But belief and practice do not always coincide. Since the late 1970s, many premillennialist fundamentalists have embraced the political activism traditionally associated with postmillennialism. There is thus a tension between the eschatological beliefs and the political acts of many current Christian fundamentalists active in the "Christian Right." This tension has often been noted by those Christian fundamentalists who continue to shun

[margin notes, handwritten:]
fundamentalist vs. evangelical

wait for the millennium

work for the millennium

political activism. These traditional fundamentalists insist that the Christian's duty is to save souls, not society. They argue that the only way to save society is by converting the people in it to their brand of Christianity, not by trying to change laws and institutions (see Thomas and Dobson 1999).

Despite the prominent political role played by the Christian Right in the last few decades of the twentieth century, there are millions of Christian fundamentalists whose militancy has remained confined to the religious and personal domain. They may be zealous in trying to convert others and in trying to conform to what they believe to be the word of God, but they are not political (see Ault 2004). How ironic, then, that these Christian fundamentalists – the only people in the world who actually call themselves fundamentalists – are thus not fundamentalists according to Marty and Appleby. And even many of the Christian fundamentalists who *are* politically active focus on moral issues like abortion, prayer in schools, homosexuality, and the teaching of "creationism," not on the reconstitution of society on the basis of Scripture. They see themselves as defending their values in the face of an onslaught of liberal, secular values. In other words, Christian fundamentalists do not see themselves as forcing their values on others. On the contrary, they see themselves as defending their values against those liberals intent on imposing liberal values on them.

True, some Christian fundamentalists in the United States do advocate the creation of a society based on strict conformity to biblical law. They are known as Christian Reconstructionists. But they constitute a small minority of the activists in the Christian Right, and they have been criticized by more moderate evangelical Christians like Ralph Reed (see Martin 1996, pp. 353–5).

Marty and Appleby have argued that there is an inherently totalitarian dimension to fundamentalism. But while Christian Reconstructionism clearly is a totalitarian ideology, it would be a mistake to argue that all Christian fundamentalists are totalitarian. Most Christian fundamentalists in the United States are firmly committed to democracy. They would deem any attempt to label their world view "totalitarian" just another example of liberal academics masking attack as analysis. Many other religious conservatives would concur (see Berger 1997; Harris 1994).

The pejorative connotations of the word "fundamentalist" have led many politically active Christian fundamentalists to refer to themselves as "Christian conservatives," a term that can include conservative Catholics and Mormons as well as "charismatic" evangelicals. Although charismatics also believe in the inerrancy of the Bible, they are more concerned with the ecstatic experience of the Holy Spirit, manifested in speaking in tongues and healing. These practices are condemned by more traditional Christian fundamentalists (see Ault 2004, pp. 56–7, 302). Even though charismatic evangelicals like Pat Robertson do not speak of themselves as fundamentalists, they share the traditional fundamentalist insistence on strict conformity to the Bible. By the end of the twentieth century, charismatics like Robertson and more traditional fundamentalists like Falwell tended to gloss over their differences for the sake of unity in the struggle against "secular humanism."

The Christian Right that emerged with the formation of Falwell's Moral Majority in 1979 was a response to the cultural transformations of the 1960s and 1970s. Fundamentalists were outraged by Supreme Court rulings that had banned prayer and the reading of the Bible in public schools. The legalization of abortion also became a major grievance, although initially this issue was primarily a Catholic one. Feminism and the increasingly permissive sexual morality that came to prevail in American culture also outraged fundamentalists, as it also did many other conservative Americans.

Another important issue was the civil rights movement, which was initially opposed by most Christian fundamentalists in the South, where fundamentalism was strongest. The Federal Government's attempts to deny tax-exempt status to many Christian schools founded to circumvent the federally mandated racial integration of public schools led many Christian fundamentalists in the South to become politically active for the first time (see Weyrich 1993).

As time passed, the racial issue receded in significance. But the issues of abortion, homosexuality, and school prayer remained prominent. In the last few decades of the twentieth century, many conservative Catholics, Mormons, and even Orthodox Jews supported Christian evangelicals in opposing what they saw as moral decay. By contrast, the issue of evolution remained primarily a fundamentalist and evangelical issue.

It is important to note that many evangelical Christians, who constitute roughly a quarter of the US population, do not support the hard-line Christian Right. There are many liberal evangelicals such as former President Jimmy Carter, who strongly disagree with many of the positions held by the Christian Right (see Wallis 2005).

Christian fundamentalism has been less politically significant outside the United States. While it has been linked with Protestant loyalism in Northern Ireland, the fundamentalist impulse in that conflict is clearly subordinate to its ethnic and nationalist dimensions, with Protestantism and Catholicism serving primarily as badges of group identity (see Bruce 2001; Buckley and Kenney 1995).

The term "Catholic fundamentalism" is sometimes used to refer to conservative Catholics. In the Preface to *Being Right: Conservative Catholics in America* Mary Jo Weaver and R. Scott Appleby describe how they have argued over this term, Weaver rejecting it and Appleby endorsing it (see Weaver and Appleby 1995, pp. vii–ix). Conservative Catholics themselves reject the term and prefer to be called "traditionalist," "orthodox," or "conservative." These Catholics, themselves not a monolithic group, do not stress the inerrancy of the Bible, as do Protestant fundamentalists. So why, then, use the term "Catholic fundamentalism"? Perhaps those who use it are more interested in attacking Catholic conservatism than in understanding it. Comparing Catholic conservatism with other forms of religious conservatism is certainly useful, but not if one starts out by labeling it a mere variant of a very different kind of conservatism. Comparing apples, oranges, and kiwis can be a useful way to determine the distinctive features of each. But if one labels the study "A Comparative Study of Apples," the oranges and kiwis being studied might well question the fairness of the exercise.

Orthodox Militancy in Israel

The term "fundamentalist" has often been applied to three main trends in Israeli Judaism: militant religious Zionism, Ashkenazi Ultra-Orthodoxy, and the Sephardic Ultra-Orthodoxy represented by the Shas party. All three groups stress the need for conformity to sacred texts – the Torah and the Talmud – and to a moral code based on these texts. These groups are also politically active. But they are called fundamentalist (in English) by their critics, not their supporters (see Lustick 1988; Sprinzak 1991). Some scholars would argue that this usage again illustrates the polemical character of the term "fundamentalist" when used outside its original Protestant context.

To understand these Israeli movements, a brief overview of Jewish recent history is needed. In the late nineteenth century some Jews concluded that the end to anti-Semitism required the creation of a Jewish state. Those who came to this conclusion were largely secular intellectuals like Theodor Herzl (1860–1904), the Viennese journalist and playwright who is often called "the father" of the modern Zionist movement.

Ever since the fall of Jerusalem's Second temple in 70 CE, most Jews had lived in the Diaspora, that is, lived dispersed from the Land of Israel (*Eretz Israel*). During their prolonged "exile" (*galut*), Jews all over the world had prayed daily for the coming of the Jewish Messiah, who would bring the Jews back to the land promised to them by God and would deliver them from their Gentile oppressors. Zionism secularized this traditional messianic theme. Instead of waiting for God and the Messiah to bring the Jews back to Israel, Zionists argued that Jews should take it upon themselves to return to the Land of Israel and recreate a Jewish society there after two millennia of dispersion. For the secular Herzl, the religious and messianic aspect of this "ingathering of the exiles" was irrelevant. The point was to create a Jewish state where the Jew would no longer be at the mercy of the Gentile (see Elon 1975).

Most Orthodox Rabbis initially condemned Zionism exactly on the grounds that it involved humans doing what only God and the Messiah were to do. In traditional Judaism the return to the Land of Israel was inseparable from the messianic redemption of the people of Israel. For humans to return to this land and create a state was to defy God's will and thereby postpone the real redemption and the real ingathering of the exiles. Moreover, Herzl and most of the early Zionist leaders were seeking to establish a secular rather than a Torah-based state.

In referring to Orthodox Judaism, one should distinguish between the "modern Orthodox" and the "Ultra-Orthodox." The modern Orthodox insist on strict conformity to Jewish law, but they have nonetheless devised ways to participate in modern society in both the Diaspora and Israel. The Ultra-Orthodox insist on strict separation from Gentiles and from those Jews who do not follow Jewish law as strictly as they do. (This emphasis on separation is reminiscent of Christian fundamentalists.) Hostility toward Zionism prevailed among both modern Orthodox and Ultra-Orthodox rabbis in the late nineteenth and early twentieth centuries, though it almost disappeared among the modern Orthodox when the Holocaust appeared to confirm the Zionist argument that Jews could be safe only in their own state.

Some modern Orthodox rabbis sought to legitimate Orthodox participation in the Zionist movement by severing it from the idea of the Messiah. Rabbi Isaac Jacob Reines (1839–1915), who founded the Mizrahi religious Zionist movement in 1902, agreed with the Ultra-Orthodox that Jews should passively await the coming of the Messiah but, unlike the Ultra-Orthodox, argued that the Zionist settlement of the land of Israel had nothing to do with the future messianic redemption of the Jews and thus did not constitute heretical defiance of God's will (see Ravitzky 1996, pp. 33–4). This view was soon displaced by the radically different view that Zionism was itself part of the gradual messianic redemption of the Jewish people and the Land of Israel. Thus the secular Zionists were doing the work of God and the Messiah but did not yet know it. This argument was made by Rabbi Avraham Kook (1865–1935) and has remained a basic theme in religious Zionism.

Religious Zionists are usually referred to as the "national religious" (*datim le'umim*) in Hebrew – a term that reflects the fusion of modern Orthodoxy with nationalism that has been the distinctive feature of religious Zionism. Unlike the Ultra-Orthodox, religious Zionists have generally been willing to cooperate with the far more numerous secular Zionists who were primarily responsible for creating the modern state of Israel. From the establishment of the modern state of Israel in 1948 until 1977, there was a close relationship between the religious Zionist parties and the Labor party that dominated Israeli politics during this period. Traditionally, the National Religious Party and its predecessors concerned themselves

modern vs. ultra orthodox

with domestic religious issues such as observance of Shabbat, and when they took positions on foreign affairs, they often took moderate and even "dovish" positions.

The Six Day War of 1967 awakened the dormant messianic dimension of religious Zionism. Many religious Zionists saw the Israeli victory as a miracle and as a major step toward the redemption of the Jewish people. East Jerusalem, the Temple Mount, and Judea – the heart of ancient Israel – were now once again in Jewish hands. To return any of this land to the Arabs would be to defy God's plan for the redemption of the Jewish people. The religious Zionists who felt this way – and not all did – began to settle in the territories occupied – or, as they saw it, liberated – in the Six Day War.   *settlements*

The militant religious Zionists in the vanguard of the settlement movement formed a movement called *Gush Emunim*, or "the Bloc of the Faithful." They clashed with the more traditional, often rather dovish, religious Zionists who still led the National Religious Party in the 1960s and 1970s. These dovish religious Zionists did believe that God had given all the Land of Israel to the Jews, but they believed that making peace and thus saving Jewish lives took priority over retaining the land. For the militant settlers, however, settling the land and preventing the Israeli Government from withdrawing from it took priority over anything else.

Militant religious Zionists do advocate the creation of a state based on strict conformity to what they consider the laws of God. But their political activities have focused primarily on settling and retaining the land won in 1967 rather than on creating a society based on strict conformity to religious law. While militant religious Zionism does have a fundamentalist dimension, it is also important to remember its nationalist dimension and its roots in the Revisionist Zionist idea that force must be used to fight the inherently anti-Semitic Gentile. Indeed, the religious Zionists tap some basic themes in mainstream Zionism, notably, the idea that the goal of Zionism is to create a Jew who will never submit to oppression. For militant religious Zionists, this conviction dictates a return to the Judaism of the Maccabees, who fought Hellenism in the second century BCE much as religious Zionists fight decadent secularism today (see Sprinzak 1991; Munson 2003).

The Ultra-Orthodox are often referred to in Hebrew as *Haredim*, or "those who tremble" in the presence of God because they are "God-fearing." Unlike the modern Orthodox, who are virtually all religious Zionists, the Haredim continue to reject Zionism, in principle at least, as a blasphemous attempt to bring about the return of the Jews to the Land of Israel by human means when God intended the return to be effected by the Messiah. In practice, this rejection of Zionism has resulted in a variety of different political positions, ranging from that of the politically insignificant Neturei Karta movement, which refuses to have anything to do with the state of Israel, to Haredi parties that sometimes determine which of Israel's major parties gets to govern (see Heilman and Friedman 1991). Israel's political system forces the major parties to make concessions to small parties in order to obtain the support of a majority of the 120 members of the Knesset, the unicameral legislature.

One should distinguish between the Ashkenazi Haredim, or the Ultra-Orthodox of Eastern European origin, and the Ultra-Orthodox of Middle Eastern origin. Unlike the religious Zionists, whose political activities since 1967 have focused primarily on settling and retaining the territories occupied in the Six Day War, the Haredi political parties have continued to concentrate on obtaining funding for their community and on enforcing conformity to their interpretation of Jewish religious law in such issues as observance of the Sabbath, conversion, dietary laws, and what the Haredim view as the desecration of the dead by archeologists. Since the Six Day War, however, most Ashkenazi Haredim have tended to support the hardline position of the militant religious Zionists on "land-for-peace" despite their continued theoretical opposition to Zionism and to the state that it has produced.

The Ashkenazi Haredim, who have traditionally withdrawn from surrounding Gentile society in the Diaspora, continue to separate themselves from mainstream Israeli society. Yet in the last few decades they have become increasingly aggressive in trying to incorporate their moral code into Israeli law. Like Christian fundamentalists in the United States, they have been torn between the desire to withdraw from society and the desire to reform it.

The third major form of Jewish militant Orthodoxy in Israel often called fundamentalist is represented by the Shas party. *Shas* is an acronym for "Sephardi Guardians of the Torah" in Hebrew. Although the term *Sephardim* originally referred to Jews of Spanish and Portuguese origin, it has come to be used to refer to Jews of Middle Eastern origin.

The Sephardim are less educated and earn less than the Ashkenazim, and many believe that Israelis of European origin discriminate against them. In addition to celebrating Sephardic identity and advocating strict conformity to God's laws, Shas provides schools and other social services for poor Sephardim. In this respect Shas is similar to some Islamic movements (see Hirschberg 1999).

Shas can be considered fundamentalist insofar as it consistently supports legislation to enforce strict conformity to Jewish religious law. But much of its popular support is rooted in the frustration, resentment, and even rage of those Jews of Middle Eastern origin who believe they are discriminated against by the Ashkenazi elite of European origin. Most Sephardim who vote for Shas do not themselves conform to the strict moral code advocated by the party. Thus Shas serves as a reminder that the movements commonly called fundamentalist often owe their political success to social grievances no less than to purely religious ones.

Islamic Fundamentalism

The subject of Islamic fundamentalism, or "Islamism," has attracted much attention ever since Iran's Islamic revolution of 1978–79. It is sometimes argued that all Muslims believe the Quran to be the literal and inerrant text of the word of God, in which case all Muslims can be considered fundamentalists in this sense. In fact, not all Muslims view the Quran this way or assume that they must conform to all the rules in it. More important, most Muslims are not ideologically committed to the idea of a state based on Islamic religious law. Only those who are should be called Islamic fundamentalists, or Islamists. Because of the Christian origins of the word "fundamentalism" and its association with fanaticism and terrorism, most scholars prefer the more neutral term "Islamism" to "Islamic fundamentalism."

In referring to the Islamic movements commonly called fundamentalist, one should bear in mind that they emerged in radically different contexts than the movements in the United States and Israel with which they are usually compared. The United States and Israel have technologically advanced, industrial economies, with democracy firmly entrenched. By contrast, the Islamic world is largely a part of the Third World, and some of the grievances that fuel Islamic fundamentalism are found in much of the rest of the Third World – notably, foreign domination and widespread economic hardship. Economic development in most of the Islamic world has not kept pace with population growth. The result has been widespread unemployment and underemployment, especially among the educated young, the very people who have been the most active in militant Islamic movements (see Munson 1988).

At the core of Islamic fundamentalism is the argument that success is a sign of God's favor and failure a sign of God's wrath. This logic is also present in conservative Christianity and Judaism. Islamic fundamentalists apply the argument as follows. When Muslims obeyed God's commandments, he enabled them to create great empires and civilizations. When they ceased to obey divine law, they became weak, and God allowed the infidels of Europe, and later of the United States and Israel, to subjugate them.

In the nineteenth and early twentieth centuries most of the Islamic world was indeed conquered and colonized by the European powers. But by the mid 1950s most predominantly Muslim countries were independent. Still, the Islamic world remained weak and underdeveloped. Muslims saw the establishment of Israel in 1948 as among the most obvious examples of their weakness vis-à-vis the West. The fundamentalists argue that if Muslims once again obey the laws of God, they will once again be strong enough to defeat not only Israel but also all the Western powers. This argument has been made, for example, by the Ayatollah Khomeini, the leader of Iran's Islamic revolution of 1978–9:

If the Muslim states and peoples had relied on Islam and its inherent capabilities and powers instead of depending on the East (the Soviet Union) and the West, and if they had placed the enlightened and liberating precepts of the Quran before their eyes and put them into practice, then they would not today be captive slaves of the Zionist aggressors, terrified victims of the American Phantoms, and toys in the hands of the accommodating policies of the satanic Soviet Union. It is the disregard of the noble Quran by the Islamic countries that has brought the Islamic community to this difficult situation full of misfortunes and reversals and placed its fate in the hands of the imperialism of the left and the right. (al-Khumaini 1977, pp. 156–7)

The resentment of Western domination that Khomeini articulates in this passage pervades Islamist rhetoric, which often has a nationalistic dimension despite the Islamists' formal condemnation of nationalism (see Munson 2004). To characterize Islamic fundamentalism as simply a rejection of secular modernity is to underestimate the extent to which Islamist movements articulate grievances once articulated by secular nationalists. Militant Islamic movements were politically significant in most Muslim countries in the late twentieth century primarily because the secular parties that had formerly articulated social and nationalistic grievances had lost credibility as a result of the failures of socialism and secular nationalism. Islamist movements also obtain some support by providing social services – schools, food for the poor, health care – that are more effective than those provided by governments (see Roy 2003).

There are considerable differences among the Islamic movements usually called fundamentalist. Many resort to violence; some do not. Some are quite radical and borrow many ideas from Marxism and socialism; others are economically conservative. Some insist that they are willing to participate in democratic political systems; others condemn democracy as un-Islamic. Most invoke anti-Semitic conspiracy theories to explain the problems of the Islamic world (see Munson 1996).

All Islamic fundamentalists insist on conformity to a code of conduct based on sacred scripture. They also insist that religion cannot be separated from politics and that religion covers all aspects of life. Like most other fundamentalists, they generally have a Manichaean world view. Messianism, which plays an important role in both Christian and Jewish fundamentalism, has been less important in most late twentieth-century Sunni fundamentalism. The abortive Mahdist (messianic) revolt in Saudi Arabia in 1979 was a throwback to the messianic revolts of past centuries and was not at all typical of the Islamic fundamentalist movements of the late twentieth century.

Puritanical revivalist movements calling for a return to the pristine Islam of the Prophet Muhammad have occurred periodically throughout Islamic history. But under the impact of Western domination in the

nineteenth and twentieth centuries, they began to take on a new polemical, apologetic character. Muslim reformists like Muhammad 'Abduh and
Jamal al-Din al-'Afghani stressed that a "return" to the rationalist Islam
which they portrayed as the pristine Islam of the Prophet Muhammad was
necessary if the Muslims were to overcome European domination. This
argument was later pushed in a more militant and fundamentalist
direction.

Conclusion

The Marty–Appleby model clearly does not fit all of the Christian, Jewish,
and Islamic movements usually called fundamentalist. Contrary to Marty
and Appleby, the mainstream Christian Right and the Orthodox movements in Israel have not sought "to replace existing structures with a
comprehensive system emanating from religious principles and embracing law, polity, society, economy, and culture" (Marty and Appleby 1991,
p. 824). One could argue that they would if they could, but their actual
agendas have remained far more limited and pragmatic. Marty and
Appleby's emphasis on the inherently political and militant character of
fundamentalism also ignores major differences among the various movements that they call fundamentalist. Their notion that fundamentalism is
above all a revolt against "modernity" overlooks the fact that many of the
movements they call "fundamentalist" are fueled, in part at least, by social
and nationalistic grievances that have nothing to do with modernity.
Many of these movements do have a fundamentalist dimension in that
they insist on strict conformity to sacred scriptures and a moral code
ostensibly based on them. But this fundamentalist impulse is not equally
significant in all cases, and it is often intertwined with other factors that
have nothing to do with religion.

It is wrong to assume that religious belief cannot induce people to
engage in political action. Yet it is also wrong to assume that religious
belief is necessarily the prime factor inducing people to join movements
that have a religious dimension. The relative weight of secular and religious grievances must be determined case by case.

Bibliography

al-Khumayni, Ruh Allah. *Durus Fi Al-Jihad Wa-Al-Rafd: Yusatiruha Al-Imam
Al-Khumayni Khilal Harakatihi Al-Nidaliyah Al-Ra'Idah*. No place of publica-
tion or publisher given. Probably published in Beirut in 1977.
Almond, Gabriel Abraham, R. Scott Appleby, and Emmanuel Sivan. *Strong

Religion: The Rise of Fundamentalisms around the World. Chicago: University of Chicago Press, 2003.

Ault, James M. Jr. *Spirit and Flesh: Life in a Fundamentalist Baptist Church*. New York: Knopf, 2004.

Berger, Peter L. "Secularism in Retreat," *National Interest* 46 (Winter 1996/97): 3–12.

Bruce, Steve. "Fundamentalism and Political Violence: The Case of Paisley and Ulster Evangelicals," *Religion* 31 (2001): 387–405.

Buckley, Anthony D., and Mary Catherine Kenney. *Negotiating Identity: Rhetoric, Metaphor, and Social Drama in Northern Ireland*. Washington, DC: Smithsonian Institution Press, 1995.

Elon, Amos. *Herzl*. New York: Holt, Rinehart and Winston, 1975.

Harris, Jay M. "'Fundamentalism': Objections from a Modern Jewish Historian," in *Fundamentalism and Gender*, ed. John S. Hawley. New York: Oxford University Press, 1994, pp. 137–73.

Heilman, Samuel C., and Menachem Friedman. "Religious Fundamentalism and Religious Jews: The Case of the Haredim," in *Fundamentalisms Observed*, eds. Martin E. Marty and R. Scott Appleby. Chicago: University of Chicago Press, 1991, pp. 197–264.

Hirschberg, Peter. *The World of Shas*. New York: Institute on American Jewish-Israeli Relations of the American Jewish Committee, 1999.

Juergensmeyer, Mark. "Why Religious Nationalists Are Not Fundamentalists," *Religion* 23 (1993): 85–92.

Lustick, Ian. *For the Land and the Lord: Jewish Fundamentalism in Israel*. New York: Council on Foreign Relations, 1988.

Marsden, George M. *Understanding Fundamentalism and Evangelicalism*. Grand Rapids, MI: Eerdmans, 1991.

Marsh, Charles. *God's Long Summer: Stories of Faith and Civil Rights*. Princeton, NJ: Princeton University Press, 1997.

Martin, William C. *With God on Our Side: The Rise of the Religious Right in America*. 1st edn. New York: Broadway Books, 1996.

Marty, Martin E., and R. Scott Appleby, eds. *Fundamentalisms Observed*. Chicago: University of Chicago Press, 1991.

Marty, Martin E., and R. Scott Appleby, eds. *Fundamentalisms and Society: Reclaiming the Sciences, the Family, and Education*. Chicago: University of Chicago Press, 1993a.

Marty, Martin E., and R. Scott Appleby, eds. *Fundamentalisms and the State: Remaking Politics, Economies, and Militance*. Chicago: University of Chicago Press, 1993b.

Marty, Martin E., and R. Scott Appleby, eds. *Accounting for Fundamentalisms: The Dynamic Character of Movements*. Chicago: University of Chicago Press, 1994.

Marty, Martin E., and R. Scott Appleby, eds. *Fundamentalisms Comprehended*. Chicago: University of Chicago Press, 1995.

Munson, Henry. *Islam and Revolution in the Middle East*. New Haven, CT: Yale University Press, 1988.

Munson, Henry. "Not all Crustaceans Are Crabs: Reflections on the Comparative Study of Fundamentalism and Politics," *Contention* 4 (1995): 151–66.

Munson, Henry. "Intolerable Tolerance: Western Academia and Islamic Fundamentalism," *Contention* 5 (1996): 99–117.

Munson, Henry. " 'Fundamentalism' Ancient and Modern," *Daedalus* (2003): 31–41.

Munson, Henry. "Lifting the Veil: Understanding the Roots of Islamic Militancy," *Harvard International Review* 25 (2004): 20–23.

Ravitzky, Aviezer. *Messianism, Zionism, and Jewish Religious Radicalism.* Chicago: University of Chicago Press, 1996.

Raychaudhuri, Tapan. "Shadows of the Swastika: Historical Reflections on the Politics of Hindu Communalism," *Contention* 4 (1995): 141–62.

Ribuffo, Leo P. *The Old Christian Right: The Protestant Far Right from the Great Depression to the Cold War.* Philadelphia: Temple University Press, 1983.

Roy, Sara. "Hamas and the Transformation(s) of Political Islam in Palestine," *Current History* 102 (2003): 13–20.

Sprinzak, Ehud. *The Ascendance of Israel's Radical Right.* New York: Oxford University Press, 1991.

Thomas, Cal, and Ed Dobson. *Blinded by Might: Can the Religious Right Save America?* Grand Rapids, MI: Zondervan, 1999.

Wallis, Jim. *God's Politics: Why the Right Gets It Wrong and the Left Doesn't Get It.* San Francisco: HarperSanFrancisco, 2005.

Weaver, Mary Jo, and R. Scott Appleby, eds. *Being Right: Conservative Catholics in America.* Bloomington: Indiana University Press, 1995.

Weyrich, Paul. "Comment on George Marsden's 'The Religious Right: A Historical Overview'," in *No Longer Exiles: The Religious New Right in American Politics*, ed. M. Cromartie. Washington, DC: Ethics and Public Policy Center, 1993, pp. 25–6.

— Chapter 14 —

Heaven and Hell

Jeffrey Burton Russell

Heaven is being in enduring joy. Hell is being in enduring misery. Heaven and hell are mutually exclusive. Those generalizations about the other life – a term that encompasses both heaven and hell – hold true for a wide variety of cultures. On a deep level they are eternalizations of the good or evil characters that people form for themselves in this life. Belief in good or evil is an almost universal concern of religions or "world views."

Heaven is characterized by joy, peace, rest, comfort, beauty, truth, happiness, communion. Hell is characterized by lack of joy. Heaven is where God's presence is most immediate. Hell is where God's presence is missing. Philosophically, God and heaven are Absolute Being. Evil and hell are close to Absolute Nonbeing. Hell is the endless, agonized longing for the reality of heaven.

Heaven and hell are usually thought of as places, but they need not exist geographically or astronomically. Nor need they exist in time, either past or future. If existence is taken to mean occupying an area of space and time, they do not in fact exist. But they certainly do exist as powerful ideas with great influence in the past and in the present, and what people believe is true usually has greater influence on their actions than what may actually be true. Another way that the other life exists is that it – especially heaven – has a perennial resonance in the depths of people's spirituality and psychology. In that sense heaven and also hell are part of the human condition. Humans can create their own heaven or hell.

At the same time the most important way that the other life can exist *is* as objective reality. Does it have external referents beyond the human mind? This chapter does not give an answer but does suggest that there are meaningful ways of investigating the question. Although materialism and scientism claim that anything that cannot be measured in space and time does not exist, that assumption is *a priori* and unprovable. Most people and most cultures have affirmed the existence of realities distinct from space and time, the central one being God, nirvana, or whatever other name one calls Absolute Reality. Some Jewish, Christian, Muslim, and Buddhist thinkers have also conceived of God and heaven as *beyond* Being. Those who define "existence" as pertaining only to material particles and forces define the other life out of existence. But there is no need to define "existence" that way. To avoid this semantic difficulty, we can use the word "subsist" instead of "exist." We can, then, say that Saturn and your shirt *exist* but that God and the other life *subsist*.

If the other life indeed subsists, how can it be studied? After all, no one has been there and back. But in fact there are ways of studying the other life. They include reports of individual human experience; philosophical and theological explorations; poetry, music, and artworks; comparative religions; psychology and sociology as to the function of belief in another life in various societies or as to what social circumstances incline people to believe; statistics as to how many persons believe in what; linguistics in terms of the realities of metaphor; history in terms of their development in civilizations; and spirituality in terms of what depths of the soul are moved by these beliefs.

To list all possible ways of studying the other life would require an encyclopedia. One must choose the best approaches. Because the subject lends itself to much abstraction, it is best first displayed in human experience. Beyond that, the best is a combination of the comparative with the historical approach.

Monotheism

The concepts of heaven and hell appear in most religions, but the concepts have had the greatest influence in the three great monotheistic religions: Judaism, Christianity, and Islam. The reason is that monotheism logically requires facing the problem of evil. Monotheism posits a God who is all powerful and all good, yet the world that we experience is not what one would expect from this kind of deity. Dualistic religions avoid the dilemma by positing two gods, one evil and the other good. Polytheistic religions usually assume a highest deity transcending various lesser ones, which take on the onus of doing good or ill. Religions beyond theism, notably Buddhism, assume ultimate harmony beyond apparent ills. Humanistic and materialistic world views assume the ability of humans to better themselves. Postmodernist world views deny that good and evil exist other than in the eye of the beholder. Since the monotheistic religions show the most strain between good and evil, and therefore between heaven and hell, it is helpful to concentrate on them.

Hell

Let us take a few examples. In ancient Egypt the god Horus threatens eternal punishment to his father's enemies:

> [You] shall be hacked in pieces, [you] shall nevermore have your being, your souls shall be destroyed. . . . My father . . . hath smitten you, he hath cut up your bodies, he hath hacked in pieces your spirits and your souls, and hath scattered in pieces your shadows. . . . [You] shall be cast down headlong into the pits of fire, and [you] shall not escape therefrom, and [you] shall not be able to flee from the flames which are in the serpent. (Bernstein 1993, pp. 16–17)

In the ancient story of Gilgamesh his companion, Enkidu, sees hell in a dream: "To the road which none leave who have entered it, On the road from which there is no way back, To the house wherein the dwellers are bereft of light, Where dust is their fare and clay their food" (Zaleski 1987, p. 15). The Psalms pronounce: "Let burning coals fall upon [the wicked]! Let them be flung into pits, no more to rise!" (Psalm 140:10). Job expects "the land of gloom and deep darkness, the land of gloom and chaos, where light is like darkness" (Job 10:21–22).

In the eleventh-century Christian "Vision of Tondal," Tondal visits hell, where the Devil "blew out and scattered the souls of the damned throughout all the regions of hell. . . . And when he breathed back in, he sucked all the souls back and, when they had fallen into the sulphurous smoke of his maw, he chewed them up" (Russell 1984, p. 215). In the *Inferno* Dante cannot even describe the horror of the lowest pit of hell, which is ice:

> O reader, do not ask of me how I
> grew faint and frozen then – I cannot write it;
> all words would fall far short of what it is. (Dante 1980, p. 294)

In the sixteenth century the English dramatist Christopher Marlowe's Satan expresses the interiority of hell:

Hell hath no limits, nor is circumscrib'd
In one selfe place: but where we are is hell,
And where hell is there we must ever be. . . .
All places shall be hell that are not heaven. (Russell 1986, p. 65)

Heaven

Visions of heaven are equally plentiful and diverse. A Tibetan describes a
blessed state: "First of all there will appear to you, swifter than lightning,
the luminous splendour of the colourless light of Emptiness, and that
will surround you on all sides. . . . Try to submerge yourself in that
light. . . . Recognize that the boundless Light of this true Reality is your
own true self" (Zaleski and Zaleski 2000, p. 49). In India the city of the
god Indra is:

> delightful with its sumptuous woods and pleasure-gardens . . . filled
> with crooning birds in pairs and drunken bees humming, and with
> celestial trees. . . . [T] here are lotus pools there. . . . [The city has] doors
> encased in sheeted gold and . . . gateways of crystal. . . . In the streets
> the wind wafts the perfume of the wreaths of fresh-blown white lilies
> fallen from the tresses of the celestial damsels. (Zaleski and Zaleski 2000,
> p. 219)

The Hebrew prophet Isaiah "saw the Lord sitting on a throne, high and
lofty; and the hem of his robe filled the temple. Seraphs . . . called to [one]
another and said: 'Holy, holy, holy is the Lord of hosts'" (Isaiah 6:1–3).
In the Book of Revelation an angel shows John "the holy city Jerusalem
coming down out of heaven from God. It has the glory of God and a radi-
ance like a very rare jewel" (Revelation 21:10–11). The third-century
Rabbi Joshua ben Levi visits Paradise: "Through . . . it flow four rivers, one
of olive oil, the other of balsam, the third of wine, and the fourth of
honey . . . and in the midst the Tree of Life" (Russell 1997, p. 111). The
fourth-century Syrian Ephraim saw a tree "whose floor is strewn with
flowers. Who has ever seen the joy at the heart of a tree, with fruits of
every taste within reach of your hand. . . . You are anointed with the sap
of the tree and inhale its perfume" (Russell 1997, pp. 13–14).

In the seventh century an angel reveals the joys of paradise to
Muhammad: "for them shall be two gardens . . . abounding in branches
. . . therein two fountains of running water . . . therein of every fruit two
kinds . . . reclining upon couches lined with brocade . . . therein maidens
restraining their glances . . . lovely as rubies, beautiful as coral . . . green,
green pastures" (Zaleski and Zaleski 2000, pp. 389–90).

Hadewijch of Antwerp, a twelfth-century spiritual writer, believed that
in heavenly love you "burn so blazingly in your oneness in all your
being . . . that for you will be nothing else than God alone. . . . [If you live

in this] being without ceasing, *the house of Jacob is a fire*" (Emerson and Feiss 2000, p. 129). Furthermore:

> With what wondrous sweetness the loved one and the Beloved dwell one in the other, and how they penetrate each other in such a way that neither of the two distinguishes himself from the other. But they abide in one another in fruition, mouth in mouth, heart in heart, body in body, and soul in soul. (Russell 1997, p. 146)

In the *Paradiso* Dante is at last invited to look directly upon God, the First Love, but only "so far as the divine glory permits," for language cannot describe the essence of heaven. He cannot remember what God did grant him to see, but "I do remember that my vision bore the intensity of the Divine ray until it joined Infinite Being and Good Itself. Ah, overflowing grace though which I could presume to fix my gaze on the Eternal Light so fully that I used up all my sight" (Russell 1997, pp. 183–4). As-Suyuti, a fifteenth-century Egyptian, reports that Allah touched him between the shoulders, "whereat I experienced such a sweetness, so pleasant a perfume, so delightful a coolness. . . . Then was I filled with joy, my eyes were refreshed, and such delight and happiness took hold of me" (Zaleski and Zaleski 2000, p. 156).

Concept and Language

These samples of experiences, while all expressing the notions of joy and torment, indicate a variety of concepts. Behind variety of concept lies variety in language. No foreign words carry the exact meanings of English "heaven" and "hell." In English the words have a history. The first appearance of "hell" is in Old English in 725, where *hel* or *helle* means the shadowy land of the dead. As the English were Christianized, the word was applied as a translation of the New Testament Greek *Geenna*, a place of torment for evil doers. Likewise Old English *heofon*, also appearing about 725, originally meant "the sky" and later was Christianized to mean where God dwells.

The conceptual differences are even greater. *Where* are heaven and hell? Heaven is a "place" of joy and so the dwelling place of God or the gods or other good spirits. It is also a place where good humans "go" and congregate with love and delight. Heaven is both theocentric – being blissfully united with Absolute Reality – and sociocentric – being with loved ones. The community is often the vehicle of salvation. Hell, by contrast, is where the evil spirit or spirits live imprisoned and torment the wicked. Hell is usually under the earth, even at the center of the earth. In some philosophies the material nature of hell is contrasted to the spiritual nature of heaven. Common metaphors for the other life imply an endless circling down into narrower and darker narcissism and ruin, or, on the heavenly side, a dynamic opening forever outward into ever greater life and joy. Thus the other life may be viewed as either static or dynamic.

Time

When are heaven and hell? In the three great monotheistic Western religions heaven and hell are usually imagined as an "afterlife," but that notion can be misleading exactly because it implies that they exist in space and time. Sometimes the other life is at the end of time, sometimes at the end of our own personal lives, sometimes both. Death itself is perceived in different ways, usually as the end of our earthly life but sometimes as a transition. Death can be morally neutral, or a great horror, or a desirable moment of passing to another life. Distinctions are sometimes made between the natural death of the earthly body and the unnatural death – damnation – reserved for the wicked.

The other life is usually permanent: the hell or heaven one makes for oneself is both in this life and thereafter. One's state may be fixed from earlier ages, by gods, fate, or the karma of one's previous lives. Some religions, particularly Buddhism, view either state as transitory: one may need to suffer in this life or in the other life (or lives) before obtaining the permanent surcease of care known as nirvana. Other views see heaven as eternal but see suffering as transitory. In Christianity a moment (or a "time") is necessary before one can enter the presence of God. That idea is concretized in medieval religion as purgatory.

Heaven can be seen as a pristine original "time" that we lost before the incarnation of our spirits, before the creation of humanity, or at the beginning of human history. The ancient Romans believed in the pristine kingdom of the god Saturn, a golden age at the beginning of humankind. The monotheistic religions postulate an initial paradise, a happy garden of joy, from which humanity was expelled through its own fault. In these religions this initial paradise can be conflated with the ultimate heaven, though theologians and poets usually seek to distinguish between them.

Good and Evil

Who, then, experiences heaven and who hell? In some societies, such as those of ancient Rome and Confucian China, one strives for civic virtue, which encompasses wisdom, justice, mercy, friendship, statesmanship, and bravery. In other societies kindness and love are more valued. Hell is either the lack of these virtues or their opposites: selfishness, cruelty, injustice, hardness of heart, weakness in statecraft, and cowardice. Hell is a state in which no friendship can exist. Though Buddhism envisions an ultimate state of being transcending good and evil, there are temporary heavens and hells in this life or in other lives that we experience before nirvana.

The other life has been perceived as bodily, as spiritual, or as both combined. Whenever the body is involved, the other life is either a perfection and extrapolation of earthly goods, needs, and wishes (heaven) or the complete lack of all of them (hell). Though some religions have held that only the spirit subsists in the other life, it has always been necessary to convey images of the other life through metaphor. Heaven and hell can be metaphors for radical good and evil.

Radical good is often expressed in terms of wisdom, mercy, generosity, and compassion, which produces happiness, harmony, fulfillment, transformation, integration, wholeness, and union with ultimate reality. An action is considered good, evil, or neutral depending on whether it is consonant with these qualities. Actions that deliberately inflict suffering on other sentient beings are deemed evil by most societies. Human beings – and often gods – are a mixture of good and evil, but those who set their course consistently in the direction of rejecting good are considered evil. Nature, nurture, fate, the gods, or free will, or all together, determine a being's character, although an act of true free will cannot by definition have a cause. Most societies assume some degree of responsibility – some freedom of choice – on the part of humans and spirits, and that human choice determines whether one is "in heaven" or "in hell."

"Nature" religions or "polytheistic" religions have been so varied that only a few observations are possible here. Beliefs in a different, greater reality than that of our everyday life appeared at least as early as the Neolithic period. Shamans, oracles, and dreams could be consulted in order to be in touch with that other life. The spirits of the dead remain with us or else enter into that other life, where we will eventually join them. Burials often included artifacts that the dead person would be able to use in the other life. In ancient Egypt cosmic order and justice (*ma'at*) were temporarily distorted by human evil. The *ka*, or the spirit of the dead person, was believed to descend into the underworld to be judged by the gods. The unjust, it was believed, would be tormented by scorching heat, whereas those living in accordance with *ma'at* would rise into the eternal realm of the gods. Ancient Mesopotamia emphasized hell more than heaven. The dead were believed to be doomed to unending gloom and wretchedness in the darkness beneath the earth. In early Greco-Roman religion the dead were believed to descend to the underworld governed by the god Hades. Originally a pale, shadowy land, Hades eventually was transformed into a pit of torment for wrongdoers. The spirits of heroes, however, rose to the Elysian Fields. Some Greek philosophers, notably Plato (427–327 BCE), argued for the immortality of the soul (a combination of basic life force with human intelligence). Cicero (106–43 BCE), the

Roman philosopher and lawyer, saw Elysium as a reward for those who had served the Roman state.

Vedic Hinduism (1500–1000 BCE) held that the dead, retaining their personal consciousness, go to a lush green place where they hear beautiful music. Those more devout dwell closer to the gods. Later the Hindu Upanishads (700–100 BCE) taught that heaven is a temporary state. True happiness consists of being freed from the illusion that this earthly life is real. Lacking a hell, the Upanishads condemn wrongdoers to cycles of reincarnation until they finally purify themselves. Then, in samadhi, consciousness of self disappears, reabsorbed into the unbounded allness of being as a drop of water merges with the sea.

Taoism (beginning about 600 BCE), originally a syncretistic religion, became increasingly philosophical, denying the existence of any world other than this one, a view that influenced Confucius (Kung Fu-Tzu, about 500 BCE). According to both Taoism and Confucianism, one achieves, or fails to achieve, harmony among self, family, state, and cosmos in this life. In Buddhism wrong arises from failure to perceive the ultimate truth that human beings have no "self." Individuals do not have souls except as part of the world soul. To be caught in the maya, or illusion, that one's self is real is to be trapped in the samsara, on cyclical flux, of reincarnations. One's actions in this life improve or worsen future lives. Temporary heavens and hells may exist, but only as transitions between lives. The "pure land," with its beautiful meadows, lakes, rivers, music, and ease, is only a prelude to true enlightenment, which ends all concerns, desires, and fears in nirvana, or the complete merging with the cosmic reality beyond human comprehension.

Dualistic world views were common in the Mediterranean and Near East in the late pre-Christian era. Two basic varieties occurred. One, associated with Platonism, espoused an opposition between matter and spirit. The more material a being, the less real and therefore the worse it is. Pure spirit is best, unformed matter worst. The other variety, associated with Iranian Mazdaism or Zoroastrianism, held to a dual opposition between warring spirits or deities. At death, it was believed, the wicked suffer terrible heat, biting cold, nauseating filth, and putrid stench in the underworld, whereas souls of the virtuous ascend toward the good spirit, Mazda, to the degree that they have transcended earthly concerns. To be trapped in a material body, it was assumed, is itself punishment. At the end of time Mazda would defeat the evil spirit Ahriman. Around 100 BCE, the two attitudes merged in Gnosticism. Most Gnostics and their successors, the Manicheans (third and fourth century CE), believe that the evil god is the lord and even the creator of matter. Matter is loathsome evil and the human body the vile prison for the human spirit, which longs to escape its bondage in order to return to the world of spirit.

Judaism and Christianity

In contrast to dualistic religions, Judaism and Christianity affirm the essential goodness of the creator, of matter in general, and of the human body in particular. Instead of a spiritual heaven, they assert the resurrection of the dead at the end of time – a resurrection like that of Jesus. But the belief is also to be found in earlier Hebrew religion: "Thus says the Lord God to these bones: I will cause breath to enter you, and you shall live. I will lay sinews on you. . . . I am going to open your graves . . . O my people; and I will bring you back to the Land of Israel" (Ezekiel 37:5–6, 12). In ancient Hebrew religion, which originated about the thirteenth century BCE, heaven was considered the dwelling place of the Lord exclusively and so was not a state that humans, with rare exceptions such as the prophet Elijah, could enter. The religion emphasized the salvation of the *qehel Adonai*, or the community faithful to the Covenant with the Lord, though individuals could also work out their characters in this earthly existence. For most humans, death would bring a shadowy existence in the underworld of Sheol, but at the end of time violators of the Covenant would suffer pains in hell (*Gehenna*), whereas those faithful to the Covenant would enjoy a blissful existence in the reign of God on earth.

Between 200 BCE and 100 CE, Hebrew religion more firmly emphasized the future reign of God on earth, which would be ushered in by the Messiah. All Jews would be resurrected in Jerusalem at the end of the world, where the faithful would enjoy the reign of God in their bodies. For all three great monotheistic religions, Jerusalem became the most powerful metaphor for heaven, the city of peace par excellence and the place where David, Jesus, and Muhammad alike trod. In the same period 200 BCE–100 CE, Jews developed a clearer picture of hell, which was believed to lie under the earth in darkness, ruled by Satan and his attendant demons.

The Christian New Testament expands the Jewish *qehel Adonai* into the idea of the salvation of all followers of God, whether Jews or Gentiles. The Christian New Testament follows the Hebrew Bible in asserting that salvation will come at the end of time, when the dead will rise in the very same, though glorified, body that they have had in this life. In the New Testament Jesus demonstrates several times that the dead rise. For nineteen centuries the ancient baptismal and creedal declaration of Christians has been: "I believe in the resurrection of the dead and the life of the world to come" (Nicene Creed, fourth century). Jesus, the Messiah, will reward those who form their character in love and will punish those who reject love. For Christians, as for Jews, heaven is the state of being in the presence of the Lord, hell the state of being in the anguish of the absence of that presence. Christ speaks of "eternal life" for those who love and of eternal banishment for those who do not.

Early Christian thought, based on Hebrew religion yet influenced by the widespread Platonism of the time, rather confusedly espoused both the resurrection of the body and the immortality of the "soul." For Christian theology from Paul onwards, "soul" did not mean pure spirit but rather a complete person composed of body and spirit together. Early Christian theologians faced the problem posed by the obvious delay between the death of an individual and the "general resurrection" at the end of time.

The Middle Ages

In popular Christian legends, story-telling, and picture-making, heaven and hell are often viewed as concrete physical places where immortal spirits go. As legend began to depart from theology as early as the third century, Hell began to be personified as one of the three evil powers – the others being Death and the Devil – that Christ had to overcome in order to save the world.

By the fifth century Christian theology of the other world was established but later varied only in detail among Western Catholic, Eastern Orthodox, and Protestant thinkers down into the seventeenth century. The theology is clearest in the work of Augustine of Hippo (354–430), for whom understanding and love fuse in heaven, surpassing all that we can know and love in this life. Humans are created with the longing to have our highest potential fulfilled, which happens in heaven, where we "rest and see, see and love, love and praise" forever (Russell 1997, p. 85). According to Augustine, the community of all lovers of God, or the communion of saints, is so blessed, yet individuals retain their conscious differentiation from other souls and from God. Resurrected body and soul are united in enjoyment of God and of one another. All of the blessed are equal in that all persons fulfill and perfect their own potential. For Augustine and other Christian theologians, damnation to hell is understood as God's judgment of the character of the person, not as God's intention. God created humanity good. Humans bent themselves through original sin, so that divine grace is needed to free them. Christ's suffering has freed them. Now they are free either to accept the goodness of our redeemed nature or to reject it. Heaven means being completely open to joy. Hell means being eternally closed to it. Just as our bodies in the other life are our own real bodies yet are even more real than our present bodies, so the fire of hell is real fire and is more real than earthly fire, having additional, eternal properties such as unquenchability. In heaven we will experience, in ascending order, the bodily vision, the imaginative vision, the spiritual vision, and the intellectual vision, the last being a direct cognition of God, which is impossible to experience in this life.

The classic poetic presentation of that theology is *The Divine Comedy* of Dante Alighieri (1265–1321). For Dante, the geographical and astronomical design of the cosmos is a metaphor of the real, ethical cosmos. Dante's cosmos is arranged in a series of concentric spheres, with the earth at the center and above it an orderly progression of spheres: the moon, Mercury, Venus, the sun, Mars, Jupiter, Saturn, and the fixed stars. Each sphere is wider and more luminous than the one it encircles. All are moved by the outermost, dimensionless sphere. That last sphere encloses the whole cosmos, but beyond it – beyond every "where" and every "when" – is the dwelling place of God. Dante's vision moved him up from sphere to brighter sphere, finally reaching the outermost sphere, where he pierced the shell of the cosmos and found himself in the eternal world, the glory of which, he wrote, could not fully be expressed, yet, once having been seen, draws us to it with unceasing love. For Dante, the essence of heaven is to broaden our vision, opening ourselves out to ever wider vistas of light, truth, and love. But when we are diverted by the illusion of self-importance, we sink downward and away from God, our vision turned within ourselves, drawn down, heavy, closed to reality, bound by ourselves to ourselves, shut in and shut off, shrouded in darkness and sightlessness, angry, hating, and isolated. Hell, like heaven, is composed of concentric circles, but the circles of hell narrow down, until in the lowest circle Satan is at the dead center, oppressed by the weight of the entire cosmos, stuck fast in the ice.

Medieval scholastic theology, drawing on Augustine and most famously represented by Thomas Aquinas (1225–74), held that heaven is the happy society of all the blessed, where all human desires for reality, goodness, and knowledge will be satisfied. Human beatitude is achieved not through wealth, fame, power, bodily pleasure, or any created good but only through the beatific vision. The beatific vision can be seen only by the intellect, and by the intellect only when divine grace has illuminated it. Even the illuminated intellect cannot understand God as he understands himself. Though the spirit may temporarily be separated from the body between our earthly death and our resurrection, the soul cannot be fulfilled until it is reunited with the body.

The leading sixteenth-century Protestant Reformers, Martin Luther and John Calvin, revived Augustine's predestinarian views. For Calvin, God predestines some to be saved and some to be damned. Other Protestant theologians argued that God predestines in the sense of knowing eternally who will be damned, but Calvin argued that God also predestines by *willing* the damned to be damned. Other Protestant Reformers believed that those who pursue worldly business are already under the power of the Devil.

Islam

Islam, founded in the 600s CE, is based upon the Qur'an and secondarily on the *hadith*, or the oral or written traditions of the practices and thoughts of Muhammad. For Muslims, the Qur'an was dictated to Muhammad word for word in Arabic by the Angel Gabriel, so that strict Muslims cannot admit of any translation or interpretation of the Scriptures. Nonetheless, many generations of Muslim scholars have used exegesis, philosophy, and metaphor as well as spirituality to understand their scripture. Traditional Islam affirms the judgment of individuals according to their deeds in this world and according to their loyalty to the teachings of the Prophet Muhammad, especially the teachings of compassion and generosity. Islam focuses on the formation of a just society on earth, but the Qur'an also asserts the resurrection of the body. At the end of time the resurrected dead will be judged and then divided into the damned and the faithful. The faithful will enter heaven, a better place than earth, yet a distinctly physical one in its attributes, including elaborate gardens, carpets, banquets, cooling drinks, sex, and other bodily comforts.

The Qur'an can be read metaphorically, and al-Ghazali in the twelfth century, along with other Muslims such as the medieval Sufis, sensed that the human mind is incapable of formulating concepts that, like heaven, are rooted in the ultimate and entire reality of the cosmos. For them, heaven meant being in the presence of the eternally just and merciful god, Allah. Islam, like Christianity, admits both divine predestination and human free will, and has as much difficulty reconciling the two. Generally, however, Muslims accept the individual's responsibility to submit to the authority of the Prophet. Some individuals, provoked by the conflict of worldly desires, reject the teachings of the Prophet and instead follow the way of apostasy, idolatry, avarice, quarreling, drinking, gluttony, or gambling. They will join Iblis, or Satan, in eternal fiery punishment.

Modernity

After reaching its peak in the early seventeenth century, Christian belief in the other life began to decline. The increasing diversity of theological views that characterized sectarian thought from the seventeenth century onwards confused and dissipated the established world view. Though conservatives continued to hold to the Scriptures and tradition, liberal theologians found the idea of the other life naive. In the late seventeenth century theology was challenged by natural science and natural philosophy. The philosopher David Hume (1711–76) argued that the only true knowledge is empirical, that religion is merely a projection of human fears, and that the existence of evil disproves the existence of a just and merciful God. To eighteenth- and nineteenth-century materialists, causation is mechanical, leaving no place for human free will and therefore none for good and evil and in turn for heaven and hell. An odd exception is Marxism, which though explicitly denying the other world, nonetheless has an analogue for heaven in the classless society that history will produce at the end of time. In the twenty-first century many people who consider themselves fully modern still believe in heaven and hell.

Bibliography

Bernstein, Alan. *The Formation of Hell: Death and Retribution in the Ancient and Early Christian Worlds.* Ithaca, NY: Cornell University Press, 1993.

Bynum, Caroline Walker. *The Resurrection of the Body in Western Christianity, 200–1336.* New York: Columbia University Press, 1995.

Clark, Stuart. *Thinking With Demons: The Idea of Witchcraft in Early Modern Europe.* Oxford: Oxford University Press, 1997.

Dante. *Inferno,* tr. Allen Mandelbaum. Berkeley: University of California Press, 1980.

Delumeau, Jean. *Que reste-t-il du paradis?* Paris: Fayard, 2000.

DeStefano, Anthony. *A Travel Guide to Heaven.* New York: Doubleday, 2003.

Emerson, Jan S., and Hugh Feiss. *Imagining Heaven in the Middle Ages.* New York: Garland, 2000.

Forsyth, Neil. *The Old Enemy: Satan and the Combat Myth.* Princeton, NJ: Princeton University Press, 1997.

Garland, Robert. *The Greek Way of Death.* Ithaca, NY: Cornell University Press, 1985.

Himmelfarb, Martha. *Ascent to Heaven in Jewish and Christian Apocalypses.* New York: Oxford University Press, 1993.

LeGoff, Jacques. *The Birth of Purgatory,* tr. Arthur Goldhammer. Chicago: Chicago University Press, 1984.

McDannell, Colleen, and Bernhard Lang. *Heaven: A History.* New Haven, CT: Yale University Press, 1988.

McGrath, Alister E. *A Brief History of Heaven.* Oxford: Blackwell, 2003.

Nickelsburg, George W. E., Jr. *Resurrection, Immortality, and Eternal Life in Intertestamental Judaism.* Cambridge, MA: Harvard University Press, 1972.

Pagels, Elaine. *The Origin of Satan.* New York: Random House, 1995.

Paterson, R. W. K. *Philosophy and the Belief in a Life After Death.* New York: St. Martin's Press, 1995.

Russell, Jeffrey Burton. *The Devil: Perceptions of Evil from Antiquity to Primitive Christianity.* Ithaca, NY: Cornell University Press, 1977.

Russell, Jeffrey Burton. *Satan: The Early Christian Tradition.* Ithaca, NY: Cornell University Press, 1981.

Russell, Jeffrey Burton. *Lucifer: The Devil in the Middle Ages*. Ithaca, NY: Cornell University Press, 1984.

Russell, Jeffrey Burton. *Mephistopheles: The Devil in the Modern World*. Ithaca, NY: Cornell University Press, 1986.

Russell, Jeffrey Burton. *The Prince of Darkness: Evil and the Power of Good in History*. Ithaca, NY: Cornell University Press, 1988.

Russell, Jeffrey Burton. *A History of Heaven: The Singing Silence*. Princeton, NJ: Princeton University Press, 1997.

Russell, Jeffrey Burton. *Paradise Mislaid: Heaven in Modern Thought*. New York: Oxford University Press, 2006.

Segal, Alan F. *Life After Death: A History of the Afterlife in Western Religion*. New York: Doubleday, 2004.

Walls, Jerry L. *Heaven: The Logic of Eternal Joy*. Oxford: Oxford University Press, 2002.

Wright, J. Edward. *The Early History of Heaven*. New York: Oxford University Press, 2000.

Zaleski, Carol. *Otherworld Journeys: Accounts of Near-Death Experience in Medieval and Modern Times*. New York: Oxford University Press, 1987.

Zaleski, Carol. *The Life of the World to Come*. Oxford: Oxford University Press, 1996.

Zaleski, Carol, and Philip Zaleski. *The Book of Heaven: An Anthology of Writings from Ancient to Modern Times*. Oxford: Oxford University Press, 2000.

— Chapter 15 —

Holy Men / Holy Women

Lawrence S. Cunningham

Peter Brown's celebrated 1971 essay on the rise and function of the holy man in late antiquity has given the phrase "holy man" a lasting currency in the field of religious studies. Brown's "holy man" not only served as a nexus between our world and the world of the Holy but, as Brown argued in subsequent studies, also served as an exemplar of religious faith as well as a carrier of cultural memory. In so doing, the holy man served as the functional equivalent of the pagan wise man in a society that was becoming ever more Christian. Whether there was a counterpart figure of the "holy woman" has been contested by feminist critics. Certainly women had little space for public action in late antiquity since most early sources about women were written by men.

Brown's research into the life and significance of the "holy man" has been so influential that entire issues of journals and at least one book (Howard-Johnston and Hayward 1999) have been dedicated to assessing or extending his insights, and at least two symposia have been held to take up the issues that he has raised. As more than one scholar has noted, if there is any study that can be called seminal, Brown's "The Rise and Function of the Holy Man in Late Antiquity" deserves that sobriquet.

One may ask whether the term "holy man" or "holy woman," redolent as it is of the distinctively Christian matrix within which Brown and his commentators have located it, provides an appropriate template for religions as diverse as indigenous ones – is the Arctic *shaman* or Central American *curandero* a holy man or woman? – or those which derive from the world of Hinduism, Buddhism, or Jainism. Dare we even use the term to discuss the Confucian ideal of the scholar-gentleman? In fact, as this chapter will argue, the term "holy man" can be used as an umbrella term, but Brown's own construal of it is too narrow to serve our needs. That the entry for "holy man" in the *Dictionary of Religion* published by the American Academy of Religion in 1995 has 117 cross-references to everything from the Islamic Sheikh to the Russian Orthodox Starets confirms the range of the phenomenon.

The adjective "holy" also presents its own problems, as does the cognate term "sacred," because of the polysemous ways in which these terms are used. For our purposes the adjective "holy" will be taken to refer to the Other understood dynamically (the Spirit world), personally (a divinity), or as an ultimate liberating goal devoid of either personality or dynamism (*Nirvana*). Some scholars prefer "sacred" to holy as the general descriptor, but "sacred" has a close association with a certain academic strand of the phenomenology of religion and, especially with Mircea Eliade's *The Sacred and the Profane* (1968). Although the term "holy" is itself in debt to Rudolph Otto's 1917 classic work, *Das Heilige*, it will be used here to provide a base point for a taxonomy of what is in fact a most complex phenomenon. To simplify what is complex, this chapter will use some common terms under which we might classify holy persons in quite different religious traditions. At the end of the chapter I will then try to present some commonalities.

The Saint

Although it is tempting to see the term holy man or holy woman as a synonym for the word "saint," the terms are not interchangeable. In Christianity the saint is a person who is recognized as such either by the rise of a spontaneous cult, as in the first millennium of Christian history, or through the process of canonization, as is practiced today in both the Roman Catholic and the Eastern Orthodox traditions. Canonization means simply that a person is put in the canon, which is to say receives public veneration in the liturgical calendar of the Christian church. The process of canonization may be either a formal procedure, as in the Roman Catholic and Eastern Orthodox Church, or an informal one, as in the Anglican, Lutheran, and other liturgical churches.

Derived from the early cult of the martyrs in Christianity, saints are those who act as intercessors in heaven for those still living on earth. The process of canonization thus demands some evidence of a miracle gained through the intercession of the saint. Saints are held up as models of religious living since they are considered virtuosi of faith and practice. Toward saints there is, then, a combination of veneration and emulation. It is from this combination that the various genres of hagiography derive.

While the understanding of Christian saints bears some family resemblance to religious virtuosi in other faith traditions, there are some clear distinctions. For example, some varieties of Judaism, such as the Hasidim, recognize holy persons ("righteous ones," or *tzaddikim*) who are venerated and whose tombs are visited but who do not function in quite the same way as saints. There is no process of canonization. Holy persons are venerated in life, and their tombs become holy places after their deaths. The same thing is true of the "Friends of God," or the *awliya*, who are mentioned in the Qur'an (10:63). The miracle-working saints in Islam and the mystics of the Sufi tradition whose tombs are visited as sacred places might have entered Islamic culture under the inspiration of Christian influence, although their origin is much debated. The main difference is that the veneration of saints in Christianity is part of mainstream practice, whereas in both Judaism and Islam the veneration of "saints" is often viewed as a form of deviant practice. Both mainstream Judaism and Sunni Islam look with some suspicion on the role of "saints."

It may be better to think of the category of "saint" in world religions as a subset of the larger phenomenon of the holy person since many functional characteristics of the saint – as model, intercessor, miracle worker – are found in other configurations in the world of religion. Figures such as the Jainist *sadhu*, who are called "great souls" because they have attained spiritual enlightenment, or the Theravada Buddhist *arahant* or the Mahayana Buddhist *bodhisattva* or the Hindu *siddha* (perfected one) can all be seen as bearing some kind of equivalency to those called "saints" in the West.

The Holy Person as Mediator

One common way in which holy persons become holy comes from their ability to serve as a conduit between the world of the transcendent and the world of the mundane. Brown saw the holy man as a kind of hinge person, whose vertical axis linked him to the realm of celestial powers and whose horizontal axis separated him from social engagement and the daily round of the quotidian. The holy person was holy both because of a vertical connection to the Holy and because of a horizontal severance from the world of the mundane through the practice of withdrawal (*anachoresis*) or asceticism. The holy man was mediator both because of the singular position vis-à-vis the world in which he lived and because of a gift or technique that linked him to god.

How that vertical mediation takes place is shaped by the very ways which a given religious tradition understands its relationship to the transcendent order. Two kinds of mediators stand out in religion: the prophet and the priest.

A *prophet* – a term found in Judaism, Christianity, and Islam – is one who claims to speak for God. Prophets are called by God to speak God's word to the people. They are mediators from the top down: from a divine source to a people. In the Hebrew Scriptures, or the Christian Old Testament, the classical, eighth-century prophets believed themselves to be called by God to deliver his message to the people of Israel. The phrases so characteristic of Hebrew prophecy are telling: "The word of the Lord came to me" or "Thus says the Lord."

The New Testament continues this characterization of the prophet. That continuity is summed up in the opening words of the Letter to the Hebrews: "Long ago God spoke to our ancestors in many and various ways through the prophets but in these last days he has spoken to us by a Son" (Hebrews 1:1–2). The precise function of the prophet is reflected in the Greek word (rendering the Hebrew *nabi*) itself: *pro-phetes*, one who speaks for another.

Islam in turn sees itself as continuing the prophetic tradition of both the Israelite and the Christian faiths. Muhammad is the final prophet and therefore the one to whom God (Allah) revealed the final revelation, which is in the *Qu'ran*. The *Qu'ran* honors the prophets of both Israel and Christianity but deems the Word of God, or Allah, coming to Muhammad as God's definitive word. Hence the fundamental creed of Islam: "There is but one God, Allah, and Muhammad is his prophet (or: messenger)."

Where the metaphorical direction of prophecy is downward, from divinity to the mediator and then to the people, the *priest/priestess* mediates upwards from the people to God. The function of the priest is to "make holy" – that is, to sacrifice (from the Latin *sacrum* [holy] + *facere* [to make]). Priests and priestesses act as surrogates for the people. They mediate by offering sacrifices from the people to God.

The priesthood is identified with sacrificial performance. Priests in indigenous religions as well as in religions ranging from Hinduism and Buddhism to Christianity are also generally regarded as ritual specialists who keep the worship place of the God intact and who perform ceremonies for the benefit of people or in honor of the gods. By reason of their duties, they themselves are regarded as "holy," as are both the places where they practice, such as in temples and churches, and the material realities, such as altars. Holiness, then, accrues in precise relationship to the object of worship. Persons, places, instruments, and times are "holy" to the degree that they approximate closeness to the divinity.

Priests may be called "technicians" of the Holy. In many religions they are expected not to be spiritual counselors or teachers but rather to be performers and preservers of the rituals to which they have been entrusted. They are guardians of the holy places where divinities dwell and to whom sacrifices are offered. Islamic mosques and Jewish synagogues are places of prayer and instruction, but no priests are present because no sacrifices are offered there.

An older generation of biblical commentators saw a tension between priestly and prophetic religion. That tension within the Hebrew Bible was supposed to be found as well between Judaism and Christianity and later between Roman Catholicism and Protestantism. But at least within the Hebrew Bible this tension does not in fact exist. There is a distinction but not an opposition, and it is between the office of priest, which is inherited, and the office of prophet, which is not. The same person can be both a priest and a prophet. The key distinction is that priests, not prophets, offer sacrifices.

The Keeper of Wisdom

Many religions single out those persons who possess and dispense secrets that result in either physical or, more commonly, spiritual liberation. In the case of physical liberation – from curses or spells that torture the mind or illnesses that weaken or threaten physical health – the holy person or the healer has a repertoire of strategies and a repository of materials that drive out alien forces and restore physical or mental health. The powers of these persons derive from a mix of primitive science and knowledge of the unseen forces in the world. The gift of healing may derive from an inherited "secret" knowledge passed on through tradition or may be acquired through some initiatory process of passage to and from the spirit world, or a combination of both. The holy person can move from the everyday world to the spirit world to overcome an alien force that is beyond the reach of the ordinary person. The combination of knowledge and power permits this transaction to take place.

One special kind of wisdom keeper is the *shaman*, who will be discussed separately. In Hinduism and Buddhism, the possessor of secret knowledge is the *guru*. Knowledge and the power to transmit this knowledge bring liberation from the grip of *karma*, the never-ending cycle of existence, resulting in liberation (*nirvana*). The acquisition of this knowledge comes from discipline. The classic text of Hinduism, the *Bhagavad Gita*, differentiates three forms of discipline (*yoga*) that can lead to liberating knowledge: the path of ascetical renunciation (*Jnana Yoga*), the path of work done without desire (*Karma Yoga*), and the path of devotion (*Bhakti Yoga*). The acquisition of knowledge liberates one from the world of illusion. Adepts can teach this knowledge to others or can guide others to attain it for themselves. In certain forms of Buddhism the person who achieves liberation may out of compassion remain in the world to help others achieve the same. These persons are known as *bodhisattvas*. The bodhisattva is both wisdom teacher and model.

The guru possesses a knowledge imparted either directly through teaching or indirectly by inducing others to emulate the guru's own life. The educational practices of the guru are not totally unlike those forms of initiation used, for example, in the Christian monastic life or in the intense life of a Jewish Yeshiva. But where the guru imparts a wisdom that is to lead to liberation, the Christian novice master aims to form a monk for life in a community based on the life of Christ, and the aim of rabbinical training is to produce a leader for the community.

Finally, one cannot discuss the wisdom tradition without consideration of the *mystic*. The word *mysticism* is a recent one in the European vocabulary. The adjective "mystical" traditionally meant that which was hidden. In Christianity it was applied to the hidden sense of Scripture, the hidden Christ in the sacrament of Holy Communion, and the hidden Spirit of God in the Church. Similarly, mystical theology meant hidden, negatively phrased discourse about God – a discourse beyond words, images, and concepts. This form of "hiddenness" also appears in Judaism in the understanding of sacred texts, in Islam as the simple intuition of God beyond words or ideas, and in the religions of India as that form of knowledge which liberates.

All the major religions of the world share the conviction that some persons attain a level of consciousness about ultimate reality that ordinary persons do not. These special persons *experience* this ultimate reality and do not simply have ideas about it. While the means of attaining these experiences vary from religion to religion, there are some commonalities: ascetic practice, a penchant for meditation, and a willingness to withdraw from the everyday world.

Mystics may seem to be out of the mainstream of any religious tradition, but their experiences in fact give assurance to ordinary believers that there is an ultimate reality. Like the *guru*, the mystic can also help others seeking the same experiential knowledge of ultimate reality. St. John of the Cross, one of the most famous of the Christian mystics, calls these persons "guides" (*guias*) or "spiritual teachers" (*maestros espirituales*). He warns against inept spiritual teachers, especially those who themselves have never had the experiences that they nevertheless seek to teach.

The Shaman

Originally observed by scholars and explorers in Siberia and Asia, the Russian *shaman* is one who is considered able to "travel" to the world of the gods or spirits. Travel occurs while the shaman is in a trance. Shamans either are trained in a long apprenticeship under a senior shaman or experience a "call" to shamanic practices. In some instances those who exhibit abnormal behavior, such as a love of solitude or the hearing of voices, are thought to have the mark of a potential shaman.

Mircea Eliade (1959) argues that the shaman makes his ecstatic journey for any of a variety of reasons: to meet gods or goddesses, to bring them gifts from the community, to bring back the spirit which has abandoned a person's body and has thereby caused sickness, to act as guide for a dead person to bring that person to a state of rest and happiness, or to help the shaman learn more about the spirit world. Clearly, the shaman's activities duplicate those of holy persons. Indeed, the term "shaman" has come to be used for holy persons in native religions. In fact, scholars of North American indigenous tribal religion have noted that the term "shaman" has been used to describe every kind of religious specialist: priest, healer, ritual specialist, and magician. What remains distinctive of someone labeled shaman is the ability to cross into another world and to interpret that world to everyone else.

The Sage

Persons of extraordinary wisdom are revered. Both Confucius (551–479 BCE) and Mencius (372–289 BCE) were revered not only for their wisdom but also for their own exemplary lives. Both figures helped others to live in ethical harmony with themselves and with their society.

The teachings of these Chinese masters developed into an elaborate system which combined study with ethical training and with ritual activity. Confucius was honored with shrines and ritual commemorations, but he was venerated more as a noble ancestor than as a god.

Sages like Confucius founded schools. In the Wisdom tradition, schools have a canon of sacred writings, a preferred form of pedagogy, and a desired goal – for example, the perfect gentleman, the humane scholar, and the wise person. As Pierre Hadot (1995) has shown, ancient Greek philosophers saw philosophy as not simply a scholastic discipline but also a way of life. It should come as no surprise that a continuity existed between Greek schools of Stoicism, Epicureanism, and Pythagoreanism and certain forms of Christian monasticism. The Cappodocian Fathers of the fourth century called the ascetic and monastic communities that they formed the "philosophical life" since for them the true Wisdom was not the Stoic-like Logos but the Logos made flesh, namely, Christ.

Holy Persons and Their Traditions

This brief survey of various typologies of holy persons should not be taken as watertight. The holy man described by Peter Brown, with which this chapter began, served as a mediator but, because of the power emanating from him, could also serve as a prophetic voice, a healer, and a reconciler of factions. Under the rubric of the Christian saint are to be found examples of almost all of the categories described in this chapter. Similarly, the shaman serves many roles. Is it possible to tease out some generic characteristics of the holy person that cuts across all of the categories described?

First, and most obviously, holy persons are those who have most deeply and fully experienced and absorbed their own religious tradition. Their lives bring their tradition alive and make transparent the promises and fruits of that tradition. Holy persons are the virtuosi of their religions.

By embodying the power of their tradition, holy persons are able to transmit that power to others. All holy persons are mediators, albeit in different ways. The Confucian sage serves to uphold the ethics of his society. The Hebrew prophet feels charged to castigate the existing society for all of its failings and to call it back to the responsibilities enunciated by the Covenant. The Buddhist *bodhisattva* actually relinquishes the claim to Nirvana in order to help others find the way. The holy person, in short, is a nexus not only to the Holy but also to the community as a whole.

The holy person also serves as a conservator of a religious tradition. The fact that the holy person experiences and transmits experience provides a kind of confirmation that the religious tradition is true. By showing how the tradition can be used to heal and to edify, the holy person attests to its power. As a conservator of a tradition, the holy person serves as well as an interpreter of that tradition. At the same time holy persons can themselves be taken as sacred "texts" who must be "read" correctly if one is to enter the world of their religion.

Bibliography

Brown, Peter. "The Rise and Function of the Holy Man in Late Antiquity," *Journal of Roman Studies* 61 (1971): 80–101.

Brown, Peter. "The Saint as Exemplar in Late Antiquity," *Representations* 2 (1983): 1–25.

Buswell, Bobert E. *The Zen Monastic Experience.* Princeton, NJ: Princeton University Press, 1992.

Cunningham, Lawrence S. *A Brief History of Saints.* Oxford: Blackwell, 2004.

Eliade, Mircea. *The Sacred and the Profane* [1959], tr. Willard R. Trask. New York: Harvest Books, 1968.

Gallagher, Winifred. *Spiritual Genius.* New York: Random House, 2000.

Hadot, Pierre. *Philosophy As a Way of Life*, tr. Arnold I. Davidson. Oxford: Blackwell, 1995.

Hawley, John Stratton, ed. *Saints and Virtues.* Berkeley: University of California Press, 1987.

Howard-Johnston, James, and Paul Anthony Hayward, eds. *The Cult of Saints in Late Antiquity and the Middle Ages.* New York: Oxford University Press, 1999.

Katz, Steven T., ed. *Mysticism and Religious Traditions.* New York: Oxford University Press, 1983.

Kieckhefer, Richard, and George Bond, eds. *Sainthood: Its Manifestation in World Religions.* Berkeley: University of California Press, 1988.

Otto, Rudolf. *The Idea of the Holy* [1917], tr. John W. Harvey. London: Oxford University Press, 1923.

Wimbush, Vincent, and Richard Valantasis, eds. *Asceticism.* New York: Oxford University Press, 1995.

— Chapter 16 —

Magic

Gustavo Benavides

Magic within Religion

Mastering the physical world has traditionally been associated with magic, whereas securing meaning or salvation has generally been associated with religion or with mysticism. In actuality, it is impossible to deal with one realm without the other – either because the one can only be understood as the rejection of the other or, more frequently, because their roots are the same. In actual usage the "mystical" and the "magical" tend to be linked, as both get pitted against institutionalized, conventional religion, and as both involve claims about access to supernatural power. For example, one finds the coexistence of the mystical with the magical in the Neoplatonic techniques used to make contact with the gods, techniques known as theurgy. The linkage is also found in Buddhism, in such canonical Mahayana texts as the *Śūraṅgamasamādhisūtra*, *Vimalakīrtinirdeśa*, and *Mahāprajñāpāramitāśātstra*, all of which deal ultimately with the achievement of enlightenment. In the first, we find references to *rddhibala*, the extraordinary power of the Buddha. In the second, it is said that through his miraculous power a bodhisattva can introduce Mt. Sumeru into a grain of mustard and the water of the four oceans into a single pore of his own skin. In the third, we find an elaborate description of the five super-knowledges, which include three kinds of *rddhi*. In Tantric Buddhism it is even more difficult to distinguish between mystical and magical pursuits. Thus in the *Mañjuśrimūlakalpa* there are references to the *vidyādhara*, "those endowed with magical powers" (see Przyluski 1923).

Even a cursory acquaintance with Roman Catholicism shows that the sacraments – instruments of salvation at the heart of this form of Christianity – rest upon an understanding of automatic ritual efficacy. The absence of a clear boundary between religion and magic has allowed members of the clergy to employ the cross or the sacraments to ward off evil in magic-like fashion, and has even enabled the laity to obtain supernatural power for its own, practical uses. The absence of a clear boundary between religion and magic has been regarded by followers of other varieties of Christianity as a betrayal of the Christian message, which for them deals primarily not with practical but with moral behavior or with the unverifiable certainty of having accepted Jesus as one's savior. Nevertheless, Jesus' reported magical activities clearly did contribute to his popularity (see Smith 1978; Aune 1980). The exegetical web spun around the purported activities of Jesus has focused effectively on the elements that have traditionally constituted the building blocks of magical efficacy: words, gestures, food, drink, and ingestion. It might even be suggested that the longevity of the Roman Church stems from its having established and maintained a link between the materiality of its ritual system and its theological speculation, including the notion of incarnation.

Legitimacy, Illegitimacy, and Efficacy

In order to account for religious activities that ordinarily would be considered magical but that must be kept apart from such risky association, Christianity distinguished between "magic" and "miracle" – the first having to do with activities that are either fraudulent or demonic, and the second having to do with the divine overruling of the divinely established natural order. What is true of Christianity is also true of Buddhism. According to the *Pātalakasūtra*, the Buddha himself distinguished between legitimate supernatural powers – *rddhi* – and spurious fraudulent, deceitful ones – *māyā*. The Buddha, while "endowed with ten powers" (see Waldschmidt 1958), emphatically denied that he was a *māyāvin*, or a "magician" in the derogatory sense of the term, even though, according to the *Upasenasūtra* of the *Samyuktāgama*, he mentioned strophes that would have prevented the monk Upasena from being poisoned by a snake.

In the Christian and in this particular Buddhist case, we see at work the anxious desire to distinguish legitimate from non-legitimate dealings with the supernatural. Perhaps, then, one can grant a distinction between the religious and the magical on the grounds of legitimacy. Hence the Anointed One and the Enlightened One perform miraculous deeds, whereas Simon Magus and Māra engage in magic. Nevertheless, the distinction is between legitimate and illegitimate agents, not between efficacious and ineffective activities. In other words, it is accepted that both religion and magic effect changes in the world through non-ordinary means.

The Christian distinction between miracle and magic, along with the Buddhist vicissitudes of *māyā* and *rddhi*, must take into account the changing meanings of such terms as *góēs*/*goēteía* and *mágos*/*mageía* in the Greek world. In the archaic period a *góēs* was a magician who functioned publicly, his power coming from his powerful personality rather than from drugs or potions. Only in the time of Plato did *goēteía* become a term of ridicule. Similarly, *mágos* could mean a ritual specialist to Herodotus and Xenophon and a "quack" or "charlatan" in tragedy (see Graf 1995, 1996; Bremmer 1999). It is not, then, unwarranted to regard "magician" and "magic" – the terms derived from *mágos* and *mageía* – as contested. They represent a conscious attempt on the part of claimants to separate their activities from the illegitimate supernatural dealings of others. But one would be doing injustice to the inchoate domain known as "religion" to reject the possibility of the presence within it of an urge to manipulate, fashion, create, and craft.

The overlapping of magic with religion is shown, furthermore, by the characterization of kings and magicians as acting like gods as well as by imagining gods who act like magicians. An example can be found in the *Sefer Yesirah*, a mid-fourth-century book in which the Jewish god creates the world by manipulating the letters of the Hebrew alphabet (see Hyman 1989). An analogous situation can be found in ancient Egypt, where Heka is the god of magic (*heka*, *hk3*); in Mesopotamia, where Enki/Ea plays the same role (see Pettinato 2001); and among the Hittites, for whom both men and gods practice magic (see Haas 1994). The difference between the Jewish and the Egyptian, Mesopotamian, and Hittite cases is that where in Judaism the connections between magic and God were suppressed, the use of magic by Heka, Thot, and other Egyptian divinities was openly acknowledged (see Kákosi 1985). The same was true of Enki/Ea and of the Hittite goddesses. Likewise where the magical aspects of Moses' and Jesus' activities were regarded with embarrassment by Jewish and Christian exegetes and so were allegorized, it was priests who were in charge of magic in ancient Egypt, a culture in which the distinction between "magic" and "religion" did not seem to apply (see Ritner 1995). An analogous situation can be found in contemporary South India, where men labeled magicians are nevertheless subordinate to their chosen deities, *Ista-devatā* (see Diehl 1956).

Furthermore, the activities of people who are believed to have access to supernatural power are by no means always considered illegal, as can be seen in ancient Egypt (see Ritner 1985). Among the Hittites, magic was an acknowledged, and not seldom feared, part of life. In Mesopotamia the deeds of the *kaššāpu/kaššaptu* ("sorcerer," "witch") were not always considered illegitimate (see Abusch 1989). Returning to India, we find that, millennia later, ambiguity is still the rule: according to medieval Indian hagiographies, religious scholars who engaged in debates can resort not only to divine help but also to "black magic," or *abhicārakriyā*, to defeat their opponents (see Granoff 1985). The recourse to either benign or malignant supernatural power is still the case in South India, where "even the Pillicūniyakāran, or performer of black magic, deals with recognized deities and divine power" (Diehl 1956, p. 366), and where traditional criteria for distinguishing between magic and religion do not apply. There is no clear demarcation between "religious" and "magical" specialists in Chinese culture either. Indeed, many of the practices one tends to associate with magic, such as the pursuit of immortality, flourished in courtly, hence religious, circles. The same applies to esoteric – Tantric – forms of Buddhism, which also found adherents in courtly circles in China and Japan. There were, to be sure, conflicts between the *fang-shih*, or magical specialists, and the Confucian establishment, but under the latter Han, for instance, Confucian scholars were familiar with esoteric literature, just as most *fang-shih* were conversant with the classics (see Ngo 1976, pp. 64–6).

As known by every reader of the *Tao Te Ching*, te (*de*) encompasses multiple meanings, including "power," "action," "life," and "virtue". That range of meanings is reflected in the various ways in which the title of the Taoist classic has been rendered in English. The bond as well as the tension between virtue as morality and virtue as ritual efficacy is present also in Japanese, a language in which virtue as moral propriety is expressed by *dōtoku*, whereas *kudoku* means virtue as efficacious power. As Ian Reader and George Tanabe point out, "While both work together, ritual power, which accesses the aid of the gods, is more potent than moral virtue and is sometimes regarded as being sufficient to relegate morality to a minor role" (Reader and Tanabe 1998, p. 112). The significance of the Japanese case goes beyond the meanings of two terms, as the Japanese religious system is built around *genze riyaku*, or the "worldly benefits" obtained through the pursuit of ritual virtue. This openness about the practical aspects of religion, which contrasts to the position ostensibly found in the contemporary West, does not go against traditional Buddhist understanding of the practical effects of meritorious behavior. On the contrary, long before Buddhism arrived in Japan, followers of the Dharma believed that physical well being was the result of righteous behavior, a belief that continues to this day throughout the Buddhist world (see Benavides 2005).

Enchantment and Disenchantment

The common roots along with the peculiar tension present in terms as distant from one other as *virtus*, *te*, and *dōtoku/kudoku* should serve as a reminder of the need to focus on the convergence as well as on the divergence between the magic-as-power and the religion-as-ethics poles. Given their shared roots, these poles have been separated through not just a political but also a conceptual struggle. Even once established, the separation can be kept in place only through continuous effort, as in the purification movements that have been a recurrent feature of Southeast Asian Buddhism, Christianity, and Islam. The opposite tendency can in turn be seen at work in the tendency of religious reform movements to develop the characteristics of the institutional bodies which they have sought to purify or from which they have attempted to separate themselves. "Re-ritualization" is found in religious bodies that have undergone a process of de-ritualization. The contemporary efforts at re-sacralization in the Roman Church only a few decades after the Second Vatican Council is a case in point.

Despite this proclivity toward enchantment, there also occurs the opposite process, namely, the questioning of the basis on which magical procedures rest. "Disenchantment," in Max Weber's sense, must constantly defend itself against re-enchantment. We have found intimations of the skeptical position in the Buddha's use of the term *māyā* and in the changing fortunes of the *góēs* and the *mágos*. We find it also in Greek verbs which, as Richard Gordon has shown, were used to undermine magical claims: "cheating, beguiling, dissembling (*kēleō*, *thelgō*, *manganeuō*)" (Gordon 1987, p. 61). The use of these verbs to refer to magical practices constitutes an example of the skepticism and naturalism with which the ancient Greeks are rightly credited (see Lloyd 1987).

An early instance of this naturalistic attitude is found in the Hippocratic treatise *On the Sacred Disease*, in which the author ridicules the claims of magicians and seeks to prove that epilepsy, "the sacred disease," is a disease like any other. But it must be remembered that, even without polemical intent, the capacity to differentiate between natural and non-natural etiologies is already present in Babylonian medical literature, where one finds the distinction between *āšipūtu* (magical practice) and *āšipu* (exorcist, magical expert) on the one hand and *asûtu* (physician's skill) and *asû* (physician) on the other (see Ritter 1965; Pettinato 2001). More generally, skepticism and disenchantment result in the "dematerialization" of religion. The consequence is that the official variety of a religion is no longer considered as able to influence the physical world and becomes limited to issues of meaning (see Benavides 1997, 1998).

It is the emergence of a complex system of symbolization that creates the gap between human beings and reality. That gap at once creates a void between oneself and the world and demands the concoction of counter-worlds and techniques to fill that void. "Mysticism" is the name generally given to attempts to deal with issues involving identity and difference, oneness and plurality. In some cases the goal of mystical practices is the reconstitution of a lost oneness. In other cases the goal is the establishment of an intimate relation with the divinity, while preserving the distinction between "self" and "other." In yet other cases the goal is retreat into an isolated self. In all of these cases some of the techniques used to achieve the mystical objectives involve practices that can also be labeled "magical."

One of those practices is asceticism, which refers to techniques of self-mastery through self-deprivation. Besides being believed to result in the attainment of the mystical goal, mystical techniques are also believed to endow the practitioner with supernatural powers. In order to understand the connection between asceticism and power, we must move away from the contemporary equation of virtue with morality. The correlation between amoral power and ascetic practices is widespread, and is found, for example, in the Scandinavian Eddas (see Kieckhefer 1989). But India is where one can observe it in its starkest form, despite scholarly efforts to explain it away or suppress it. In fact, the warnings against its misuse demonstrates that *siddhis* or *vibhūtis* are central to yoga, just as *abhijñas* are an integral part of Buddhism (see Pensa 1969). The connection between self-deprivation and magical power can also be seen in the tena-ciousness with which the Roman Church clings to the doctrine of clerical celibacy. Clinging to an *ex opere operato* understanding of the sacraments – the *raison d'être* of the Church, after all – requires the maintenance of a repository of ritual power, which must be fed through sexual or often ascetic practices.

Magic Language

Given the central role of language in establishing and maintaining distance between humans and reality, while also making it possible to achieve the social complexity necessary to master reality, it is language that lies at the core of the cluster named "religion." Indeed, that which makes possible the preservation of the symbolic split is also charged with overcoming it. Language and its counterpart, silence, play a role in all aspects of religion – in official liturgies, in mystical speculation, and in secret incantations. It is nevertheless difficult to distinguish among religious, magical, and mystical uses, for what is assumed to be characteristic of one kind of linguistic practice can be found in another. Magic, for example, frequently resorts to formulas in dead, alien, or made-up languages and even, in the case of Indian *dhāranī* or of Greek *Ephesia grammata*, to strings of sounds with no semantic content. But it must be remembered that besides functioning in a magical manner, *dhāranī* are used as support in the practice of meditation. Likewise in official liturgies the language used publicly may be also one that hardly anyone understands – including, in the case of Sanskrit and Latin, barely literate priests in India and pre-industrial Europe and, in the case of Arabic, most clerics in non-Arabic speaking areas of the Muslim world. In all of these cases incomprehensibility, which is not infrequently accompanied by ritualized gestures and dance, seems to intensify the portentousness and above all the effectiveness of the utterance. In some cases the use of mild incomprehensibility may not suffice to classify a linguistic practice as magical, but even in these instances it is possible to discern the rhetorical, power-related purpose of linguistic obscureness. The Roman Catholic Church's persistent use in these post-Latin days of terms such as *magisterium* and *mandatum* serves to elicit a degree of awe, however mild, among the theologians subject to such *magisterium* and *mandatum* – that is, to the teaching authority claimed by the Roman Church and to the authority to teach granted by the bishop to those who teach theology at institutions under his jurisdiction.

Difficult as the differentiation of magical from religious language is, it can be said that magical language is used not to represent reality but rather to intervene upon reality. In most cases the presumed intervention involves the semantic or phonic components of language, or a combination of both. In other cases, such as in ancient Egypt, the written form harbors a magical function. In still other cases, it is the very materiality of the text – papyrus, parchment, book, engraved stone, inscribed pottery – that is believed to be efficacious. Hence the Gospel of John is used as a pillow in order to cure headaches, as advised by Augustine. Or a book is opened at random for divinatory purposes. Or liquid used to wash a magical text is drunk, as attested in ancient Egypt, Greece, medieval Europe, and Sudanese Islam. The boundaries among these practices are fluid.

Insofar as the function of everyday language is not purely representational, there are points of contact between ordinary and magical language. The overlap can be seeing in situations in which to say is to do and even to make. For example, in religious or nonreligious contexts an utterance – usually involving also gestures, touch, and assorted objects or substances – creates a state of affairs or a change in status, as in baptisms, naming ceremonies, the conferring of degrees or honors, and inaugurations. These "speech acts" constitute examples of benign nonrepresentational uses of language on the part of those who claim access to legitimate power (see Tambiah 1985; Todorov 1973). Their malignant, but still legitimate, counterparts can be found in public condemnation and ritual cursing. Oaths constitute an ambiguous case, as they involve conditional self-cursing. Through an oath, one in effect calls divine punishment upon oneself in case one does not fulfill one's promise: one makes oneself conditionally *sacer*, that is, liable to be killed by anybody. Like traditional speech acts, oaths are generally intensified analogically through nonverbal means. In the seventh century BCE the inhabitants of Thera uttered an oath as they left their city in order to found the city of Cyrene. The Therans "moulded wax images and burnt them while they uttered the following imprecation, all of them, men and women, boys and girls: 'May he, who does not abide by this agreement but transgresses it, melt away and dissolve like the images, himself, his seed and his property'"(Faraone 1993, p. 61).

Private instances of speech acts usually do not have the backing of institutionalized power and therefore tend to slide into the realm of illegitimacy that is associated with magic. But public rituals – for example, the Babylonian royal curses upon those who violated oaths or trespassed boundaries; the Theran colonists' conditional self-imprecation; and the Roman *evocatio*, whereby the gods of an enemy city were enticed away, leaving the city unprotected – can be distinguished from private nefarious ones only in terms of the brute power behind them. The same applies to the relationship between the solemn excommunication ceremonies of the Roman Church and a private curse. What we find in the cases mentioned can be arranged on a grid built upon the criteria of legitimacy and presumed efficacy. According to this arrangement, Theran oath, Roman *evocatio*, Roman Catholic excommunication, and eucharistic consecration, all of which rank high in the presumed efficacy and in the legitimacy axes, would not be regarded as magic by Therans, Roman rulers, Roman Catholics or, in the case of the *evocatio*, by the inhabitants of the cities besieged by the Romans inasmuch as the inhabitants of these cities shared the Roman belief in the efficacy of bellicose rituals. Yet especially in situations of religious ferment, some committed Protestants would regard Catholic sacramental claims as illegitimate and therefore as magic or superstition. Indeed, regarding those sacramental claims as blasphemous was an important component of what made one a Protestant.

While issues of legitimacy, social location, and political power are important in magic, it is necessary once again not to lose sight of magic as efficacious. Through magical language one seeks to act upon the world by establishing a link between reality and the manipulation of analogies and differences (see Tambiah 1985; Todorov 1973; Versnel 1996), of made-up languages, and of pure sounds. A remarkable example of the magical effects of the interaction among agency, plenitude, and analogy is found in the "act of truth" (*satyakriyā*), attested in India and in ancient Ireland. The act of truth consists in uttering in a solemn manner an absolute truth concerning one's life (see Brown 1972). The absolute identity of language with reality embodied in the utterance allows the speaker to have unhindered mastery of reality, so that the utterance can be used as a magical spell.

In the self-referential manner of poetic language, magical formulas point to their own efficacy. Ultimately, metaphors and metonymies are pushed beyond their ordinary role. They are made to perform deeds within the incantations to make the incantations efficacious. A paradigmatic deed (*historiola*) may be mentioned at the beginning of an incantation in order to charge analogically what one's incantation seeks to accomplish. As in poetic language in general, in verbal magic there is a conscious attempt to establish distance from ordinary language by foregrounding its formal aspects. This effect is achieved by focusing on the extreme forms of phonic, morphological, syntactic, and semantic aspects of the language. Syntax may become rigid or left behind; meaning may be intensified or abandoned; and one can play with rhythm, rhyme, and alliteration without losing concern with semantic content (see Michalowski 1981;Versnel 1996). Eventually, sounds may be used in an onomatopoetic manner or may become ends in themselves, having a hypnotic effect on the person to be affected as well as on the performing priest or magician. The techniques, in all of which the very substance of the text is made to act efficaciously, can be found in Sumerian "carminative poetics" as well as in the magic charms collected in contemporary Bosnia-Herzegovina, Croatia, Serbia, Macedonia, Bulgaria, and Russia (see Conrad 1983, 1987, 1989) and in Czech lands (see Kent 1983). Thus in a Sumerian incantation against an intestinal affliction that is equated with a snake and with a fire that must be extinguished, the repetition of the word *ze* functions as a "powerful onomatopoetic device which captures the hissing sound shared by the snake, the fire and the 'Gall'" (Michalowski 1981, p. 10). A preferred technique in Slavic magic is reverse counting, in which the movement toward zero in the formula is believed to bring about the diminution of the symptoms one seeks to cure (see Conrad 1983, 1987; Versnel 1996). The arousing, disruptive use of sexual imagery is also used to induce strength and fertility.

The Body in Magic

Besides the linguistic underpinnings of magical practices, there are the bodily ones, including the role played by natural attraction and aversion (see Rozin and Nemeroff 1990). Magically, one seeks either to transform the body or to render it immortal, either to make it invulnerable or to cure it. Magically, the body can be hurt or obliterated; it can be fed; it can be made sexually irresistible; it can be seduced or possessed; it can be freed; and it can be bound. Binding is central among magical practices. We find it in the Greek verb *théō* (to bind strongly, magically); in Latin *fascinum* (charm, malefice), related to *fascia* (bundle), and also in *ligare* (to bind) and *ligatura* (the action of binding, charm) (see Annequin 1973, p. 19). It is significant that Christian apologists such as Lactantius and Augustine have sought to derive *religio* from *religare*. Linguistically unjustified as such derivation is, there is some metaphorical justification in this association, insofar as *ligare* has to do with the sovereign agency of a god, whereas *religere*, the most likely etymology of *religio*, refers to a scrupulous attitude toward ritual practices. As in the case of linguistic practices, we find that in the Greco-Roman world and in the Middle Ages private rituals involving ligatures, which rank high in the presumed efficacy axis but low in legitimacy, are considered as magic. By contrast, the kind of binding referred to in the Gospel of Matthew 16:19 and 18:18, which validates ritual practices such as Roman Catholic marriage, consecration, and confession, is commonly regarded as religious.

If it is not clear whether the legitimacy axis applies in a given culture, then the label of "magic" will have to be discarded for that culture. Thus the ancient Egyptian rituals of execration, which consisted of destroying an image of the god Seth (see Frankfurter 1994) or a large number of clay vases inscribed with the names of enemies, will have to be considered as feared but not as illegitimate. Another legitimate ritual of execration, the Neo-Assyrian magical series *Maqlû*, which involved the burning of effigies of natural or supernatural enemies of the king, seems to have originated as a private ritual (see Faraone 1991; Pettinato 2001). Echoes of these rituals can be discerned in the executions *in effigie* that took place in Europe until the seventeenth century. Here the power of the state rendered legitimate the vicarious hanging, burning, beheading, drowning, or quartering of the king's enemies.

It tends to be forgotten that in a world ruled by scarcity, much of what human bodies do is work. As we saw at the beginning of this chapter, the various components clustered under the label "religion" are as involved in coming to terms with oneness and multiplicity, with union and separation, as in coming to terms with power and powerlessness, abundance and lack. The scarcity that engenders labor also engenders utopian dreams about realms of leisure and plenty, be they as resolutely physical as the Land of Cockaigne or as rarefied as the Buddhist Pure Lands. Scarcity also gives rise to magical practices, which seek to intensify the efficacy of one's labor or to procure supernaturally that which in reality can be obtained only through labor. But the image of limited goods also sets in motion feelings of envy toward those whose work appears to produce richer rewards than one's own, which in turn gives rise to magical attempts to steal, destroy, or damage what one's neighbors' efforts have produced. In Rome, fear of having one's harvest magically stolen seems to have been so common that legislation was passed against it. The reverse can be found in magical attempts to protect oneself from others' envy through apotropaic rituals. Rituals and frequently phallic amulets against the "evil eye" can be found in the pagan and early Christian Mediterranean world as well as in modern Italy, Spain, and the Balkans.

But it should not be forgotten that, as widespread as these practices have been, since the appearance of stratified societies the preferred way of satisfying one's needs without having to work has been through the extraction of labor from others. Religion has played a crucial role in sanctifying the mechanisms of extraction as well as in providing the means of transcending in an imaginary manner the degradation of being subject to need. This process of extraction can be carried one step further by magically dreaming up those who will free us from want by working for us. Examples of magical workers go back to Old and Middle Kingdom Egypt, where we can identify statuettes that represent laborers buried with their masters in order to save them from having to work in the other world. Eventually, those statuettes were replaced by the *ushabti*, which represented not laborers but the deceased himself, who, by entrusting an alter ego with work, was able to rest eternally (see Kákosi 1985). The same concern is at work in the lead figurines found in poorer tombs in Han dynasty China. The figurines substituted for the deceased in netherworld corvée (see Poo 1998). In the Egyptian and Chinese practices we witness what at one remove the gods did according to the Mesopotamian myth of Atramhasis, namely, to create, first, lesser gods and then human beings in order to save themselves from back-breaking labor. Comparing the *ushabti*, the lead figurines, with the Atramshasis myth, we encounter once again the common roots of religion and magic, for in order to free themselves from the servitude of labor, gods as much as humans fashion lesser gods, human beings, imaginary servants, and even images of themselves. In the end, as shown by the *ushabti*, by the Atramhasis myth, and by the rituals that mimic ordinary work, ancient Egyptians and Mesopotamians, while trying to escape from labor, demonstrated its inescapability (see Benavides 2000). This point applies to all the cases of magic-religion-mysticism surveyed in this chapter. In seeking release, power, or plenitude, human beings point to the unavoidable nature of the constraints that constitute us. The more imaginative and the more desperate the attempts to escape or to master reality, the more that reality reveals its hold.

Bibliography

Abusch, Tzvi. "The Demonic Image of the Witch in Standard Babylonian Literature: The Reworking of Popular Conceptions by Learned Exorcists," in *Religion, Science, and Magic in Concert and in Conflict*, eds. Jacob Neusner, Ernest S. Frerichs, and Paul V. Flesher. New York: Oxford University Press, 1989, pp. 27–58.

Annequin, Jacques. *Recherches sur l'action magique et ses représentations (Ier et IIième siècles après J.C.)*. Paris: Les Belles Lettres, 1973.

Aune, David E. "Magic in Early Christianity," in *Aufstieg und Niedergang der römischen Welt*, II.23.2, ed. Wolfgang Haase. Berlin: De Gruyter, 1980, pp. 1507–57.

Benavides, Gustavo. "Magic, Religion, Materiality," *Historical Reflections/ Réflexions historiques* 23 (1997): 301–30.

Benavides, Gustavo. "Modernity," in *Critical Terms for Religious Studies*, ed. Mark C. Taylor. Chicago: University of Chicago Press, 1998, pp. 186–204.

Benavides, Gustavo. "Towards a Natural History of Religion," *Religion* 30 (2000): 229–44.

Benavides, Gustavo. "Economy," in *Critical Terms for the Study of Buddhism*, ed. Donald S. Lopez, Jr. Chicago: University of Chicago Press, 2005, pp. 77–102.

Bremmer, Jan N. "The Birth of the Term 'Magic'," *Zeitschrift für Papyrologie und Epigraphic* 126 (1999): 1–12.

Brown, W. Norman. "Duty as Truth in India," *Proceedings of the American Philosophical Society* 116 (1972): 252–68. Reprinted in his *India and Indology*. Delhi-Varanasi-Patna: Motilal Banarsidass, 1978, pp. 102–19.

Conrad, Joseph L. "Magic Charms and Healing Rituals in Contemporary Yugoslavia," *Southeastern Europe/L'Europe du sud-est* 10 (1983): 99–120.

Conrad, Joseph L. "Bulgarian Magic Charms: Ritual, Form, and Content," *Slavic and East European Journal* 31 (1987): 548–62.

Conrad, Joseph L. "Russian Ritual Incantations: Tradition, Diversity, and Continuity," *Slavic and East European Journal* 33 (1989): 422–44.

Diehl, Carl Gustav. *Instrument and Purpose: Studies on Rites and Rituals in South India*. Lund: Gleerup, 1956.

Faraone, Christopher A. "Binding and Burying the Forces of Evil: The Defensive Use of 'Voodoo Dolls' in Ancient Greece," *Classical Antiquity* 10 (1991): 165–205.

Faraone, Christopher A. "Molten Wax, Spilt Wine and Mutilated Animals: Sympathetic Magic in Near Eastern and Early Greek Oath Ceremonies," *Journal of Hellenic Studies* 113 (1993): 60–80.

Flint, Valerie I. J. *The Rise of Magic in Early Medieval Europe*. Princeton, NJ: Princeton University Press, 1991.

Frankfurter, David. "The Magic of Writing and the Writing of Magic: The Power of the Word in Egyptian and Greek Traditions," *Helios* 21 (1994): 189–221.

Gordon, Richard. "Aelian's Peony: The Location of Magic in Graeco-Roman Tradition," *Comparative Criticism* 9 (1987): 59–95.

Graf, Fritz. "Excluding the Charming: The Development of the Greek Concept of Magic," in *Ancient Magic and Ritual Power*, eds. Marvin Meyer and Paul Mirecki. Leiden: Brill, 1995, pp. 20–42.

Graf, Fritz. *Gottesnähe und Schadenzauber: Die Magie in der griechisch-römischen Antike*. Munich: Beck, 1996.

Granoff, Phyllis. "Scholars and Wonder-Workers: Some Remarks on the Role of the Supernatural in Philosophical Contests in Vedānta Hagiographies," *Journal of the American Oriental Society* 105 (1985): 459–67.

Haas, Volkert. *Geschichte der hethitischen Religion*. Leiden: Brill, 1994.

Hyman, Peter. "Was God a Magician? Sefer Yesira and Jewish Magic," *Journal of Jewish Studies* 40 (1989): 225–37.

Kákosy, László. *La Magia in Egitto ai tempi dei faraoni*. Modena: Edizioni Panini, 1985.

Kent, George P. "The Poetic Order of Healing in a Czech Incantation Against Erysipelas," *Southeastern Europe/L'Europe du sud-est* 10 (1983): 121–49.

Kieckhefer, Richard. *Magic in the Middle Ages*. Cambridge: Cambridge University Press, 1989.

Lloyd, G. E. R. *The Revolutions of Wisdom: Studies in the Claims and Practice of Ancient Greek Science*. Berkeley: University of California Press, 1987.

Michalowski, Piotr. "Carminative Magic: Towards an Understanding of Sumerian Poetics," *Zeitschrift für Assyriologie und vorderasiatische Archäologie* 71 (1981): 1–18.

Ngo, Van Xuyet. *Divination, magie et politique dans la Chine ancienne*. Paris: Presses Universitaires de France, 1976.

Pensa, Corrado. "On the Purification Concept in Indian Tradition, with Special Regard to Yoga," *East and West* 19 (1969): 194–228.

Pettinato, Giovanni. *Angeli e demoni a Babilonia. Magia e mito nelle antiche civiltà mesopotamiche*. Milan: Mondadori, 2001.

Poo, Mu-chou. *In Search of Personal Welfare: A View of Ancient Chinese Religion*. Albany: State University of New York Press, 1998.

Przyluski, Jean. "Les Vidyārāja: Contribution à l'histoire de la magie dans les sectes mahāyānistes," *Bulletin de l'École française d'Extrême-Orient* 23 (1923): 301–18.

Reader, Ian, and George J. Tanabe. *Practically Religious: Worldly Benefits and the Common Religion of Japan*. Honolulu: University of Hawaii Press, 1998.

Ritner, Robert K. "Egyptian Magical Practice Under the Roman Empire: The Demotic Spells and their Religious Context," in *Aufstieg und Niedergang der römischen Welt*, II.18.5, ed. Wolfgang Haase. Berlin: De Gruyter, 1985, pp. 3333–79.

Ritner, Robert K. "The Religious, Social, and Legal Parameters of Traditional Egyptian Magic," in *Ancient Magic and Ritual Power*, eds. Marvin Meyer and Paul Mirecki. Leiden: Brill, 1995, pp. 43–60.

Ritter, Edith K. "Magical-Expert (= Ašipu) and Physician (= Ašu): Notes on Two Complementary Professions in Babylonian Medicine," *Studies in Honor of Benno Landsberger on his Seventy-Fifth Birthday, April 21, 1965*. Chicago: University of Chicago Press, 1965, pp. 299–321.

Rozin, Paul, and Carol Nemeroff. "The Laws of Sympathetic Magic: A Psychological Analysis of Similarity and Contagion," in *Cultural Psychology: Essays on Comparative Human Development*, eds. James W. Stigler, Richard A. Shweder, and Gilbert Herdt. Cambridge: Cambridge University Press, 1990, pp. 205–32.

Smith, Morton. *Jesus the Magician*. San Francisco: Harper and Row, 1978.

Tambiah, Stanley J. *Culture, Thought, and Social Action: An Anthropological Perspective*. Cambridge, MA: Harvard University Press, 1985.

Todorov, Tzvetan. "Le discours de la magie," *L'Homme* 13.4 (1973): 38–65.

Versnel, H. S. "Some Reflections on the Relationship Magic-Religion," *Numen* 38 (1991): 177–97.

Versnel, H. S. "Die Poetik der Zaubersprüche," in *Die Macht des Wortes* [Eranos NF 4], eds. Tilo Schabert and Rémi Brague. Munich: Wilhelm Fink Verlag, 1996, pp. 233–97.

Waldschmidt, Ernst. "Ein zweites Daśabalasūtra," *Mitteilungen des Instituts für Orientforschung* 6 (1958): 382–405. Reprinted in his *Von Ceylon bis Turfan: Schriften zur Geschichte, Literatur, Religion und Kunst des indischen Kulturraumes.* Göttingen: Vandenhoeck und Ruprecht, 1967, pp. 347–70.

— Chapter 17 —

Modernity and Postmodernity

Colin Campbell

Modernity

At its simplest, "modernity" refers to the ideas and attitudes associated with the period since the Middle Ages. The term is associated with the replacement of traditional by new institutions, practices, and ways of thought. Considered in this light, "modernity" implies that the present represents a decisive break with the past. Precisely when this break occurred and therefore when the modern age commenced remains a matter of dispute. Some place the break as far back as the "ancient" period. The use of the Latin term *modernus* by St. Augustine is cited as evidence for this precocious dating. Others emphasize the recovery of classical texts and the emergence of humanism that occurred in the Renaissance. Most take the tendency in the eighteenth-century Enlightenment to identify the modern with the present as the turning point. For the term "modern" now became employed as a term of praise and was associated with that which was innovative, progressive, and up-to-date (see Lukacs 1970).

As Krishan Kumar has observed, "modernity" is at heart a contrast concept: its meaning comes as much from what it denies as from what it affirms (see Kumar 1993, p. 391). Hence "modern" depends on the contrast to "traditional." "Modernity" is commonly formulated in terms of processes that are regarded as marking the transition from the traditional to the new. "Modernity" is associated with the nation state, industrialization, secularization, rationalization, bureaucracy, and urbanism. As Robert Hollinger expresses it, "Generally, 'modernity' means the rise of industry, cities, market capitalism, the bourgeois family, growing secularization, democratization, and social legislation" (Hollinger 1994, p. 25).

Understanding these developments, and coming to terms with "modernity" in general, was the principal concern of the major social theorists of the nineteenth century – including Emile Durkheim, Karl Marx, Georg Simmel, Ferdinand Tönnies, and Max Weber. Although all of them noted that a differentiated, industrial, mechanical, urban, scientific, and technical society was replacing an agrarian-based model, each emphasized somewhat aspects of this process. In this sense each could be said to have a different theory of the modern. Thus Durkheim portrayed the change largely in terms of a move from a society with little or no occupational specialization to one with an extensive division, or specialization, of labor. For Marx, the key lay in the change from feudal to capitalistic modes of production. Weber emphasized the role played by progressive rationalization and secularization. Tönnies stressed the shift from close intimate face-to-face relationships based on family and guild to largely impersonal and indirect forms of interaction based on rationality and calculation.

In addition to identifying those distinctive features and processes that now mark societies, "modernity" is also a central concept in the history of ideas. That is to say, it is a philosophical concept as well as a historical and sociological category. Viewed in this way, "modernity" constitutes a particular view of the possibilities and direction of human social life, one with utopian overtones and a faith in rational thought, science, and technology. It is in this connection that "modernity" is sometimes labeled an ideology and identified with "The Enlightenment Project" (see Habermas 1981).

Modernism

"Modernity" is conventionally distinguished from "modernism," which refers to an international cultural movement, sometimes called "the modern movement," that arose in poetry, fiction, drama, music, painting, and architecture in the West in the late nineteenth and early twentieth centuries. This movement signified a break with the European representational and realist tradition, in which art had been viewed as equivalent to holding up a mirror to nature. By contrast, modernism evinced an obsession with form rather than with content. Form was viewed as in effect autonomous in a way that content was not. Modernism embraces such artistic movements as symbolism, impressionism, cubism, DADA, and surrealism.

Jochen Schulte-Sasse has observed that modernism can be seen as the "cultural precipitate" of "modernity" (Schulte-Sasse 1986, p. 24). Modernism corresponds at the level of beliefs, ideas, and attitudes to the physical, economic, and social changes, such as industrialization and urbanism, that typify the process of modernization. Certainly a case can be made for claiming that modernism and "modernity" – viewed as an ideology – share such features as an emphasis on self-awareness and a critical reflexivity. It is more usual to regard modernism as at best ambivalent toward "modernity" and as more commonly opposed to it, such that modernism is seen as carrying forward the Romantics' disenchantment with the rationalism and empiricism of the Enlightenment. Ironically, then, modernism can be taken as the antithesis of modernity. Modernism is rebelliously anti-bourgeois, anti-rational, and anti-scientific, so that contemporary intellectual life is viewed as involving a clash of "two cultures" or a "cultural contradiction" (see Snow 1969; Bell 1976).

Postmodernism

What is postmodernism?

Postmodernism is an exceptionally difficult phenomenon to pin down, so much so that some have even suggested that it does not have a determinate meaning can even be dismissed as "meta-twaddle" (Gellner, cited in Beckford 1996, p. 302). As Alex Callinicos has suggested, the term is certainly something of a "floating signifier" (Callinicos 1989, p. 169) and consequently, in Tom Docherty's words, "hovers uncertainly in most current writings between a difficult philosophical concept and a simplistic notion of a certain nihilistic tendency in contemporary culture" (Docherty 1993, p. 1). When first used, the term did have a largely accepted and determinate meaning, but it has since become "an irredeemably contested concept" (Turner 1990, p. 1).

The term was actually used as long ago as 1947 by Arnold Toynbee to designate a new cycle in Western civilization. The term became more widely used in the late 1950s and early 1960s to refer to a particular configuration of art and architecture – one that could be considered either to have succeeded modernism or to be a reaction against modernism. At this point it was relatively easy to identify the referent for the term, which in effect was an experimental tendency in architecture, painting, music, the novel, poetry, and drama.

In the 1970s and 1980s the term was no longer employed in this relatively restricted sense but began to take on a much broader range of connotations. Above all, it came to be applied to a philosophical position and to a body of social and political thought distinguished by a critical stance vis-à-vis modern theories of knowledge and epistemology. The key proponents of this new intellectual movement were nearly all French. The most notable were Jean-François Lyotard and Jean Baudrillard, together with poststructuralist thinkers such as Jacques Lacan, Roland Barthes, Michel Foucault, and Jacques Derrida. Largely as a consequence of the growing influence of these thinkers, the term also became widely used to indicate a new cultural epoch, one that has come after the modern age. In this context that postmodernity became linked with the notion of a "post-industrial society," in which knowledge has displaced property as the prime source of power and status (see Bell 1973). This assumption that contemporary Western society differs significantly from modern, industrial society has led in turn to the assumption that all aspects of contemporary society are postmodern.

Postmodernism maintains that recent decades have seen the collapse of "The Enlightenment Project," once manifest in the great modern creeds of socialism and communism, together with the intellectual tradition of Marxism. The suggestion that "the postmodern condition" prevails in the contemporary West means that the optimism concerning the future which had been contained in the "grand narratives" of "modernity" has finally been dissipated. Along with hope for a better future has gone any sense of a meaningful past. The "end of history" is a necessary consequence of the claimed "incredulity toward meta-narratives." In turn, one of the most distinctive features of postmodern thought is its character as intellectual and conceptual "bricolage," or an assemblage of ideas taken from many different sources. As David Harvey has expressed it:

> Eschewing the idea of progress, postmodernism abandons all sense of historical continuity and memory, while simultaneously developing an incredible ability to plunder history and absorb whatever it finds there as some aspect of the present. Post-modern architecture, for example, takes bits and pieces from the past quite eclectically and mixes them together at will. (Harvey 1989, pp. 54–5)

This loss of temporal meaning is matched by a loss of ontological meaning, or certainty about the true nature of the real. The result is that bricolage and the imitation of a variety of styles are matched by a stress on the image or copy as having a reality independent of any referent. The collapse of a modernist philosophy is seen as leading to an emphasis on such cultural characteristics as the willingness to combine symbols from disparate codes and the celebration of spontaneity, fragmentation, playfulness, and irony – all of them postmodern virtues.

Regarded as a body of philosophical speculation and social theory, post-modernism, like "modernity," can be considered a "contrast concept," taking its meaning as much from what it rejects as from what it espouses. Here the concept denied is that of "modernity" itself. The starting point for almost all the postmodern theorists named is the assumption that "modernity" has been "problematized," or called into question. Although each theorist tends to define the nature of this problem differently, all agree that "modernity" is no longer a credible world view. For Lyotard, for example, "modernity" is no longer capable of functioning as an adequate and satisfying historical meta-narrative (see Lyotard 1984). For Jurgen Habermas, the problem is a "crisis of legitimation" (see Habermas 1975).

Postmodernism maintains that people in the West today do not believe that the practices, institutions, and values of "modernity" are meaningful. Postmodern thought, while centering on a discussion of the epistemological and ontological problems thrown up by the collapse of a modernist outlook, also focuses on the social and cultural consequences of this sense of meaninglessness – mainly, a postulated personal and collective crisis of identity. Postmodern writings can variously be categorized as simply describing this crisis, as arguing for accepting that it is no longer possible to provide a satisfying system of meaning in the modern world, or as asserting that all forms of meaning are equally meaningful and legitimate.

At the heart of postmodernism lies a philosophical debate about the nature of truth, beauty, and morality. Modernity, rooted as it is in the Enlightenment Project, involves the assumption that truth, beauty, and morality exist "out there" in the world and can be discovered through the use of science and other objective methods. Postmodernists claim that these ideals do not have an existence "out there" but instead are created, or constructed, by us. They are the products of how we think, write, and talk about them.

Consequently, postmodernists tend to reject "logocentricism," or the idea that reality can be successfully named and represented in language, together with the associated idea that only that which can be articulated is knowable. This argument is advanced with various degrees of forcefulness, amounting in Barbara Epstein's terminology to the difference between "strong" and "weak" versions of postmodernity (see Epstein 1997). The "strong" position claims that there exists no objective truth. There are only truth claims, and "since there is nothing against which these claims can be measured, they all have the same standing" (Epstein 1997, p. 136). There are only words, or words put together as discourses. "Strong" postmodernists use terms such as "essentialism" and "foundationalism" to condemn any notion of a reality external to us. By contrast, "weak" postmodernists accept that the perception of reality is mediated but do not maintain that all claims to truth have equal status. They are not, like strong postmodernists, relativists.

It is widely recognized that there is a paradox at the heart of all postmodern positions. For while all attack on the philosophy of "modernity," all also depend on that philosophy for their *raison d' être*. Consequently some commentators, noting modernity itself as a reaction to tradition, see postmodernism as more of a development of an essentially modernist impulse rather than as a new movement in its own right – a development that extends not invents, a critical, questioning, reflexive, and self-referential tendency. It is in this sense that postmodernism has been called "the Enlightenment gone mad" (Rosen, quoted by Hollinger 1994, p. 8). Postmodernism has become the subject of its own "heretical imperative" (see Berger 1980).

Postmodernism as a contested concept

However postmodernism is characterized, it remains a contested concept in at least three ways. First, the empirical claim that "modernity" has given way to postmodernity or that contemporary society is characterized by "the postmodern condition" has been regularly challenged. Second, the ideological and philosophical critique launched by postmodernists against a modernist world view has been countered by those who seek to defend "modernity" (see Habermas 1981). Third, some argue that postmodernism itself is a conservative rather than a radical force – that it serves to legitimate rather than to undermine existing society. Marxists have understandably been in the fore in arguing that postmodernism endorses, glorifies, and even aggravates those trends in postindustrial society most closely associated with capitalism (see Lash and Urry 1987; Callinicos 1989). Postmodernism, by rejecting any kind of meta-narrative, rejects one that could serve as the basis for a critique of society. Postmodernism also endorses modern consumer society through an apparent celebration of pastiche, image, diversity, and the "construction" of the self. But if some Marxists consider postmodernity the ideology of postindustrial late capitalism, others see postmodernism as offering new possibilities for a radical critique of society. For example, Ernesto Laclau and Chantal Mouffe (1985) employ post-Marxism to argue for a program of radical social reform that relies on individualistic rather than institutional change, an approach that has been labeled "micro-politics" or "postmodern politics" (see Best and Kellner 1991, p. 165).

North American postmodernism

Postmodernism can also be viewed as a cultural phenomenon in its own right, something especially noticeable in North America. As Barbara

Epstein notes, "By the early 80s an intellectual subculture was emerging in the U.S. which tended to use the term postmodernism to describe its outlook. Though it was primarily located in the universities, it had links to avant-garde developments in art and architecture and a strong interest in experimental trends in popular culture" (Epstein 1997, p. 135). In fact, this subculture consisted of a loose alliance of several distinct movements with the common aim of achieving change in some aspect of culture. These movements represent the interests of groups who believe that the orthodoxy of "modernity" oppresses them in some way. The movements include feminism, the gay and lesbian movement, the political left, Marxist or neo-Marxist organizations, and non-Western ethnic and religious groups. Binding them together is "identity politics," in which postmodern theoretical perspectives have been enlisted to advance the causes concerned.

What makes this North American branch of postmodernism so different from its European counterpart is the context in which it emerged. For while European postmodernism can be found in the political disillusionment experienced by left-wing academics and intellectuals following the events of 1968, no such pessimism arose in North America. Thus where in France theories were developed to explain how the vast impersonal structures of language and culture had so managed to imprison people that radical political change was now impossible, post-1960s developments in North America took a very different direction. As Paul Berman, the American social theorist, puts it, "The sixties revolt against liberalism in America was more a matter of action than of theory" (Berman 1992, p. 11). At the same time there was never the same expectation in America that a political, as opposed to a cultural, revolution was imminent.

Consequently, the belief that real change was still possible persisted, together with a continuing belief in the liberty and autonomy of the individual. This optimism about change, together with the emphasis on technique, developed into the North American version of postmodernism. This North American version of postmodernism is often overlooked, for it generally goes by the name "identity politics," "race/class/gender-ism" (Berman 1992, p. 14). North American postmodernism, in contrast to European, believes that progressive change can be achieved. The emphasis is less on all-powerful structures that serve to constrain the individual than on the manner in which the culture of one powerful group dominates all others. This culture is usually called Eurocentric or "phallologocentric" and is said to have been created by "DWEMs," or Dead White European Males. Where European postmodernism sees culture as a giant, hidden, all-powerful oppressive structure that effectively stifles dissent, North American postmodernism sees oppression as simply the present domination by a single group. North American postmodernists believe that, by successfully challenging the dominance of this group through a rejection of its culture, other groups can obtain full expression for their own identity in what can then become a truly multi-cultural civilization. This aim is being pursued through changes in school, college, and university curricula, together with changing the orthodox cultural canon in all its forms, and not least through the replacement of "biased and repressive" linguistic nouns and expressions by ones that do not privilege the dominant group.

Postmodernism and religion

At first glance, "the postmodern condition" would not appear to favor religion. After all, this term was first coined by Lyotard to refer to an "incredulity toward meta-narratives" (Lyotard 1984, p. xxiv). Given that there can hardly be more all-encompassing meta-narratives than those offered by Christianity and Judaism, both of which trace the history of humanity back to the first humans and forward to the coming of the Messiah, the turn to postmodernism would appear to presuppose a collapse of religious faith. Yet as we have seen, the turn has also served to work against those secular ideologies, or "secular religions," that had largely come to fulfill the function of providing meaning formerly provided by traditional religions. Therefore the postmodern condition can be said *not* to favor secularity. While postmodernism certainly offers no endorsement of any claim to absolute truth, including that by religion, it is equally dismissive of the skepticism and disdain toward traditional "superstitions" that marks the Enlightenment-inspired ideology of modernity. Postmodernism adopts a skeptical attitude toward skepticism, thereby favoring a "post-secular" environment in which any form of belief, including religious belief, can thrive. As Lyotard himself has expressed it, "The postmodern condition is as much a stranger to disenchantment as it is to the blind positivity of delegitimation" (Lyotard 1984, p. xxiv). The sociologist Zygmunt Bauman goes even further, claiming that postmodernity actually restores to the world what "modernity" had taken away: "a *re-enchantment* of the world that 'modernity' tried hard to *disenchant*" (Bauman 1992, p. x). For if postmodernists rejects all absolutist and exclusivist claims to truth, it thereby permits truth claims of all kinds, including religious ones.

Alienation from traditional religion but widespread interest in all kinds of New Age spirituality characterizes the postmodern religious scene. Alienation from traditional religion has spurred some to label the contemporary scene as "post-Christian," which, as the English theologian Don Cupitt puts it, is one in which modern sensibilities have moved "beyond faith" (see Cupitt 1998). The English scholar of religion Paul Heelas provides a description of the various responses that fall under the heading "New Age":

For some, the disintegration of the certainties of "modernity" has left a situation in which postmodern religion – Gnostic or New Age spirituality – can develop. For others, the distressing certainties of "modernity" have resulted in the valorization of a premodern past. Yet for others, postmodern religion belongs to that great counter-current of modernity, namely the Romantic Movement. And then there are those who associate postmodern religion with changes taking place within the mainstream of capitalistic modernity. (Heelas 1998, p. 1)

Among the alternatives that Heelas outlines is the suggestion that postmodern religion involves a return to a premodern past. This redirection can be seen as the logical consequence of a movement that, in rejecting modernity, is bound to rehabilitate the outlook associated with a largely agrarian and medieval past. It is therefore hardly surprising to find that some self-declared postmodernists, after condemning "modern spirituality" for being "dualistic and supernaturalistic," advocate a postmodernity that involves "a return to a genuine spirituality that incorporates elements from premodern spiritualities" (Griffin 1988, p. 2).

Whether a postmodern society can be said to favor religion is, however, a different question from whether those religious movements that do exist in contemporary society ought to be labeled "postmodern." This issue is the subject of a lively and ongoing debate, especially in connection with the New Age movement. In his original study of the New Age movement (1996) Heelas rejected the suggestion that the New Age movement can be described as postmodern. Instead, he emphasizies its continuity with the counter-Enlightenment Romantic Movement (see Heelas 1996, p. 216). However, in subsequent writings he seems prepared to employ the postmodern label, as in identifying "Gnostic or New Age spirituality" with "postmodern religion." Yet even prior to 1996 he had noted that "much of the New Age bears the marks of post-modern consumer culture" (Heelas 1993, p. 108).

On the one hand it is hard to see how religion, with its clear commitment to an absolute, can truly be postmodern. On the other hand it is undeniable that many contemporary religious or at least spiritual movements do indeed appear to manifest the characteristic hallmarks of postmodernism noted. Contemporary movements tend to be culturally eclectic and syncretic, taking beliefs, myths, symbols, and practices from various traditions. At the same time epistemological individualism prevails, with individuals asserting their right to interpret teachings as they think fit in the course of pursuing their own personal spiritual paths. Those assertions accord with postmodern presuppositions and with the typical characteristics of a consumer society.

Conclusion

Whether "modernity" really has been replaced by postmodernity remains an open question. For dynamism and change were always an essential feature of the modern, with growth, development, and innovation a necessary concomitant of any society that qualified for that appellation. Almost all of those features identified as postmodern have obvious precursors in what is conventionally considered the modern age, especially in the movement of modernism. As Krishnan Kumar notes, "Much of what appears as 'postmodernity' first found its expression in the cultural revolt against 'modernity' which marked the movement of modernism" (Kumar 1993, p. 392). It is unquestionable that certain of the verities of "modernity" are no longer widely accepted, especially faith in reason and the power of science to produce a better world. So too, has faith in the former great secular religion of Communism dissolved. Whether this loss of faith suffices to justify describing the contemporary age as "postmodern" is highly debatable, as is the suggestion that all grand narratives are now rejected as incredible. But then it is typical of postmodern theorists to reject as hopelessly modern any conventional notions of logic, proof, and verification. Consequently, it is hard to know how these issues are ever likely to be resolved. Finally, insofar as the term "modern" does actually mean "of the moment," it is indeed probably true to say, as Lyotard does, that "A work can [now] only be modern if it is first postmodern" (Lyotard 1984, p. 79).

Bibliography

Bauman, Zygmunt. *Intimations of Postmodernity*. London: Routledge, 1992.

Beckford, James. "Postmodernity, High Modernity and New Modernity: Three Concepts in Search of Religion," in *Postmodernity, Sociology and Religion*, eds. Kieran Flanagan and Peter C. Jupp. New York: St. Martin's Press, 1996, pp. 30–47.

Bell, Daniel. *The Coming of Post-Industrial Society: A Venture in Social Forecasting.* New York: Basic Books, 1973.

Bell, Daniel. *Cultural Contradictions of Capitalism*. London: Heinemann, 1976.

Berger, Peter. L. *The Heretical Imperative: Contemporary Possibilities of Religious Affirmation.* Garden City, NY: Doubleday, 1980.

Berman, Paul, ed. *Debating P.C.: The Controversy Over Political Correctness on College Campuses.* New York: Dell, 1992.

Best, Steven, and David Kellner. *Postmodern Theory: Critical Interrogations.* London: Macmillan, 1991.

Callinicos, Alex. *Against Postmodernism: A Marxist Critique.* Cambridge: Polity Press, 1989.

Cupitt, Don. "Post-Christianity," in *Religion, Modernity and Postmodernity*, ed. Paul Heelas. Oxford: Blackwell, 1998, pp. 218–32.

Docherty, Thomas, ed. *Postmodernism: A Reader.* New York: Columbia University Press, 1993.

Foster, Hal, ed. *The Anti-Aesthetic: Essays on Postmodern Culture.* Seattle: Bay Press, 1983.

Epstein, Barbara. "Postmodernism and the Left," *New Politics* 6 (1997): 130–44.

Featherstone, Mike. *Consumer Culture and Postmodernism.* London: Sage, 1991.

Griffin, David Ray. *The Reenchantment of Science: Postmodern Proposals.* Albany: State University of New York Press, 1988.

Habermas, Jurgen. *Legitimation Crisis*, tr. Thomas McCarthy. Boston: Beacon Press, 1975.

Habermas, Jurgen. "Modernity versus Post Modernity," *New German Critique* 22 (1981): 3–14.

Harvey, David. *The Condition of Postmodernity.* London: Blackwell, 1989.

Heelas, Paul. "The New Age in Cultural Context: The Premodern, the Modern and the Postmodern," *Religion* 23 (1993): 103–16.

Heelas, Paul. *The New Age Movement: The Celebration of the Self and the Sacralization of Modernity.* Oxford: Blackwell, 1996.

Heelas, Paul, ed. *Religion, Modernity and Postmodernity.* Oxford: Blackwell, 1998.

Hollinger, Robert. *Postmodernism and the Social Sciences: A Thematic Approach.* Thousand Oaks, CA: Sage, 1994.

Kaplan, Ann. *Postmodernism and Its Discontents: Theories, Practices.* London: Verso, 1988.

Kroker, Arthur, and David Cook. *The Postmodern Scene.* New York: St. Martin's, 1986.

Kumar, Krishnan. "Modernity," in *The Blackwell Dictionary of Twentieth-Century Social Thought*, eds. William Outhwaite and T. B. Bottomore. Oxford: Blackwell, 1993, pp. 391–2.

Laclau, Ernesto, and Chantal Mouffe. *Hegemony and Socialist Strategy. Towards a Radical Democratic Politics*, trs. Winston Moore and Paul Cammack. London: Verso, 1985.

Lash, Scott, and John Urry. *The End of Organised Capitalism.* Cambridge: Polity Press, 1987.

Lukacs, John. *The Passing of the Modern Age.* New York: Harper and Row, 1970.

Lyotard, Jean-François. *The Postmodern Condition: A Report on Knowledge* [1979], trs. Geoffrey Bennington and Brian Massumi. Manchester: Manchester University Press, 1984.

Rosen, Stanley. "A Modest Proposal to Rethink Enlightenment," in his *Ancients and Moderns.* New Haven, CT: Yale University Press, 1988, pp. 1–21.

Schulte-Sasse, Jochen. "Modernity and Modernism, Postmodernity and Postmodernism," *Culture Critique* 5 (1986): 23–49.

Snow, C. P. *Two Cultures and the Scientific Revolution* [1957]. Cambridge: Cambridge University Press, 1969.

Smart, Barry. *Postmodernity.* London: Routledge, 1993.

Turner, Bryan. "Periodization, and Politics in the Postmodern," in *Theories of Modernity and Postmodernity,* ed. Bryan Turner. London: Sage, 1990, pp. 1–13.

— Chapter 18 —

Mysticism

Jeffrey J. Kripal

Mysticism is a modern comparative category that has been used in a wide variety of ways to locate, describe, and evaluate individuals' experiences of communion, union, or identity with the sacred. Among the many connotations of the term are esoteric strategies of textual interpretation and ritual knowledge; nonrational, immediate, or intuitive modes of cognition; the temporary loss of egoic subjectivity, often symbolized by complexly gendered images of sexual ecstasy and death; an ambiguous relationship to both social ethics and religious orthodoxy; a radical relationship to language expressed through forms of poetic and philosophic writing that subvert or deconstruct the grammatical stabilities and metaphysical substances of normative doctrine and practice; the attainment of supernormal or psychical powers; and a heightened sense of meaning both in the objective universe and in the scriptural texts or myths of the tradition. Many scholars have sought to distance mysticism from one or another of these associations. But the linkage of mysticism to folklore, hagiography, mythology, poetry, the ritual transformation of consciousness, visionary phenomena, and the production of richly evocative texts and iconic artifacts has ineluctably kept it tied to the human imagination and its culturally sensitive mediation of religious experience (see Hollenback 1996).

Mysticism and Modernity

Like other terms that seem to be natural or eternal, "mysticism" in fact is fundamentally a project of modernity, coming into wide use as a noun only in the twentieth century, and then primarily in a theologically liberal context. Convinced by the findings of biblical criticism, which rendered a literal faith difficult to maintain, and eager to forge a more ecumenical vision of the world within increasingly pluralistic societies, scholars turned to the categories of "mysticism" and "experience" (hence "mystical experience") to rethink religion itself.

Undeniably, the term mysticism, particularly as a more humble adjective, does reach further back in the history of the West. The word is derived from the Greek verbal root *muo-*, to close (the eyes, ears, or lips – a kind of sensual silence), which in turn probably derives from the more ancient Indo-European root *mu-*, which lies behind such words as the English mutter, mum, mute, and mystery as well as the Sanskrit *muni* (the "silent one" or sage). Most scholars trace the religious use of the word mysticism back as far as the Greek mystery religions, where the adjective *mustikos* ("hidden," "secret") was used to signal the secret meanings of the ritual symbols and activities that most likely had to do with the mystery of agricultural and human fertility. The early Church Fathers adopted the same adjective to describe the "hidden" universe of meaning that the Scriptures secretly revealed through Christ (see Bouyer 1980). Here, then, the mystical was a kind of scriptural treasure that could be discovered with the proper hermeneutical method. At the same time the sacramental life of the Church was characterized by a set of precious "mysteries" that possessed "mystical" meanings. That association can still be heard in the English version of the Catholic Latin mass: "By the mystery of this water and wine."

From these ancient Greek and early Christian practices the term, while still always an adjective, developed a distinctly "apophatic" tone, which is to say one that sought to deconstruct, or "say away" (*apo-phasis*), the literal meaning (see Sells 1994; Cupitt 1998). Only in the early modern period did the term become a noun, the French *la mystique*. As the French historian Michel de Certeau has pointed out, by the sixteenth and seventeenth centuries "mysticism" was understood to refer to a realm of subjective experience independent of religious tradition and now open to rational and systematic exploration. In effect, a new tradition of what would be called "mystics" had been created, with "mysticism" understood "as an obscure, universal dimension of man, perceived or experienced as a reality hidden beneath a diversity of institutions, religions, and doctrines" (de Certeau 1992, p. 14). Mysticism was now primarily a modern psychological category open to everyone rather than a monopoly more or less controlled by the Church.

Born anew within Anglo-American discourse during the English Enlightenment and later among Transcendentalist Unitarian thinkers in the United States, the category eventually came to function alternately as a liberal polemic against religious excess and enthusiasm especially associated with women, as a developing philosophy of religious pluralism, and as a Romantic sign of a new kind of constructive liberal theology (see Schmidt 2003). The nineteenth and especially the twentieth centuries witnessed further transformations, as Christian theologians came into greater contact with people of other faiths. Certainly by the turn of the twentieth century it was common for commentators to note the virtual identity of mystical experience across cultures and times. Mysticism was becoming an implicitly ecumenical sign.

At the same time the category was subjected to scrutiny by the new discipline of psychology, which had also turned its eye to mystical phenomena in the first decades of the twentieth century. Psychologists noted that pathological and mystical phenomena often display similar psychophysical dynamics. If mysticism had become an ecumenical sign, it had also become a psychological symptom.

Experience, Essentialism, and Epistemology

The history of the modern study of religion has witnessed numerous approaches to mysticism that we might alliteratively name experience, essentialism, and epistemology.

There are important predecessors of the rhetoric of personal experience in some of the medieval and late medieval Catholic writers. Bernard of Clairvaux (1090–1153) is sometimes cited as the first writer to identify the category through his invocation of the "book of experience." This turn to experience as a source of mystical truth was clearly in place by the time of St. Teresa of Avila (1515–82), who wrote extensively of her own visions and states in a self-reflexive way and who often struggled to reconcile them with the authority of Church doctrine. Important as well were the Reformers' stress on the priesthood of all believers and on the privileging of the individual as reader of the biblical text.

It was the German Protestant theologian Friedrich Schleiermacher who, in his *On Religion: Speeches to Its Cultured Despisers* (1799), initiated the first phase of the modern history of mysticism with his focus on deeply felt piety, on individual experience, and on emotion as the place to locate a legitimate religious life for modern skeptics. This same focus on experience rather than creed was developed by the American psychologist and philosopher William James in his *The Varieties of Religious Experience* (1902), by the British writer Evelyn Underhill in her *Mysticism* (1911), and by the German comparativist of religion Rudolf Otto in his *The Idea of the Holy* (1917).

By the middle of the twentieth century this psychological discourse had developed into a well-formed, more or less conscious essentialism which saw as its goal the identification of a "common core" of mysticism universally – a perennial philosophy (*philosophia perennis*). The term "perennial philosophy" was probably coined by Agostino Steuco in 1540 to capture the similarly universalizing spirit of the Italian Renaissance and its recovery of Neoplatonic and Hermeticist texts (see Sedgwick 2004). It was now asserted that all "true" or "genuine" mystics were saying the same thing. This "same thing" was usually expressed in abstract monistic terms that were nevertheless in fact indebted to a very small number of religious traditions – some form of Sufism, Neo-Vedanta, or (mostly Mahayana) Buddhism being the most commonly cited. The French intellectual and anti-modernist René Guénon, the Sinhalese art critic Ananda Coomaraswamy, the Swiss esotericist Frithjof Schuon, the American philosopher Walter Stace, the Islamicist Sayyed Hussein Nasr, the Anglo-American novelist Aldous Huxley, and the American comparativist of religion Huston Smith are probably the best-known exponents of this thesis.

This same mystical essentialism had a tremendous impact on the New Age, which inherited many of the thought forms and symbols of Western mysticism but which radically revised them through the modern lenses of democratic individualism, secularism, and capitalism (see Hanegraaff 1998). Other forms of perennialism, however, had been present since the eighteenth and nineteenth centuries, in such important nonacademic movements as German and English Romanticism, American Transcendentalism, occultism, and theosophy. Perennialism was also to be found in certain strands of European fascism, perhaps most dramatically represented in the writings of the Italian metaphysician Julius Evola, who functioned as a kind of inspired metaphysical propagandist for both Hitler and Mussolini.

Although perennialism had its eloquent ethical and typological critics early on – foremost among them Albert Schweitzer, R. C. Zaehner, and Gershom Scholem – it was not effectively challenged in academic discourse until 1978, when the American historian of Judaism Steven Katz published his seminal essay, "Language, Epistemology, and Mysticism," in his edited volume, *Mysticism and Philosophical Analysis*. Katz offered a position that would come to be known as "contextualism," the strong form of which states that there are no unmediated "pure" mystical experiences

and that instead every mystical experience, like every other mental phenomenon, is mediated through complexly coded linguistic, doctrinal, and
cultural filters that shape experience itself. Interpretation, is not something that comes *after* the experience, as the essentialists had argued, but
rather *is* experience. We are back in a way to Bernard's *book* of experience.
Drawing on Kant's epistemological insight that human knowledge is intimately structured by the *a priori* categories of the mind and therefore
cannot know the thing-in-itself, Katz offered a similar critique of traditional mystical and, more important, of modern academic claims about
the ontological fit between knowing and being. Contrary to exponents of
perennialism, Katz argued that mystics do not have any direct, unmediated access to reality. Accordingly, scholars would more productively spend
their energies not on some assumed ideological oneness but on the differences of language, religious history, ritual, and doctrine among cases of
mysticism worldwide. Katz's methodological revolution has been challenged on a variety of grounds, with Robert K. C. Forman's edited *The
Problem of Pure Consciousness* (1997) standing out as the most heavily
cited. Nevertheless, Katz's epistemological shift of the discourse has permanently altered the field, rendering it far more sensitive to historical
context and far more skeptical of essentialist positions.

From Schleiermacher's attempt to enlist personal piety before the
Infinite to rescue religion from its cultured despisers, to the universalizing
trajectories of the perennial philosophy, to Katz's contextualizing epistemology – the modern discussion of "mysticism" has been transformed
several times over the last two centuries. And the discussion has hardly
ended. Recent turns have taken the category of mysticism in decidedly
postmodern and postcolonial directions that promise to transform the
discursive field yet again, this time calling the field to own up to its own
colonial pasts and to question its now normative Kantian epistemological
commitments through a deeper and more radical engagement with Asian
philosophical and meditative traditions, many of which cogently deconstruct the models of consciousness, knowing, and the individual that have
subtly controlled most scholarship on "mysticism" in the modern period
(see King 1999).

Paradox, Mysticism, and Mythology

If there is a single epistemological requirement for understanding mystical
literature, it is probably the ability, or at least the willingness, to think
dialectically, even paradoxically – that is, beyond the law of noncontradiction, in the realm of the both-and and the mediating third. In this respect,
mysticism shares the structure of mythology delineated by the French
anthropologist Claude Lévi-Strauss. Like any set of myths for Lévi-Strauss,

mystical literature is forever trying to say two things, often seemingly opposite things, at one and the same time, uniting in the process orders of being that appear to be quite distinct and in the process generating an immense corpus of texts and experiences that never quite resolve the initial contradiction. As Schleiermacher had long observed, human beings possess contradictory desires: a desire to be a separate, distinct individual and a desire to merge with a greater Whole.

These dual desires carry over into the linguistic structures of mysticism. From the Zen *koan*, or meditative riddle, to the Tantric use of *sandha-bhasa*, or doubly intentional language to speak simultaneously of sexual and spiritual realities, to Western monotheistic forms of apophaticism, to the famous "You are that" (*tattvamasi*) of the ancient Indian Upanisads, mystical literature often strives for a kind of literary *coincidentia oppositorum*, a coincidence of opposites that collapses linear thought and speech into a sudden paradoxical revelation of unity or communion with the sacred order. This literary mimicking of the mystical moment is what Michael Sells has called a "meaning event," a complexly coded grammatical structure that can catalyze a similarly sudden revelation in the reader of the text (see Sells 1994). In general, methods that either turn these structurally paradoxical relationships into pure metaphors – as if, for example, there are no real relations between sexual and religious experiences – or collapse them into simple identities – as if religious experience were nothing but a kind of distorted sexual expression – are less effective than those that preserve the structural paradoxes of mystical speech and textuality.

Beyond the Ego: The Psychology of Mysticism

Following theology, which had already begun to engage and help create the new field of "mysticism" early in the eighteenth and nineteenth centuries, one of the first disciplines to take a serious and prolonged look at mysticism was the young field of psychology. Sigmund Freud had dedicated much of his writing to the subject of religion, accepted the epistemological reality of telepathy, and knew more than a little about mysticism, mostly through his correspondence with the French playwright and self-confessed mystic Romain Rolland (see Parsons 1999). C. G. Jung, whom a frustrated Freud once dismissed as a "mystic," was even more committed to ideas and practices – archetypal realities, the Self, individuation, active imagination, synchronicity, and the paranormal, for example – that in an earlier age would have been construed as "mystical." Not only the Austrian Freud and the Swiss Jung but also many early American and French psychologists had much to say about the subject, notably, William James,

James Leuba, Edwin Starbuck, Jean-Martin Charcot, Pierre Janet, Henri Delacroix, Richard Bucke (a Canadian and mystic himself), and Henri Bremond.

Exactly what these psychologists saw when they looked at mystical literature depended on their own theories, but all agreed that mysticism usually involves a temporary loss of self that, in psychoanalytic terms, involves the temporary elimination or transcendence of the socialized ego. Freud wondered whether the classical experience of unity was not a regressive return to the infant's narcissistic bond with the mother. Charcot and Janet noted the uncanny similarities between the symptoms of hysterics and the behavior of saints. James, drawing on the category of the subliminal developed by the British psychical researcher F. W. H. Myers, speculated about a divine More that could be accessed through the door of the subconscious. Jung postulated a collective unconscious and universal archetypes. Bucke wrote enthusiastically about a cosmic consciousness that he himself had experienced and that he believed was the ultimate goal of evolution. For all these figures, whatever mysticism was, it was definitely not a function of the ego. The mystical was that which entered from elsewhere, from the unconscious depths of the psyche. All the usual religious tropes of passivity and surrender, of transcendence, and of sudden revelation were "psychologized," with the unconscious replacing the divine. The category of "experience," moreover, was now paramount. Ritual, institution, and doctrine had faded into the background.

"Exactly as If It Were Female Orgasm": The Mystical as the Erotic

The psychological insight that mysticism draws on forces beyond the conscious self finds more than a little support in the traditions themselves, where the mystical process is routinely depicted in images that signal a dramatic loss of normal consciousness and where symbolic expressions of annihilation, suffering, death, drunkenness, emptiness, flight, absorption, melting, and most remarkably sexual ecstasy or orgasm are the order of the day (or night). In the language of the French philosopher Georges Bataille, it is death and sensual rapture that speak most effectively and accurately to the human experience of becoming one with a greater whole. Accordingly, it is to death and eroticism that we must turn in order better to understand mysticism, for both death and eroticism appear along the same recognizable spectrum of human possibilities (see Bataille 1986). The English theologian Don Cupitt's mischievous terms put it well: "Union with God is described [by male mystics] *exactly* as if it were female orgasm, by people who are not merely of the wrong sex, but not supposed to have any personal experience of such things anyway" (Cupitt 1998, p. 25). Certainly it is no accident that the first writer to employ the English term "mysticism," Henry Coventry (ca. 1710–52), identified the phenomenon as distinctly female, saw "disappointed love" as the deepest source of mystical devotion, and worked toward what we would today call a theory of sublimation to explain the obvious eroticism of the religious phenomena he sought to explain by the term "mysticism" (see Schmidt 2003, pp. 277–8). From the earliest historical use of the English term, "mysticism" has thus been understood to be a form of eroticism. Little wonder, then, that recent scholars have explored questions concerning the female gendering, or *jouissance*, of mystical language (see Clément 1994; Hollywood 2002) and the relationship of mystical language to sexual orientation, social repression, and sublimation (see Kripal 2001).

The connection of the mystical to death and to eroticism can be found in mystical traditions themselves. The Kabbalistic and Sufi traditions, understand the adept's physical death to be his marriage to the divine. The Hindu god Siva is both master of deathly asceticism – traditionally represented by sacred ash, cremation grounds, and skulls – and lord of the phallic *lingam*, his sacred icon. So, too, in Tibetan Vajrayana, where the central symbol of the tradition, the *vajra*, or diamond-like thunderbolt, often takes on explicitly phallic meanings and where the rich iconography envisions the highest state of empty enlightenment as an ecstatic sexual embrace between a Buddha and his consort. In Christian bridal mysticism the mystic, male or female, becomes the bride of Christ. There is an Indian counterpart in the many elaborate Vaishnava theological and devotional traditions in which the human soul becomes a female attendant or even a lover of the beautiful blue god Krishna.

By no means do all the traditions that we might call mystical, stress love or death. Advaita Vedanta and Theravada and Zen Buddhism, for example, rely on other primary metaphors. And the many that do depend upon the sexual register reveal just how diverse sexually the traditions actually are. Whether or not ontological oneness is one, the human experience of divine love definitely is not. Accordingly, what we actually see when we look closely enough are different kinds of bodies with different kinds of desires desiring differently gendered deities, who often manifest themselves in differently embodied, desiring human beings. The gender and sexual complexities of these traditions quickly approach the mind-boggling: male mystics posing as women in order to love male gods (Christian bridal mysticism and many forms of Vaishnavism), male mystics arousing a male God by engaging in sexual intercourse with women (Kabbalah), male mystics seeing a male God in the beauty of young boys (ancient Greek Platonism and medieval Persian Sufism), male and female mystics sexually uniting to effect the union of a god with a goddess or of a male with a female principle (many forms of South Asian Tantra), same-sex communities (monasteries and convents), cross-dressing practices, castration images and practices, and androgynous models of deity.

This sexual diversity alone argues against the perennialist assumptions of mystical uniformity. Indeed, it is remarkable just how few bodies there are in perennialist approaches to mysticism. We hear of many essences and many minds, but seldom do we hear of actual skin, of genitals and sexual fluids, of fingers and toes, or of faces and smiles and groans – in short, of genuinely gendered bodies. Whether or not all true mystics experience the same ontological essence and whether every mystical experience is mediated through historical context are questions that must be left open. But the human body is an indubitable universal in the history of mysticism, for *every* historical mystic has a gendered body. Here, however, we find ourselves within the dialectic of comparison, for the body is never simply biological. It is always cultural as well, its most intimate processes elaborately influenced, if not determined, by historically conditioned cultural practices, ranging from childrearing arrangements and marriage rituals to funerary customs. Much like the sexual body in contemporary gender theory, even the mystical body displays the intricacies of human culture and the marks of human language.

On the (Ab)Uses of Oneness and Transgression: Mysticism and Ethics

Both the early psychological hermeneutic and the traditional sexualization of mystical experience likened to death have profound, if usually unrecognized, implications for the ethical import of those classes of experiences that we now gather under the umbrella of "mysticism." The study of mysticism was quite comfortable with such insights at the end of the nineteenth and at the beginning of the twentieth century, particularly within Jean-Martin Charcot's Salpêtriére circle and the later French and American psychologies of religion. No doubt deeply influenced by Charcot, who had offered his own understanding of hysteria as "a scientific explanation for phenomena such as demonic possession states, witchcraft, exorcism, and religious ecstasy" and had even applied his idea to medieval art (see Herman 1997), Freud made the link early on. In his correspondence with his original co-theorist, Wilhelm Fliess, he commented on the uncanny similarity between the sexual symptomatology of hysteria and the demonic possessions of medieval witchcraft that depicted in sexual terms a splitting of consciousness that we now recognize as dissociation. Similarly, the American psychologist James Leuba mused that "[N]ot one of the prominent representatives of mysticism lived a normal married life" (Leuba 1925, p. 119). The observation remains both astonishingly accurate and richly suggestive of the traumatic subtexts of mystical literature that now constitute one of the persistent nodes of study in the field (see Kripal 1995; Hollywood 2002).

To their great credit, early scholars of religion such as Schleiermacher and Otto were careful not to confuse either a pious feeling of oneness with the Infinite (Schleiermacher) or a paradoxical experience of terrifying allure before the holy (Otto) with the ethical. In its more astute moments, the modern study of mysticism has done the same. In its lazier moments it has all but conflated the sacred with the moral, arguing that a mystical experience of oneness is the ontological origin of ethics. Hence the sacred is still a *mysterium*, but it has lost almost all of its *tremendum*. The traditional violence and the annihilating death of the mystical are rationalized away as something impossible within a more or less monistic world view. After all, where everything and everyone are one, how can oneness be bad? The discourse, in other words, has suffered from a recurring moral perennialism, even after it has more or less abandoned an ontological one. Certainly not every scholar would accept this reading, but it remains true that the one indubitable feature of the relationship of mysticism to social ethics is that this relationship has been debated endlessly (see Barnard and Kripal 2002).

The historical evidence is by no means all negative. Cupitt and Sells have demonstrated that one of the most recurring elements of mystical writings is the attempt to deconstruct orthodox discourse, to deny traditional authority, and to transgress the social norms of their own conservative cultures, often for reasons that we might now recognize as profoundly ethical. In this sense, at least, "mysticism" can be taken as a kind of individualist counter-culture working to deconstruct the hegemonic forces of oppression and the theological necessity of divine transcendence that constitute the heart of so many religions. Here mysticism becomes a kind of "dangerous writing" that seeks to melt down the oppressive structures of tradition in order to effect a state of religious happiness in the reader (see Cupitt 1998).

Ecstasy and Empowerment: Mysticism and the Psychical

Unusual powers, from reported flight and telepathy to telekinesis and the ability to heal, are a part of mystical writings around the globe. The almost total neglect of them in the modern study of mysticism – with F. W. H. Myers' *Human Personality and Its Survival of Bodily Death* (1904), Freud's private correspondence on telepathy (see Jones 1953–57), and Herbert Thurston's *The Physical Phenomena of Mysticism* (1952) as the most impressive exceptions – has at least two sources: the traditional, quite two-

faced demeaning of their importance in some varieties of religious literature, which inevitably extol their presence even as they deny the relevance
of such phenomena, and the embarrassment that scholars routinely feel
when they encounter things that cannot be integrated into their own
positivistic world views.

Jess Byron Hollenback's *Mysticism: Experience, Response, and
Empowerment* (1996) stands virtually alone in its contemporary insistence that, however we interpret them, folklore, hagiography, and mystical
literature of all types are clear that the ability to transcend the ego – or in
mythological terms, to leave the body – often brings in its wake a series of
psychic powers. In Hollenback's terms, these events witness to an "empow-
ered imagination" that, if we are to believe the innumerable accounts of
such phenomena, somehow has the ability to make contact with extra-
psychic information and veridical sources of knowledge. It remains to be
seen whether anyone will take Hollenback's lead, or return to Myers,
Freud, and Thurston. Doing so would certainly have considerable ramifications for the study of mysticism.

Reality as Interpreted: Mysticism as Hermeneutics

Central to Katz's contextualist revolution is the notion that interpretation
and experience are inseparable. Interpretation is central to all forms of
human experiencing, not least the mystical. This focus on interpretation
takes us back to some of the earliest meanings of the term *mustikos*, that
is, to the early Christian writings, where the mystical signals a particular
kind of hermeneutical practice that can reveal the secret Christological
meanings of the sacred Scriptures or bestow on one a salvific *gnosis*.
Particularly within the early Gnostic communities, interpretation *was* this
gnosis. Hence the Gospel of Thomas opens with Jesus' saying that "Whoever
discovers the interpretation of these sayings will not taste death" (Meyer
1992, p. 23, v. 2), and Clement can describe the evangelist Mark as possessing secret teachings and "certain sayings of which he knew the interpretation would, as a mystagogue, lead the hearers into the innermost
sanctuary of that truth hidden by seven [veils]" (Smith 1973, p. 15). So
too, in Jewish Kabbalah, where the interpretation of the Torah catalyzes
and guides the mystical process, hermeneutical activity is itself a mystical
discipline (see Wolfson 1994).

Moreover, it is often the mystic who offers creative "misreadings" of
traditional texts that veer the tradition off in new directions – for example,
the effect of Paul's experience of the risen Christ on his understanding of
the Torah; Kabbalistic interpretations of biblical texts as the elaborate

dynamics of the *sefirot*; or the Tibetan Buddhist use of *terma*, or hidden textual treasures destined to be "discovered" at a time when the tradition requires them for its survival or renewal. Experience, in other words, can catalyze new interpretation, just as interpretation can catalyze new experience. Thus mysticism can be seen as a creative hermeneutics, as an experience of the divine through an interpretation of texts that can alter, sometimes radically, the original tradition. Perhaps it is no accident, after all, that the discipline of hermeneutics seems to be named after Hermes, that polymorphous, often phallic deity (the erotic returns) of Western thought who, as Hermes, Mercury, or Hermes Trismegistus, has presided for so long over the divine acts of speech and interpretation, of alchemy and magic, and of the very Renaissance esoteric traditions that gave us the expression "perennial philosophy."

These traditional linkages of hermeneutical activity, creativity, and mystical practice are reflected in the modern study of religion. Scholars have come to approach mystical texts as predecessors of a kind of postmodern deconstruction of theological literalisms (see Cupitt 1998), as a mystical practice involving the apophatic use of language that "says away" the reifying structures of grammar (see Sells 1994), or as a potent site for the mystical experiences of the scholarly hermeneuts themselves (see Kripal 2001). Here, too, we might identify Jorge Ferrer's and Cyril O'Regan's different critiques of "experientialism," or the focus on intrasubjective experience as the sole locus of the spiritual, as well as their analogous turns to relationships and events outside the person as the richer and more adequate site of the mystical. Ferrer, for example, writes of the "transpersonal participatory event" that might precipitate an "experience" in an individual who participates in that event but that cannot be reduced to the phenomenology of any individual's experience (see Ferrer 2002). Similarly, O'Regan approaches the texts of Jacob Boehme not as simple descriptors of the writer's psychology but as a "discursive event" with far-ranging effects on the history of Western religious and philosophical thought (see O'Regan 2002). Nowhere is the link between mystical experience and writing more apparent than in the psychical phenomenon of "automatic writing," an altered state of consciousness in which a text flows spontaneously from the pen of an inspired writer. Here the mystical state literally produces the text, and the text is said to possess the capacity within itself to lead the reader back to the same state of consciousness. Consciousness produces text produces consciousness in a never-ending cycle of text and interpretation.

On the Paradoxical Practice of
Comparative Mysticism

Finally, then, we can see that "mysticism," very much like "mythology," "sexuality," and "religion" itself, is an explicitly comparative and modern term that accomplishes certain kinds of intellectual work. At the same time we can also see that it possesses a long complex history and presently encodes at once a liberal pluralist theology, a democratic political economy, and a certain individualistic ethics. Some of these features, such as the geopolitics of colonialism that played into the construction of the mystical East, appear now as immoral. Others, such as democracy, individualism, and intellectual freedom, appear much more as nonnegotiable fundamentals without which the critical study of religion would cease to exist.

Put differently, it is one thing to show that something like "sexuality" and "homosexuality" are modern constructs unknown to the ancient Greeks (see Halperin 1990). It is quite another to suggest, overtly or implicitly through historical relativism, the moral desirability of a polity that privileges a small elite group of free men who penetrate – both literally and politically – younger men, women, or slaves within a hierarchical system of dramatic social inequalities. The modern category of "sexuality," which underlies all modern theoretical and ethical gains regarding gender and sexual orientation, can easily be seen as a philosophical boon in a comparative context.

So, too, with "mysticism" and "religion." It is one thing to show that these are modern constructs that privilege Western notions of individualism for the separation of the sacred from the secular (they do) or that they have sometimes interacted with the construction and practice of Western colonialism (they have). It is quite another to opt, through postmodern relativism or postcolonial guilt, for hierarchical or theocratic polities that privilege small elite groups of men who subordinate lower class men and all women through traditional purity codes, religious privilege, and elaborate metaphysical systems, as does almost any major religion, from Tibetan Buddhism and Islam to Roman Catholicism and Hinduism. Once again, a category such as "mysticism," which at its best wants to put in scare quotes almost any traditional religious claim and every socialized ego, looks very much like an intellectual gain here, a radical practice uniquely suited to the scholar's vocation both to understand and to doubt.

Bibliography

Barnard, G. William, and Jeffrey J. Kripal, eds. *Crossing Boundaries: Essays on the Ethical Status of Mysticism.* New York: Seven Bridges Press, 2002.

Bataille, Georges. *Erotism: Death and Sensuality.* Tr. Mary Dalwood. San Francisco: City Lights Books, 1986.

Bouyer, Louis. "Mysticism: An Essay on the History of the Word," in *Understanding Mysticism,* ed. Richard Woods. Garden City, NY: Image Books, 1980.

Clément, Catherine. *Syncope: The Philosophy of Rapture.* Minneapolis: University of Minnesota Press, 1994.

Cupitt, Don. *Mysticism After Modernity.* Oxford: Blackwell, 1998.

de Certeau, Michel. "Mysticism," *Diacritics* 22 (1992): 11–25.

Ferrer, Jorge N. *Revisioning Transpersonal Theory: A Participatory Vision of Human Spirituality.* Albany: State University of New York Press, 2002.

Forman, Robert K. C., ed. *The Problem of Pure Consciousness: Mysticism and Philosophy.* New York: Oxford University Press, 1997.

Halperin, David. *One Hundred Years of Homosexuality and Other Essays on Greek Love.* New York: Routledge, 1990.

Hanegraaff, Wouter. *New Age Religion and Western Culture: Esotericism in the Mirror of Secular Thought.* Albany: State University of New York Press, 1998.

Herman, Judith. *Trauma and Recovery: The Aftermath of Violence – From Domestic Abuse to Political Terror.* New York: Basic Books, 1997.

Hollenback, Jess Byron. *Mysticism: Experience, Response, and Empowerment.* University Park: Pennsylvania State University Press, 1996.

Hollywood, Amy. *Sensible Ecstasy: Mysticism, Sexual Difference, and the Demands of History.* Chicago: University of Chicago Press, 2002.

Jones, Ernest. *The Life and Work of Sigmund Freud,* 3 vols. London: Hogarth Press, 1953–7.

Katz, Steven T., ed. *Mysticism and Philosophical Analysis.* London: Oxford University Press, 1978.

King, Richard. *Orientalism and Religion: Postcolonial Theory, India and "the Mystic East."* London: Routledge, 1999.

Kripal, Jeffrey J. *Kali's Child: The Mystical and the Erotic in the Life and Teachings of Ramakrishna.* Chicago: University of Chicago Press, 1995.

Kripal, Jeffrey J. *Roads of Excess, Palaces of Wisdom: Eroticism and Reflexivity in the Study of Mysticism.* Chicago: University of Chicago Press, 2001.

Leuba, James H. *The Psychology of Mysticism.* London: Kegan Paul, Trench, Trubner, 1925.

Meyer Marvin, ed. and tr., *The Gospel of Thomas: The Hidden Sayings of Jesus.* New York: HarperSanFrancisco, 1992.

Myers, Frederic W. H. *Human Personality and Its Survival of Bodily Death.* London: Longmans, Green, 1904.

O'Regan, Cyril. *Gnostic Apocalpyse: Jacob Boehme's Haunted Narrative.* Albany: State University of New York Press, 2002.

Parsons, William B. *The Enigma of the Oceanic Feeling: Revisioning the Psychoanalytic Study of Mysticism.* New York: Oxford University Press, 1999.

Schmidt, Leigh Eric. "The Making of Modern 'Mysticism'," *Journal of the American Academy of Religion* 71 (2003): 273–302.

Sedgwick, Mark J. *Against the Modern World: Traditionalism and the Secret Intellectual History of the Twentieth Century.* New York: Oxford University Press, 2004.

Sells, Michael. *Mystical Languages of Unsaying.* Chicago: University of Chicago Press, 1994.

Smith, Morton. *The Secret Gospel: The Discovery and Interpretation of the Secret Gospel According to Mark.* San Francisco: Harper and Row, 1973.

Thurston, Herbert. *The Physical Phenomena of Mysticism.* London: Burns Oates, 1952.

Wolfson, Elliot R. *Through a Speculum That Shines: Vision and Imagination in Medieval Jewish Mysticism.* Princeton, NJ: Princeton University Press, 1994.

— Chapter 19 —

Myth

Robert A. Segal

In *Paradise Lost* (1667) John Milton combines riveting descriptions of hell and paradise as places "out there" in the world with characterizations of them as states of mind. On the one hand Hell, into which Satan and his retinue land after their fall from heaven, is a lake of fire, the light from which only makes the place darker. The beach is itself on fire and offers no respite from the heat:

> At once as far as Angels' ken he [Satan] views
> The dismal Situation waste and wild,
> A Dungeon horrible, on all sides round
> As one great Furnace flam'd, yet from those flames
> No light, but rather darkness visible
> Serv'd only to discover sights of woe,
> Regions of sorrow, doleful shades, where peace
> And rest can never dwell, hope never comes
> That comes to all; but torture without end
> Still urges, and a fiery Deluge, fed
> With ever-burning Sulphur unconsum'd:
> Such place Eternal Justice had prepar'd

> For those rebellious, here thir Prison ordained
> In utter darkness, and thir portion set
> As far remov'd from God and light of Heav'n
> As from the Center thrice to th' utmost Pole. (I.59–74)

On the other hand hell is a state of mind. Satan, upon awakening in hell, actually boasts that both heaven and hell are the product of mind and can therefore be established anywhere at will:

> Is this the Region, this the Soil, the Clime,
> Said then the lost Arch-Angel, this the seat
> That we must change for Heav'n, this mournful gloom
> For that celestial light? Be it so, since he
> Who now is Sovran can dispose and bid
> What shall be right.
>
>   Farewell happy Fields
> Where Joy for ever dwells: Hail horrors, hail
> Infernal world, and thou profoundest Hell
> Receive thy new Possessor: One who brings
> A mind not to be chang'd by Place or Time.
> The mind is its own place, and in itself
> Can make a Heav'n of Hell, a Hell of Heav'n. (I.241–55)

Later, Satan says the same, but now in self-doubt rather than arrogance, as he recognizes what he has lost and recognizes that, as evil, he turns everything into hell:

> Me miserable! which way shall I fly
> Infinite wrath, and infinite despair?
> Which way I fly is Hell; myself am Hell. (IV.73–75)

It is not just Satan the character who makes hell and paradise mental states. As author, Milton writes of Satan that:

>   from the bottom stir
> The Hell within him, for within him Hell
> He brings, and round about him, nor from Hell
> One step no more than from himself can fly
> By change of place. (IV.19–21)

What for Milton is true of hell is also true of paradise. On the one hand it is a place "out there," lovingly and lushly described:

> Beneath him with new wonder now he [Satan] views
> To all delight of human sense expos'd
> In narrow room Nature's whole wealth, yea more,
> A Heaven on Earth: for blissful Paradise

Of God the Garden was, by him in the East
Of Eden planted; Eden stretch'd her Line
From Auran Eastward to the Royal Tow'rs
Of Great Seleucia, built by Grecian Kings,
Or where the Sons of Eden long before
Dwelt in Telassar: in this pleasant soil
His far more pleasant Garden God ordain'd;
Out of the fertile ground he [God] caus'd to grow
All Trees of noblest kind for sight, smell, taste.

        Thus was this place,
A happy rural seat of various view:
Groves whose rich Trees wept odorous Gums and Balm,
Others whose fruit burnisht with Golden Rind
Hung amiable, Hesperian Fables true,
If true, here only, and of delicious taste. (IV.205–51)

On the other hand the archangel Michael consoles Adam with knowledge of the virtues that human beings can acquire only in the wake of the fall: Faith, Patience, Temperance, Love, and Charity. Concludes Michael:

        then wilt thou not be loath
To leave this Paradise, but shalt possess
A paradise within thee, happier far. (XII.585–87)

Among modern theorists of myth, C. G. Jung is especially eager to trace the psychologizing of the world all the way back to ancient Gnostics and in turn to medieval alchemists. But for him the twentieth century is distinctive in its *separation* of the psychological from the physical and the metaphysical – the separation of the inner from the outer. By contrast, Milton somehow combines the two. Rather than reducing hell and paradise to states of mind, Milton somehow makes them at once physical places and states of mind. That position is distinct from the nineteenth- as well as from the twentieth-century one.

Myth as the Primitive Counterpart to Science

Nineteenth-century theories of myth, if one can generalize, saw myth as entirely about the physical world. The two most famous nineteenth-century theorists were the English anthropologist E. B. Tylor, whose chief work, *Primitive Culture*, first appeared in 1871, and the Scottish classicist and anthropologist J. G. Frazer, the first edition of whose main opus, *The Golden Bough*, was published in 1890. For both Tylor and Frazer, myth is a religious explanation of a physical event. For example, a myth says that rain falls because a god decides to send it. The myth often goes into detail about how the god comes to be responsible for rain and how the god exercises that responsibility. The explanation is personalistic: rain falls because a divine personality decides to send it.

For Tylor, myth provides knowledge of the physical world as an end in itself. For Frazer, the knowledge that myth provides is a means to an end, which is control over the physical world. For both Tylor and Frazer, myth is the "primitive" counterpart to science, which is exclusively modern. "Modern myth" is a contradiction in terms. By science is meant natural science, not social science. The events explained by myth are ones like the falling of rain and the rising of the sun. Myths that explain laws, customs, institutions, and other social phenomena are secondary.

For Tylor, myth is as rational as science. In fact, "primitives" create myth through the scientific-like processes of observation (noticing the regularity of rain), hypothesis (conjecturing that, by analogy to human actions, actions in the physical world are caused by the decisions of super-human personalities), and generalization (generalizing from the cause of one event in the physical world to the cause of others). (Tylor has an old-fashioned, inductivist notion of science.) Myth and science are identical in function as well as in origin. Both serve to account for all events in the physical world. Those events include not only events in the world around us but also physical events in humans such as birth and death. Just as it rains because a god decides to send rain, so a human being dies because the personality in it – its soul – decides to leave the body.

In function, then, science renders myth redundant. But science does more. It renders myth impossible. For both myth and science offer *direct* accounts of events. According to myth, the rain god, let us suppose, collects rain in buckets and then chooses to empty the buckets on some spot below. According to science, meteorological processes cause rain. One cannot reconcile the accounts by stacking a mythological account atop a scientific account, for the rain god does not utilize meteorological processes but acts instead of them. In short, it is impossible to accept both myth and science. Taking for granted that moderns have science, Tylor obliges them to reject myth as false, if still fully rational.

Again, science means natural, not social, science. For Tylor, personalistic explanations of *human* actions are not unscientific, and the social sciences readily provide them. The same holds for us today. The heyday of behaviorism in the social sciences has long passed, and cognitive science shows constraints on decisions rather than rules them out. Above all, the relationship of the mind to the body remains an openly scientific question. Whatever the mix of personalistic and impersonal ingredients in contemporary explanations of *human* actions, it is personalistic explanations of events in the *physical* world that are usually considered unscientific. There is thus a disjunction between the kinds of explanations permitted of human behavior and the kinds permitted of the behavior of the physical world. In myth, there is no disjunction. The physical world operates the same way the human world does, simply on a grander scale.

For Frazer, myth is not only false but also irrational. For it is tied to magic, which stems from the failure to make basic logical distinctions. As epitomized by voodoo, magic fails to distinguish between a symbol and what it symbolizes: a voodoo doll is assumed by practitioners to be identical with the person of whom it is an image rather than merely symbolic of the person. Otherwise what one did to the doll would not affect the person. Magic works by imitating on the doll what one wants to happen to the person.

Magic puts myth into practice in the form of ritual, which is a vain attempt to gain control over the physical world, especially over crops. Typically, the king plays the role of the god of vegetation, the chief god of the pantheon, and acts out the key part of the myth, or biography, of the god: his death and rebirth. As in voodoo, imitating the death and rebirth of the god of vegetation is believed to cause the same to happen to the god. And as the god goes, so go the crops. For Frazer, the cause of the rebirth of crops is, strictly, not here a decision by the god, as it would be for Tylor, but the physical condition of the god: a revived god automatically spells revived crops. The ritual is performed at the end – the desired end – of winter, presumably when stored-up provisions are running low. For Frazer, myth still explains the state of the crops, as for Tylor, but for the purpose of reviving them, not just for the purpose of explaining their revival.

To be sure, Frazer offers an alternative scenario, according to which the king, now himself divine, is actually killed at the first sign of weakening and is immediately replaced. The restoration to health of the god of vegetation residing within the incumbent is thereby ensured. Here, too, as the god goes, so go the crops.

For Frazer, myth, together with ritual, is the primitive counterpart to *applied* science rather than, as for Tylor, the primitive counterpart to *theoretical* science. Myth is even more conspicuously false for Frazer than for Tylor because it fails to deliver the goods.

In the twentieth century Tylor's and Frazer's theories have been spurned by fellow theorists of myth on many grounds: for pitting myth against science and thereby precluding both traditional myths and modern ones, for subsuming myth under religion and thereby precluding secular myths, for deeming the function of myth explanatory, for deeming the subject matter of myth the physical world, and for deeming myth false. Nevertheless, Tylor's and Frazer's theories have remained central to the study of myth, and subsequent theories can be taken as rejoinders to them.

The overarching twentieth-century rejoinder to Tylor and Frazer has been the denial that myth is the primitive counterpart to modern science and that myth must therefore go when science comes. Twentieth-century theorists have not defended myth by challenging science as the reigning explanation of the physical world. They have not, for example, relativized science, "sociologized" science, or made science "mythic." Postmodern wariness of science has not arisen. The physical world has been conceded to science. Instead, myth has been recharacterized as other than a literal explanation of that world. Either myth has been taken as other than an explanation, in which case its function diverges from that of science, or myth has been read other than literally, in which case it does not even refer to the physical world. Either the function or the subject matter of myth has been reconceived to accommodate science. Or both have been reconceived. The issue has not been whether "primitives" can have myth. It has been taken for granted that they can and do. The issue has been whether moderns, who by definition have science, can also have myth.

Myth as Other Than an Explanation of the Physical World

The most important reinterpreters of the function of myth have been Bronislaw Malinowski (1926) and Mircea Eliade (1968), both of whom still read myth literally. It is not clear whether for Malinowski, the Polish anthropologist who spent most of his career in England, moderns as well as primitives have myth. What is clear is that for him primitives have science as well as myth, so that myth cannot be the primitive counterpart to modern science, theoretical or applied. For Malinowski, primitives use science, however rudimentary, both to explain and to control the physical world. They use myth to do the opposite: to reconcile themselves to aspects of the world that cannot be controlled, such as natural catastrophes, illness, old age, and death. Myths root these woes in the irreversible, primordial actions of gods or humans. According to one myth, humans age because a forebear did something foolish that introduced old age irremediably into the world: "The longed-for power of eternal youth and the faculty of rejuvenation which gives immunity from decay and age, have been lost by a small accident which it would have been in the power of a child and a woman to prevent" (Malinowski 1926, p. 104). Myth pronounces the world not the best possible one but, in the wake of unalterable events, the sole possible one. Still, the world, seen through myth, is less capricious than it would otherwise be.

Even more important than reconciling humans to physical unpleasantries is the role of myth in reconciling humans to social unpleasantries – to the imposition of laws, customs, and institutions. Far from unalterable, these unpleasantries *can* be cast off. Myth helps ensure that they are not, by rooting them, too, in a hoary past, thereby conferring on them the clout of tradition. If for Malinowski moderns have myth, then a myth about fox hunting would trace the activity back as far as possible, thereby making it a traditional part of country life. If for Malinowski moderns do not have myth, then the modern counterpart to myths about social phenomena would be ideology, as myth is for Roland Barthes (1972).

Insofar as myth for Malinowski deals with the social world, it turns its back on the physical world. But even when myth deals with the physical world, its connection to that world is limited. Myth may explain how flooding arose – a god or a human brought it about – but science, not myth, explains why flooding occurs whenever it does. And science, not myth, says what to do about it. Indeed, myth says that nothing can be done about it. Malinowski never works out how the mythic explanation is compatible with the scientific one, but at least he tries to keep the two apart and therefore compatible.

For Mircea Eliade, the Romanian-born historian of religions who eventually emigrated to the United States, myth explains the origin of both physical and social phenomena, just as for Malinowski. And the explanation, as for Malinowski, is that a god – for Eliade, never a mere human – brought it about. Myth, as for Tylor and Frazer, is part of religion. But the pay-off of myth is not, as for Malinowski, reconciliation to the unpleasantries of life. The pay-off is the opposite: escape from the world and return to the time of the origin of whatever phenomenon is explained. Myth is like a magic carpet. Because all religions, according to Eliade, believe that gods were closer at hand in days of yore than now, to be whisked back in time is to be able to brush up against god – the ultimate pay-off. Myth is a medium for encountering god.

Eliade ventures beyond not only Malinowski but, more important, Tylor and Frazer in proclaiming myth panhuman and not merely primitive. He cites modern plays, novels, and movies with the mythic theme of yearning to escape from the everyday world into another, often earlier one:

> A whole volume could well be written on the myths of modern man, on the mythologies camouflaged in the plays that he enjoys, in the books that he reads. . . . Even reading includes a mythological function . . . particularly because, through reading, the modern man succeeds in obtaining an 'escape from time' comparable to the 'emergence from time' effected by myths. (Eliade 1968, p. 205)

If even moderns, who for Eliade are professedly atheistic and therefore anti-mythic, harbor myths, then myth must be universal.

Alas, Eliade's attempt to make myth modern sidesteps the problem. Instead of showing how myth is compatible with science – here social scientific or natural scientific – he simply enlists example after example of what he calls modern myth. But not all modern plays, movies, and novels even take place in the past, much less describe the origin of some phenomenon, let alone attribute that origin to the handiwork of a god. A story of the origin of, say, a great nation can elevate the founders to a superhuman status, but can the retelling or re-enacting of their feat carry the audience back in time? True, one can get lost in a play, movie, or novel and forget where one is. Horror movies are scary exactly because moviegoers imagine themselves up there on the screen, as the monster's next victim. But once the movie is over, and the lights come on, one usually remembers all too abruptly where one really is. Even if the memory of the experience of the film lingers, the memory is of feeling *as if* one had been part of the action. Sane persons do not think they really had been.

Myth as Other Than Literal in Meaning

The most prominent reinterpreters of not the *function* but the *meaning* of myth have been the German New Testament scholar Rudolf Bultmann (1953) and the German-born philosopher Hans Jonas (1963), who eventually settled in the United States. Both were followers of the philosopher Martin Heidegger and offer existentialist readings of myth. While they limit themselves to their specialties, Christianity and Gnosticism, they apply a theory of myth *per se*.

Bultmann acknowledges that, read literally, myth is about the physical world and is incompatible with science. When taken literally, myth should rightly be rejected as uncompromisingly as Tylor and Frazer reject it. But unlike both Malinowski and Eliade as well as Tylor and Frazer, Bultmann proposes reading myth symbolically. Read symbolically, or "demythologized," myth is no longer about the external world. It is now about the place of human beings in the world. Myth no longer explains but describes, and describes not the world itself but humans' experience of the world: "The real purpose of myth is not to present an objective picture of the world as it is, but to express man's understanding of himself in the world in which he lives. Myth should be interpreted not cosmologically, but anthropologically, or better still, existentially" (Bultmann 1953, p. 10). Myth ceases to be primitive and becomes universal. It ceases to be false and becomes true. It becomes a statement of the human condition.

Read literally, the New Testament describes a cosmic war between good and evil superhuman figures for control of the physical world, just as in *Paradise Lost* and just as for Tylor and Frazer. These figures intervene miraculously not only in the operation of nature, as for Tylor and Frazer, but also in the lives of human beings. God directs humans to do good; Satan tempts, even compels, them to do evil.

Read symbolically, the New Testament still refers in part to the physical world, but now to a world ruled by a single, transcendent God, who does not look like a human being and who does not intercede miraculously in the world. Satan does not even exist and instead symbolizes the evil disposition of humans. There is no longer any physical hell, which, after all, has not quite been detected by geologists. Hell symbolizes despair over the absence of God. Likewise heaven refers not to a place in the sky, which should have been visible to astronauts, but to joy in the presence of God. The imminent end of the world predicted by the Gospels – a prediction that has proved false and must therefore similarly be demythologized to be acceptable to historically minded moderns – refers not to a set point in time but to the moment when one accepts God. The Kingdom comes not outwardly, with all kinds of cosmic upheavals, but inwardly, whenever one embraces God. The Kingdom refers less to one's state of mind – a psychological interpretation – than to the state of the world once one believes God to be present in it – an existentialist interpretation. Because Bultmann is a religious existentialist rather than, like Jean-Paul Sartre and Albert Camus, an atheistic one, the human condition for him is not that of permanent alienation from the world. Alienation is the condition of humanity prior to finding god. At-homeness in the world is the condition upon finding god. Alienation means what it is like to live in a world in which one cannot count on the crops to grow when needed. At-homeness means what it is like to live in a world in which, thanks to a solicitous God, one can.

Like Eliade, Bultmann desperately wants moderns to have myth. Both want to make myth universal and not merely primitive. But unlike Eliade, Bultmann actually tries to make myth acceptable to scientifically minded moderns. Even when demythologized, however, the New Testament still refers to God, albeit of a nonphysical form. One must continue to believe in God to accept the mythology.

Like Bultmann, Hans Jonas seeks to show that ancient myths retain a meaning for moderns rather than, like Eliade, that moderns have myths of their own. For Jonas, as for Bultmann, myth read symbolically describes the alienation of humans from the world as well as from their true selves prior to their acceptance of God. Because ancient Gnosticism, unlike mainstream Christianity, sets the soul against body and immateriality against matter, humans remain alienated from the physical world and from their bodies even after they have found the true God. In fact, the true God can be found only by rejecting the false god of the physical world. Gnostics overcome alienation from this world only by transcending it.

Unlike Bultmann, who strives to bridge the gap between Christianity and modernity, Jonas acknowledges the divide between Gnosticism and modernity. He translates Gnostic myths into existentialist terms to demonstrate only the similarity, not the identity, between the ancient Gnostic outlook and the modern, secular existentialist one: "the essence of existentialism is a certain dualism, an estrangement between man and the world. . . . There is only one situation . . . where that condition has been realized and lived out with all the vehemence of a cataclysmic event. That is the gnostic movement" (Jonas 1963, p. 325). In Gnosticism, the state of estrangement is temporary, at least for those who eventually find God. In modernity, which Jonas interprets from the standpoint of secular existentialism, alienation is permanent. It is the human condition. Jonas does not attempt to demythologize Gnostic metaphysics. He isolates the Gnostic description of how the world is experienced prior to the revelation and parallels it to the secular existentialist description of how the world is experienced permanently.

Without trying to make Gnosticism palatable to moderns, as Bultmann does for Christianity, Jonas strives to show how a mythology that far exceeds even Milton's in the scale of its worlds and its deities can still speak to moderns – and not to modern believers, as for Bultmann, but to modern skeptics. Gnostic mythology can do so because, rightly grasped, it addresses not the nature of the world but the nature of the experience of the world. Like Bultmann, Jonas seeks to reconcile myth with science by recharacterizing the subject matter of myth.

In concentrating on the meaning of myth, both Bultmann and Jonas bypass the issue of the function of myth. Suppose their existentialist interpretations of myth were acceptable to moderns. Would moderns need myth? There are theorists of myth, such as the French philosopher Paul Ricoeur (1967) and the American philosopher Philip Wheelwright (1968), for whom the meaning of myth is somehow untranslatable into non-mythic terms, in which case myth is indispensable for expressing and even revealing its contents. But Bultmann and Jonas can hardly claim the same since they take their interpretive cues from Heidegger. For them, modern philosophy unlocks myth, not vice versa. They are thereby left with a theory that makes myth at best palatable to moderns but not thereby necessary for them. Myth for Bultmann and Jonas is what myth would be for Tylor and Frazer if it were compatible with science: superfluous.

Myth as Both Other Than Explanatory and Other Than Literal

The most radical departures from Tylor and Frazer have transformed both the explanatory function and the literal meaning of myth. The most influential theorists here have been the Austrian physician Sigmund Freud (1965) and the Swiss psychiatrist C. G. Jung (1968). For both, the subject matter of myth is conspicuously a state of mind – and not a conscious state, as for Milton, but an unconscious one. For Freud, the function of myth is to vent the unconscious. For Jung, the function is to encounter the unconscious. For neither Freud nor Jung does myth make the unconscious conscious. On the contrary, myth ordinarily operates unconsciously and for Freud must operate unconsciously. Freud and Jung differ sharply over the nature of the unconscious and in turn over the reason that myth is needed to express it.

Because the Freudian unconscious is composed of repressed, anti-social drives, myth releases those drives in a disguised way, so that neither the myth maker nor the reader of the myth ever confronts its meaning and thereby the myth maker's or the reader's own true nature. Myth, like other aspects of culture, serves simultaneously to reveal and to hide its unconscious contents. Myth is a "compromise formation." The classical Freudian approach to myth takes myth as wish fulfillment. Focusing on myths of male heroes, Freud's one-time disciple Otto Rank (1914) sees these myths as providing a partial fulfillment of, above all, Oedipal drives. By unconsciously identifying oneself with the named hero, one gains a vicarious, mental fulfillment of one's own lingering desires. Myths serve neurotic adults who are stuck, or fixated, at their Oedipal stage: "Myths are, therefore, created by adults, by means of retrograde childhood fantasies, the hero being credited with the myth-maker's personal infantile [i.e., childhood] history" (Rank 1914, p. 82). The real hero of the myth is not the named hero but the myth maker or reader. The true subject matter of the myth is the fantasized life of that myth maker or reader. At heart, myth is not biography but autobiography.

Spurred by the emergence of ego psychology, which has broadened psychoanalysis from a theory of abnormal personality to a theory of normal personality, contemporary Freudians see myth as contributing to psychological development and not just to neurosis. For them, myth helps one grow up rather than, like Peter Pan, remain a child. Myth abets adjustment to society and to the physical world rather than childish flight from them. Myth may still serve to release repressed drives, but it serves even more to sublimate them and to integrate them. It serves the ego and the superego, not merely the id. Moreover, myth serves everyone, not only neurotics. To quote the American psychoanalyst Jacob Arlow:

> Psychoanalysis has a greater contribution to make to the study of mythology than [merely] demonstrating, in myths, wishes often encountered in the unconscious thinking of patients. The myth is a particular kind of communal experience. . . . [T]he myth can be studied from the point of view of its function in psychic integration – how it plays a role in warding off feelings of guilt and anxiety, how it constitutes a form of adaptation to reality and to the group in which the individual lives, and how it influences the crystallization of the individual identity and the formation of the superego. (Arlow 1961, p. 375)

In his book *The Uses of Enchantment* (1976) the better-known Freudian Bruno Bettelheim says much the same, but he insistently says it of fairy tales rather than of myths, which he oddly interprets in a classically Freudian way.

The telling phrase from Arlow is "adaptation to reality." Myth for contemporary Freudians, no less than for classical ones, presupposes a divide between the individual, which means the individual's drives, and reality. For classical Freudians, myth functions to satisfy in fantasy what cannot be satisfied in reality. For contemporary Freudians, myth functions to help one accept the inability to be satisfied in reality. For both varieties of Freudians, myth is not about reality – that is, the external world. It is about the individual, who comes smack up against reality. It is about the clash between the pleasure principle and the reality principle. Myth either shields the individual from reality – the classical view – or foments acceptance of reality – the contemporary view. Rather than explaining reality, myth takes reality for granted and reacts to it, either negatively (classical) or positively (contemporary). To explain reality, one turns to natural science, just as for Tylor and Frazer. Myth taken literally is incompatible with science, in the same way that it is for Tylor and Frazer. Myth psychologized is compatible with science because it is no longer about reality – outer reality.

Tylor and Frazer have a psychology of their own, and it is incorporated in their theory of myth. But for them myth does not arise from any confrontation between individual and reality. It arises from the experience of reality, which one wants either to explain (Tylor) or to manipulate (Frazer). Whatever role the individual plays in creating myth, the subject matter of myth is still the world, not the individual. Even though for Tylor especially, mythic explanations stem from the analogy that primitives draw between human behavior and that of the world, myth is still about the world, not about humans. And Tylor is not even fazed by the subsequent kinship between humans and the world – an issue for those who, like Bultmann and Jonas, are concerned with attitudes toward the world. Frazer, for his part, attributes mythic explanations not to an analogy with human behavior but to despair over the ability to control the world – a despair which leads to the assumption that the world operates at the behest of gods. The world is thereby experienced as hard to control, but myth is still about the world itself, not about the experience of it.

For Freudians, and also for Jungians, myths project human nature onto the world in the form of gods or god-like heroes. To understand the world is exactly to withdraw those projections. The world really operates according to mechanical laws rather than according to the wills of a divine family. There is no parallel between humans and the world. Even hero myths involve projection: the plot of hero myths is the expression of fantasized family relations. Heroism itself is more fantasy than reality. There are no heroes in the real world, at least ones elevated to superhuman status. There are only human beings, some better than others.

For Jungians as well as for Freudians, myths project human nature onto the world in the form of gods and god-like heroes. To understand the world is, similarly, to withdraw those projections and to recognize the world as it really is. Jungian projections are more elusive than Freudian ones because they cover a far wider range of the personality. There are an almost endless number of sides of the personality, or archetypes. Anything in the world can be archetypal – that is, can provide a hook for the projection of an archetype.

Unlike Freudians, Jungians have taken myth positively from the outset. For them, the unconscious expressed in myth is not the Freudian repository of repressed, unacceptable drives but a storehouse of innately unconscious archetypes that have simply never had an opportunity at realization: "Contents of an archetypal character . . . do not refer to anything that is or has been conscious, but to something essentially unconscious" (Jung 1968, p. 156). Myth is one means of encountering this unconscious. The function of myth is less that of release, as for classical Freudians, than that of growth, as for contemporary ones. But where even contemporary Freudians see myth as a means of adjustment to the demands of the outer world, Jungians see myth as a means of the cultivation of the inner world. The pay-off is not adjustment but self-realization. Myth is a circuitous, if still useful, means of self-realization because it involves projection: one encounters oneself *through* the world. Ordinarily, projections are recognized and thereby withdrawn only in the course of analysis – a point that holds for Freudians no less than for Jungians. If for either Freudians or Jungians myth can still be employed once the projection has been recognized, then the middle man – the world – has conveniently been eliminated.

Freud and Jung alike bypass the power of myth at the conscious, usually literal, level. While both appreciate the need to be moved by the life of the named hero or protagonist, that figure is a mere hook onto which to hang the autobiography. The story is moving only when it becomes one's own. As Freud states, Oedipus' "destiny moves us only because it might have been ours – because the oracle laid the same curse [i.e., the Oedipus complex] upon us before our birth as upon him" (Freud 1965, p. 296). Jung would concur. For both, myth is autobiography. No theory of myth is more solipsistic than theirs, with Jung's even more solipsistic than Freud's.

To be sure, Jung does return to the world through the concept of synchronicity, developed with the physicist Wolfgang Pauli. Synchronicity restores a link between humanity and the world that the withdrawal of projections still insisted upon by Jung removes. Synchronicity refers to the coincidence between our thoughts and the behavior of the world, between what is inner and what is outer. As Jung writes of his favorite example of synchronicity, that of a resistant patient who was describing a dream about a golden scarab when a scarab beetle appeared: "at the moment my patient was telling me her dream a real 'scarab' tried to get into the room, as if it had understood that it must play its mythological role as a symbol of rebirth" (Jung 1973–4, II, p. 541). Here the world apparently responds to the patient's dream; but understood synchronistically, the world merely, if most fortuitously, *matches* the patient's dream rather than is *effected* by it. The patient's conscious attitude, which dismisses the notion of an unconscious, is "out of sync" with the world. While synchronicity is not itself myth, which would be an account of a synchronistic experience,

Jung's fascination with the concept shows that even he, who psychologizes myth (and everything else) more relentlessly than anyone else, cannot resist the allure of the external world. Nevertheless, when he analyzes myth, he analyzes it as about oneself, not the world.

Myth as Variation on Tylor or Frazer

Ironically, some of the most recent theorizing about myth has been a variation on either Tylor or Frazer. Led by the French anthropologist Pascal Boyer (1994), "cognitivists" follow Tylor in deeming myth a primitive explanation of the world, but they are concerned with how the mind constrains mythic explanations rather than, like Tylor, with the explanations themselves. They analyze the mental processes that shape thinking, and those processes are far more constrictive than Tylor's loose sequence of observation, hypothesis, and generalization.

Similarly, the German classicist Walter Burkert (1996) and the French literary critic René Girard (1972) have given new twists to Frazer's myth-ritualism. Where in Frazer's alternative scenario myth is the script for the ritualistic killing of the king, whose death and replacement ensure the rebirth of crops, for Burkert myth reinforces the ritual that commemorates the past hunting of animals for food. The function of myth is not physical but psychological and social: to cope with the guilt and anxiety that members of society feel toward their own aggression.

Where in the same alternative scenario of Frazer's the king is willing to die for the sake of his subjects, for Girard the king (or someone else) is selected as a scapegoat to blame for the violence in society. Rather than directing the ritualistic killing, myth arises afterwards to cover up the deed by turning the victim into a criminal and then into a hero. The function of myth is social: to preserve the ethos of sociability by hiding not only the killing but also the violence endemic to society – violence ultimately stemming from the "mimetic" nature of human beings.

While Boyer, Burkert, and Girard do offer revivals of the theories of Tylor and Frazer, the variations they introduce do not bring myth back to the external world. For all three, myth is about human nature, not about the nature of the external world. The three are therefore examples of the twentieth-century rejoinder to Tylor and Frazer rather than exceptions to it.

Myth as Again Primitive Science

Of all twentieth-century theorists, the one who has most fully brought myth back to the world is the French anthropologist Claude Lévi-Strauss

(1978). At first glance, Lévi-Strauss seems a throwback to Tylor. For myth is for Lévi-Strauss, as for Tylor, an exclusively primitive, yet nevertheless rigorously intellectual, enterprise. In declaring that primitives, "moved by a need or a desire to understand the world around them, . . . proceed by intellectual means, exactly as a philosopher, or even to some extent a scientist, can and would do" (Lévi-Strauss 1978, p. 16), Lévi-Strauss seems indistinguishable from Tylor. Yet he is in fact severely critical of Tylor, for whom primitives concoct myth rather than science because they think less critically than moderns. For Lévi-Strauss, primitives concoct myth because they think differently from moderns.

Primitive, or mythic, thinking is concrete. Modern thinking is abstract. Primitive thinking focuses on the observable, sensory, qualitative aspects of natural phenomena rather than, like modern thinking, on the unobservable, nonsensory, quantitative ones. Yet myth for Lévi-Strauss is no less scientific than modern science. It is simply part of the "science of the concrete" rather than part of the science of the abstract. Myth *is* primitive science, but it is not inferior science.

If myth is an instance of mythic thinking because it deals with concrete, tangible phenomena, it is an instance of thinking *per se*, modern and primitive alike, because it classifies phenomena. According to Lévi-Strauss, all humans think in the form of classifications, specifically pairs of oppositions, and project them onto the world. Many cultural phenomena express these oppositions. Myth is distinctive in resolving or, more accurately, tempering the oppositions it expresses. While the oppositions experienced in the world are reducible to the consummately existential tension between nature and culture, the pay-off from the diminution of the oppositions is purely intellectual: myth serves not to make life more bearable, as for Malinowski, but to solve a logical conundrum – the oppositions amounting to contradictions. Because myth presents and diminishes contradictions at the level of "structure" rather than of plot, Lévi-Strauss renders superficial the issue of a literal or symbolic reading of the plot.

Yet for all Lévi-Strauss' bold efforts at reviving the nineteenth-century view of myth as scientific-like, myth for him, as for his nineteenth-century predecessors, is supplanted by, if not science *per se*, then modern science. Myth may not be at odds with modern science, focused as the two are on different aspects of the world, but moderns have modern science and not myth. Moreover, the contradictions tempered by myth lie in the mind, which simply projects them onto the world and then confronts them as if they were inherent in the world. Myth is thus not really about the world even for primitives.

Of course, there are other structuralists besides Lévi-Strauss, and some of them have analyzed modern myths. Notably, the French semiotician Roland Barthes (1972) takes as myths various cultural artifacts and shows how they serve to justify the bourgeois outlook of postwar France. But then the function of myth becomes ideological, and myth ceases to have anything to do with the physical world. Similarly, the French classicists inspired by not only Lévi-Strauss but also Louis Gernet – Jean-Pierre Vernant (1983), Marcel Detienne (1977), and Pierre Vidal-Naquet (1981) – have examined the ideological function of myth. But then again, myth, while not merely primitive, is still not about the physical world.

Myth as Again About the External World

Is there a way of bringing myth back to the world? I think there is, through the approach of the English child psychiatrist and psychoanalyst D. W. Winnicott (1982, 1987). Winnicott does not himself analyze myth, but his analysis of play and of its continuation in adult make-believe provides one road back to the world.

For Winnicott, play is *acknowledged* as other than reality: children grant that they are just playing. But play is no mere fantasy or escapism. It is the construction of a reality that has personal meaning. To pretend that a spoon is a train is to take a spoon and turn it into a train. Far from the projection of oneself onto the world, as for Freud and Jung, play is the construction of a distinct world. As Winnicott continually declares, play is "creative." Far from the confusion of itself with reality, play demarcates the difference. Play grants itself the right to treat a spoon as a train, and a parent is barred from asking whether the spoon really is a train. Once play is over, the train is again a mere spoon.

To use Winnicott's term, play is a "transitional" activity. It provides a transition not merely from childhood to adulthood but also from the child's inner world of fantasy to outer reality: "play can easily be seen to link the individual's relation to inner reality with the same individual's relation to external or shared reality" (Winnicott 1987, p. 145). Play links the realms by constructing an external world to fit the fantasy: play transforms a spoon into a train. Play combines a mental state with the external world – not simply by juxtaposing the two, as Milton does, but by connecting them. At the same time play does not deny the difference between the inner and the outer worlds, for only during play is the spoon a train. On the one hand play is recognized as make-believe: outside of play the spoon is conceded to be only a spoon. On the other hand the make-believe is taken seriously: within play the spoon really is a train.

A transitional activity or object, such as a teddy bear, does not confuse the symbol with the symbolized, the way, by contrast, magic for Frazer does. The child knows that the teddy bear is not Mommy or Mommy's breast, even while clutching it as if it were. The child knows that play is not "reality" but pretends that it is.

A transitional activity or object is transitional in several respects. First, the activity or object straddles the inner and the outer worlds. It partakes of both, while remaining distinct from both. (In Lévi-Straussian terms, it mediates the opposition between the worlds.) A child uses materials from the outer world – a spoon – to create a world with inner meaning – a train. A child creates a living teddy bear out of cloth and stuffing. The meaning constitutes the transformation of the outer world to suit the inner. Second, a transitional object or activity is transitional in that it is experienced *in* the outer world. Play can occur anywhere.

As adult extensions of play, Winnicott names gardening and cooking, in both of which one creates a world with personal meaning out of elements from the external world. Winnicott also names art and religion, in both of which as well one creates one's own world out of any number of elements from the external world, though with a far deeper meaning to it:

> It is assumed here that the task of reality-acceptance is never completed, that no human being is free from the strain of relating inner and outer reality, and that relief from this strain is provided by an intermediate area of experience which is not challenged (arts, religion, etc.). This intermediate area is in direct continuity with the play area of the small child who is "lost" in play. (Winnicott 1982, p. 13)

I propose taking myth as a case of modern, adult make-believe.

It would be preposterous to suggest that all myths are held as make-believe. Doubtless there is a spectrum. Some myths are taken and perhaps can only be taken as unassailable truths – for example, myths about the coming end of the world. Biblical myths, if still espoused literally, would fall here. Other myths are taken and perhaps can only be taken as make-believe – for example, hagiographical biographies of heroes. In between would lie myths that can be taken either way – for example, ideologies and world views, such as Marxism, the belief in progress, and psychoanalysis itself. Taken as make-believe, these myths would serve as *guides* to the real world rather than as *depictions* of the world.

The "rags-to-riches" myth, which claims that America is a land of boundless opportunity, would fall in this in-between state. Undeniably, the credo can be held as an unassailable truth, and can lead to frustration and recrimination when it does not pan out. But it can also be held as "make-believe" – not as a false characterization of American life but as a hoped-for one. Here America is seen *as if it were* a haven of opportunity. Contentions that race, class, gender, or religion stymies opportunity are here recognized but fended off, rationalized away as excuses for personal failure. In the wake of the civil rights movement, the feminist movement, and multiculturalism, these "excuses," far from being acknowledged as legitimate, are dismissed even more sharply than before: whether or not in generations past, at least by now, America is believed to offer equal opportunity to all. The present-day epitome of this myth is Anthony Robbins, salesman par excellence for success. What, according to Robbins, keeps persons from succeeding? Not trying. Where there is a will, there most certainly is a way. Taking the rags-to-riches myth as make-believe means trusting Tony Robbins – not because he is indisputably right but because one wants him to be right.

To view a myth as make-believe is not to dismiss it as a delusion. To do so would be to revert to the present either/or option, according to which myth, to be acceptable to moderns, either must be true about the external world or, if false about the external world, must concern itself instead with the mind or society in order still to be true. To view myth as make-believe is to allow for a third way of characterizing myth. The choice is not simply either delusion or reality. The third option is make-believe. Taken as make-believe, myth can again be true about the world, and not just about the social world but even about the physical world.

The deification of celebrities, above all of Hollywood stars, turns them into superhuman figures, into "gods." They are credited with extraordinary accomplishments in not only the social world – ending poverty, cancelling Third World Debt – but also in the physical world – saving species, ending pollution. Their power often exceeds that of even heads of state. The devotion of fans amounts to "worship." At the same time that worship is in the form of make-believe. Hagiographical biographies of celebrities constitute myths.

Bibliography

Arlow, Jacob. "Ego Psychology and the Study of Mythology," *Journal of the American Psychoanalytic Association* 9 (1961): 371–93.

Barthes, Roland. *Mythologies*, tr. Annette Lavers. New York: Hill and Wang; London: Cape, 1972.

Bettelheim, Bruno. *The Uses of Enchantment*. New York: Knopf, 1976.

Boyer, Pascal. *The Naturalness of Religious Ideas*. Berkeley: University of California Press, 1994.

Bultmann, Rudolf. "New Testament and Mythology" [1944], in *Kerygma and Myth*, ed. Hans-Werner Bartsch, tr. Reginald H. Fuller. London: SPCK, 1953. Vol. 1, pp. 1–44.

Burkert, Walter. *Creation of the Sacred*. Cambridge, MA: Harvard University Press, 1996.

Detienne, Marcel. *The Gardens of Adonis*, tr. Janet Lloyd. Hassock: Harvester Press; Atlantic Highlands, NJ: Humanities Press, 1977.

Eliade, Mircea. *The Sacred and the Profane* [1959], tr. Willard R. Trask. New York: Harvest Books, 1968.

Frazer, James George. *The Golden Bough*. Abridged edn. London: Macmillan, 1922 [first unabridged edn. 1890].

Freud, Sigmund. *The Interpretation of Dreams* [1900], tr. James Strachey. New York: Avon Books, 1965 [1953].

Girard, René. *Violence and the Sacred*, tr. Peter Gregory. London: Athlone Press; Baltimore: Johns Hopkins University Press, 1972.

Jonas, Hans. "Gnosticism, Existentialism, and Nihilism" [1952], in his *The Gnostic Religion* [1958], 2nd edn. Boston: Beacon Press, 1963, pp. 320–40.

Jung, C. G. *The Archetypes and the Collective Unconscious* [1959], 2nd edn. Collected Works of C. G. Jung, eds. Sir Herbert Read et al., trs. R. F. C. Hull et al., vol. 9, pt. 1. Princeton, NJ: Princeton University Press, 1968.

Jung, C. G. *Letters*, eds. Gerhard Adler and Aniela Jaffé, tr. R. F. C. Hull. Princeton, NJ: Princeton University Press, 1973–4.

Lévi-Strauss, Claude. *Myth and Meaning.* Toronto: University of Toronto Press, 1978.

Malinowski, Bronislaw. *Myth in Primitive Psychology.* London: Kegan Paul; New York: Norton, 1926.

Rank, Otto. *The Myth of the Birth of the Hero.* 1st edn. Trs. F. Robbins and Smith Ely Jelliffe. Nervous and Mental Disease Monograph Series, no. 18. New York: Journal of Nervous and Mental Disease Publishing, 1914.

Ricoeur, Paul. *The Symbolism of Evil*, tr. Emerson Buchanan. New York: Harper and Row, 1967.

Tylor, Edward Barnett. *Primitive Culture.* 2 vols. 1st edn. London: Murray, 1871.

Vernant, Jean-Pierre. *Myth and Thought among the Greeks*, tr. not given. London: Routledge and Kegan Paul, 1983.

Vidal-Naquet, and Jean-Pierre Vernant. *Myth and Tragedy in Ancient Greece*, tr. Janet Lloyd. Brighton: Harvester Press, 1981.

Wheelwright, Philip. *The Burning Fountain* [1954]. Rev. edn. Bloomington: Indiana University Press, 1968.

Winnicott, D. W. "Transitional Objects and Transitional Phenomena" (1951), in his *Playing and Reality* [1971] (London and New York: Routledge, 1982), ch. 1. Also in Winnicott, *Through Paediatrics to Psychoanalysis* [1958] (London: Karnac Books, 1992), ch. 18.

Winnicott, D. W. *The Child, the Family and the Outside World* [1964]. Reading, MA: Addison-Wesley, 1987.

— Chapter 20 —

Nationalism and Religion

Mark Juergensmeyer

The extraordinary events of September 11, 2001, provided a dramatic demonstration of the resurgence of politicized religion in the contemporary age. Though politics have been an aspect of every religion throughout history, a particularly strident form began to assert itself shortly before the dawn of the twenty-first century. Even before the Twin Towers of New York City's World Trade Center crumbled into dust, the al-Qaida network of Osama bin Laden had been implicated in a series of terrorist incidents, most of them aimed at the global military and economic power of the United States. Other movements of religious activism, from the Ayatollah Khomeini's Islamic revolution in Iran to the Khalistani movement of Sikhs in northern India, targeted the political leaders of their own countries. In bin Laden's case the goal was transnational. In most other instances of religious politics, including the Iranian and Sikh cases, the goal was a new form of religious nationalism. Both movements rejected the secular nationalism that had been the central feature of European Enlightenment since the eighteenth century.

In most cases the new religious movements were reactions to the spread worldwide of secular modernity. They were responses to the insufficiencies of what is often touted as the world's global political standard: the secular, Westernized constructs of nationalism that are found not only in the West but also in many parts of the former Third World as vestiges of colonialism. These secular nationalisms, weakened by globalization, have been under siege. Their vulnerability has enabled new ethnic and religious politics to step into the breach and shore up national identities in their own distinctive ways. Yet these identities have often had international and transnational aspects of their own. Thus some forms of ethnic and religious politics have been global, some virulently anti-global, and still others stridently nationistic. Yet all have preyed upon the weakened state of secular nationalism in the present period of late modernity.

The Assault on Secular Nationalism

Born as a stepchild of the European Enlightenment, the idea of the modern nation-state is at once profound and simple: the state is created by the people within a given national territory. Secular nationalism – the ideology that originally gave the nation-state its legitimacy – contends that the authority of a nation is based on the secular idea of a social compact of equals rather than on ethnic ties or sacred mandates. It is a compelling idea, one with claims to apply universally. It reached its widest extent of worldwide acceptance in the first half of the twentieth century.

But the second half of the century turned out to be a different story. The secular nation-state proved to be a fragile artifice, especially in those many areas of the world where nations had been created by retreating colonial powers – in Africa by Britain, Portugal, Belgium, and France; in Latin America by Spain and Portugal; in South and Southeast Asia by Britain, France, the Netherlands, and the United States; and in Eurasia by the Soviet Union. In some cases boundary disputes led to conflicts between neighboring nations. In others the very idea of the nation caused suspicion.

Many of these imagined nations – some with invented names such as Pakistan, Indonesia, and Yugoslavia – were not accepted by all within their territory. In other cases the tasks of administration became difficult to perform. The newly created nations had only brief histories of prior colonial control to unite them, and after independence they had only the most modest of economic, administrative, and cultural infrastructures to hold the disparate regions within them together.

By the 1990s these ties had begun to fray. The global economic market undercut national economies, and the awesome military technology of the United States and NATO reduced national armies to border patrols. More significant, the rationale for the nation-state came into question.

With the collapse of the Soviet Union and the postcolonial, post-Vietnam critique of Western democracy, the secular basis for the nation-state seemed increasingly open to criticism. In cases such as Yugoslavia, when the ideological glue of secular nationalism began to dissolve, the state fell apart.

The effect of what I have elsewhere called "the loss of faith in secular nationalism" was devastating (see Juergensmeyer 1993). It seemed that nationalism was being challenged everywhere, and the scholarly community joined in the task of trying to understand the concept in a post-Cold War and transnational era (see Kotkin 1994; Smith 1995). Part of the reason for the shaky status of nationalism was that it was transported to parts of the world in the cultural baggage of what Jurgen Habermas has called "the project of modernity" – a trust in reason that was by now considered obsolete. In a multicultural world, where a variety of views of modernity are in competition, the very concept of a universal model of secular nationalism became highly debatable.

Globalization has challenged the modern idea of nationalism in a variety of ways. These challenges have been varied because globalization is multifaceted. The very term "globalization" refers not to any one thing but to a series of processes. It embraces not only the global reach of transnational businesses but also their labor supply, currency, and financial instruments. In a broader sense globalization also refers to the planetary expansion of media and communications technology, popular culture, and environmental concerns. Ultimately, it also includes a sense of global citizenship and a commitment to world order.

Globalization has affected societies in differing ways. Some countries that have been brought into contact with economic globalization – by supplying labor for the commodity chains of globalized production – have not experienced the globalization of culture and citizenship. In fact, the advent of economic globalization has threatened local identities in such a way as to encourage the protection of local cultures and social identities, sometimes in hostile and defensive ways. This effect has been observed by Benjamin Barber, who notes that the "McWorld" of contemporary Westernized culture has assaulted the public consciousness in various parts of the world. In extreme forms the reaction has been the "Jihad" of militant tribalism (see Barber 1995). Some of the most intense movements of ethnic and religious nationalism have arisen in nations which have felt themselves exploited by the global economy, such as in Iran and Egypt, or else have believed that somehow the benefits of economic globalization are passing them by (see Juergensmeyer 1993, 2000). The global shifts in economic and political power that occurred following the breakup of the Soviet Union and the sudden rise and subsequent fall of Japanese and other Asian economies in the last decade of the twentieth century have also had significant social repercussions. The public sense of insecurity that came in the wake of these changes was felt especially in areas economically devastated by the changes, including those nations that had been under the dominance of the Soviet Union.

These shifts led to a crisis of national purpose in less developed nations as well. Leaders such as India's Jawaharlal Nehru, Egypt's Gamal Abdel Nasser, and Iran's Riza Shah Pahlavi had tried to create their own versions of America – or else a cross between America and the Soviet Union. But a new, postcolonial generation no longer believed in the Westernized vision of Nehru, Nasser, or the Shah. Rather, it wanted to complete the process of decolonialization by asserting the legitimacy of their countries' own traditional values in the public sphere and by constructing a national identity based on indigenous culture. This eagerness became all the more keen with the global media assault of Western music, videos, and films – an assault that has threatened to obliterate local and traditional forms of cultural expression.

In other cases it was a different kind of globalization – the emergence of multicultural societies through global migrations and the suggestion of global military and political control in a "new world order" – that caused fear. Perhaps surprisingly, this response was most intense in the most developed countries, which in other ways seemed to be the paradigm of globalization. In the United States, for example, the Christian Identity movement and militia organizations were fueled by fears of a massive global conspiracy of liberal American politicians and the United Nations. In Japan a similar conspiracy theory motivated leaders of the Aum Shinrikyo movement to predict a catastrophic World War III, which their nerve gas assault in the Tokyo subways was meant to emulate.

As farfetched as the idea of a "new world order" of global control may be, there is some truth to the notion that the globalization of culture has brought the world closer together. Although it is unlikely that a cartel of malicious schemers plotted this global trend, its effect on local societies and national identities has nonetheless been profound. Globalization has undermined the modern idea of the nation-state by providing nonnational and transnational forms of economic, social, and cultural interaction. The global economic and social ties of the inhabitants of contemporary global cities are linked together in a way that supersedes the Enlightenment notion that peoples in particular regions are naturally linked together by a social contract. In a global world it is hard to say where one region ends and another begins. In fact, it is hard to say how the "people" of a particular nation should even be defined.

Religion and ethnicity have stepped in to redefine public communities. The fading of the nation-state and of old forms of secular nationalism has produced both the opportunity and the need for new nationalisms. The opportunity has arisen because the old orders have become so weak. The need for national identity persists because no single alternative form of social cohesion and affiliation has yet appeared to dominate public life, the way the secular nation-state did in the twentieth century. In a curious way traditional forms of social identity have helped to rescue the idea of national societies. In the continuing absence of any other demarcation of national loyalty and commitment, these old staples – religion, ethnicity, and traditional culture – have become resources for national identification.

Religion in Support of New Nationalisms

Today religious rather than secular nationalism has provided a solution to the problem of Western-style secular politics in a non-Western and multicultural world. As secular ties have begun to unravel in the post-Soviet and postcolonial era, local leaders have searched for new anchors to ground their social identities and political loyalties. Many have turned to ethnicity and religion. What is ideologically significant about these ethnic and religious movements is their creativity. Although many of the framers of the new nationalisms have reached back in history for ancient images and concepts that will give them credibility, theirs are not efforts simply to resuscitate old ideas. These are contemporary ideologies that meet present-day social and political needs.

In the modern context the notion that indigenous culture can provide the basis for new political institutions, including resuscitated forms of the nation-state, is revolutionary. Movements that have supported ethnic and religious nationalism have therefore often been confrontational and violent. They have rejected the intervention of outsiders and at the risk of being intolerant have pandered to indigenous cultural bases and have enforced traditional social boundaries. It is no surprise, then, that they have gotten into trouble with one another and with defenders of the secular state. Yet even these conflicts with secular modernity have served a purpose for the movements. They have helped define who they were as a people and who they were not – for example, not secularists.

Since secularism has often been targeted as the enemy, that enemy has most easily been symbolized by things American. The United States has taken the brunt of religious and ethnic terrorist attacks in recent years, in part because it so aptly symbolizes the transnational secularism that the religious and ethnic nationalists loathe and in part because the United States does indeed promote transnational and secular values. For instance, the United States has a vested economic and political interest in shoring up the stability of regimes around the world. This interest often puts the United States in the position of defending secular governments. Moreover, the United States supports a globalized economy and a modern culture. In a world where villagers in remote corners of the world increasingly have access to MTV, Hollywood movies, and the Internet, the images and values that have been projected globally have been American.

It is thus understandable that the United States is disdained. What is perplexing to many Americans is why their country is so severely hated, even caricatured. The demonization of the United States by many ethnic and religious groups in fact fits into a process of delegitimizing secular authority. In order to delegitimize the public authority, the religious groups have had to shore up their own pillars of authority. In doing so, they have appropriated traditional religious images, especially that of cosmic war. In this scenario, competing religious groups are seen as foes and scapegoats, and the secular state is viewed as the enemy of religion. This "satanization" is aimed at reducing the power of opponents by discrediting them. By humiliating them – by making them subhuman – religious groups assert the superiority of their own moral power.

During the early days of the Persian Gulf War in 1991, the Hamas movement issued a communique stating that the United States "commands all the forces hostile to Islam and the Muslims" and singled out then-President George Bush as not only "the leader of the forces of evil" but also "the chief of the false gods." As late as 1997, Iranian politicians, without a trace of hyperbole, described America as the "Great Satan." This rhetoric first surfaced in Iran during the early stages of the Islamic revolution, when both the Shah and President Jimmy Carter were referred to as Yazid ("agent of Satan"). "All the problems of Iran," the Ayatollah Khomeini elaborated, are "the work of America" (Khomeyni 1977, p. 3). He meant not only political and economic problems but also cultural and intellectual ones, fostered by "the preachers they planted in the religious teaching institutions, the agents they employed in the universities, government educational institutions, and publishing houses, and the Orientalists who work in the service of the imperialist states" (Khomeini 1985, p. 28). The scope and power of this conspiratorial network could only be explained by its supernatural force.

The Global Agenda of Religious Nationalism

Although the members of many radical religious groups fear globalization as a whole, what they distrust specifically are the secular aspects of globalization. They are afraid that global economic forces and cultural values will undercut the legitimacy of their own bases of identity and power. By contrast, other aspects of globalization – technical and economic – are often perceived as neutral and even useful.

Some groups have a global agenda of their own, a transnational alternative to political nationalism. Increasingly, terrorist wars have been waged on an international and transnational scale. When the World Trade Center was demolished in the dramatic aerial assaults of September 11, 2001, it was not just the United States that was targeted but also the power of the global economic system that the buildings symbolized. Osama bin Laden's al-Qaida network was itself a global structure. The Gamaa i-Islamiya group, related to al-Qaida, literally moved its war against secular powers abroad when its leader, Sheik Omar Abdul Rahman, moved from Egypt to Sudan to Afghanistan to New Jersey. It was from the Jersey City location that his followers organized the 1993 bombing attack on the World Trade Center that killed six and injured a thousand. Osama bin Laden's operative, Ramzi Youssef, also convicted of complicity in the 1993 World Trade Center bombing, masterminded the "Bojinka Plot" that would have destroyed a dozen US commercial planes over the Pacific during the mid-1990s. Youssef moved from place to place throughout the world, including Pakistan and the Philippines. Algerian Muslim activists brought their war against secular Algerian leaders to Paris, where they have been implicated in a series of subway bombings in 1995. Hassan Turabi in Sudan has been accused of orchestrating Islamic rebellions in a variety of countries, linking Islamic activists in common cause against what is seen as the great Satanic power of the secular West. Osama bin Laden, from his encampment in Afghanistan, is alleged to have ordered many of these acts of terrorism around the world.

These worldwide attacks may be seen as skirmishes in a new Cold War or, more apocalyptically, a "clash of civilizations," as Samuel Huntington has termed it (see Huntington 1996). It is possible to imagine this clash if one assumes that Islam and other religions are civilizations comparable with the modern West, or if one regards secular nationalism as, in the words of one of the leaders of the Iranian revolution, "a kind of religion." Those religious opponents of secular nationalism who regard it as religious often describe it as a religion that is peculiar to the West, a point echoed by leaders of the Muslim Brotherhood in Egypt.

Behind this image of a clash of cultures and civilizations is a certain vision of social reality, one that involves a series of concentric circles. The smallest are families and clans; then come ethnic groups and nations; the largest and most important are religions. Religions here are not just bodies of doctrine and communities of believers but shared world views that span great expanses of time and space. They are global civilizations. Among these are Islam, Buddhism, and what some who hold this view call "Christendom," "Western civilization," or "Westernism." The so-called secular culture of places such as Germany, France, and the United States stand as subsets of Christendom/Western civilization. Similarly, Egypt, Iran, Pakistan, and other nations are subsets of Islamic civilization. From this vantage point it is both a theological and a political error to suggest that Egypt or Iran should be thrust into a Western frame of reference. By this view of the world they are intrinsically part of Islamic, not Western, civilization, and it is an act of imperialism to think of them otherwise. Proponents of Islamic nationalism often see themselves as a part of a larger, global encounter among Western, Islamic, and yet other cultures.

This view of a "clash of civilizations" is not confined to the imaginations of either Samuel Huntington or a small number of Islamic extremists but has animated much of the political unrest at the dawn of the twenty-first century.

An even more extreme version of this global cultural clash has been an apocalyptic one, in which contemporary politics has been seen as fulfilling an extraordinary religious vision. Some Messianic Jews, for instance, think the Kingdom that will arise with the coming of the Messiah is close at hand. It will occur when the biblical lands of the West Bank are returned to complete Jewish control and when the Jerusalem Temple described in the Bible is restored on its original site, one presently occupied by the Muslim Dome of the Rock. Several Jewish activists have been implicated in plots to blow up the shrine in order to hasten the coming of the Kingdom. One who served time in prison for his part in such a plot said that the rebuilding of the Temple was not just a national obligation but an obligation for redemption of the world.

Religious activists such as Millennarian Christians and Shi'ite Muslims, who have a strong sense of the historical fulfillment of prophecy, also look to a religious apocalypse that will usher in a new age. American Christian political activists such as Pat Robertson and the late Jerry Falwell are exercised by the idea that the political agenda of a righteous America will help to usher in an era of global redemption. The leader of Aum Shinrikyo, borrowing Christian ideas from the sixteenth-century French astrologer Nostradamus, proclaimed the coming of Armegeddon in 1999. Those who survived this World War III – mostly members of his own movement – would create a new society in 2014, one led by Aum-trained "saints."

Activists in other religious traditions have seen a righteous society established in a less dramatic manner. Some Sunni Muslims, Hindus, and Buddhists have in their own ways articulated hopes for a political fulfillment of a religious society. They believe that "dhammic society can be established on earth," as one activist Buddhist monk in Sri Lanka put it, by creating a religious state. These forms of religious politics are more than nationalist because they envision the world as caught up in a cosmic confrontation, albeit one that will ultimately lead to a peaceful world order constructed by religious nations. The result of this process will be a global order radically different from secular versions of globalization, but it will still be an ideological confrontation on a global scale.

The Future of Religious Nationalism

The goal of other religious activists is the revival of a nation-state that avoids the effects of globalization. Where new religious states have emerged, they have tended to be isolationist. In Iran, for instance, the ideology of Islamic nationalism that emerged during and after the 1979 revolution from the Ayatollah Khomeini and his political theoretician, Ali Shari'ati, was intensely parochial. It was not until some twenty years later that new movements of moderate Islamic politics encouraged its leaders to move out of their self-imposed international isolation. The religious politics of Afghanistan, especially after Taliban militants seized control in 1995, were even more strongly isolationist. Led by members of the Pathan ethnic community who were former students of Islamic schools, the religious revolutionaries of the Taliban established a self-contained autocratic state with strict adherence to traditional Islamic codes of behavior. Only after the collapse of the Taliban in 2001, following the al-Qaida terrorist attacks, did Afghanistan become more open to the wider world.

Other movements of religious nationalism have not been quite so isolationist. In India, when Hindu nationalists in the Bharatiya Janata Party (BJP), or "Indian People's Party," came to power in 1998 – a victory that was consolidated in the national elections of 1999 – some observers feared that India would become isolated from world opinion. The testing of nuclear weapons as one of the BJP's first acts in power did little to dispel these apprehensions. But in many other ways, including its openness to economic ties and international relations, the BJP has maintained India's active role in the world community. Credit for this openness may go in part to the moderate leadership of the former BJP Prime Minister, Atal Bihari Vajpayee, one of the country's most experienced and temperate politicians.

It is an open question whether movements of religious and ethnic nationalism elsewhere in the world, if they ever come into power, will behave like the Taliban or like the BJP. The movements in Pakistan, Egypt, and Algeria could go either way. When Abdurrahman Wahid, a Muslim cleric, edged past the daughter of Indonesia's founder to become the country's Prime Minister in 1999, observers wondered whether he would usher in an era of religious nationalism. In this case the fears were unfounded. The actions of his government showed Wahid's brand of Islam to be moderate and tolerant, one committed to bringing Indonesia into the world community and the global economic market.

In other regions of the world it has not been the creation of new religious states that has been at issue but instead the breakdown of old secular states with no clear political alternative. In some instances religious activists have contributed to these anarchic conditions. In the former Yugoslavia, for instance, the bloodshed in Bosnia and Kosovo was caused as much by the collapse of civil order as by the efforts to create new ethnic and religious regions. Because these situations have been threats to world order, they have prompted the intervention of international forces such as NATO and the UN.

It is, however, world order itself that many of these religious nationalists have opposed. They note that the increasingly multicultural societies

of most urban communities around the world have undermined traditional cultures and their leaders. They have imagined the United States
and the United Nations to be agents of an international conspiracy, one
hell-bent on forming a homogenous world society and a global police
state. It was this specter, graphically described in the novel *The Turner
Diaries* by Andrew Macdonald, that one of the novel's greatest fans,
Timothy McVeigh, had hoped to forestall by attacking a symbol of Federal
control in America's heartland. His assault on the Oklahoma City Federal
building, and other terrorist attacks around the world such as Osama bin
Laden's alleged bombing of US embassies in Africa in 1998 and of the *USS
Cole* in Yemen in 2000, were acts of what might be considered "guerrilla
antiglobalism."

Ultimately, however, it seems likely that despite these efforts to ignore
or reject the forces of globalization, transnational cultures will expand,
and that among them will be elements of religion and ethnicity. One future
form of religious transnationality may emerge from the international relations of kindred religious states. According to one theory of global Islamic
politics that circulated in Egypt in the 1980s and 1990s, local movements
of Muslim politics were meant to be only the first step in creating a larger
Islamic political entity – a consortium of contiguous Muslim nations. By
this scenario, religious nationalism would be the precursor of religious
transnationalism. Transnational Islam would lead to Islamic versions of
such secular consortia as NAFTA and the European Community. In the
Islamic model, however, the divisions among states would eventually
wither away, and a greater Islamic union would arise.

A second kind of transnational association of religious and ethnic
activists has developed in the diaspora of cultures around the world. Rapid
Internet communication allows members of ethnic and religious communities to maintain a close association despite geographic dispersion.
These "e-mail ethnicities" are not limited by political boundaries or
national authorities. Expatriate members of separatist communities such
as India's Sikhs and both Sinhalese and Tamil Sri Lankans have provided
funding for their compatriates' causes. In the case of Kurds their "nation"
is spread throughout Europe and the world, united through a variety of
modern communications. In some cases these communities long for a
nation-state of their own. In other cases they are prepared to maintain
their non-state national identities for the indefinite future.

Each of these futures harbors a paradoxical relationship between the
national and the globalizing aspects of religious politics. This relationship
suggests that there is a symbiotic relationship between certain forms of
globalization and religious nationalism. It may appear ironic, but the glo-
balism of culture and the emergence of transnational political and economic institutions enhance the need for local identities. They create the
desire for a more localized form of authority and social accountability. In
an era of globalization the crucial problems are identity and control. The

two problems are linked, in that a loss of a sense of belonging leads to a feeling of powerlessness. At the same time what has been perceived as a loss of faith in secular nationalism is experienced as a loss of agency as well as of identity. For all these reasons the assertion of traditional forms of religious identities is tied to attempts to reclaim personal and cultural power. In this sense the vicious outbreaks of religious terrorism that have occurred at the turn of the century can be seen as tragic attempts to regain social control.

Bibliography

Anderson, Benedict. *Imagined Communities: Reflections on the Origin and Spread of Nationalism*. London: Verso, 1983.

Barber, Benjamin R. *Jihad Vs. McWorld*. New York: Times Books, 1995.

Casanova, José. *Public Religions in the Modern World*. Chicago: University of Chicago Press, 1994.

Hedetoft, Ulf, and Mette Hjort. *The Postnational Self: Belonging and Identity*. Minneapolis: University of Minnesota Press, 2002.

Huntington, Samuel P. *The Clash of Civilizations and the Remaking of World Order*. New York: Simon and Schuster, 1996.

Juergensmeyer, Mark. *The New Cold War? Religious Nationalism Confronts the Secular State*. Berkeley: University of California Press, 1993.

Juergensmeyer, Mark. *Terror in the Mind of God: The Global Rise of Religious Violence*. Berkeley: University of California Press, 2000.

Juergensmeyer, Mark. *Global Religions: An Introduction*. Oxford: Oxford University Press, 2003.

Juergensmeyer, Mark, ed. *Religion in Global Civil Society*. New York: Oxford University Press, 2005.

Khomeini, Imam [Ayatollah]. *Islam and Revolution: Writings and Declarations* [1981], tr. Hamid Algar. London: Routledge and Kegan Paul, 1985.

Khomeyni, Imam [Ayatollah]. *Collection of Speeches, Position Statements* [translations from "Najaf Min watha 'iq al-Imam al-Khomeyni did al-Quwa al Imbiriyaliyah wa al-Sahyuniyah wa al-Raj'iyah" ("From the Papers of Imam Khomeyni Against Imperialist, Zionist, and Reactionist Powers")]. Translations on Near East and North Africa, Number 1902. Arlington, VA: Joint Publications Research Service, 1977.

Kotkin, Joel. *Tribes: How Race, Religion, and Identity Determine Success in the New Global Economy*. New York: Random House, 1994.

Lie, John. *Modern Peoplehood*. Cambridge, MA: Harvard University Press, 2004.

Rudolph, Susanne Hoeber, and James Piscatori, eds. *Transnational Religion and Fading States*. Boulder, CO: Westview Press, 1997.

Smith, Anthony D. *Nations and Nationalism in a Global Era*. London: Polity Press, 1995.

Westerlund, David, ed. *Questioning the Secular State: The Worldwide Resurgence of Religion in Politics*. London: Hurst, 1996.

— Chapter 21 —

New Religious Movements

Lorne L. Dawson

The study of "new religious movements," more popularly known as "cults," is a relatively new endeavor, expanding rapidly since the 1970s. To be sure, these groups have long been studied, if only because the great religious traditions of the world began as new religious movements, and many of the periods of greatest social and religious turbulence have been marked by the emergence of new forms of religious life – for example, of Buddhism in India in the fifth century BCE and of Protestantism in the sixteenth century. But the term "new religious movements" (hereafter cited as NRMs) is closely associated with the recent research of those historians and sociologists of religion who were responding to the public perception, in North America and Western Europe, that cults were becoming a social problem. New religions have always been the source of controversy in society (see Jenkins 2000), but beginning in the 1960s a new and more widespread fear of these groups received substantial media attention and set off a series of attempts to suppress them. Sensing that these measures were largely born of misunderstanding and were potentially harmful to the state of religious liberty, scholars of religion began to investigate more systematically the nature of the new religions in their midst. That effort has resulted in thousands of publications and a remarkable expansion of our understanding of many of the most basic aspects of contemporary religious life, including the processes of conversion and recruitment, religious innovation, organization, resource mobilization, the origins of religious violence, and the future of religion in advanced industrial society (see Bromley and Hadden 1993; Dawson 1998; Lewis 2004). Still, only a small fraction of the thousand or more NRMs estimated to be operating in North America and Europe, let alone elsewhere, have been studied at all.

The study of NRMs, together with the change in cultural mores that it has helped stimulate, is starting to reduce the stigma associated with new and different kinds of religions. Still, scholars in the field operate under a cloud of suspicion. The study of deviant expressions of religiosity is suspected to stem from sympathy for these groups. In actuality, the study of NRMs is approached with some trepidation because researchers are required to become familiar with unorthodox beliefs and practices as well as with some unusual persons. They must contend at once with fanatics present in the religions and their equally fervent opponents. The quest for neutrality remains a live issue in the study of NRMs, in part because the findings can have real implications for individuals and groups in legal proceedings and government investigations.

In the first section of this chapter the difficulty of defining NRMs is discussed. The second section summarizes the results of the investigation of the process of conversion to NRMs and the tendency toward violence in some NRMs. The third section examines how these movements change with time and the factors that help to determine whether they will succeed. The fourth and final section considers the significance of NRMs, discusses other issues addressed by scholars of NRMs, and examines the kind of research required to advance the field.

What Is a New Religious Movement?

No more of a consensus exists on the definition of a cult or new religious movement than a consensus exists on the definition of religion itself. The term "cult" has a long popular and academic usage associated with practices of intense ritual devotion within religious traditions, as in the cult of the Virgin Mary in Catholicism or in the cult of Krishna in Hinduism. But the term is also associated with the many small and largely ritualistic religious groups from the Middle East and elsewhere that were popular in Rome at the time of the rise of Christianity – for example, the cult of Isis. Consequently, within the predominantly Jewish and Christian context of the West there has always been a tinge of negativity associated with the term. The label implies an element of heresy or unhealthy fanaticism, and in the early twentieth century that is how the term was employed in many well-known texts written to warn American Christians against the dangerous theological errors of such NRMs as the Mormons, Seventh Day Adventists, and Jehovah's Witnesses.

In the sociology of religion a cult is a form of religious organization that is neither a church nor a sect. In 1904 the German sociologist Max Weber (1958) drew a distinction between churches and sects that was later developed by his theological colleague Ernst Troeltsch (1931). Churches are large, inclusive organizations, with heterogenous memberships, that have accommodated themselves to the values of the societies in which they exist. Sects are small, exclusive organizations, with homogenous memberships, born of schisms in churches and protesting against the norms in both churches and society as a whole. It was Troeltsch who introduced a third kind of religious organization, called spiritual and mystical religion, which has many parallels to contemporary cults. His analysis, however, has been largely overlooked.

The category "cult" was introduced to sociology by Howard Becker (see Von Wiese and Becker 1932, pp. 627–8) as a way of identifying the amorphous forms of spiritual and mystical practice of some individuals and small groups in Western societies that resisted easy categorization as either churches or sects. A cult is an even smaller group than most sects. It is free of any direct association with a preceding church, is intensely focused on various religious experiences, and is relatively unconcerned with the social and political issues of the society in which it exists.

Ideally, religions could now be classified as churches, sects, or cults. But with the onset of the "cult scare" of the 1970s and 1980s, the term cult started to be applied indiscriminately to the bewildering array of new forms of religious activity rising in Western societies, with the intent once again of calling the legitimacy of these religions into doubt (see Enroth 1977). Seeking to dissociate their research from the overwhelmingly pejorative connotation of the word "cult" in the public mind, sociologists of religion struck upon the more neutral term "new religious movements."

Yet even this term is not free of difficulties. Many of the most prominent and controversial NRMs are no longer so new. For example, the Unification Church was founded in 1958. Others, including Krishna Consciousness, were never really new, except in a Western context. Likewise many NRMs no longer are or never were movements in the strict sociological sense – for example, the Church Universal and Triumphant and the Raelians. Whether some groups should even be called religions has also been raised – for example, of Scientology and Transcendental Meditation. In recent years some scholars have consequently begun to speak simply of "new religions."

Part of the definitional problem stems from the sheer diversity of groups commonly encompassed by the term. New religions can be classified in many ways. From a strictly descriptive perspective it might be said that there are at least five different family groups of NRMs. First are the groups based on various East Asian and Southeast Asian religious traditions, be they philosophical, mystical, meditative, or devotional. Examples are Soka Gakkai, Siddha Yoga, Krishna Consciousness, Brahma Kumaris, and the Divine Light Mission. Second are groups based largely on aspects of the American Human Potential Movement in psychology. Examples are Scientology, est, Silva Mind Control, and Synanon. Third are groups based on various aspects of Western pre-Christian folklore and neo-Christian esoteric traditions. Examples are Wicca and neo-paganism, Rosicrurians, I AM, Solar Temple, Ordo Templi Astartes, and Satanism. Fourth are groups based on aspects of Judaism, Christianity, or Islam. Examples are Jews for Jesus, Children of God/The Family, The Way International, the International Churches of Christ, the Nation of Islam, Bahai, and the Bawa Muhaiyaddeen Fellowship. Fifth and last are groups based on UFOs and the teachings of space aliens. Examples are the Aetherius Society, Heaven's Gate, Urantia, and the Raelians.

This list could be subdivided or extended. There are many spin-offs from other, less prominent religions. Examples of spin-offs are Santeria, Rastafarians, Subud, and Unio Do Vegetal. There also are groups that defy easy categorization because they are the product of syncretism – for example, Cao Dai and Vajradhatu/Shambhala. Other groups blur the boundaries between religious and secular activities – for example, the Rajneesh/Osho Foundation and the Unification Church. Still others have origins that are even more idiosyncratic – for example, New Age channeling groups such as A Course in Miracles and Ramtha. This blending of diverse religious and cultural legacies prevents any simple classification of many of these new religions, yet also makes it important to understand them, for many of these groups reflect the processes of cultural transplantation, transformation, and globalization that are reshaping the West.

Efforts have been made to devise more abstract and analytical typologies of NRMs. Some have focused on the ideologies of different NRMs. Others have focused on their mode of organization, their criteria for membership, or their relations with the dominant society. But most of these efforts have been defeated by the sheer range of groups under consideration.

In one of the most popular and influential typologies, British sociologist Roy Wallis (1984) proposed a dvision into world-affirming, world-rejecting, and world-accommodating cults:

A new movement may embrace the world, affirming its normatively approved goals and values; it may reject that world, denigrating those things held dear within it; or it may remain as far as possible indifferent to the world in terms of its religious practice, accommodating to it otherwise, and exhibiting only mild acquiescence to, or disapprobation of, the ways of the world. (Wallis 1984, p. 4)

Each orientation to the world, argues Wallis, gives rise to a distinctive social structure for the religion.

Alternatively, the American sociologists Rodney Stark and William Sims Bainbridge (1985) have proposed differentiating among audience cults, client cults, and cult movements. This distinction is based on the mode of membership displayed by groups and their consequent organization. Audience cults are the least organized yet most pervasive aspect of cult activity in contemporary societies. They consist of loose networks of persons who absorb the lectures and books of spiritual teachers such as Krishnamurti and Deepak Chopra. These audience cults sometimes develop into client cults, in which followers enter into a more regular and contractual-like relationships with their spiritual leaders, signing up for sessions of counselling, meditation, communication with the dead, and other exotic undertakings. Cults of this kind – for example, est, Scientology, and New Age groups – require a higher level of organization. But the clients are not welded to a social movement. They maintain independent lives, which may involve ties to other religious organizations. By contrast, cult movements are full-fledged religious organizations. They seek to meet all the religious needs of their members, to sever their ties with competing groups, and to change the world by converting others. Examples are Krishna Consciousness and Soka Gakkai.

The American sociologist Thomas Robbins and American psychologist Dick Anthony (1987) suggest differentiating cults according to their teachings and the ramifications of those teachings for the "moral indeterminacy" of modern mass societies. They divide groups into dualistic movements, which promote an absolute dichotomy of good and evil forces in the world, and monistic movements, which teach the ultimate unity of all things and moral relativism. This distinction is then correlated with a distinction between unilevel and multilevel religions. Unilevel groups tend to be literalistic in their approach to language and texts. Multilevel groups display a higher appreciation of the symbolic and metaphorical aspects of language and regard spiritual teachings as encompassing various levels of meaning. When this distinction is combined with a further distinction between subtypes of monism – technical movements, which offer procedures for manipulating consciousness, and charismatic movements, which stress the emulation of a spiritual leader – an elaborate array of classificatory possibilities unfolds.

Much has been learned from these attempts to classify NRMs. The classifications have highlighted key structural and motivational differences among NRMs. More work of this kind is strongly recommended. But typologies like those of Robbins and Anthony are often too complex for the research needs of others, whereas those of Wallis and of Stark and Bainbridge are too simplistic. Typologies are introduced here to call attention to some of the features of NRMs and to demonstrate a frustrating fact of the study of NRMs: for every generalization proposed, there are important exceptions.

With that caution in mind, let it still be proposed that NRMs, or cults, tend to have the following features: (1) they are more concerned than churches or sects with meeting the needs of their individual members; (2) they lay claim to some esoteric knowledge that has been lost, repressed, or newly discovered; (3) they offer their believers some kind of ecstatic or transfiguring experience that is more direct than that provided by traditional modes of religious life; (4) unlike established faiths, they often display no systematic orientation to the broader society and usually are loosely organized; and (5) they are almost always centered on a charismatic leader and face disintegration when the leader dies or is discredited.

Curiously, most of the NRMs studied in depth in response to the latest "cult scare" are fairly atypical. If most NRMs are short-lived, small, and obscure, Scientology, Krishna Consciousness, and the Unification Church are relatively long-lived, large, and well known. They are more highly organized than most NRMs and are more ideologically and practically sophisticated in their relations with the rest of society. With the exception of the Unification Church, whose founder is still alive, they have also survived the death of their charismatic leader. Originally, each of these groups displayed all of the traits of a cult or NRM. But with time they have become more sect-like. However, they continue to display many cult-like attitudes and practices, such as the emphasis on esoteric teachings and on the needs of individual members. Perhaps another category is needed, parallel to the notion of "established sects" like the Jehovah's Witnesses. With time some NRMs do become "established cults." Most of the thousands of groups we are considering, however, fit our profile of cults quite well. Even with these established cults, the difference is one of degree. It is an open question when a group ceases to be a NRM.

Conversion and Violence

The coercive conversion controversy

Much of the research on NRMs has focused on the processes of affiliation, recruitment, and conversion. This is because public authorities have been preoccupied with the accusations of brainwashing made by the opponents of various NRMs. Critics claim that NRMs use systematic techniques of brainwashing to recruit the young and naive or the socially weak and marginal. This accusation originated in the legal need to overcome the guarantee of freedom of religious expression accorded Americans by the First Amendment to the Constitution of the United States. In the late 1970s some of the parents of the young adults who had abandoned their families to join The Children of God, Hare Krishna, the Unification Church, and other NRMs turned to the courts for help. Invoking the laws of conservatorship on the books in such states as California, parents argued that their adult children should be returned temporarily to their custody because they were no longer competent to handle their own affairs, so fully brainwashed had they become. The key stipulation was that their children's constitutional right of religious freedom could be abrogated since their conversions had been involuntary. Lawyers enlisted various psychologists and psychiatrists who derived the idea of brainwashing from a handful of books prompted by the experiences of some American prisoners during the Korean war (see Singer 1995; Lifton 1961). These studies examined the fate of these prisoners in the light of similar campaigns of political re-education and indoctrination in the Soviet Union and in Communist China.

The initial success of this argument permitted the forced "deprogramming" of many cult members. By the mid to late 1980s, however, the courts were becoming unsympathetic to this line of reasoning, as more reliable sociological and psychological studies of NRMs began to question the scientific credibility of the brainwashing thesis and as judges began to fear that even more conventional forms of religious expression were being placed in jeopardy (see Young and Griffiths 1992). Today most experts reject the plausibility of brainwashing as a process and therefore reject its practice in NRMs.

In addition, studies of NRMs revealed a social profile for those who joined NRMs that was at odds with the stereotypes promoted by the anti-cult movement (see Dawson 1998, pp. 103–27). In the process, significant advances were made in understanding the nature of religious conversions. It is increasingly apparent that the process of conversion can be explained using conventional ideas from social psychology, such as deconditioning and resocialization, and that contrary to the implications of brainwashing, people are not so much converted to a religious world view as convert themselves. Conversions are the result of the active participation of converts in the negotiation of a new identity (see Richardson 1993).

The literature on brainwashing in NRMs is largely anecdotal and non-falsifiable. Aspects of the original and highly speculative theories of brainwashing are used in a selective, indiscriminate, and sometimes misleading manner. Discrepancies in their very psychological premises are ignored – for example, the differences between psychoanalytic and behaviorist approaches – as are important qualifications in the findings. The association of brainwashing with NRMs often displays an ethnocentric bias against non-Western forms of religion or a categorical suspicion of any mode of consciousness falling outside the scope of ordinary wakefulness – for example, religiously motivated meditative and trance states. The brainwashing scenario turns out to be a pseudo-scientific ideological device with dehumanizing implications for converts to NRMs.

Contrary to the claims for pervasive brainwashing, it is now clear that cults suffer from extremely low rates of recruitment and high rates of defection. Roughly 90 percent of members leave voluntarily within two years (see Barker 1984). Therefore if coercive persuasion is at work, it is not very effective. Certainly there is no evidence that persons have ever been held physically against their will – a prerequisite for all of the classical theories of brainwashing. Finally, though the results of numerous psychological studies are somewhat inconclusive, none of the members and ex-members of NRMs tested has scored outside the normal range, contrary to the expectations of the anti-cultists, and there is some evidence that individuals receive a therapeutic benefit from their involvement (see Saliba 1993).

Converts to NRMs are not the weak, vulnerable, and suggestive souls first presupposed by the anti-cult movement. At the same time it cannot be claimed, as some leaders of the anti-cult movement later proposed (see Singer 1995), that everyone is susceptible to being recruited, for the social profile of those who have joined is fairly specific. Research has shown, in descending order of pertinence, that converts tend to be young (in their early twenties), better educated than the general public (quite notably in some groups), disproportionately from the middle and upper middle classes, relatively unattached socially, ideologically unaligned, and with a history of seekership – that is, with a history of investigating different religious and spiritual options. In the words of Rodney Stark and William Sims Bainbridge, the research suggests that contemporary NRMs "skim more of the cream of society than the dregs" (Stark and Bainbridge 1985, p. 395). This fact alone may account for much of the stiff opposition to NRMs. Of course, there are interesting exceptions to these generalizations. The age profile of some NRMs is changing as the membership ages, and groups such as Scientology and Soka Gakkai have always attracted a larger number of older followers.

Lastly, it is apparent now that most persons join NRMs through pre-existing social networks and favorable social interactions with cult members. Converts help to convert friends, family members, classmates, and neighbors. Converts repeatedly say that they were influenced foremost by the warmth, genuineness, and sense of purpose that they had detected in the members they met. Few conversions are the result of solitary encounters in public spaces. Ironically, then, NRMs acquire new members in much the same way that mainstream religions do (see Dawson 1998, pp. 79–90).

Table 1 Cult tragedies

NRM	Location and date	Number of deaths
Peoples Temple	Jonestown, Guyana, November 1978	914 (mostly suicide)
Branch Davidians	Waco, Texas, April 1993	80 (murder-suicide)
Solar Temple	Switzerland, October 1994	53 (murder-suicide)
	France, December 1995	16 (suicide)
	Quebec, March 1997	5 (suicide)
Aum Shinrikyo	Tokyo, Japan, May 1995	12 (murdered on subway and 1,000 s injured)
		23 (or more previous murders)
Heaven's Gate	San Diego, California, March 1997	39 (suicide)
Movement for the Restoration of the Ten Commandments	Uganda, March 2000	780 (murder-suicide)

NRMs and incidents of mass violence

The other issue that has galvanized public concern about NRMs is their potential for violence. There have been six tragic incidents of mass violence involving NRMs in the last several decades, resulting in the deaths of almost 2,000 persons (see Table 1). Most of these deaths were religiously inspired suicides, though murders of cult members and others (opponents and law enforcement officers) have also occurred. But only in the cases of the Japanese group Aum Shinrikyo and perhaps of the African group, The Movement for the Restoration of the Ten Commandments were the murders fully premeditated and religiously sanctioned. The details of each incident are complex, and accurate information is scarce. But again, contrary to the fears raised by cult critics, most NRMs have shown no proclivity for violence. The rareness of violence makes it all the more important to understand what went so grievously wrong in the few instances of violence (see Hall 2000; Bromley and Melton 2002).

Each tragedy is the result of a unique combination of factors. In some cases external factors – for example, threatening actions undertaken by law enforcement agents – played a consequential role in instigating violence. In other cases internal factors, such as the social background of members, played a prominent role. Still, there are four common internal factors for violence to erupt. Each of these factors was present in the six incidents of mass violence, though none, on its own or in combination, is sufficient to account for the violence. The first factor is the presence of strong apocalyptic beliefs. The second factor is strong commitment to a charismatic leader and a charismatic mode of authority. The third factor is a process of social encapsulation. The fourth factor is a strong sense of perceived persecution. The presence of these factors heightens the likelihood that the relations between a religious movement and the dominant society will become hostile.

When they do, either the movement or the society may engage in actions that prompt a combative or self-destructive response from the NRM. It is the pattern of the interaction between the parties that is crucial, and in most of the tragedies in question we can trace a pattern of deviance amplification. Relatively minor sources of conflict escalate into situations in which movements or societies think that "the requisite conditions for maintaining their core identity and collective existence are being subverted" and that the only tolerable response is "a project of final reckoning" to restore "what they avow to be the appropriate moral order" (Bromley 2002, p. 11). The process is relatively slow and incremental, as the cycle of movement radicalization and mounting public hostility feeds the fears of both sides, but the final reckoning often comes suddenly, as a result of the destabilizing effects of the resultant polarization (see Robbins and Anthony 1995; Dawson 1998, pp. 128–57; Bromley 2002). This reckoning can, however, be averted with the appropriate intervention.

The apocalyptic beliefs in these groups had significant behavioral consequences in terms of providing the groups with a transcendental and urgent mandate for their actions, diminishing the impact of existing social standards, facilitating the demonization of opponents, and initiating a process of socialization that prepares members for extreme events. The beliefs set the psychological stage for strong reactions to minor but seemingly important symbolic signs of God's will in the world. These proclivities can be aggravated by the strategies initiated by some cult leaders who are struggling with the precarious legitimacy of their charismatic modes of authority (see Dawson 2002, pp. 80–98). In striving to maintain just the right level of exposure to their followers, to avoid the rise of alternative sources of authority or other dissipations of their personal power within their movements, and to maintain an aura of ever more success, some ambitious charismatic leaders will instigate changes in policy designed to undermine rivals. Leaders will prompt crises, real or imagined, to test the loyalty of the group. With time, however, these maneuvers can get out of hand and destabilize the group. The actions can also foster an equally deleterious homogenization of the membership. When all dissent disappears, a rigid social solidarity is achieved at the expense of coping with environmental challenges or resisting the dangerous demands of an unbalanced or simply demoralized leader (see Dawson 1998, pp. 132–48).

One of the strategies frequently invoked by charismatic cult leaders seeking to perpetuate their personal power is to increase the isolation of their followers, both physically and socially. This isolation serves to cut off negative feedback to the group from the larger society. But social systems cannot operate effectively without a measure of criticism and difference of opinion, and an unintended consequence can be the implosion or encapsulation of the group. In isolation, the tendencies to rigidity and homogeniety are magnified, and the normal restraints on the desires, ideals, or delusions of the leaders are diminished. The measure of conformity achieved facilitates acting on extreme suggestions without regard for the consequences (see Dawson 1998, pp. 148–52). In each of the recent incidents of mass violence, all of these factors were aggravated by an ongoing struggle with real or perceived enemies. The resulting persecution complex played a significant role in the demise of the cults, as various acts of seeming opposition to their cause triggered the fatal denouements. The quickest way for authorities to intervene effectively in situations of potential violence involving a NRM is through displays of restraint and sympathy that can defuse the fear of persecution.

Detailed research on each of these processes has just begun. How certain beliefs, patterns of authority and social relations, and shared psychological reactions in these groups have contributed to their violent behavior has just started to be studied. New efforts will doubtless follow from the further episodes of religiously inspired violence that are bound to occur.

Change and Success in New Religious Movements

To date, much of the research on NRMs has focused on the description of the beliefs, practices, and organizational histories of groups that rose to prominence after the 1960s. It is important to recognize that these groups have changed with the passing decades. In fact, NRMs provide scholars with natural laboratories for the observation of religious change.

Reflecting on her three decades of research on NRMs, the English sociologist Eileen Barker (1995) has discussed some significant changes in the characteristics of those NRMs that have survived and grown. First, there has been an organizational shift from familial forms of association to more bureaucratic forms of organization, with a corresponding increase in the division of labor and in the rules governing relations among members. Likewise the range of ways of organizing their movements has expanded, creating a greater, not lesser, diversity of kinds of NRMs.

Second, there has been a significant shift in the composition of the membership of many groups, as the balance of young to old and of new to long-term members changes. Rising birthrates among members have reduced the need to engage in aggressive proselytizing but have also introduced new kinds of demands on the organizations and shifts in priorities. In Barker's words, "It does not take much imagination to recognize that a movement comprised of enthusiastic and inexperienced young converts with few if any responsibilities will differ fundamentally from one in which middle-aged adults, with 10 to 20 years experience of the movement, have a large number of dependent children" (Barker 1995, p. 169).

Third, the day-to-day activities and the financial dealings of NRMs have shifted with the need to socialize a second generation of members. The children born into the movement may call for changes in policies and practices. Marked diversity is evident in how specific NRMs have actually responded to this challenge.

Fourth, there tends to be significant change in the nature of leadership, with a shift from charismatic to more traditional and rational modes of authority. Often the result is a diffusion of power and responsibilities, "increased accountability for decisions," and "more room for [the] interpretation and negotiation" of beliefs and practices (Barker 1995, p. 171).

Fifth, the belief systems of these NRMs have become more elaborate, in part because they also tend to become more qualified and less extreme. Millennial beliefs, for example, are muted in the face of the postponement of the predicted end of the world. A greater diversity of interpretive positions is tolerated.

Sixth, there has been a weakening of lifestyle requirements and a corresponding softening of the distinction between insiders and outsiders. Groups that were strictly communal and adamant in their rejection of important aspects of the larger society such as higher education start to institutionalize varying levels of acceptable membership, "ranging from the totally committed . . . through the rank-and-file faithful to fringe members who accept the beliefs but do not want to commit their whole lives to the movement . . . and, finally, sympathizers who may owe allegiance to another religion" (Barker 1995, p. 174). Similarly, extreme stances on issues like sex and gender relations have drifted "toward the social norm," and the groups have sought active alliances with other groups in society in the support of various causes.

The moderating effect of these changes is what sociologists and historians would expect. With time, argues Barker, the differences between most NRMs and the wider society will decrease. But ironically, in light of the highly pluralistic character of contemporary Western society, the differences among the NRMs may well increase, as each group accommodates itself to a different set of accepted norms (see Barker 1995, pp. 165,

179). This fact may also partially account for the emergence of "established cults" as a new order of religious life in the contemporary religious environment.

In a similar analysis Rodney Stark has argued that the cumulative body of research now shows that NRMs will succeed insofar as:

1. They retain cultural continuity with the conventional faiths of the societies within which they seek converts.
2. Their doctrines are non-empirical.
3. They maintain a medium level of tension with the surrounding environment – are strict, but not too strict.
4. They have legitimate leaders with adequate authority to be effective.
   (4a) Adequate authority requires clear doctrinal justifications for an effective and legitimate leadership.
   (4b) Authority is regarded as more legitimate and gains in effectiveness to the degree that members perceive themselves as participants in the system of authority.
5. They generate a highly motivated, volunteer, religious labor force, including many willing to proselytize.
6. They maintain a level of fertility sufficient to at least offset member mortality.
7. They compete against weak, local conventional religious organizations within relatively unregulated religious economies.
8. They sustain strong internal attachments, while remaining an open social network, able to maintain and form ties to outsiders.
9. They continue to maintain sufficient tension with their environment – remain sufficiently strict.
10. They socialize the young sufficiently well as to minimize both defection and the appeal of reduced strictness. (Stark 1996, pp. 144–5)

If Stark is correct, then some of the changes that Barker has observed in the larger and more controversial NRMs may be detrimental to their success in the long run. For example, if strictness contributes to the competitive edge of a group, then accommodation may harm it. But accommodation to the dominant society seems advantageous in other ways. Success hinges on sustaining a delicate balance of these elements in the face of known and unknown contingencies. The play of ideological and social factors awaits further research.

Other Research Issues

In many respects the "cult scare" of the 1970s and 1980s that spurred so much of the contemporary study of NRMs has impaired the social sci-

entific analysis of this phenomenon. Studies of NRMs have been disproportionately opportunistic in focusing on the controversy surrounding
conversion in particular. Too much of the information available on NRMs
provides only a snap shot of one group or a segment of a group at one
time or on one issue. Moreover, research has concentrated on a handful
of relatively large and well-known groups. Thousands of smaller and less
organized groups have been neglected. Furthermore, the study of NRMs
has concentrated on North America and Western Europe. In time these
limitations may be rectified as younger scholars seek out new groups to
study. But research in the field remains unsystematic and insufficiently
comparative. More longitudinal studies of the development of groups are
needed.

To this end, Susan Pitchford, Christopher Bader, and Rodney Stark
(2001) have proposed an agenda for generating a truly comparable and
cumulative database. They present a persuasive argument for the future
codification of data dealing with crucial aspects of the history and the
demographics of groups, their methods and rates of recruitment and
defection, and their doctrines and rituals. Data are needed on the levels,
styles, and costs of commitment to the groups, the sources of funds and
kinds of expenditures, the nature and exercise of leadership, the mental
states and criminal activities of some leaders, the growth curve of the
organizations, and the impact of groups on surrounding religious
cultures.

Data about the growth and impact of NRMs are central to the determination of their cultural significance. Why should we bother to study these
groups in the first place, especially if they tend to be small and short-lived?
Every study offers at least an implicit and partial answer, but the analysis
remains fragmentary (see Dawson 2004). I have argued that most sociologists of religion think of the cultural significance of NRMs in terms of
the role they play in the debate over secularization. NRMs perhaps point
to the rebirth of religiosity in a secular age. With the rise of so many
NRMs, scholars find themselves asking whether these developments
challenge the conventional association of modernity with the demise of
religion or are ephemeral and confirm the triumph of secular society
over religion.

The efflorescence of NRMs may point beyond secularization to even
more sweeping changes in the very structure of contemporary life.
There is an apparent, though still unexplored, affinity among three
phenomena studied by sociologists: the new religious sensibilities of
large numbers of North Americans and Europeans, the spiritual innovations and styles of many NRMs, and certain larger institutional
changes.

But this is only one of many lines of research currently being pursued
in the study of NRMs. Other important work is being done on such issues
as defection and apostasy, health and healing, sex and gender relations,

the response to failed prophecies, the impact of the Internet, church–state relations, and the social and political activism of these groups (see Lewis 2004). In these and many other ways, contemporary NRMs provide a unique and manageable way to investigate the dialectic of social and religious forces that construct the worlds of ultimate meaning in which people place their faith.

Bibliography

Barker, Eileen. *The Making of a Moonie: Choice or Brainwashing?* Oxford: Blackwell, 1984.

Barker, Eileen. "Plus ça change . . . ." *Social Compass* 42 (1995): 165–80.

Bromley, David G. "Dramatic Denouements," in *Cults, Religion and Violence*, eds. David G. Bromley and J. Gordon Melton. Cambridge: Cambridge University Press, 2002, pp. 11–41.

Bromley, David G., and Jeffrey K. Hadden, eds. *The Handbook on Cults and Sects in America, Part A and B.* Religion and the Social Order Series, Vol. 3, Greenwich, CT: JAI Press, 1993.

Bromley, David G., and J. Gordon Melton, eds. *Cults, Religion and Violence.* Cambridge: Cambridge University Press, 2002.

Dawson, Lorne L. *Comprehending Cults: The Sociology of New Religious Movements.* Toronto: Oxford University Press, 1998.

Dawson, Lorne L. "Crises of Charismatic Legitimacy and Violent Behavior in New Religious Movements," in *Cults, Religion and Violence*, eds. David G. Bromley and J. Gordon Melton. Cambridge: Cambridge University Press, 2002, pp. 80–101.

Dawson, Lorne L. "The Socio-Cultural Significance of New Religious Movements," in *The Oxford Handbook on New Religious Movements*, ed. James R. Lewis. New York: Oxford University Press, 2004, pp. 68–98.

Enroth Ronald. *Youth, Brainwashing, and the Extremist Cults.* Grand Rapids, MI: Zondervan, 1977.

Hall, John R. *Apocalypse Observed: Religious Movements and Violence in North America, Europe, and Japan.* New York: Routledge, 2000.

Jenkins, Phillip. *Mystics and Messiahs: Cults and New Religions in American History.* New York: Oxford University Press, 2000.

Lewis, James, R., ed. *The Oxford Handbook of New Religious Movements.* New York: Oxford University Press, 2004.

Lifton, Robert J. *Thought Reform and the Psychology of Totalism.* New York: Norton, 1961.

Pitchford, Susan, Christopher Bader, and Rodney Stark. "Doing Field Studies of Religious Movements: An Agenda," *Journal for the Scientific Study of Religion* 40 (2001): 379–92.

Richardson, James T. "A Social Psychological Critique of 'Brainwashing' Claims about Recruitment to New Religions," in *The Handbook on Cults and Sects in America, Part A and B*, eds. David G. Bromley and Jeffrey K. Hadden. Religion and the Social Order Series, Vol. 3, Greenwich, CT: JAI Press, 1993, pp. 75–97.

Robbins, Thomas, and Dick Anthony. "New Religions and Cults in the United States," in *The Encyclopedia of Religion*, ed. Mircea Eliade. 1st edn. New York: Macmillan, 1987, Vol. 10 pp. 394–405.

Robbins, Thomas, and Dick Anthony. "Sects and Violence: Factors Enhancing the Volatility of Marginal Religious Movements," in *Armageddon in Waco: Critical Perspectives on the Branch Davidian Conflict*, ed. Stuart Wright. Chicago: University of Chicago Press, 1995, pp. 236–59.

Saliba, John A. "The New Religions and Mental Health," in *The Handbook on Cults and Sects in America, Part A and B*, eds. David G. Bromley and Jeffrey K. Hadden. Religion and the Social Order Series, Vol. 3. Greenwich, CT: JAI Press, 1993, pp. 99–113.

Singer, Margaret T. *Cults in Our Midst: The Hidden Menace in our Everyday Lives.* San Francisco: Jossey-Bass, 1995.

Stark, Rodney. "Why Religious Movements Succeed or Fail: A Revised General Model," *Journal of Contemporary Religion* 11 (1996): 133–46.

Stark, Rodney, and William Sims Bainbridge. *The Future of Religion: Secularization, Revival, and Cult Formation.* Berkeley: University of California Press, 1985.

Troeltsch, Ernst. *The Social Teachings of the Christian Churches*, tr. Olive Wyon. 2 vols. London: Allen and Unwin; New York: Macmillan, 1931.

Von Wiese, Leopold, and Howard Becker. *Systematic Sociology.* New York: Wiley, 1932.

Wallis, Roy. *The Elementary Forms of the New Religious Life.* London: Routledge and Kegan Paul, 1984.

Weber, Max. *The Protestant Ethic and the Spirit of Capitalism* [1904/5/20], tr. Talcott Parsons. New York: Scribner, 1958.

Weber, Max. *The Sociology of Religion* [1922], tr. Ephraim Fischoff. Boston: Beacon Press, 1964.

Young, John L., and Ezra E. H. Griffiths. "A Critical Evaluation of Coercive Persuasion as Used in the Assessment of Cults," *Behavioral Sciences and the Law* 10 (1992): 89–101.

— Chapter 22 —

Pilgrimage

Simon Coleman

Pilgrimage is an activity found in all major religions. Rather than declining in the face of modernity and apparent secularization, pilgrimage appears to be on the increase, even if it has been transformed to accommodate the economic, social, and technological developments evident at the beginning of the twenty-first century. Within the last few years, pilgrimage has occasioned some of the largest gatherings of human beings ever. The 1989 Kumbh Mela in Allahabad – a Hindu festival held every twelve years – brought together fifteen million pilgrims, and the 2001 event attracted even more, including around 100,000 visitors from outside India. The official government Kumbh Mela website (http://www. kumbhallahabad.com) went as far as to declare that "the world stands divided into two – those who witnessed it and those who missed it." Despite the hyperbole of this claim, the self-confidence expressed has some justification. For instance, daily updates on the 2001 event were shown on UK television, extending the viewing of the event to an audience far beyond Allahabad itself.

Despite its ubiquity, magnitude, and longevity, pilgrimage harbors something of a paradox as an object of study. It has retained prominence and popularity across religions, yet has failed to receive much scholarly attention. In this chapter, I intend to consider definitions of pilgrimage, to comment on the academic debates that pilgrimage has prompted, to trace some of the reasons that it has not been studied more, and to show why it is finally coming to the fore as a topic of academic interest.

Pilgrimage Defined

At first sight, pilgrimage seems to be a relatively discrete activity. Its key components can swiftly and easily be listed. Using the model of, say, Jerusalem as a city sacred to Jews, Christians, and Muslims, one might say that pilgrimage involves leaving one's home to go on a journey to a distant and holy place, then returning home, often after having undergone a powerful spiritual experience. There is certainly much truth in this view. As Richard Barber notes, "Pilgrimage, the journey to a distant sacred goal . . . is a journey both outwards, to new, strange, dangerous places, and inwards, to spiritual improvement, whether through increased self-knowledge or through the braving of physical dangers" (Barber 1991, p. 1). While this definition is a usable shorthand summary of pilgrimage, almost every part of it raises questions. How distant should a goal be from one's home? How is the sacred to be defined? Do all religions make a distinction between the inner and the outer, at least in the way described, or does Barber's definition reveal distinctly Christian assumptions about the self? Need a pilgrimage be dangerous? In order to provide a brief guide through these questions, I shall examine three elements of pilgrimage: place, movement, and motivation.

Let us start with *place*. The anthropologist Jill Dubisch argues that pilgrimage depends on "(1) the association created within a particular religious tradition of certain events and/or sacred figures with a particular field of space, and (2) the notion that the material world can make manifest the invisible spiritual world at such places" (Dubisch 1995, p. 38). In other words, at the center of pilgrimage is a site – a shrine, a part of the landscape, such as a river confluence or a mountain perhaps even a whole town – that draws to it not only pilgrims but also historical, theological, and mythical associations and resonances. The "marking" of a place as special can occur, especially with major shrines, through the connections that the site is said to have with the origins and the founders of a faith. For instance, the "Holy Land" provides a charged landscape that commemorates the sacred landscapes of the Old and New Testaments, including the paths trodden by Moses and Jesus. Mecca is revered by Muslims not only as the location of the origin of the world but also as the birthplace and site of many of the activities of the Prophet Muhammad. The Buddha prescribed certain places of pilgrimage, choosing sites linked to key events in his life. According to Hindu tradition, Benares (Varanasi) was founded at the dawn of creation and is the earthly home of Lord Shiva.

Just as sacred figures provide a bridge between this world and the next, so the pilgrim can come closer to the divine through re-inhabiting the places associated with them. Indeed, the Hindu word *tirtha* is a Sanskrit-derived term that encompasses a number of meanings, including those of a ford, a holy man, and even Scripture. What unites these associations is the notion of crossing over, of moving between the realm of humanity and the realm of the gods (see Coleman and Elsner 1995, pp. 137–8).

Places that are marked as having particular power are often subject to physical as well as ideological competition among adherents of different religions or even of the same religion. Thus the Indian town of Ayodhya is considered the birthplace of the Hindu God Rama but is also sacred to Muslims, and the mosque constructed in the town became the site of numerous attacks as each side attempted to appropriate the sacred ground for its own faith. Jerusalem is the paradigmatic example of a contested space both among and within religions. The Muslim Dome of the Rock was placed on the site of the Jewish Temple by the Caliph Abd al-Malik in the seventh century CE. The Church of the Holy Sepulchre in Jerusalem houses competing Christian factions who look after and control separate parts of the Church.

Yet we should not fall into the trap of assuming that pilgrimage is only about the time spent at the site itself. Pilgrims often spend more time journeying to and from a given site than actually at the site, and their travel is part of the religious experience itself. Pilgrimage thus often involves as much the traversing of boundaries – of cultures, territories, even religions – as the reaching of an area bounded by its sanctity. There are even cases of sacred travel where no end point is specified. Some early Celtic monks spent their lives in virtually perpetual motion, set on no final destination. Bawa Yamba, describing the lives of contemporary West African Muslims in Sudan, calls his informants "permanent pilgrims," for they live as if they are on their way to Mecca but never actually embark on the final journey to the place itself (Yamba 1995, pp. 1–2). Most of the inhabitants of "pilgrim villages" in Sudan are third-, fourth-, and even fifth-generation immigrants who have lived all their lives in the country yet who still regard themselves as being in transit, consequently constructing temporary homes rather than buildings of bricks, and subscribing to what Yamba calls "the ideology of pilgrim-ness" (Yamba 1995, p. 120).

Stephen Glazier's case study of Christian baptists in Trinidad is equally striking. The religious journeys carried out by these believers are largely about demonstrating commitment to a church leader and raising funds. Since the divine is not associated with any particular location, the busload itself becomes a "moving hierophany" (Glazier 1992, p. 140). One might argue that Glazier's baptists are simply not pilgrims. But more conventional examples of pilgrimages also show a similar detachment from place. Richard Stirrat's (1991) account of Sinhala Catholic pilgrimage traces a fascinating shift in emphasis over the last few decades. While in the nineteenth century the great sites of pilgrimage in Sri Lanka consisted of a series of shrines, more recently the centrality of place has been challenged by focusing instead on holy men, who are seen as imbued with the power of the divine, personalizing it and removing it from the institutional shackles of the Church.

The assumption that pilgrimage is fundamentally oriented toward a single place also proves unwarranted. Clearly, in most cases the activity must be about home *in relation to* the place toward which one travels, and both Ann Gold's (1988) work on Rajasthani Hindu pilgrims and Carol Delaney's (1990) work on Turkish *hajjis*, or pilgrims to Mecca, provide vivid examples of the dialogue between home and distant place, and potentially of places in between, that can occur in the minds of pilgrims, as well as showing that a full understanding of a pilgrimage must incorporate the journey "back" as well as the journey "to." We can see why the anthropologists Victor and Edith Turner deploy the encompassing metaphor of a "field" to describe all the sacred aspects of a pilgrimage, including numerous routes, personnel, and rituals (see Turner and Turner 1978, p. 22). More broadly, Surinder Bhardwaj's (1973) work on Hindu places of pilgrimage in India draws on concepts drawn from cultural geography to show how shrines should not be seen as autonomous but instead frequently form hierarchies of sacred centers – hierarchies that range from local to regional to national and to even international complexes. This tendency is evident in many pilgrimage systems, though Bhardwaj argues that there are likely to be differences between Hinduism, where no single, explicit organizational mechanism exists, and the formally more clearly delineated authorities found in Roman Catholicism (see Bhardwaj 1973, p. 7). One might add that, in all of the world religions, powerful shrines tend to become replicated in new landscapes. Thus in the nineteenth century the American University of Notre Dame constructed a series of shrines, including replicas of the French grotto to Our Lady of Lourdes and of the Italian shrine at Loreto. The shrine at Loreto was allegedly the original holy house inhabited by Jesus, Mary, and Joseph and had miraculously been transported to Europe (see McDannell 1995, pp. 154–60).

Inevitably, I have already referred to forms of *movement*, the second of my elements of pilgrimage. There are three different ways in which this activity can be conceptualized and realized. Obviously, there is pilgrimage to and from a site as well as the ideologies of permanent movement noted. Nancy Frey (1998), writing on Santiago de Compostela, focuses almost entirely on the journeys across Europe to the site rather than on what happens when pilgrims arrive. She matches the gradations of perceived authenticity with different modes of transport. In contemporary society, given that so many relatively cheap, safe, and comfortable forms of travel are available, the decision to walk to the shrine from abroad takes on a new significance that may be rooted in notions of spiritual self-abnegation but may equally reflect more general feelings of attuning the body to a rhythm that is self-consciously non-modern or even anti-modern. Walking is seen as more authentic than cycling, and cycling more authentic than driving a car. Movement in pilgrimage is thus linked not only to place but also to novel forms of experiencing time: the reliving of the medieval past through following the old pathways of the *Camino de Santiago* (the Road of St. James) is combined with seemingly more intense, "grounded" connections with locality.

Movement *at* a site must also be taken into account. A remarkably common feature of pilgrimage across the world religions is circumambulation. That is, once the destination has been reached, linear movement toward a given point is replaced by moving around a given object or place, often in liturgically marked ways – for instance, only clockwise, in combination with other pilgrims, or even while prostrate on the ground. We cannot assume that what looks like a similar action will have the same meaning across faiths. Collective circumambulation of the *Ka'aba*, or centrally located sacred building, is in effect a prescribed part of the *hajj* to Mecca, but it is more nearly optional and individualized in other cases, and the significance ascribed to this act is likely to vary.

The third and final element of pilgrimage is that of *motivation*. No matter what theological orthodoxy might state, the actual motivations for going on pilgrimages are myriad and cannot be encapsulated by such all-encompassing phrases as "exteriorized mysticism" (Turner and Turner 1978, p. 7). The Turners' characterization, while intriguing, parallels the inner-outer distinction made by Barber. That distinction does not hold for all the world religions. Similar skepticism may be expressed toward Michael Carroll's (1986) attempt to use psychoanalytic theory to understand Roman Catholic devotion to the Virgin Mary – a devotion that necessarily involves pilgrimage. How useful is it to "explain" Marianism in terms of the presence of masochism and a desire for "the mother" in contexts where so-called "father-ineffective" families prevail?

Pilgrimage may be spurred by a search for self-consciously ascetic other-worldliness or by a strictly down-to-earth plea for a better job. It may evince piety on the part of the pilgrim or be a punishment for a moral infraction. While the search for physical healing is a common factor, even this activity contains ambiguities and tensions. Drawing on his experiences at Lourdes, John Eade (1991) notes the contrast between sacrificial and miraculous perspectives among those present at the shrine. Sacrifice is emphasized more by clergy, who point to the redemptive benefits of suffering associated with Christ. For them, healing is likely to occur only symbolically, in reconciling of the self with pain. The idea of a miracle is more likely to be invoked by lay visitors, who seek immediate, physical relief from their impairments.

Pilgrimage Lost

Pilgrimage "lost" might seem like an odd subtitle. By it, I mean first to reiterate that, as a topic, pilgrimage has not received sufficient attention from scholars, and second, to argue that some of the theoretical approaches adopted, no matter how useful in reviving interest in sacred travel, have sometimes tended to constrain further debate.

Why has pilgrimage been neglected? One possible reason is the spatial open-endedness and temporal ephemerality of a pilgrimage. For a social scientist, pilgrimage presents some tricky methodological problems. How does the researcher engage in sustained contact with pilgrims who by definition are on the move and are likely to be at a site for only a short time? Gathering data exclusively at a shrine necessarily means that one fails to cover the journeys to and from home. Of course, these problems are not insurmountable, but they have made the study of pilgrimage look anomalous within disciplines, especially within anthropology, that have until recently tended to focus on in-depth studies of single locales.

The other possible reason is the ambiguous status of pilgrimage as a religious act. For at least the Christian theologian and also perhaps the traditional historian, the decidedly populist, often unorthodox, character of much pilgrimage has not commended it as a subject of study. Thus David Blackbourn writes of older styles of historical research: "If the role of religion in modern Europe was generally neglected, popular religious phenomena were truly the lost souls of historiography. They were usually passed over, and what attention they did receive was slighting" (Blackbourn 1993, p. 13). Furthermore, the writings of political and religious elites are usually easier to recover than the voices of ordinary people, so that tracing the unrecorded views of ordinary pilgrims can be difficult for disciplines primarily dependent on texts for their data.

What, however, of the work that has been produced? Robert Hertz's (1983) work on the Alpine site of St. Besse was first published in 1913 but did not act as a catalyst for further researches, perhaps because it suffered in relation to his other work, which was on death. The landmark in pilgrimage studies was not to emerge for another seventy years, and it was Victor and Edith Turner's *Image and Pilgrimage in Christian Culture* (1978). The authors had developed a Christian faith that came to inform their work. As the title of their book suggests, the case studies on which they focus – drawn largely from Mexico, England, Ireland, France, and Italy – are of Roman Catholic pilgrimages. Nevertheless, their generalizations have been applied elsewhere, and much of their own writing on pilgrimage constitutes a dialogue with their earlier fieldwork among the Ndembu of Central Africa.

For the Turners, pilgrimage, an activity specifically carried out within the "historical religions," shares certain similarities to rites of passage, which are evident in many cultures around the world but which are most marked in tribal contexts such as that of the Ndembu. In common with ritual novices, pilgrims become initiates into religious processes that remove them from everyday life and expose them to powerful symbols and experiences. On their return to the mundane world, they will have changed in some way – possibly in how they are viewed by others but almost certainly in their perceptions of themselves. Both pilgrimages and rites of passage invoke contrasts between the "structure" of everyday life and the "anti-structure" – the reversals of everyday assumptions and statuses – involved in temporarily removing oneself from mainstream society. In other words, displacement from the mundane is cultivated during experiences that are highly charged.

Yet the Turners warn against simply equating tribal initiation with pilgrimage. Initiation is *liminal*: it involves transitions between states that are usually socially obligatory for the initiates. Pilgrimage is more likely to be *liminoid*: it constitutes a voluntary form of release from more flexibly organized industrial societies and thus is part of the wider genre of leisure activities that include the arts and sports. According to this view, even the *hajj* provides so many possibilities of extenuating circumstances that it has some elements of choice, at least by comparison with tribal ritual.

The Turners argue that in the pilgrimages they describe the moral unit is the individual, whose goal is release from the sins of the structural world. In tribal initiation the moral unit is the social group, and the goal is attainment of a new status (see Turner and Turner 1978, pp. 8–9). Yet one of their most influential concepts, that of *communitas*, refers to a kind of dialectic between the individual and the group that emerges in pilgrimage and other anti-structural contexts. When travelers have reached their sacred goal, they are likely to find themselves in the midst of a vast throng of other visitors, with whom they share the identity of pilgrim but no further ties. The homogenization of status that is produced, according to which everyday hierarchies become irrelevant and humans encounter one other directly, can be put in Christian terms: "It is only through the power ascribed by all to ritual, particularly to the Eucharistic ritual . . . that likeness of lot and intention is converted into commonness of feeling, into 'communitas'" (Turner and Turner 1978, p. 13).

The Turners' approach to pilgrimage put the study of sacred travel on the scholarly map. It gave pilgrimage a distinctive profile yet also located it within such historical processes as colonialism, the Protestant

Reformation, and the nineteenth-century development of ideologies of secularism. Above all, it deployed a theoretical vocabulary – that of structure, anti-structure, communitas, and the liminoid – that could readily be used in the study of other religious activities.

Many scholars were strongly influenced by the Turners as they came to study pilgrimage in other world religions, leading to something of an intellectual irony. Yamba summed up the situation by arguing that the structure/anti-structure model ultimately came to inhibit rather than encourage creative approaches to the topic. In other words, scholars felt that they had to wrestle with the Turners' approach before they could produce their own studies of sacred travel (see Yamba 1995, p. 9). Furthermore, studies of Islamic pilgrimage (see Eickelman 1976), Hinduism (see Van der Veer 1984), and even Christianity in Latin America (see Sallnow 1992) have found pilgrimage to be rather more heterogeneous than the image of communitas might have implied. Erik Cohen (1992) has also isolated what he considers to be a particularly Catholic conception of pilgrimage. He argues that Catholicism maintains an institutionalized separation between the political and the religious spheres, so that the authorities of Pope and /Ruler can be separated, whereas religious centers are ideally less likely to become domains of political power (see Cohen 1992, p. 35). But in other faiths, such as those of the East, religion and politics are more readily combined, so that the model of a pilgrimage center lying "out there" beyond the concerns of mundane society does not hold.

The Turners' approach is in fact rather more subtle than many commentators have allowed, since it recognizes that different forms of communitas exist and that in practice conflict is often endemic in the historical and contemporary appropriation of sites. However, the very power of the broad model as it has been perceived by scholars is evidenced in probably the most significant alternative theoretical approach to have emerged, one that pits itself directly against communitas. The origins of this alternative approach are worthy of note. In 1988, an interdisciplinary conference was held in London at the Roehampton Institute on the broad subject of pilgrimage. Despite the apparently common interests of those present, clear methodological divisions emerged along disciplinary lines (see Bowman 1988, pp. 20–3). "Religionists" were concerned with how to draw pilgrims to sites and then to socialize them into orthodoxy. Historians were chiefly interested in how studies of shrines could contribute to the wider task of reconstructing a largely European past. Anthropologists were keen to produce analyses critical of the Turnerian legacy – providing what Glenn Bowman calls a kind of "Oedipal rectification" of the previous model (Bowman, 1988, p. 21). The edited volume that resulted from the conference (Eade and Sallnow 1991) was called *Contesting the Sacred*, thus directly substituting a metaphor of conflict for the Turners' image of communion. The volume confined itself to Christian cases.

John Eade and Michael Sallnow's new agenda for pilgrimage studies seeks to depict the power of a shrine as a kind of "religious void, a ritual space capable of accommodating diverse meanings and practices" that were brought to them by diverse constituencies and interest groups (Eade and Sallnow 1991, p. 15). Accordingly, shrines cannot be divorced from political or economic structures but must be seen as places where varying discourses and modes of authority may actually become more visible by being juxtaposed in ritually charged spaces. Thus at Lourdes, lay and clergy can be shown to display contrasting attitudes to the body and to the likelihood of the miraculous. At Jerusalem, different groups of Christian pilgrims appropriate different spaces, in line with their theological assumptions and ritual practices.

A new course was thus set in pilgrimage studies. Yet the logic of the Eade and Sallnow position contains a particular sting in its theoretical tail. If pilgrimage is made up of varying discourses and practices, it appears to lack any basic unifying elements as an institution, even within Christianity. Pilgrimage is thus "lost" in a new sense, as it disappears into a postmodern haze or at least into a mass of conflicting interpretations. As Eade and Sallnow put it, "If one can no longer take for granted the meaning of a pilgrimage for its participants, one can no longer take for granted a uniform definition of the phenomenon of 'pilgrimage' either" (Eade and Sallnow 1991, p. 3).

In fact, the paradigms of communitas and contestation are not altogether at odds (see Coleman 2002). First, both provide perspectives drawn from fieldwork among Christian pilgrims that nonetheless appear to have wider resonances and that have been drawn upon by scholars working on other religions. Second, the Turners were in fact willing to accept the position that symbols and sites can be interpreted differently by different constituencies. Their view resonates with their own work on the functions of ritual symbols among the Ndembu. Third, just as the Turners posited a kind of vacuum at the center of pilgrimage – the stripping off of identities involved in the emergence of communitas – so Eade and Sallnow have deployed the image of a void at the symbolic center of a shrine, though of course they have gone on to trace how the void was filled by contending forces. Fourth, it is not clear that Eade and Sallnow have actually "deconstructed" pilgrimage, such that it is no longer a meaningful sociological entity. By referring to the ways in which major shrines displayed a "capacity to absorb and reflect a multiplicity of religious discourses" (Eade and Sallnow 1991, p. 15), they have in effect implied that a constant function of pilgrimage shrines can be discovered. In addition, they have themselves suggested that Christian, and possibly other, pilgrimages appear generally to involve interactions among the elements of person, place, and text.

The legacy left by the Turners and by Eade and Sallnow, including the contributions to Eade and Sallow's edited volume, is a powerful one. Both sets of authors place pilgrimage at the center of rich theoretical debates, and both combine theory with ethnographic, historical, and even theo-logical detail. Still, pilgrimage must not be confined to the analytical frames that they have produced. It should not be allowed to leap without reservation from the frying pan of communitas into the fire of contesta-tion, thus becoming re-constrained by a new body of theory. As we shall see in the next section, recent studies have indicated that the resurgence of interest in pilgrimage is likely to go beyond these particular debates.

Pilgrimage Regained

The way forward for pilgrimage studies is likely to be along many divergent paths. Eade and Sallnow's emphasis on discrepant discourses was itself a product of an academic world characterized by the intellectual fragmenta-tion within many disciplines from the 1980s. It may be significant that some of the most stimulating recent work on pilgrimage manages to cross academic boundaries without laying down doctrinaire theoretical pro-nouncements. Thomas Tweed (1997) hails from the field of religious studies but has produced an ethnographically informed book on the importance of a shrine in Florida to Cuban exiles who have been forced to reconstruct their religion and national identity through diasporic net-works of connection. David Blackbourn (1993) writes as an historian on apparitions of the Virgin Mary in nineteenth-century Germany, but the detail and vividness of his account are likely to appeal to many disciplines.

Even anthropologists, who have been closest to the theoretical debates discussed, have produced valuable work in which the Turners' and post-Turners' legacies have been of minimal importance. Jill Dubisch's (1995) study shows how reflections on Orthodox pilgrimage to the Greek island of Tinos can be a means less of detecting the presence or absence of *com-munitas* than of weaving together ideas about identity, gender, and suffer-ing. Nancy Tapper (1990) has also explored the links among voluntary movement, gender relations, and reciprocity in a Turkish community.

There is also an underlying social reason for continued interest in pil-grimage. As many authors have observed, scholars of the humanities and human sciences have increasingly been forced to contend with globalizing processes of migration, tourism, transnational social movements, and the explosion of mass media. Often it is difficult to separate out these processes in real-life case studies. Tweed's study, for example, is as much about migration as about pilgrimage. Nancy Frey's (1998) description of visitors to Santiago de Compostela reveals that for many the journey is neither about conventional spirituality nor about escape from the banalities of a package holiday. It thus challenges and recombines conventional views of both pilgrimage and tourism. If a few decades ago the study of multi-sited phenomena appeared anomalous in the social sciences, it is becoming, if not the norm, then at least a central part of contemporary research. Furthermore, historians and theologians are becoming less afraid of popular culture than they once were. The future for studies of pilgrimage therefore looks bright, since it encapsulates the restless movement so characteristic of peoples in many parts of the contemporary world.

Bibliography

Barber, Richard. *Pilgrimages*. Woodbridge: Boydell Press, 1991.

Bhardwaj, Surinder. *Hindu Places of Pilgrimage in India: A Study in Cultural Geography*. Berkeley: University of California Press, 1973.

Blackbourn, David. *Marpingen: Apparitions of the Virgin Mary in Nineteenth-Century Germany*. Oxford: Clarendon Press, 1993.

Bowman, Glenn. "Pilgrimage Conference," *Anthropology Today* 4 (1988): 20–3.

Carroll, Michael. *The Cult of the Virgin Mary: Psychological Origins*. Princeton NJ: Princeton University Press, 1986.

Cohen, Erik. "Pilgrimage Centers: Concentric and Excentric," *Annals of Tourism Research* 19 (1992): 33–50.

Coleman, Simon. "Do You Believe in Pilgrimage?: *Communitas*, Contestation and Beyond," *Anthropological Theory* 2 (2002): 355–68.

Coleman, Simon, and John Elsner. *Pilgrimage Past and Present in the World Religions*. Cambridge, MA: Harvard University Press, 1995.

Delaney, Carol. "The Hajj: Sacred and Secular," *American Ethnologist* 17 (1990): 513–30.

Dubisch, Jill. *In a Different Place: Pilgrimage, Gender, and Politics at a Greek Island Shrine*. Princeton, NJ: Princeton University Press, 1995.

Eade, John. "Order and Power at Lourdes: Lay Helpers and the Organization of a Pilgrimage Shrine," in *Contesting the Sacred: The Anthropology of Christian Pilgrimage*, eds. John Eade and Michael Sallnow. London: Routledge, 1991, pp. 51–76.

Eade, John, and Michael Sallnow. Introduction to *Contesting the Sacred: The Anthropology of Christian Pilgrimage*, eds. John Eade and Michael Sallnow. London: Routledge, 1991, pp. 1–29.

Eickelman, Dale. *Moroccan Islam*. Austin: University of Texas Press, 1976.

Frey, Nancy. *Pilgrim Stories: On and Off the Road to Santiago*. Berkeley: California University Press, 1998.

Glazier, Stephen. "Pilgrimages in the Caribbean: A Comparison of Cases from Haiti and Trinidad," in *Sacred Journeys: The Anthropology of Pilgrimage*, ed. Alan Morinis. Westport, CT: Greenwood Press, 1992, pp. 135–47.

Gold, Ann. *Fruitful Journeys: The Ways of Rajasthani Pilgrims*. Berkeley: University of California Press, 1988.

Hertz, Robert. "Saint Besse: A Study of An Alpine Cult" [1913], in *Saints and Their Cults: Studies in Religious Sociology, Folklore and History*, ed. Stephen Wilson. Cambridge: Cambridge University Press, 1983, pp. 55–100.

McDannell, Colleen. *Material Christianity: Religion and Popular Culture in America*. New Haven, CT: Yale University Press, 1995.

Sallnow, Michael. "Communitas Reconsidered: The Sociology of Andean Pilgrimage," *Man* 16 (1992): 163–82.

Stirrat, Richard. "Place and Pilgrimage in Sinhala Catholic Pilgrimage," in *Contesting the Sacred: The Anthropology of Christian Pilgrimage*, eds. John Eade and Michael Sallnow. London: Routledge, 1991, pp. 122–36.

Tapper, Nancy. "*Ziyaret*: Gender, Movement, and Exchange in a Turkish Community," in *Muslim Travellers: Pilgrimage, Migration, and the Religious Imagination*, eds. Dale Eickelman and James Piscatori. London: Routledge, 1990, pp. 135–47.

Turner, Victor, and Edith Turner. *Image and Pilgrimage in Christian Culture*. New York: Columbia University Press, 1978.

Tweed, Thomas. *Our Lady of the Exile: Diasporic Religion at a Cuban Catholic Shrine in Miami*. New York: Oxford University Press, 1997.

Van der Veer, Peter. "Structure and Anti-Structure in Hindu Pilgrimage to Ayodhya," in *Changing South Asia: Religion and Society*, eds. Kenneth Ballhatchet and David Taylor. London: Asian Research Service for the Centre of South Asian Studies, School of Oriental and African Studies, University of London, 1984, pp. 59–67.

Yamba, Bawa. *Permanent Pilgrims: The Role of Pilgrimage in the Lives of West African Muslims in Sudan*. Edinburgh: Edinburgh University Press, 1995.

— Chapter 23 —

Ritual

Catherine Bell

Soon after the destruction of the World Trade Center towers in New York City on September 11, 2001, photographs of missing relatives were put up at local hospitals and buildings used by rescue services. As hope faded that the missing might be found alive, these posters gave way to memorials. All around New York City, people posted messages to individuals who had died, and many fashioned small altars that allowed them to share something of their distress and bewilderment. In one community an altar for the dead soon incorporated pictures of neighbors who, one by one, were determined to have been among those killed. Strangers brought flowers and joined impromptu prayers. At the site itself – "Ground Zero" – workers and community leaders orchestrated a series of *ad hoc* rituals over the course of the following months, from brief honor parades given to the remains of dead firemen found in the debris to the closure sought by the final, solemn escort for an empty stretcher and the last steel girder.

While churches, synagogues, and mosques across the city held innumerable funeral and prayer services, the public spaces marked by street altars and other expressions of personal sentiments were also the focus of attention. They were the places where average New Yorkers felt part of an encompassing community united in grief. Families left tokens of personal significance, visitors posted messages of solidarity, and school children contributed class projects of indiscriminate tribute. After nine months, most of the memorials were taken down as the clean-up of the area expanded, but on the wrought iron fences of a nearby church there remained a layered and increasingly weathered display – of grief, gratitude, and, here and there, hope. While the communal solace evoked by these memorials was intense, it was also clear that people were casting about for ways to come to grips with the enormity of the event. The memorials were emotionally moving to create, display, and observe, and yet they were rough, tentative, debated, and eventually collected as historical artifacts.

In these various activities a repertoire of customary rituals was integral to how people dealt publicly with their experiences. Yet these makeshift rites differ significantly from the models that most persons would use when thinking about ritual. Certainly the history of scholarship on ritual long took the nature of ritual for granted. Only in the last few decades have scholars regularly asked just what *is* ritual and proposed new definitions or classifications. Yet we frequently wonder why these public acts are performed, how much religion is the key motivation, and how innovation figures in ritual traditions.

General Overview

Definitions of ritual abound. Most stress the formality and traditionalism of ritual action. Some attempt to articulate the elusive quality that can make even quotidian activities seem ritualistic, such as a routine for brushing one's teeth or a precisely timed trip to the pub to meet friends. Today the emphasis is on how people *ritualize*, that is, on how they set apart an activity in striking ways and then make that activity distinctive for what is done, for when and where it is done, for how it is done, and by whom it is done. While this approach to ritual is better able to address changes in how people ritualize, it also suggests that the exact repetition of a supposedly age-old ceremony is unlikely, even though the claim of scrupulous faithfulness to an ancient prototype is among the commonest ways of differentiating ritual activities from other activities. In the case of both newer and older rites, people choose *what* to ritualize – for example, the Sabbath with a special dinner at sundown or the alignment of Jupiter and Mars with a dawn picnic on the California coast – and then *how* to ritualize – for example, with a traditional model or deliberate innovating.

Just as there have been many definitions of ritual, so there have been numerous classifications of rituals. These classifications have ranged from the simple to the elaborate. The French sociologist Emile Durkheim distinguished between negative rites (taboos) and positive rites (communion rites) (see Durkheim 1965, p. 337). Others have worked out more detailed classifications. A pragmatic approach suggests six open-ended categories: calendrical rites; rites of passage; rites of exchange and communion; rites of affliction; feasting, fasting, and festivals; and political rites (see Bell 1997, p. 94). Yet even these six categories do not exhaust the ways in which people act ritually.

The term "ritual" comes from the Latin words *ritus* and *ritualis*, which refer, respectively, to the prescribed ceremonial order for a liturgical service and to the book that lays out this order. Interchangeable in English with ceremony or liturgy, the term "ritual" began to be used in an anthropological sense early in the twentieth century as part of the exploration of the origin of religion. While ritual was taken to be something common to all religions, most of these early discussions of ritual focused on so-called "primitive" religion. Therefore while the term "ritual" began to evoke a more even-handed appreciation of the commonalities in all religions, the focus on primitive ritual helped to distance these studies from Christianity, which was assumed to be superior. Nevertheless, some early scholars wrote about primitive ritual in a way that made the parallelism with the rites of Christianity hard to overlook (see Beidelman 1974).

Among the many attitudes toward ritual in the history of religion is the Protestant distrust of rites. That distrust is taken furthest by groups like the Quakers, who shun any kind of orchestrated activity. Even today, a self-consciously "modern" attitude tends to equate a full ritual system with a "primitive" form of religiosity. This cultural continuation of a Protestant aversion to ritual tends to equate heavily ritualized practices with Catholic excesses and with the Catholic corruption of a prior, pristine period (see Douglas 1968). These inconsistent assessments of ritual – ritual as a merely primitive activity versus ritual as excessively priestly pomp – avoided expose by being applied to different religions in different parts of the world. Hence primitive religion was to be found in illiterate Africa and corrupted Buddhism in literate Asia. Despite sensitivity to these tendencies, some argue that there remain subtle biases. "Ritualistic" still connotes thoughtless and dogmatic.

Models

Ritual became an object of study in its own right only in the late nineteenth century. Since then, it has come to be studied in many disciplines, including anthropology, religious studies, history, sociology, and psychology. Today theoretical approaches to ritual cut across these disciplines. The main approaches are functionalism, psychoanalysis, phenomenology, structuralism, culturalism, performance studies, and practice theory, as well as cognitive, ethological, and sociobiological methods. Furthermore, many specific studies combine approaches and thereby defy simple classification. Since the 1980s, when allegiance to a particular school of theory became less important, scholars from all these persuasions have drawn on a common body of studies. Although other figures are invoked, including Jacques Derrida and Georges Bataille, the theorists to be described have most shaped our understanding of ritual.

Both William Robertson Smith (1846–94) and James George Frazer (1854–1941) argued for the centrality of ritual in religion, or at least in "primitive" religion. Robertson Smith saw religion, and civilization itself, as originating in the communal bond instilled by participation in the ritual sacrifice of the community's divine totem. He saw ritualistic sacrifice as centered not on gifts of homage, as had previously been assumed, but on the expression of love between humans and their totems, who were eaten by their worshipers (see Smith 1969). Frazer followed Smith in making sacrifice the key religious ritual. He argued that the fundamental sacrificial ritual was that in which the god of fertility, who had been killed, was resurrected. Through his rebirth came the rebirth of crops (see Frazer 1922). The "myth and ritual" school of classicists known as the Cambridge Ritualists proceeded to use Frazer's "dying and rising god" pattern to analyze literature. For example, Lord Raglan identified a universal hero myth that corresponded to Frazer's pattern (see Segal 1998). Ritual meant activities communally organized and executed, the script and meaning of which could later float free to create literature. Most myth ritualists, who professionally were largely classicists and anthropologists, did not examine the rituals of their own day.

These early scholars saw ritual not simply as a religious activity but also as a *social* activity. Subsequent scholars no longer focused on the social *origin* of religious rituals but instead on the social *function* of religions rituals. Foremost here was Emile Durkheim (1858–1917), for whom rituals are the rules of conduct governing human activity in the face of the sacred, or those "things set apart and forbidden" (see Durkheim 1965, pp. 52–3). Durkheim proposed that periodic gatherings to venerate symbols of the sacred enabled people to experience a "collective effervescence," an emotional state through which they came to identify themselves with their gods. In actuality, their gods were a "figurative expression of the society" itself, which was internalized through the ritual (see Durkheim 1965, p. 258). For Durkheim it is through ritual activities directed to the sacred that a society becomes simultaneously a moral community, the heart of the individual's sense of self, and a fundamental constituent about reality.

As the reputed father of sociology, Durkheim is also the father of a functional approach to social phenomena. Ritual is explained by how it functions to maintain society. The British anthropologist Mary Douglas (1921–2007), a Durkheimian who nevertheless moved beyond simple functionalism, helped retire notions of a distinctively primitive form of religion by showing that standard European analyses of so-called magical (primitive) rituals were shaped by a distinctly Protestant disdain for ritual in general (see Douglas 1966, pp. 18–19). In her work on magical rites and purity taboos, Douglas argues that these symbolic activities reflect particular forms of social organization. Rituals act as a form of communication that has a constraining effect on social behavior.

Two students of Durkheim, Henri Hubert (1872–1927) and Durkheim's nephew Marcel Mauss (1873–1950), wrote a short monograph, *Sacrifice*, (1898), that offered a provocative new element to the sociology of ritual. For Hubert and Mauss, it is not the effervescence of the ritual experience that is important, as Durkheim had suggested, but the structured sequence of the rite itself. The sacrificial ritual consecrates the offering, enabling it to act as a medium of communion between the human and the divine realms. After this communion, everything must be desacralized in order to re-establish the necessary distinctions between the human and the divine, the profane and the sacred. For Hubert and Mauss, sacrifice is a special form of ritual, for it alone involves sacralization and the all-important sense of union with the sacred. They demonstrated that ritual is fundamental to the creation and maintenance of a sacred realm distinct from the human – the very foundation of religion.

Sacrifice has traditionally meant killing an animal and then offering it to the gods and to those present. It figures prominently in the Bible, where there is the classification of sacrifices in Leviticus, the sacrifice sealing the covenant with Abraham (Genesis 15 : 9–18), and even the representation of Christ's death (Hebrews 9 : 12–14). Well before Hubert and Mauss, and even before classicists began studying Greek rites of animal offerings, sacrifice was taken as the pre-eminent form of ritual. For Robertson Smith, for example, ritual is the heart of religion and sacrifice the heart of ritual. Ritual represents "a unique process, time, and place in which desire and order, the individual and the universal, are conjoined" (Herrenschmidt 1982, p. 25). In this view sacrifice mediates relations between human beings and the gods. The priority of sacrifice appeared to be confirmed when scholars began to explore the Vedic (Brahmanic) system of sacrifices in ancient India, most exhaustively analyzed by Frits Staal (1983). With biblical, classical, and then comparative textual evidence, sacrifice dominated the early study of ritual.

René Girard (b. 1923), trained as a literary theorist, has incorporated the approaches of both Frazer and Freud in focusing on a primordial sacrifice. But he continually underscores the differences between himself and them. He argues that religion arose to counter the violent social effects of "mimetic desire," or the desire for what someone else has. In effect, primordial rites of collective violence achieved social cohesion by involving everyone in the killing of a designated scapegoat. Girard's "generative" theory of the ritual expulsion and killing of the scapegoat evokes Freud's attempt to root his Oedipal theory in supposed patricide at the dawn of humanity and also depends on Frazer's claim of the actual killing of a human for the sake of the community. Yet even more than they, Girard makes violence the subject of ritual, the function of which is nevertheless reconciliation (see Girard 1987).

This emphasis on sacrifice and violence as the root of human history is also found in the theory of the German classicist Walter Burkert (b. 1931). He suggests that the origins of society lie in hunting – a pre-agricultural stag – that is recalled, and perpetuated, in all rituals. For Burkert, sacrifice is not just one category of ritual. Rather, all rituals are disguised sacrifices and are acts of aggression. Burkert invokes the work of the ethologist Konrad Lorenz, who attempted to demonstrate the roots of human aggression in animal behavior such as the ritual-like patterns found in animal courtship and the pack's hunting activities. More recently, using the approach known as sociobiology, or biological anthropology, Burkert has described the "creation of the sacred" in human evolution, suggesting that ritual was a pre-verbal form of communication and a matter of fixed behavioral patterns characterized, as Freud suggested, by obsessive repetition (see Burkert 1996, pp. 19–20).

The phenomenology of religion has creatively drawn on Frazer, Freud, and C. G. Jung, among others. Phenomenologists such as Mircea Eliade (1907–86) and Jonathan Z. Smith (b. 1938) have contributed a distinctive angle on ritual experience. In ritual, Eliade argued, people symbolically perform the acts of the gods that are recounted in myths about how they brought order (cosmos) to the primordial chaos. Myth recounts these divine acts, and ritual re-enacts them. Every time the creation is repeated in ritual, there is a fresh victory over the forces of chaos since "the ritual makes creation over again" (Eliade 1963, p. 346).

Breaking with those who argued for the priority of ritual, Eliade also broke with Frazer's view that the primitive or archaic ritual is concerned only with fertility. He argued for the importance of the complete cosmogonic myth with its "models" for many levels of ritualistic activity, such as the preparation of medicinal agents. Eliade's influential analysis of New Year rituals paid particular attention to the distinction between the past and the present that is then overcome by ritually created experiences of chaos followed by order – chaos and cosmos. He also gave fresh significance to the repetition of ritual through the renewal bestowed by the cosmogonic myth – a welcome alternative to the harsher, psychological judgments of Freud's theory of neurotic obsession (see Eliade 1954; Freud 1963).

Recent Formulations

In a series of studies drawing on both historical and ethnographic data, Jonathan Z. Smith has recast Eliade's ideas with a fresh concern for the context of any comparative project, but ritual articulates something more than its real context and historical detail. Ritual is a dramatization of how things should be, not of how they actually are. To keep chaos from overwhelming cosmos, ritual regularly reaffirms the right order of things. Ritual acts as an opportunity, a kind of "focusing lens," for seeing what is of value (Smith 1982, p. 65). Like Eliade, Smith does not concern himself with how ritual functions in society. He is concerned instead with how the religious imagination understands what it is doing in performing a rite. In particular, Smith suggests that ritual is a mechanism for repairing the fragmentation of human experience and the breakdown of cosmic coherence.

The ethnologist Arnold van Gennep (1873–1957) was one of the first theorists of ritual *not* to focus on sacrifice. In his classic work *The Rites of Passage* (1909) he addressed life-crisis rites, or those rites accompanying a change in social status, such as initiation and marriage. He argued that rites of passage orchestrate a change in status by means of a three-part structure: first, separation, in which the person is removed from the person's immediate social group, such as that of young girls; second, transition, in which the person is kept in a temporary, in between, "liminal" state, such as a cohort group of girls being confined in an isolated, womb-like hut at the far edge of the village; and third, incorporation, in which the person is given a new status in another social grouping – for example, that of marriageable adult women. Van Gennep found that this three-part structure could be as simple as passing through gates and portals, or as complicated as one involving multiple sub-rites and long transition periods. Working with van Gennep's model, Bruce Lincoln (1991) has provided examples of women's coming-of-age rites, and Ronald Grimes (2000) has written about life-crisis rites in America today.

The British anthropologist Victor Turner (1920–83) modified van Gennep's three-part structure theory to develop a view of ritual as a social process with a dramatic structure. The "ritual process" puts structural elements of society, such as its hierarchical associations and kinship relations, into dialectical interplay with society's anti-structural elements, such as various egalitarian groupings of men or women as well as symbols of paradox or transgressive playfulness (see Turner 1969). Van Gennep's stages of separation, transition, and reincorporation become Turner's stages of structure, anti-structural liminality, and revised structure. The liminal, transitional stage, marked by experiences of what he calls *communitas*, both differentiates changes in structure and facilitates them. In other words, ritual simultaneously affirms the social order and changes it.

Chaotic inversions of the social order found in the symbols and activities of the liminal phase of *communitas* maintain the structure that they invert in the same way that a door maintains the boundaries of one room by creating passage to another one.

Turner's analysis of *communitas* found a wide readership. Not unlike Eliade's description of the anarchy that separates the old year from the new, Turner depicted *communitas* in terms of symbols that invert or subvert the social structure. For example, in the course of his coronation, a king is deliberately humbled. Turner then turned to exploring the performative aspects of ritual and in turn the links between ritual and theater (see Turner 1982).

During the same period the American anthropologist Clifford Geertz (1935–2006) formulated a description of religion as a "cultural system." Symbols and symbolic actions influence people's attitudes by formulating coherent conceptions of the general order of existence. "In a ritual the world as lived and the world as imagined, fused under the agency of a single set of symbolic forms, turns out to be the same world" (Geertz 1973, p. 112). Ritual is the way that people at once affirm and embody social values. These values of coherence make experiences beyond the rite more manageable and meaningful. Like Turner, Geertz encouraged thinking of ritual not only in terms of established religious traditions, such as the Javanese communal feast known as the *slametan*, but also in terms of the *ritual-like* qualities of secular activities, such as cock fighting. While Turner has been influential for his analysis of what happens within a ritual event, Geertz has been influential for his articulation of the role of ritual within an elastic definition of religion. Both Turner and Geertz have helped to create a consensus that the system of meanings embodied in a ritual can be related to larger social and psychological processes. Ritual can no longer be taken as it had initially been taken – as a wholly discrete, isolated event.

In what is apt to be called a linguistic approach, the focus is on how the symbolic action of the ritual – primarily but not exclusively the verbal action of speaking – does not simply communicate but also accomplishes specific goals. For example, a marriage ceremony does not simply communicate a change in the social status of the man and woman but actually produces this change. This focus on linguistic "performatives" makes clear that ritual is more than the simple acting out of beliefs. Other recent studies have been concerned with the relationship of belief and ritual, arguing that the "sacred postulates" of a community emerge within performative aspects of ritual. What is claimed is that the oral and bodily gestures performed in the ritual generate "statements" about reality that communicate both information and attitudes, especially acquiescence to the reality so defined (see Rappaport 1999; Humphrey and Laidlaw 1994).

Practice theory and performance theory attempt to articulate how what is done in a ritual – the gestures, words, and physical delineations of space and time – actually accomplishes what a ritual is thought to do, namely, shape attitudes. Anthropologist Sherry Ortner (1978) has analyzed the symbols and rituals of the Himalayan Sherpas. Theater scholar Richard Schechner has painstakingly explored the body language of ritualized performances and performed rituals, ranging from cross-cultural facial expressions to the elaborate dramas of the Ram *lila* in Northern India (see Schechner and Appel 1989; Hughes-Freeland and Crain 1998). In my own work I have looked at ritual in the context of social action in general, not as something set apart either in theory or in actuality (see Bell 1992, 1997). I attempt to determine what is distinctive about this way of acting when compared with other ways of acting.

Several ideas emerge from this new perspective. All action is strategic and situational – that is, construes its context in ways that are advantageous to the actors. Ritualized action construes its situation for the advantages of promoting images and relationships in which there is overt deference to the authority of otherworldly sources of power as well as of those of human beings believed to speak for these powers. Central to the strategy of ritualizing activity is deft bodily movement. As the body moves about, marking off space and time, it defines even the most complex ritual environment by simple acts such as kneeling, circumambulation, and procession. These bodily movements of gesture and sound generate a series of oppositional schemes that structure the environment in a redundant sequence of analogies: upper/lower, inner/outer, right hand/left hand, divine/human, older/younger, male/female, pure/impure, and so on. Mobilizing or deploying these oppositions, the body first *defines* the ritual space and then more dramatically *reacts* to it. The shaped and qualified environment gives those in it an experience of the objective reality of the schemes that have defined it. Participants do not so much see how they and their ritual leaders have generated this environment as feel its impact on them.

Taken as a form of social practice, ritual has as its ultimate goal the creation of a ritualized body (ritual mastery), a body in which the ritual schemes (higher is divine, lower is humble; inner is soul, outer is corporeal body) are fully absorbed, enabling a person to mold situations that occur outside the rite itself (see Bell 1992). In the still practiced Chinese practice of daily domestic offerings of incense to the ancestors, the scripted aspect of the ritual distinguishes it from other domestic routines. With a few simple moves, the body can define a totalizing cosmic orientation at the heart of the home. As the grandmother of the house "lights incense and distributes the sticks in their various pots, she does not [actually] see herself reconstructing a complex cultural system of binary categories": living descendants/dead ancestors, benevolent gods/malevolent ghosts, family deities/community deities, higher status/lower status, superior/ inferior, and a female's routine care/the male's formal ceremony. "Yet performance analysis suggests that the particular efficacy of her actions as action lies in how she creates and modifies such realities while never quite seeing the creation of the system as such" (Bell 1998, p. 216). A practice approach attempts to answer the question why ritual is deemed to be the effective thing to do in a particular situation. An emphasis on the performative aspects of ritual (script, drama, roles) attempts to discern how these qualities can have both social and individual effects.

The potential of a focus on ritual for understanding religion and society was argued with fresh energy in the late 1970s, when Ronald Grimes coined the designation "ritual studies" and pushed for the recognition of the new field with the founding of the *Journal of Ritual Studies* (see Grimes 1995). The study of religion, long focused on sacrifice, at last began to pay attention to the more broadly conceived notion of ritual. Apart from a new interdisciplinary ethos, which widened the scope of material considered relevant to religion, the emergence of a focus on culture in such fields as anthropology and literary studies suggested that study of the social dimensions of religion need not be so reductive as an earlier generation of scholars had feared.

Today, scholars may be at the point of relinquishing the idea that there can be a single theory of ritual, for ritual may not be any one thing. While some characteristics recur in activities readily identified as ritualistic – for example, formality, repetition, and limited vocabulary – how these activities are construed by participants varies greatly.

The Contemporary Ritual Scene

The place of ritual in contemporary European and US communities is the subject of much discussion. For many communities the last few decades have brought dramatic changes to ritual life. For Catholics, the Second Vatican Council (1963) modified the Roman Rite, which had been performed since the sixteenth century, by streamlining the liturgy and replacing Latin with the vernacular. Anglicans in the United Kingdom and around the globe saw major revisions in the *Book of Common Prayer*, which had originally been adopted in 1662. Orthodox Jewish communities, stressing careful observance of the many rites of a Torah-centered life, grew with converts and a high birth rate. Reform Jewish communities experimented with restoring some discarded rites in order to counter their gentle decline in numbers. In fact, all mainstream religious communities lost membership in the last few decades, whereas evangelical churches, featuring large and lively services, which is to say rituals, saw their congregations swell. Questions about the use of culturally specific symbols and music became more pressing as Christian communities in Africa and Asia joined conversations about liturgical reform and as Christianity began to spread dramatically when Scripture and the Liturgy were translated into native languages. Urban centers everywhere became more culturally diverse, exposing people to a richer spectrum of ritual practices than ever before. The dramatic changes in the ritual life of the churches and the development of independent ritual communities sent both theologians and self-taught liturgists to ritual theory to understand and to orchestrate ritual practices. Thomas Driver (1997) has explored the transformative qualities of communal ritual. Ronald Grimes (2000) has suggested how people might, in a more entrepreneurial spirit, adapt older patterns to fit new ritual needs.

Ever since Turner suggested that the dialectic of ritual structure and anti-structure can effect social change, there has been great interest in the way that a ritual tradition, hitherto considered static, can appropriate new elements and discard old ones. There are now many studies of the alteration of rituals in situations of sudden stress, such as the rapid economic and social changes that accompany urbanization or the sudden development of lucrative tourism. Eric Hobsbawn and Terence Ranger's 1983 collection, *The Invention of Tradition*, shows how rituals that generate an aura of great age can in fact be rather recent creations. Less common are studies of social changes that ritual traditions are *unable* to meet.

Apart from the issue of tradition and change, one key recent topic in the study of ritual is the role of the body. Focus on the body is intended to counter the tendency to over-intellectualize ritual. In some cases interest in the body has taken the form of attempts to analyze the way that ritual can effect changes of disposition or mental orientation, even to the extent of providing healing. It has been suggested that the personal agency afforded by rites enables individuals to deal more effectively with other aspects of their lives. This impression, which has become an explicit principle in the use of ritual by family therapists, is also expressed in studies that show how collective rites can fortify a whole community against violence and neglect (see Imber-Black *et al.* 1988; Thomas 1999). Similarly, studies of women's rituals often argue for the creative impact of domestic ritualizing on personal and public identities (see Northrup 1997).

Spurred at once by new historical models and by alarming instances of religious violence, some studies have looked at the contributions of ritual to group psychology, ideological training, and playful transgressions of revered symbols. These studies suggest, if not always pursue, a darker dimension to ritual, lodged perhaps in the conformity of group participation and the submission rendered to powers that transcend the rational (see Davis 1975; McNeill 1995). Studies of political rites illustrate the temporal reach of the sacredness defined by ritual symbols (see Kertzer 1988).

Recent research has noted shifts in the dominant sites of ritual behavior, suggesting that religion and social change are not simply a matter of newly modified rites but more deeply a change in which elements of life are ritualized. For example, in the contemporary individualized forms of spirituality called the New Age, ritual activity has moved from the public domain to the more private one. At the same time studies of the ritual aspects of consumer behavior and of organized sports suggest that the transfer of some ritual activity may be linked to the creation of new forms of community that integrate different aspects of life (see MacAloon 1984).

Most of the popular literature on ritual, of which a great deal is published every year, promotes self-created rituals, especially rites of passage. There are books to help individuals, families, and small groups design their own ceremonies for critical events in life such as adolescence, marriage, divorce, childbirth, and menopause. Manuals encourage readers to bring more ritual into their lives – for example, by adopting the shamanic curing rites or the vision quest (with sweat lodge) of the American Plains Indians. The accompanying ethnographies are decidedly romanticized. For the main events of life, Americans and Britons alike tend to return to mainstream churches.

The public acts of shared mourning witnessed in the aftermath of the destruction of the World Trade Center echo earlier urban displays. In the last thirty years the United States and the United Kingdom have seen many examples of an evolving routine – mainly the embellishment of an urban site memorializing the deceased with flowers, messages, and private objects. Some date the first of these large public displays to the death of John Lennon in 1980, others back to that of John F. Kennedy in 1963. Some see roots in Latin and Hispanic practices to placate the souls of youth killed on the streets, including memorial "walls" painted by graffiti artists turned community entrepreneurs. Still others suggest the influence of the Mexican peasant practice of erecting a roadside shrine at the site of a fatal car accident (see Zeitlin and Harlow 2001, pp. 192–5).

Not too long ago there was a scholarly debate over the Japanese practice of buying and inscribing *ema*, on small wooden tablets with requests for the gods. Was this practice religious or secular (see Anderson and Reader 1991)? The exchange illuminated, once again, the difficulty in identifying or locating ritual. Does ritual behavior need to be concerned with the religious imagery of gods, ancestors, and human afterlife, or is any symbolic sequence of standardized gestures a ritual? The prudent answer is probably to follow the word usage of the culture itself. Whether we look to the majestic Easter rites of the Greek Orthodox Church or to the Chinese dragon dance at the lunar New Year, there are links to a religious cosmos of powers beyond the human. Yet those writers who have pushed the boundaries of this limited definition to show the rituals in daily hygiene routines, in professional wrestling, and in operatic theater have contributed to our understanding of how the English-speaking world distinguishes what Durkheim called the sacred from what he calls the profane.

The creation of a small altar out of plywood and colored paper exteriorizes grief, love, and hope. Facing this altar, one is comforted by the external reinforcement for the feelings that created it. On the altar one sees love, hope, and grief. When these feelings are recognized by others, and so shared, they can steady personal identities and reinforce communities. Ritual has been described as an encounter between imagination and memory translated into the physical acts of the body. People may perform these acts of the body with enthusiasm or boredom, yet either way ritual appears to be a bit of psychosocial alchemy as nimble and as inexhaustible as our imaginations and our memories.

Bibliography

Anderson, Richard W., and Ian Reader. "What Constitutes Religious Activity? I and II," *Japanese Journal of Religious Studies* 18 (1991): 369–76.

Beidelman, T. O. *W. Robertson Smith and the Sociological Study of Religion.* Chicago: University of Chicago Press, 1974.

Bell, Catherine. *Ritual Theory, Ritual Practice.* New York: Oxford University Press, 1992.

Bell, Catherine. *Ritual: Perspectives and Dimensions.* New York: Oxford University Press, 1997.

Bell, Catherine. "Performance," in *Critical Terms for Religious Studies*, ed. Mark C. Taylor. Chicago: University of Chicago Press, 1998, pp. 205–24.

Burkert, Walter. *Homo Necans: The Anthropology of Ancient Greek Sacrificial Ritual and Myth*, tr. Peter Bing. Berkeley: University of California Press, 1983.

Burkert, Walter. *Creation of the Sacred: Tracks of Biology in Early Religions.* Cambridge, MA: Harvard University Press, 1996.

Davis, Natalie Z. *Society and Culture in Early Modern France: Eight Essays.* Stanford, CA: Stanford University Press, 1975.

Douglas, Mary. *Purity and Danger: An Analysis of Concepts of Pollution and Taboo.* London: Routledge and Kegan Paul, 1966.

Douglas, Mary. "The Contempt of Ritual," *New Blackfriars* 49 (1968): 475–82, 528–35.

Douglas, Mary. *Natural Symbols: Explorations in Cosmology.* 1st edn. Harmondsworth: Penguin, 1970.

Driver, Thomas F. *Liberating Rites: Understanding the Transformative Power of Ritual* [1994]. Boulder, CO: Westview Press, 1997.

Durkheim, Emile. *The Elementary Forms of the Religious Life* [1912], tr. Joseph Ward Swain. New York: Free Press, 1965 [1915].

Eliade, Mircea. *The Myth of the Eternal Return [Cosmos and History]*, tr. Willard R. Trask. Princeton, NJ: Princeton University Press, 1954.

Eliade, Mircea. *Patterns in Comparative Religion* [1958], tr. Rosemary Sheed. New York: Meridian Books, 1963.

Frazer, James George. *The Golden Bough: A Study in Magic and Religion*. Abridged edn. London: Macmillan, 1922.

Freud, Sigmund. "Obsessive Acts and Religious Practices" [1907], in his *Character and Culture*, ed. Philip Rieff. New York: Collier Books, 1963, pp. 17–26.

Geertz, Clifford. *The Interpretation of Cultures*. New York: Basic Books, 1973.

Girard, René. *Things Hidden since the Foundation of the World* [1978], trs. Stephan Bann and Michael Metteer. Stanford, CA: Stanford University Press, 1987.

Grimes, Ronald L. *Beginnings in Ritual Studies* [1982], rev. edn. Columbia: University of South Carolina Press, 1995.

Grimes, Ronald L., ed. *Readings in Ritual Studies*. Upper Saddle, NJ: Prentice-Hall, 1996.

Grimes, Ronald L. *Deeply into the Bone: Re-Inventing Rites of Passage*. Berkeley: University of California Press, 2000.

Herrenschmidt, Oliver. "Sacrifice: Symbolic or Effective," in *Between Belief and Transgression: Structuralist Essays in Religion, History and Myth*, eds. Michel Izard and Pierre Smith, tr. John Levitt. Chicago: University of Chicago Press, 1982, pp. 24–42.

Hobsbawn, Eric, and Terence Ranger, eds. *The Invention of Tradition*. Cambridge: Cambridge University Press, 1983.

Hubert, Henri, and Marcel Mauss. *Sacrifice: Its Nature and Functions* [1898], tr. W. D. Hall. Chicago: University of Chicago Press, 1964.

Hughes-Freeland, Felicia, and Mary M. Crain. *Recasting Ritual: Performance, Media, Identity*. London: Routledge, 1998.

Humphrey, Caroline, and James Laidlaw. *The Archetypal Actions of Ritual*. Oxford: Clarendon Press, 1994.

Imber-Black, Evan, Janine Roberts, and Richard A. Wittig, eds. *Ritual in Families and Family Therapy*. New York: Norton, 1988.

Kertzer, David I. *Ritual, Power and Politics*. New Haven, CT: Yale University Press, 1988.

Lincoln, Bruce. *Emerging from the Chrysalis: Rituals of Women's Initiation* [1981]. Rev. edn. New York: Oxford University Press, 1991.

MacAloon, John J. "Olympic Games and the Theory of Spectacle in Modern Societies," in *Rite, Drama, Festival, Spectacle: Rehearsals Towards a Theory of Cultural Performance*, ed. John J. MacAloon. Philadelphia: Institute for the Study of Human Issues, 1984, pp. 241–80.

McNeill, William H. *Keeping Together in Time: Dance and Drill in Human History*. Cambridge, MA: Harvard University Press, 1995.

Northrup, Lesley A. *Ritualizing Women: Patterns of Spirituality*. Cleveland: Pilgrim Press, 1997.

Ortner, Sherry B. *Sherpas Through Their Rituals*. Cambridge: Cambridge University Press, 1978.

Rappaport, Roy A. *Ritual and Religion in the Making of Humanity*. Cambridge: Cambridge University Press, 1999.

Sanneh, Lamin. *Translating the Message: The Missionary Impact on Culture.* Maryknoll, NY: Orbis, 1989.

Schechner, Richard, and Willa Appel, eds. *By Means of Performance: Intercultural Studies of Theater and Ritual.* Cambridge: Cambridge University Press, 1989.

Segal, Robert A., ed. *The Myth and Ritual Theory.* Oxford: Blackwell, 1998.

Smith, Jonathan Z. *Imagining Religion: From Babylon to Jonestown.* Chicago: University of Chicago Press, 1982.

Smith, Jonathan Z. *To Take Place: Toward Theory in Ritual.* Chicago: University of Chicago Press, 1987.

Smith, William Robertson. *Lectures on the Religion of the Semites: The Fundamental Institutions* [1889], 3rd edn. New York: KTAV, 1969 [1927].

Staal, Frits. *Agni: The Vedic Fire Ritual.* Berkeley: Asian Humanities Press, 1983.

Thomas, Linda Elaine. *Under the Canopy: Ritual Process and Spiritual Resilience in South Africa.* Columbia: University of South Carolina Press, 1999.

Turner, Victor. *The Ritual Process: Structure and Antistructure.* Ithaca, NY: Cornell University Press, 1969.

Turner, Victor. *From Ritual to Theatre: The Human Seriousness of Play.* New York: Performing Arts Journal Publications, 1982.

Van Gennep, Arnold. *The Rites of Passage* [1909], trs. Monika B. Vizedom and Gabrielle L. Caffee. Chicago: University of Chicago Press, 1960.

Zeitlin, Steve, and Illana Harlow. *Giving a Voice to Sorrow: Personal Responses to Death and Mourning.* New York: Penguin Putnam, 2001.

Chapter 24

Secularization

Steve Bruce

The peoples of pre-industrial Europe were deeply religious. The extent to which they were orthodox Christians varied, but most understood the world through basically Christian lenses. Most knew the Lord's Prayer and the Hail Mary and could make the sign of the cross. They knew the Ten Commandments, the four cardinal virtues, the seven deadly sins, and the seven works of mercy. They paid tithes, brought babies for baptism, and married in church. They believed sufficiently in hell and in the status of Holy Writ for the swearing of oaths on the Bible to be a means of control. They avoided blaspheming. They paid large sums for priests to say Mass on their behalf. Most knew that they had to make reparation to God for their sins, in this life or in the next. When the clergy complained of irreligion, they were complaining not that people were secular but that they were persisting in pre-Christian superstitions and were using the Church's rituals in a magical manner (see Bruce 2002, pp. 45–59).

As societies became industrialized, people became divided into those who were well-informed true believers and those who fell away. The once pervasive religious world view gave way to an increasingly secular public culture. By the middle of the nineteenth century religion had become so separated from everyday life that its supporters could be counted. Whether we count membership, church attendance, religious ceremonies to mark rights of passage, or indices of belief, we find that across the industrial world there has been a major decline in all religious indices (see Bruce 2002).

Understanding Secularization

Explaining the decline in the power, prestige, and popularity of religion has exercised so many scholars that we can represent their work as a "secularization paradigm." Figure 1 represents a synthesis from a variety of sources of the trend toward secularization. Some of the scholars cited would dissent from other elements of the synthesis, but we will forgo examining these discussions here.

Monotheism (R1)

Following Max Weber, the American sociologist of religion Peter Berger (1967) has argued that the monotheism of Judaism and Christianity contributed to the rationality of the West. Where the Egyptian world was embedded in a cosmic order that embraced the entire universe, with no sharp distinction between the human and the non-human, the Jewish God was remote. He would one day end the world that he had created, but in the interim it had its own structure and logic. He made consistent ethical demands and was beyond magical manipulation. We had to learn his laws and to obey them. We could not bribe, cajole, or trick him. As the Christian Church evolved, the cosmos was re-mythologized with angels and semi-divine saints. The idea that God could be manipulated through ritual, confession, and penance undermined the tendency to regulate behavior with a standardized, or rationalized, ethical code. But this trend was reversed anew as the Protestant Reformation again demythologized the world by eliminating the ritual and sacramental manipulation of God and by restoring the process of ethical rationalization.

Making formal what pleased God made it possible for ethics to become detached from beliefs about the supernatural. Codes could be followed for their own sake and could even attract alternative justifications. In that sense the rationalizing tendency of Christianity created space for secular alternatives.

The Protestant Ethic (E1)

Weber argues that the Reformation inadvertently created new attitudes toward work and toward the accumulation of capital (see Weber 1976).

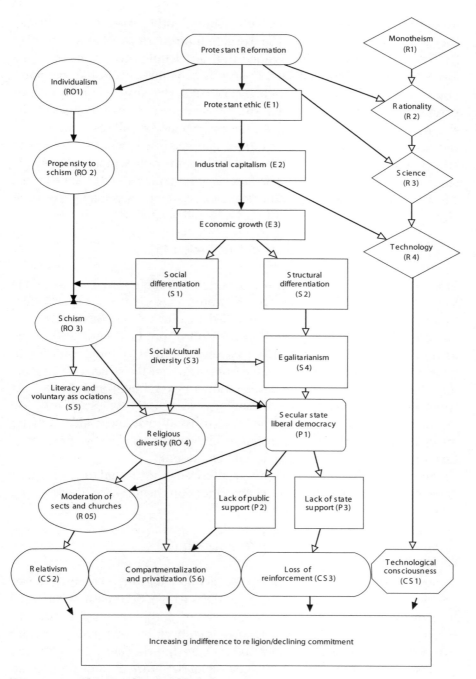

Figure 1 The trend toward secularization

Previously, the most pious people displayed "other-worldly asceticism": they cut themselves off from the world in monasteries and in hermitages. By contrast, Martin Luther argued that any legitimate occupation, performed diligently, glorified God. By arguing against confession, penance, and absolution, Reformers such as Luther deprived people of a way of periodically wiping away their sins. The reformers thus increased the strain of trying to live a Christian life and made work all the more important as a way of avoiding temptation. The result was what Weber called "this-worldly asceticism": an ordered, diligent, and temperant life well suited to rational capitalism. The link E2 to E3 represents the fact that the countries that first adopted industrial capitalism prospered ahead of their rivals. As we will see, prosperity weakens religiosity.

Structural differentiation (S2)

Modernization involves structural or functional differentiation: social life fragments as specialized roles and institutions are created for specific features or functions previously embodied in one role or institution (see Parsons 1964). The family was once a unit of production as well as the institution through which society was reproduced. With industrialization, economic activity became separated from the home. It also became increasingly informed by its own values, as shown by the link from R2 to S2. At work, we are supposed to be rational, instrumental, and pragmatic. We are also supposed to be universalistic: to treat customers alike, paying attention only to the matter in hand. The private sphere, by contrast, is taken to be expressive, indulgent, and emotional.

Increased specialization directly secularized many social functions that were once dominated by the church: education, health care, welfare, and social control.

Social differentiation (SI)

As society fragments, so do the people. Economic growth created an ever greater range of occupations and situations which, because accompanied by growing egalitarianism, led to an increasing separation of classes. In feudal societies, masters and servants lived cheek-by-jowl. This proximity was possible because the gentry had no fear that the lower orders would get ideas "above their station." As the social structure became more fluid, those who could afford to do so replaced the previously effective *social* distance with a *literal* one.

The plausibility of a single moral universe in which all people have a place depends on the stability of the social structure. With new social roles and increasing social mobility, communal conceptions of the moral and supernatural order fragmented. As classes became more distinctive, each created a system of salvation better suited to its interests. The great pyramid of pope, bishops, priests, and laity reflected the social pyramid of king, nobles, gentry, and peasants. Independent small farmers and the rising business class preferred a more democratic religion. Hence their attraction to such Protestant sects as the Presbyterians, Baptists, and Quakers.

Modernization was not simply a matter of the *response* of religion to social, economic, and political changes. Religion was itself a cause of change, as a step back to the links among the Reformation, the rise of individualism, and schism will show.

Individualism (ROI)

The English sociologist of religion David Martin has noted a major effect of the Reformation: "The logic of Protestantism is clearly in favour of the voluntary principle, to a degree that eventually makes it sociologically unrealistic" (Martin 1978, p. 9). Belief systems differ greatly in their propensity to fragment. Put simplistically, some religions claim a unique path to salvation, whereas others allow for many ways to salvation. The Catholic Church claims that Christ's authority was passed to Peter and then fixed in the office of Pope. It claims a monopoly on access to salvation and on the right to decide disputes about God's will. If those claims are accepted, the Church is relatively immune to fission. The rejection of those claims involves extreme upheavals, such as the French Revolution. Thus as Catholic countries modernize, they split internally into the religious and the secular. Hence Italy, Spain, and France have at once conservative Catholic traditions and powerful Communist parties.

Protestantism was vulnerable to schism because it rejected institutional mechanisms to settle disputes. To assert that all can discern God's will is to invite schism. Tradition, habit, respect for learning, and admiration for piety perhaps restrained division, but they could not prevent it. The Reformation produced not one church purified and strengthened but competing churches.

We might add a secular version of RO1. Individualism gradually developed an autonomous dynamic as the egalitarianism located in the diagram as S4. Egalitarianism is placed there to stress that individualism and the closely associated social reality of diversity (S3) could develop only in propitious circumstances – ones of structural differentiation (S2) and economic growth (E3).

The link between modernization and inequality is paradoxical. Industrialization produced at once greater social distance and greater egalitarianism (S4). The Reformers themselves were hardly democrats, but they inadvertently caused a major change in the relative importance of community and individual. By removing the special status of the priesthood and the possibility that religious merit could be transferred – by, for example, saying masses for the souls of the dead – they reasserted what had been implicit in early Christianity: that we are all equal in the eyes of God. Initially, that equality lay in our sinfulness, but the idea could not indefinitely be confined to duty. Equal obligations eventually became equal rights.

Wide-ranging equality was made possible by changes in the economy (see Gellner 1991). Economic development brought change and the expectation of further change. It also brought occupational mobility. As it became more common for people to better themselves, it also became more common for them to think better of themselves. However badly paid, the industrial worker did not see himself as a serf. Where the serf occupied just one role in an all-embracing hierarchy, and where that role shaped his entire life, a tin miner in Cornwall in 1800 might be oppressed at work but in the late evening and on Sunday could change clothes to become a Baptist preacher – a man of prestige. This alternation marks a crucial change. Once social status became task-specific, people could occupy different positions in different hierarchies. That variability made it possible to distinguish between the role and the person who played the role. Roles could still be ranked and accorded very different degrees of power or status, but the persons behind the roles could be seen as in some sense equal.

Societalization

"Societalization" is the term that the English sociologist of religion Bryan Wilson has given to the way in which "life is increasingly enmeshed and organized, not locally but societally (that society being most evidently, but not uniquely, the nation state)" (Wilson 1982, p. 154). If social differentiation (S1) and individualism (RO1) are blows to small-scale communities from below, societalization is the attack from above. Closely knit, integrated communities gradually lost power and presence to large-scale industrial and commercial enterprises, to modern states coordinated through massive and impersonal bureaucracies, and to cities. This community-to-society transition was classically delineated by the German sociologist Ferdinand Tönnies (1955).

Following Durkheim, Wilson argues that religion draws its strength from the community. As the society rather than the community became the locus of the individual's life, religion was denuded. The church of the Middle Ages baptized, christened, married, and buried. Its calendar of services mapped onto the seasons. It celebrated and legitimated local life. In turn, it drew strength from being frequently reaffirmed by the local people. In 1898 almost all members of my Scottish boyhood village celebrated the harvest by bringing tokens of their produce to the church. In 1998 a very small number of people in my village, and only one of them a farmer, celebrated by bringing to the church vegetables and tinned goods (many of foreign provenance) bought in a supermarket.

Instead of celebrating the harvest, the service thanked God for all his creation. Broadening the symbolism solved the problem of relevance but lost direct contact with the lives of those involved. When the all-embracing community of like-situated people working and playing together gave way to the dormitory town or suburb, there was little left in common to celebrate.

Differentiation and societalization reduced the plausibility of any single overarching religious system and thus encouraged competing religions. While religions might have had much to say to private experience, they could have little connection to the performance of social roles or the operation of social systems because they were not society-wide – that is, as extensive as the social roles and systems. Religion retained what Berger calls its "subjective plausibility" for some, but it lost its objective taken-for-grantedness. Religion was now a preference, not a necessity.

Again it is worth stressing the interaction of social and cultural forces. The fragmentation of Western Christianity that began with the Reformation (RO3) hastened the development of the religiously neutral state (P1). A successful economy required a high degree of integration, which involved effective communication, a shared legal code to enforce contracts, and a climate of trust (see Gellner 1991). This integration required an integrated national culture. Where there was consensus, a national "high culture" could be provided through the dominant religious tradition. The clergy could continue to be the school teachers, historians, propagandists, public administrators, and military strategists. Where there was little consensus (RO4), the growth of the state was secular.

Schism and sect formation (RO3)

The Reformation stimulated literacy (S5). With everyone required to answer to God individually, lay people needed to be able to meet that new responsibility. Hence the translation of the Bible into vernacular languages, the rapid advance in printing, the spread of literacy, and the start of mass education. Competition among sects was a further spur. And as the English anthropologist Ernest Gellner and others have argued, the spread of education was both a necessity for economic growth and the consequence of it. The sectarian competitive spirit of the RO line interacted with the requirements of the E and S line to produce a literate and educated laity, which in turn encouraged the general emphasis on the importance and rights of the individual and the growth of both egalitarianism (S4) and liberal democracy (P1).

Protestant sects also had a direct influence on P1 by providing a new model for social organization. Reformed religion was individualistic, but it encouraged individuals to band together for encouragement, edification, evangelism, and social control. As an alternative to the organic community, in which every position was inherited and assigned, the sectarians established the voluntary association of like-minded individuals coming together to pursue common goals.

Social and cultural diversity (S3)

Diversity created the secular state. Modernization brought with it increased cultural diversity in three ways. First, peoples moved and brought their language, religion, and social mores into their new setting. Second, the expansive nation-state encompassed new peoples. Third, economic modernization, especially common in Protestant settings, created classes that in turn created competing sects. Hence the paradox: at the same time that the nation-state was trying to create a unified national culture out of thousands of small communities, it was having to come to terms with increasing religious diversity. The solution was an increasingly neutral state. Religious establishments were either abandoned altogether, as in the United States, or neutered, as in the United Kingdom. While freedom from entanglements with secular power allowed churches to become more clearly "spiritual," their removal from the center of public life reduced their contact with the general population and thereby their relevance (P2 and P3).

Separation of church and state was one consequence of diversity. Another was the break between the community and the religious world view. In sixteenth-century England every significant event in the life cycle of the individual and the community was celebrated in church and was given a religious gloss. The techniques of the church were used to bless the sick, sweeten the soil, and increase animal productivity. Testimonies, contracts, and promises were reinforced by oaths sworn on the Bible and before God. But beyond the special events that saw the parish troop into the church, the credibility of the religious world view was confirmed through everyday interaction and conversation. People commented on the weather by saying "God be praised" and on parting wished each other "God Speed" or "Goodbye" (an abbreviation of "God be with you").

Diversity also called into question the certainty that believers could have of their religion (see Berger 1980). Ideas are most convincing when they are shared. The elaboration of alternatives provides a profound challenge. True, believers need not fall on their swords when they find that others disagree with them. Where clashes of ideologies occur in the context of social conflict, or when alternatives are promoted by people who need not be taken seriously, the cognitive challenge can be dismissed (see Berger and Luckmann 1966, p. 133). But the proliferation of alternatives does remove the sense of inevitability. When the oracle speaks with a single clear voice, it is easy to believe it to be the voice of God. When it speaks with twenty different voices, it is tempting to look behind the screen.

Compartmentalization and privatization (S6)

Believers may respond to the fact of variety by supposing that all religions are in some sense the same (RO5). Another possibility, quite compatible with that relativism, is to confine one's faith to a particular compartment of social life (S6). With compartmentalization comes privatization. As the German sociologist of religion Thomas Luckmann puts it:

> This development reflects the dissolution of *one* hierarchy of significance in the world view. Based on the complex institutional structure and social stratification of industrial societies different "versions" of the world view emerge. . . . With the pervasiveness of the consumer orientation and the sense of autonomy, the individual is more likely to confront the culture and the sacred cosmos as a "buyer". Once religion is defined as a "private affair", the individual may choose from the assortment of "ultimate" meanings as he sees fit. (Luckmann 1970, pp. 98–9)

The American sociologist of religion José Casanova (1994) argues that differentiation need not cause privatization. The major churches, having now accepted the rules of liberal democracy, can regain a public role – not, as before, by establishing a compact between a dominant church and the state but by acting as pressure groups in civil society. Casanova is right, but he misses a key point: religious interest groups are now required to present their case in *secular* terms. For example, whatever the source of their motives, conservative Christians who oppose abortion must now do so not on the grounds that it violates biblical teachings but on the grounds that it violates the universal human right to life.

The secular state and liberal democracy (PI)

Social innovations, once established, can have an appeal that goes far beyond the initial spur to innovate. Secular liberal democracy evolved as a necessary response both to the egalitarianism (S4) made possible by structural differentiation (S2) and to the diversity (S3) created by a combination of the "fissiparousness" of Protestantism (RO2) and social differentiation (S1). But secular liberal democracy became attractive in its own right, and in the late nineteenth century societies that had no great need for democracy introduced it as part of wider political reforms. Despite its confinement of dissent to viewpoints within the Lutheran tradition, the introduction of representative democracy and the weakening of the monarchy (or Grand Duchy) in the Nordic countries was accompanied by a weakening of the Church, which managed to retain its diverse social functions only by presenting them as secular social services.

The moderation of sects and churches (RO5)

The American theologian and sociologist of religion H. Richard Niebuhr (1962) elaborated a small but important element of the trend toward moderation in his extension of Ernst Troeltsch's comments on the evolution of sects. Niebuhr noted that initially radical sects such as the Quakers and the Methodists tended to become comfortable denominations, on easy terms with the world. Commitment was inevitably reduced as inheritance replaced personal choice. Most sectarians prospered ahead of the average, partly because of the "Protestant Ethic" as elaborated by Weber (E1) and partly because of their asceticism, which made them widely trusted. Most of the British banking system developed from family firms run by Quakers, including the Barclays, Backhouses, Trittons, and Gurneys. Increased wealth, and the social status and public acceptance that came with it, increased the costs of asceticism, and consequently most sectarians moderated.

The Italian political scientist Robert Michels (1962) identified a further source of moderation in his study of oligarchy in leftwing trade unions and political parties. Most sects began as primitive democracies, with little formal organization, but gradually acquired a professional leadership. Especially after the founder died, there was a need to educate and train the preachers and teachers who would sustain the movement. In turn, there was a need to coordinate a growing organization. There were assets to be safeguarded and books to be published. With organization came paid officials, who had a vested interest in reducing tension between the sect and the wider society. Nonconformist ministers could also compare themselves with the clergy of the state church and, even if for the sake of their faith rather than for themselves, desire the same level of training, remuneration, and status.

If a sect can isolate itself from the wider society, so that its culture forms the taken-for-granted backcloth to life, then it can sustain itself. The Amish, Hutterites, and Doukobhors are examples. But usually a sect is only slightly insulated and cannot avoid the social and psychological effects of diversity. Having failed to win over the bulk of the people and thus having to come to terms with being only a "saved remnant," the sect finds good reasons to moderate its claims and comes to see itself not as the sole embodiment of God's will but as just one expression of that will.

The moderation of sects is mirrored in the moderation of churches. Faced with widespread defection and the loss of authority, most churches tempered their claims and came to view themselves as just one church among others. The change was not always made willingly, but by the start of the twentieth century most state churches were cooperating with other Christian organizations. By the end of the twentieth century most state churches were presenting themselves as the senior spokesman for *all* religions against a largely secular climate.

Economic growth (E3)

The effect of prosperity on Protestants sects can be generalized: increasing affluence reduces religious fervor and religious traditionalism (see Inglehart 1997). Religion often provides solace for the dispossessed. As these religions prosper, the faith is rewritten and loses much of its power. American Pentecostals such as Oral Roberts grew up in impoverished conditions, which made it both easy and satisfying to denounce flashy clothes, make-up, Hollywood movies, social dancing, and television (see Harrell 1985). But once they could afford what had previously been the work of the Devil, they compromised their principles. For example, divorce, though still regretted by American Pentecostals, has become widely accepted. It is not that Pentecostals are thereby becoming less religious but that the erosion of distinctive ways of life makes the maintenance of distinctive beliefs harder (see Shibley 1996).

Science (R3) and technology (R4)

Critics of the secularization thesis misrepresent it by assuming that it elevates science to a central position. It is "science that has the most deadly implications for religion," declare Rodney Stark and Roger Finke (2000, p. 61). True, this zero-sum notion of knowledge, with rational thought and science conquering territory from superstition, was carried into early sociology by Auguste Comte and Karl Marx, but it is not part of the modern secularization paradigm. Proponents of the paradigm recognize that modern people are quite capable of believing untruths, so that decreasing plausibility cannot be explained simply by the introduction of more plausible ideas – here scientific ones. The crucial connections are more subtle and complex than those implied in a battle between science and religion.

One line was drawn by the American sociologist of science Robert Merton in his work on Puritan scientists (1970). He argued that many seventeenth-century Protestant scientists were inspired to undertake natural science by a desire to demonstrate the glory of God's creation, by the rationalizing attitude of the Protestant ethic, and by a commitment to control the corrupt world. The result was the same irony that followed from the rationalization of ethics. By demonstrating the fundamentally rule-governed nature of the material world, the Puritan scientists allowed their heirs to do science without framing their work within the assumption that orderliness shows God's glory.

More important to secularization than science has been the development of effective technologies. Religion is often practical. Holy water purportedly cures ailments, and prayers purportedly improve crops. Bryan Wilson has argued that technology secularizes the world by reducing the occasions on which persons need recourse to religion. Farmers did not stop praying to save their sheep from maggots because the invention of an effective sheep dip persuaded them that God was not scientifically up to date. Rather, they needed to appeal to God less often to save their sheep. More generally, as David Martin puts it, with the growth of science and technology "the general sense of human power is increased, the play of contingency is restricted, and the overwhelming sense of divine limits which afflicted previous generations is much diminished" (Martin 1969, p. 116).

Technological consciousness (CSI)

In exploring the psychology of modern work, Peter Berger, Brigitte Berger, and Hansfried Kellner (1974) have argued that even if we are unaware of it, modern technology brings with it a "technological consciousness" that is difficult to reconcile with a sense of the sacred. An example is "componentiality." Modern work assumes that the most complex entities can be broken down into parts that are infinitely replaceable. Likewise actions can be reduced to elements that can be indefinitely repeated. This attitude is carried over from industrial work to workers (a management style known after its heroic promoter as "Fordism") and then to bureaucracy generally. While there is no obvious clash between these assumptions and the teachings of most religions, there are serious incompatibilities of approach. There is little opportunity for the eruption of the divine.

To summarize the R line, the effects of science and technology on the plausibility of religious belief are often misunderstood. Any direct clash is less significant than the subtle impact of naturalistic ways of thinking. Science and technology have not made us atheists, but their underlying rationality makes us less likely than our forebears to entertain the notion of the divine.

Relativism (CS2)

Finally, we come to the bottom line. The Christian Church of the Middle Ages was firmly authoritarian and exclusivistic in its attitude toward knowledge. There was a single truth, and the Church knew what it was. Increasingly social and cultural diversity has combined with egalitarianism to undermine all claims to certain knowledge. While compartmentalization can serve as a holding operation, it is difficult to live in a world that treats as equally valid a large number of incompatible beliefs and that shies away from authoritative assertions without coming to question the existence of any one truth. We may continue to prefer our world view, but we find it hard to insist that what is true for us must also be true for everyone else. The tolerance that is necessary for harmony in diverse egalitarian societies weakens religion by forcing us to live as if we cannot be sure of God's will. The consequence, visible over the twentieth century in liberal democracies, has been a decline in the commitment of church adherents and then in the number of church adherents. Relativism debilitates faith by removing the best reason to ensure that one's children are socialized in the faith. If all faiths offer a road to God, and if there is no hell to which heretics get sent, then there is no need to ensure the transmission of orthodoxy.

Retarding Tendencies

The secularization thesis suggests that social and structural differentiation, societalization, rationalization, individualism, egalitarianism, and diversity all combine to undermine religion. However, most proponents would add an important qualification: except where religion finds or retains work to do other than connecting individuals to the supernatural. The many and varied instances of that work can be summarized under the headings of cultural transition and cultural defence.

Cultural transition

Where social identity is threatened in the course of major social transitions, religion may help to negotiate these changes or assert a new claim to a sense of worth. Religious and ethnic groups can ease the move between homeland and new world. The church offers a supportive group that speaks one's language and shares one's values but that also has contacts with the new social milieu.

There is another manifestation of the tendency for religion to retain significance or even temporarily to grow in significance, and that is in the course of modernization itself. Modernization disrupted communities, traditional employment patterns, and status hierarchies. By extending the range of communication, modernization made the social peripheries and hinterlands more aware of the manners and mores of the center and vice versa. Those at the center of the society were motivated to proselytize the rest, seeking to assimilate them by socializing them in "respectable" beliefs and practices. Sectors of the periphery in turn were motivated to embrace the models of respectable performance offered to them, especially when they themselves were already in the process of upward mobility and self-improvement (see Brown 1987). Industrialization and urbanization gave rise to revival and reform movements.

Cultural defense

Religion often acts as a guarantor of group identity. Where culture, identity, and sense of worth are challenged by a source promoting either an alien religion or rampant secularism, and where that source is negatively valued, secularization will be inhibited. Religion can provide resources for the defense of a national, local, ethnic, or status group culture. Two examples are the role of Catholicism in Irish opposition to Protestant settlers and in Polish national resistance to Soviet Communism.

In the process of functional differentiation the first sphere to become freed of cultural encumbrances is the economy, but religious and ethnic identity can constrain even that trend. Employers often hire "their own," and even in consumption religion may override rationality. Northern Ireland's small towns often have a Protestant butcher and a Catholic butcher even when the market can profitably sustain only one. At times of heightened tension, Protestants and Catholics boycott each other's businesses and travel considerable distances to engage in commerce with their own sort.

Cultural defense also inhibits societalization. A beleaguered minority may try to prevent the erosion of the community. Those who order their lives in the larger society rather than in the community may be regarded as treacherous and may be punished accordingly. In ethnic conflicts – Bosnia and Northern Ireland, for example – those who marry across the divide are frequent targets for vigilantes.

Finally, religious and ethnic conflict mutes the cognitive consequences of pluralism because the prevalence of invidious stereotypes allows a much more thorough stigmatizing of alternative cultures. The openness to relativism as a way of accommodating those with whom we differ depends on our taking others seriously. Where religious differences are strongly embedded in ethnic identities, the cognitive threat from others is relatively weak. Scottish Protestants in the nineteenth century deployed caricatures of the social vices of the immigrant Irish Catholics as a way of avoiding having to consider them as Christians.

The Rational Choice Alternative

There is a radically different reading of the consequences of diversity. The American sociologist of religion Rodney Stark has argued that the religious vitality of the United States is to be explained by its having a free market in religious goods and considerable competition among the providers of these goods. Diversity allows all to find a religion that suits their interests, keeps costs down, and thus makes easier the creation of new religions. Also, it provides the clergy with incentives to recruit a following.

There is evidence from some specific cases to support this "rational choice," or supply-side, model but it mostly comes from studies produced by Stark (2000) and his associates. Attempts to replicate that work, either by the comparison of religious vitality and diversity for different areas within one society or by cross-cultural comparison, fail to find positive effects of diversity. Across Europe church adherence is far higher in countries dominated by one religion – Poland and Ireland, for example – than in diverse cultures such as the United Kingdom. In the Baltic states of Lithuania, Latvia, and Estonia, overwhelmingly Catholic Lithuania has a far higher rate of church adherence than have the more mixed Latvia and Estonia.

A detailed critique of the supply-side approach can be found elsewhere (see Bruce 1999; Jelen 2002). I will make just two points. First, whatever support the supply-side model finds by comparing diversity and religious vitality in different places at the same time is overwhelmed by the conclusions drawn from looking at one place over time. Whether we take Canada, Australia, Norway, Scotland, or Holland, we find that religion was far more popular and powerful in 1850, 1900, or 1950 than at the end of the twentieth century. As these countries have become more diverse, they have become more secular.

Second, rational choice works best for fields where general demand is high but "brand loyalty" low. We are not socialized into a culture that bans us from buying a certain car: we are free to maximize. But for most of the world, religion is not a preference; it is an inherited social identity, closely tied to other shared identities. It can be changed only at considerable personal cost. Hence this paradox: only in largely secular societies, where there is little religious behavior left to explain, will people have the attitude to religion supposed by the rational choice model.

The Irreversibility of Secularization

Of course, it is always possible that the secularization of the twentieth-century West is merely temporary. Many thinkers believe the human condition to be such that we will always need religion: that the desire for the supernatural and its benefits is somehow "hard-wired" into our constitution. Long-term and widespread secularization is therefore deemed impossible. If one religious tradition declines, another will arise.

This conviction neglects the role of culture. It supposes that individual needs translate into outcomes in an unmediated fashion. It misses the point that biological and psychological drives are shaped by a particular culture. Even if there are basic questions that most people will ask themselves, such as what the meaning of life is, we cannot assume that large numbers will on their own frame the question in the same terms, let alone embrace the same answer. On the contrary, the authority of the autonomous individual precludes consensus. While it is common to ascribe to

individualism every manner of social vice and to yearn for a more communal way of life, there is no sign that the people of the West are willing
to give up their autonomy. The communalist always wants everyone else
to get back to the communalist's basics.

Stated bluntly, shared belief systems require coercion. The survival of
religion requires that individuals be subordinated to the community. In
some settings, such as religious and ethnic conflicts, individual autonomy
is constrained by shared identities. In the stable affluent democracies of
the West the individual asserts the rights of the sovereign autonomous
consumer. Just as we choose our electrical goods, so we choose our gods.
Unless we can imagine some social forces that will lead us to give up that
freedom, we cannot imagine the creation of detailed ideological consensus. It is not enough to suggest that some calamity may disrupt our com-
placency. Without a pre-existing common culture, large numbers will not
interpret a disaster in the same way and therefore will not respond collectively. When the common culture of a society consists of operating principles that allow the individual to choose, no amount of vague spiritual
yearning will generate shared beliefs.

To conclude, the secularization thesis argues that the decline of religion
in the West is not an accident but is an unintended consequence of a
variety of complex social changes that we can summarily call modernization. It was not inevitable. But unless we can imagine a reversal of the
increasing cultural autonomy of the individual, secularization is
irreversible.

Bibliography

Berger, Peter L. *The Sacred Canopy: Elements of a Sociological Theory of Religion.*
    Garden City, NY: Doubleday, 1967.
Berger, Peter L. *The Heretical Imperative: Contemporary Possibilities of Religious
    Affirmation.* Garden City, NY: Doubleday, 1980.
Berger, Peter L., Brigitte Berger, and Hansfried Kellner. *The Homeless Mind.*
    Harmondsworth: Penguin, 1974.
Berger, Peter L., and Thomas Luckmann. "Secularization and Pluralism,"
    International Yearbook for the Sociology of Religion 2 (1996): 73–84.
Brown, Callum. *The Social History of Religion in Scotland Since 1730.* London:
    Methuen, 1987.
Bruce, Steve. *Religion in the Modern World: From Cathedrals to Cults.* Oxford:
    Oxford University Press, 1996.
Bruce, Steve. *Choice and Religion: A Critique of Rational Choice Theory.* Oxford:
    Oxford University Press, 1999.
Bruce, Steve. *God Is Dead: Secularization in the West.* Oxford: Blackwell, 2002.
Casanova, José. *Public Religions in the Modern World.* Chicago: University of
    Chicago Press, 1994.

Gellner, Ernest. *Plough, Sword and Book: The Structure of Human History.* London: Paladin, 1991.

Harrell, David E. *Oral Roberts: An American Life.* Bloomington: Indiana University Press, 1985.

Inglehart, Robert. *Modernization and Postmodernization: Cultural, Political and Economic Change in Forty-three Societies.* Princeton, NJ: Princeton University Press, 1997.

Jelen, Ted, ed. *Sacred Markets, Sacred Canopies: Essays on Religious Markets and Religious Pluralism.* Lanham, MD: Rowman and Littlefield, 2002.

Luckmann, Thomas. *The Invisible Religion: The Problem of Religion in Modern Society.* New York: Macmillan, 1970.

Martin, David. *The Religious and the Secular.* London: Routledge and Kegan Paul, 1969.

Martin, David. *The Dilemmas of Contemporary Religion.* Oxford: Blackwell, 1978.

Merton, Robert K. *Science, Technology and Society in the Seventeenth Century* [1938]. New York: Fetting, 1970.

Michels, Robert. *Political Parties: A Sociological Study of the Oligarchic Tendencies of Modern Democracy* [1911], trs. Eden and Cedar Paul. New York: Free Press, 1962 [1915].

Niebuhr, H. Richard. *The Social Sources of Denominationalism.* New York: Holt, 1929.

Parsons, Talcott. "Evolutionary Universals in Society," *American Journal of Sociology* 29 (1964): 339–57.

Shibley, Mark A. 1996. *Resurgent Evangelicalism in the United States: Mapping Cultural Change Since 1970.* Columbia: University of South Carolina Press.

Stark, Rodney, and Roger Finke. *Acts of Faith: Explaining the Human Side of Religion.* Berkeley: University of California Press, 2000.

Tönnies, Ferdinand. *Community and Association* [1887], tr. C P. Loomis. London: Routledge and Kegan Paul, 1955.

Weber, Max. *The Protestant Ethic and the Spirit of Capitalism* [1904–5/1920], tr. Talcott Parsons. London: Allen and Unwin, 1930.

Wilson, Bryan R. *Religion in Sociological Perspective.* Oxford: Oxford University Press, 1982.

Bibliography

Abusch, Tzvi. "The Demonic Image of the Witch in Standard Babylonian Literature: The Reworking of Popular Conceptions by Learned Exorcists," in *Religion, Science, and Magic in Concert and in Conflict*, eds. Jacob Neusner, Ernest S. Frerichs, and Paul V. Flesher. New York: Oxford University Press, 1989, pp. 27–58.

al-Khumayni, Ruh Allah. *Durus Fi Al-Jihad Wa-Al-Rafd: Yusatiruha Al-Imam Al-Khumayni Khilal Harakatihi Al-Nidaliyah Al-Ra'Idah*. No place of publication or publisher given. Probably published in Beirut in 1977.

Allport, Gordon W. *The Individual and His Religion: A Psychological Interpretation*. New York: Macmillan, 1950.

Almond, Gabriel Abraham, R. Scott Appleby, and Emmanuel Sivan. *Strong Religion: The Rise of Fundamentalisms around the World*. Chicago: University of Chicago Press, 2003.

Alston, William. *Perceiving God*. Ithaca, NY: Cornell University Press, 1991.

Ammerman, Nancy. *Congregation and Community*. New Brunswick, NJ: Rutgers University Press, 1997.

Anderson, Benedict. *Imagined Communities: Reflections on the Origin and Spread of Nationalism*. London: Verso, 1983.

Anderson, Richard W., and Ian Reader. "What Constitutes Religious Activity? I and II," *Japanese Journal of Religious Studies* 18 (1991): 369–76.

Annequin, Jacques. *Recherches sur l'action magique et ses représentations (Ier et IIème siècles après J.C.)*. Paris: Les Belles Lettres, 1973.

Anscombe, Elizabeth. "Modern Moral Philosophy," in *Virtue Ethics*, eds. Roger Crisp and Michael Slote. Oxford: Oxford University Press, 1997, pp. 26–44.

Aristotle. *The Complete Works of Aristotle: The Revised Oxford Translation*, ed. Jonathan Barnes. 2 vols. Princeton, NJ: Princeton University Press, 1985.

Aristotle. *Nicomachean Ethics*, tr. Terence Irwin, 2nd edn. Indianapolis: Hackett Books, 1999.

Arlow, Jacob. "Ego Psychology and the Study of Mythology," *Journal of the American Psychoanalytic Association* 9 (1961): 371–93.

Arnold, Matthew. *Literature and Dogma* [1873]. London: Macmillan, Popular edn, 1895.

Arnold, Matthew. *God and the Bible* [1875], ed. R. H. Super. Ann Arbor: University of Michigan Press, 1971.

Asad, Talal. *Genealogies of Religion: Discipline and Reasons of Power in Christianity and Islam*. Baltimore: Johns Hopkins University Press, 1993.

Ashton, Rosemary. *The German Idea: Four English Writers and the Reception of German Thought, 1800–1860*. Cambridge: Cambridge University Press, 1980.

Ault, James M. Jr. *Spirit and Flesh: Life in a Fundamentalist Baptist Church*. New York: Knopf, 2004.

Aune, David E. "Magic in Early Christianity," in *Aufstieg und Niedergang der römischen Welt*, II.23.2, ed. Wolfgang Haase. Berlin: De Gruyter, 1980, pp. 1507–57.

Ayer, A. J. *Language, Truth and Logic*. London: Gollancz, 1936.

Balthazar, Hans Urs von. *Two Say Why*, tr. John Griffiths. London: Search Press, 1973.

Balthazar, Hans Urs von. *The Glory of the Lord*, ed. and tr. John Riches, 7 vols. Edinburgh: Clark, 1982–89.

Barber, Benjamin R. *Jihad Vs. McWorld*. New York: Times Books, 1995.

Barber, Richard. *Pilgrimages*. Woodbridge: Boydell Press, 1991.

Barker, Eileen. *The Making of a Moonie: Choice or Brainwashing?* Oxford: Blackwell, 1984.

Barker, Eileen. "Plus ça change . . . ," *Social Compass* 42 (1995): 165–80.

Barnard, G. William. "Diving into the Depths: Reflections on Psychology as a Religion," in *Religion and Psychology: Mapping the Terrain*, eds. Diane Jonte-Pace and William B. Parsons. London: Routledge, 2001, pp. 297–318.

Barnard, G. William, and Jeffrey J. Kripal, eds. *Crossing Boundaries: Essays on the Ethical Status of Mysticism*. New York: Seven Bridges Press, 2002.

Barth, Karl. *Church Dogmatics III/4: Doctrine of Creation*, trs. Geoffrey Bromiley and Thomas Torrance. Edinburgh: Clark, 1961.

Barthes, Roland. *Mythologies*, tr. Annette Lavers. New York: Hill and Wang; London: Cape, 1972.

Bataille, Georges. *Erotism: Death and Sensuality*. San Francisco: City Lights Books, 1986.

Bateson, Gregory. *Mind and Nature: A Necessary Unity*. London: Wildwood Press, 1977.

Batson, C. Daniel, and W. Larry Ventis. *The Religious Experience: A Social-Psychological Perspective*. New York: Oxford University Press, 1982.

Bauman, Zygmunt. *Intimations of Postmodernity*. London: Routledge, 1992.

Bauman, Zygmunt. *Mortality, Immortality*. London: Polity Press, 1992.

Beaty, Michael, and Charles Taliaferro. "God and Concept Empiricism," *Southwest Philosophy Review* 6 (1990): 97–105.

Becker, Lawrence, and Charlotte Becker, eds. *Encyclopedia of Ethics* [1992], 2nd edn. London: Routledge, 2001.

Beckford, James. *The Trumpet of Prophecy*. Oxford: Blackwell, 1975.

Beckford, James. "Postmodernity, High Modernity and New Modernity: Three Concepts in Search of Religion," in *Postmodernity, Sociology and Religion*, eds. Kieran Flanagan and Peter C. Jupp. New York: St. Martin's Press, 1996, pp. 30–47.

Beidelman, T. O. *W. Robertson Smith and the Sociological Study of Religion*. Chicago: University of Chicago Press, 1974.

Beit-Hallahmi, Benjamin. "Psychology of Religion 1880–1930: The Rise and Fall of a Psychological Movement," *Journal of the History of the Behavioral Sciences* 10 (1974): 84–90.

Beit-Hallahmi, Benjamin, and Michael Argyle. *The Psychology of Religious Behaviour, Belief and Experience*. London: Routledge, 1997.

Bell, Catherine. *Ritual Theory, Ritual Practice*. New York: Oxford University Press, 1992.

Bell, Catherine. *Ritual: Perspectives and Dimensions*. New York: Oxford University Press, 1997.

Bell, Catherine. "Performance," in *Critical Terms for Religious Studies*, ed. Mark C. Taylor. Chicago: University of Chicago Press, 1998, pp. 205–24.

Bell, Daniel. *The Coming of Post-Industrial Society: A Venture in Social Forecasting*. New York: Basic Books, 1973.

Bell, Daniel. *Cultural Contradictions of Capitalism*. London: Heinemann, 1976.

Bellah, Robert N. "Civil Religion in America," *Daedalus* 96 (1967): 1–21.

Benavides, Gustavo. "Magic, Religion, Materiality," *Historical Reflections/Réflexions historiques* 23 (1997): 301–30.

Benavides, Gustavo. "Modernity," in *Critical Terms for Religious Studies*, ed. Mark C. Taylor. Chicago: University of Chicago Press, 1998, pp. 186–204.

Benavides, Gustavo. "Towards a Natural History of Religion," *Religion* 30 (2000): 229–44.

Benavides, Gustavo. "Economy," in *Critical Terms for the Study of Buddhism*, ed. Donald S. Lopez, Jr. Chicago: University of Chicago Press, 2005, pp. 77–102.

Benedict, Ruth. *Patterns of Culture* [1934]. Boston: Houghton Mifflin, 1959.

Berger, Peter L. *The Sacred Canopy: Elements of a Sociological Theory of Religion*. Garden City, NY: Doubleday, 1967.

Berger, Peter L. *A Rumor of Angels: Modern Society and the Rediscovery of the Supernatural*. Garden City, NY: Doubleday, 1969.

Berger, Peter L. *The Heretical Imperative: Contemporary Possibilities of Religious Affirmation*. Garden City, NY: Doubleday, 1980.

Berger, Peter L. "Secularism in Retreat," *National Interest* 46 (Winter 1996/97): 3–12.

Berger, Peter L. "Epistemological Modesty: An Interview with Peter Berger," *Christian Century* 114 (1997): 972–8.

Berger, Peter L., ed. *The Desecularization of the World: Resurgent Religion and World Politics*. Grand Rapids, MI: Eerdmans, 1999.

Berger, Peter L., and Thomas Luckmann. *The Social Construction of Reality: A Treatise on the Sociology of Knowledge*. Garden City, NY: Doubleday, 1996.

Berger, Peter L., and Thomas Luckmann. "Secularization and Pluralism," *International Yearbook for the Sociology of Religion* 2 (1996): 73–84.

Berger, Peter L., Brigitte Berger, and Hansfried Kellner. *The Homeless Mind*. Harmondsworth: Penguin, 1974.

Berman, Paul, ed. *Debating P.C.: The Controversy Over Political Correctness on College Campuses*. New York: Dell, 1992.

Bernstein, Alan. *The Formation of Hell: Death and Retribution in the Ancient and Early Christian Worlds*. Ithaca, NY: Cornell University Press, 1993.

Best, Steven, and David Kellner. *Postmodern Theory: Critical Interrogations*. London: Macmillan, 1991.

Bettelheim, Bruno. *The Uses of Enchantment*. New York: Knopf, 1976.

Bhardwaj, Surinder. *Hindu Places of Pilgrimage in India: A Study in Cultural Geography*. Berkeley: University of California Press, 1973.

Blackbourn, David. *Marpingen: Apparitions of the Virgin Mary in Nineteenth-Century Germany*. Oxford: Clarendon Press, 1993.

Blair, Hugh. *Sermons*, 2 vols. London: Baynes, 1824.

Bloch, Maurice. *Prey into Hunter*. Cambridge: Cambridge University Press, 1992.

Boas, Franz. "The Limitations of the Comparative Method of Anthropology" [1896], in his *Race, Language and Culture*. New York: Macmillan, 1940, pp. 270–80.

Borgerhoff Mulder, Monique, Margaret George-Cramer, Jason Eshleman, and Alessia Ortolani. "A Study of East African Kinship and Marriage Using a Phylogenetically Based Comparative Method," *American Anthropologist* 103 (2001): 1059–82.

Bouyer, Louis. "Mysticism: An Essay on the History of the Word," in *Understanding Mysticism*, ed. Richard Woods. Garden City, NY: Image Books, 1980.

Bowie, Andrew. *Aesthetics and Subjectivity from Kant to Nietzsche*. Manchester: Manchester University Press, 1990.

Bowie, Fiona. *The Anthropology of Religion*. Oxford: Blackwell, 2000.

Bowie, Fiona. "Belief or Experience: The Anthropologist's Dilemma," in *Contemporary Conceptions of God: Interdisciplinary Essays*, ed. Cyril G. Williams. Lewiston, ME: Edwin Mellen, 2003, pp. 135–60.

Bowman, Glenn. "Pilgrimage Conference," *Anthropology Today* 4 (1988): 20–3.

Boyarin, Daniel. *Dying for God: Martyrdom and the Making of Christianity and Judaism*. Stanford, CA: Stanford University Press, 1999.

Boyer, Pascal. *The Naturalness of Religious Ideas*. Berkeley: University of California Press, 1994.

Boyer, Pascal. *Religion Explained: The Evolutionary Origins of Religious Thought*. New York: Basic Books, 2001.

Bremmer, Jan N. "The Birth of the Term 'Magic'," *Zeitschrift für Papyrologie und Epigraphic* 126 (1999): 1–12.

Brody, Baruch. "Morality and Religion Reconsidered," in *Readings in the Philosophy of Religion*, ed. Baruch Brody, 2nd edn. Englewood Cliffs, NJ: Prentice Hall, 1992, pp. 491–503.

Bromley, David G. "Dramatic Denouements," in *Cults, Religion and Violence*, eds. David G. Bromley and J. Gordon Melton. Cambridge: Cambridge University Press, 2002, pp. 11–41.

Bromley, David G., and Jeffrey K. Hadden, eds. *The Handbook on Cults and Sects in America, Part A and B*. Religion and the Social Order Series, Vol. 3. Greenwich, CT: JAI Press, 1993.

Bromley, David G., and J. Gordon Melton, eds. *Cults, Religion and Violence*. Cambridge: Cambridge University Press, 2002.

Brown, Callum. *The Social History of Religion in Scotland Since 1730*. London: Methuen, 1987.

Brown, Callum. *The Death of Christian Britain*. London: Routledge, 2001.

Brown, Peter. "The Rise and Function of the Holy Man in Late Antiquity," *Journal of Roman Studies* 61 (1971): 80–101.

Brown, Peter. "The Saint as Exemplar in Late Antiquity," *Representations* 2 (1983): 1–25.

Brown, Peter. *The Body and Society: Men, Women, and Sexual Renunciation in Early Christianity*. New York: Columbia University Press, 1988.

Brown, W. Norman. "Duty as Truth in India," *Proceedings of the American Philosophical Society* 116 (1972): 252–68. Reprinted in his *India and Indology*. Delhi-Varanasi-Patna: Motilal Banarsidass, 1978, pp. 102–19.

Bruce, Steve. *Religion in the Modern World: From Cathedrals to Cults*. Oxford: Oxford University Press, 1996.

Bruce, Steve. *Choice and Religion: A Critique of Rational Choice Theory*. Oxford: Oxford University Press, 1999.

Bruce, Steve. "Fundamentalism and Political Violence: The Case of Paisley and Ulster Evangelicals," *Religion* 31 (2001): 387–405.

Bruce, Steve. *God Is Dead: Secularization in the West*. Oxford: Blackwell, 2002.

Brundage, James. *Medieval Canon Law*. London: Longman, 1995.

Brush, Stephen. "Should the History of Science Be X-Rated?" *Science* 183 (1974): 1164–72.

Buckley, Anthony D., and Mary Catherine Kenney. *Negotiating Identity: Rhetoric, Metaphor, and Social Drama in Northern Ireland*. Washington, DC: Smithsonian Institution Press, 1995.

Bultmann, Rudolf. "New Testament and Mythology" [1944], in *Kerygma and Myth*, ed. Hans-Werner Bartsch, tr. Reginald H. Fuller. London: SPCK, 1953. Vol. 1, pp. 1–44.

Burkert, Walter. *Homo Necans: The Anthropology of Ancient Greek Sacrificial Ritual and Myth*, tr. Peter Bing. Berkeley: University of California Press, 1983.

Burkert, Walter. *Creation of the Sacred: Tracks of Biology in Early Religions*. Cambridge, MA: Harvard University Press, 1996.

Buswell, Bobert E. *The Zen Monastic Experience*. Princeton, NJ: Princeton University Press, 1992.

Butler, Judith. *Bodies That Matter*. London: Routledge, 1993.

Bynum, Caroline Walker. *Fragmentation and Redemption: Essays on Gender and the Human Body in Medieval Religion*. New York: Zone Books, 1991.

Bynum, Caroline Walker. *The Resurrection of the Body in Western Christianity, 200–1336*. New York: Columbia University Press, 1995.

Byrne, Peter, and Peter Clarke. *Definition and Explanation in Religion*. Basingstoke: Macmillan, 1993.

Cahill, Lisa. *Love Your Enemies: Discipleship, Pacifism, and Just War Theory*. Minneapolis, MN: Augsburg Fortress, 1994.

Callinicos, Alex. *Against Postmodernism: A Marxist Critique*. Cambridge: Polity Press, 1989.

Capps, Donald, ed. *Freud and Freudians on Religion: A Reader*. New Haven, CT: Yale University Press, 2001.

Carroll, Michael. *The Cult of the Virgin Mary: Psychological Origins*. Princeton, NJ: Princeton University Press, 1986.

Casanova, José. *Public Religions in the Modern World*. Chicago: University of Chicago Press, 1994.

Chantepie de la Saussaye, Pierre Daniel. *Manual of the Science of Religion* [1887], tr. Beatrice Colyer-Fergusson. New York: Longmans, Green, 1891.

Chateaubriand, François René Auguste de. *The Genius of Christianity* [1802], tr. Charles White. Baltimore, 1856.

Chatwin, Bruce. *The Songlines*. New York: Penguin, 1987.

Clark, Stuart. *Thinking With Demons: The Idea of Witchcraft in Early Modern Europe*. Oxford: Oxford University Press, 1997.

Clément, Catherine. *Syncope: The Philosophy of Rapture*. Minneapolis: University of Minnesota Press, 1994.

Coakley, Sarah, ed. *Religion and the Body*. Cambridge: Cambridge University Press, 1997.

Cohen, Erik. "Pilgrimage Centers: Concentric and Excentric," *Annals of Tourism Research* 19 (1992): 33–50.

Coleman, James S. *Foundations of Social Theory*. Cambridge: Belknap Press of Harvard University Press, 1990.

Coleman, Simon. "Do You Believe in Pilgrimage? *Communitas*, Contestation and Beyond," *Anthropological Theory* 2 (2002): 355–68.

Coleman, Simon, and John Elsner. *Pilgrimage Past and Present in the World Religions*. Cambridge, MA: Harvard University Press, 1995.

Coleridge, Samuel Taylor. *Confessions of an Inquiring Spirit*, 2nd edn, ed. H. N. Coleridge, 1849.

Coleridge, Samuel Taylor. *Biographia Literaria* [1817], ed. John T. Shawcross, 2 vols. Oxford: Oxford University Press, 1907.

Coleridge, Samuel Taylor. *Lay Sermons* [1816–17], ed. R. J. White. Princeton, NJ: Princeton University Press, 1972.

Collins, David. *An Account of the English Colony of New South Wales* [1796], 2nd edn. London, 1804.

Comte, Auguste. *The Positive Philosophy* [1830], ed. and tr. Harriet Martineau. London: Bell, 1896.

Conrad, Joseph L. "Magic Charms and Healing Rituals in Contemporary Yugoslavia," *Southeastern Europe/L'Europe du sud-est* 10 (1983): 99–120.

Conrad, Joseph L. "Bulgarian Magic Charms: Ritual, Form, and Content," *Slavic and East European Journal* 31 (1987): 548–62.

Conrad, Joseph L. "Russian Ritual Incantations: Tradition, Diversity, and Continuity," *Slavic and East European Journal* 33 (1989): 422–44.

Cook, Michael. *Commanding Right and Forbidding Wrong in Islamic Thought.* Cambridge: Cambridge University Press, 2000.

Crisp, Roger, and Michael Slote, eds. *Virtue Ethics.* Oxford: Oxford University Press, 1997.

Csordas, Thomas J. "Somatic Modes of Attention," *Cultural Anthropology* 8 (1993): 135–56.

Csordas, Thomas J. *The Sacred Self: A Cultural Phenomenology of Healing.* Berkeley: University of California Press, 1997.

Csordas, Thomas. "Asymptote of the Ineffable: Embodiment, Alterity, and the Theory of Religion," *Current Anthropology* 42 (2004): 1–23.

Cunningham, Lawrence S. *A Brief History of Saints.* Oxford: Blackwell, 2004.

Cupitt, Don. *After God: The Future of Religion.* New York: Basic Books, 1997.

Cupitt, Don. *Mysticism After Modernity.* Oxford: Blackwell, 1998.

Cupitt, Don. "Post-Christianity," in *Religion, Modernity and Postmodernity*, ed. Paul Heelas. Oxford: Blackwell, 1998, pp. 218–32.

Curran, Charles. *The Catholic Moral Tradition Today.* Washington, DC: Georgetown University Press, 1999.

Daly, Mary. *Pure Lust: Elemental Feminist Philosophy.* Boston: Beacon Press, 1984.

Daly, Mary. *Gyn/Ecology: The Metaethics of Radical Feminism.* Boston: Beacon Press, 1990.

Dante. *Inferno*, tr. Allen Mandelbaum. Berkeley: University of California Press, 1980.

Danto, Arthur. *Mysticism and Morality: Oriental Thought and Moral Philosophy.* New York: Basic Books, 1972.

Davie, Grace. *Religion in Britain Since 1945: Believing Without Belonging.* Oxford: Blackwell, 1994.

Davie, Grace. *Religion in Modern Europe.* Oxford: Oxford University Press, 2000.

Davie, Grace. *Europe, the Exceptional Case.* London: Darton, Longman and Todd, 2002.

Davies, Douglas J. *Death, Ritual and Belief.* London: Continuum, 2002.

Davies, Douglas J. *Anthropology and Theology.* Oxford: Berg, 2002.

Davies, Paul. *God and the New Physics.* London: Penguin Books, 1983.

Davis, G. Scott. "Tradition and Truth in Christian Ethics," in *The Wisdom of the Cross: Essays in Honor of John Howard Yoder*, eds. Stanley Hauerwas, Chris Hubner, Harry Hubner, and Mark Thiessen Nation. Grand Rapids, MI: Eerdmans, 1999, pp. 278–305.

Davis, Natalie Z. *Society and Culture in Early Modern France: Eight Essays.* Stanford, CA: Stanford University Press, 1975.

Dawkins, Richard. Letter to *The Independent*, March 20, 1993. Reprinted in *A World Religions Reader*, ed. Ian Markham. Oxford: Blackwell, 2000. pp. 22–3.

Dawson, Lorne L. *Comprehending Cults: The Sociology of New Religious Movements.* Toronto: Oxford University Press, 1998.

Dawson, Lorne L. "Crises of Charismatic Legitimacy and Violent Behavior in New Religious Movements," in *Cults, Religion and Violence*, eds. David G. Bromley and J. Gordon Melton. Cambridge: Cambridge University Press, 2002, pp. 80–101.

Dawson, Lorne L. "The Socio-Cultural Significance of New Religious Movements," in *The Oxford Handbook on New Religious Movements*, ed. James R. Lewis. New York: Oxford University Press, 2004, pp. 68–98.

de Certeau, Michel. "Mysticism," *Diacritics* 22 (1992): 11–25.

Delaney, Carol. "The Hajj: Sacred and Secular," *American Ethnologist* 17 (1990): 513–30.

Delumeau, Jean. *Que reste-t-il du paradis?* Paris: Fayard, 2000.

Dennett, Daniel. *Consciousness Explained.* New York: Little, Brown, 1991.

DeStefano, Anthony. *A Travel Guide to Heaven.* New York: Doubleday, 2003.

Detienne, Marcel. *The Gardens of Adonis*, tr. Janet Lloyd. Hassock: Harvester Press; Atlantic Highlands, NJ: Humanities Press, 1977.

Diehl, Carl Gustav. *Instrument and Purpose: Studies on Rites and Rituals in South India.* Lund: Gleerup, 1956.

Docherty, Thomas, ed. *Postmodernism: A Reader.* New York: Columbia University Press, 1993.

Doniger, Wendy, and Brian K. Smith, trs. *The Laws of Manu.* Harmondsworth: Penguin Books, 1991.

Douglas, Kelly Delaine Brown. "Womanist Theology: What Is its Relationship to Black Theology?" in *Black Theology*, eds. James H. Cone and Gayraund S. Wilmore. Maryknoll, NY: Orbis, 1993, pp. 290–9.

Douglas, Mary. *Purity and Danger: An Analysis of Concepts of Pollution and Taboo.* London: Routledge and Kegan Paul, 1966.

Douglas, Mary. "The Contempt of Ritual," *New Blackfriars* 49 (1968): 475–82, 528–35.

Douglas, Mary. *Natural Symbols: Explorations in Cosmology.* 1st edn. Harmondsworth: Penguin, 1970.

Douglas, Mary. *Implicit Meanings* [1975], 2nd edn. London: Routledge, 1998.

Driver, Thomas F. *Liberating Rites: Understanding the Transformative Power of Ritual* [1994]. Boulder, CO: Westview Press, 1997.

Dubisch, Jill. *In a Different Place: Pilgrimage, Gender, and Politics at a Greek Island Shrine.* Princeton, NJ: Princeton University Press, 1995.

Durkheim, Emile. *The Elementary Forms of the Religious Life* [1912], tr. Joseph Ward Swain. London: Allen and Unwin; New York: Free Press, 1965 [1915].

Durkheim, Emile. *The Elementary Forms of the Religious Life* [1912], tr. Karen E. Fields. New York: Free Press, 1995.

Eade, John. "Order and Power at Lourdes: Lay Helpers and the Organization of a Pilgrimage Shrine," in *Contesting the Sacred: The Anthropology of Christian Pilgrimage*, eds. John Eade and Michael Sallnow. London: Routledge, 1991, pp. 51–76.

Eade, John, and Michael Sallnow. Introduction to *Contesting the Sacred: The Anthropology of Christian Pilgrimage*, eds. John Eade and Michael Sallnow. London: Routledge, 1991, pp. 1–29.

Eggan, Fred. "Social Anthropology and the Method of Controlled Comparison," *American Anthropologist* 56 (1954): 743–6.

Eickelman, Dale. *Moroccan Islam*. Austin: University of Texas Press, 1976.

Eilberg-Schwartz, Howard. *God's Phallus and Other Problems for Men and Monotheism*. Boston: Beacon Press, 1994.

Eisenstadt, Shmuel. "Multiple Modernities," *Daedalus* 120 (2000): 1–30.

Elford, R. John. *The Pastoral Nature of Theology*. London: Cassell, 1999.

Elford, R. John. *The Ethics of Uncertainty: A New Christian Approach to Moral Decision-Making*. Oxford: Oneworld, 2000.

Eliade, Mircea. *The Myth of the Eternal Return [Cosmos and History]*, tr. Willard R. Trask. Princeton, NJ: Princeton University Press, 1954.

Eliade, Mircea. *The Sacred and the Profane* [1959], tr. Willard R. Trask. New York: Harvest Books, 1968.

Eliade, Mircea. *Patterns in Comparative Religion* [1958], tr. Rosemary Sheed. New York: Meridian Books, 1963.

Eliot, T. S. "Tradition and the Individual Talent" [1919], in his *Selected Essays*. London: Faber, 1932, pp. 13–22.

Elon, Amos. *Herzl*. New York: Holt, Rinehart and Winston, 1975.

Ember, Carol. "Cross-Cultural Research," in *Encyclopedia of Cultural Anthropology*, eds. David Levinson and Melvin Ember. New York: Holt, 1996, vol. I, pp. 261–5.

Ember, Melvin. "The Logic of Comparative Research," *Behavior Science Research* 25 (1991): 143–53.

Ember, Melvin, and Carol R. Ember. "Cross-Cultural Studies of War and Peace: Recent Achievements and Future Possibilities," in *Studying War: Anthropological Perspectives*, eds. S. P. Reyna and R. E. Downs. Langhorne, PA: Gordon and Breach, 1994, pp. 185–208.

Ember, Melvin, and Keith F. Otterbein. "Sampling in Cross-Cultural Research," *Behavior Science Research* 25 (1991): 217–33.

Emerson, Jan S., and Hugh Feiss. *Imagining Heaven in the Middle Ages*. New York: Garland, 2000.

Enroth Ronald. *Youth, Brainwashing, and the Extremist Cults*. Grand Rapids, MI: Zondervan, 1977.

Epstein, Barbara. "Postmodernism and the Left," *New Politics* 6 (1997): 130–44.

Erikson, Erik H. *Young Man Luther: A Study in Psychoanalysis and History*. New York: Norton, 1958.

Erikson, Erik H. *Gandhi's Truth*. New York: Norton, 1969.

Evans-Pritchard, E. E. *Theories of Primitive Religion*. Oxford: Oxford University Press, 1965.

Evans-Pritchard, E. E. "The Comparative Method in Social Anthropology," in *The Position of Women in Primitive Societies and Other Essays in Social Anthropology*, ed. E. E. Evans-Pritchard. New York: Free Press, 1965, pp. 13–36.

Evans-Pritchard, E. E. *Witchcraft, Oracles and Magic among the Azande* [1937]. Abridged edn, ed. Eva Gillies. Oxford: Clarendon Press, 1976.

Faraone, Christopher A. "Binding and Burying the Forces of Evil: The Defensive Use of 'Voodoo Dolls' in Ancient Greece," *Classical Antiquity* 10 (1991): 165–205.

Faraone, Christopher A. "Molten Wax, Spilt Wine and Mutilated Animals: Sympathetic Magic in Near Eastern and Early Greek Oath Ceremonies," *Journal of Hellenic Studies* 113 (1993): 60–80.

Farber, Marvin. *The Foundation of Phenomenology: Edmund Husserl and the Quest for a Rigorous Science of Philosophy*. 3rd edn. Albany: State University of New York Press, 1968.

Featherstone, Mike. *Consumer Culture and Postmodernism*. London: Sage, 1991.

Featherstone, Mike, and Bryan S. Turner. *The Body: Social Process and Cultural Theory*. London: Sage, 1991.

Featherstone, Mike, and Bryan S. Turner. "Body and Society: An Introduction," *Body and Society* 1 (1995): 1–12.

Ferrer, Jorge N. *Revisioning Transpersonal Theory: A Participatory Vision of Human Spirituality*. Albany: State University of New York Press, 2002.

Feuerbach, Ludwig. *The Essence of Christianity* [1841], tr. George Eliot. New York: Harper Torchbooks, 1957.

Fingarette, Herbert. *Confucius: The Secular as Sacred*. New York: Harper and Row, 1972.

Finke, Roger, and Rodney Stark. *The Churching of America, 1776–1990: Winners and Losers in Our Religious Economy*. New Brunswick, NJ: Rutgers University Press, 1992.

Fletcher, Joseph. *Situation Ethics: The New Morality*. Philadelphia: Westminster, 1966.

Flint, Valerie I. J. *The Rise of Magic in Early Medieval Europe*. Princeton, NJ: Princeton University Press, 1991.

Flood, Gavin. *Beyond Phenomenology: Rethinking the Study of Religion*. London: Cassell, 1999.

Forman, Robert K. C., ed. *The Problem of Pure Consciousness: Mysticism and Philosophy*. New York: Oxford University Press, 1997.

Forsyth, Neil. *The Old Enemy: Satan and the Combat Myth*. Princeton, NJ: Princeton University Press, 1997.

Foster, Hal, ed. *The Anti-Aesthetic: Essays on Postmodern Culture*. Seattle: Bay Press, 1983.

Foucault, Michel. *The Birth of the Clinic: An Archaeology of Medical Perception* [1963], tr. A. M. Sheridan Smith. New York: Vintage, 1975.

Foucault, Michel. *Discipline and Punish: The Birth of the Prison*, tr. Allan Sheridan. London: Allen Lane, 1977.

Frankena, William. *Ethics* [1963], 2nd edn. Englewood Cliffs, NJ: Prentice-Hall, 1973.

Frankfurter, David. "The Magic of Writing and the Writing of Magic: The Power of the Word in Egyptian and Greek Traditions," *Helios* 21 (1994): 189–221.

Frazer, James George. *The Golden Bough*, 1st edn, 2 vols. London: Macmillan, 1890. 2nd edn, 3 vols. London: Macmillan. 3rd edn, 12 vols. London: Macmillan, 1911–15. Abridged edn. London: Macmillan, 1922.

Frazer, James George. *Garnered Sheaves*. London: Macmillan, 1931.

Frei, Hans W. *The Eclipse of Biblical Narrative: A Study in Eighteenth and Nineteenth Century Hermeneutics*. New Haven, CT: Yale University Press, 1974.

Freud, Sigmund. *Beyond the Pleasure Principle* [1920–22], tr. C. J. Hubback. London: International Psychoanalytic Press, 1922.

Freud, Sigmund. *The Future of an Illusion* [1927], tr. W. D. Robson-Scott, rev. James Strachey. Garden City, NY: Doubleday, 1961.

Freud, Sigmund. "Obsessive Acts and Religious Practices" [1907], in his *Character and Culture*, ed. Philip Rieff. New York: Collier Books, 1963, pp. 17–26.

Freud, Sigmund. *The Interpretation of Dreams* [1900], tr. James Strachey. New York: Avon Books, 1965 [1953].

Freud, Sigmund. *The Origins of Religion*, tr. James Strachey, Penguin Freud Library, vol. 13 (1907–39). London: Penguin, 1990.

Freud, Sigmund. *Civilization, Society and Religion*, tr. James Strachey, Penguin Freud Library, vol. 12 (1908–33). London: Penguin, 1991.

Frey, Nancy. *Pilgrim Stories: On and Off the Road to* Santiago. Berkeley: University of California Press, 1998.

Gallagher, Winifred. *Spiritual Genius*. New York: Random House, 2000.

Garland, Robert. *The Greek Way of Death*. Ithaca, NY: Cornell University Press, 1985.

Geertz, Clifford. *Islam Observed: Religious Development in Morocco and Indonesia*. Chicago: University of Chicago Press, 1968.

Geertz, Clifford. "Religion as a Cultural System," in *Anthropological Approaches to the Study of Religion*, ed. Michael Barton. London: Tavistock, 1973, pp. 1–46.

Geertz, Clifford. *The Interpretation of Cultures*. New York: Basic Books, 1973.

Geertz, Clifford. *Local Knowledge: Further Essays in Interpretive Anthropology*. New York: Basic Books, 1988.

Geertz, Clifford. *Available Light: Anthropological Reflections on Philosophical Topics*. Princeton, NJ: Princeton University Press, 2000.

Gellner, Ernest. *Plough, Sword and Book: The Structure of Human History*. London: Paladin, 1991.

George, Robert. *Making Men Moral: Civil Liberties and Public Morality*. Oxford: Oxford University Press, 1993.

George, Robert. *The Clash of Orthodoxies: Law, Religion, and Morality in Crisis*. Wilmington, DE: ISI Books, 2001.

Gifford, Paul. *African Christianity: Its Public Role*. London: Hurst, 1998.

Gilhus, Ingvild Saelid. "Is a Phenomenology of Religion Possible? A Response to Jeppe Sinding Jensen." *Method and Theory in the Study of Religion* 6 (1994): 163–71.

Gill, Anthony. *Rendering unto Caesar*. Chicago: University of Chicago Press, 1998.

Girard, René. *Violence and the Sacred*, tr. Peter Gregory. London: Athlone Press; Baltimore: Johns Hopkins University Press, 1972.

Girard, René. *Things Hidden since the Foundation of the World* [1978], trs. Stephan Bann and Michael Metteer. Stanford, CA: Stanford University Press, 1987.

Glazier, Stephen. "Pilgrimages in the Caribbean: A Comparison of Cases from Haiti and Trinidad," in *Sacred Journeys: The Anthropology of Pilgrimage*, ed. Alan Morinis. Westport, CT: Greenwood Press, 1992, pp. 135–47.

Godin, Henri, and Yvan Daniel. *La France, pays de mission*. Paris: Les Éditions du Cerf, 1943.

Gold, Ann. *Fruitful Journeys: The Ways of Rajasthani Pilgrims*. Berkeley: University of California Press, 1988.

Good, Byron J. *Medicine, Rationality and Experience: An Anthropological Perspective*. Cambridge: Cambridge University Press, 1994.

Gordon, Richard. "Aelian's Peony: The Location of Magic in Graeco-Roman Tradition," *Comparative Criticism* 9 (1987): 59–95.

Graf, Fritz. "Excluding the Charming: The Development of the Greek Concept of Magic," in *Ancient Magic and Ritual Power*, eds. Marvin Meyer and Paul Mirecki. Leiden: Brill, 1995, pp. 20–42.

Graf, Fritz. *Gottesnähe und Schadenzauber: Die Magie in der griechisch-römischen Antike*. Munich: Beck, 1996.

Granoff, Phyllis. "Scholars and Wonder-Workers: Some Remarks on the Role of the Supernatural in Philosophical Contests in Vedānta Hagiographies," *Journal of the American Oriental Society* 105 (1985): 459–67.

Gregor, Thomas A., and Donald Tuzin. "Comparing Gender in Amazonia and Melanesia: A Theoretical Orientation," in *Gender in Amazonia and Melanesia: An Exploration of the Comparative Method*, eds. Thomas A. Gregor and Donald Tuzin. Berkeley: University of California Press, 2001, pp. 1–16.

Griffin, David Ray, ed. *The Reenchantment of Science: Postmodern Proposals*. Albany: State University of New York Press, 1988.

Griffiths, Paul. *On Being Buddha*. Albany: State University of New York Press, 1994.

Grimes, Ronald L. *Beginnings in Ritual Studies* [1982], rev. edn. Columbia: University of South Carolina Press, 1995.

Grimes, Ronald L., ed. *Readings in Ritual Studies*. Upper Saddle, NJ: Prentice-Hall, 1996.

Grimes, Ronald L. *Deeply into the Bone: Re-Inventing Rites of Passage*. Berkeley: University of California Press, 2000.

Gustafson, James. *Protestant and Roman Catholic Ethics: Prospects for Rapprochement*. Chicago: University of Chicago Press, 1978.

Gutierrez, Gustavo. *A Theology of Liberation: History, Politics, Salvation*, trs. C. Inda and John Eagleson. Maryknoll, NY: Orbis Books, 1973.

Haas, Volkert. *Geschichte der hethitischen Religion*. Leiden: Brill, 1994.

Habermas, Jurgen. *Legitimation Crisis*, tr. Thomas McCarthy. Boston: Beacon Press, 1975.

Habermas, Jurgen. "Modernity versus Post Modernity," *New German Critique* 22 (1981): 3–14.

Hadaway, Kirk, Penny Marler, and Mark Chaves. "A Symposium on Church Attendance," *American Sociological Review* 63 (1998): 111–45.

Haddad, Yvonne H., and Adair T. Lummis. *Islamic Values in the United States: A Comparative Study.* Oxford: Oxford University Press, 1987.

Hadot, Pierre. *Philosophy As a Way of Life*, tr. Arnold I. Davidson. Oxford: Blackwell, 1995.

Hailes, N. Katherine. *How We Became Posthuman: Virtual Bodies in Cybernetics, Literature and Informatics.* Chicago: University of Chicago Press, 1999.

Hall, John R. *Apocalypse Observed: Religious Movements and Violence in North America, Europe, and Japan.* New York: Routledge, 2000.

Halperin, David. *One Hundred Years of Homosexuality and Other Essays on Greek Love.* New York: Routledge, 1990.

Hamilton, Sir William. *Lectures on Metaphysics and Logic*, eds. Henry Mansel and John Veitch. 2 vols. Edinburgh: Blackwood, 1877.

Hanegraaff, Wouter. *New Age Religion and Western Culture: Esotericism in the Mirror of Secular Thought.* Albany: State University of New York Press, 1998.

Haraway, Donna J. *Modest_Witness@Second_Millennium: FemaleMan©_Meets_OncoMouse™.* New York: Routledge, 1997.

Harrell, David E. *Oral Roberts: An American Life.* Bloomington: Indiana University Press, 1985.

Harris, Jay M. "'Fundamentalism': Objections from a Modern Jewish Historian," in *Fundamentalism and Gender*, ed. John S. Hawley. New York: Oxford University Press, 1994, pp. 137–73.

Harrison, Peter. *"Religion" and the Religions in the English Enlightenment.* Cambridge: Cambridge University Press, 1990.

Harvey, David. *The Condition of Postmodernity.* London: Blackwell, 1989.

Harvey, Peter. *An Introduction to Buddhist Ethics: Foundations, Values and Issues.* Cambridge: Cambridge University Press, 2000.

Hauerwas, Stanley. *The Hauerwas Reader*, eds. John Berkman and Michael Cartwright. Durham, NC: Duke University Press, 2001.

Hauerwas, Stanley, Chris Hubner, Harry Hubner, and Mark Thiessen Nation, eds. *The Wisdom of the Cross: Essays in Honor of John Howard Yoder.* Grand Rapids, MI: Eerdmans, 1999.

Hawley, John Stratton, ed. *Saints and Virtues.* Berkeley: University of California Press, 1987.

Hedetoft, Ulf, and Mette Hjort. *The Postnational Self: Belonging and Identity.* Minneapolis: University of Minnesota Press, 2002.

Heelas, Paul. "The New Age in Cultural Context: The Premodern, the Modern and the Postmodern," *Religion* 23 (1993): 103–16.

Heelas, Paul. *The New Age Movement: The Celebration of the Self and the Sacralization of Modernity.* Oxford: Blackwell, 1996.

Heelas, Paul, ed. *Religion, Modernity and Postmodernity.* Oxford: Blackwell, 1998.

Hegel, Georg Wilhelm Friedrich *The Phenomenology of Mind* [1807], tr. J. B. Baillie. New York: Harper and Row, 1967.

Hegel, Georg Wilhelm Friedrich. *Aesthetics: Lectures on Fine Arts* [1835–38], tr. T. M. Knox, 2 vols. Oxford: Clarendon Press, 1975.

Heidegger, Martin. *Being and Time* [1927], trs. John Macquarrie and Edward Robison. New York: Harper and Row, 1962.

Heilman, Samuel C., and Menachem Friedman. "Religious Fundamentalism and Religious Jews: The Case of the Haredim," in *Fundamentalisms Observed*, eds. Martin E. Marty and R. Scott Appleby. Chicago: University of Chicago Press, 1991, pp. 197–264.

Heisig, James. "Psychology of Religion," in *Encyclopedia of Religion*, ed. Mircea Eliade. 1st edn. New York: Macmillan; London: Collier Macmillan, 1989, vol. 12, pp. 57–66.

Hepburn, Ronald W. "From World to God," *Mind* 72 (1963): 40–50.

Herman, Judith. *Trauma and Recovery: The Aftermath of Violence – From Domestic Abuse to Political Terror*. New York: Basic Books, 1997.

Herrenschmidt, Oliver. "Sacrifice: Symbolic or Effective," in *Between Belief and Transgression: Structuralist Essays in Religion, History and Myth*, eds. Michel Izard and Pierre Smith, tr. John Levitt. Chicago: University of Chicago Press, 1982, pp. 24–42.

Hertz, Robert. "A Contribution to the Study of the Collective Representation of Death" [1907], in his *Death and the Right Hand*, eds. and trs. Rodney Needham and Claudia Needham. New York: Free Press, 1960, pp. 27–86.

Hertz, Robert. "Saint Besse: A Study of an Alpine Cult" [1913], in *Saints and Their Cults: Studies in Religious Sociology, Folklore and History*, ed. Stephen Wilson. Cambridge: Cambridge University Press, 1983, pp. 55–100.

Hervieu-Léger, Danièle. *La Religion en miettes ou la question des sectes*. Paris: Calman-Lévy, 2001.

Hervieu-Léger, Danièle, and Jean-Paul Willaime. *Sociologies et religion*. Paris: Presses Universitaires de France, 2001.

Hick, John. *Evil and the God of Love*. 1st edn. London: Macmillan, 1966.

Hick, John. *God and the Universe of Faiths*. London: Macmillan, 1973.

Hick, John, ed. *The Myth of God Incarnate*. London: SCM Press, 1977.

Hicks, Douglas. *Inequality and Christian Ethics*. Cambridge: Cambridge University Press, 2000.

Himmelfarb, Martha. *Ascent to Heaven in Jewish and Christian Apocalypses*. New York: Oxford University Press, 1993.

Hirschberg, Peter. *The World of Shas*. New York: Institute on American Jewish-Israeli Relations of the American Jewish Committee, 1999.

Hobart, Mark. "Summer's Days and Salad Days: The Coming of Age of Anthropology?" in *Comparative Anthropology*, ed. Ladislav Holy. Oxford: Blackwell, 1987, pp. 22–51.

Hobbes, Thomas. *Leviathan* [1651]. Chicago: Regnery, 1956.

Hobsbawn, Eric, and Terence Ranger, eds. *The Invention of Tradition*. Cambridge: Cambridge University Press, 1983.

Hocart, Arthur Maurice. *The Life-giving Myth and other Essays*, ed. Lord Raglan. London: Methuen, 1952.

Hohfeld, Wesley Newcomb. *Fundamental Legal Concepts as Applied to Judicial Reasoning.* New Haven, CT: Yale University Press, 1919.

Holdrege, Barbara A. "Body Connections: Hindu Discourses of the Body and the Study of Religion," *International Journal of Hindu Studies* 2 (1998): 341–86.

Hollenback, Jess Byron. *Mysticism: Experience, Response, and Empowerment.* University Park: Pennsylvania State University Press, 1996.

Hollinger, Robert. *Postmodernism and the Social Sciences: A Thematic Approach.* Thousand Oaks, CA: Sage, 1994.

Hollywood, Amy. *Sensible Ecstasy: Mysticism, Sexual Difference, and the Demands of History.* Chicago: University of Chicago Press, 2002.

Holy, Ladislav, ed. *Comparative Anthropology.* Oxford: Blackwell, 1987.

Homans, Peter. "Psychology and Religion Movement," in *Encyclopedia of Religion,* ed. Mircea Eliade. 1st edn. New York: Macmillan; London: Collier Macmillan, 1989, vol. 12, pp. 66–75.

Hood, Ralph, *et al. The Psychology of Religion: An Empirical Approach* [1985]. 2nd edn. New York: Guilford Press, 1996.

Horton, Robin. *Patterns of Thought in Africa and the West.* Cambridge: Cambridge University Press, 1994.

Houlden, Leslie. "The Creed of Experience," in *The Myth of God Incarnate,* ed. John Hick. London: SCM Press, 1977, pp. 125–32.

Hourani, George F. *Islamic Rationalism: The Ethics of 'Abd Al-Jabbar.* Oxford: Oxford University Press, 1971.

Howard-Johnston, James, and Paul Anthony Hayward, eds. *The Cult of Saints in Late Antiquity and the Middle Ages.* New York: Oxford University Press, 1999.

Hubert, Henri, and Marcel Mauss. *Sacrifice: Its Nature and Functions* [1898], tr. W. D. Hall. Chicago: University of Chicago Press, 1964.

Hughes-Freeland, Felicia, and Mary M. Crain. *Recasting Ritual: Performance, Media, Identity.* London: Routledge, 1998.

Hume, David. *Inquiry Concerning Human Understanding* [1748]. New York: Macmillan, 1962.

Humphrey, Caroline, and James Laidlaw. *The Archetypal Actions of Ritual.* Oxford: Clarendon Press, 1994.

Huntington, Samuel P. *The Clash of Civilizations and the Remaking of World Order.* New York: Simon and Schuster, 1996.

Husserl, Edmund. *Logical Investigations* [1900], tr. John. N. Findlay. 2 vols. London: Routledge and Kegan Paul, 1970.

Husserl, Edmund. *Ideas* [1913], tr. W. R. Boyce Gibson. New York: Humanities Press, 1976.

Husserl, Edmund. "Phenomenology," *Encyclopaedia Britannica.* 14th edn. [1927], vol. 17, pp. 699b–702b.

Husserl, Edmund. *Experience and Judgment* [1948], trs. J. S. Churchill and Karl Ameriks. Evanston, IL: Northwestern University Press, 1973.

Hyman, Peter. "Was God a Magician? Sefer Yesira and Jewish Magic," *Journal of Jewish Studies* 40 (1989): 225–37.

Iannaccone, Laurence R. "Why Strict Churches Are Strong," *American Journal of Sociology* 99 (1994): 1180–211.

Iannaccone, Laurence R. "Risk, Rationality, and Religious Portfolios," *Economic Inquiry* 33 (1995): 285–95.

Imber-Black, Evan, Janine Roberts, and Richard A. Wittig, eds. *Ritual in Families and Family Therapy*. New York: Norton, 1988.

Inglehart, Robert. *Modernization and Postmodernization: Cultural, Political and Economic Change in Forty-three Societies*. Princeton, NJ: Princeton University Press, 1997.

Ingold, Tim, ed. *Companion Encyclopaedia of Anthropology* [1994]. 2nd edn. London: Routledge, 2002.

Introvigne, Massimo, and Rodney Stark. "Religious Competition and Revival in Italy," *Interdisciplinary Journal of Research on Religion* 1 (2005): www.bepress.com/ijrr.

Isambert, François-André, and Jean-Paul Terrenoire. *Atlas de la pratique religieuse des catholiques en France*. Paris: Presses de la Fondation nationale des sciences politiques; Editions du CNRS, 1980.

James, George Alfred. *Interpreting Religion: The Phenomenological Approaches of Pierre Daniel Chantepie de La Saussaye, W. Brede Kristensen, and Gerardus van der Leeuw*. Washington, DC: Catholic University of America Press, 1995.

James, William. *The Varieties of Religious Experience*. 2nd edn. New York: Longmans, Green, 1902.

Jankowiak, William, ed. *Romantic Passion: A Universal Experience?* New York: Columbia University Press, 1995.

Jelen, Ted, ed. *Sacred Markets, Sacred Canopies: Essays on Religious Markets and Religious Pluralism*. Lanham, MD: Rowman and Littlefield, 2002.

Jenkins, Philip. *Mystics and Messiahs: Cults and New Religions in American History*. New York: Oxford University Press, 2000.

Jenkins, Philip. *The Next Christendom: The Coming of Global Christianity*. Oxford: Oxford University Press, 2002.

Jensen, Jeppe Sinding. "Is a Phenomenology of Religion Possible? On the Ideas of a Human and Social Science of Religion." *Method and Theory in the Study of Religion* 5 (1993): 109–33.

Jobling, J'annine. *Restless Readings*. Aldershot: Ashgate, 2002.

Jonas, Hans. "Gnosticism, Existentialism, and Nihilism" [1952], in his *The Gnostic Religion* [1958], 2nd edn. Boston: Beacon Press, 1963, pp. 320–40.

Jones, Ernest. *The Life and Work of Sigmund Freud*, 3 vols. London: Hogarth Press, 1953–7.

Jones, Gareth. *Critical Theology*. Cambridge: Polity Press, 1995.

Jonte-Pace, Diane. "Analysts, Critics, and Inclusivists: Feminist Voices in the Psychology of Religion," in *Religion and Psychology: Mapping the Terrain*, eds. Diane Jonte-Pace and William B. Parsons. London: Routledge, 2001, pp. 129–46.

Jonte-Pace, Diane, and William B. Parsons, eds. *Religion and Psychology: Mapping the Terrain*. London: Routledge, 2001.

Juergensmeyer, Mark. *The New Cold War? Religious Nationalism Confronts the Secular State*. Berkeley: University of California Press, 1993.

Juergensmeyer, Mark. "Why Religious Nationalists Are Not Fundamentalists," *Religion* 23 (1993): 85–92.

Juergensmeyer, Mark. *Terror in the Mind of God: The Global Rise of Religious Violence*. Berkeley: University of California Press, 2000.

Juergensmeyer, Mark. *Global Religions: An Introduction*. Oxford: Oxford University Press, 2003.

Juergensmeyer, Mark, ed. *Religion in Global Civil Society*. New York: Oxford University Press, 2005.

Jung, C. G. *The Archetypes and the Collective Unconscious* [1959], 2nd edn. Collected Works of C. G. Jung, eds. Sir Herbert Read *et al.*, trs. R. F. C. Hull *et al.*, vol. 9, pt. 1. Princeton, NJ: Princeton University Press; London: Routledge and Kegan Paul, 1968.

Jung, C. G. *Psychology and Religion: West and East* [1958], 2nd edn. Collected Works of C. G. Jung, vol. 11. Princeton, NJ: Princeton University Press; London: Routledge and Kegan Paul, 1969.

Jung, C. G. *Letters*, eds. Gerhard Adler and Aniela Jaffé, tr. R. F. C. Hull. Princeton, NJ: Princeton University Press, 1973–4.

Kákosy, László. *La Magia in Egitto ai tempi dei faraoni*. Modena: Edizioni Panini, 1985.

Kant, Immanuel. *Metaphysical Foundations of Natural Science* [1790–1803] in *Philosophy of Material Nature*, tr. James W. Ellington. Indianapolis, IN: Hackett, 1985.

Kaplan, Ann. *Postmodernism and Its Discontents: Theories, Practices*. London: Verso, 1988.

Katz, Steven T., ed. *Mysticism and Philosophical Analysis*. London: Oxford University Press, 1978.

Katz, Steven T., ed. *Mysticism and Religious Traditions*. New York: Oxford University Press, 1983.

Kent, Edward A., ed. *Law and Philosophy: Readings in Legal Theory*. New York: Appleton Century Crofts, 1970.

Kent, George P. "The Poetic Order of Healing in a Czech Incantation Against Erysipelas," *Southeastern Europe/L'Europe du sud-est* 10 (1983): 121–49.

Kerr, Fergus. "Simplicity Itself: Milbank's Thesis" [1992], reprinted in *Theology and Sociology*, ed. Robin Gill, new edn. London: Cassells, 1996, pp. 429–34.

Kertzer, David I. *Ritual, Power and Politics*. New Haven, CT: Yale University Press, 1988.

Khomeyni, Imam [Ayatollah]. *Collection of Speeches, Position Statements* [translations from "Najaf Min watha 'iq al-Imam al-Khomeyni did al-Quwa al Imbiriyaliyah wa al-Sahyuniyah wa al-Raj'iyah" ("From the Papers of Imam Khomeyni Against Imperialist, Zionist, and Reactionist Powers")]. Translations on Near East and North Africa, Number 1902. Arlington, VA: Joint Publications Research Service, 1977.

Khomeini, Imam [Ayatollah]. *Islam and Revolution: Writings and Declarations* [1981], tr. Hamid Algar. London: Routledge and Kegan Paul, 1985.

Kieckhefer, Richard. *Magic in the Middle Ages*. Cambridge: Cambridge University Press, 1989.

Kieckhefer, Richard, and George Bond, eds. *Sainthood: Its Manifestation in World Religions*. Berkeley: University of California Press, 1988.

Kierkegaard, Søren. *The Concept of Irony, with Continual Reference to Socrates* [1841], eds. and trs. Howard V. Hong and Edna H. Hong. Princeton, NJ: Princeton University Press, 1989.

Kierkegaard, Søren. *Fear and Trembling*, tr. Walter Lowrie [1941]. Princeton, NJ: Princeton University Press, 1989.

King, Richard. *Orientalism and Religion: Postcolonial Theory, India and "the Mystic East."* London: Routledge, 1999.

Kotkin, Joel. *Tribes: How Race, Religion, and Identity Determine Success in the New Global Economy*. New York: Random House, 1994.

Kramer, David. *The Meanings of Death in Rabbinic Judaism*. London: Routledge, 2000.

Kripal, Jeffrey J. *Kali's Child: The Mystical and the Erotic in the Life and Teachings of Ramakrishna*. Chicago: University of Chicago Press, 1995.

Kripal, Jeffrey J. *Roads of Excess, Palaces of Wisdom: Eroticism and Reflexivity in the Study of Mysticism*. Chicago: University of Chicago Press, 2001.

Kristensen, William Brede. *The Meaning of Religion*, tr. John B. Carman. The Hague: Martinus Nijhoff, 1960.

Kroker, Arthur, and David Cook. *The Postmodern Scene*. New York: St. Martin's, 1986.

Kumar, Krishnan. "Modernity," in *The Blackwell Dictionary of Twentieth-Century Social Thought*, eds. William Outhwaite and T. B. Bottomore. Oxford: Blackwell, 1993, pp. 391–2.

Laclau, Ernesto, and Chantal Mouffe. *Hegemony and Socialist Strategy: Towards a Radical Democratic Politics*, trs. Winston Moore and Paul Cammack. London: Verso, 1985.

Lacoue-Labarthe, Philippe, and Jean-Luc, Nancy. *The Literary Absolute: The Theory of Literature in German Romanticism* [1978], trs. Philip Barnard and Cheryl Lester. Albany: State University of New York Press, 1988.

Lambert, Johann Heinrich. *Neues Organon*. 2 vols. Leipzig: Johann Wendler, 1764.

Lane Fox, Robin. *Pagans and Christians*. London: Viking, 1986.

Lash, Scott, and John Urry. *The End of Organised Capitalism*. Cambridge: Polity Press, 1987.

Lawson, E. Thomas, and Robert N. McCauley. *Rethinking Religion: Connecting Cognition and Culture*. Oxford: Oxford University Press, 1990.

Ledbetter, Shannon. "Vocation and Our Understanding of God," *Modern Believing* 4 (2001): 38–49.

Leeuw, Gerardus van der. *Religion in Essence and Manifestation: A Study in Phenomenology* [1933], tr. J. E. Turner. Princeton, NJ: Princeton University Press, 1986.

LeGoff, Jacques. *The Birth of Purgatory*, tr. Arthur Goldhammes. Chicago: Chicago University Press, 1984.

Lerner, Ralph, and Muhsin Mahdi, eds. *Medieval Political Thought*. Ithaca, NY: Cornell University Press, 1963.

Lett, James. "Science, Religion, and Anthropology," in *Anthropology of Religion: A Handbook*, ed. Stephen D. Glazier. Westport, CT: Greenwood, 1997, pp. 103–20.

Leuba, James H. *The Psychology of Mysticism*. London: Kegan Paul, Trench, Trubner, 1925.

Lévi-Strauss, Claude. *Myth and Meaning*. Toronto: University of Toronto Press, 1978.

Lévy-Bruhl, Lucien. *How Natives Think* [1910], tr. Lilian A. Clare, with introduction by C. Scott Littleton. Princeton, NJ: Princeton University Press, 1985 [original publication of tr. 1926].

Lévy-Bruhl, Lucien. *The Notebooks on Primitive Mentality* [1949], tr. Peter Rivière. Oxford: Blackwell, 1975.

Lewis, James, R., ed. *The Oxford Handbook of New Religious Movements*. New York: Oxford University Press, 2004.

Liddell, Henry George, and Robert Scott. *A Greek-English Lexicon*. New York: Harper, 1846.

Lie, John. *Modern Peoplehood*. Cambridge, MA: Harvard University Press, 2004.

Lifton, Robert J. *Thought Reform and the Psychology of Totalism*. New York: Norton, 1961.

Lincoln, Bruce. *Emerging from the Chrysalis: Rituals of Women's Initiation* [1981]. Rev. edn. New York: Oxford University Press, 1991.

Lindbeck, George. *The Nature of Doctrine: Religion and Theology in a Postliberal Age*. Philadelphia: Westminster Press, 1984.

Lloyd, G. E. R. *The Revolutions of Wisdom: Studies in the Claims and Practice of Ancient Greek Science*. Berkeley: University of California Press, 1987.

Locke, John. *A Letter Concerning Toleration* [1689], in his *Treatise of Civil Government and A Letter Concerning Toleration*, ed. Charles L. Sherman. New York: Appleton Century Crofts, 1965.

Lofland, John, and Rodney Stark. "Becoming a World-Saver: A Theory of Conversion to a Deviant Perspective," *American Sociological Review* 30 (1965): 862–75.

Luckmann, Thomas. *The Invisible Religion: The Problem of Religion in Modern Society*. New York: Macmillan, 1970.

Luhrmann, Tarya. *Persuasions of the Witch's Craft*. Oxford: Blackwell, 1989.

Lukacs, John. *The Passing of the Modern Age*. New York: Harper and Row, 1970.

Lustick, Ian. *For the Land and the Lord: Jewish Fundamentalism in Israel*. New York: Council on Foreign Relations, 1988.

Lyotard, Jean-François. *The Postmodern Condition: A Report on Knowledge* [1979], trs. Geoffrey Bennington and Brian Massumi. Manchester: Manchester University Press, 1984.

MacAloon, John J. "Olympic Games and the Theory of Spectacle in Modern Societies," in *Rite, Drama, Festival, Spectacle: Rehearsals Towards a Theory of Cultural Performance*, ed. John J. MacAloon. Philadelphia: Institute for the Study of Human Issues, 1984, pp. 241–80.

MacIntyre, Alasdair. "The Idea of a Social Science," in *Rationality*, ed. Bryan R. Wilson. Oxford: Blackwell, 1970, pp. 112–30.

MacIntyre, Alasdair. *After Virtue: A Study in Moral Theory*. London: Duckworth, 1981.

MacIntyre, Alasdair. *Whose Justice? Which Rationality?* Notre Dame, IN: University of Notre Dame Press, 1988.

MacIntyre, Alasdair. *The MacIntyre Reader*, ed. Kelvin Knight. Notre Dame, IN: University of Notre Dame Press, 1998.

Mackie, John L. *The Miracle of Theism*. Oxford: Clarendon Press, 1985.

Malinowski, Bronislaw. *Myth in Primitive Psychology*. London: Kegan Paul; New York: Norton, 1926.

Malinowski, Bronislaw. *Magic, Science and Religion and Other Essays*, ed. Robert Redfield. Garden City, NY: Doubleday, 1948.

Manguel, Alberto. *A History of Reading*. New York: HarperCollins, 1996.

Marion, Jean-Luc. *God Without Being: Hors-Texte*, tr. Thomas K. Carlson. Chicago: University of Chicago Press, 1991.

Markham, Ian. *A Theology of Engagement*. Oxford: Blackwell, 2004.

Marsden, George M. *Understanding Fundamentalism and Evangelicalism*. Grand Rapids, MI: Eerdmans, 1991.

Marsh, Charles. *God's Long Summer: Stories of Faith and Civil Rights*. Princeton, NJ: Princeton University Press, 1997.

Marsh, Clive. *Christianity in a Post-Atheist Age*. London: SCM Press, 2002.

Martin, Bernice. "The Pentecostal Gender Paradox: A Cautionary Tale for the Sociology of Religion," in *The Blackwell Companion to the Sociology of Religion*, ed. Richard Fenn. Oxford: Blackwell, 2002, pp. 52–66.

Martin, David. *The Religious and the Secular*. London: Routledge and Kegan Paul, 1969.

Martin, David. *The Dilemmas of Contemporary Religion*. Oxford: Blackwell, 1978.

Martin, David. *Tongues of Fire*. Oxford: Blackwell, 1990.

Martin, David. *Reflections on Sociology and Theology*. Oxford: Clarendon, 1997.

Martin, David. *Pentecostalism: The World Their Parish*. Oxford: Blackwell, 2002.

Martin, Michael. *Atheism*. Philadelphia: Temple University Press, 1990.

Martin, William C. *With God on Our Side: The Rise of the Religious Right in America*. 1st edn. New York: Broadway Books, 1996.

Marty, Martin E. "Churches as Winners, Losers," *Christian Century* (January 27, 1993): 88–9.

Marty, Martin E., and R. Scott Appleby, eds. *Fundamentalisms Observed*. Chicago: University of Chicago Press, 1991.

Marty, Martin E., and R. Scott Appleby, eds. *Fundamentalisms and Society: Reclaiming the Sciences, the Family, and Education*. Chicago: University of Chicago Press, 1993.

Marty, Martin E., and R. Scott Appleby, eds. *Fundamentalisms and the State: Remaking Politics, Economies, and Militance*. Chicago: University of Chicago Press, 1993.

Marty, Martin E., and R. Scott Appleby, eds. *Accounting for Fundamentalisms: The Dynamic Character of Movements*. Chicago: University of Chicago Press, 1994.

Marty, Martin E., and R. Scott Appleby, eds. *Fundamentalisms Comprehended*. Chicago: University of Chicago Press, 1995.

Maslow, Abraham. *Religions, Values, and Peak Experiences*. Columbus: Ohio State University Press, 1964.

Mauss, Marcel. "Body Techniques" [1936], in his *Sociology and Psychology: Essays*, tr. Ben Brewster. London: Routledge and Kegan Paul, 1979, pp. 95–123.

McCall, Raymond J. *Phenomenological Psychology*. Madison: University of Wisconsin Press, 1983.

McCormick, Richard, and Paul Ramsey, eds. *Doing Evil to Achieve Good: Moral Choice in Conflict Situations*. Chicago: Loyola University Press, 1978.

McCutcheon, Russell T. *Manufacturing Religion: The Discourse on Sui Generis Religion and the Politics of Nostalgia*. Oxford: Oxford University Press, 1997.

McDannell, Colleen. *Material Christianity: Religion and Popular Culture in America*. New Haven, CT: Yale University Press, 1995.

McDannell, Colleen, and Bernhard Lang. *Heaven: A History*. New Haven, CT: Yale University Press, 1988.

McFague, Sallie. *Models of God*. Minneapolis, MN: Augsberg Fortress Press, 1993.

McGrath, Alister E. *A Brief History of Heaven*. Oxford: Blackwell, 2003.

McNeill, William H. *Keeping Together in Time: Dance and Drill in Human History*. Cambridge, MA: Harvard University Press, 1995.

Mehler, Jacques, and Emmanuel Dupoux. *What Infants Know: The New Cognitive Science of Early Development* [1990], tr. Patsy Southgate. Oxford: Blackwell, 1994.

Mellor, Philip, and Chris Shilling. *Re-Forming the Body: Religion, Community and Modernity*. London: Sage, 1997.

Merton, Robert K. *Science, Technology and Society in the Seventeenth Century* [1938]. New York: Fetting, 1970.

Meyer Marvin, ed. and tr., *The Gospel of Thomas: The Hidden Sayings of Jesus*. New York: HarperSanFrancisco, 1992.

Michalowski, Piotr. "Carminative Magic: Towards an Understanding of Sumerian Poetics," *Zeitschrift für Assyriologie und vorderasiatische Archäologie* 71 (1981): 1–18.

Michels, Robert. *Political Parties: A Sociological Study of the Oligarchic Tendencies of Modern Democracy* [1911], trs. Eden and Cedar Paul. New York: Free Press, 1962 [1915].

Milbank, John. *Theology and Social Theory: Beyond Secular Reason*. Oxford: Blackwell, 1990.

Mill, John Stuart. "What Is Poetry?" [1833], in *Mill's Essays on Literature and Society*, ed. J. B. Schneewind. New York: Collier Books; London: Collier-Macmillan, 1965, pp. 102–17.

Mitchell, Basil, ed. *The Philosophy of Religion*. Oxford: Oxford University Press, 1971.

Moran, Dermot. *Introduction to Phenomenology*. London: Routledge, 2000.

Morris, T. V., ed. *The Concept of God*. Oxford: Oxford University Press, 1987.

Munson, Henry. *Islam and Revolution in the Middle East*. New Haven, CT: Yale University Press, 1988.

Munson, Henry. "Not All Crustaceans Are Crabs: Reflections on the Comparative Study of Fundamentalism and Politics," *Contention* 4 (1995): 151–66.

Munson, Henry. "Intolerable Tolerance: Western Academia and Islamic Fundamentalism," *Contention* 5 (1996): 99–117.

Munson, Henry. " 'Fundamentalism' Ancient and Modern," *Daedalus* (2003): 31–41.

Munson, Henry. "Lifting the Veil: Understanding the Roots of Islamic Militancy," *Harvard International Review* 25 (2004): 20–3.

Murdock, George P., and Douglas R. White. "Standard Cross-Cultural Sample," *Ethnology* 8 (1969): 329–69.

Myers, Frederic W. H. *Human Personality and Its Survival of Bodily Death*. London: Longmans, Green, 1904.

Naroll, Raoul. "Galton's Problem," in *A Handbook of Method in Cultural Anthropology*, eds. Raoul Naroll and Ronald Cohen. New York: Columbia University Press, 1970, pp. 974–89.

Newman, John Henry. *Essays Critical and Historical*, 2 vols. London: Longmans, Green, 1846.

Newman, John Henry. *Lectures on Certain Difficulties Felt by Anglicans*, 2nd edn. London: Burns and Lambert, 1850.

Newman, John Henry. *Apologia Pro Vita Sua*. London: Longmans, Green, 1864.

Ngo, Van Xuyet. *Divination, magie et politique dans la Chine ancienne*. Paris: Presses Universitaires de France, 1976.

Nickelsburg, George W. E., Jr. *Resurrection, Immortality, and Eternal Life in Intertestamental Judaism*. Cambridge, MA: Harvard University Press, 1972.

Niebuhr, H. Richard. *The Social Sources of Denominationalism*. New York: Holt, 1929.

Nietzsche, Friedrich. *The Twilight of the Idols and the Anti-Christ*, ed. and tr. R. J. Hollingdale. Penguin, 1968.

Nineham, Dennis. *The Use and the Abuse of the Bible*. London: Macmillan, 1976.

Noll, Mark A. *The Old Religion in a New World*. Grand Rapids, MI: Eerdmans, 2002.

Northrup, Lesley A. *Ritualizing Women: Patterns of Spirituality*. Cleveland: Pilgrim Press, 1997.

Nygren, Anders. *Eros and Agape*, tr. Philip A. Watson. London: SPCK, 1953.

Okin, Susan Moller. *Is Multiculturalism Bad for Women?*, eds. Joshua Cohen, Matthew Howard, and Martha Nussbaum. Princeton, NJ: Princeton University Press, 1999.

Ong, Walter J. *Orality and Literacy: The Technologizing of the Word*. London: Methuen, 1982.

O'Regan, Cyril. *Gnostic Apocalypse: Jacob Boehme's Haunted Narrative*. Albany: State University of New York Press, 2002.

Ortner, Sherry B. *Sherpas Through Their Rituals*. Cambridge: Cambridge University Press, 1978.

Otto, Rudolf. *The Idea of the Holy: An Inquiry into the Non-rational Factor in the Idea of the Divine and its Relation to the Rational* [1917], tr. John W. Harvey. London: Oxford University Press, 1923.

Outka, Gene, and Paul Ramsey, eds. *Norm and Context in Christian Ethics*. New York: Scribner's, 1968.

Pagels, Elaine. *The Origin of Satan*. New York: Random House, 1995.

Palmer, Michael. *Freud and Jung on Religion*. London: Routledge, 1997.

Panikkar, Raimon. *The Intrareligious Dialogue*. New York: Paulist Press, 1999.

Parsons, Talcott. "Evolutionary Universals in Society," *American Journal of Sociology* 29 (1964): 339–57.

Parsons, William B. *The Enigma of the Oceanic Feeling: Revisioning the Psychoanalytic Study of Mysticism*. New York: Oxford University Press, 1999.

Parsons, William B. "Themes and Debates in the Psychology – Comparativist Dialogue," in *Religion and Psychology: Mapping the Terrain*, eds. Diane Jonte-Pace and William Parsons. London: Routledge, 2001, pp. 229–53.

Paterson, R. W. K. *Philosophy and the Belief in a Life After Death*. New York: St. Martin's Press, 1995.

Peirce, Charles Sanders. *Collected Papers*, eds. Charles Hartshorne and Paul Weiss. Vol. 1: *Principles of Philosophy*. Vol. 2: *Elements of Logic*. Vol. 5: *Pragmatism and Pragmaticism*. Cambridge, MA: Harvard University Press, 1974.

Pensa, Corrado. "On the Purification Concept in Indian Tradition, with Special Regard to Yoga," *East and West* 19 (1969): 194–228.

Percy, Martyn. *The Salt of the Earth: Religious Resilience in a Secular Age*. Sheffield: Sheffield Academic Press, 2001.

Pettinato, Giovanni. *Angeli e demoni a Babilonia. Magia e mito nelle antiche civiltà mesopotamiche*. Milan: Mondadori, 2001.

Phillips, D. Z. *Religion Without Explanation*. Oxford: Blackwell, 1976.

Phillips, D. Z. "Wittgensteinianism: Logic, Reality, and God," in *The Oxford Handbook of Philosophy of Religion*, ed. William Wainwright. Oxford: Oxford University Press, 2005, pp. 447–71.

Pitchford, Susan, Christopher Bader, and Rodney Stark. "Doing Field Studies of Religious Movements: An Agenda," *Journal for the Scientific Study of Religion* 40 (2001): 379–92.

Plantinga, Alvin. *God and Other Minds*. Ithaca, NY: Cornell University Press, 1967.

Plantinga, Alvin. *The Nature of Necessity*. Oxford: Oxford University Press, 1974.

Plato, *Complete Works*, ed. John Cooper. Indianapolis, IN: Hackett, 1997.

Polanyi, Michael. *Personal Knowledge: Towards a Post-Critical Philosophy*. London: Routledge, 1958.

Polkinghorne, John. *Reason and Reality*. London: SPCK, 1991.

Poo, Mu-chou. *In Search of Personal Welfare: A View of Ancient Chinese Religion*. Albany: State University of New York Press, 1998.

Pratt, James. B. *The Religious Consciousness: A Psychological Study*. New York: Macmillan, 1920.

Prickett, Stephen. *Romanticism and Religion: The Tradition of Wordsworth and Coleridge in the Victorian Church*. Cambridge: Cambridge University Press, 1976.

Prickett, Stephen. *Words and the Word: Language, Poetics, and Biblical Interpretation*. Cambridge: Cambridge University Press, 1986.

Prickett, Stephen. *Origins of Narrative: The Romantic Appropriation of the Bible*. Cambridge: Cambridge University Press, 1996.

Prickett, Stephen. *Narrative, Religion and Science: Fundamentalism versus Irony, 1700–1999*. Cambridge: Cambridge University Press, 2002.

Przyluski, Jean. "Les Vidyārāja: Contribution à l'histoire de la magie dans les sectes mahāyānistes," *Bulletin de l'École française d'Extrême-Orient* 23 (1923): 301–18.

Pui-lan, Kwok. *Introducing Asian Feminist Theology*. Sheffield: Sheffield Academic Press, 2000.

Pyysiäinen, Ilkka. "Phenomenology of Religion and Cognitive Science: The Case of Religious Experience." *Temenos* 35–36 (1999–2000): 125–54.

Quinn, Philip L., and Charles Taliaferro, eds. *The Blackwell Companion to Philosophy of Religion*. Oxford: Blackwell, 1997.

Quinn, Philip L., and Kevin Meeker, eds. *The Philosophical Challenge of Religious Diversity*. Oxford: Oxford University Press, 2000.

Radcliffe-Brown, A. R. *The Andaman Islanders*. Cambridge: Cambridge University Press, 1922.

Radcliffe-Brown, A. R. "The Comparative Method in Social Anthropology," *Journal of the Royal Anthropological Institute* 81 (1951): 15–22.

Rank, Otto. *The Myth of the Birth of the Hero*. 1st edn. Trs. F. Robbins and Smith Ely Jelliffe. Nervous and Mental Disease Monograph Series, no. 18. New York: Journal of Nervous and Mental Disease Publishing, 1914.

Ranke-Heinemann, Uta. *Eunuchs for Heaven: The Catholic Church and Sexuality*, tr. John Blownjobs. London: Deutsch, 1990.

Rappaport, Roy A. "Logos, Liturgy, and the Evolution of Humanity," in *Fortunate the Eyes That See: Essays in Honor of David Noel Freedman*, eds. Astrid Beck *et al.* Grand Rapids, MI: Eerdmans, 1995, pp. 601–32.

Rappaport, Roy A. *Ritual and Religion in the Making of Humanity*. Cambridge: Cambridge University Press, 1999.

Ravitzky, Aviezer. *Messianism, Zionism, and Jewish Religious Radicalism*. Chicago: University of Chicago Press, 1996.

Rawls, John. *A Theory of Justice* [1971]. Rev. edn. Cambridge, MA: Harvard University Press, 1999.

Raychaudhuri, Tapan. "Shadows of the Swastika: Historical Reflections on the Politics of Hindu Communalism," *Contention* 4 (1995): 141–62.

Reader, Ian, and George J. Tanabe. *Practically Religious: Worldly Benefits and the Common Religion of Japan*. Honolulu: University of Hawaii Press, 1998.

Ribuffo, Leo P. *The Old Christian Right: The Protestant Far Right from the Great Depression to the Cold War*. Philadelphia: Temple University Press, 1983.

Richardson, James T. "A Social Psychological Critique of 'Brainwashing' Claims about Recruitment to New Religions," in *The Handbook on Cults and Sects in America, Part A and B*, eds. David G. Bromley and Jeffrey K. Hadden. Religion and the Social Order Series, Vol. 3. Greenwich, CT: JAI Press, 1993, pp. 75–97.

Ricoeur, Paul. *The Symbolism of Evil*, tr. Emerson Buchanan. New York: Harper and Row, 1967.

Ritner, Robert K. "Egyptian Magical Practice Under the Roman Empire: The Demotic Spells and Their Religious Context," in *Aufstieg und Niedergang der römischen Welt*, II.18.5, ed. Wolfgang Haase. Berlin: De Gruyter, 1985, pp. 3333–79.

Ritner, Robert K. "The Religious, Social, and Legal Parameters of Traditional Egyptian Magic," in *Ancient Magic and Ritual Power*, eds. Marvin Meyer and Paul Mirecki. Leiden: Brill, 1995, pp. 43–60.

Ritter, Edith K. "Magical-Expert (= *Āšipu*) and Physician (= *Ašu*): Notes on Two Complementary Professions in Babylonian Medicine," *Studies in Honor of Benno Landsberger on his Seventy-Fifth Birthday, April 21, 1965*. Chicago: University of Chicago Press, 1965, pp. 299–321.

Robbins, Thomas, and Dick Anthony. "New Religions and Cults in the United States," in *The Encyclopedia of Religion*, ed. Mircea Eliade. New York: Macmillan, 1987, Vol. 10, pp. 394–405.

Robbins, Thomas, and Dick Anthony. "Sects and Violence: Factors Enhancing the Volatility of Marginal Religious Movements," in *Armageddon in Waco: Critical Perspectives on the Branch Davidian Conflict*, ed. Stuart Wright. Chicago: University of Chicago Press, 1995, pp. 236–59.

Roberts, Richard H. *Religion, Theology and the Human Sciences*. Cambridge: Cambridge University Press, 2001.

Robison, John. "Philosophy." *Encyclopaedia Britannica*. 3rd edn. [1798], one-volume edition, pp. 586–8.

Roscoe, Paul B. "The Perils of 'Positivism' in Cultural Anthropology," *American Anthropologist* 97 (1995): 492–504.

Rosen, Stanley. "A Modest Proposal to Rethink Enlightenment," in his *Ancients and Moderns*. New Haven, CT: Yale University Press, 1988, pp. 1–21.

Rosenzweig, Franz. *The Star of Redemption* [1921], tr. William W. Hallo. London: Routledge and Kegan Paul, 1971.

Rowe, William. "The Problem of Evil and Some Varieties of Atheism," *American Philosophical Quarterly* 16 (1979): 335–41.

Rowe, William. *Can God Be Free?* Oxford: Clarendon Press, 2004.

Roy, Sara. "Hamas and the Transformation(s) of Political Islam in Palestine," *Current History* 102 (2003): 13–20.

Rozin, Paul, and Carol Nemeroff. "The Laws of Sympathetic Magic: A Psychological Analysis of Similarity and Contagion," in *Cultural Psychology: Essays on Comparative Human Development*, eds. James W. Stigler, Richard A. Shweder, and Gilbert Herdt. Cambridge: Cambridge University Press, 1990, pp. 205–32.

Rudolph, Susanne Hoeber, and James Piscatori, eds. *Transnational Religion and Fading States*. Boulder, CO: Westview Press, 1997.

Russell, Jeffrey Burton. *The Devil: Perceptions of Evil from Antiquity to Primitive Christianity*. Ithaca, NY: Cornell University Press, 1977.

Russell, Jeffrey Burton. *Satan: The Early Christian Tradition*. Ithaca, NY: Cornell University Press, 1981.

Russell, Jeffrey Burton. *Lucifer: The Devil in the Middle Ages*. Ithaca, NY: Cornell University Press, 1984.

Russell, Jeffrey Burton. *Mephistopheles: The Devil in the Modern World*. Ithaca, NY: Cornell University Press, 1986.

Russell, Jeffrey Burton. *The Prince of Darkness: Evil and the Power of Good in History*. Ithaca, NY: Cornell University Press, 1988.

Russell, Jeffrey Burton. *A History of Heaven: The Singing Silence*. Princeton, NJ: Princeton University Press, 1997.

Russell, Jeffrey Burton. *Paradise Mislaid: Heaven in Modern Thought*. New York: Oxford University Press, 2006.

Ryan, Alexandra E. *Our Only Uniform Is the Spirit: Embodiment, Tradition and Spirituality in British Taijiquan*. Unpublished PhD dissertation, Lancaster University, 2002.

Ryan, John A. *A Living Wage*. New York: Macmillan, 1906.

Ryba, Thomas. *The Essence of Phenomenology and its Meaning for the Scientific Study of Religion*. New York: Peter Lang, 1991.

Ryba, Thomas. "Why Revisit the Phenomenology of Religion?" *Temenos* 35–36 (1999–2000): 155–82.

Ryba, Thomas. "Manifestation." In *Cassell's Guide to the Study of Religion*, eds. Russell McCutcheon and Willi Braun. London: Cassell, 2000, pp. 168–89.

Ryba, Thomas. "Comparative Religion, Taxonomies and 19th Century Philosophies of Science: Chantepie de la Saussaye and Tiele." *Numen* 48 (2001): 309–38.

Sagovsky, Nicholas. *Between Two Worlds: George Tyrrell's Relationship to the Thought of Matthew Arnold*. Cambridge: Cambridge University Press, 1983.

Saler, Benson. "Comparison: Some Suggestions for Improving the Inevitable," *Numen* 48 (2001): 267–75.

Saliba, John A. "The New Religions and Mental Health," in *The Handbook on Cults and Sects in America, Part A and B*, eds. David G. Bromley and Jeffrey K. Hadden. Religion and the Social Order Series, Vol. 3. Greenwich, CT: JAI Press, 1993, pp. 99–113.

Sallnow, Michael. "Communitas Reconsidered: The Sociology of Andean Pilgrimage," *Man* 16 (1992): 163–82.

Samuel, Geoffrey D. *Mind, Body and Culture: Anthropology and the Biological Interface*. Cambridge: Cambridge University Press, 1990.

Sanneh, Lamin. *Translating the Message: The Missionary Impact on Culture*. Maryknoll, NY: Orbis, 1989.

Scharfstein, Ben-Ami. *Mystical Experience*. Indianapolis, IN: Bobbs-Merrill, 1973.

Schechner, Richard. "The Future of Ritual," in his *The Future of Ritual: Writings on Culture and Performance*. London: Routledge, 1993, pp. 228–65.

Schechner, Richard, and Willa Appel, eds. *By Means of Performance: Intercultural Studies of Theater and Ritual*. Cambridge: Cambridge University Press, 1989.

Schimmel, Annemarie. *My Soul Is a Woman: The Feminine in Islam*. New York: Continuum, 1997.

Schipper, Kristofer. *The Taoist Body*. Berkeley: University of California Press, 1993.

Schlegel, Friedrich. *Lucinde and the Fragments* [1799], tr. Peter Firchow. Minneapolis: University of Minnesota Press, 1971.

Schleiermacher, Friedrich. *On Religion: Speeches to its Cultured Despisers* [1799], tr. Richard Crouter. Cambridge: Cambridge University Press, 1988.

Schmidt, Leigh Eric. "The Making of Modern 'Mysticism'," *Journal of the American Academy of Religion* 71 (2003): 273–302.

Schneewind, Jerome. *The Invention of Autonomy: A History of Modern Moral Philosophy*. Cambridge: Cambridge University Press, 1998.

Schulte-Sasse, Jochen. "Modernity and Modernism, Postmodernity and Postmodernism," *Culture Critique* 5 (1986): 23–49.

Searle, John. "The World Turned Upside Down." In *Working through Derrida*, ed. Gary B. Madison. Evanston, IL: Northwestern University Press, 1993, pp. 170–83.

Sedgwick, Mark J. *Against the Modern World: Traditionalism and the Secret Intellectual History of the Twentieth Century*. New York: Oxford University Press, 2004.

Segal, Alan F. *Life After Death: A History of the Afterlife in Western Religion*. New York: Doubleday, 2004.

Segal, Robert A., ed. *The Myth and Ritual Theory*. Oxford: Blackwell, 1998.

Segal, Robert A. "In Defense of the Comparative Method," *Numen* 48 (2001): 339–73.

Segovia, Fernando F. "Aliens in the Promised Land: The Manifest Destiny of U. S. Hispanic American Theology," in *Hispanic/Latino Theology: Challenge and Promise*, eds. Ada María Isasi-Díaz and Fernando F. Segovia. Minneapolis, MN: Fortress Press, 1996, pp. 15–44.

Sells, Michael. *Mystical Languages of Unsaying*. Chicago: University of Chicago Press, 1994.

Sessions, Lad. *The Concept of Faith: A Philosophical Investigation*. Ithaca, NY: Cornell University Press, 1994.

Sherkat, Darren E., and John Wilson. "Preferences, Constraints, and Choices in Religious Markets: An Examination of Religious Switching and Apostasy," *Social Forces* 73 (1995): 993–1026.

Shibley, Mark A. 1996. *Resurgent Evangelicalism in the United States: Mapping Cultural Change Since 1970*. Columbia: University of South Carolina Press.

Sidgwick, Henry. *The Methods of Ethics* [1874], 7th edn. London: Macmillan, 1907.

Singer, Margaret T. *Cults in Our Midst: The Hidden Menace in our Everyday Lives*. San Francisco: Jossey-Bass, 1995.

Singer, Peter, ed. *A Companion to Ethics*. Oxford: Blackwell, 1991.

Singer, Peter. *Practical Ethics* [1979], 2nd edn. Cambridge: Cambridge University Press, 1993.

Smart, Barry. *Postmodernity*. London: Routledge, 1993.

Smart, J. J. C., and Bernard Williams. *Utilitarianism: For and Against*. Cambridge: Cambridge University Press, 1973.

Smith, Adam. *An Inquiry into the Nature and Causes of the Wealth of Nations* [1776]. 2 vols. Indianapolis: Liberty Fund, 1981.

Smith, Anthony D. *Nations and Nationalism in a Global Era*. London: Polity Press, 1995.

Smith, Jonathan Z. *Imagining Religion: From Babylon to Jonestown*. Chicago: University of Chicago Press, 1982.

Smith, Jonathan Z. *To Take Place: Toward Theory in Ritual*. Chicago: University of Chicago Press, 1987.

Smith, Morton. *The Secret Gospel: The Discovery and Interpretation of the Secret Gospel According to Mark*. San Francisco: Harper and Row, 1973.

Smith, Morton. *Jesus the Magician*. San Francisco: Harper and Row, 1978.

Smith, William Robertson. *Lectures on the Religion of the Semites: The Fundamental Institutions* [1889], 3rd edn. New York: KTAV, 1969 [1927].

Snow, C. P. *Two Cultures and the Scientific Revolution* [1957]. Cambridge: Cambridge University Press, 1969.

Sobel, Howard. *Logic and Theism*. Cambridge: Cambridge University Press, 2004.

Spilka, Bernard. "Psychology of Religion: Empirical Approaches," in *Religion and Psychology: Mapping the Terrain*, eds. Diane Jonte-Pace and William B. Parsons. London: Routledge, 2001, pp. 30–42.

Spong, John Shelby. *Why Christianity Must Change or Die*. San Francisco: HarperSanFrancisco, 1998.

Sprinzak, Ehud. *The Ascendance of Israel's Radical Right*. New York: Oxford University Press, 1991.

Staal, Frits. *Agni: The Vedic Fire Ritual*. Berkeley: Asian Humanities Press, 1983.

Stark, Rodney. *The Rise of Christianity: A Sociologist Reconsiders History*. Princeton, NJ: Princeton University Press, 1996.

Stark, Rodney. "Why Religious Movements Succeed or Fail: A Revised General Model," *Journal of Contemporary Religion* 11 (1996): 133–46.

Stark, Rodney. *For the Glory of God: How Monotheism Led to Reformations, Science, Witch-Hunts, and the End of Slavery*. Princeton, NJ: Princeton University Press, 2003.

Stark, Rodney. *Exploring the Religious Life*. Baltimore: Johns Hopkins University Press, 2004.

Stark, Rodney. *The Victory of Reason: How Christianity Led to Freedom, Capitalism, and Western Success*. New York: Random House, 2005.

Stark, Rodney, and William Sims Bainbridge. *The Future of Religion: Secularization, Revival, and Cult Formation*. Berkeley: University of California Press, 1985.

Stark, Rodney, and William Sims Bainbridge. *A Theory of Religion*. New York: Peter Lang, 1987.

Stark, Rodney, and Roger Finke. *Acts of Faith: Explaining the Human Side of Religion*. Berkeley: University of California Press, 2000.

Steedly, Mary Margaret. *Hanging Without a Rope: Narrative Experience in Colonial and Postcolonial Karoland*. Princeton, NJ: Princeton University Press, 1993.

Steiner, George. *Real Presences: Is There Anything In What We Say?* London: Faber, 1989.

Stirrat, Richard. "Place and Pilgrimage in Sinhala Catholic Pilgrimage," in *Contesting the Sacred: The Anthropology of Christian Pilgrimage*, eds. John Eade and Michael Sallnow. London: Routledge, 1991, pp. 122–36.

Stoller, Paul, and Cheryl Olkes. *In Sorcery's Shadow*. Chicago: University of Chicago Press, 1989.

Strenski, Ivan. "Original Phenomenology of Religion: A Theology of Natural Religion." In *The Comity and Grace of Method*, eds. Thomas Ryba, George Bond, and Herman H. Tull. Evanston, IL: Northwestern University Press, 2004, pp. 5–16.

Stuart, Elizabeth. *Just Good Friends: Towards a Lesbian and Gay Theology of Relationships*. London: Mowbray, 1995.

Swinburne, Richard. *The Coherence of Theism*. Oxford: Clarendon Press, 1977.

Swinburne, Richard. *The Existence of God*. Oxford: Clarendon Press, 1979.

Swinburne, Richard. *Providence and the Problem of Evil*. Oxford: Oxford University Press, 1998.

Synnott, Anthony. *The Body Social: Symbolism, Self and Society*. London: Routledge, 1993.

Taliaferro, Charles. *Consciousness and the Mind of God*. Cambridge: Cambridge University Press, 1994.

Taliaferro, Charles. *Contemporary Philosophy of Religion*. Oxford: Blackwell, 1998.

Taliaferro, Charles. *Evidence and Faith: Philosophy and Religion since the Seventeenth Century*. Cambridge: Cambridge University Press, 2005.

Tambiah, Stanley J. *Culture, Thought, and Social Action: An Anthropological Perspective*. Cambridge, MA: Harvard University Press, 1985.

Tapper, Nancy. "*Ziyaret*: Gender, Movement, and Exchange in a Turkish Community," in *Muslim Travellers: Pilgrimage, Migration, and the Religious Imagination*, eds. Dale Eickelman and James Piscatori. London: Routledge, 1990, pp. 135–47.

Thomas, Cal, and Ed Dobson. *Blinded by Might: Can the Religious Right Save America?* Grand Rapids, MI: Zondervan, 1999.

Thomas, Linda Elaine. *Under the Canopy: Ritual Process and Spiritual Resilience in South Africa*. Columbia: University of South Carolina Press, 1999.

Thurston, Herbert. *The Physical Phenomena of Mysticism*. London: Burns Oates, 1952.

Tiele, Cornelius Petrus. *Elements of the Science of Religion*. 2 vols. London: Blackwood, 1899.

Tillich, Paul. *The Courage to Be*. New Haven, CT: Yale University Press, 1952.

Todorov, Tzvetan. "Le discours de la magie," *L'Homme* 13.4 (1973): 38–65.

Tönnies, Ferdinand. *Community and Association* [1887], tr. C. P. Loomis. London: Routledge and Kegan Paul, 1955.

Troeltsch, Ernst. *The Social Teachings of the Christian Churches*, tr. Olive Wyon. 2 vols. London: Allen and Unwin; New York: Macmillan, 1931.

Turner, Bryan. "Periodization and Politics in the Postmodern," in *Theories of Modernity and Postmodernity*, ed. Bryan Turner. London: Sage, 1990, pp. 1–13.

Turner, Bryan S. *The Body and Society: Explorations in Social Theory* [1984]. London: Sage 1996.

Turner, Edith. *Experiencing Ritual: A New Interpretation of African Healing*. Philadelphia: University of Pennsylvania Press, 1992.

Turner, Victor. *The Ritual Process: Structure and Antistructure*. Ithaca, NY: Cornell University Press, 1969.

Turner, Victor. *From Ritual to Theatre: The Human Seriousness of Play*. New York: Performing Arts Journal Publications, 1982.

Turner, Victor, and Edith Turner. *Image and Pilgrimage in Christian Culture*. New York: Columbia University Press, 1978.

Tweed, Thomas. *Our Lady of the Exile: Diasporic Religion at a Cuban Catholic Shrine in Miami*. New York: Oxford University Press, 1997.

Tylor, Edward Burnett. "On a Method of Investigating the Development of Institutions; Applied to Laws of Marriage and Descent," *Journal of the Royal Anthropological Institute* 18 (1889): 245–72.

Tylor, Edward Burnett. *Primitive Culture*, 2 vols. 1st edn, London: Murray, 1871. 5th edn, London: Murray, 1913. Reprint of 5th edn. New York: Harper, 1958.

Tyrrell, George. *The Faith of the Millions: A Selection of Past Essays*. 2nd Series. London: Longmans, Green, 1902.

Van der Veer, Peter. "Structure and Anti-Structure in Hindu Pilgrimage to Ayodhya," in *Changing South Asia: Religion and Society*, eds. Kenneth Ballhatchet and David Taylor. London: Asian Research Service for the Centre of South Asian Studies, School of Oriental and African Studies, University of London, 1984, pp. 59–67.

Van Gennep, Arnold. *The Rites of Passage* [1909], trs. Monika B. Vizedom and Gabrielle L. Caffee. Chicago: University of Chicago Press, 1960.

Van Inwagen, Peter. "The Magnitude, Duration, and Distribution of Evil: A Theodicy," *Philosophical Topics* 16 (1998): 161–87.

Vernant, Jean-Pierre. *Myth and Thought among the Greeks*, tr. not given. London: Routledge and Kegan Paul, 1983.

Versnel, H. S. "Some Reflections on the Relationship Magic-Religion," *Numen* 38 (1991): 177–97.

Versnel, H. S. "Die Poetik der Zaubersprüche," in *Die Macht des Wortes* [Eranos NF 4], eds. Tilo Schabert and Rémi Brague. Munich: Wilhelm Fink Verlag, 1996, pp. 233–97.

Vidal-Naquet, Pierre and Jean-Pierre Vernant. *Myth and Tragedy in Ancient Greece*, tr. Janet Lloyd. Brighton: Harvester Press, 1981.

Volf, Miroslav. *Work in the Spirit: Toward a Theology of Work*. New York: Oxford University Press, 1991.

Von Wiese, Leopold, and Howard Becker. *Systematic Sociology*. New York: Wiley, 1932.

Waaijman, Wees. "Towards a Phenomenological Definition of Spirituality," *Studies in Spirituality* 3 (1993): 5–57.

Waardenburg, Jacques. *Reflections on the Study of Religion.* The Hague: Mouton, 1978.

Wainwright, William, ed. *The Oxford Handbook of Philosophy of Religion.* Oxford: Oxford University Press, 2005.

Waldschmidt, Ernst. "Ein zweites Daśabalasūtra," *Mitteilungen des Instituts für Orientforschung* 6 (1958): 382–405. Reprinted in his *Von Ceylon bis Turfan: Schriften zur Geschichte, Literatur, Religion und Kunst des indischen Kulturraumes.* Göttingen: Vandenhoeck und Ruprecht, 1967, pp. 347–70.

Wallis, Jim. *God's Politics: Why the Right Gets It Wrong and the Left Doesn't Get It.* San Francisco: HarperSanFrancisco, 2005.

Wallis, Roy. *The Elementary Forms of the New Religious Life.* London: Routledge and Kegan Paul, 1984.

Walls, Jerry L. *Heaven: The Logic of Eternal Joy.* Oxford: Oxford University Press, 2002.

Walter, Tony. *The Revival of Death.* London: Routledge, 1994.

Ward, Graham. *True Religion.* Oxford: Blackwell, 2003.

Ward, Keith. *Reason and Revelation.* Oxford: Oxford University Press, 1994.

Ward, Keith. *Religion and Revelation.* Oxford: Oxford University Press, 1996.

Weaver, Mary Jo, and R. Scott Appleby, eds. *Being Right: Conservative Catholics in America.* Bloomington: Indiana University Press, 1995.

Weber, Max. *General Economic History,* tr. Frank H. Knight. London: Allen and Unwin, 1927.

Weber, Max. *The Protestant Ethic and the Spirit of Capitalism* [1904–05/1920], tr. Talcott Parsons. London: Allen and Unwin, 1930.

Weber, Max. *The Sociology of Religion* [1922], tr. Ephraim Fischoff. Boston: Beacon Press, 1963.

Weber, Max. *Economy and Society: An Essay in Interpretative Sociology,* eds. Guether Roth and Claus Wittich, trs. Ephraim Fischoff *et al.* 2 vols. Berkeley: University of California Press, 1978.

West, William. *Psychotherapy and Spirituality: Crossing the Line between Therapy and Religion.* London: Sage, 2000.

Westerlund, David, ed. *Questioning the Secular State: The Worldwide Resurgence of Religion in Politics.* London: Hurst, 1996.

Weyrich, Paul. "Comment on George Marsden's 'The Religious Right: A Historical Overview'," in *No Longer Exiles: The Religious New Right in American Politics,* ed. Michael Cromartie. Washington, DC: Ethics and Public Policy Center, 1993, pp. 25–6.

Wheeler, Kathleen M. (ed.), *German Aesthetic and Literary Criticism.* Cambridge: Cambridge University Press, 1984.

Wheelwright, Philip. *The Burning Fountain* [1954]. Rev. edn. Bloomington: Indiana University Press, 1968.

Whewell, William. *The Philosophy of the Inductive Sciences Founded on Their History* [1840]. 2 vols. New York: Johnson Reprint Company, 1967.

Whiting, Beatrice B. *Paiute Sorcery*. New York: Viking Fund, 1950.

Whiting, John W. M. "Effects of Climate on Certain Cultural Practices," in *Explorations in Cultural Anthropology*, ed. Ward H. Goodenough. New York: McGraw Hill, 1964, pp. 511–44.

Whiting, John W. M., Richard Kluckholn, and Albert S. Anthony. "The Function of Male Initiation Ceremonies at Puberty," in *Readings in Social Psychology*, eds. Eleanor E. Maccoby, Theodore M. Newcomb, and Eugene L. Hartley. New York: Holt, 1958, pp. 359–70.

Wilkins, John, ed. *Considering "Veritatis Splendor."* Cleveland: Pilgrim Press, 1994.

Willaime, Jean-Paul. *Sociologie des religions*. Paris: Presses Universitaires de France, 1995.

Wilson, Bryan R. *Religion in Sociological Perspective*. Oxford: Oxford University Press, 1982.

Wimbush, Vincent, and Richard Valantasis, eds. *Asceticism*. New York: Oxford University Press, 1995.

Winch, Peter. *The Idea of a Social Science*. London: Routledge and Kegan Paul, 1958.

Winnicott, D. W. *The Child, the Family and the Outside World* [1964]. Reading, MA: Addison-Wesley, 1987.

Winnicott, D. W. "Transitional Objects and Transitional Phenomena" [1951], in Winnicott, *Playing and Reality* [1971] (London and New York: Routledge, 1982), ch. 1. Also in Winnicott, *Through Paediatrics to Psychoanalysis* [1958] (London: Karnac Books, 1992), ch. 18.

Wolfe, Alvin W. "Social Structural Bases of Art," *Current Anthropology* 10 (1969): 3–29.

Wolfson, Elliot R. *Through a Speculum That Shines: Vision and Imagination in Medieval Jewish Mysticism*. Princeton, NJ: Princeton University Press, 1994.

Woodhead, Linda. "Women and Religion," in *Religions in the Modern World*, eds. Linda Woodhead, Paul Fletcher, Hiroko Kawanami, and David Smith. London: Routledge, 2002, pp. 332–56.

Wright, J. Edward. *The Early History of Heaven*. New York: Oxford University Press, 2000.

Wulff, David M. *Psychology of Religion: Classic and Contemporary*, 2nd edn. New York: Wiley, 1997.

Yamba, Bawa. *Permanent Pilgrims: The Role of Pilgrimage in the Lives of West African Muslims in Sudan*. Edinburgh: Edinburgh University Press, 1995.

Yandell, Keith. *The Epistemology of Religious Experience*. Cambridge: Cambridge University Press, 1993.

Yegenoglu, Meyda. *Colonial Fantasies: Towards a Feminist Reading of Orientalism*. Cambridge: Cambridge University Press, 1998.

Yoder, John Howard. *The Royal Priesthood*, ed. Michael Cartwright. Grand Rapids, MI: Eerdmans, 1994.

Young, John L., and Ezra E. H. Griffiths. "A Critical Evaluation of Coercive Persuasion as Used in the Assessment of Cults," *Behavioral Sciences and the Law* 10 (1992): 89–101.

Young, Lawrence A., ed. *Rational Choice Theory and Religion: Summary and Assessment.* New York: Routledge, 1997.

Zaleski, Carol. *Otherworld Journeys: Accounts of Near-Death Experience in Medieval and Modern Times.* New York: Oxford University Press, 1987.

Zaleski, Carol. *The Life of the World to Come.* Oxford: Oxford University Press, 1996.

Zaleski, Carol, and Philip Zaleski. *The Book of Heaven: An Anthology of Writings from Ancient to Modern Times.* Oxford: Oxford University Press, 2000.

Zeitlin, Steve, and Illana Harlow. *Giving a Voice to Sorrow: Personal Responses to Death and Mourning.* New York: Penguin Putnam, 2001.

Index